D1242972

Federal Land Series

Federal Land Series

A CALENDAR OF ARCHIVAL MATERIALS
ON THE LAND PATENTS ISSUED BY THE
UNITED STATES GOVERNMENT, WITH
SUBJECT, TRACT, AND NAME INDEXES

Volume 3 • 1810-1814

Clifford Neal Smith

F51509

AMERICAN LIBRARY ASSOCIATION · CHICAGO 1980

Library of Congress Cataloging in Publication Data

Smith, Clifford Neal.
    Federal land series.

    CONTENTS: v. 1.   1788-1810.--v. 2.   Federal bounty-
land warrants of the American Revolution, 1799-1835.--
v. 3.   1810-1814.
    1. Land grants--United States.   I. Title.
KF5675.A73S6   333.1'6'0973   72-3238
ISBN 0-8389-0278-2 (v. 3)

Copyright ©   1980 by the American Library Association

    All rights reserved. No part of this publication
    may be reproduced in any form without permission
    in writing from the publisher, except by a reviewer
    who may quote brief passages in a review.

        Printed in the United States of America

Contents

Maps

Acknowledgments

I wish to express my gratitude to Mr. Edwin C. Bixby, administrator of the Copper Queen Hospital, Bisbee, Arizona, for his kind permission to use the hospital's computer for the indexing of this volume of the *Federal Land Series*. In addition, I have had the very efficient assistance of Messrs. John E. Myers and Gary L. Vertrees of the hospital staff for the programming of the computer. Their patience and cooperation is much appreciated.

Introduction

Volume Three of the *Federal Land Series* takes up where Volume One left off--Volume Two having dealt entirely with the special records of land granted in the United States Military District of Ohio for military service during the American Revolution. Unlike the first volume, in which material from a number of manuscript sources was presented, the entries in the third volume are abstracted entirely from National Archives Microcopy no. 25, entitled *Miscellaneous Letters Sent by the General Land Office, 1796-1889* (Record Group 49, "Records of the Bureau of Land Management"). Volume Three completes rolls 4 and 5 of the microcopy, covering the period 1 June 1810 to 17 August 1814.

The 1810-1814 period was one of increasing land-office activity, despite renewed hostilities with the British during the War of 1812 and consequent Indian unrest. Even though Detroit was occupied by British forces,[1] the southern half of Ohio was rapidly filling up with settlers; nor did the vulnerability of New Orleans to attack deter American settlement in the Alabama-Mississippi-Louisiana region of the country, as will be noted from the increasing number of land grants made there. Genealogical researchers encountering surnames of interest to them in Volume Three will want to consider them in the light of the historical events of the period.

Ethnically, one notes a change: The surnames of the grantees in Volume One were almost exclusively British or French in origin. Volume Three shows a large number of German surnames, no doubt reflecting the migration into Ohio of German families from Pennsylvania, rather than direct immigration from Germany.

In the seven years since publication of the first volume of the *Federal Land Series*, the compiler has had numerous occasions to lecture on the land records of the United States and believes their usefulness to genealogical researchers is now generally recognized. (It is a source of personal satisfaction to the compiler that, in major centers of research, the first two volumes of the *Series* appear dilapidated by constant use.) However, there is some doubt that, as tools of research, the volumes have been fully exploited by everyone. As a consequence, the compiler makes the following observations:

Almost automatically, researchers finding ancestral names of interest in the volumes of the *Federal Land Series* should check Phillip W. McMullin's *Grassroots of America*[2] which indexes the nine-volume subseries on private land claims set forth in the *American State Papers*,[3] covering nearly 80,000 claims to land in the trans-Appalachian and trans-Mississippian regions asserted prior to American sovereignty over these territories. A cursory comparison of the index to the third volume of the *Federal Land Series* with *Grassroots of America* discloses considerable concord, particularly for preemption claimants. The volumes of the *American State Papers*, to which the researcher then has access, are an extraordinary mine of genealogical information—not merely on land ownership—for a period which antedates nearly all other available sources. Frequently, lineages can be carried back several generations on the basis of information recited by claimants under oath to the land commissioners regarding claims in areas where no census enumerator had ever ventured.

The finding of an ancestral name among the lists of grantees in volumes of the *Federal Land Series* should be the *beginning* of a further inquiry into the ancestor's land ownership, rather than the ending of it. There are numerous uncalendared records supporting entries in these volumes to be found in the National Archives and in corresponding state archives. Some of these records are of great potential value. In this regard the thorough researcher will try to answer a series of questions:

Where was the grant located? The entries in the volumes of the Series are precise, but it may not always be obvious which is the correct location among several similar-appearing land descriptions, particularly for lands in Ohio, where the numbering of ranges and townships was exceedingly complex. The first line of inquiry is to consult the maps for the appropriate land office district, as presented in these volumes. When all else fails, the State Auditor's Office, State Capitol Building, Columbus, Ohio 43215, may be able to clarify doubt by naming the corresponding county and township names. It must be added that few, perhaps five percent, of the early Ohio patents were ever recorded in county records; thus, evidence of the earliest land ownership only appears circumstantially, when land was later sold by deed or transferred to heirs.[4]

Where did the grantee live at the time of application or purchase of the land? The distinguished specialist in Ohio genealogical research, Carol Willsey Flavell, C.G., reports that the records of the district land offices in Ohio usually reveal the former places of residence of the grantees. Thus, an ancestor purchasing land in Ohio, found through an entry in the *Federal Land Series*, can be traced back to a prior residence further east--information of crucial importance to the researcher.[5] Flavell has prepared for publication her gleanings from the Steubenville Land Office records, 1800-1820, and projects similar extracts from the Marietta Land Office records, 1801-1818, and from the Zanesville Land Office records, 1804-1888.[6] Margaret R. Waters has published monographs on Indiana land grants made through the Cincinnati and Vincennes land offices. The Vincennes monograph lists the residences of grantees; the Cincinnati monograph does not.[7] Mayburt S. Riegel has published a compilation, entitled *Early Ohioans' Residences from the Land Grant Records*, listing the names of some grantees, but the monograph is by no means exhaustive in coverage.[8] Lowell M. Volkel has recently published entries from the Shawneetown, Illinois, Land Office records on file in the Illinois State Archives.[9] His monograph, too, contains the residences of grantees.

What were the circumstances of purchase? Most sales of land were credit sales, and there are land office receivers' records showing time, places of residence, and amounts of each installment payment. These entries are likely to contain incidental data, or even circumstantial clues, useful to the researcher. If the grantee took his land under right of preemption, having settled upon the land before the federal government commenced its granting of patents in the area, the particulars of this prior settlement are possibly recorded in the field notes of the surveyors, proven in the hearings of the boards of land commissioners set up in some regions, recorded in the surviving register of Symmes Purchase deeds, or mentioned in the various receipt books recording payments for land.

When did the ancestor settle on the land? There is no certain way to determine the precise date of settlement, but a close study of all the various records relating to the land transaction may give an approximate answer, when outside sources--censuses, tax lists, and contemporary unofficial papers--are silent or missing. The first official census of Ohio (1810), for example, was almost totally destroyed by fire in Washington, D.C., and the early Ohio tax levies were made only after the fifth year of settlement.[10] Researchers will want to consult Carol Willsey Flavell's *Ohio Genealogical Guide* for an overview of Ohio census and tax information,[11] Esther W. Powell's *Early Ohio Tax Records*,[12] Ronald V. Jackson's *Index to Ohio Tax Lists, 1800-1813*,[13] and Gerald M. Petty's *Ohio 1810 Tax Duplicate*.[14]

Who were the grantee's neighbors? Researchers ought to consider an ancestor's neighbors. If several families settled near one another about the same time, they may have migrated together from further east for mutual help and protection. Researchers should use the tract indexes to the volumes of the *Federal Land Series* to establish the identities of all contemporaneous landowners within a radius of three to five miles of an ancestor's place of settlement. From these circles of acquaintance came the marriage partners for their children and the recruits for new church, political, and social organizations. In this context local histories and directories, and especially newspaper obituaries, may be of aid. In a few cases, a prominent individual may have purchased large tracts of land in a locality, later to be sold by deed to members of particular religious or ethnic groups.[15] In such cases, the private papers of the original purchaser could be of considerable value. They may sometimes be located through the volumes of the *National Union Catalog of Manuscript Collections*,[16] an annual publication of the

Library of Congress available in any self-respecting research library.

Presumably, proven descendants of Ohio settlers, recorded in volumes of the *Federal Land Series* so far published, would be eligible to join First Families of Ohio, a commemorative organization sponsored by the Ohio Genealogical Society.[17]

Arrangement of the *Federal Land Series*

As has been stated in Volume One, the mass of data included in the *Federal Land Series* requires a precise, somewhat cryptic, format for the entries. As a rule, all names and addresses (excepting those of district land office personnel), tract descriptions, and subject matter are set forth in the entries. Within each entry information is placed in a specific position in order to conserve space and eliminate ambiguity. Most entries follow the format described in figure 1.

Land descriptions used in the Series differ in the following manner from descriptions found in the correspondence itself:

Land office prefixes. Prefixes have been added to denote the district land office where the application for land was originally made and in whose records the details of payment, survey, and the like, are presumed to be located.

Transposed order of citation. The land descriptions are shown in an order reverse to those normally found in deeds. For example, one usually finds a tract of land described by section, township, range, and meridian, in that order. When looking for the tract on a map, however, one has first to transpose the description, finding first the meridian, then the range, then the township, then the section, necessitating an awkward mental somersault. It has been

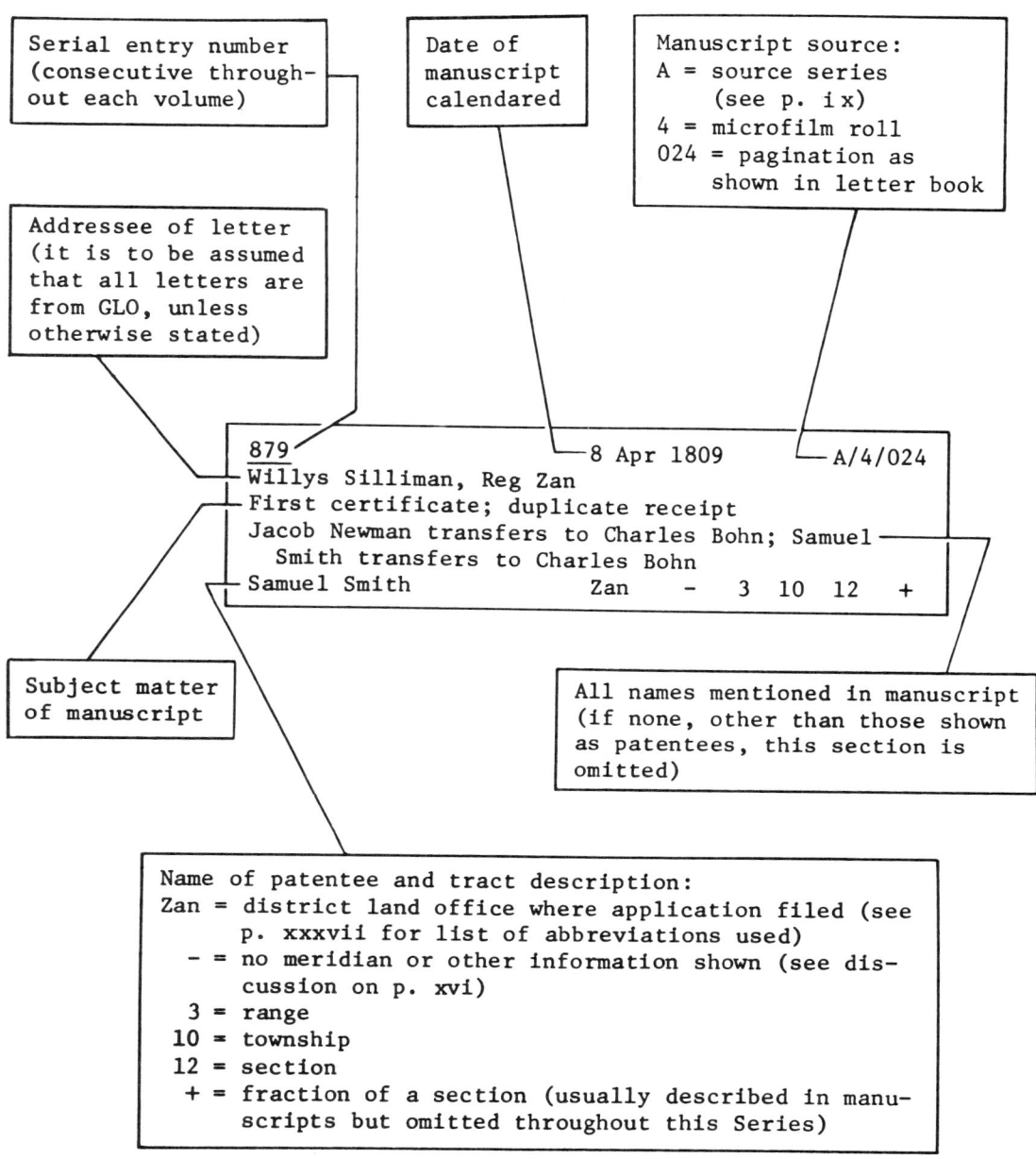

Serial entry number (consecutive through-out each volume)

Addressee of letter (it is to be assumed that all letters are from GLO, unless otherwise stated)

Date of manuscript calendared

Manuscript source:
A = source series (see p. ix)
4 = microfilm roll
024 = pagination as shown in letter book

879   8 Apr 1809   A/4/024
Willys Silliman, Reg Zan
First certificate; duplicate receipt
Jacob Newman transfers to Charles Bohn; Samuel
    Smith transfers to Charles Bohn
Samuel Smith   Zan   -   3 10 12   +

Subject matter of manuscript

All names mentioned in manuscript (if none, other than those shown as patentees, this section is omitted)

Name of patentee and tract description:
Zan = district land office where application filed (see p. xxxvii for list of abbreviations used)
  - = no meridian or other information shown (see discussion on p. xvi)
  3 = range
 10 = township
 12 = section
  + = fraction of a section (usually described in manuscripts but omitted throughout this Series)

Fig. 1. Serial entry format

thought more convenient to the researcher to arrange land descriptions in the latter order, particularly since it would be the normal one by which a computer would read the descriptions from input tape. Thus, the *Federal Land Series* shows land descriptions in this order:

District Land Office Where Application Papers Were Filed	Meridian	Range	Township	Section	Fraction or Lot
Zan	Mil	1	1	3	9
Cin	Pre	4	2	8	+
Chl	WS	21	11	34	+
Stu	–	2	3	6	–

Since meridians and base lines were not used in the earliest Ohio land descriptions, except in the Cincinnati Land Office district, the meridian column above has been frequently used to note other facts of interest, as follows:

Zan Mil. The Zanesville land description shown above indicates that the patentee received land in exchange for a military bounty-land warrant. Although these warrants were freely bought and sold and, thus, frequently used by persons who were not themselves veterans of the Revolutionary War, genealogists will want to consider the possibility that patentees of interest may have been veterans. If so, a military service record should be sought elsewhere in the National Archives collections.

Cin Pre. The Cincinnati preemption notation shown above indicates very early settlement. Patentees receiving land under rights of preemption were likely to have been settlers on the land before it was surveyed by the federal government. In the eyes of officials, they were "squatters" or "intruders," occasionally with solemn consequences (see entries 2524 and 2525 of Volume One for cases in point). Later laws recognized the preemptive rights of such early settlers. In the Cincinnati Land Office district a *Pre* notation

can also indicate governmental confirmation of land purchased before
1801 from John Cleeves Symmes by the settlers.

Chl WS. In three small areas of the Chillicothe Land Office district, land descriptions bear survey notations (Langham's Survey,
Matthew's Survey, Worthington's Survey).

Plus (+) sign. Complete land descriptions would specify the
fraction of a section (as, for example, the north half of the south-
east quarter of section 3). These fractional parts of a section
have been indicated in the *Federal Land Series* simply by a plus sign
(+) in the fraction or lot column to conserve space and minimize
transcription errors. Persons who have found the section in question
can refer to the original microfilm source for the fractional description, if needed. Copies of the microfilm rolls are readily available
from the National Archives.

Frequently, a number will be shown in the fraction or lot
column of a land description. If the land described is within the
United States Military District of Ohio or within the Refugee Tract
(also Ohio), the number indicates a lot. A number placed in this
column in any other land office district indicates a complete, but
fractional, section--one which, because of natural topographic
features (usually a river), is less than the standard 640 acres in
size. Under the original land laws, such fractional sections could
only be purchased by persons buying an adjacent full section.

Locating Land Descriptions

In Volume One of the *Federal Land Series* a map of the state
of Ohio, divided into three plates, was included as an aid in locating land descriptions mentioned in the text. These three plates
are repeated in Volume Three and summarized in the Orientation Map

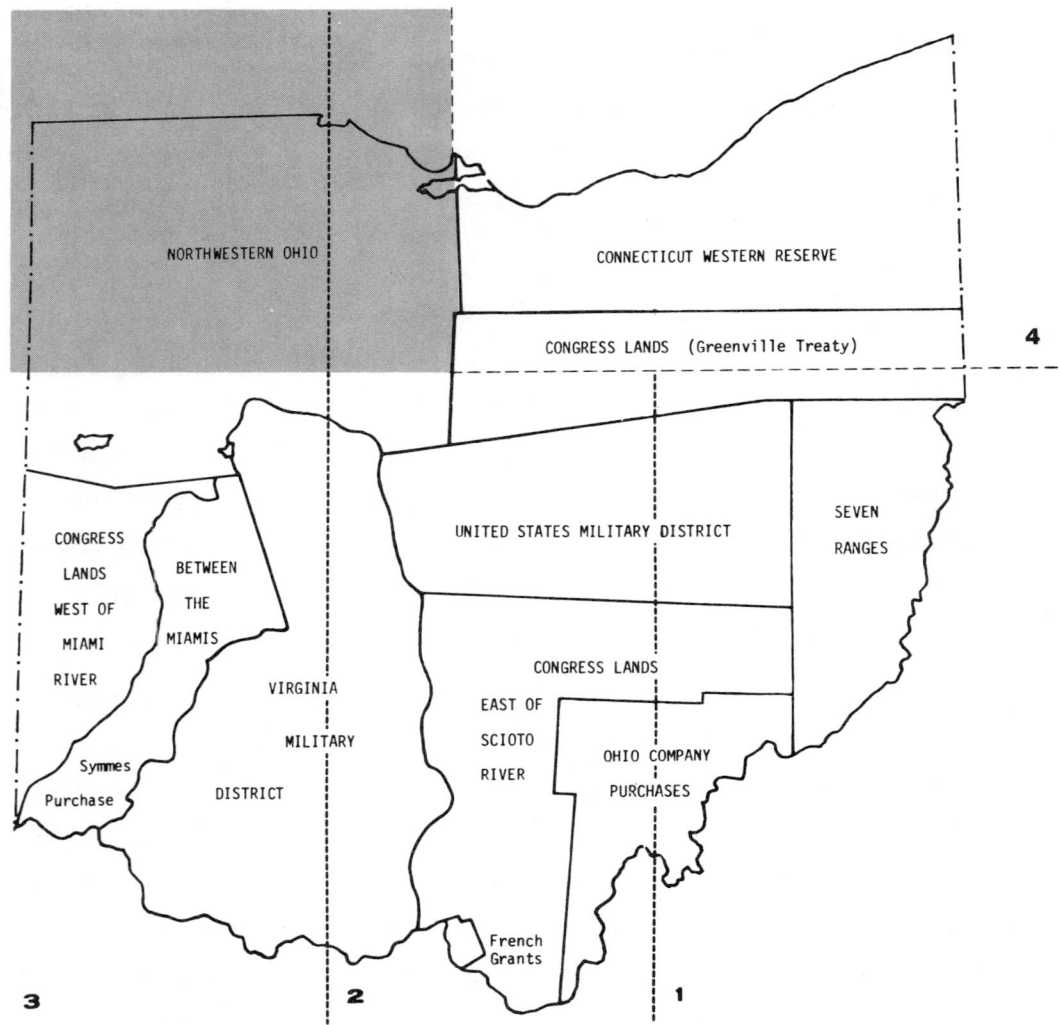

Orientation map of Ohio: Details of the areas numbered 1-4 are shown on the four plates numbered to correspond. Shaded area indicates the part of the state of Ohio that is not shown on the plates.

of Ohio. In addition, the increasing activities of the Canton Land Office require the inclusion of a fourth Ohio plate. Further maps reflecting the beginning activities of land offices in Indiana, Illinois, Alabama, Mississippi, and Louisiana are also provided.

Plate 1. Southeastern Ohio

The plate covers the Seven Ranges, the eastern third of the United States Military District, the eastern "panhandle" of the Congress Lands East of the Scioto River, and the eastern half of the Ohio Company Purchases.

(a) *Seven Ranges*. Volume One of the *Federal Land Series* contains the record of land auctions pertaining to this tract. All other grants within the tract were made through the Steubenville or Marietta land offices. Ranges are numbered 1 through 7 (in roman numerals in Plate 1), from east to west, beginning at the Ohio-Pennsylvania boundary. Townships are numbered from south to north, beginning at the Ohio River. Land descriptions bear the *Stu* or *Mar* prefix.

(b) *United States Military District*. The larger land grants within the United States Military District have been covered in Volume Two of this series, but a number of grants were also recorded in the books of nearby land offices. These entries will usually be found among the records of the Zanesville Land Office; some grants were also recorded by the Chillicothe Land Office, but it appears that this practice was discontinued, when the Zanesville office became well-enough established to take over the eastern portion of the area formerly served by Chillicothe. During the 1810-1814 period, however, it seems likely that there was still some overlapping, with both Chillicothe and Zanesville registering grants in the same area. When identifiable, military land grants have been given a *Mil* prefix or suffix, as follows:

```
Chl Mil   -   -   -   -
Zan Mil   -   -   -   -
Mil   -   -   -   -   -
```

Ranges in the United States Military District were numbered from east to west. Plate 1 covers ranges 1 through 6 (shown in roman numerals along the southern boundary of the Military District, beginning in Guernsey County). The townships were numbered from south to north, 1 through 10, in Plate 1. Section numbers 1 through 25 are also shown on the plate, with smaller land units (lots) indicated, where so subdivided. The counties partially covered in the Plate 1 portion of the Military District are Coshocton, Guernsey, Holmes, Muskingum, and Tuscarawas.

(c) *Congress Lands East of the Scioto River.* The lands within the eastern "panhandle" of the Congress Lands were under the jurisdiction of the Zanesville Land Office (excepting for Range 8 which was distributed by the Steubenville Land Office), but, again, it may have been that some of the earlier grants were made by the more distant Chillicothe Land Office, whose activities antedate those of the Zanesville office.

The ranges within the portion shown in Plate 1 are numbered from 8 to 13 (in roman numerals), beginning in the northeastern corner. The townships appear almost to bear random numbers in each range, but, in fact, they are numbered consecutively from the Ohio River northward, beginning in the Ohio Company Purchases tract. Counties partially included in the Congress Lands "panhandle" are the southernmost tip of Guernsey, Morgan, Muskingum, Noble, and Washington. Land descriptions bear the *Chl*, *Stu*, or *Zan* prefix, depending upon land office of issuance. Certain descriptions in small areas in ranges 21 and 22 also bear survey designators, as previously mentioned, of which there were three in the Chillicothe Land Office district.

(d) *Ohio Company Purchases*. The eastern half of the Ohio Company Purchases, shown in Plate 1, was within the Marietta Land Office district. Most of the land grants seem to have been recorded very early; they appear numerously in Volume One of this series, but infrequently in Volume Three. Most entries were made before the federal administration took over at Marietta. For prior records, researchers are referred to the Ohio Company records in the archives of Marietta College and to Albion M. Dyer's *First Ownership of Ohio Lands*.[18]

Ranges within the Marietta Land Office district are shown in Plate 1 running numerically from east to west, beginning with Range 8 to Range 13 (being the same as for the Congress Lands "panhandle" described in (c) above). The office also distributed land in the southern portion of the Seven Ranges. Townships are numbered from south to north, beginning at the Ohio River. Counties partially included in the eastern half of the Ohio Company Purchases are Athens, Gallia, Lawrence, Meigs, and Washington. Land descriptions bear the *Mar* prefix.

Plate 2. South Central Ohio

The western limits of Plate 2 bisect the Virginia Military District and include the western two-thirds of the United States Military District, the Refugee Tract, the bulk of the Congress Lands East of the Scioto River, and the Western half of the old Ohio Company Purchases.

(a) *Virginia Military District of Ohio*. No land entries in the district are included in the first three volumes of this series, because they were recorded in separate registers generated by officials of the state of Virginia. These records will be the subject of several forthcoming volumes, as time permits.

(b) *United States Military District*. Land grants within the Military District have been the subject of Volume Two of the *Federal Land Series*. However, transactions were also recorded in the general records of both the Chillicothe and Zanesville Land Offices, as described in section b, Plate 1.

Plate 2 covers ranges 7 through 18 (shown in roman numerals). As in Plate 1, townships are numbered from south to north, 1 through 10, at most. Section numbers vary according to the subdivisions established by Congress, some being from 1 to 4 only, others being from 1 to 25. Counties entirely or partially included in the Plate 2 portion of the Military District are Coshocton, Delaware, Franklin, Holmes, Knox, Licking, Marion, Morrow, and Muskingum. As stated in section c, Plate 1, land descriptions bear *Mil* prefix or suffix.

(c) *Refugee Tract*. The tract was a narrow strip of land running eastward from present-day Columbus. (It is not shown in the Orientation Map of Ohio.) All claimants for land in the Refugee Tract have been listed in Volume One of this series; only a few entries in Volume Three pertain to the area. Land descriptions bear the *Ref* prefix.

(d) *Congress Lands East of the Scioto River*. As stated in section c, Plate 1, most land entries will have been recorded at the Chillicothe Land Office, with others recorded at the Zanesville Land Office, especially in the northeastern portion of the Congress Lands. Since the Chillicothe office antedates the Zanesville office by some years, one would expect to find the earliest claims registered at Chillicothe, even though later claimants for neighboring lands may have been recorded at Zanesville.

The ranges, within that portion of the tract illustrated by Plate 2, are numbered in roman numerals from east to west, 13 (east of Zanesville) through 22 (around Columbus). Townships are numbered from south to north, beginning at the Ohio River. Counties wholly or partially within the Congress Lands include Fairfield, Franklin, Gallia, Hocking, Jackson, Lawrence, Morgan, Muskingum, Perry, Pickaway, Pike, Ross, Scioto, and Vinton. Land descriptions bear the *Chl* or *Zan* prefix, depending upon land office of issuance.

(e) *Ohio Company Purchases*. See the comments pertaining to this tract in section d, Plate 1. Plate 2 includes ranges 13 through 15 only, covering portions of Athens, Gallia, Lawrence, and Meigs counties. Land descriptions bear the *Mar* prefix.

Plate 3. Southwestern Ohio

As will be seen from the Orientation Map of Ohio, Plate 3 bisects the Virginia Military District and contains three major tracts of land: the old Symmes Purchase, the Region Between the Two Miami Rivers, and the Congress Lands West of the [Great] Miami River.

(a) *Symmes Purchase*. Judge Symmes's scheme to sell land around Cincinnati (parts of Butler, Hamilton, and Warren counties) had been superseded about 1801[19] by the federal government's distribution of land in the area. Ranges 1 and 2 and a southern fractional range around Cincinnati--about nine townships in all--bordering upon the three rivers (Ohio, Great Miami, and Little Miami rivers) were numbered from south to north, as shown in Plate 3. All federal transactions were recorded in the Cincinnati Land Office, including the lots sold within the original town itself. Records of Judge Symmes's prior sales were thought to have been entirely lost in a fire, but one register may be held by the Cincinnati Public Library. It has not been seen by this writer. Cincinnati Land Office land descriptions often bear the prefixes *Cin EML* and *Cin WML*. These refer to a meridian line drawn through fractional Range 2 (south from the town of Hamilton).[20] Land descriptions for town lots in Cincinnati have the prefix *Cin Twn*.

(b) *Congress Lands West of the [Great] Miami River.* Between the Great Miami River and the border with Indiana is a large tract of land in which grants were distributed through the Cincinnati Land Office. Ranges are numbered from 1 through 8 (in roman numerals), west to east (on Plate 3 these ranges are shown beginning between Union City and Fort Recovery). Parts of the following counties are within the tract: Butler, Darke, Hamilton, Logan, Mercer, Miami, Montgomery, Preble, Shelby, and Warren. Land descriptions bear the *Cin ---* prefix.

Plate 4. Ohio Congress Lands (Greenville Treaty)

As will be seen from the Orientation Map of Ohio, there was a long tract of land in north central Ohio stretching from the eastern boundary with Pennsylvania to approximately the middle of the state of Ohio. During the 1810-1814 period it was open to settlement, and a considerable number of grants were made through the Canton Land Office. The ranges in the district were numbered from 1 through 21 (in roman numerals on Plate 4), beginning at the eastern boundary of the state. The townships in each range were numbered from south to north, as shown in Table 1. The counties later organized in the tract include all or portions of Ashland, Carroll, Columbiana, Crawford, Ford, Holmes, Mahoning, Morrow, Richland, Stark, and Wayne. Land descriptions bear the *Can* prefix.

Maps 5, 6, and 7. Indiana

Three maps of the state of Indiana are presented herein. Map 5 shows the boundaries of the various land office districts as they eventually became about two decades after the period covered in Volume Three of the *Federal Land Series*. In 1810-1814 only the southern third of the state was open for settlement. Map 6 depicts

Table 1. Townships in the Congress Lands (Greenville Treaty)

Range	Township Numbers	Total Twps.
1	6 through 9	4
2	10 through 13	4
3	13 through 16	4
4	14 through 17	4
5	15 through 18	4
6	16 through 19	4
7	17 through 20	4
8	9 through 12	4
9	9 through 12	4
10	10* through 12	2+
10	1** through 2**	2
11	14* through 18	4+
12	14* through 18	4+
13	13* through 17	4+
14	17* through 21	4+
15	19* through 23	4+
16	19* through 23	4+
17	20* through 25	5+
18	18* through 23	5+
19	18* through 23	5+
20	17* through 22	5+
21***	13* through 18	5+

*Fractional township at southern boundary.

**No explanation given as to why these townships are so numbered; they correspond to 13 and 14, if sequentially numbered.

***Fractional range along western boundary of the tract.

the range-township numbering system which was instituted. Map 7 supplements the two preceding maps by showing the counties which were eventually organized in each of the districts.

(a) *Eastern Indiana Lands*. It will be seen from Map 5 that two wedge-shaped tracts on the eastern border of the state were distributed through the Cincinnati Land Office. Many grants in these tracts are to be found in the third volume of this series;

Table 2.   Summary of Ohio Maps

Land Office	Plate 1	Plate 2	Plate 3	Plate 4
Canton (*Can*)				
a. Congress Lands (Greenville Treaty)	–	–	–	Rg 1-21
Chillicothe (*Chl*)				
a. U.S. Military District (*Chl Mil*)	Rg 1-7	Rg 7-18*	–	–
b. Congress Lands East of Scioto River (*Chl ---*)	Rg 8-13	Rg 13-22*	–	–
Cincinnati (*Cin*)				
a. Symmes Purchase & Cincinnati town lots (*Cin EML, Cin WML, Cin Twn*)	–	–	Rg 1-2+	–
b. Region Between Two Miami Rivers & Daytown lots (*Cin MR, Cin Pre, Cin Day*)	–	–	Rg 3-14	–
c. Congress Lands West of Great Miami River (*Cin ---*)	–	–	Rg 1-8	–
Marietta (*Mar*)				
a. Ohio Company Purchases	Rg 8-13	Rg 13-15	–	–
b. Seven Ranges	Rg 1-7**	–	–	–
Steubenville (*Stu*)				
a. Seven Ranges	Rg 1-7**	–	–	–
b. Congress Lands East of Scioto River (*Stu*)	Rg 8	–	–	–
Zanesville (*Zan*)				
a. U.S. Military District (*Zan Mil, Mil ---*)	Rg 1-7	Rg 7-18*	–	–
b. Congress Lands East of Scioto River (*Zan ---*)	Rg 8-13	Rg 13-22*	–	–

*Chillicothe and Zanesville Land Offices distributed lands in the same tracts; applicants for land made entries in the nearest office.

**Both the Marietta and Steubenville Land Offices distributed land in Seven Ranges.

only relatively few in the first volume. Ranges are from 11 East through 15 East of the Second Principal Meridian (ranges shown in roman numerals in Map 5) and Township 1 North through 19 North for the eastern "wedge" (numbers directly on the Ohio boundary) and 10 North through 23 North for the "wedge" to the west of it. Land descriptions in these tracts bear the prefix *Cin Two*, referring to ranges east of the Second Principal Meridian. A few land descriptions bearing the *Cin Two* prefix, if correct, appear to be far to the west of the two "wedges," in lands later under the jurisdiction of the Indianapolis Land Office.

(b) *Jefferson District Lands*. Map 5 shows the extent of the district, including ranges 1 East through 6 East of the Second Principal Meridian (in roman numerals in Map 6), just west of Clark's Grant and the town of Jeffersonville itself, then continuing to 13 East in the northeastern corner of the district. The townships are numbered 1 South through 6 South of an east-west base line. Above that base line, the district included lands in township 1 North through 9 North (or 11 North in its northeastern corner) in range 1 East through 13 East (again, refer to Map 6 for greatest clarity).

In the tract index to Volume Three, some Jeffersonville land descriptions are shown as *Jef Two*, whereas most of the remainder are simply shown as *Jef ---*. Both prefixes cover the same areas; in some descriptions officials thought to include reference to the Second Principal Meridian, in others it was omitted.

(c) *Vincennes District Lands*. This large land office district covered ranges 1 West through 15 West, extending westward from the Second Principal Meridian to the Wabash River boundary with the state of Illinois. The townships were numbered 1 South of a base line through 8 South on the Ohio River, and townships 1 North of the base line through 16 North. As in the Jeffersonville case, the Vincennes Land Office may have made some early grants north and east of its final boundary in areas assigned to the Crawfordsville and Jeffersonville Land Offices. Map 7 shows the counties organized in the Vincennes Land Office district. Land descriptions bear the *Vin* prefix.

Maps 8 and 9. Illinois

Two maps of the state of Illinois are presented herein. Map 8 shows the boundaries of the various land office districts as they eventually became two or more decades after the period covered in Volume Three of the *Federal Land Series*. In the 1810-1814 period only the southern fourth of the state was legally open to settlement through the federal land-granting system (note, however, that Chicago and Peoria were long-established settlements outside the southern area). Map 9 depicts the range-township numbering system which was instituted. During the period covered by the third volume, neither the Kaskaskia nor Shawneetown Land Offices had completed any grants, although the first applications for land had been received.

(a) *Shawneetown District Lands*. The Shawneetown district will be most clearly seen from Map 8, bounded on the north by a base line, on the east and south by the Ohio River, and on the west by the Third Principal Meridian. The ranges run from 1 East through fractional 11 East of that Meridian. Townships are numbered from north to south, 1 South through 16 South of the base line. In the northeastern corner, around the town of Mount Carmel, the ranges are numbered 12 West through 14 West of the Second Principal Meridian; included therein are three complete townships and five fractional ones on the Wabash River. Although Map 9 does not show the counties included within the district, the main settlements and watercourses

are shown, which should give sufficient orientation for the researcher to compare with modern county maps.

(b) *Kaskaskia District Lands*. Map 8 clearly shows the extent
of the district, and Map 9 shows settlements and watercourses
therein. From the Third Principal Meridian on the east, ranges are
numbered 1 West through 10 West, with a fractional eleventh and
twelfth ranges on the Mississippi River northwest of the Kaskaskia
settlement. Townships run from 1 South through 17 South on the
Ohio River at Cairo. The Kaskaskia district had ancient settlements
of mainly French-speaking inhabitants. Their land claims, being
based upon grants from French and British sovereigns, were investi-
gated by a board of land commissioners. The results of hearings
conducted were published in the *American State Papers* and reindexed
in McMullin's *Grassroots of America*.

Maps 10 and 11. Alabama

Map 10 depicts the federal land office boundaries as they
became some decades after the 1810-1814 period covered in Volume
Three of the *Federal Land Series*. Map 11 shows the range-township
numbering system instituted in the state, as well as the major
watercourses and early settlements. For the period in question,
only the Huntsville Land Office district and the St. Stephens Land
Office district were active.

(a) *Old Madison County*. This county, at the northern boundary
of the state, was among the first areas in which grants were made.
Some of these grants were apparently made from temporary offices
in Nashville, Tennessee (not a land state), while the land office
being opened in Huntsville was still in its organizing stage.
Land descriptions in the county bear the prefixes *Mad* or *Nas*, and

all grants appear to have been near the town of Huntsville. Somewhat later, the descriptions in the county begin to bear the prefixes *Hun ---*, *Hun EML*, and *Hun WML*; all five prefixes refer to land in the same district.

(b) *Huntsville District Land*. As will be seen from both maps, the district extended both east and west of Huntsville Basis Meridian. The ranges are numbered 1 East to 13 East (eventually including the Cherokee and Creek concessions) and 1 West through 16 West to the boundary with the state of Mississippi. Townships are numbered from the Tennessee line southward through Township 22. At a later time, as will be seen from Map 10, parts of the district were split off to make the Coosa, Tallapoosa, and Tuscaloosa Land Office districts. Land descriptions carry the prefixes *Hun ---*, *Hun EML*, *Hun WML*, and as mentioned above, occasionally the prefixes *Mad* and *Nas*; all five prefixes refer to land in the same district, being merely the various ways in which early land officials expressed themselves before nomenclature was standardized.

(c) *St. Stephens District Land*. Map 11 discloses the original extent of the district; Map 10 shows the later divisions into Cahaba, Sparta, and Tallapoosa districts. Ranges were numbered east and west of St. Stephens Basis Meridian, close to the meandering course of the Tombigbee (Tombeckbee) River. Townships are numbered from south to north, 1 through 24. Map 11 shows these tract designations most clearly. In the 1810-1814 period there appear to have been no completed land grants in the district, although correspondence is reported.

Maps 12 and 13. Mississippi

The two maps for the state of Mississippi both postdate the 1810-1814 period by some decades. Only the two original districts--District West of Pearl River and District East of Pearl River--are of interest in the earliest period. Map 12 shows the various land office districts south of the Chickasaw Line with greater clarity than 13, which on the other hand is useful because it includes the counties.

(a) *District West of Pearl River*. The seat of the land office for the District West of Pearl River was at Washington in Adams County. As will be seen most clearly from Map 13, ranges ran from 1 West to 5 West on the Mississippi River and from 1 East to 14 East on the Pearl River. Townships are numbered from south to north, 1 through 18, ending just north of the mouth of the Yazoo River. Volume Three of this series reports a number of grants in the district; the land descriptions bear the prefixes *WPR* and *Wsh*; some descriptions will be seen to be defective, because they do not state whether the ranges are east or west of the base line. These omissions reflect the initial inexperience of early land office clerks and can only be clarified by search of later deeds and wills, to be found among the records of the appropriate counties.

(b) *District East of Pearl River*. The seat of the land office for the District East of Pearl River was first at Augusta, later at Paulding in Perry County. During the 1810-1814 period, there seems to have been difficulty in engaging competent officials for the land office, and certainly the amount of business transacted there was small in comparison with other offices. Ranges were numbered 5 through 18 east to west from the Alabama boundary to the Pearl River. Townships were numbered 1 South through 10 South (below Pass Christian) and from 1 North through 10 North. Land descriptions bear the *EPR* prefix. In Volume Three there are a number of *EPR* grants described as being in ranges 1 West and 2 West. These are thought to be in the area later organized into the

Choctaw Land Office district (Jackson), as they do not describe land in the District East of Pearl River. All other land descriptions in the district appear to be defective to one extent or another.

Maps 14 and 15. Louisiana

Volume One and Volume Three of the *Federal Land Series* have only scattered references to matters concerning the land offices in the state of Louisiana. During the 1810–1814 period, land office affairs at New Orleans reflected the uncertainties of the War of 1812, apparent corruption of officials, and the need for establishing the validity of land claims made under French and Spanish sovereigns. The Southwestern Land Office district (Opelousas), Southeastern Land Office district (New Orleans), and St. Helena Land Office district (Greensburg) were being organized, but there appear to have been no completed grants during the period, although correspondence is reported.

Map 14 shows the land office districts in Louisiana (some organized several decades after the time period covered in Volume Three), and Map 15 includes the parishes, making it possible for researchers to determine where later land records might be found.

Notes

1. During the period that the Detroit Land Office was closed down by the British occupants, land claims continued to be recorded and processed in Washington, although the patents were not issued until the Americans reentered the region.

2. Phillip W. McMullin, *Grassroots of America: A Computerized In-*

dex to the American State Papers: Land Grants and Claims (1789-1837) . . . (Salt Lake City, Utah: Gendex Corporation, 1972).

3. The *American State Papers* are official documents of the federal government, although privately printed in the period before the founding of the Government Printing Office. Since only 750 copies of the Gales & Seaton edition were printed, most libraries have microform copies, rather than the original volumes.

4. Communication from Carol Willsey Flavell, who has made a study of the land records of Columbiana County, one of the earliest counties organized in Ohio.

5. It should be understood that the purchasers' places of residence given in land office records are those which pertained at the time of the original application for the land and may not be the places of their birth. Thus, temporary or short-term residences--the most illusive of all for the genealogical researcher-- are often revealed.

6. Researchers interested in these prospective publications should contact Carol Willsey Flavell at 4649 Yarmouth Lane, Youngstown, Ohio 44512, for further information.

7. Margaret R. Waters, *Indiana Land Entries* (place and date of publication not given). Volume 1 thereof is subtitled *Cincinnati Land Office, 1801-1840* and covers all or parts of the following Indiana counties: Dearborn, Fayette, Franklin, Jay, Ohio, Randolph, Switzerland, Union, and Wayne. Volume II, Part I, is subtitled *Vincennes Land Office, 1807-1877* and covers the Indiana counties of Daviess, Gibson, Knox, Martin, and Pike, plus half of Monroe and Lawrence. These publications are available through Ye Olde Genealogie Shoppe, 9430 Vandergriff Road, Indianapolis, Indiana 46239.

8. Mayburt S. Riegel, *Early Ohioans' Residences from the Land Grant Records* (place and date of publication not given). This monograph is available through the Ohio Genealogical Society, Post Office Box 2625, Mansfield, Ohio 44906.

9. Lowell M. Volkel, *Shawneetown [Illinois] Land Office Records, 1814-1820* (Springfield, Ill.: privately printed, n.d.). It is available from the compiler, Post Office Box 635, Springfield, Illinois 62705.

10. Communication from the Ohio State Auditor's Office to Carol Willsey Flavell.

11. Carol Willsey Flavell, *Ohio Genealogical Guide* (Youngstown, Ohio: privately printed, 1978), pp. 58-63.

12. Esther W. Powell, *Early Ohio Tax Records* (Akron, Ohio: privately printed, 1971). It may be obtained from the compiler, 36 North Highland Avenue, Akron, Ohio 44303. The contents of this publication are listed in detail in Flavell, *op.cit.*, p. 37.

13. Ronald V. Jackson and others, *Ohio Tax List, 1800-1818* (Bountiful, Utah: Accelerated Indexing Systems, 1977). It may be obtained from the publisher, 3346 South Orchard Drive, Bountiful, Utah 84010.

14. Gerald M. Petty, *Ohio 1810 Tax Duplicate* (Columbus, Ohio: privately printed, 1977). It may be obtained from the compiler, 48 Chatham Road, Columbus, Ohio 43214.

15. For example, the land purchases of John H. Brinton of Philadelphia, a well-known lawyer, may eventually have been re-sold to Quaker purchasers.

16. *National Union Catalog of Manuscript Collections, 1959-* (Hamden, Conn.: Shoe String Press, 1959-). Although privately

published, this is an official publication of the Library of Congress which acts as clearinghouse for archival collections throughout the United States. The contents of state archives are not included, however.

17. Membership in the Ohio Genealogical Society is a further prerequisite to membership in First Families of Ohio. For the details, write to the Ohio Genealogical Society, Post Office Box 2625, Mansfield, Ohio 44906.

18. Albion M. Dyer, *First Ownership of Ohio Lands* (1911. Reprint Baltimore: Genealogical Publishing Company, 1969). Originally published in the *New England Historical and Genealogical Register*, volumes 64-65 (1910-1911). All in *Register* reprints, volume 37. Contains names of more than 1,000 proprietors of the Ohio Company, 1788-1792 [Filby No. 2699].

19. *Federal Land Series*, Volume One, entry 2580.

20. Ohio Cooperative Topographic Survey, *Original Ohio Land Subdivisions*, volume 3 (Ohio State Reformatory Press, 1925), p. 74. The complications of tract designations in the Cincinnati Land Office district are best described in chapter 6 of this publication, to which the researcher will wish to refer for further information.

Abbreviations

Can   Canton (Ohio) land office district

Chl   Chillicothe (Ohio) land office district

Cin   Cincinnati (Ohio) land office district

Day   Dayton, Ohio

Det   Detroit (Michigan) land office district

E   East

ELA   Land office for the eastern district of the State of Louisiana

EML   East Meridian Line; East of Meridian Line

EOr   East Orleans land office district; office located at New Orleans, Louisiana

EPR   East Pearl River land office district; office located at Fort St. Stephen

frac   Fraction; fractional section (*see also* +)

GLO   General Land Office, Washington, D. C.

Hun   Huntsville (Alabama) land office district

Jef   Jeffersonville (Indiana) land office district

Kas   Kaskaskia (Illinois) land office district

LS	Langham's Survey; this could also refer to Ludlow's Survey in some instances, but no distinction was made in the correspondence
LO	District land office
M	Meridian
Mad	Madison County (Mississippi Territory) land office district
Mar	Marietta (Ohio) land office district
Mil	United States Military District of Ohio, if appearing in the land office column of a tract description; if appearing in the meridian column of a tract description, it indicates that the tract was obtained under a military bounty land warrant
MR	Miami rivers; Miami Reserve; between the two Miami rivers
MS	Matthew's Survey
N	North
NA	National Archives, Washington, D. C.
Nas	Nashville (Tennessee) land office district
NOL	New Orleans, Louisiana
Opl	Opelousas, Louisiana
Pre	Preemption; claimed under preemption right
Rec	Receiver of public monies, the official having the responsibility for accepting payments for land; each land office had such an appointed official
Ref	Canadian and Nova Scotian Refugee Tract (Ohio)
Reg	Register, the official in charge of a district land office
Rg	Range
S	South
Sec	Section (usually 640 acres)

SG	Surveyor General of the United States
Shw	Shawneetown (Illinois) land office district
Stu	Steubenville (Ohio) land office district
Twp	Township; town
Unk	Unknown; used where land office district could not be determined from context or addressee of letter; researchers can often determine from other evidence (such as cross-indexed names) the probable land office where tract application was made
Vin	Vincennes (Indiana) land office district
W	West
WLA	Land office for the western district of the State of Louisiana
WML	West Meridian Line; West of Meridian Line
WOr	West Orleans land office district; office located at Opelousas, Louisiana
WPR	West Pearl River land office district; office located at Washington, Mississippi Territory
WS	Worthington's Survey
Wsh	Washington (Mississippi Territory) land office district (*see also* WPR)
Zan	Zanesville (Ohio) land office district
+	Plus sign in tract description indicates fraction of a section
−	Minus sign after the section means entire section was included

CALENDAR OF
ARCHIVAL MATERIAL

1   1 Jun 1810   A/4/142
John Williams, Waterford, Loudon County, Virginia
Transmits patents at request of James Ratchkin
John Heston   Stu - 6 13 30 SW
James Ratchkin   Stu - 7 15   1 NW
James Ratchkin   Stu - 7 15   1 SW
James Ratchkin   Stu - 7 15   1 SE

2   1 Jun 1810   A/4/143
Haris? Wiley, St. Clairsville, Ohio
Transmits patent
Haris? Wiley   Stu - 4   6   6 SE

3   4 Jun 1810   A/4/143
John R. Mills, Cincinnati
Transmits patents, per instruction of Hon. Jera-
    [miah?] Morrow
John R. Mills   Cin? EML 1   1 30   -
John R. Mills   Cin? EML 1   1 31 +*
    *"fraction, the island adjoining"

4   5 Jun 1810   A/4/143
LO Zan
Tranmits patents
William Adams   Mil - 10 3   1   E
Jonah Adams   Mil - 10 3   1 SW
Jonah Adams   Mil - 10 3 10 NW
Jonah Adams   Mil - 10 3   1 NW
Joshua W. Satterthwaite   Mil -   3 1 21 SE
Jonah Adams   Mil - 10 4 21 SE
Jonah Adams   Mil -   7 3 19 NE

5   5 Jun 1810   A/4/143-144
LO Stu
Transmits patents
Lindley [Lindsey?] Cannon   Stu - 2 11 26 NE
Daniel Crawford   Stu - 2 10 11 SE
Robert Parks   Stu - 7 12   3 SE
John Bockins   Stu - 5 13 23 NE
Ulrey [Ulrich] Shiveley   Stu - 7 19 29 NE
George Schultz   Stu - 4 11   8 NW
Henry Schooley   Stu - 6 14 28 SW
Thomas Neal   Stu - 4 14   1   W
Jacob Shenenberger   Stu - 8 11 35 NW
Thomas Cowgill   Stu - 2 11 14 NW
Benjamin Borton   Stu - 7 10   7 SW
Daniel Bair   Stu - 5 11   6 SE
Benjamin Borton   Stu - 7 10 13 SE
George Kerns   Stu - 1   9   7   -
Martin Houser   Stu - 7 20 20 SW
Adam Werner   Stu - 8 11 27   N

6   6 Jun 1810   A/4/144
LO Cin
Transmits patents
John Williams, heirs of   Cin MR 10 4   8   S
Samuel Phillips   Cin MR   5 2 26 NW
John Jay   Cin MR   5 3   8 NW
John Simmons   Cin MR 11 2 36 NE
Jacob Koutz   Cin MR   4 2 12 +*
Charles Null   Cin MR   4 3 11 NE
William P. Smith   Cin EML 2 7   2 SE
Joseph Trotter, Junior   Cin EML 2 7 36 SE
Joseph Conkling   Cin EML 1 4 14 SW
James Ludgrove   Cin EML 4 3   3   E
Peter Newcorner [Newcomer?] Cin EML 1 1   9 SW
John Brower   Cin EML 3 5 33 NE

Daniel Bowser   Cin EML 5 3 30 NE
William Sivisker   Cin EML 3 5 23 NW
Albert Bonta [Banta?]   Cin EML 4 3 31 SW
Robert Patterson & William
    Lindsey   Cin EML 6 1   6 +**
Philip Nagley   Cin EML 5 2 18   -
William Allenworth &
    William Ramey? [Rainey?] Cin WML 1 7 13   W
Abraham Bledso   Cin WML 1 8   9 SE
    *"E[ast] part of Fr[action]."
    **"Fractions 3, 4, 5, 9, 10."

7   6 Jun 1810   A/4/144-145
James Moore, Front Royal, Frederick County, Virginia
Acknowledges receipt of $75 for account of Edward
    Wilson; Wilson has not paid third installment, due
    14 Jun 1809
Edward Wilson   Zan - 9   1 13 SE

8   7 Jun 1810   A/4/145
J. H. Brinton, 279 Market Street, Philadelphia
Acknowledges receipt of $722.35 for several tracts
    of land, as mentioned in Brinton's letter of 4 Jun
    1810 to Treasurer of the United States. [These
    tracts not otherwise described, excepting "16
    cents on account of Mr. Candy's land"; see entry
    12 for listing.]

9   15 Jun 1810   A/4/145
LO Stu
Transmits patents
Isaac Miller   Stu - 4 12 28 SW
Abraham Wildman   Stu - 7 20 24 SE
Peter Kail   Stu - 5 11 18 NW
Samuel Jones   Stu - 2 11   5 SE
Benjamin Johnston   Stu - 6 11 10 SW
Robert Johnson   Stu - 7 20   1 SE
John Johnson   Stu - 6 11 27 NW
William Johnson   Stu - 6 10 18 NW
Hugh Davison   Stu - 9   9 14 NW
James Alman   Stu - 5   8 29 NE
Daniel Dunlevy   Stu - 2   6 25 NW
Richard Schooley   Stu - 4 15 17 SE
Jacob Bair   Stu - 8 11   3 SE

10   15 Jun 1810   A/4/146
LO Cin
Transmits patents
Joab Comstock   Cin EML 1 2 12 NE
Hugh Karr   Cin EML 1 1   9 SE
Christian Waggaman   Cin EML 4 5 25 SE
Silas Gregg   Cin EML 3 4 14 SW
John Weymire   Cin EML 5 5 25 NW
James Ocheltree   Cin EML 1 6 11 SW
John Trimble   Cin EML 5 8 13 SW
Joseph Kingery   Cin EML 1 6 32 NW
Joseph Kingery   Cin EML 1 6 32 NE
Aaron Tullis   Cin EML 6 5 20 NE
Isaac Bear   Cin EML 4 4 31 NW
Jacob Dilts   Cin EML 6 7 29 SE
Abraham Deter   Cin EML 5 5 17 NE
Francis Johnston   Cin EML 5 8 12 NE
Henry Obfal   Cin EML 5 5 20 NW
Henry Oler   Cin EML 4 3   8 NE
Andrew Hood   Cin EML 5 4   3 NE
Jonathan Justice   Cin EML 5 5 35 NE
Thomas Henderson   Cin WML 2 9 33 NW
David Hollingsworth   Cin WML 2 11 27 NE

John Keever	Cin	MR	4	4	29	SE
Michael Halberstall	Cin	MR	7	3	9	SE

11   15 Jun 1810   A/4/146
Peter Wilson [Rec Stu]
Encloses duplcate receipt for $722.35 paid by John
   H. Brinton "on account of sundry tracts of land
   in your district" [see entry 12 for listing]

12   15 Jun 1810   A/4/147
John H. Brinton, 279 Market Street, Philadelphia
Encloses receipt for $722.35 for following tracts:

--	$ 158.50	Stu	-	7	18	24	N
--	84.00*	Stu	-	8	10	20	SW
--	85.79	Stu	-	6	16	19	SW
--	79.04	Stu	-	7	17	23	NW
--	82.22	Stu	-	7	15	12	SW
--	154.99	Stu	-	6	16	12	E
--	77.51	Stu	-	6	16	12	SW
	722.35**					

  *"Including 16 cents for Mr. Candy."
  **Adds to $722.05.

13   15 Jun 1810   A/4/147
Jesse Spencer, Reg Chl
Transmits patent

John McMullen	Chl	-	17	18	14	S*

  * Half secton.

14   15 Jun 1810   A/4/147
John Dunkin, Post Office Middleburgh, Loudon County,
   Virginia
Transmits patent

John Dunkin	Stu	-	3	14	18	NE

15   15 Jun 1810   A/4/148
William Stevenson, Post Office, Baltimore
Transmits patent

William Stevenson	Chl	-	?	15	18	N

16   18 Jun 1810   A/4/148
Jesse Spencer, Reg Chl
Obstacles remain for patenting of Chl WS 21 9 34 NW
   to Edward Shirlock, because 2/3 of land already
   conveyed to Michael Senff, and because there is
   no certification that William McCoy was executor
   to Jane Mitchell. Encloses following receipts
   from Treasurer of the United States:

Nathan Wood	$ 92.12	Chl	-	14	8	12	SW
Thomas Ijams	´268.32	Chl	-	17	17	34	N

17   18 Jun 1810 A/4/148-149
Wyllys Silliman, Reg Zan
Requests final certificates for following:

Samuel Hill	Zan	-	12	13	3	NE
Adam Smith	Zan	-	10	1	22	SE
Adam Smith	Zan	-	10	1	21	NW
Adam Smith	Zan	-	10	1	19	NW
Adam Smith	Zan	-	10	1	19	NE

Also encloses receipts from Treasurer of the United
   States for the following:

Frederick Salmon	$ 186.21	Zan	-	1	9	1	NE
Philip Shutt	148.48	Zan	-	4	8	12	NE
Edward Wilson	75.00	Zan	-	9	1	13	SE

18   18 Jun 1810   A/4/149
Daniel Symmes, Reg Cin
Requests final certificate for Cin EML 3 6 33 SW in
   favor of Joseph Terrence. New patent for Jacob
   Hay transmitted [land description not given], as
   former patent was erroneous. Forwards following
   Treasury receipts:

Felix Welton [Walton?]	Cin	-	10	5	9	SE
Peter Ingleman	Cin	-	3	4	12	NW
Felix Wilton	Cin	-	10*	5	17	NE

   *[Could read Cin - 1 5 17 NE]

19   22 Jun 1810   A/4/150
John Kantner, Reading, Pennsylvania
Acknowledges receipt of papers "relative to claim of
   Peter Hoofnagle to bounty land, with his power of
   attorney to George Hoofnagle." To be forwarded to
   the Secretary of War.

20   22 Jun 1810   A/4/150
Isaac Ozman [Ozmeier?], Lawrenceville, Tuscarawa
   County, Ohio
Acknowledges receipt of letter and will forward to
   Secretary of War; James Sherwood and Nicholas
   Brown mentioned. [Apparently concerning bounty-
   land warrant.]

21   25 Jun 1810   A/4/150
LO Cin
Transmits patents

Joseph Burrowes	Cin	MR	7	2	11	NE
Benjamin Pearson	Cin	EML	5	7	33	NE
James Steel	Cin	MR	9	5	13	NW
Robert Richardson	Cin	EML	4	2	11	SE
William Swaford	Cin	EML	2	6	34	SE
Frederick Sheffer	Cin	EML	4	3	8	SE
Thomas Ramsey	Cin	EML	2	5	27	SE
John Bern?	Cin	EML	4	3	27	NE
Joseph Kingery	Cin	EML	1	6	31	SE
Knowles Shaw	Cin	EML	2	3	32	SE
Jacob Slifer	Cin	EML	4	4	10	SW
Alexander Cochran	Cin	EML	5	7	33	W
Valentin Giphart	Cin	EML	5	3	2	-
Robert Orbison	Cin	EML	3	3	31	W
Philip & Jacob Kemp, fl?	Cin	EML	4	2	15	-
Philip & Jacob Kemp, fl?	Cin	EML	4	2	16	-
William Jones	Cin	EML	3	3	17	SE

22   27 Jun 1810   A/4/151
LO Stu
Transmits patents

Christian Storch	Stu	-	8	10	12	SW
John Smith	Stu	-	1	6	18	SE
Christian Shively	Stu	-	5	17	35	-
John Shaw	Stu	-	7	18	12	SE
Nicholas Stump	Stu	-	9	9	10	SW
Jacob Smyer	Stu	-	4	10	6	SW
John Sluss?	Stu	-	7	18	19	SW
John Sluts	Stu	-	4	11	12	SW
Adam Schaeffer	Stu	-	8	11	23	NW
Aaron Stanton	Stu	-	6	19	11	NW
James Stanton	Stu	-	6	19	12	NW
John Moore	Stu	-	2	3	32	NE
John Lamb	Stu	-	6	10	12	SW
John Pugh	Stu	-	6	11	10	NE
Micajah Macy	Stu	-	5	18	33	NE
John Stokesberry	Stu	-	2	11	14	SW

Benjamin Murphy	Stu	–	6	9	10	NW
Conrad Simmerman	Stu	–	4	15	23	SE
Thomas Hailey	Stu	–	8	11	29	NW
John Ruff	Stu	–	8	11	23	SW
John Ruff	Stu	–	8	11	26	NW
George Starbuck	Stu	–	6	8	23	SW

23   27 Jun 1810   A/4/152
Samuel Russell, Hillsborough, Loudon County, Virginia
Transmits patent

Samuel Russell	Stu	–	2	10	11	NW

24   27 Jun 1810   A/4/152
John Anspach or David Sleighter, Chambersburg, Pennsylvania
Transmits patent

James Taylor & Robert McConnell	Zan	–	6	1	7	W

"N.B.: John Anspach on the 6th August 1810 produced the above patent, and a transfer of the land to him, W. Jones, dated 26 May 1807; and had the patent altered at Dept. in favor of J. Gardiner, George & John Anspach."

25   27 Jun 1810   A/4/152
Daniel Symmes, Reg Cin
Encloses first certificate and receipt

John Zeller*	Cin	EML	5	3	32	NW

*Endorsed to Henry Houtz.

26   5 Jul 1810   A/4/153
LO Cin
Transmits patents

Samuel Moore [Moorer?]	Cin	WML	1	8	10	SE
Benjamin Owen	Cin	EML	6	2	6	SE
Amos Butler	Cin	WML	2	9	29	SW
Caleb Esterling	Cin	WML	2	12	11	NW
Ephraim Owen	Cin	EML	5	4	1	NW
Mary Everton	Cin	WML	1	13	9	SW
Robert Richardson	Cin, Square 3, Lot 4					–
Andrew Fouts	Cin	EML	4	4	23	SW
John Stedham	Cin	EML	5	7	32	SW
Robert Blackburn	Cin	EML	1	2	13	NE
Henry Steddam	Cin	WML	1	13	2	NE
Daniel Crissman [Cripman?]	Cin	EML	3	4	11	NE

27   5 Jul 1810   A/4/153
LO Stu
Transmits patents

John Woods	Stu	–	6	19	8	NW
Ephraim Holloway	Stu	–	2	11	5	NW
Thomas Rowland	Stu	–	3	9	24	NE
William Ewing	Stu	–	8	10	2	SE
Daniel Easley	Stu	–	7	11	18	SE
George Ramsey	Stu	–	7	17	10	NW
James Caldwell	Stu	–	5	8	26	NE
Henry Carver	Stu	–	5	9	27	SE
William Chapman	Stu	–	8	11	1	SW
George Nees	Stu	–	8	10	30	NE
Robert Cunningham	Stu	–	3	14	32	SW
James Hanna	Stu	–	4	10	35	SE
Peter Hack	Stu	–	8	10	25	NW

28   5 Jul 1810   A/4/154
LO Jef
Transmits patents

Adam Bower	Jef	N 9E	1	15	NE
George Shannon	Jef	N10E	4	36	SW
John McMillan	Jef	N10E	4	33	NE
David Glass	Jef	N 4E	2	9	SW
George Shannon	Jef	N 9E	3	24	NW

29   5 Jul 1810   A/4/154
Messrs. Bohn, Slingluff, & Deardorff, Baltimore
Transmits patents

Bohn, Slingluff, & Deardorff Mil*	–	3	8	3	NE
Bohn, Slingluff, & Deardorff Mil*	–	3	8	2	NW
Bohn, Slingluff, & Deardorff Mil*	–	3	8	1	NE

*Zanesville

30   5 Jul 1810   A/4/154
Robert Russell, Swicker's Gap, Loudon County, Virginia
Transmits patent

Robert Russell	Stu	–	6	10	14	SE

31   6 Jul 1810   A/4/155
John Brinton, Philadelphia
Gives amounts due on each of following tracts [dollar amounts omitted herein]

––	Unk	–	9	9	26	–
––	Unk	–	9	9	5	–
––	Unk	–	9	9	6	–
––	Unk	–	9	9	8	–
––	Unk	–	9	9	22	–
––	Unk	–	10	1	4	–
––	Unk	–	10	1	9	–
––	Unk	–	10	1	5	–
––	Unk	–	10	1	6	–
––	Unk	–	7	15	14	E
––	Unk	–	9	9	2	SE
––	Unk	–	9	9	3	NW
––	Unk	–	9	9	4	SW
––	Unk	–	9	9	23	NW
––	Unk	–	4	17	4	SE
––	Unk	–	4	17	4	SW
––	Unk	–	4	17	9	NW
––	Unk	–	4	17	14	NW
––	Unk	–	5	17	13	SW
––	Unk	–	6	17	10	NE
––	Unk	–	6	18	34	NE
––	Unk	–	6	18	34	NW
––	Unk	–	6	18	34	SW
––	Unk	–	7	20	25	NE

32   6 Jul 1810   A/4/156
Col. James Taylor, Newport, Kentucky
Transmits patents

James Taylor	Mil	–	16	7	4	8
James Taylor	Mil	–	15	1	3	13
Oldham & Taylor	Mil	–	16	7	4	13
Oldham & Taylor	Mil	–	16	7	4	14
Oldham & Taylor	Mil	–	16	7	4	15

33   6 Jul 1810   A/4/156
George Nigh, Hagerstown, Maryland
Transmits patent

George Nigh	Chl	–	20	12	9	SE

34   9 Jul 1810   A/4/156
Peter Wilson, [Rec Stu]
Reports overpayment and sends refund

Joshua Antrim   [Stu] -   7 20 23 SE

35   16 Jul 1810   A/4/157
Obadiah Jennings, Stu
Acknowledges receipt of final certificate in favor
  of John Way, assignee of the administrators of
  John Hough, original purchaser of Stu? - 6 19
  5 NW.
Also instructs that patent in name of George Kernes
  for Stu - 1 9 7 -, already forwarded to Stu,
  should be returned, because it should not have
  issued to a deceased person; new patent to issue
  in name of heirs.

36   10 Jul 1810   A/4/157
Wyllys Silliman, [Reg Zan]
Returns document purporting to transfer Zan - 1
  3 8 NW from William Welch to James Welch, Junior, for lack of signature.

37   23 Jul 1810   A/4/157
Samuel Hill, Gettysburg, Adams County, Pennsylvania
Small amount remains due on purchase
Samuel Hill   Zan - 12 13   3 NE

38   23 Jul 1810   A/4/157
Wyllys Silliman, [Reg Zan]
Transmits Treasury receipt
Samuel Hill   Zan - 12 13   3 NE

39   23 Jul 1810   A/4/157
Jesse Spencer, [Reg Chl]
Transmits Treasury receipts
Jacob Claypoole   [Chl] - 19 15 21 SE
David Bussard   [Chl] - 16 17   4 SE

40   23 Jul 1810   A/4/158
David Sample, Lewistown, Pennsylvania
Transmits Treasury receipt
David Sample   Cin -*   2   6 30 NW
*EML, per entry 48.

41   23 Jul 1810   A/4/158
David Hoge, [Reg Stu]
Transmits certificates and Treasury receipts
Isaac Walker   [Stu] -   4 17 10 SE
John Wilson   [Stu] -   5 18   9 NW
John Wilson   [Stu] -   5 18   9 NE

42   23 Jul 1810   A/4/158
Daniel Symmes, [Reg Cin]
Transmits first certificate
David Sample   Cin -*   2   6 30 NW
*EML, per entry 48.

43   23 Jul 1810   A/4/158
John Badollet, [Reg Vin]
Transmits certificate and Treasury receipt
Jacob Funk   [Vin] - 2E 5S   2 +

44   8 Aug 1810   A/4/158
T. H. Brinton, Market Street, Philadelphia

Regarding outstanding balance due
--   Stu -   7 20 25 NW

45   7 Aug 1810   A/4/159
Charles Robertson, Post Office, Zanesville
Encloses lengthy list of vacant lots remaining in
  the [United States] Military District. [This list
  not reproduced herein.]

46   10 Aug 1810   A/4/160
William Reynolds, Canton, [Ohio]
Transmits patent
Philip Slusser   Unk -   8 10 10 SE

47   10 Aug 1810   A/4/160
Isaac Vanhorne, Rec Zan
Requests information regarding payment by Hugh
  McCaully for land [not described] bought origin-
  ally by Daniel Converse.

48   20 Aug 1810   A/4/161
Daniel Symmes, [Reg Cin]
Reports payment made by
David Sample   Cin EML   2   6 30 NW
Also, transmits certificates for
David Osborne, assignee   Cin MR   12   5   9 SE
David Osborne, assignee   Cin MR   12   5   9 NW
Dennis Boyse, assignee   Cin EML   2   5 19 NW
David Reese   Cin WML   1   5 20 W
David Reese   Cin WML   1   5 19 NE
David Reese   Cin WML   1   5 21 -
David Reese   Cin WML   1   5 22 +
David Reese   Cin WML   1   5 23 +
Philip Corner? [Comer?]   Cin MR   12   3   8 NE

49   21 Aug 1810   A/4/161
John Pigott, care of Dr. Heaton, near Waterford,
  Loudon County, Virginia
Transmits patent
John Pigott?   Stu -   5   9 26 NW

50   22 Aug 1810   A/4/162
LO Cin
Transmits patents
John Kaylor   Cin EML   6   1 17 +
John Kaylor   Cin EML   6   1 18 +
John Kaylor   Cin EML   5   3 13 +
J. Smith, heirs & devisees Cin EML   2   6 28 E
Thomas Ewing   Cin EML   1   1 21 -
Thomas Ewing   Cin EML   1   1 22 +
Thomas Ewing   Cin EML   1   1 27 -
Thomas Ewing   Cin EML   1   1 28 +
David Patty   Cin EML   5   5   8 NW
John Price, Junior   Cin EML   2   5   8 SE
Peter Parham   Cin EML   2   7   2 NW
Jacob Kercher   Cin EML   4   4 24 SE
Jacob Kercher   Cin EML   4   4 24 NE
Joseph Seller   Cin EML   2   7 10 NE
Robert Dixon   Cin EML   5   7   7 NW
Boston Hoblet   Cin EML   6   2   1 SW*
Mathias Roll   Cin EML   4   4 34 +*
Charles Hilliar   Cin EML 11   1 30 +*
John Weaver   Cin EML   6   1 17 +*
John Craft   Cin EML   5   3   1 +*
John Weaver   Cin EML   6   1 18 +*
John Willson   Cin EML   5   3   4 +*

George Holman	Cin	WML	1	13	17	NE
John Stoneberger	Cin	MR	12	4	31	SE
John Wolf	Cin	MR	12	3	30	W

*Pre-emptions.

51 22 Aug 1810 A/4/162
LO Stu
Transmits patents

Martin Hammon	Stu	-	7	18	5	SW
Elizabeth Toole, Senior	Stu	-	5	10	20	NW
Thomas Conn	Stu	-	5	18	25	SE
James Watson	Stu	-	1	8	21	NE
Abram Betz	Stu	-	3	10	31	-
Abram Betz	Stu	-	3	10	25	-
George Shidler	Stu	-	7	19	13	S

52 22 Aug 1810 A/4/163
LO Chl
Transmits patents

Henry Drum	Chl	-	20	11	4	SW
James Chambers	Chl	-	19	12	6	NW
Abraham Plummer	Chl	-	20	15	31	NE
Jared Graham	Chl	WS	21	9	6	SE
Thomas Crow	Chl	WS	21	10	25	SW
Jared Graham	Chl	WS	21	10	34	NE
Martin Kettry? [Kelly?]	Chl	-	20	14	10	SE
Gideon Gairy	Chl	-	18	16	6	E
Gideon Gairy	Chl	-	18	16	6	NW
Edward Teal	Chl	-	17	18	31	E
Christian Grumrine	Chl	-	16	17	32	NE
George Gaul	Chl	-	19	11	9	NW
William Kendal *et al*	Chl	-	17	2	32	+
Michael Senff	Chl	WS	21	9	34	NW
Peter Ruffner, heirs & legal representatives of	Chl	-	17	17	32	-
Elisha Decker	Chl	MS	21	10	10	SE

53 22 Aug 1810 A/4/163
LO Zan
Transmits patents

William Reynolds	Zan	-	11	13	2	SE
Daniel Horne	Zan	-	15	17	36	SE
Samuel Ream	Zan	-	15	17	31	SW
John Hendricks	Zan	-	15	17	17	NW
Nathan Hawthorne	Zan	-	15	17	31	NW
George & Thomas Ritchie	Zan	-	8	8	6	SE
David Stokely	Zan	-	14	15	34	SW
Jacob Hammer	Zan	-	15	17	32	NE
Robert Caldwell	Zan	-	9	6	3	NE
William Ford	Zan	-	14	15	34	NE
Robert Mossman	Zan	-	8	4	10	NE
John Watermire	Zan	-	14	15	26	NW

54 30 Aug 1810 A/4/164
Isaac Vanhorne, [Rec Zan]
Transmits Treasury receipt

| Levi Deaver | Zan | - | ? | 14 | 36 | NW |

55 31 Aug 1810 A/4/164
Jesse Spencer, [Reg Chl]
Reports chain of title incomplete for tract
  Chl - 20 2 16 + whereby certificate transferred from Alexander Burnside & Andrew Poole to Amos Wheeler, John Hatch, & John Taylor. Defective papers acknowledged before John Brown.

56 4 Sep 1810 A/4/164
LO Cin
Transmits patents

Samuel Boogher	Cin	Pre	7	2	25	SE
Isaac Ward	Cin	Pre	5	3	13	-
William Irwin	Cin	Pre	6	2	3	NW+
John Paul	Cin	Pre	7	3	7	-
John Paul	Cin	Pre	7	3	25	SE
Jacob Coy	Cin	Pre	7	3	25	W
Peter Layman	Cin	Pre	7	2	27	NE
William Bruce	Cin	EML	2	8	34	SE
William Bruce	Cin	EML	2	7	3	-
Abraham Hartzell	Cin	EML	3	3	25	W
Peter Raker	Cin	EML	5	3	30	SE
Othniel Looker	Cin	EML	1	2	20	NW
William Law	Cin	EML	6	3	19	NW
David Krater	Cin	EML	4	6	24	NE
John Rench	Cin	EML	5	5	19	SW
William McKinstry	Cin	EML	2	4	3	NW
John Hancock	Cin	EML	1	4	1	SE
George Roudebush	Cin	EML	4	4	29	SW
Levi Jennings	Cin	EML	4	2	31	-
Levi Jennings	Cin	EML	4	2	32	+
Levi Jennings	Cin	EML	4	2	33	+
Thomas Henderson	Cin	WML	2	9	32	W
William Russell	Cin	WML	1	7	11	E
John Myers	Cin	WML	1	11	36	NE
Robert McConnell	Cin	WML	1	6	14	SE
George Gillespie	Cin	MR	4	3	29	NE
James Galloway, Junior	Cin	MR	7	4	29	+
Ichabod Corwin	Cin	MR	4	4	26	SE

57 4 Sep 1810 A/4/165
LO Stu
Transmits patents

Matthew Worstell	Stu	-	3	15	25	NW
George Adam Hantz	Stu	-	8	11	19	NW
Adam Wise	Stu	-	7	19	24	-
David Smith	Stu	-	6	8	1	NW
Charles Hay? [Hoy?]	Stu	-	1	6	35	NW
Michael Zahner	Stu	-	5	16	2	-
Joel Judkins	Stu	-	6	8	27	NE
Carolus Judkins	Stu	-	6	8	27	SE
Richard Carle	Stu	-	4	16	10	SW
William Scott	Stu	-	3	11	32	NE
John & Andrew Kepler	Stu	-	9	12	17	E
John Endsley	Stu	-	5	11	17	SW
William Rippith	Stu	-	7	14	5	NE
George Warschler	Stu	-	9	12	24	NW
Joseph Reeves	Stu	-	3	15	22	NW
Adam Fost	Stu	-	4	17	1	SW
Daniel Long	Stu	-	7	9	33	SW
John Crawford	Stu	-	2	9	34	NW
Nicholas Miller	Stu	-	4	15	24	NE
Benjamin Scattergood	Stu	-	2	11	31	NW
Samuel Hatchinson	Stu	-	5	10	13	NE

58 4 Sep 1810 A/4/166
John H. Brinton, Merchant, Philadelphia
Encloses Treasurer's receipts for undescribed lands
  in Stu district.

59 4 Sep 1810 A/4/166
Obadiah Jennings, Stu
Transmits patent

| Baltzer Young? | Stu | - | 4 | 7? | 12 | E |

60   12 Sep 1810   A/4/167
William Mallery, Harper's Ferry
Comments on Treasurer's receipt sent to Cin LO and
   assignment from James Hendricks.

61   12 Sep 1810   A/4/167
Jesse Spencer, [Reg Chl]
Reports payment deficiency

Solomon Cox	Chl	-	20	8	34	-

62   12 Sep 1810   A/4/167
John N. Cummings, Newark, New Jersey
Transmits copy of patent

John N. Cummings, John Burnet, & George William Burnet	Mil	-	12	2	4*	-

*Described as a "quarter."

63   2 Sep 1810   A/4/167
Joseph Nourse, Reg Washington
Communication respecting Thomas Worthington from
   John G. Jackson, Clarksburg. Asks about land
   transaction at falls of Hockhocking [Ohio] and
   the mileage Colonel Worthington charged as U.S.
   Senator.

64   12 Sep 1810   A/4/168
J. G. Jackson
Reply by J. Nourse to preceding letter. Land is in
   Chl - 17 14 10 E, originally purchased by
   Henry Massie and assigned by him to Worthington,
   to whom it was patented. Comments laconically on
   amount paid for Senator Worthington's travel expenses to Washington.

65   14 Sep 1810   A/4/169
Samuel Gwathmey, [Reg Jef]
Notes an error in land description:

Thomas Montgomery (per certificate)	Jef	-	9E	2N	12	SW
Thomas Montgomery (per application)	Jef	-	8E	2N	12	SW

66   12 Sep 1810   A/4/169
Obadiah Jennings, Stu
Corrects patent issued to Thomas Mills to Thomas
   Miles.

67   14 Sep 1810   A/4/169
Daniel Symmes, [Reg Cin]
Transmits Treasurer's receipts for:

Dennis Boyse	Cin	-	2E	5	18	SE
Samuel Bond	Cin	-	1	5	9	SW
Samuel Bond	Cin	-	1	5	9	SE
Samuel Bond	Cin	-	1	5	5	SE
Samuel Bond	Cin	-	1	5	19	SW
William Cummings	Cin	-	2	6	36	SW

Requires further authentication on following certificates:

Robert Patterson & John Clark	Cin EML	3E	3	26	W
Abijah Jones	Cin EML	6	3	30	SE
George Brenner	Cin EML	4	5	12	SE

Notes discrepancies in following accounts and requests clarification:

Peter Dill	Cin	-	4E	3	30	NW
James Alexander	Cin	-	1W	14	36	NW
James Ireland	Cin	-	1W	14	36	SW
Beal Butler	Cin	-	1W	12	18	NW

68   15 Sep 1810   A/4/170
Wyllys Silliman, [Reg Zan]
Land description to be corrected:

Martin Overholder	Zan	-	8	3	12*	NW

*Erroneous, as this is a lot number.

69   15 Sep 1810   A/4/170
Peter Wilson, [Rec Stu]
Transmits Treasurer's receipts

John H. Brinton	Stu	-	9	9	22	-
John H. Brinton	Stu	-	10	1	4	-
John H. Brinton	Stu	-	10	1	9	-
John H. Brinton	Stu	-	7	15	14	E
John H. Brinton	Stu	-	9	9	2	SE
John H. Brinton	Stu	-	9	9	3	NW
John H. Brinton	Stu	-	9	9	4	SW
John H. Brinton	Stu	-	9	9	23	NW
John H. Brinton	Stu	-	4	17	4	SE
John H. Brinton	Stu	-	4	17	4	SW
John H. Brinton	Stu	-	4	17	9	NW
John H. Brinton	Stu	-	4	17	14	NW
John H. Brinton	Stu	-	5	17	13	SW
John H. Brinton	Stu	-	6	17	10	NE
John H. Brinton	Stu	-	6	18	34	NE
John H. Brinton	Stu	-	6	18	34	NW
John H. Brinton	Stu	-	6	18	34	SW
John H. Brinton	Stu	-	7	20	25	NE
Obed Pierpoint	Stu	-	6	18	14	SW
Francis Pierpoint	Stu	-	6	18	5	NW

70   15 Sep 1810   A/4/170
Jesse Spencer, [Reg Chl]
Transmits Treasury receipts for:

George Dove & George Shoemaker	Chl	-	20*	15	6	NW
Jesse Gause	Chl	-	18	16	7	NE
Edward Berry	Chl	-	18	16	13	SE
Jacob Ruse	Chl	-	21	11	1	SE

Transmits first certificates for:

[George] Dove & [George] Shoemaker, assignees	Chl	-	18*	15	6	NW
Jesse Gause	Chl	-	18	16	7	NE
Edward Berry	Chl	-	18	16	13	SE
Jacob Ruse	Chl	MS	21	11	1	SE

*Note discrepancy in land description; but see also
   following entry.

71   15 Sep 1810   A/4/171
Bryan Thompson, Merchant, Alexandria, [Virginia]
Transmits Treasury receipt

George Dove & George Shoemaker	Chl	-	20	15	6	NW

72   17 Sep 1810   A/4/171
Daniel Symmes, [Reg Cin]
Transmits assignment from Zachariah Hole to John Eckman and notes error in land description

John Eckman [correct]	Cin	-	3E	7	23	SW
John Eckman [erroneous]	Cin	-	3E	7	23	NW

73
David Hoge, [Reg Stu]   25 Sep 1810   A/4/171
Patent originally sent to Adam Siebert at Winchester,
Virginia, but returned addressee unknown. Letter
now received from J. G. Hening of Stu asking that
patent be transmitted to you
Adam Siebert   Stu? -   4   8   9   -

74   25 Sep 1810   A/4/171
Joseph Vance, Franklinton, Ohio
Lot desired has already been patented to another
  person.

75   27 Sep 1810   A/4/172
Jesse Spencer, [Reg Chl]
Requires further authentication for various transac-
tions involving Zane family. Mentions Elizabeth
  Sprigg; Thomas Rees (an original purchaser);
  Ludwick Wolsley; Zebulon Warner, Hugh Boyle, &
  Adam Weaver (all magistrates); John Zane's will.
Noah Zane & William Wells   Chl - 17 17 23   -
Noah Zane   Chl - 19 14 11   -
Noah Zane   Chl - 19 14 12 E?

76   25 Sep 1810   A/4/172
LO Cin
Transmits patents
Christopher Wilter   Cin WML 1 11 13 SW
John Allen   Cin WML 1   8 29 NW
John Melholland   Cin WML 2   8   3 SE
Jonathan Cox   Cin EML 6   2   6 NW
Jesse Kenworthy   Cin EML 3   4 32 NW
Samuel Brown, Senior   Cin EML 5   8 19 SE
Stephen McFarland   Cin EML 1   4 24 SE
John Varshimman?   Cin EML 5   4 32 NE
Ephraim Scudder   Cin EML 1   4 13 NW
John Bake   Cin EML 3   3 23 NE
Samuel Martin   Cin EML 5   7 12 NE
James Hellaugh   Cin EML 2   6 29 SE
Frederick Miller   Cin EML 3   6 34   -

77   28 Sep 1810   A/4/173
LO Stu
Transmits patents
John Way   Stu -   6 19   5 NW
Joseph Reeves   Stu -   3 15 15 SW
Joseph Reeves   Stu -   3 15 15 SE
Peter Fornig   Stu -   6 13   8 NW
John McDonald   Stu -   2 10 27 SE

78   28 Sep 1810   A/4/173
John Badollet, [Reg Vin]
Transmits patents
Eli Wright   Vin - 4E 4S   4 NE
George Humphreys   Vin - 11W 1S 34 NE
George Doup   Vin - 3E 3S 35 SE*
*Sent to Reg Jef.

79   28 Sep 1810   A/4/173
Samuel Gwathmey, [Reg Jef]
Transmits patent, per Doup's instruction
George Doup   Vin - 3E 3S 35 SE

80   28 Sep 1810   A/4/173
Henry Houtz, Lebanon, [Pennsylvania?]

Henry Houtz   Cin EML 5   3 31 NW

81   28 Sep 1810   A/4/173
Jesse Spencer, [Reg Chl]
Transmits patent
Isaac Evans   Chl WS 21 11 26 N

82   28 Sep 1810   A/4/173
LO Can
Transmits patents
Henry Hauger   Can - 13 13 10 SE
David Smith   Can - 13 15   6 NE

83   28 Sep 1810   A/4/173
David Osborne, Shepherds Town, Virginia
Transmits patent
David Osborne   [Cin] [MR*] 12   5   9 NW
David Osborne   [Cin] [MR*] 12   5   9 SE
*"Between the Great Miami River and the Virginia
  reservation."

84   3 Oct 1810   A/4/174
LO Cin
Transmits patents
John Ewing   Cin WML 2 10 17 SE
Henry Florey?   Cin EML 5   5 32 SE
Henry Florey?   Cin EML 5   5 32 SW

85   3 Oct 1810   A/4/174
LO Chl
Transmits patents
David Augustus   Chl MS 22   4 14 SW
Thomas Evans   Chl - 20 13   2 NE
Daniel Stevenson   Chl MS 21 11 13 SE
Charles Rairy?   Chl MS 21 11 33 S
Jacob Hautz   Chl - 17 17 13 SE
Jacob Broomback   Chl - 19 16 28 NW
John Ford   Chl - 20 15   1 SW
Isaac Larick   Chl - 19 11   7 NE
Benjamin Tallman   Chl - 20 15 19 SW
Jacob Alspack, Junior   Chl - 19 15   2 NW
William Ewing   Chl MS 21 10 34 SE
William Ewing   Chl MS 21   9   3 NE
John Dunckall   Chl - 19 11 23 NE
William Davidson   Chl - 17   1   5 +
David Bright   Chl MS 21 10 14 NE

86   3 Oct 1810   A/4/174
Philip Comer, Shenandoah County, Virginia
Transmits patent
Philip Comer   [Cin?] [MR*] 12   3   8 NE
*Between the great Miami River and the Virginia reser-
  vation.

87   8 Oct 1810   A/4/175
David Hoge, [Reg Stu]
Certificate returned for insufficient payment:
   James Sinclair, Senior   Stu -   5   7 18   -
Certificate and Treasury receipt forwarded:
   Jacob Hosteller   Stu -   6 17 36 NE
   Jacob Hosteller   Stu -   5 16 31 NW

88   8 Oct 1810   A/4/175
Jesse Spencer, [Reg Chl]

Transmits first certificates and Treasury receipts:

John Kerlin	Chl	–	17 17	21	NE
John Peden	Chl	–	16 17	2	NW

89   8 Oct 1810   A/4/175
Daniel Symmes, [Reg Cin]
Transmits certificates

John Groves*	Cin	MR	10 4	15	SE
George Logan**	Cin	MR	7 4	24	+

  *Transferred from John Chandler.
  **Transferred from William Logan.

90   8 Oct 1810   A/4/175
Jared Mansfield, [Surveyor General]
Surveying errors suspected in following tracts:

--	Cin	–	1W 14	36	–*
--	Cin	–	4E 3	30	–*

*Surveyed by Ludlow in 1800, 1801.

91   22 Oct 1810   A/4/176
LO Cin
Transmits patents

Eli Cook	Cin	EML	2 5	11	NW
James Charlton	Cin	EML	1 3	33	NW
John Croll	Cin	EML	5 3	5	SE
James Brown	Cin	EML	1 6	24	SE
Nathan Seller	Cin	EML	2 7	10	SW
Joseph Hollingsworth	Cin	EML	5 4	1	NE
Ebenezer Elliot	Cin	EML	1 6	26	SE
George Sinks	Cin	EML	5 5	2	SE
Thomas Williams	Cin	WML	2 9	19	SE
Moses Lyon	Cin	WML	1 7	14	NE
Aaron Martin	Cin	WML	1 13	30	NE
John Star	Cin	WML	1 12	9	NW
Henry Eisinger?	Cin	WML	5 3	31	SW
Henry Stansell	Cin	WML	5 3	34	+*
Benjamin Evans	Cin	WML	4 4	14	SW*
Jacob Coy	Cin	WML	7 2	7	SE*
Elisha Harbour	Cin	MR	12 4	20	NE
Ralph French	Cin	MR	9 2	25	NE
Elisha Harbour	Cin	WML	11 4	18	NE*

*Preemption.

92   22 Oct 1810   A/4/176
John Wilson, Hopewell Township [state not given]
Transmits patents

John Wilson	Stu	–	5 18	9	NE
John Wilson	Stu	–	5 18	9	NW

93   24 Oct 1810   A/4/176
John Cox Stockston, Zaneville
Returns military bounty land warrant 462 in favor
  of Thomas Mitchell, "a fifer in the late Rhode
  Island line," for proper endorsement and a power
  of attorney whereby Mitchell authorized Elisha
  Matthewson to sell the warrant.

94   24 Oct 1810   A/4/176
LO Chl
Transmits patents

John Good, Senior	Chl	–	17 18	17	SE
Jacob Huver	Chl	MS	21 9	5	SE
John Davis	Chl	–	17 16	2	SW

95   24 Oct 1810   A/4/177

Wyllys Silliman, [Reg Zan]
Transmits first certificates and Treasury receipts

Samuel Mandenhall*	Zan	–	9 3	13	W
Samuel Mandenhall*	Zan	–	9 3	19	NW
Samuel Mandenhall*	Zan	–	9 3	18	E
Samuel Mandenhall*	Zan	–	9 3	13	SE

*[Probably should read Mendenhall.]

96   24 Oct 1810   A/4/177
Jesse Spencer, [Reg Chl]
Transmits certificates and Treasury receipts

John Dunkle	Chl	–	19 11	24	NW
John Dunkle	Chl	–	21 11	8	NE
Samuel Noble*	Chl	–	20 11	2	NW

97   24 Oct 1810   A/4/177
John Sloane, [Rec Can]
Transmits Treasury receipts

William Hough	Can	–	16 21	26	NE
William Hough	Can	–	16 21	26	SE
William Hough	Can	–	16 21	26	SW
William Hough	Can	–	16 21	25	NW
William Hough	Can	–	16 21	24	SW

98   24 Oct 1810   A/4/177
David Sample, Lewistown [state not given]
Notifies him that no receipt from him has been received by Cin Rec; therefore, patent cannot be
  issued.

99   7 Nov 1810   A/4/178
Jesse Spencer, [Reg Chl]
John Gochnour applied to Treasury intending to pay
  arrears and interest on land, "but since he had
  not inhabited and cultivated the land, nor any
  person for him, he was not entitled to the privi-
  lege. The present intention, therefore, is that,
  if the land should be sold when the sales of such
  kind of forfeitures take place, the tract may be
  entered in his name."

John Gochnour	Chl	–	19 16	8	N

100   21 Nov 1810   A/4/178
LO Stu
Transmits patents

George Snider	Stu	–	7 19	7	N
James Caldwell	Stu	–	6 8	15	SE
John Haycock	Stu	–	7 18	1	N
James Dallas	Stu	–	5 8	27	SE
Jacob Ong?	Stu	–	3 9	11	–
John Gardner	Stu	–	4 9	22	SE
John Gardner	Stu	–	4 9	22	NE
Zebediah Cox	Stu	–	5 11	20	S
John Bowman	Stu	–	5 8	17	–

101   21 Nov 1810   A/4/178
LO Cin
Transmits patents

Archibald Burns	Cin	EML	1 4	28	SW
Andrew Cornelison	Cin	EML	3 3	23	SE
Seth Goodwine	Cin	EML	1 3	6	NE
Henry Garner	Cin	EML	2 3	6	NW
Willis Whitson	Cin	EML	2 5	12	NW
Christopher Folker	Cin	EML	6 8	25	SE
James Barber	Cin	EML	1 4	31	NW
John Burns	Cin	EML	1 4	28	SE

John Arnold	Cin EML	4	5	1?	NE
Abraham Holderman	Cin EML	3	5	28	S
Abraham Holderman	Cin EML	3	5	32	E
James Dunn	Cin EML	2	3	11	-
James Dunn	Cin EML	2	3	14	+
John Whistler	Cin EML	6	4	5	SW
John Creek	Cin WML	1	11	32	NW
David B. Close	Cin WML	1	4	34	NE
William G. Eads	Cin WML	2	8	2	NW
Lewis Jones	Cin WML	1	2	27	NE
Lazarus Whitehead	Cin WML	1	13	31	NW
William Sparks	Cin WML	2	11	34	SE
Joseph Siers	Cin WML	1	8	11	NE
Chistley Norman	Cin MR	12	4	31	NW
Christopher Weaver	Cin MR	10	4	12	SW
Matthew Caldwell	Cin MR	12	1	5	SW
Francis Brook	Cin MR	5	2	11	NW

102   7 Dec 1810   A/4/179
David Hoge, [Reg Stu]
Transmits certificates and Treasury receipts, "gentlemen of Congress having the charge of obtaining the patent[s]"

George Wilson	Stu	-	8	9	8	S
John Rife?	Stu	-	9	9	2	SW

103   8 Dec 1810   A/4/179
Jesse Spencer, [Reg Chl]
Transmits first certificate*

Andrew Forster	Chl	-	17	18	33	SW
Andrew Forster	Chl	-	17	18	29	SW
Andrew Forster	Chl	-	17	18	19	SW

*Presented by Daniel Bussard, agent for William Forster, father of Andrew Forster.

104   8 Dec 1810   A/4/180
Christian Especk, New Philadelphia, Ohio
Describes documents received, encompassing the following transactions:
(a) Official discharge from General [George] Washington granted to Tunis Covert, formerly a private in the New Jersey Regiment;
(b) Assignment of all rights under Covert's discharge to Nicholas Perrine, 7 Feb 1784;
(c) Assignment by Covert of Congressional bonus? to Perrine;
(d) Assignment by Perrine of rights thereunder to Peter Snider;
(e) Reassignment by Snider to Abraham Shane?;
(f) [Footnote remarks that Peter Covert had also assigned his rights to Jacob Helter and that bounty-land warrant 8206 was issued to Helter, as assignee, on 20 Sep 1791].

105   10 Dec 1810   A/4/181
Isaac Vanhorne, [Rec Zan]
Assures Robert Henderson that patents for three quarter sections of land will be issued in due course.

106   10 Dec 1810   A/4/181
Wyllys Silliman, [Reg Zan]
Transmits Treasury receipts and certificates, at request of gentlemen of Congress

Samuel Hill	Zan	-	12	13	3	NE
William Gladden	Mil	-	5	1	13	NW
William Gladden	Mil	-	5	1	18	NW

George Custard	Mil	-	1	9	11	SE
George Custard	Mil	-	1	9	13	SE
Daniel Custard	Mil	-	1	9	10	NW

107   10 Dec 1810   A/4/181
Daniel Symmes, [Reg Cin]
Inquires regarding final certificate, " a gentleman of Congress having made very pressing application for the patent"

Jeremiah Gustin? [Austin?]	Cin Pre	4	3	9	-

108   10 Dec 1810   A/4/182
John Morrow, Shepherds Town, Virginia
Transmits patent

John Vanausdle	[Cin] EML	3	5	15	SW

109   10 Dec 1810   A/4/182
Jesse Spencer, [Reg Chl]
Transmits certificate and questions discount given

Henry Liteanaker	Chl	-	19	16	35	NE

110   28 Dec 1810   A/4/182
[not stated]
Transmits Treasury receipts

W. Akinson	[Stu?]	-	5	16	26	NW
J. B. Candy*	[Stu?]	-	6	16	17	SW
J. Burson	[Stu?]	-	3	14	18	NW

*Mentioned in entry 12 supra.

111   2 Jan 1811   A/4/183
Hon. John Smilie
Transmits patents

John Gilchrist	[Unk]	-	5	10	14	SW
Daniel McDowell	[Unk]	-	5	10	20	NE
John McDowell	[Unk]	-	5	9	23	NE
John McDowell	[Unk]	-	5	9	36	NE

112   3 Jan 1811   A/4/183
David Sample, Lewistown, Pennsylvania
Transmits patent

David Sample	Cin EML	2	6	3	NW

113   3 Jan 1811   A/4/183
Hon. William Crawford
Transmits patents

Jacob Hosteller?	[Stu*]	-	6	17	36	NE
Jacob Hosteller?	[Stu*]	-	5	16	31	NW

*Per entry 81 supra.

114   5 Jan 1811   A/4/183
LO Cin
Transmits patents

James Wright	Cin MR	9	6	17	SE
James Wright	Cin MR	9	6	17	SW
Michael Unger	Cin MR	5	2	30	S
John Riddle	Cin MR	2	3	11	R+
Daniel Hawn	Cin MR	4	3	29	NW
John Taylor	Cin MR	6	2	26	SW
Samuel Yeaman	Cin MR	4	4	26	SW
Jacob Hosier*	Cin MR	6	2	8	NW
John L. Wilson	Cin MR	5	3	11	NE
John Edwards	Cin Pre	6	2	19	Lt3
John Edwards	Cin Pre	6	2	19	Lt2
Leonard Petro?	Cin Pre	5	2	14	W

-- Bigger & -- White	Cin Pre	6	2	15	-
William Layton	Cin Pre	9	3	2	Lt1
James Patterson	Cin Pre	6	2	17	-
Adam Garbrick	Cin Pre	7	2	10	Lt1
George Folk	Cin Pre	8	3	7	-

*Entry entirely crossed out.

---

115 5 Jan 1811 A/4/184
LO Cin
Transmits patents

Samuel Walker	Cin WML	1	13	9	NE
John Endsley	Cin WML	2	13	36	NE
Amos Butler	Cin WML	2	9	29	SE
Amos Butler	Cin WML	2	9	20	SW
Benjamin McCarty	Cin WML	2	9	21	NW
Jonas Urner	Cin EML	3	5	29	S
Samuel Tait?	Cin EML	2	7	36	W
Enoch Pearson	Cin EML	6	4	20	NW
John Kemp	Cin EML	4	3	32	S
Benjamin Bishop	Cin EML	2	6	25	SW
Zachariah Hole	Cin EML	3	7	27	E
James Boyse	Cin EML	1	6	17	S
Henry Taylor	Cin EML	2	5	36	-
Jesse Gerrard	Cin EML	6	4	3	+
Henry Sefton?	Cin EML	1	2	12	SW
George Stetler	Cin EML	4	3	5	S

---

116 5 Jan 1811 A/4/184
LO Stu
Transmits patents

Jacob Shively	Stu	-	7	18	8	NW
Jacob Shively	Stu	-	6	18	30	SW
Samuel Shaw	Stu	-	4	15	31	W
David Dierdorff	Stu	-	9	10	34	S
John Gardner	Stu	-	5	16	25	SW
George Grous	Stu	-	8	10	5	SE
Daniel Easley	Stu	-	6	10	27	NW
George Grous	Stu	-	8	9	11	-
Daniel Easley	Stu	-	7	11	17	NE
Daniel Easley	Stu	-	6	10	8	NE

---

117 5 Jan 1811 A/4/185
Hon. Joseph Lewis
Reports as follows:
(a) Thomas Parker, late a captain in Virginia
    line, received bounty-land warrant 1742,
    used to locate land in [Mil?] - 17 7 4
    lots 3, 4, & 5;
(b) Warrant 1741 "was issued to Richard Platt,
    the assignee of another Thomas Parker, Cap-
    tain in the Virginia line, which appears to
    have been assigned to the Ohio Company;
(c) Returns letter from a Mr. -- Mills.

---

118 7 Jan 1811 A/4/185
Thomas Gibson, [Reg Can]
Encloses certificates and Treasury receipts

David Lane*	Can	-	17	23	31	NW
Isaac Hatcher	Can	-	19	19	31	SE
Isaac Hatcher	Can	-	18	18	2	NE

*"Pressingly called for by gentleman in Congress."

---

119 7 Jan 1811 A/4/186
Wyllys Silliman, [Reg Zan]
Transmits certificates; requests prompt delivery of
  Gladden, Custard, and Hill patents*

Jacob Buchman	Zan	-	8	4	4	SE
Samuel Heuslie & James Williams **	Zan	-	9	1	19	NW
John Wade	Zan	-	3	10	16	SW
Isaac Deardorff	Zan	-	3	10	19	NW

 *See entry 106, *supra*.
**Transferred to George Grant.

---

120 7 Jan 1811 A/4/186
David Hoge, [Reg Stu]
Transmits certificates and Treasury receipts

James Clay*	Stu	-	8	11	35	SE
Thomas Sands	Stu	-	5	16	27	NE
Price Kieth	Stu	-	5	16	24	NE
John Glass	Stu	-	2	13	22	NW

*Assigned to Moses Nellson.

---

121 7 Jan 1811 A/4/187
Jesse Spencer, [Reg Chl]
Transmits certificates and Treasury receipts

Benjamin Crisman	Chl	-	20	12	18	SE
William Black	Chl	-	16	15	19	SW
Philemon Needless*	Chl	-	19	15	21	SE
Joel Posey	Chl	-	14	8	19	NW
Benjamin Bowman	Chl	-	20	13	22	SW

*Treasury receipt for this land is in name of Jacob
  Claypoole.

---

122 7 Jan 1811 A/4/187
Daniel Symmes, [Reg Cin]
Transmits certificates and Treasury receipts

James Bishop	Cin MR	10	5	3	SE
John Mills & Seth Mills*	Cin MR	9	2	22	SE
Alexander C. Lanier**	Cin EML	2	7	11	SW
Jacob Humbert	Cin EML	5	3	22	SW

 *Treasury receipt in name of Abraham Studebaker.
**Assigned to John Lock.

---

123 9 Jan 1811 A/4/188
Thomas M. Thompson, Stu
Thompson's request that his military bounty-land warrant 426 be located on a given lot [description
  partially illegible] cannot be granted, as it is
  already patented to another person.

---

124 10 Jan 1811 A/4/188
Joseph Vance, Franklinton, Ohio
Vance's reques that military bounty-land warrants
  6163 and 336 be located on Mil - 19 7 2 1
  and Mil - 16 7 2 35 cannot be granted, as
  these lots have been patented to other persons.
Transmits patents

Thomas Swan	Mil	-	16	7	2	35
William Dennison	Mil	-	6	2	1	33
Daniel McKay	Mil	-	17	7	2	7
Daniel McKay	Mil	-	17	7	2	8

---

125 10 Jan 1811 A/4/188
John Miller, Union Town, Pennsylvania
Answers inquiry regarding delay in patent issuance

Adam Brown	Chl	-	17	18	24	SW

---

126 11 Jan 1811 A/4/189
Wyllys Silliman, [Reg Zan]
Asks return of certificate

Jacob Yoke*	Zan	-	8	8	12	SE

*Assignee of Archibald Woods.

127   11 Jan 1811   A/4/189
Daniel Symmes, [Reg Cin]
Asks return of certificates

| -- Mallery & -- Taylor* | Cin | MR | 12 | 5 | 10 | SW |
| -- Mallery & -- Taylor* | Cin | MR | 12 | 5 | 10 | E |

*Originally purchased by James Hendricks.

128   11 Jan 1811   A/4/189
Jesse Spencer, [Reg Chl]
Transmits certificates and Treasury receipts; mentions Jacob Humbert, but without giving corresponding land description

John Sharp	Chl	-	21	11	33	N
John Sharp	Chl	-	20	12	19	NE
John Sharp	Chl	-	20	12	20	NW

129   15 Jan 1811   A/4/190
Jesse Spencer, [Reg Chl]
Transmits patent

| Alexander McClintock, *et al* | Chl | - | 20 | 8 | 8 | - |

130   15 Jan 1811   A/4/190
LO Cin
Transmits patents

Eli Henderson	Cin	WML	2	11	24	SW
Benjamin Wilson	Cin	WML	2	4	23	NE
Peter Fleming	Cin	WML	1	13	1	NE
Thadeus Cooley	Cin	WML	1	6	27	NE
Samuel Scott & Charles Scott	Cin	WML	2	8	3	SW
Jesse Hendly	Cin	WML	1	12	7	SE
John Rhode	Cin	WML	2	13	36	NW
John Vance	Cin	EML	3	7	33	SE
George Kunse	Cin	EML	2	2	6	NW
Jacob Honer?	Cin	MR	6	2	8	NW

131   15 Jan 1811   A/4/190
LO Stu
Transmits patents

Joseph Shields	Stu	-	5	17	11	NE
John Gilson	Stu	-	5	17	19	SW
Eli Davis	Stu	-	1	7	28	NE
Zebediah Cox	Stu	-	5	11	19	NW
William Leeper & Samuel Leeper	Stu	-	7	17	20	SE
Nathaniel Gilmore	Stu	-	7	12	24	SE
Roger Toothaker	Stu	-	5	10	19	SE
Michael Reed	Stu	-	8	10	3	NE
Martin Bradstone	Stu	-	3	14	19	SW
John Hall	Stu	-	7	9	13	NE
John Hall	Stu	-	7	9	7	NE
Thomas Gilham	Stu	-	5	8	23	SE
Robert Huston	Stu	-	1	8	35	SW

132   23 Jan 1811   A/4/191
LO Zan
Transmits patents

Martin Chandler	Zan	-	12	13	12	SW
Samuel Thompson	Zan	-	15	16	18	SE
Samuel Ream & Jacob Ream	Zan	-	14	15	27	SE
Robert Henderson	Zan	-	15	17	13	SW
Nathan Hall	Zan	-	15	17	28	NE
Robert Manly	Zan	-	15	18	15	NW
James Lewis	Zan	-	13	12	10	NW
George Mathews	Zan	-	14	15	11	SE
Joseph Pierce	Zan	-	12	13	17	SE
Joseph Pierce	Zan	-	12	13	18	NE
Joseph Pierce	Zan	-	12	13	8	SW
Jonathan Addison	Zan	-	14	15	2	SW
Jacob Gaddes	Zan	-	14	14	32	SE
Henry Shepler	Zan	-	11	13	13	SE
Nicholas Bush	Zan	-	15	17	36	SW
Nicholas Bush	Zan	-	15	16	2	NE
John Bush	Zan	-	14	15	9	NE
William Bizand	Zan	-	14	15	3	NW
John McClaray	Zan	MY	1	9	2	SE
John Bowers	Zan	MY	7	1	10	SE
John Stuart	Zan	MY	1	3	14	SE
John Stuart	Zan	MY	1	3	14	NE
Adam Smith	Zan	MY	10	1	21	NW
Adam Smith	Zan	MY	10	1	19	NW
Adam Smith	Zan	MY	10	1	19	NE
Adam Smith	Zan	MY	10	1	22	SE
Joseph Vernon	Zan	MY	7	1	10	SW
James Wilson	Zan	MY	5	1	11	NW
John Low	Zan	MY	1	1	2	SW
Jane Hursey	Zan	MY	10	1	22	SW
John Nicholls	Zan	MY	7	5	1	SW

133   23 Jan 1811   A/4/191
General [Thomas] Worthington
Transmits patents

| Daniel McFarlane | Chl | - | 21 | 8 | 8 | SW |
| William Gass | Chl* | - | 12 | 7 | 25 | SW |

*Military District.

134   23 Jan 1811   A/4/192
LO Stu
Transmits patents

Joseph Hobson	Stu	-	3	10	14	NE
Joseph Holloway	Stu	-	5	9	23	SE
Daniel Easley	Stu	-	7	12	19	SE
Isaac Johnson	Stu	-	1	7	20	NE
Joshua Dickerson	Stu	-	5	10	19	NE
Peter Hesser	Stu	-	3	9	30	SE
Benjamin Harrison	Stu	-	5	16	13	NE
William Straughan	Stu	-	4	17	27	NW
William Lisle	Stu	-	5	11	8	NW
Richard Kenny	Stu	-	5	7	26	NE
Thomas Farquhar	Stu	-	5	16	36	E
Daniel Hardman	Stu	-	2	12	15	NW
George Brown	Stu	-	1	8	34	SW
George Brown	Stu	-	1	7	3	NW
William Stuart	Stu	-	2	13	3	-
John Andrews	Stu	-	3	10	6	-
Isaac Bachtel	Stu	-	8	11	34	SW
Abraham Brokaw	Stu	-	6	10	3	NE
Peter Cook	Stu	-	2	13	18	SW
George Macenterfer	Stu	-	7	18	1	SW
John McCoy	Stu	-	4	12	14	SW
Samuel Davis	Stu	-	4	17	29	NE
John Piggott	Stu	-	5	7	29	SE
Samuel Laferty	Stu	-	6	10	9	NW
Nathaniel Paramour	Stu	-	5	10	19	SW
John Hare	Stu	-	7	20	1	NE
Hugh McBean	Stu	-	2	10	34	SW
Thomas Gibson	Stu	-	5	17	19	SE
Richard Rice	Stu	-	5	7	30	NE
Richard Rice	Stu	-	5	8	25	SE
John Pugh	Stu	-	6	11	2	SW

135   23 Jan 1811   A/4/193
LO Cin
Transmits patents

| Robert Ewing | Cin | EML | 5 | 5 | 9 | SW |
| Samuel Teil | Cin | EML | 3 | 4 | 4 | SW |

Robert Quin	Cin	EML	3	6	31	SE
Joseph Layton	Cin	EML	6	5	28	SW
John Tilman	Cin	EML	3	7	12	SE
Peter Ridenhour	Cin	EML	1	6	33	W
Samuel Pearson	Cin	EML	6	4	20	NE
Christopher Emrick	Cin	EML	3	6	20	NE
Francis Ott	Cin	EML	3	7	29	NE
Lewis Long, John Heaston, & Daniel Heaston	Cin	EML	5	3	3	-
Samuel Huston	Cin	EML	1	6	31	SW
William Cooper	Cin	EML	1	8	34	N
George Gillespie	Cin	EML	6	4	11	+
George Gillespie	Cin	EML	6	4	14	-
Peter Grumrine	Cin	EML	4	5	13	NW
Robert Scott	Cin	EML	5	5	14	NE
Richard Cornell	Cin	EML	3	2	18	SE
John Gripe	Cin	EML	5	4	26	-
John Day	Cin	EML	2	8	24	SW
William Jones	Cin	EML	1	6	25	SE
William P. Smith	Cin	EML	2	7	12	SW
Lydia Pemberton	Cin	EML	5	7	31	SW
Gabriel McCall	Cin	EML	5	7	29	NW

---

136 22 Jan 1811 A/4/194
Hon. Philip Reed
Transmits patent

Daniel Smith, heirs of	Mil	-	9	7	3	14

---

137 22 Jan 1811 A/4/194
Hon. Jonathan Robinson
Transmits patent

Edward Bates & Nathaniel Bates	Mil	-	3	8	4	19

---

138 22 Jan 1811 A/4/194
Messrs. Slingluff & Fahnestock, N. Howard St., Baltimore
Transmits patents

Bohn & Slingluff	Mil	-	3	7	1	9
Bohn & Slingluff	Mil	-	3	7	1	19
Bohn & Slingluff	Mil	-	3	7	1	20
Bohn & Slingluff	Mil	-	3	7	1	21
Bohn & Slingluff	Mil	-	5	9	3	1
Bohn & Slingluff	Mil	-	5	9	3	6
Bohn & Slingluff	Mil	-	5	9	3	7
Bohn & Slingluff	Mil	-	5	9	3	10
Bohn & Slingluff	Mil	-	5	9	3	11
Bohn & Slingluff	Mil	-	3	8	4	3
Slingluff & Fahnestock	Mil	-	3	8	4	16
Slingluff & Fahnestock	Mil	-	3	8	4	20
Slingluff & Fahnestock	Mil	-	3	8	4	21

---

139 25 Jan 1811 A/4/195
Hon. Joseph Lewis
Answers inquiry

Patented under bounty-land warrant 1742	[Mil]	-	17	7	4	3
Ditto	[Mil]	-	17	7	4	4
Ditto	[Mil]	-	17	7	4	5
Still unpatented	[Mil]	-	16	7	2	3
Ditto	[Mil]	-	16	7	2	4
Ditto	[Mil]	-	16	7	2	5

---

140 25 Jan 1811 A/4/195
LO Jef
Transmits patents

Lewis Fouts	Jef	-	9E	2N	31	NE
Matthew Coffin	Jef	-	4E	2N	3	SW
William Robinson	Jef	-	4E	1S	10	NW
Francis Giltner	Jef	-	9E	2N	33	SW
Lewis Fouts	Jef	-	9E	2N	30	SE
Matthew Coffin,	Jef	-	4E	2N	4	SW
John Reese	Jef	-	9E	1N	5	NW
Roger Thompson	Jef	-	4E	2N	1	SW
John Buckhanan	Jef	-	11E	6N	34	SE
George Shannon	Jef	-	9E	4N	9	NE
George Shannon	Jef	-	9E	3N	24	NE
George Shannon	Jef	-	9E	4N	9	SE
James Maxwell	Jef	-	1E	2N	5	SE

---

141 25 Jan 1811 A/4/195
LO Chl
Transmits patents

Henry Orts?	Chl	-	18	16	8	NW
Henry Bowman	Chl	-	17	18	17	NW
John McArthur	Chl	-	19	15	5	SE
Henry Mongold	Chl	-	19	15	2	NE
Reuben Newkirk	Chl	-	20	14	36	E
Nimrod Bright	Chl	-	20	14	6	SE

---

142 25 Jan 1811 A/4/196
LO Cin
Transmits patents

Jacob Fare	Cin	EML	6	4	28	SE
Jacob Kercker	Cin	EML	4	4	24	SW
Benjamin Vancleife	Cin	EML	3	3	13	SW
John Kemp	Cin	EML	4	3	27	W
William Cooper	Cin	EML	1	8	34	SE
Joseph Singer	Cin	EML	3	7	34	W
William Crawford	Cin	WML	1	10	12	SW
Benjamin Wilson*	Cin	WML	2	10	24	NW
Richard Rue	Cin	WML	1	13	30	SE
Philip Lybrook	Cin	WML	1	12	36	N
John Clark	Cin	MR	5	1	7	+
Robert Buckhannon, heirs of	Cin	MR	4	3	31	Lt3
George Harner?	Cin	MR	7	3	17	E
Charles Starrett	Cin	MR	8	6	5	N
Thomas Hamilton	Cin	MR	11	1	2	SW
Andrew D. Brien	Cin	MR	11	3	28	SE
Benjamin Wallinford	Cin	MR	9	6	23	SE
George Gillespie	Cin	MR	4	2	11	SW
William Davis	Cin	MR	10	3	36	SE
Amos Crane	Cin	MR	4	4	29	SW
Isaac Miller	Cin	MR	6	2	11	SW

*Entire entry marked through.

---

143 28 Jan 1811 A/4/196
General [Thomas] Worthington
Transmits patents

Daniel McFarlane	[Mil*]	-	21	8	8	SW
William Gass	[Mil*]	-	12	7	25	SW

*Chl LO.

---

144 28 Jan 1811 A/4/197
Wyllys Silliman, [Reg Zan]
Transmits final certificates

Daniel Custard	Mil	-	1	9	10	NW*
Samuel Hill	Zan?	-	12	13	3	NE

*Returned for correction; erroneously showed NE.

---

145 28 Jan 1811 A/4/197
Jonathan Carlisle, Junior, Post Office Brookville, Montgomery County, Maryland
Transmits patents

Jonathan Carlisle, Junior	Zan	-	13	11	7	S+
Jonathan Carlisle, Junior	Zan	-	13	11	8	S+

146   28 Jan 1811   A/4/197
Jesse Spencer, [Reg Chl]
Transmits patents

Joshua Hedges	Chl	MS	21	9	9	-
Mary Hedges	Chl	MS	21	9	19	W
Solomon Cox	Chl	-	20	8	34	-

147   28 Jan 1811   A/4/197
Hon. John Rea
Transmits patent

George Wilson	Stu	-	8	9	8	S

148   28 Jan 1811   A/4/198
Hon. W. Findley
Transmits patents

Conrad Knappenberger	Mil	-	3	9	9	E
Conrad Knappenberger	Mil	-	3	9	1	W

149   30 Jan 1811   A/4/198
Hon. Jonathan Jennings
Transmits patent

George P. Torrence	[Cin*]	[MR]	9	3	8	+

*"Between the Great Miami River and the Virginia Reservation."

150   30 Jan 1811   A/4/198
Hon. John Smilie
Transmits patents

Jacob Longaneker	Chl	-	18	16	1	E
Jacob Longaneker	Chl	-	17	18	6	SW

151   30 Jan 1811   A/4/198
General [Thomas] Worthington
Transmits patent

William Blocksom?	Chl	-	17	18	32	SE

152   30 Jan 1811   A/4/198
Jesse Spencer, [Reg Chl]
Transmits patents

John Bicken & Moses Wright	Chl	-	21	10	18	NE

153   31 Jan 1811   A/4/199
LO Cin
Transmits patents

Jesse Jenkins	Cin	EML	6	4	10	+
Michael Pierce	Cin	EML	2	8	26	SW
James Lister	Cin	EML	2	4	13	SE
William Caldwell	Cin	EML	3	2	17	W
Elijah Mendenhall	Cin	EML	5	6	32	SW
John Clem	Cin	EML	1	4	1	SW
Robert Swan	Cin	EML	2	11	22	SW
William Swisher	Cin	EML	3	7	33	NE
Benjamin Pearson	Cin	EML	6	4	30	NW
George Coon	Cin	EML	3	6	24	NE
Jacob Kunse	Cin	EML	5	4	4	NW
William Jenkins	Cin	EML	6	4	17	NE
William Cooper	Cin	EML	1	7	9	NE
Thomas Pearson	Cin	EML	6	4	17	SE
David Cox	Cin	EML	5	5	35	NW
Christopher Emrick	Cin	EML	4	3	35	NW

Joseph Mendenhall	Cin	EML	5	6	32	NE
David McDill	Cin	EML	1	6	35	NW
Joseph Ridenhour	Cin	EML	1	6	29	S
Richard Goodwin	Cin	EML	3	4	17	SE
John Zeller	Cin	EML	3	6	29	NE
Samuel Teil	Cin	EML	3	4	4	NW

154   31 Jan 1811   A/4/199
Jesse Spencer, [Reg Chl]
Error in computation of interest, etc.

Noah Zane	Chl	-	17	17	23	-
Noah Zane	Chl	-	19	14	12	W
Noah Zane	Chl	-	19	14	12	11+

155   2 Feb 1811   A/4/200
Hon. John Smilie
Transmits patent; mentions Daniel Custard & David Lane

George Custard	[Mil]	-	1	19	11	SE
George Custard	[Mil]	-	1	9	13	SE

156   4 Feb 1811   A/4/200
Wyllys Silliman, [Reg Zan]
Inquires regarding certificates for Joseph Darrah, John Fedrow, James Wimans, Nicholas Pierce

Samuel Hill	Zan	-	12	13	3	NE

157   15 Feb 1811   A/4/200
Hon. Thomas Worthington
Transmits patents

Noah Zane	[Chl]	-	19	14	11	-
Noah Zane	[Chl]	-	19	14	12	W+
Robert F. Slaughter	[Chl]	-	19	14	9	W
James Trindle	[Chl]	-	18	17	23	NE

158   15 Feb 1811   A/4/201
Adam Brown, [no address given]
Transmits patent

Adam Brown	Chl	-	17	18	24	SW

159   15 Feb 1811   A/4/201
LO Chl
Transmits patents

Philamon Beecher	Chl	-	18	15	7	W
John Busby	Chl	-	20	13	2	NW
Joseph Harness?	Chl	-	20	8	19	NW

160   15 Feb 1811   A/4/201
[Addressee not given]
Transmits patent

Frederick Geiger	Unk	-	3E	6S	4	+
Frederick Geiger	Unk	-	3E	6S	5	+

161   18 Feb 1811   A/4/201
Jonathan Dayton
Transmits patents

Jonathan Dayton	Cin	WML	1	4	14	+
Jonathan Dayton	Cin	WML	1	4	15	+
Jonathan Dayton	Cin	WML	1	4	16	-

162   18 Feb 1811   A/4/201
Hon. Aaron Lyle
Transmits patent

John Swearingen	Stu	-	1	6	33	-

163	18 Feb 1811	A/4/202

LO Cin
Transmits patents

William Fouts	Cin WML	1	13	13	NE
Daniel Fouts	Cin WML	1	12	18	NE
Daniel Feather	Cin EML	5	5	29	NW

164	18 Feb 1811	A/4/202

Hon. Thomas Worthington
Transmits patents

Zaccheus? A. Beatty	Zan	-	3	2	4	NE
Zaccheus? A. Beatty	Zan	-	3	2	13	NW
Zaccheus? A. Beatty	Zan	-	3	2	15	NE

165	18 Feb 1811	A/4/202

Hon. Jeremiah Morrow
Transmits patent

Alexander Speer	Zan	-	4	2	22	NW

166	20 Feb 1811	A/4/202

Hon. Thomas Worthington
Transmits patents

Philamon Needles	Chl	-	20	15	31	NW
Philamon Needles	Chl	-	20	15	31	SE

167	20 Feb 1811	A/4/202

Hon. William Jennings
Transmits patents

Z. A. Beatty	Zan	-	3	2	8	SW
Z. A. Beatty	Zan	-	3	2	14	NW

168	20 Feb 1811	A/4/202

Michael Harner, Lebanon, Pennsylvania
Transmits patent

Michael Harner	[Cin] WML	2	4	11	NW

169	21 Feb 1811	A/4/203

Hon. William Helms
Transmits patents

Robert Lynn? in trust for heirs of John Harding	Unk	-	16	7	4	Lt12
Ditto	Unk	-	16	7	4	Lt11

170	21 Feb 1811	A/4/203

Hon. Thomas Worthington
Transmits patent

Amos Stackhouse	Unk	-	4	4	3	Lt14

171	23 Feb 1811	A/4/203

LO Cin
Transmits patents

Andrew Weaver	Cin WML	1	14	27	NW
Andrew Weaver	Cin WML	1	14	28	NE
Andrew Weaver	Cin WML	1	14	29	SE
David Reese	Cin WML	1	5	19	NE
David Reese	Cin WML	1	5	20	W
David Reese	Cin WML	1	5	21	-
David Reese	Cin WML	1	5	22	+
David Reese	Cin WML	1	5	23	+

172	23 Feb 1811	A/4/203

Levi Baker, Esq., Mar
Transmits patent; mentions the Hon. Dr. -- Campbell

Philip Trichler	Mar	-	14	4	11	-

173	23 Feb 1811	A/4/203

William Mallery, Harper's Ferry
Transmits patent

William Mallery	Cin MR	12	5	10	E

174	23 Feb 1811	A/4/204

Hon. Dr. -- Crawford
Transmits patents

George Kortman	Mil*	-	2	7	13	NE
Samuel Hill	Zan	-	12	13	3	NE

*LO Zan.

175	23 Feb 1811	A/4/204

Hon. Jeremiah Morrow
Transmits patent

James Hammet	Zan	-	15	17	12	SE

176	23 Feb 1811	A/4/204

Hon. -- Jennings
Transmits patent

Jacob Gomlar?	Mil*	-	3	2	3	SW

*LO Zan.

177	23 Feb 1811	A/4/204

Hon. John Smilie
Transmits patent

Daniel Custard	Mil*	-	1	9	10	NW

*LO Zan.

178	25 Feb 1811	A/4/204

Samuel Gwathmey, [Reg] Jef
Transmits certificate

Jonathan Lindley	Jef	-	1E	1N	8	SE

179	26 Feb 1811	A/4/204

Hon. Jeremiah Morrow
Transmits patent

David Moore	Mil*	-	2	1	1	NE
Thomas Speer	Mil*	-	5	1	1	SE

*LO Zan.

180	26 Feb 1811	A/4/205

John Lock, Frederick Town
Transmits patent

John Lock	Cin EML	2	7	11	SW

181	26 Feb 1811	A/4/205

Benjamin Crisman, Post Office, Bedford, Pennsylvania
Transmits patent

Benjamin Crisman	Chl	-	20	12	18	SE

182	26 Feb 1811	A/4/205

LO Cin
Transmits patents

John Taylor	Cin MR	12	5	10	SW
David Hartman	Cin EML	4	5	27	NE
Peter Solman	Cin EML	2	4	19	S
Andrew Heimleck	Cin EML	3	5	19	NW
Isaac Pedrick	Cin EML	5	6	19	-
Benjamin Blue	Cin WML	1	9	25	SE

James Seal & William Seal	Cin WML	1	9	31	SE
Andrew Cornelianson	Cin WML	1	10	32	SW
Henry Burch	Cin EML	1	3	10	SW
F? Nieswanger & S. Nies-wanger	Cin EML	4	6	23	E
David Cox	Cin EML	5	5	35	NW
Elijah Paine	Cin EML	1	7	5	NE

183
LO Can   26 Feb 1811   A/4/205
Transmits patents

| Andrew Johnstone | Can | - | 14 | 20 | 24 | SW |
| David H. Knox | Can | - | 13 | 13 | 11 | NE |

184
LO Chl   [26 Feb 1811]   A/4/205
Transmits patents

| Roger Seldon | Chl | - | 17 | 2 | 19 | - |
| John Carlisle | Chl | MS | 22 | 2 | 36 | SW |

185
LO Vin   26 Feb 1811   A/4/205
Transmits patents

Jacob Conrad	Vin	-	4E	3S	32	SW
Jacob Conrad	Vin	-	4E	3S	32	SE
Russell Hewitt	Vin	-	10W	7S	11	NW

186
LO Zan   26 Feb 1811   A/4/205
Transmits patents

Isaac Van Horne	Zan	-	13	12	6	E+
George Grant	Mil	-	9	1	19	NW
Robert Henderson	Zan	-	15	17	4	SE
Jacob Baker	Zan	-	14	15	31	NW
Benjamin Feikle	Zan	-	15	17	10	SE
John Reddick	Zan	-	14	15	18	SW
M. Porter & S. Porter	Zan	-	14	14	10	NW

187
LO Cin   27 Feb 1811   A/4/206
Transmits patents

George Kunse	Cin EML	5	4	19	SE
Joseph Davis	Cin EML	1	7	33	SW
Jesse Lane	Cin EML	2	6	35	NE
Lewis Davis	Cin EML	3	6	29	SW

188   27 Feb 1811   A/4/206
General [Thomas] Worthington
Transmits patent; mentions Raynal [Regnal?] Green

| Alexander McClintock | Chl | - | 21 | 8 | 14 | NW |
| Solomon Cox* | Chl | - | 20 | 8 | 34 | - |

*Previously transmitted.

189   1 Mar 1811   A/4/206
General [Thomas] Worthington
Answers inquiry regarding Israel Ruland's status as
a refugee; he was so declared in a Commissioners'
report of 2 Apr 1806 with recommendation that he
be awarded 960 acres of land.

190   1 Mar 1811   A/4/207
Hon. William McKinley
Answers inquiry regarding certificates [names of
grantees not given]

191   2 Mar 1811   A/4/207
General [Thomas] Worthington
Transmits patent

| Regnal Green | Chl | - | 19 | 14 | 18 | E |

192   3 Mar 1811   A/4/207
Hon. David Garland, New Glasgow, Amherst County, Virginia
Transmits patent in name of Benjamin Hawkins for
military services [land description not given].

193   3 Mar 1811   A/4/207
Jacob Bachman, Post Office, Westminster, Maryland
Transmits patent

| Jacob Bachman | Mil* | - | 8 | 4 | 4 | SE |

*LO Zan.

194   3 Mar 1811   A/4/208
William Black, Post Office, Lewistown, Mifflin
County, Pennsylvania
Transmits patent

| William Black | Chl | - | 16 | 15 | 19 | SW |

195   6 Mar 1811   A/4/208
LO Cin
Transmits patents

| William McKinstry | Cin EML | 2 | 4 | 4 | NE |
| David Patty | Cin EML | 4 | 9 | 33 | NE |

196   11 Mar 1811   A/4/208
Daniel Symmes, [Reg Cin]
Transmits patent and certificate

| David Miller | Cin EML | 5 | 7 | 6 | NE |
| Laurence Bousman | Cin MR | 12 | 4 | 21 | S |

197   11 Mar 1811   A/4/208
Thomas Sands, Post Office, Leesburgh, Virginia
Transmits patent

| Thomas Sands | Stu | - | 5 | 16 | 27 | NE |

198   11 Mar 1811   A/4/209
Moses Nelson, Post Office, Hagars Town [Maryland]
Transmits patent

| Moses Nelson | Stu | - | 8 | 11 | 35 | SE |

199   11 Mar 1811   A/4/209
Price Keith, Post Office, Middleburgh, Loudon County,
Virginia
Transmits patent

| Price Keith | Stu | - | 5 | 16 | 24 | NE |

200   11 Mar 1811   A/4/209
LO Chl
Transmits patent

| Joseph Miller | Chl | MS | 21 | 11 | 28 | SW |

201   12 Mar 1811   A/4/209
John Misseillius? Hagerstown, Maryland
Transmits patent

| John Misseillius? | Chl | - | 20 | 15 | 20 | SW |

202		12 Mar 1811		A/4/210

Joseph Wood, [Reg Mar]
Answers inquiry regarding patent issuances; mentions
    Benjamin Ives Gillman, assignee of Peleg Mason,
    and Daniel Sheldon, agent

-- Lockwood & -- Coleman*	Mar	-	3	4	6	SE
William Skinner*	Mar	-	5	1	17	+
William Skinner*	Mar	-	5	1	23	N

*Delivered to G. Meigs, Esq., 21 Jun 1809.

203	12 Mar 1811	A/4/210

Thomas Gibson, [Reg Can]
Answers inquiry; mentions David Lane?

204	12 Mar 1811	A/4/211

Alexander Macomb, Esq., New York
Transmits statement of lands forfeited by -- Edgar
    & -- Macomb.

205	14 Mar 1811	A/4/211

Daniel Symmes, [Reg Cin]
Inquires regarding transfer (Mills patent) and
    transmits Treasury receipts

John Mills & Seth Mills*	Cin	MR	9	2	22	SE
Jacob Humbert	Cin	?	3	5	22	NW
Jacob Humbert	Cin	?	3	5	15	-
Jacob Humbert	Cin	?	5	4	15	N
Jacob Humbert	Cin	?	4	4	5	-
William McClelland	Cin	?	6	2	11	NW

*Transferred to Abraham Rudebaker.

206	15 Mar 1811	A/4/211

Peter Audrain, [Reg Det]
Signature required on patent certificate in favor
    of Charles Rouleau.

207		15 Mar 1811		A/4/211

Samuel Gwathmey, [Reg Jef]
Unpaid balance outstanding

William West	Jef	-	9E	3N	2	NE

208		15 Mar 1811		A/4/212

David Hoge, [Reg Stu]
Through error, two patents pertaining to LO Ch1 were
    forwarded to you on 4 Feb 1809

Jacob Shoemaker*	Ch1	-	20	11	18	-
Jacob Spitler*	Ch1	-	18	15	10	SE

*See *Federal Land Series*, volume 1, entry 825.

209		15 Mar 1811		A/4/212

Isaac Vanhorne, [Rec Zan]
Comments on discrepancies noted, transmits Treasury
    receipts

Joseph Reeve	Zan	-	8	10	10	NE
John Lock*	Zan	-	1	8	8	SE

*"Lives at or near Frederick Town, Md."

210		15 Mar 1811		A/4/212

Wyllys Silliman, [Reg Zan]
Returns certificate with discrepancies noted

John Willey	Zan	-	30*	12	7	SE
John Heckewelder	Zan	-	2	7	12	NW

*Range number is erroneous.

211		15 Mar 1811				A/4/213

Jesse Spencer, [Reg Ch1]
Transmits patent

-- Miller & -- Vangundy	Ch1	WS	21	10	36	NW

212		16 Mar 1811			A/4/213

LO Cin
Transmits patents

Andrew Hoover	Cin	WML	1	14	28	W
Andrew Hoover	Cin	WML	1	14	28	SE
Elias Baldwin	Cin	EML	2	3	6	SW
Robert Wilson	Cin	EML	5	5	35	SE
Joshua Piggot	Cin	WML	1	14	20	NE
William Lees	Cin	EML	3	7	28	SE
William Harbour	Cin	MR	12	4	14	SE
Nicholas Gift	Cin	EML	3	4	3	SE
William Marshall	Cin	MR	11	1	22	NW
Isaac Barker	Cin	WML	1	14	8	SW
Abraham Jones	Cin	WML	1	10	36	SW
Benjamin Youngs	Cin	EML	2	4	4	SW
John Small	Cin	WML	1	14	29	NE
Henry Freeman	Cin	MR	12	1	15	NE
Amos Embree	Cin	EML	2	8	33	NE
John Hall	Cin	MR	12	4	35	NE
John Kribe?	Cin	EML	5	4	31	SW
John Simmons	Cin	MR	11	2	35	NE

213		16 Mar 1811			A/4/213

Peter Mills, Esq., Zan
Transmits patents

Peter Mills	Mil	-	16	6	1	1
Peter Mills	Mil	-	16	6	1	2
Alexander Parker	Mil	-	16	6	1	21
Alexander Parker	Mil	-	16	6	1	22
Alexander Parker	Mil	-	16	6	1	23
Alexander Parker	Mil	-	16	6	1	31
Alexander Parker	Mil	-	7	4	2	4*
Alexander Parker	Mil	-	7	4	2	19*
Alexander Parker	Mil	-	7	4	2	32*
Alexander Parker	Mil	-	7	4	2	33*

*[Manuscript is somewhat ambiguous and these loca-
tions may be in error.]

214		16 Mar 1811		A/4/213

John Cox Stockton, Zan
Transmits patent

John Cox Stockton	Mil	-	5	3	3	17

215	16 Mar 1811	A/4/213

William Craig, Post Office, Leesburgh, Virginia
Transmits patent

William Craig	Stu	-	4	15	30	NE

216	16 Mar 1811	A/4/214

Charles Roberts, Zan
Transmits patents for four military land warrants
    [not described].

217		16 Mar 1811		A/4/214

Thomas M. Thompson, Stu
Transmits patents

Thomas M. Thompson, assignee						
of Abraham Greenewald	Mil	-	8	9	2	7
Thomas M. Thompson, assignee						
of John Steele	Mil	-	8	9	2	3

Thomas M. Thompson, assignee
  of John Steele   Mil -   8   9   2   4
Thomas M. Thompson, assignee
  of John Steele   Mil -   8   9   2   5
Thomas M. Thompson, assignee
  of James Burns   Mil -   8   9   2   8
James Barnet*   Mil -   8   9   3   7
*"Place of residence is not known here."

218   19 Mar 1811   A/4/214
Jesse Spencer, [Reg Chl]
Transmits corrected patent
John McMullin   Chl - 17 18 14   W*
*[Corrected; formerly shown as W.]

219   19 Mar 1811   A/4/214
David Hoge, [Reg Stu]
Transmits certificates and Treasury receipts
Abraham Golloday   Stu -   9   9   3   NE
Richard Ewers   Stu -   5   7 13   NW

220   19 Mar 1811   A/4/214
James Creegan, Springfield, Hampshire County, Virginia
Transmits patent
James Creegan   [Cin] [MR*] 12   1 21   NE
*"Between the Miami River and the Virginia reservation."

221   20 Mar 1811   A/4/215
LO Cin
Transmits patents
Thomas Dougherty   Cin EML   1   6 33   NE
Samuel Wood   Cin EML   1   9   4   NW

222   20 Mar 1811   A/4/215
LO Mar
Transmits patents
John McBride   Mar -   3   1 26   -
Augustine Webster   Mar - 12   4   8   NW
William Nixon   Mar -   7   2 35   NW

223   20 Mar 1811   A/4/215
LO Zan
Transmits patents
Jacob Yoho   Zan -   8   8 12   SE
William Robinson   Mil -   5   4 24   NW
John Tadron? [Fadron?]   Zan - 14 15   7   SW

224   23 Mar 1811   A/4/215
LO Cin
Transmits patents
Abraham Stetler   Cin EML   6   6 31   NW
Eliazar Dunham   Cin EML   1   4   6   SW
Samuel Stubbs   Cin EML   2   6 36   SE
John Spaight   Cin EML   2   8 34   SW
Abraham Hapner   Cin EML   3   7 20   SW
James Howard   Cin EML   1   3 24   SE
Christopher? Emrick   Cin EML   3   6 33   NW
Francis Ott   Cin EML   3   7 20   SE

225   23 Mar 1811   A/4/215
LO Chl
Transmits patent
John Pickens   Chl MS 21 10 18   NE

226   25 Mar 1811   A/4/215
LO Chl
Transmits patents
-- Sterret & -- Baldwin   Chl - 18 14   5   -
-- Sterret & -- Baldwin   Chl - 18 14   6   +

227   25 Mar 1811   A/4/215
Isaac Vanhorne, [Rec Zan]
Transmits patent
John Smith   Zan - 14 16   8   NE

228   25 Mar 1811   A/4/216
Samuel Annin, Esq., Paymaster, Harper's Ferry
Transmits patent
Joseph Huffman   [Cin] [MR*] 14   2   4   W
*"Between the Great Miami River and the Virginia
   Reservation."

229   28 Mar 1811   A/4/216
Wyllys Silliman, [Reg Zan]
Transmits certificate and Treasury receipt
Henry Davy   Mil -   1   9   2   SW

230   3 Apr 1811   A/4/216
Peter Audrain, [Reg Det]
Returns certificates for signature; mentions Louis
   Vassiere, Junior, and André Viger.

231   5 Apr 1811   A/4/216
Henry Eagle, Hagerstown, Maryland
Transmits patent
Edward Berry   Chl - 18 16 13   SE

232   5 Apr 1811   A/4/217
LO Stu
Transmits patent
Jacob Crouse   Stu -   4 15 25   SW

233   5 Apr 1811   A/4/217
LO Mar
Transmits patent
John Starr   Mar -   7   8 33   NE

234   5 Apr 1811   A/4/217
LO Cin
Transmits patents
Amos Embree   Cin EML   3   4 23   NW
David Jenkins   Cin EML   6   4   5   SE
James Price   Cin WML   1   8 18   SW
Jacob Bloyd   Cin WML   2 10 17   NE
Robert Bennet   Cin WML   1 12 20   SW
John Vincent   Cin WML   2   9 19   SW
William Norris   Cin WML   2 11 28   SE
Jacob R. Compton   Cin WML   1   6   2   SE

235   15 Apr 1811   A/4/217
David Hoge, [Reg Stu]
Requests final certificate
Morris Albaugh   Stu -   8 12 17   E

236   15 Apr 1811   A/4/217
John F. Mansfield, Esq.
Transmits patent

William Harris   Mil   -   11   6   1   35

---

237   18 Apr 1811   A/4/217
Wyllys Silliman, [Reg Zan]
Transmits patent
Philip Baker, assignee
   of Jacob Ayers   Zan   -   12   12   8   +

238   25 Apr 1811   A/4/218
Wyllys Silliman, [Reg Zan]
Transmits additional set of books.

239   29 Apr 1811   A/4/218
LO Chl
Transmits patents
James Bell   Chl MS 21 9 23 NW
Jacob Shoup   Chl MS 21 9 27 SE
John Wilson & Christian Gundy   Chl - 19 16 33 W
Frederick Peterson   Chl MS 21 11 23 N
Isaac Bury   Chl - 17 16 29 NE
John Dindore   Chl - 19 14 24 NW
John Dunkil   Chl - 24 11 8 NW
George White   Chl - 19 12 29 NE
Boston Lanert? & Jacob Houser   Chl - 19 16 26 NE
James Henderson   Chl - 17 18 27 NW
Jacob Ruse   Chl MS 21 11 1 SE
David Rees   Chl - 19 15 24 -
John Heller   Chl MS 22 2 36 NW

240   2 May 1811   A/4/218
LO Chl
Transmits patents
Joshua Hobbs   Chl WS 21 10 13 E
William Kendall   Chl - 17 2 30 +
William Kendall   Chl - 17 2 31 -?
Daniel Glick   Chl MS 21 10 36 NE
Daniel Cleck   Chl MS 21 10 25 E
Daniel Cleck   Chl MS 21 10 25 NW
Stephen Ross   Chl - 20 9 7 N
John King   Chl - 17 18 35 W
Philip Cleck   Chl - 18 16 30 N
Zephaniah Drake   Chl - 20 14 23 W
John Flick   Chl - 18 15 22 SW

241   2 May 1811   A/4/219
LO Can
Transmits patents
Reasin Beale   Can - 17 23 26 SE
Reasin Beale   Can - 10 12 3 SE
Reasin Beale   Can - 18 21 21 SW
Reasin Beale   Can - 18 19 5 SE
Reasin Beale   Can - 13 15 3 SW

242   2 May 1811   A/4/219
LO Cin
Transmits patents
James Turner   Cin MR 12 5 17 NE
James Turner   Cin MR 6 2 28 +*
*North half of Lot 1.

243   2 May 1811   A/4/219
LO Vin
Transmits patent
Samuel Jones   Vin - 13W 7S 5 SW

---

244   2 May 1811   A/4/219
LO Stu
Transmits patents
Alexander Lee   Stu - 5 13 17 NW
Morris Albaugh   Stu - 5 12 18 SE

245   2 May 1811   A/4/219
Isaac Vanhorne, [Rec Zan]
Transmits patent, certificate and Treasury receipt
William Moore   Zan - 13 11 10 N+
William Foy, Senior   Zan - 2 2 20 NE

246   2 May 1811   A/4/219
Isaac Hatcher, to be left at Captain Thomas Grigg's
   store, near Leesburg, Virginia
Transmits patents
Isaac Hatcher   Can - 19 19 31 SE
Isaac Hatcher   Can - 18 18 6 NE

247   2 May 1811   A/4/220
Thomas Gibson, [Reg Can]
Transmits certificates and Treasury receipts; mentions David Lane
William Hough   Can - 16 21 24 SW
William Hough   Can - 16 21 25 NW
William Hough   Can - 16 21 26 NE
William Hough   Can - 16 21 26 SE
William Hough   Can - 16 21 26 SW
Jacob Kent   Can - 15 20 5 SE
Jacob Kent   Can - 15 20 4 SW

248   2 May 1811   A/4/220
Jesse Spencer, [Reg Chl]
Transmits certificate and Treasury receipt
Thomas Ijams   Chl - 17 17 34 N

249   2 May 1811   A/4/220
William Dickson, Reg Nsh
Asks for missing January returns, as it has probably
   miscarried in the mails.

250   2 May 1811   A/4/221
David Hoge, [Reg Stu]
Transmits certificate and Treasury receipt
Andrew Whisler   Stu - 9 10 35 NW

251   9 May 1811   A/4/221
LO Chl
Transmits patents
John Keller   Chl MS 22 2 36 NE
Jacob Gardner   Chl - 20 13 27 W
George Renick   Chl MS 22 3 22 NW
George Renick   Chl MS 22 3 21 -

252   8 May 1811   A/4/221
John Badollet, [Reg Vin]
Transmits patent for correction
John Anderson   Vin - 12W 35 4* SE
*Incorrectly shown as section 3.

253   9 May 1811   A/4/222
LO Chl
Transmits patents
Thomas Watson   Chl - 18 16 23 SE

Thomas Crow	Chl	WS	21	10	25	SE
Jacob Boobs	Chl	-	20	14	30	SE
George Benetum	Chl	-	20	14	14	NE
Abraham Dumbold	Chl	-	16	17	7	NW
John Beacher*	Chl	MS	21	10	10	NE
John Peacher*	Chl	MS	21	10	2	SW
John Peacher*	Chl	MS	21	10	3	SE
John Peacher*	Chl	MS	21	10	11	NW
John Peacher*	Chl	MS	21	10	5	SE

*So spelled.

254   14 May 1811   A/4/222
LO Chl
Transmits patents

Jonathan Looker	Chl	-	20	15	9	NE
John Ritter	Chl	MS	21	10	24	NW
Daniel Snyder	Chl	-	17	18	33	NW
Philip Lamb	Chl	-	20	14	23	SE
H. Trusbaugh & John Ely	Chl	WS	21	11	34	SE
David Cochran	Chl	-	17	17	36	SE
John Cochran	Chl	-	17	17	36	SW
James Looker	Chl	-	20	15	15	SE
James Looker	Chl	-	20	15	14	NW
James Looker	Chl	-	20	15	10	S

255   14 May 1811   A/4/222
Messrs. G. Dove & G. Shoemaker, care of Bryam Hampson, Merchant, Alexandria [Virginia]
Transmits patent

G. Dove & G. Shoemaker	Chl	-	20	15	6	NW

256   14 May 1811   A/4/223
Jesse Gause, Wilmington, Delaware
Transmits patent

Jesse Gause	Chl	-	18	16	7	NE

257   21 May 1811   A/4/223
LO Stu
Transmits patents

Joseph Patterson	Stu	-	6	8	13	NE
Zebediah Cox	Stu	-	5	11	19	SE
Samuel Hicklen	Stu	-	6	19	4	SW
Samuel Meck	Stu	-	7	16	36	NW
Peter Wise	Stu	-	17*	19	6	SW
John Fife	Stu	-	2	10	18	SW
Thomas Dunn	Stu	-	6	9	18	NW
Horton Howard	Stu	-	4	17	31	SE
William Patterson	Stu	-	6	8	20	NW
Isabella Haggerty	Stu	-	5	11	3	SW
Ezekiel Vance	Stu	-	7	9	10	SE
Abraham Warrington, Junior	Stu	-	4	17	12	W
John Batten	Stu	-	6	19	5	E
William Barnhill	Stu	-	5	11	4	SE
Jacob Anspach	Stu	-	9	9	13	NW
Mary Stinger? [Slinger?]	Stu	-	5	12	6	SE
George Snider	Stu	-	7	19	7	SE
James Caldwell	Stu	-	6	8	22	SW
William McCreery	Stu	-	5	11	24	NE
David Brown	Stu	-	6	19	11	NE
Jonathan Sayrs	Stu	-	6	11	27	NE
Isaac Clay	Stu	-	7	19	5	NW
Jonah Wildman	Stu	-	7	20	1	SW
John Nichols	Stu	-	8	10	27	NE
Ezekiel Vance	Stu	-	7	9	4	SW

*Could be Range 7.

258   25 May 1811   A/4/224
Wyllys Silliman, [Reg Zan]

Thomas Kelly, assignee of M. Young	Mil	-	7	1	9	SE

259   25 May 1811   A/4/224
LO Stu
Transmits patents

William Meck	Stu	-	3	5	36	SE
David Craig	Stu	-	3	9	22	NE
David Craig	Stu	-	3	9	22	SE
Joshua Cowpland	Stu	-	3	13	6	NE
Demay? Johnson	Stu	-	7	20	11	SE
George Wirick	Stu	-	7	18	14	NE
Henry Miser	Stu	-	5	12	31	NE
George Herrimer	Stu	-	5	11	14	NE
Peter Wise	Stu	-	7	19	6	SE
Peter Wise	Stu	-	7	19	17	SW
Peter Wise	Stu	-	7	19	29	SW
Peter Wise	Stu	-	8	11	11	NE
Thomas Rowland	Stu	-	3	9	30	SW

260   28 May 1811   A/4/224
Fisher A. Blocksom, New Lisbon, Columbia County, Ohio
Transmits patent

John McMillan	Unk	-	2	11	32	NE

261   30 May 1811   A/4/225
LO Cin
Transmits patents

Joseph Beard	Cin	EML	3	3	12	E
Lucy Ramsey	Cin	EML	1	4	34	NW
Abijah Jones	Cin	EML	6	3	30	NE
Joseph Owen	Cin	EML	5	5	23	SW
Gideon Wilkinson	Cin	EML	1	4	3	NW
Jacob Cooper	Cin	EML	1	7	27	NW
Joel Williams	Cin	EML	2	4	34	SE
George Carr	Cin	EML	6	4	8	S
John Coppock	Cin	EML	5	6	5	SE
John Henry Treber	Cin	EML	2	5	35	NE
John Morrow	Cin	WML	1	14	27	SW
Jeremiah Cox	Cin	WML	1	14	32	SE
Jeremiah Cox	Cin	WML	1	14	33	SW

262   31 May 1811   A/4/225
LO Chl
Transmits patents

William Brown	Chl	MS	21	9	23	NE
George Givens	Chl	-	21	5	32	SW
Jacob Thomas	Chl	-	16	6	36	NW
Moses Scott	Chl	WS	21	10	33	NE
Henry Culp	Chl	-	18	16	13	SW

263   6 Jun 1811   A/4/226
LO Chl
Transmits patents

Jesse Spencer	Chl	-	20	2	16	-
Jacob Martz	Chl	-	20	15	10	NE
Daniel Ulm	Chl	-	20	9	31	SE
Simon Christ	Chl	-	20	14	35	NE
Jesse Huff	Chl	-	21	5	27	SW
Henry Valentine	Chl	MS	22	4	25	E
Horatio Clark	Chl	-	20	14	33	W
Conrad Hite	Chl	-	18	16	20	-
John Swinehart	Chl	-	16	17	19	SE
Jeremiah Conaway	Chl	-	16	16	23	SE
Matheus Rinebold	Chl	-	17	18	26	W
Stephen Cole	Chl	IS	1	9	4	W

George Miller	Chl	– 17	17	4	NE
Jacob Miller	Chl	– 16	16	3	NW

264 12 Jun 1811 A/4/226
Daniel Symmes, [Reg Cin]
Inquires regarding final certificate

Peter Inglemar	Cin EML	3	4	12	NW

265 12 Jun 1811 A/4/226
Samuel Finley, [Rec Chl]
Transmits Treasury receipt

Christian Houtz, assignee of Henry Zeller	Chl	– 17	14	6	SW

266 12 Jun 1811 A/4/227
Peter Ingleman, Staunton, Augusta County, Virginia
Explains delay in issuing patent.

267 12 Jun 1811 A/4/227
Jesse Spencer, [Reg Chl]
Transmits papers regarding a claim in the Virginia
  military reservation in which emendations are required. Also transmits certificate and Treasury
  receipt

Jacob Powers	Chl	– 16	17	28	SW

268 13 Jun 1811 A/4/227
LO Stu
Transmits patents

Peter Boghart	Stu	– 5	13	23	SE
William Rogers	Stu	– 5	10	28	NW
Christian Herr, heirs of	Stu	– 6	13	8	SE
William Rogers	Stu	– 5	10	34	SE
Joseph Milner	Stu	– 4	15	28	NW
James Fisher	Stu	– 5	11	4	NW
Daniel Hardman	Stu	– 2	12	15	NE
George Brown	Stu	– 4	15	21	SW
Thomas Hartford	Stu	– 8	10	17	SE
Alexander Moore	Stu	– 5	11	25	SW
Nathan Galbraith	Stu	– 4	16	29	NW
Peter Ward	Stu	– 6	17	13	NW
John Glen	Stu	– 2	10	2	SE
Henry Smart	Stu	– 6	19	13	NE
John Ruff	Stu	– 6	17	6	–
William Arnst	Stu	– 4	11	36	SE
William Gardner	Stu	– 4	10	22	SW
William Copeland	Stu	– 7	20	23	NE
Henry Hare	Stu	– 5	18	20	NE

269 13 Jun 1811 A/4/228
LO Chl
Transmits patents

S. Ruffner & J. Ruffner	Chl	– 17	18	19	NE
Jacob Bumgarner	Chl	– 21	5	32	SE
David Williamson	Chl	WS 21	9	29	–
Rudolph Vitcher	Chl	– 20	14	24	E
Garret Bootes	Chl	– 21	8	32	SW
Michael John James Bacus* & Christian Bacus	Chl	– 20	2	23	+
Henry Neff	Chl	– 16	2	35	NE
John Barr	Chl	MS 22	3	11	–
John Sunday	Chl	MS 21	10	13	SE
John Kile	Chl	MS 21	11	17	SE
Andrew Doherty	Chl	– 20	15	3	SW
Nicholas Kelley	Chl	– 20	8	19	SW
William Glen	Chl	– 16	7	25	NW

Samuel R. Holcomb	Chl	– 16	7	24	SW
Thomas Gray	Chl	MS 21	11	4	SE
Thomas Gray	Chl	MS 22	4	35	SW

*It is not clear whether one, or several, persons is
meant.

270 14 Jun 1811 A/4/229
LO Chl
Transmits patents

William A. McNeal	Chl	WS 21	11	6	SE
Thomas McNeal	Chl	WS 21	11	7	SE
Christian Wolf	Chl	– 18	13	10	SE
Conrad Hite	Chl	– 18	16	7	NW
Herbert Winegarder*	Chl	– 18	16	12	NW
John Helser	Chl	– 16	17	30	SW
John Moler	Chl	MS 22	3	26	NW
Jacob Fast	Chl	– 17	16	24	SW
Peter Hendricks	Chl	– 16	17	33	NE
Mason Dean	Chl	– 16	17	26	SE
John Christy	Chl	– 20	13	35	SW
John Philips	Chl	– 17	11	34	SE
George Akert, Junior	Chl	– 18	13	23	SE
George Akert, [Senior?]	Chl	– 18	13	14	SW
George Akert, Junior	Chl	– 18	13	23	NW
George Akert, Junior	Chl	– 18	13	23	SE
George Akert, Junior	Chl	– 18	13	23	NE
Michael Kraner	Chl	– 20	15	4	SW
Jacob Carne	Chl	– 17	14	17	NW
Henry Carne	Chl	– 17	14	17	SE
Jacob Kraner	Chl	– 16	16	32	NE

*So spelled in manuscript.

271 24 Jun 1811 A/4/228
LO Zan
Transmits patents

Archibald Allison	Zan	– 12	13	18	NW
David Harvey	Zan	– 13	12	8	NE
William Comvill?	Zan	– 13	12	11	NE
Frederick Secrist	Zan	– 9	8	10	NW
Thomas Heneboard	Zan	– 15	18	12	NE
John Hendricks	Zan	– 15	17	17	NE
John Hendricks	Zan	– 15	17	18	NE
John Conden	Zan	– 14	15	34	SE
John Brush	Zan	– 15	17	24	SW
James Porter	Zan	– 14	15	33	SW
William Ford	Zan	– 14	15	34	NW
Christian Spangler	Zan	– 13	12	2	SW
-- Gaddis & -- Springer	Zan	– 14	14	9	SE

272 28 Jun 1811 A/4/230
Richard Flowers, Morrisville, Pennsylvania
Transmits Treasury receipt

Richard Flowers	Zan	– 14	16	8	SW

273 2 Jul 1811 A/4/230
Christian Houtz, Lebanon, Pennsylvania
Gives accounting of payments since 1806

Christian Houtz	Chl	– 17	14	6	SW

274 3 Jul 1811 A/4/231
Samuel Finley, Rec Chl
Transmits Treasury receipts

Christian Houtz	Chl	– 17	14	6	SW

275 — 11 Jul 1811 — A/4/231
Thomas Gibson, Reg Can
Transmits patent

Adam Groundz	Can	- 10	11	23	NE

276 — 11 Jul 1811 — A/4/231
LO Jef
Transmits patents

Jesse Connell	Jef	- 10E	2N	6	NE
John Taylor	Jef	- 10E	4N	34	SW
George Kindle	Jef	- 11E	5N	29	SE
Henry Wyman	Jef	- 4E	1S	3	NW
Michael? Smith	Jef	- 4E	1N	31*	SW
Thomas Carr	Jef	- 4E	2N	13	NE

*Could read section 37.

277 — 11 Jul 1811 — A/4/232
Thomas Gibson, Reg Can
Transmits patent

Michael? Waxler	Can	- 11	15	12	NE

278 — 11 Jul 1811 — A/4/232
Daniel Symmes, Reg Cin
Transmits patent

John Coppock	Cin EML	5	6	7	NE

279 — 11 Jul 1811 — A/4/232
LO Vin
Transmits patents

-- Anderson & -- Calton	Vin	- 12E	3S	4	NW
John Hollowell	Vin	- 3E	1S	15	NW

280 — 17 Jul 1811 — A/4/233
LO Jef
Transmits patents

John Burger	Jef	- 5E	2S	27	SW
Frederick Phillips	Jef	- 1E	2N	12	NW
James West	Jef	- 10E	2N	17	+
James West	Jef	- 10E	2N	20	+
John West	Jef	- 10E	2N	30	SE
Joshua Carter	Jef	- 1E	2N	1	NW
John Eddleman	Jef	- 5E	2S	19	SW
Thomas Montgomery	Jef	- 8E	2N	12	SW
Thomas Hopper	Jef	- 2E	2N	32	SE
Jacob Stucker	Jef	- 9E	2N	12	SW

281 — 17 Jul 1811 — A/4/233
LO Stu
Transmits patents

Arthur Burbick	Stu	- 3	14	27	SW
Job Lewis	Stu	- 5	9	28	NE
William Waddel	Stu	- 4	12	9	SW
John Metz	Stu	- 8	11	23	NE

282 — 17 Jul 1811 — A/4/233
Joseph Wood, Reg Mar
Transmits patent

John Sharp & John Mitchell	Mar	- 7	3	31	SW

283 — 25 Jul 1811 — A/4/233
LO Zan
Transmits patents

George Dills? [Dilts?]	Zan	- 15	17	4	NE
John Evansdant?	Zan	- 15	18	3	SE

Frederick Salmon	Zan Mil	1	9	1	NE
John Le Leivre	Zan	- 9	8	7	E
John Adams	Zan Mil	8	4	12	SW
George Leinenger	Zan Mil	4	8	1	SW
Nicholas Bright	Zan Mil	8	2	20	SW
George Leinenger	Zan Mil	4	8	1	SE
Christian Walhammer?	Zan Mil	3	8	2	NE
Christian Yollen?	Zan Mil	5	9	20	NW

284 — 20 Jul 1811 — A/4/234
LO Vin
Transmits patents

John Wallace	Vin	- 7W	2N	9?	NE
John Fisher	Vin	- 11W	1S	36	NE
Thomas Jones	Vin	- 1E	5S	3	+
Thomas Jones	Vin	- 1E	5S	4	+
Robert Anderson	Vin	- 12W	3S	5	NE
William Patterson	Vin	- 11W	1S	35	SE
Samuel Adams	Vin	- 11W	1S	24	SW
Levi Compton	Vin	- 12W	1N	24	NE
Smith Maunce?	Vin	- 12W	3S	24	SW
John A. Miller	Vin	- 11W	1S	26	NE
John Warrick	Vin	- 11W	3S	4	SW
Thomas Jones	Vin	- 14W	8S	7	+
Toussaint Dubois	Vin	- 12W	1N	12	+
Jacob Yulstar	Vin	- 2E	5S	23	+
Jacob Lapp	Vin	- 2E	5S	25	+
Jacob Lapp	Vin	- 2E	5S	26	+

285 — 26 Jul 1811 — A/4/234
William Silliman, Reg Zan
Transmits patent

Jacob Kreger	Zan Mil	4	8	16	NE

286 — 26 Jul 1811 — A/4/234
LO Chl
Transmits patents

Jacob Lutz	Chl	- 20	10	6	NE
Jacob Lutz	Chl	- 20	10	6	SE
Elizabeth Ramsey	Chl	- 17	18	28	SE
William Bogle	Chl	- 16	17	9	NW
William Bogle	Chl	- 16	17	9	NE
William Bogle	Chl	- 16	17	3	SE

287 — 26 Jul 1811 — A/4/235
David Hoge, [Reg Stu]
Transmits patent

Thomas Stephenson	Stu	- 1	6	20	SE

288 — 2 Aug 1811 — A/4/235
LO Cin
Transmits patents

Adam Blair?	Cin Pre	4	3	5	E
Owen Davis	Cin Pre	8	5	32	+
Arthur Johnston	Cin Pre	8	3	4	NW
Arthur Johnston	Cin Pre	8	3	4	NE
William Millikan	Cin Pre	4	4	13	NE
John M. Gillespie	Cin Pre	4	3	27	NW
John Bradford	Cin Pre	6	2	28	E*
David Werman?	Cin Pre	7	2	31	SW

*250 acres therein.

289 — 8 Aug 1811 — A/4/235
LO Cin
Transmits patents

Francis Jer? [Ier?]	Cin Pre	4	3	5	W

Peter Smith	Cin Pre	11	4	23	SE
Henry Pence	Cin Pre	11	4	36	NE
Joseph Pence	Cin Pre	11	5	33	SE
William Holmes	Cin Pre	9	3	22	NW
John Steddem	Cin Pre	4	4	14	SE
Levin Hatfield	Cin Pre	5	3	12	NE

290 7 Aug 1811 A/4/235
Isaac Vanhorne, [Rec Zan]
Transmits Treasury receipts

| Jacob Bachman | Zan | – | 8 | 4 | 4 | SE |
| Richard Flowers | Zan | – | 4 | 16 | 8 | SW |

291 7 Aug 1811 A/4/236
Daniel Symmes, [Reg Cin]
Transmits Treasury receipts

David Huston	Cin MR	8	2	26	SW
James Miller	Cin Pre	7	2	22	E
James Miller	Cin Pre	7	2	22	SW
Jacob Humbert	Cin EML	5	3	22	SW
John Buchanan*	Cin	–	5	6	14	NW
Dennis Boyse*	Cin	–	2	5	18	SE
John Lock	Cin	–	3	7	26	SW
Ludwick Kemp	Cin	–	7	2	22	E
Ludwick Kemp	Cin	–	7	2	22	SW
Christian Bleakenstaff	Cin	–	6	4	27	SE
Jacob Humbert	Cin	–	5	5	22	SW
Jacob Humbert	Cin	–	3	5	15	NW
Jacob Humbert	Cin	–	3	5	22	NW
Jacob Humbert	Cin	–	4	4	5	–
Jacob Humbert	Cin	–	5	4	15	N
Samuel Bond	Cin	–	1	5	19	SW
Samuel Bond	Cin	–	1	5	5	SE
Samuel Bond	Cin	–	1	5	9	SE
Samuel Bond	Cin	–	1	5	9	SW
Enos Matson	Cin	–	8	2	26	SW

*Multiple receipts. Letter contains amounts and
dates, not transcribed here.

292 7 Aug 1811 A/4/236
Jesse Spencer, [Reg Chl]
Transmits Treasury certificates

John Martin Fulkamore	Chl	–	21	5	5	+
John Martin Fulkamore	Chl	–	21	5	16	+
Isaac Clowburg	Chl WS	21	11	11	E
Christian Houtz	Chl	–	17	14	6	SW

293 7 Aug 1811 A/4/237
Christian Houtz, Lebanon, Pennsylvania
Returns certificate and requests new assignment from
Adam Spitler

| Henry Zeller? [Keller?] | Chl | – | 17 | 14 | 6 | SW |

294 7 Aug 1811 A/4/237
David Hoge, [Reg Stu]
Transmits Treasury certificate

Jacob Conkle*	Stu	–	1	7	32	SW
John Shover	Stu	–	3	10	15	NE
Jacob Smith	Stu	–	4	11	22	NE
-- Myers & -- Lowman	Stu	–	8	12	30	NW

*Assigned to John Davis.

295 7 Aug 1811 A/4/237
Horton Howard, St. Clairsville, Ohio
Reports sending patent to LO Stu

| John Piggot | Stu | – | 5 | 7 | 29 | SE |

296 8 Aug 1811 A/4/238
Thomas Gibson, [Reg Can]
Transmits certificates

Philip Slusher	Can	–	10	12	14	NE
Joseph Friend	Can	–	17	21	3	NE
Thomas Eagle	Can	–	15	21	23	NW
Zephaniah Beale	Can	–	10	1	27	SE
David Lane	Can	–	17	23	31	NW

297 8 Aug 1811 A/4/238
Charles Bohn, Baltimore
Transmits patents

C. Bohn & -- Slingluff*	Mil	–	3	8	4	31
C. Bohn & -- Slingluff**	Mil	–	3	8	4	7
Christian Deardorff***	Mil	–	3	8	4	18

* Assignees of Isaac Lane.
** Assignees of Tippits F. Hopkins.
*** Assignee of Josiah Willcox.

298 8 Aug 1811 A/4/238
James Findlay, [Rec Cin]
Inquires regarding following accounts, dating from
1806

Christopher Hansel	Cin WML	1	10	25	NE
John Young	Cin EML	2	5	10	–
Asaiah Rance*	Cin EML	5	7	20	SE

*Note says "probably Roe."

299 13 Aug 1811 A/4/239
Richard Forrest, [U.S.] Department of State
Returns corrected patent for signature

| Robert Swan | [Cin?] WML* | 2 | 11 | 22 | SW |

*Doubt as to whether EML or WML.

300 14 Aug 1811 A/4/239
Samuel Finley, [Rec Chl]
Requests submission of quarterly accounts for audit.

301 14 Aug 1811 A/4/239
William Dixon, Reg Hun
Acknowledges receipt of July 1811 monthly return for
LO Nsh.

302 15 Aug 1811 A/4/239
Thomas Gibson, Reg Can
Returns certificates for signature.

303 15 Aug 1811 A/4/240
Daniel Symmes, [Reg Cin]
Corrected patent transmitted

| Robert Swan | Cin EML | 2 | 11 | 22 | SW |

304 16 Aug 1811 A/4/240
Daniel Symmes, [Reg Cin]
Payments made

| -- | Cin EML | 4 | 4 | 34 | – |

305 17 Aug 1811 A/4/240
LO Stu
Transmits patents

Robert Huston	Stu	–	6	10	17	NW
John Fisk	Stu	–	8	10	21	N
Philip Smith	Stu	–	2	9	35	NW

William Morrison	Stu	–	2	10	3	SW
James Devore	Stu	–	5	11	9	SE
Thomas Fife	Stu	–	4	14	1	SE
William Bevard	Stu	–	7	9	30	NW
Hugh Anderson	Stu	–	2	9	28	SE
Philip Ream	Stu	–	8	10	1	E
Christian Bowman	Stu	–	2	11	26	SW
Jacob Easterday	Stu	–	6	13	27	NE
Bezaliel Wells	Stu	–	4	10	3	SW
Bezaliel Wells	Stu	–	8	10	5	NW
Bezaliel Wells	Stu	–	7	18	5	NE
Bezaliel Wells	Stu	–	7	18	7	NW
Bezaliel Wells	Stu	–	7	18	9	SW
Bezaliel Wells	Stu	–	7	18	4	NW
Bezaliel Wells	Stu	–	7	18	7	NE
Bezaliel Wells	Stu	–	8	10	4	NE

306   17 Aug 1811   A/4/241
James Findlay, [Rec Cin]
Descrepancies in land descriptions in audit of 1806
    accounts; mentions: Elijah Brush & Jacob Burnet;
    Emanuel Vantrees; Henry C. Smith of Pennsylvania;
    Thomas Miller, assignee of Joseph Mays; Peter
    Shutt [Shull?]

307   17 Aug 1811   A/4/241
Parke Walton, Rec Wsh
Transmits receipt for pre-emption land for Daniel
    Williams

308   18 Aug 1811   A/4/241
David Hoge, [Reg Stu]
Acknowledges receipt of Jul 1811 returns.

309   18 Aug 1811   A/4/241
Postmaster, Harper's Ferry
Patent sent to postoffice for Joseph Hoffman or --
    Annin should be handed to the latter.

310   18 Aug 1811   A/4/242
Samuel Gwathmey, [Reg Jef]
Acknowledges receipt of packet.

311   18 Aug 1811   A/4/242
Samuel Finley, [Rec Chl]
Correction of reports.

312   18 Aug 1811   A/4/242
John Sloane, [Rec Can]
Requests monthly reports.

313   18 Aug 1811   A/4/242
Peter Audrain, [Reg Det]
Returns certificates for the following persons:
    Alexander Harrow; John, William, & David McComb;
    Louis Bernard dit Lajoye; George Cotterall; George,
    Henry, John, James, & David Cotterall; Nicholas
    Patenode; Alexander Grant
Certificate of legal heirs of Joseph Noyer incom-
    pletely assigned to Henry B. Broovoock. Heirs
    mentioned were Charles Noyer & Therrier Ecuyer
Certificate of widow and heirs of Battiste Chovan
    transferred by widow to one heir only. Was there
    only one heir?

314   18 Aug 1811   A/4/243
LO Stu
Transmits patents

Stacy Bevan	Stu	–	5	9	29	NW
Thomas Moore, Senior	Stu	–	1	6	4	SE
William McCreary	Stu	–	7	15	29	SW
Bezaliel Wells	Stu	–	8	10	6	NE
Stacy Bevan	Stu	–	6	10	3	SE
John Spiller	Stu	–	2	8	6	+
Ebenezer Altman	Stu	–	9	9	4	NW
Ebenezer Altman	Stu	–	9	9	4	NE
Ebenezer Altman	Stu	–	9	10	33	SW
Ezekiel Vunce? [Vance?]	Stu	–	7	9	5	SW
Robert Bell	Stu	–	6	10	11	NE
Jacob Click & Jacob Brougher	Stu	–	8	10	25	SW

315   20 Aug 1811   A/4/243
John Badollet, Reg Vin
Returns for Jul 1811 received.

316   20 Aug 1811   A/4/243
Daniel Symmes, [Reg Cin]
Returns certificates for correction or clarification

Daniel C. Cooper*	Cin	MR	7	2	11	NW
John Smiley**	Cin	EML	2	4	30	SE
John Miller***	Cin	WML	1	10	1	E
Jonas Randle****	Cin	WML	1	13	6	NE
John Rue#	Cin	MR	9	4	35	NW
James Findlay##	Cin	–	5	3	29	NE
George Newcorn###	Cin	MR	9	2	13	SW
James Wills####	Cin	Pre	4	4	22	SW
Diana Ewam§						
Samuel Beck§§	Cin	–	6	6	7	NW
Samuel Beck§§	Cin	–	2	6	7	NW

*Assigned to Isaac Spinning & Alexander Tillford;
    the latter reassigned South half to Adam Garbuck,
    although he had only an undivided half-interest in
    the quarter section.
**Assigned to James Wettherell? by administrators of
    estate, Christiana & John Smiley, Junior.
***Assignee of Cornelius Wiely.
****Transferred to Jeremiah Meek.
#Assigned by Rue's attorney, Samuel Smith, to Nathan-
    iel Williams.
##Assigned to John Harris.
###Assignee's name illegible to GLO.
####Section was apportioned as follows: James Wills
    & -- Graham, 190 acres; Henry Brandenbourg, 50
    acres; Peter Kever, 109 acres; Stephen Vineyard,
    309 acres.
§Name mentioned but without land description.
§§Land description incorrect; land transferred to
    -- Horner.

317   21 Aug 1811   A/4/245
Samuel Gwathmey, [Reg Jef]
Returns erroneous certificates for correction

James Kundell	Jef	–	5E	2S	6	NE
Jacob Copple	Jef	–	9E	1N	3	NW
Jacob Copple	Jef	–	9E	2N*	3	NW
Richard Gillstrape	Jef	–	3E	1N	12	NE
John C. Laurence**	Jef	–	9E	1N	5	NE

*Township 2N is correct description.
**Assigned to Bailey Johnston.

318   21 Aug 1811   A/4/245
Wyllys Silliman, [Reg Zan]

Erroneous certificates returned for correction

John Paxton	Zan Mil	2	3	1	SW	
Jacob Bowers	Zan Mil	7	1	7	SE	
Jacob Bowers	Zan Mil	6*	1	7	SE	
Abraham Messer	Zan **	12	13	6	SE	
Jacob Titerack	Zan Mil	1	3	15	SE	
Jacob Titerack	Zan Mil	1	3	15	SW***	
James Wilson	Zan -	14	16	8	SW	
James Wilson	Zan -	15#	16	8	SW	
R-- Flowers	Zan -	14	16	8	SW	
James Falherty, Richard & Andrew McBride	Zan -	14	15	1	NE	
David Calhoon	Zan Mil	1	1	23	NW	
David Calhoon	Zan Mil	5##	1	23	NW	
Daniel Wilkin	Zan Mil	11	3	16	SW	
Daniel Wilkin	Zan Mil	11	3	16	NW###	
Abraham Clements	Zan Mil	2	2	8	SE	

*Range 6 is erroneous description.
**Erroneously read "Military" in original descrip-
   tion; assigned to George Messer.
***SW is correct description.
#Range 15 is correct description.
##Range 5 is correct description.
###NW quarter is correct description.

319   21 Aug 1811   A/4/246
Jesse Spencer, [Reg Chl]
Certificates returned for correction

Thomas Barr*	Chl WS	21	10	28	W	
Abraham Lorance**	Chl -	21	5	33	SE	
James O'Hara***	Chl -	20	12	10	NW	
William Crosin	Chl -	17	16	13	NE	
Thomas George Fayette#	Chl -	20	15	32	NW	
Samuel Lee	Chl -	20	14	7	SE	
Samuel Drake##	Chl -	20?	14	20	NE	
William Enterken	Chl WS	21	10	34	SW	
Anthony Rapenholst###	Chl -	21?	9	31	NW	
Philip Hoy§						
Isaac Temboss	Mil? -	19	7	19	SE	
John McNeal§§	Chl WS	21	11	18	NW	
Joseph Shoots & James Roads§§§	Chl MS	21	9	9	SE	
Benjamin Yates¶						

*Transfer to James Ferguson incomplete.
**Transfer to Jacob Bumgarner acknowledged by John
   Lorance.
***Assigned to John Christ acknowledged by Joseph
   Tiffin, instead of Edward Tiffin.
#Assignment not signed by F. & G. Fayette.
##Assignee of John Corn.
###Assignee of William Asher.
§Assignee of James Lambert; land description not
   given.
§§"John, the assignee of Thomas McNeal."
§§§"The land is assigned to Waiser, the final certi-
   ficate calls him Waider. There is wanted the
   acknowledgement of Gallaspy's transfer. . . ."
¶Assigned to Jacob Saltsgaver.

320   21 Aug 1811   A/4/247
Samuel Finley, [Rec Chl]
Discusses differences in calculation of interest.

321   28 Aug 1811   A/4/247
N. Tiltan, Reg Wsh
Regarding mistake noted.

322   27 Aug 1811   A/4/248
R[ichard] Forrest, U.S. Department of State

Asks for transmission of patent

Reasin Beall	Stu -	3	14	22	NW	

323   27 Aug 1811   A/4/248
LO Stu
Transmits patents

James Armstrong	Stu -	4	15	30	SW	
Moses Campbell	Stu -	5	8	34	SW	
James Wright	Stu -	5	9	32	SE	
David Spence	Stu -	2	10	4	SE	
Joseph Rutter	Stu -	6	14	25	NE	
Jacob Troxell	Stu -	7	18	6	NE	
-- Coburn & -- Perry	Stu -	1	6	18	NW	
Thomas Hanna	Stu -	6	19	17	SW	
Alexander Rogers	Stu -	5	17	34	-	
Alexander Rogers	Stu -	2	11	9	SW	
Littleberry Stanley	Stu -	4	16	6	SW	
William Stalcup	Stu -	1	6	20	NW	
Aaron Street	Stu -	4	17	7	SW	
William Harbough	Stu -	2	11	32	SE	
George Adam Rex?	Stu -	8	11	28	SE	

324   29 Aug 1811   A/4/249
Jared Mansfield, SG
Requests survey of an area too indefinite for patent-
   ing; 100-acre tract assigned by Blackford to John
   Terril adjacent to the following

John Blackford	Cin Pre	5	3	19	+	

325   29 Aug 1811   A/4/249
Jesse Spencer, Reg Chl
Transmits certificate

William Claypoole*	Chl -	16	17	4	NE	

*Assigned to -- Harris; reassigned to -- Reasler;
   reassigned to Danniel Bussard.

326   5 Sep 1811   A/4/250
James Findlay, [Rec Cin]
Discrepancy in account of Peter Atherton.

327   5 Sep 1811   2/4/250
Jesse Spencer, [Reg Chl]
Reports on cases in process

William Bogle	Chl -	16	17	9	SW	
George Glaze	Chl -	21	10	19	NW	
George Glaze*	Chl -	21	10	27	S	
-- Valentine**	Chl -	17	18	31	W	

*Transferred from James Bell; Peter Apple, magistrate.
**Transferred by Edward Teal, attorney, for Peter
   Hush.

328   5 Sep 1811   A/4/251
Jared Mansfield, SG
Requests survey for 61.43 acres in NW corner of

Philip Siler	Unk Pre	9	2	18	+	

329   5 Sep 1811   A/4/251
Daniel Symmes, [Reg Cin]
Cases requiring further clarification

John Knoop	Cin Pre	10	1	4	+*	-
William Bruce	Cin EML	4	3	23		
Abraham Hanes**	Cin EML	4	4	30	SW	
Amos Durragh***	Cin MR	8	2	8	2	
John Freeman	Cin MR	4	2	26	NE	
John Campbell#	Cin -	1	2	1	NE	
William Jones##	Cin WML	1	13	26	N	

John Chribe & Samuel
  Chribe (should
  read Gripe)   Cin EML 5 4 35   -
*"Excepting 100 acres in NE corner."
**Assigned to Jacob Miller.
***Assigned to Jacob White.
#Assignee of William Smith Briggs.
##Assigned to John Clark; Nathan Stubbs & Griffin
  Yeatman, magistrates.

330   18 Sep 1811   A/4/252
Joseph Wood, [Reg Mar]
Recports for Jan, Feb, Mar 1810 not received.

331   18 Sep 1811   A/4/252
Jesse Spencer, [Reg Chl]
Certificates returned for correction

Bazil Alecks	Chl	MS	22	3	36	NE
William Rollins*	Chl	LS	20	2	18	NW
James Converse & Simon Converse**	Chl	-	20	13	9	NE
Jacob Cagey***	Chl	-	18	16	26	NE
Christian Whiteman#	Chl	MS	21	9	6	NW
Richard Wilson	Chl	-	17	16	24	NW
John Overmire##	Chl	-	16	16	4	SW
Daniel Finkhauser	Chl	MS	21	10	14	SE
George W. Selby	Chl	-	20	13	3	SW
Thomas Worthington	Chl	-	17	14	5	NW
Jacob Switzer, Senior & Junior	Chl	-	19	15	15	NE

*Assignee of John Edwards; Elias Langham's survey
  of 1799 and James Denny's subdivision of 1806 mentioned.
**Assigned to George Walters.
***Assignee of Robert Chalfant.
#Assignee of Mordecai Williams.
##Assignee of Christian Deal.

332   20 Sep 1811   A/4/253
Jesse Spencer, [Reg Chl]
Returns certificates for correction

Levi Midges*	Chl	-	19	13	32	NE
Richard Harpur**	Chl	-	17?	14	4	SW
John McDougall & Robert F. Slaughter						
John Kerr***	Chl	-	17	16	2	NW
Daniel Deffenbaugh	Chl	-	19	12	17	SW
David Shallenberger#	Chl	-	17	16	10	W
Samuel Ramsay##	Chl	-	16	17	10	NE
John Sunday###	Chl	-	19	11	23	NW
William Morgan's assignee§	Chl	WS	21	10	18	W

*Transferred to Samuel Friend and Henry Buzzard.
**Assigned to David Garringer; Elnathan Scofield,
  magistrate.
***Possibly transferred to John Ross; then to Wil-
  liam Alexander; then to Jacob Graffis.
#Assignment by Schallenberger's administrators to
  Joseph Zeile?; Emanuel Carpenter, Junior, attorney.
##Transferred to James Stewart.
###Assigned to Thomas Armstrong. John Kraisher men-
  tioned; George Will, magistrate.
§Mary Morgan, administratrix; David Shelby, magistrate.

333   21 Sep 1811   A/4/254
William Ruffin, Cincinnati
Reports on patent

William Robinson*	[Cin]	WML	3	1	5	-
William Robinson*	[Cin]	WML	3	1	6	-

*To be patented in names of -- Craig & -- Bledsoe.
  Robinson's name so spelled; see entry 334 below.

334   21 Sep 1811   A/4/255
R[ichard] Forrest, [U.S. Department of State]
Patent obtained by fraud returned for cancellation

William Robertson*	[Cin]	WML	3	1	5	-
William Robertson*	[Cin]	WML	3	1	6	-

*So spelled; see entry 333 above.

335   21 Sep 1811   A/4/255
Samuel Gwathmey, [Reg Jef]
Certificate returned for correction

Andrew Maiden*	Jef	-	8E	2N	23	SE

*Assigned to Jacob Fouts; Charles Johns, magistrate.

336   23 Sep 1811   A/4/255
[Daniel] Symmes, [Reg Cin]
Returns certificates for correction

William Taylor	Cin	-	10	6	9	+
William Taylor	Cin	-	10	6	15	+

337   25 Sep 1811   A/4/256
Jesse Spencer, [Reg Chl]
Certificates returned for correction

Winn Winship & Samuel Finley	Chl	-	20	14	3	NW
James Pierce	Chl	-	18	14	14	NW
Peter Apple	Chl	-	20	12	6	+
Winn Winship*	Chl	-	20	11	5	SW
Elizabeth Taylor? [Saylor?]**	Chl	-	20	12	17	SW
Adam Kinser***	Chl	WS	21	10	24	SW
Samuel Thomas & Benjamin Warner#	Chl	-	18	16	7	SE
Philip Shartle##	Chl	MS	21	10	33	NE
Andrew Friend & Augustine Friend###	Chl	-	20	10	2	E
Peter Apple§	Chl	-	20	12	7	N
Samuel Ream§§	Chl	-	17	18	9	SE
Walter Hews§§§	Chl	-	20	14	30	SW
Adam C. Ford¶	Chl	-	20	15	14	NE
Christian Hoover¶¶	Chl	-	17	18	10	SW
John Hunter & Peter Rever¶¶¶	Chl	MS	21	9	18	NE
John Houser^	Chl	-	19	16	10	SW
Henry Culp^^	Chl	-	19	16	26	SW
David Philips^^^	Chl	-	17	14	9	SE
Thomas W. Swearingen£	Chl	-	20	14	35	SE
Joseph Lane££	Chl	-	20	11	30	NW
Joseph Lane£££	Chl	-	21	11	30	NW
Valentine Keffer	Chl	MS	21	11	18	SW
Thomas Townsend	Chl	Mil	14	8	21	NW
Peter Miller	Chl	WS	21	10	36	SE

*Assigned to Jacob Helm; reassigned to Francis Her-
  ron, acknowledged by Joseph Tiffin, magistrate;
  reassigned to Robert Clendinin.
**Assigned to Peter Wolf, acknowledged by Jacob Shoe-
  maker, magistrate.
***Assigned to Henry Haller.
#"A chain of assignments conveys land to Abraham
  Boughman [variously spelled in documents]."
##Assigned to Thomas Reber (also Reaver); Elnathan
  Scofield, magistrate.
###Assigned to John Purdee; reassigned to John Ebert.
§Assigned to John Bonheiner.
§§Assigned to Jacob Kemper & Daniel Kemper.
§§§Assigned to Jacob Brobs; A. V. Courtright, magis-
  trate.
¶Assigned to Michael Kraner.

¶¶Assigned to Isaac Kemper; Mordecai Chalfant,
   magistrate.
¶¶¶Peter Rever's portion assigned to John Hunter;
   Elnathan Scofield, magistrate.
^Assigned to Daniel Funkhauser.
^^Assigned to Daniel May; John Thompson, magistrate.
^^^Assigned to William Philips.
£Assigned to Theodorus Williamson; Jesse Hedges,
   magistrate.
££Assigned to Frederick Fiederrolf?; David Shelby,
   magistrate; discrepancy in description, either
   range 20 or 21.

338   30 Sep 1811   A/4/258
LO Mar
Transmits patents
Daniel Thomas   Mar -   4   5   3 NE
-- Moore & -- Brewer   Mar -   5   2   3 -
-- Moore & -- Brewer   Mar -   5   2   2 +

339   30 Sep 1811   A/4/258
LO Chl
Transmits patents
Jacob Beery   Chl - 17 16 19 W
-- Miller & -- Fenn?
  [Finn? Linn?]   Chl - 19 12   7 NW
George W. Williams   Chl MS 22   4 11 SW
Jacob Rough   Chl - 19 16 27 NE
Jacob Pebler?   Chl - 19 16   1 S
Daniel Crouse   Chl MS 21 10   1 NE
John Branson   Chl - 20 10   6 SW
Samuel Wiseman   Chl - 18 16 12 SE
John Pickens   Chl - 21   8 21 SW
Solomon Huffort? [Haffort?] Chl - 17 16 34 NW
William Wilker   Chl WS 21 11   3 NW
Jesse D. Courtright   Chl MS 21 11 25 SE
William McCormick   Chl - 17 17 24 -
Christian Whiteman   Chl MS 21   9 27 NE
Ludwick Kreamer   Chl - 20 15 19 SE+
Michael Boyer   Chl - 16 17 27 NE
Conrad Pitser   Chl WS 21   9   3 NE
Thomas Wheeler   Chl WS 21   9 35 NW
Peter Glick   Chl WS 21   9   2 SW
Ludwick Kreamer   Chl - 20 15 30 NE
Henry Culp   Chl - 18 15 15 NW
Moses Boggs   Chl - 21 10 30 NW

340   4 Oct 1811   A/4/259
Richard Forrest, [U.S. Department of State]
Requests patent signature
Isaac Clendennin*   Stu -   5   7 33 NE
*Land sold and purchaser threatens to sue for deliv-
ery of patent.

341   4 Oct 1811   A/4/259
J. W. Condy, Philadelphia
Discusses accounts
J. W. Condy   [Stu]* -   7 17 14 SW
J. W. Condy   [Stu]* -   8 10 29 NW
J. W. Condy   [Stu]* -   7   7 14 SE
*Determined on basis of entry 1192 of Federal Land
Series, volume 1.

342   7 Oct 1811   A/4/259
Daniel Symmes, [Reg Cin]
Transmits Treasury receipts
John Kershner*   Cin Pre 8   3   1 SE
*Assignee of Martin Baum.

343   7 Oct 1811   A/4/260
Jesse Spencer, [Reg Chl]
Transmits Treasury receipt
Daniel Poorman   Chl - 16 16 29 NW

344   8 Oct 1811   A/4/260
John Kerr, Chilicothe
Transmits patent
A. McLaughlin & John Kerr Chl - 21   7   1 SW

345   8 Oct 1811   A/4/260
LO Stu
Transmits patent
John Prior   Stu -   4   6 35 SW

346   8 Oct 1811   A/4/260
James Bowland, Burgetts Town, Washington County,
   Pennsylvania
Transmits patent
James Bowland   Stu -   4 12   1 SE

347   8 Oct 1811   A/4/260
LO Cin
Transmits patents
Robert Scott   Cin -   5   3 24 NW
James Petticrew   Cin -   4   3 24 SE
Jonathan Kershman?
  [Hershman?]   Cin -   7   2 22 NW
George Harlin, Junior   Cin -   5   3 25 NE+*
Nicholas Angle   Cin -   4   3 23 W
*"W[est] end of a tract of 200 acres on NE corner."

348   8 Oct 1811   A/4/260
S. Pleasonton, U.S. Department of State
Encloses copy of patent
Stephen Vail   -

349   8 Oct 1811   A/4/261
LO Chl
Transmits patents
John Foht & Jonas Foht   Chl - 16 17 33 SE
Thomas Waddle   Chl MS 21   9 27 SW
Daniel Conrod   Chl - 20 13 15 SE
Thomas Cole   Chl - 20 14 31 SE
Christian Gruber   Chl WS 21 11 35 SW
John Thomas Twigg   Chl - 20 15   1 SE
Robert Skinner   Chl - 16 16   2 SW
Daniel McIntire   Chl - 17 16   9 NW
Jacob Minehart   Chl - 19 16   5 NW

350   11 Oct 1811   A/4/261
LO Cin
Transmits patents
William Frost   Cin MR 12   1 20 SE
Isaac Lindly   Cin EML 1   4 12 SE
Christian Harter   Cin EML 4   3   2 W
Daniel Crissman   Cin EML 3   5   4 W
John Treber & Henry Treber Cin EML 3 6 32 SW
Daniel Repp   Cin EML 3   5   7 NE
Daniel Yount   Cin EML 6   3 30 NW
Matthias Swartsell   Cin EML 4   4 25 SW
Alex Stout   Cin MR   2   5 20 -
Richard D. Hall   Cin EML 3   4 14 NE

351   11 Oct 1811   A/4/261
William Ruffin, Cincinnati
Tranmits patents

Benjamin Craig & Isaac Bledsoe*	Cin WML	3	1	5	+
Benjamin Craig & Isaac Bledsoe*	Cin WML	3	1	6	+

*Assignees of William Robertson.

352   11 Oct 1811   A/4/262
LO Chl
Transmits patents

Jeremiah Runkle	Chl	-	20	15	33	NE
John Radcliffe	Chl	-	19	10	30	NW

353   14 Oct 1811   A/4/262
David Hoge, [Reg Stu]
Transmits Treasury receipts

J. W. Condy	Stu	-	7	17	14	SW
J. W. Condy	Stu	-	8	10	29	NW

354   14 Oct 1811   A/4/262
J. W. Condy, Philadelphia
Transmits Treasury receipts

J. W. Condy	Stu	-	7	17	14	SW
J. W. Condy	Stu	-	8	10	29	NW

355   14 Oct 1811   A/4/262
LO Stu
Transmits patents

Jacob McKay	Stu	-	6	10	7	SE
Thomas Stanley	Stu	-	5	17	1	E
John Worley	Stu	-	7	16	11	NE
Jacob Macenterfer	Stu	-	7	20	32	SW
Joshua Wood	Stu	-	6	10	7	SW
Ullery Shively	Stu	-	7	19	23	E
Benjamin Walton	Stu	-	4	15	17	NW
John Ebi	Stu	-	8	11	24	N
John Weaver	Stu	-	2	11	30	NE
Peter Beam	Stu	-	6	13	28	NW
John Moore	Stu	-	5	18	32	N
Mathias Springer	Stu	-	8	11	29	SE
George Grate	Stu	-	1	7	1	NW
Hugh McClaron	Stu	-	2	11	17	SE
Michael Spangler	Stu	-	8	11	27	SW
Michael Spangler	Stu	-	8	11	34	NE
Abraham Bair	Stu	-	7	18	19	NE
Thomas Creighton	Stu	-	1	6	15	SW
William Cook	Stu	-	10	2	35	SE
James Ratekin	Stu	-	7	15	8	NW
Christian Knagg	Stu	-	5	12	25	NW

356   16 Oct 1811   A/4/263
LO Cin
Transmits patents

Prudence McMun	Cin EML	6	3	18	SW
Stephen Dixon	Cin EML	1	7	10	NE
Anthony Cobble	Cin EML	6	3	18	NW
John Compton	Cin EML	5	6	8	SW
George Hunt	Cin EML	2	12	1	SE
Benjamin Owen	Cin EML	5	4	1	SE
John Quillen	Cin EML	5	5	4	NW
John Lea	Cin EML	1	3	34	W
John Levingstone	Cin WML	2	4	10	NE
Thomas Willson	Cin MR	5	3	11	SE
John Simmons	Cin MR	11	1	12	NE
Joseph Pence	Cin MR	11	5	33	NE
Job Martin	Cin MR	12	5	34	NE
Levi Rouze	Cin MR	11	4	25	NW
Esther Coleman	Cin MR	10	2	33	SE
Arthur Forbes	Cin MR	8	5	27	SE
Francis Best	Cin MR	9	4	4	NE
Nathan Darnold	Cin MR	11	4	25	SW

357   16 Oct 1811   A/4/264
LO Cin
Transmits patents

Aaron Tullis	Cin EML	6	5	21	+
Aaron Tullis	Cin EML	6	5	22	+
Eleizar Purviance	Cin EML	1	9	29	NW
Robert Blackburn	Cin EML	1	2	12	SE
John Wilson	Cin EML	6	7	7	NE
John Stockton	Cin EML	4	2	8	NW
James Martin	Cin EML	2	5	21	SW
Frederick Nutts	Cin EML	5	7	7	NE
Samuel Martin	Cin EML	6	5	6	-
John Hartman	Cin EML	4	3	10	NW
William Waggaman	Cin EML	4	5	36	NE
Joseph Dungan	Cin EML	1	4	36	SE
-- Sutherland & -- Brown	Cin EML	6	2	3	SE

358   16 Oct 1811   A/4/264
LO Stu
Transmits patents

John Hugus	Stu	-	7	19	17	N
Henry Zahner	Stu	-	7	19	3	NE
Mahlon Smith*	Stu	-	5	8	10	-

*". . . Smith, assignee of William Meredith, has
written pressingly for a patent. . . . It does not
appear that the final certificate has been received.
. . ."

359   17 Oct 1811   A/4/264
LO Cin
Transmits patents

John Todd	Cin EML	6	5	32	NW
David Mills	Cin EML	4	9	26	W
Joel Williams	Cin EML	2	3	5	SE
Samuel Trotter	Cin EML	5	8	24	SE
William Barber	Cin EML	6	5	28	NE
John Manning	Cin EML	6	6	17	+
Cornelius Voorhes	Cin EML	6	4	5	NW
Joseph Baird	Cin EML	3	3	12	SW
Robert Vanhorn	Cin EML	5	6	3	SW
Phineas McCray	Cin EML	4	3	35	NE
Esther Pemberton	Cin EML	5	6	7	NW
Alexander Cothran	Cin EML	5	7	32	NE
Benjamin Harris	Cin EML	1	7	10	NW
Peter Hashman	Cin EML	2	8	9	NW
James Jusco	Cin EML	5	5	1	SW
Rosannah Russell	Cin EML	6	4	20	SW
Richard Watts	Cin EML	2	7	12	NE
Samuel Beakley	Cin EML	5	8	31	NE
Joseph Hartin? [Martin?]	Cin EML	2	6	29	SW
John Harvey	Cin EML	1	9	17	NE
Henry Coate	Cin EML	5	6	6	SW

360   18 Oct 1811   A/4/265
Isaac Vanhorne, Rec Zan
Transmits Treasury receipts

Richard Burrel	Zan	-	3	10	25	NW
John Wade	Zan	-	3	10	16	SW
John Wade	Zan	-	3	10	18	SE

361   21 Oct 1811   A/4/265
Jesse Spencer, [Reg Chl]
Transmits certificate

James Lambert	Chl	-	20	15	6	NE

362   22 Oct 1811   A/4/266
David Hoge, [Reg Stu]
Requests final certificate

Robert Hanna*	Stu	-	4	7	30	SE

*Assignee of Andrew Armstrong.

363   25 Oct 1811   A/4/266
John Graham, [Chief Clerk, U.S. Department of State]*
Transmits patents

Neal Meahan	[Chl]	MS	22	4	11	NW
Lucas Sullivant	[Chl]	MS	22	4	3	NE
Lucas Sullivant	[Chl]	MS	22	4	3	SE

*Identified in entry 962, *Federal Land Series*, volume 1.

364   25 Oct 1811   A/4/266
LO Chl
Transmits patents

John Sunday	Chl	MS	21	10	24	NE
Ludwick Brand	Chl	-	16	16	14	NW
Jonathan Hays	Chl	-	20	13	9	NW
Benjamin Barnett	Chl	-	20	12	33	SE

365   29 Oct 1811   A/4/267
R[ichard] Forrest, [U.S. Department of State]
Requests patent

Thomas Ramsey	Stu	-	16	19	23	S

366   29 Oct 1811   A/4/267
Jesse Spencer, [Reg Chl]
Transmits certificate

Abraham Peters	Chl	-	20	12	10	E

367   29 Oct 1811   A/4/267
LO Cin
Transmits patents

Peter Swank	Cin	EML	4	5	12	SW
Isaac Hosier	Cin	EML	6	3	27	NE
Samuel Patterson	Cin	EML	1	6	30	SW
David Prestley	Cin	EML	1	7	28	NW
John Morris	Cin	EML	1	4	17	NE
David Kenworthy	Cin	EML	5	6	3	NW

368   30 Oct 1811   A/4/268
Daniel Symmes, [Reg Cin]
Account overcharged

Andrew McCalla	Cin	EML	6	2	20	-
Andrew McCalla	Cin	EML	6	2	21	+
Andrew McCalla	Cin	EML	6	2	22	+

369   1 Nov 1811   A/4/268
Solomon Vauss, Romney Postoffice, Hampshire County, Virginia
Transmits patents

Solomon Vauss	[Cin]	MR	11	6	35	NE
Solomon Vauss	[Cin]	MR	11	6	36	+
James Foley	[Cin]	MR	10	5	3	W
Peter A. Banta*	[Cin]	EML	3	3	14	NE

*This entire line crossed out.

370   2 Nov 1811   A/4/268
R[ichard] Forrest [U.S. Department of State]
Patents for correction; mentions John Alliman and
  Henry Alliman for land in Steubenville district

Thomas Hunford*	[Stu]	-	8	10	17	SE
William Hamilton	[Stu]	-	5	9	32**	NE
William Bogle	[Stu]	-	16	17	2***	SE

*Formerly read Hartford.
**Formerly read section 35.
***Formerly read section 9.

371   2 Nov 1811   A/4/269
LO Chl
Transmits patents

Joas Miller	Chl	WS	21	9	33	NW
Samuel Brombaugh	Chl	-	19	16	4	NW

372   2 Nov 1811   A/4/269
LO Cin
Transmits patents

Philip Kiser	Cin	MR	10	4	30	SW
Joseph Parks	Cin	EML	2	6	30	SW
Christian Houtz	Cin	EML	4	3	14	SW
William Bumberger	Cin	EML	6	2	3	SW
Elisha Landan	Cin	EML	1	4	8	NW
Caspar Bartorf	Cin	EML	2	7	34	NW
Jonas Pearson	Cin	EML	5	6	36	SE
Edward Dyer	Cin	EML	2	4	8	SE
Thomas Burkel	Cin	EML	1	8	17	SW
Joseph Miller	Cin	EML	6	3	19	NE
John Jay	Cin	EML	5	6	36	NE
Thomas Jay	Cin	EML	5	5	2	NE
Robert Scott & Richard Scott	Cin	EML	2	5	21	SE
Joel Hollingsworth	Cin	EML	4	7	2	SW

373   2 Nov 1811   A/4/269
LO Stu
Transmits patents

Daniel Mosser	Stu	-	8	11	25	NE
Nicholas Murray	Stu	-	8	11	6	SE
Hugh Rose	Stu	-	2	9	30	-
Andrew Adams	Stu	-	2	10	28	SW
Nicholas Murray	Stu	-	7	19	33	NW
William R. Dickinson	Stu	-	8	10	27	W
James McCullough	Stu	-	7	19	9	-

374   2 Nov 1811   A/4/270
David Hoge, [Reg Stu]
Transmits Treasury receipt

Robert Watson	Stu	-	6	1	28	SW

375   2 Nov 1811   A/4/270
Wyllys Silliman, [Reg Zan]
Transmits Treasury receipt

David Baker	Zan	Mil	5	8	20	NE

376   2 Nov 1811   A/4/270
Jesse Spencer, [Reg Chl]
Transmits corrected patent

William Bogle	Chl	-	16	17	2	SW

377   2 Nov 1811   A/4/270
Daniel Symmes, [Reg Cin]
Requests final certificate

Frederick Baker	Cin	EML	5	3	30	SW

378   2 Nov 1811   A/4/290
LO Stu
Transmits patents
William Hamilton   Stu -   5   9 32 NE
Moses Gilson   Stu -   5 17 19 NW
Andrew Newman   Stu -   7 18   5 NW
Jacob Ritter   Stu -   3 12 33 NE
Thomas Hurford   Stu -   8 10 17 SE
Peter Anspach   Stu -   9   9 10 SE
Baltzer Koontz   Stu -   9   9   3 SW
Alexander Campbell   Stu -   7   9   4 NE
John Smith   Stu -   2   9 35 SW

379   2 Nov 1811   A/4/271
H. & J. Alliman, Middletown, Dauphin County, Penn-
    sylvania
Transmits patents
Henry Alliman   Stu -   6 10 27 NE
John Alliman   Stu -   6 10 33 NE

380   5 Nov 1811   A/4/271
LO Stu
Transmits patents
John Tintsman   Stu -   2 13   1   -
William Lowther, Senior Stu - 8 12 35 W
James Ratckin? [Ratekin?] Stu - 6 14 28 NE
James Lyon   Stu -   1   6   8   -
Jonathan Grayble   Stu -   9 12 23 W
John Fife   Stu -   2 10 17 NW
Benjamin Henyard   Stu -   4 11 15 NW
Joseph Walker   Stu -   2   8 15 NW
John Emreg? [Emrey?] Stu -   5 17 13 E
Stephen Ford   Stu -   4 11 31   -
James Ratekin   Stu -   6 14 34 SE

381   5 Nov 1811   A/4/271
Jesse Spencer, [Reg Chl]
Transmits certificates
Samuel Lewis   Chl MS 21 10 31 NE
Samuel Lewis   Chl MS 21 10 31 SE

382   7 Nov 1811   A/4/272
R[ichard] Forrest, [U.S. Department of State]
Transmits request of "the Honorable General Brown
    from Pennsylvania" for patent
John Heckewelder   Zan Mil 2   7 12 NW

383   7 Nov 1811   A/4/272
Thomas Gibson, Reg Can
Transmits certificates and patent
William Hough   Can - 16 21 24 SW
William Hough   Can - 16 21 25 NW
William Hough   Can - 16 21 26 NE
William Hough   Can - 16 21 26 SE
William Hough   Can - 16 21 26 SE
John Cook*   Can - 19 18   5 NE
John Smith   Can - 11 10   4   -
Frederick Stump   Can - 10 12 34 SW
*Patented.

384   7 Nov 1811   A/4/272
LO Stu
Transmits patents
Jacob Knaggy   Stu -   5 12 32 NW
Jacob Mushrush   Stu -   2   8 31 NW
Richard Hart   Stu -   1   7 34 SW

John Mercer   Stu -   5   8 30 NE
John Howell   Stu -   5   8 30 NW
Esther Holse   Stu -   4   6   5 NE
Asa Holloway   Stu -   5   7 10 SE
William Hardesty   Stu -   4 15 35 SW
Peter Kesser? [Keyser?] Stu - 3   9 29 NE
John Velte   Stu -   8 10 11 NE
Peter Pontius   Stu -   8 12 19 NW
John McAdams   Stu -   5   9 24 NW
James D. Stanley   Stu -   5 18 24 NW
Michael Engle   Stu -   7 18 32 NE
John Ewers   Stu -   5   7   8 NE
Thomas Parkinson   Stu -   3 11 27 SE
John Smith   Stu -   5   7 11 SW
James Hogeland   Stu -   5 11 33 NE
George Wertenberger   Stu -   7 19 18 S
Nathan Johns   Stu -   1   7   9 SE
Thomas Gordon   Stu -   5 10 25 SW
David Custard   Stu -   5 12   7 NE
Ezekiel Marsh   Stu -   6 18 33 S
Richard Fawcett   Stu -   6 19 25 S
Daniel Linn   Stu -   8 10 29 SW
John Street   Stu -   6 19   9 NE
Philip Arhart   Stu -   4 15 35 N
Daniel Raper? [Roper?] Stu - 9 12 24 SE

385   8 Nov 1811   A/4/273
Wyllys Silliman, [Reg Zan]
Transmits certificates
--   Zan - 13 12 15 E+
--   Zan - 14 16 15 NE
--   Zan - 14 15   3 SE
George Korbman   Zan -   2   7 13 NE

386   8 Nov 1811   A/4/273
Daniel Symmes, [Reg Cin]
Transmits patent and certificates
Christian Harter*   Cin EML 3   5 36 SW
--   Cin EML 5   4 20 SW
--   Cin Pre 5   3 30 NE
--   Cin Pre 5   4 34 NE
--   Cin Pre 6   1   7 SW
--   Cin MR 10   1   8   +
--   Cin MR   7   2   2 NE
--   Cin EML 2   4 11 NE
*Patented.

387   8 Nov 1811   A/4/274
Richard Forrest, [U.S. Department of State]
Patents requested by members of Congress
Eli Wright   Jef --
James Bruce   Jef --
Solomon Bower   Jef --
A. Halberstadt   Cin --
H. March   Stu --
A. Brooks   Stu --
J. N. Brock   Stu --

388   9 Nov 1811   A/4/274
Thomas Marshel, Postoffice, Baltimore
Replies to inquiry regarding land purchased in the
    Cincinnati land district

389   9 Nov 1811   A/4/274
Jesse Spencer, [Reg Chl]
Transmits certificate
Robert Mitchell   Chl - 16 15 31 SW

390		9 Nov 1811				A/4/274

Wyllys Silliman, [Reg Zan]
Transmits certificate

Jacob Albright	Zan	–	4	8	6	NW

391		9 Nov 1811				A/4/275

James Anderson, Postoffice, St. Clairsville, Ohio
Transmits patent

James Anderson	Zan Mil	1	4	24	SW

392		9 Nov 1811				A/4/275

Daniel Symmes, [Reg Cin]
Patent requested by member of Congress

David Longhead	Cin	–	5	3	23	–
David Longhead	Cin	–	5	3	24	+
David Longhead	Cin	–	6	1	19	+
David Longhead	Cin	–	6	1	20	+
David Longhead	Cin	–	6	1	29	+

393		9 Nov 1811				A/4/275

John Heckewelder, Bethlehem, Pennsylvania
Transmits patent

John Heckewelder	Zan Mil	2	7	12	NW

394		9 Nov 1811				A/4/275

LO Zan
Transmits patents

Elijah Shriver & Adam Shriver	Zan Mil	3	1	19	NE
Ralph Hardisty	Zan Mil	5	1	14	SE
John Hardisty	Zan Mil	9	3	12	SW
John Hardisty	Zan Mil	8	4	22	SE
John Spangler	Zan Mil	5	8	19	NW
G. C. Spangler, Junior	Zan Mil	5	8	19	SW

395		9 Nov 1811				A/4/275

Hon. -- Laycock
Assignment defective in certificate "you left in the Land Room this day"

Talbot Townsend*	Stu	–	4	17	31	NW
William Henry**	Can	–	10	12	9	SE

*Assigned to Isaac Townsend; reassigned to Moses Mendenhall.
**Assigned to Thomas Henry.

396		12 Nov 1811				A/4/276

Hon. Thomas Worthington
Transmits patent

George Renick	[Cin?] MR?	2	2	22	NW

397		12 Nov 1811				A/4/276

Hon. Andrew Gregg
Transmits patent

Conrad Dulman	Stu	–	9	12	23	SE

398		12 Nov 1811				A/4/276

LO Stu
Transmits patents

Peter Mottice	Stu	–	7	18	30	NW
John Jewel	Stu	–	2	11	25	SW
Andrew Scott	Stu	–	3	14	28	NW
Jesse Baily	Stu	–	7	20	24	NW

399		12 Nov 1811				A/4/276

LO Zan
Transmits patent and certificate

Adam Rider	Zan	–	14	14	10	NE
Joseph Keifer? [Kiefer?]	Zan Mil	3	10	24	SE

400		12 Nov 1811				A/4/276

LO Chl
Transmits patents

Andrew Hite, Senior	Chl	–	17	18	29	NW
Henry Einsell	Chl	–	18	14	36	NW
John Luke	Chl	–	21	8	11	NE
Jordan Manring	Chl	–	16	6	29	NE
John Riley	Chl	WS	21	11	2	SW
Lewis Sites	Chl	–	19	16	12	N

401		13 Nov 1811				A/4/277

Thomas Gibson, [Reg Can]
Transmits Treasury receipts

John Stump	Can	–	10	12	28	N
Frederick Stump	Can	–	10	12	33	NW

402		13 Nov 1811				A/4/277

LO Chl
Transmits patents

Stephen Freeman	Chl	–	17	17	4	SE
Daniel Baum	Chl	WS	21	10	35	SW
Henry Moore	Chl	–	20	12	30	NE
Nathaniel Wilson	Chl	–	20	15	12	NE
Paul Brickley	Chl	–	19	15	12	E
George Losley?	Chl	–	16	16	9	NW
John Evans	Chl Mil	14	8	19	S

403		13 Nov 1811				A/4/277

Hon. -- Jennings
Transmits patents

Clement Nance	Unk*	–	5E	3S	15	NW
Patrick Shields	Unk*	–	5E	2S	33	NE
John Harberson	Unk*	–	5E	3S	19	SE
Tice Licht	Unk*	–	4E	3S	25	SE
Samuel Bell	Unk*	–	4E	3S	18	SE

*Either Jeffersonville or Vincennes.

404		13 Nov 1811				A/4/277

Charles Roberts, Zanesville
Acknowledges receipt of [bounty] land warrants 362 & 484; mentions Mesheck Walker.

405		13 Nov 1811				A/4/277

Richard Forrest, [U.S. Department of State]
Transmits patent for signature

Isaac Patton	Stu	–	5	7	32	NE

406		13 Nov 1811				A/4/278

Jesse Spencer, [Reg Chl]
Transmits certificate

Frederick Divert	Chl	–	20	?	1	SW

407		13 Nov 1811				A/4/278

Joseph Wood, [Reg Mar]
Statement of account

Samuel Edgarton	Mar	–	5	6	34	NE

408   14 Nov 1811   A/4/278
Daniel Symmes, [Reg Cin]
Transmits certificates and Treasury receipts

John Smith*	Cin Pre	10	1	18	+
James Smith	Cin Pre	12	4	22	SE
Robert Donavan	Cin Pre	11	5	20	SW
Robert Donavan	Cin Pre	11	5	36	SE

*Transferred to Richard Carr.

409   14 Nov 1811   A/4/278
Richard Forrest, [U.S. Department of State]
Transmits certificate

| [John Smith]* | Cin Pre | 10 | 1 | 18 | + |

*See entry 408 above.

410   14 Nov 1811   A/4/278
LO Stu
Transmits patents

Andrew Dickson	Stu	–	3	10	24	W
Jacob Keyser	Stu	–	8	9	20	SW
Reasin Beall	Stu	–	3	14	22	NW
Martin Houser	Stu	–	7	20	29	N
John Nimmon	Stu	–	8	10	32	E

411   14 Nov 1811   A/4/279
LO Cin
Transmits patents

| Isaac Ingle | Cin MR | 6 | 2 | 11 | SE |
| John Rogers | Cin MR | 6 | 2 | 29 | NW |

412   14 Nov 1811   A/4/279
Jesse Spencer, [Reg Chl]
Transmits certificates; mentions John Graham's will,
Michael Ernest; John Mitten, Joshua Mitten, John
Clark; Thomas Cole; Christian Kromlegh

413   14 Nov 1811   A/4/279
Joseph Wood, [Reg Mar]
Transmits patent

| John Burres | Mar | – | 6 | 2 | 2 | SE |

414   14 Nov 1811   A/4/279
LO Chl
Transmits patents

John Miller	Chl MS	21	9	36	NE
Broad Cole	Chl MS	21	10	27	NW
Peter? Robenault	Chl	–	20	14	9	NW
P. Dunn	Chl	–	17	17	3	SW
Philip Christ	Chl	–	17	18	24	NW

415   15 Nov 1811   A/4/280
Thomas Gibson, [Reg Can]*
Transmits certificate; "pressing application of a
gentleman of Congress"

| Reasin Beall | Can | – | 13 | 15 | 1? | SW |

*Note states "not sent."

416   15 Nov 1811   A/4/280
Hon. Thomas Worthington
Reports final certificate sent to Canton land dis-
trict for signature

| Reasin Beall | Can | – | 13 | 15 | 1 | SW |
| Reasin Beall | Can | – | 3 | 14 | 22 | NW* |

*Land description erroneous, as it does not exist,
according to letter.

417   15 Nov 1811   A/4/280
Peter Wilson, [Rec Stu]
Searching for final certificate sent to predecessor,
Zaccheus Biggs, on 13 May 1807

| William Meredith* | Stu | – | 5 | 8 | 10 | – |

*Transferred to Mahlon Smith, St. Clairsville, "who
has repeatedly written for his patent."

418   15 Nov 1811   A/4/280
LO Stu
Transmits patents

Peter Dehuff	Stu	–	5	12	12	SE
James Parkhill	Stu	–	3	9	29	SW
John Edmonson	Stu	–	1	7	9	NW
Ezekiel Vance	Stu	–	7	9	11	SE

419   15 Nov 1811   A/4/281
Jesse Spencer, [Reg Chl]
Inquires regarding case of David Bussard; transmits
certificates

Isaac Vanmetre, Felix Renick, & George Harness*	Chl	–	21	2	17	–
Isaiah Willis	Chl MS	21	9	19	SE
Isaiah Willis	Chl MS	21	9	19	NE

*Transferred to George Harness.

420   15 Nov 1811   A/4/281
LO Cin
Transmits patents

Benjamin Nutter?	Cin WML	1	12	33	SE
Abia B. Martin	Cin MR	11	2	9	NW
Henry Yount	Cin EML	5	5	24	SW
James Young	Cin EML	1	6	5	NW

421   15 Nov 1811   A/4/281
Hon. -- Jennings
Transmits patent

| James Bruce | Vin | – | 4E | 3S | 34 | SE |

422   15 Nov 1811   A/4/281
Hon. -- Laycock
Transmits patent

| John Bever | Can | – | 13 | 15 | 9 | NE |

423   15 Nov 1811   A/4/281
Hon. -- Lyle
Transmits patents

| Robert McLaughlin | Stu | – | 5 | 13 | 6 | NE |
| James McLaughlin | Stu | – | 4 | 13 | 31 | NW |

424   15 Nov 1811   A/4/281
Israel French, New Market, Maryland
Transmits patent

| Isaac Patton | Stu | – | 5 | 7 | 32 | NE |

425   16 Nov 1811   A/4/282
John Johnston, Esq., Picqua Town, Miami County, Ohio
Transmits patents

James Johnston*	[Cin] EML	5	8	12	NW
George Moffett	[Cin] EML	5	8	11	E
George Moffett	[Cin] EML	5	8	12	SW
-- Scudder	[Cin] MR	12	1	27	+
-- Scudder	[Cin] MR	12	1	33	+

*Assignee of George Moffett.

426		16 Nov 1811		A/4/282				
Hon. -- Jennings								
Transmits patents								
John Warrick		Vin	- 11W	3S	4	NW		
John Wilson		Vin	- 11W	3S	19	NW		
Abraham? Garrison		Vin	- 14W	8S	1	NE		

427		18 Nov 1811		A/4/282			
Wyllys Silliman, [Reg Zan]							
Requests final certificate							
Charles Bohn*		Zan Mil	3	10	12	SE	

*Mentions an assignment from -- Newman.

428		19 Nov 1811		A/4/282			
Daniel Symmes, [Reg Cin]							
Inquires regarding patents							
William Ward		Cin	- -	-	24	SW+*	
Benjamin Daniels**		Cin Pre	5	3	19	+	

*Thirty acres "to be twice as long from North to
 South as it is in width from East to West, and so
 as to include Simon Kenton's Mills or Mill Seat on
 the east branch of Mad River."
**Assigned to Benjamin Daniels by John Daniels, but
 from another assignment patent should have issued
 to John Keever.

429		19 Nov 1811		A/4/283			
Hon. Thomas Worthington							
Transmits patent							
Jesse Spencer		Chl	- 16	16	1	E	

430		19 Nov 1811		A/4/283			
LO Chl							
Transmits patents							
Herbert Winegardner		Chl	-	7	17	21	SE
John Ulrich		Chl	-	19	16	34	SE
Daniel Glick		Chl	MS	21	10	27	NE
Michael Knayer		Chl	-	20	13	11	NE
Valentine Rever? [Kever?]		Chl	-	19	11	8	SE
Edward Miller		Chl	-	16	1	32	+
Edward Miller		Chl	-	16	1	33	+
Elihu Short		Chl	-	16	16	26	NE
John Greave		Chl	-	20	8	35	SW
Henry Douse?		Chl	-	20	15	30	SW
George Brinker		Chl	MS	21	9	3	SE
David Dawson		Chl	-	19	11	24	NE
Daniel Firestene		Chl	-	19	15	5	NE
John Goldthwait		Chl	-	18	16	26	NW
Levi Moore		Chl	-	20	14	5	NE
John Herman		Chl	WS	21	4	25	NE
Elias Decker		Chl	-	20	15	29	SW
Anthony Rapeholst		Chl	-	20	9	31	NE
Christian Wolf		Chl	-	18	13	14	SE
William Pyle		Chl	-	21	8	1	NE
John Good		Chl	-	17	18	10	NW
John Koontz		Chl	-	16	6	25	SW
Robert Hunter		Chl	-	20	13	31	-
Joel Berry		Chl	-	17	18	30	SW
Edward Ricketts		Chl	-	20	15	23	NE
Ludwick Zehring		Chl	-	17	16	3	SE

431		20 Nov 1811		A/4/283			
R[ichard] Forrest, [U.S. Department of State]							

Requests signature of patent; "he wants to convey
 the said tract to another person"

John Shoemaker		Chl	-	20	15	20	NW

432		21 Nov 1811		A/4/284			
William Cummins, Kishicoquilis Valley, Mifflin							
County, Pennsylvania							
Transmits duplicate receipt							
William Cummins		Cin	-	2	5	1	NW

433		21 Nov 1811		A/4/284			
LO Cin							
Transmits patents							
Leonard Haines		Cin Pre	9	2	1	NE	
Nicholas Sintz		Cin Pre	9	4	10	+	
Thomas Stafford		Cin Pre	10	3	31	NW	
James McGrew		Cin Pre	6	1	4	NW*	
Arthur Vandever		Cin MR	10	2	10	NE	
Joseph Reynolds		Cin MR	10	4	36	NW	
Joseph Reynolds		Cin MR	11	4	15	W	
Joseph Reynolds		Cin MR	11	4	32	SE	
Esther Thomas		Cin MR	3	3	11	SW	
David H. Morris		Cin Pre	9	2	23	N	
Thomas R. Ross		Cin Pre	10	1	3	SW	
Stephen White		Cin Pre	6	2	20	NE	
Casper Bottorf		Cin EML	3	5	8	SW	
James Stewart		Cin MR	3	3	8	SE	
Arthur Vandeveer		Cin MR	10	2	10	NW	
James Stewart		Cin MR	3	3	11	NE	
Arthur Vandeveer		Cin MR	10	2	10	SW	

*Corner.

434		21 Nov 1811		A/4/284			
LO Chl							
Transmits patents							
Isaac Terboss		Chl Mil	19	7	22	NW	
Isaac Waltman		Chl MS	21	10	18	NW	
Abraham Inskeep		Chl MS	22	4	34	SW	
John Shoemaker		Chl	-	20	11	4	SE
William Marquis		Chl Mil	12	7	25	SE	
Andrew Hayes		Chl WS	21	9	34	NE	
Ignatius Hardin		Chl	-	16	16	28	NE
James English		Chl MS	21	11	17	SW	

435		21 Nov 1811		A/4/284			
Daniel Symmes, [Reg Cin]							
Transmits certificate							
William Hamar*		Cin Pre	7	2	20	NE	
Matthias Scudder		Cin MR	12	1	23	+	
Matthias Scudder		Cin MR	12	1	27	+	

*Assigned to James Gillespie.

436		21 Nov 1811		A/4/285			
James Findlay, [Rec Cin]							
Discrepancies in account; transmittal of certificate							
William Cummins		Cin EML?	2	5	1	NW	
Peter Atherton		Cin EML	1	2	2	-	

437		21 Nov 1811		A/4/285			
Joseph Vance, Franklintown, Ohio							

The military land warrant sent cannot be used on
 Unk* - 20 6 3 19 "as that fraction was not
 designated when the quarter townships were subdivided into lots. . . ."
*[Probably the U.S. Military District is meant.]

438		21 Nov 1811		A/4/285			
David Moodey, Esq., Steubenville							
Certificate forwarded incomplete							
Sterling Johnson		[Stu?]	-	4	7	7	NW

439   22 Nov 1811   A/4/285
Hugh Rose, Steubenville
Patent transmitted to Land Office
Hugh Rose   [Stu?]   -   2   9   30   -

440   23 Nov 1811   A/4/286
LO Stu
Transmits patents
Isaac Hillard, heirs of   Stu   -   8   12   28   NW
Joseph Yunker   Stu   -   2   11   30   NW
John Shover   Stu   -   3   10   15   NE
Joseph Rogers   Stu   -   7   9   20   SE
Robert Kelly   Stu   -   4   10   29   NE
John Davis   Stu   -   1   7   32   SW
Jacob Smith   Stu   -   4   11   22   NE
John Duvall   Stu   -   6   18   11   SW
Matthew Howell   Stu   -   3   5   18   NE
William Anderson   Stu   -   5   11   13   NE
Jacob Newman   Stu   -   8   11   2   SE
Philip Sutar?   Stu   -   7   15   29   NE
Daniel Pettit   Stu   -   2   12   22   SE
Thomas Thorn   Stu   -   7   20   13   S
Samuel Rogers   Stu   -   7   9   4   SE
-- Myers & -- Lowman   Stu   -   8   12   30   NW

441   23 Nov 1811   A/4/286
Peter Wilson, [Rec Stu]
Transmits Treasury receipt
Jonathan W. Condy   Stu   -   6   16   17   SW

442   25 Nov 1811   A/4/286
Hon. Joseph Lefevre
Transmits corrected patent
George Akert, Junior   Chl   -   18   13   23   SE

443   25 Nov 1811   A/4/286
Hon. -- Pope
Final certificate defective
Thomas Helm*   Cin   -   3   8   24   +
Thomas Helm*   Cin   -   3   8   25   -
*Assignee of Peyton Short, via agency of -- Van
   Cleve.

444   25 Nov 1811   A/4/287
Wyllys Silliman, [Reg Zan]
Transmits certificate
Gerrud? [Gerard?] Topkin   Zan Mil   5   1   9   NW

445   25 Nov 1811   A/4/287
William Dickson, [Reg Nas]
Discrepancies in accounts
George Dilworth   Nas   -   1   2*   33   SE
George Dilworth   Nas   -   1   3*   33   SE
Robert Thompson**   Nas   W   1   2   12   SE
*Discrepancy in township designation to be resolved.
**Assignee of Thomas Bibb.

446   25 Nov 1811   A/4/288
Jonathan W. Condy
Clarification of accounts
Jonathan W. Condy   Stu   -   6   16   17   SW
Jonathan W. Condy   Stu   -   8   10   29   NW
Jonathan W. Condy   Stu   -   7   7   14   S

447   25 Nov 1811   A/4/288
LO Stu
Transmits patents
John Johnson   Stu   -   1   8   36   SE
Peter Wise   Stu   -   8   10   1   NW
John Snyder   Stu   -   8   11   26   SE
David Cunningham   Stu   -   5   9   36   NW
John Warnock   Stu   -   4   6   12   SE
Watson Atkinson   Stu   -   5   16   26   NW
Hanes Yerk   Stu   -   9   12   25   SE

448   25 Nov 1811   A/4/288
LO Cin
Transmits patents
Isaac Burnet   Cin   MR   7   2   29   SE
Jacob Wilson   Cin   MR   9   2   13   E
Joseph Eddy   Cin   MR   3   4   11   SE
John Carlough   Cin   MR   8   5   18   SW
Christian Judy   Cin   EML   4   3   19   E
John Snodgrass   Cin   MR   6   2   8   SE
James Cummins   Cin   EML   6   7   19   E
Silas Johnson   Cin   MR   12   3   9   SW
John Simmons   Cin   MR   11   2   36   S
John Davis   Cin   EML   2   5   6   N
David Hoover   Cin   EML   5   5   10   E
John Knoops   Cin   MR   11   2   19   W
James Popenoe   Cin   MR   6   3   29   +
John Paul   Cin   MR   9   3   29   N
William Berry   Cin   MR   12   1   23   +

449   26 Nov 1811   A/4/289
Daniel Symmes, [Reg Cin]
Returns defective certificates; mentions Daniel C.
Cooper
William Swisher   Cin   EML   3   4   2   -
Jacob Gates   Cin   MR   11   1   4   SE
Peter Banta*   Cin   MR   6   1   19   NE
George Wilson   Cin   MR   10   3   36   N
*Gave assignment to person unnamed herein.

450   27 Nov 1811   A/4/289
Felix Wilton, Moorfields, Virginia
Explains delays in issuing patents
Felix Wilton   Cin   MR   10   5   9   SE
Felix Wilton   Cin   MR   10   5   17   NE

451   28 Nov 1811   A/4/290
-- Annin, Harpers Ferry
Transmits patents
Joseph Hoffman & the heirs
   of George Hoffman   Chl   MS   22   2   34   +
Joseph Hoffman & the heirs
   of George Hoffman   Chl   MS   22   2   35   +

452   28 Nov 1811   A/4/290
Hon. Gen. [Thomas] Worthington
Transmits patents
Jesse Spencer   Chl   WS   21   10   10   NW
John Pancake   Chl   -   20   7   26   +
Benjamin Spencer   Chl   -   16   16   12   NE
Mary Deffenbaugh   Chl   -   19   12   17   SW
Jesse Spencer   Chl   -   20   12   2   SE
Jesse Spencer   Chl   -   16   16   12   NW
Frederick Miers   Chl   -   12   7   25   NW
Alexander Fleming   Chl   MS   21   9   31   SE
Frederick Fredderolf   Chl   WS   21   11   30   NW

453		28 Nov 1811			A/4/290

Jared Mansfield, [SG]
Discusses pre-emptions of John Terril and Philip Siler.

454		28 Nov 1811					A/4/290

Wyllys Silliman, [Reg Zan]
Returns defective certificate & comments on overpayment

Philip Kuhn	Zan	Mil	2	8	25	NE

455		28 Nov 1811				A/4/291

David Hoge, [Reg Stu]
Calls attention to defective transfers

Isaac Osbun*	Stu	–	4	10	21	SE
John Smith	Stu	–	5	7	20	NE
Isaac Bachtel**	Stu	–	8	10	3	SW
Michael Jenkins	Stu	–	5	9	19	–

*Assigned to a person unnamed herein.
**Assignee of Jacob Newman.

456		29 Nov 1811					A/4/292

Jesse Spencer, [Reg Chl]
Discrepancies in certificates

James Neely	Chl	–	19	15	6	NE
Jacob Cagy*	Chl	–	18	16	26	NE
Peter Swineford**	Chl	–	20	12	4	W
Joseph Bogle	Chl	–	16	16	13	NE
Joseph Bogle	Chl	–	16	17***13	NE
Jacob Pickle#	Chl	–	19	12	6	SE
William Williamson & John Williamson##	Chl	MS	21	9	29	SE
George Anthony###	Chl	MS	21	11	24	NW
John Moore & Hester Moore§	Chl	–	20	2	15	SW

*Assignee of Robert Chalfant.
**"Originally purchased by yourself [Jesse Spencer]" and assigned to James Lamb; reassigned to Swineford.
***Section 17 is correct.
#Assignee of John Miller.
##Assigned to person unnamed herein.
###Defective assignment to person unnamed herein.
§Mentions assignment of 25 acres to Nicholas Moore; assignment to -- Burnsides; Justice Marshal mentioned; case so defective that it should be begun anew.

457		29 Nov 1811				A/4/293

Daniel Symmes, [Reg Cin]
Return of defective documents

Adam McPherson	Cin	Pre	9	3	13	+
John Fryback	Cin	EML	6	3	23	+
John Fryback	Cin	EML	6	3	24	+
Susannah Butler	Cin	WML	2	13	12	NE
James Johnson	Cin	EML*	3	4	25	SW
James Johnson	Cin	WML*	3	4	25	SW
William C. Shenck & Obadiah Shenck**	Cin	EML	4	3	36	NW
Elijah Lymps***	Cin	MR	5	2	30	NW
Elmow Williams**	Cin	EML	4	3	26	SE

*Erroneous; should read West.
**Assigned to person unnamed herein.
***Assignee of Enoch Lymps.

458		30 Nov 1811			A/4/293

Jesse Spencer, [Reg Chl]
Transmits Treasury receipts

Samuel Lewis	Chl	MS	21	10	31	SE
Samuel Lewis	Chl	MS	21	10	31	NE

459		30 Nov 1811				A/4/293

LO Cin
Transmits patents

James Boyse	Cin	EML	1	6	7	E
Edwin Smith	Cin	MR	6	1	2	W
William Ward	Cin	MR	11	5	21	NW
Andrew Kreitzer	Cin	MR	6	2	18	SW
Joseph Miller	Cin	MR	5	8	29	NW
Casper Bartorf	Cin	MR	2	7	26	NE
Elisha Hammer	Cin	MR	2	5	5	SE
Abraham Yeazel? [Yeagel?]	Cin	MR	10	6	31	NW
Abraham Harner	Cin	EML	4	4	1	SE
George Harter	Cin	EML	3	5	28	N
Michael? Angle	Cin	EML	5	8	20	NE
James Boyse	Cin	EML	1	6	8	W
Michael Wolf	Cin	EML	3	5	9	NW
James Hollingsworth	Cin	EML	5	6	29	NW
Peter Kreitzer	Cin	EML	5	4	10	SW
William Gallaway	Cin	MR	8	4	26	SW
David? [Daniel?] McClung	Cin	EML	6	5	19	SE
Henry Landers	Cin	EML	3	5	33	W

460		2 Dec 1811			A/4/294

Jonathan W. Condy
Acknowledges receipt of payment; mentions -- Simpson's draft.

461		2 Dec 1811				A/4/294

David Hoge, [Reg Stu]
Discrepancies in certificates

John Votaw	Stu	–	3	14	7	NW
Isaac Bachtel*	Stu	–	8	10	3	NW

*Assignee of John Hammon.

462		2 Dec 1811				A/4/294

Wyllys Silliman, [Reg Zan]
Asks whether following patents have been received in LO Zan

Samuel Mendenhall	Zan	Mil	9	3	13	W
Samuel Mendenhall	Zan	Mil	9	3	18	E
Samuel Mendenhall	Zan	Mil	9	3	19	NW
Samuel Mendenhall	Zan	Mil	9	3	13	SE

463		2 Dec 1811				A/4/294

Daniel Symmes, [Reg Cin]
Transmits certificates

Samuel Bond	Cin	WML	1	5	5	SE
Samuel Bond	Cin	WML	1	5	19	SW
Samuel Bond	Cin	WML	1	5	9	SE
Samuel Bond	Cin	WML	1	5	9	SW

464		2 Dec 1811				A/4/295

John Badollet, [Reg Vin]
Discrepancy in certificate

Thomas Jones*	Vin	–	13W	7S	7	+

*Assignee of William Wick.

465		3 Dec 1811				A/4/295

LO Cin
Transmits patents

Ezekiel Ross	Cin	EML	1	4	23	NE
Thomas McIntire	Cin	MR	12	4	30	NE

Cornelius Blue	Cin	MR	11	4	33	SE
Edward Covington	Cin	MR	13	3	5	NE
Robert McImpsey	Cin	EML	6	5	33	SE
John Miller	Cin	EML	4	9	35	NE
Jacob Grenwell	Cin	EML	3	5	23	NE
Stephen Gard	Cin	EML	2	8	26	NW
Samuel Pears	Cin	EML	5	6	10	NE
John Lister	Cin	EML	2	8	35	NE
George Stump	Cin	EML	3	6	36	NE
David Miller	Cin	EML	5	5	17	SE
Daniel Repp	Cin	EML	3	5	7	NW

466   3 Dec 1811   A/4/295
Jonathan W. Condy
Further explanation of account

| Jonathan W. Condy | [Stu] | - | 6 | 16 | 17 | SW |

467   3 Dec 1811   A/4/295
Jesse Spencer, [Reg Chl]
Asks return of transfers

| James Ferguson, Senior* | Chl | WS | 21 | 10 | 28 | W |

*Assigned by Thomas Barr to James Denny; reassigned
  by Denny to Ferguson.

468   4 Dec 1811   A/4/296
Hon. Gen. [Thomas] Worthington
Certificates returned for correction; mentions Wil-
  liam Wells, Peyton S. Symmes.

469   5 Dec 1811   A/4/296
William Simmons, Esq.
Transmits patent

| Lawrence Bowsman | [Cin] | MR | 12 | 4 | 21 | S |

470   5 Dec 1811   A/4/296
LO Cin
Transmits patents

James Smith	Cin	MR	10	6	31	NE
Jesse Wilson	Cin	MR	5	3	26	NE
Felix Rock	Cin	MR	12	4	9	NE
George Gieseman	Cin	MR	9	2	25	NW
William Wells	Cin	MR	12	1	29	+
Nicholas? Lintz	Cin	MR	9	4	23	NW
William Concannon	Cin	MR	11	2	36	NW
George Gordon	Cin	MR	5	4	30	SW
Joseph Brown	Cin	MR	12	1	22	SE
Philip Snysor	Cin	MR	12	1	22	SW
Andrew Black	Cin	MR	10	3	25	SE
Jacob Server	Cin	MR	13	4	25	SE
Jacob Eulas? [Enlas?]	Cin	MR	5	3	26	SE
George Newcom	Cin	MR	8	2	30	NW

471   5 Dec 1811   A/4/297
Peter Wilson, [Rec Stu]
Transmits Treasury receipts

| Mordecai Lee | Stu | - | 6 | 18 | 9 | NW |
| Mordecai Lee | Stu | - | 6 | 18 | 8 | NE |

472   5 Dec 1811   A/4/297
LO Chl
Transmits patents

Mary Deffenbaugh	Chl	-	19	12	17	SW
John Pancake	Chl	-	20	7	26	+
Frederick Fredderrolf	Chl	WS	21	11	30	NW

473   6 Dec 1811   A/4/297
LO Stu
Transmits patents

Michael Yoke	Stu	-	8	10	36	NE
Joseph Bursen	Stu	-	7	14	18	NW
William Armstrong	Stu	-	8	10	29	SE
Benjamin Hall	Stu	-	2	5	8	NE
William Craig	Stu	-	6	12	34	SW
William Craig	Stu	-	6	12	33	NE
Michael Yoke	Stu	-	7	18	31	NW
Daniel Keyser	Stu	-	8	9	20	NW
Henry Crabs	Stu	-	3	11	27	NE
Jacob Crabs	Stu	-	8	11	20	NE
Walter Craig	Stu	-	6	12	27	SE

474   6 Dec 1811   A/4/297
LO Stu
Transmits patents

Samuel Davis	Stu	-	4	17	28	NW
Israel Wilson	Stu	-	6	10	35	SE
Nathan Hole	Stu	-	1	7	18	SE
Barnabas Weller	Stu	-	8	12	29	NW
Jacob Wilker	Stu	-	2	11	33	SW
Daniel Mathias	Stu	-	7	19	3	SE
Hu[gh?] Gilliland	Stu	-	6	9	19	SW
Jesse Hains	Stu	-	5	10	37	NE
Jesse Williams	Stu	-	2	12?	12	NE
George Rogers	Stu	-	5	17	20	SE
John Milligan	Stu	-	6	19	12	SE
Amos Janney	Stu	-	8	9	23	SW
Leonard Barnes	Stu	-	4	14	14	NW
Jacob Harter	Stu	-	8	11	8	SE
Francis Holmes	Stu	-	4	10	11	SW

475   9 Dec 1811   A/4/298
Daniel Symmes, [Reg Cin]
Certificates returned because of discrepancies

John Hall	Cin	EML	2	4	14	SE
Hezekiah Broadberry	Cin	EML	2	5	35	-
Duvalt Leatherman*	Cin	EML	4	9	24	NE
Jacob Beal	Cin	MR	8	3	2	S
Henry French**	Cin	EML	3	5	1	SE
Simeon Broadberry	Cin	--***				
Tobias Tilman#	Cin	EML	3	7	12	SW
David Broadstreet##	Cin	Pre	5	3	33	NE
Martin Weightbright	Cin	-	5	4	8	S

*Assigned to Joseph Leatherman; acknowledged by
  Salome Swinehart, Jonathan Leatherman, Elizabeth
  Leatherman, and Hannah Leatherman.
**Assignee of Albert Banta.
***Erroneous land description.
#Assigns to George Harlass and John Tilman "to be
  equally divided between them." John Tilman assigns
  North end to George Rector, who reassigns to --
  Gavel, who reassigns to -- Swisher, who reassigns
  to -- Simonton.
##Mentions Daniel Kelsey.

476   9 Dec 1811   A/4/299
Jesse Spencer, [Reg Chl]
Documents returned for correction

Alexander Berry	Chl	-	20	11	28	+
George White	Chl	-	19	12	29	NW
John Graham*	Chl	-	20	12	23	SE
John Hampson	Chl	-	20	9**	29	SW

*Transferred to James Reynolds by Elijah Friend,
  agent for Graham.
**Probably township 8 is meant.

477	10 Dec 1811	A/4/299					

David Hoge, [Reg Stu]
Notes discrepancy and forwards Treasury receipt

Samuel Dorans*	Stu	–	4	12	4	–
Levi Housley	Stu	–	9	12	35	SE
Levi Housley	Stu	–	9	12	36	SW

*Assignee of Robert Whitehill, Junior, who was an assignee of Henry Lape.

| **478** | 12 Dec 1811 | A/4/299 |

LO Chl
Transmits patents

John Miller	Chl	MS	21	9	36	NE
John Hanaway	Chl	–	20	13	11	SW
Jacob Kettleborough	Chl	–	17	16	9	SW
George Shimp	Chl	–	19	16	9	NE
Joseph C. Clayton	Chl	–	16	16	13	SE
Isaac Greave	Chl	–	20	8	27	SE
Samuel Bechtell	Chl	MS	21	9	34	NE
George Hosher	Chl	MS	21	11	2	SW
James Dean	Chl	–	16	17	34	NW
Samuel Miller	Chl	–	19	16	9	SE
Christian Cagy	Chl	–	18	16	14	SW
Low Curtz	Chl	–	20	14	31	SW
Edward Hathaway	Chl	–	20	15	18	SW
Barnet Van Kirk	Chl	MS	21	9	29	SW
John Snyder	Chl	–	20	10	32	SW
Jacob Audrick	Chl	–	20	14	6	NW
David Pugh	Chl	–	16	16	12	SE
James Looker	Chl	–	20	15	11	SW
Jacob Corbman? [Corfman?]	Chl	–	18	15	22	SE
Jacob Bibler	Chl	–	18	16	18	NE
Jacob Hooper	Chl	–	19	18	19	SE
Jacob Allbright	Chl	–	21	11	24	SE
Herbert Winegardner	Chl	–	17	18	27	SW

| **479** | 13 Dec 1811 | A/4/300 |

William Cummins
Error in payment

| William? Cummins* | [Cin] | EML | 2 | 5 | 1 | SW |

*"Purchased by your son."

| **480** | 13 Dec 1811 | A/4/300 |

Wyllys Silliman, [Reg Zan]
Inquired regarding certificate and send Treasury receipt

Henry B. Goe?*	Zan	–	12	12	5	+
Henry B. Goe?*	Zan	–	12	12	8	+
William Wilson	Zan	–	11	3	17	NW

*Assignee of Joseph T. Munro.

| **481** | 13 Dec 1811 | A/4/301 |

Henry B. Goe
Vouchers for patents have been requested of the Zan LO.

| **482** | 13 Dec 1811 | A/4/301 |

David Hoge, [Reg Stu]
Transmits certificates and Treasury receipts

| George Prince | Stu | – | 8 | 10 | 15 | NE |
| John Piggot | Stu | – | 6 | 10 | 2 | SE |

| **483** | 13 Dec 1811 | A/4/301 |

Jesse Spencer, [Reg Chl]
Transmits certificate

| John Kerlin | Chl | – | 17 | 17 | 21 | NE |

| Aquilla Fishpaw | Chl | – | 20 | 15 | 25 | W |

| **484** | 14 Dec 1811 | A/4/301 |

Daniel Symmes, [Reg Cin]
Transmits certificate

| Joseph Bigger | Cin | – | 5 | 2 | 12 | SE* |

*West half thereof; intended to be assigned to Frederick Fox.

| **485** | 14 Dec 1811 | A/4/301 |

LO Cin
Transmits patents

Able Stout	Cin	EML	2	5	20	–
John Tickell	Cin	EML	3	6	32	NW
Samuel Duncan	Cin	EML	5	6	10	NW
William Hays	Cin	EML	1	6	20	SW

| **486** | 14 Dec 1811 | A/4/302 |

LO Vin
Transmits patents

William Hargrove	Vin	–	11W	1S	36	SW
John Coleman	Vin	–	7W	2N	20	SW
John Boyse	Vin	–	2E	1S	35	SE
J. J. Gary & J. M. Gary	Vin	–	12W	3S	2	SW
J. C. Veale	Vin	–	7W	2N	17	NW
Daniel Rhoads	Vin	–	8W	7S	9	W
William Gamble	Vin	–	4E	2S	1	NW
Joshua Kernsby	Vin	–	5W	4S	10	SW

| **487** | 14 Dec 1811 | A/4/302 |

LO Chl
Transmits patents

John Bear	Chl	–	20	14	24	SW
John Cooke	Chl	–	14	8	21	NE
Benjamin Rush	Chl	–	13	7	12	SE
Peter Wolf	Chl	–	20	12	17	SW
John Ebert	Chl	–	20	10	2	E
Samuel Fowler	Chl	–	20	11	29	–
John Binheimer	Chl	–	20	12	6	E
John Hunter	Chl	MS	21	9	18	NE
J. Kemper & D. Kemper	Chl	–	17	18	9	SE

| **488** | 14 Dec 1811 | A/4/302 |

Hon. -- Jennings
Transmits patents

| James Blair* | Stu | – | 3 | 10 | 8 | SW |
| Henry Berkshire | Vin | – | 5E | 2S | 34 | NW |

*". . . by your brother directed to be given to you."

| **489** | 14 Dec 1811 | A/4/302 |

LO Stu
Transmits patents

John Russell	Stu	–	2	5	5	SE
John Bene?	Stu	–	2	5	8	NW
A. Holloway	Stu	–	6	19	17	SE
Martin Bughtel	Stu	–	8	12	18	NW
John Abrams	Stu	–	4	11	8	SW
John P. Bond	Stu	–	4	10	30	NE
Zeb Cox	Stu	–	6	11	1	NW
John Dixon	Stu	–	6	19	25	NW
Adam Simmons	Stu	–	4	11	30	SW
Mathew? Wood	Stu	–	5	7	19	SW
Henry Kelton?	Stu	–	2	8	23	SW
John Kennedy	Stu	–	6	10	9	SE

490   15 Dec 1811 A/4/303

Wyllys Silliman, [Reg Zan]
Documents returned for correction

William Smith	Zan	-	15 18	6	NW
William Smith	Zan	-	15 18	6	SW
John Adams*	Zan Mil	8	2	7	SW
John Adams*	Zan Mil	8	2	1	SW
Joseph Reaves & John Vorhies	Zan Mil	8	8	10	SE
Batson Ditrick**	Zan Mil	15	16	14	SW
Batson Ditrick**	Zan Mil	14	16	14	SW
John Pritchard	Zan	--			
George Lapp	Zan Mil	10	7	5	SE
James Rusk (or Bush)***	Zan	-	15 16	9	SE

*Assignee of Levi Cooper.
**Assignee of Godfrey Weymer.
***"According to the original returns this person's name seems to be James Bush. The true name ought to be clearly ascertained before patent is issued."

491   15 Dec 1811 A/4/303

Thomas Gibson, [Reg Can]
Assignments missing

John Christmass*	Can	--

*Assignee of John Bever.

492   17 Dec 1811 A/4/303

LO Cin
Transmits patents

Barnabas Blue	Cin	MR	11	2	28	NE
Ezekiel Patty	Cin	MR	12	5	21	SW
James Pearse	Cin	MR	10	6	14	SE
John Irwin	Cin	MR	8	4	26	NE
Henry Price	Cin	EML	3	6	6	NE

493   17 Dec 1811 A/4/303

LO Stu
Transmits patents

Joseph Rhodes	Stu	-	4	15	32	SW
Caleb Engle	Stu	-	4	6	28	NW
John Hamlin	Stu	-	7	20	24	NE

494   17 Dec 1811 A/4/304

James Findlay, [Rec Cin]
Transmits Treasury receipts

Jacob Humbert	Cin	-	3	5	15	NW
Jacob Humbert	Cin	-	3	5	22	NW
Jacob Humbert	Cin	-	4	4	5	S
Jacob Humbert	Cin	-	5	4	15	N

495   17 Dec 1811 A/4/304

Daniel Symmes, [Reg Cin]
Requests further information

John Wolf	Cin	-	8	3	15	-*
Christian Fogalgasang**	Cin	EML	4	4	13	-
Jonathan Higgens***	Cin	EML	5	2	31	-

*"Except 50 acres in SW corner thereof."
**To be patented to the heirs: Christian, George, Jacob, & Catharina Fogalgasang. . . ."
***Assigned to Zebulon Berkalaw; James Ewing, justice of the peace.

496   17 Dec 1811 A/4/304

LO Vin
Transmits patents

Thomas Waters	Vin	- 12W	3S	4	NE
Chris. Shock	Vin	- 4E	4S	3	NW
David Farnsley	Vin	- 5E	4S	10	NE
William Gamble	Vin	- 6E	4S	6	+
William Gamble	Vin	- 6E	4S	7	+

497   19 Dec 1811 A/4/305

LO Cin
Transmits patents

William Gesserman	Cin	MR	9	2	19	NW
Daniel Aguabraugh	Cin	MR	9	2	28	SE
James Steel	Cin	MR	9	5	19	NE
Samuel Yeaman	Cin	MR	4	4	26	NW
Samuel Still	Cin	MR	8	4	26	SE

498   19 Dec 1811 A/4/305

Jesse Spencer, [Reg Chl]
Returns documents for correction

Clemuel Green*	Chl	-	19	16	31	W

*Assigned one half to Joseph Latchaw; Latchaw assigns East half to Peter Wotrines. Green by a second assignment transfers rights to 51 acres in SW quarter of the half section to Peter Wotrines, according to a survey of Eli Manvill; by a third assignment [Green] assigns all his remaining rights to the same person [Peter Wotrines]. Finally, Wotrines assigns his title to George Fenstermecker. All these assignments defective; issues instructions as to method of correction.

499   20 Dec 1811 A/4/306

Thomas Gibson, [Reg Can]
Transmits Treasury receipt for monies paid by William Hough.

500   20 Dec 1811 A/4/306

LO Vin
Transmits patents

Samuel Aldridge	Vin	- 13W	7S	6	SW
Absalom Lynn	Vin	- 11W	1S	36	NW
Robert Mosely	Vin	- 11W	1S	24	NE

501   21 Dec 1811 A/4/306

Daniel Vanmetre
Transmits patents

Daniel Vanmetre	Chl	-	9	14	30	SE
Daniel Vanmetre	Chl	-	18	14	9	NW
Daniel Vanmetre	Chl	-	18	14	9	NE
Daniel Vanmetre	Chl	-	18	14	10	NE
Daniel Vanmetre	Chl	-	20	13	24	SE
Daniel Vanmetre	Chl	-	20	13	25	W
Daniel Vanmetre	Chl	-	19	14	30	W
Daniel Vanmetre	Chl	-	20	13	25	SE
Daniel Vanmetre	Chl	-	18	14	10	NW

502   24 Dec 1811 A/4/306

J. Jenkinson, Steubenville
Patent of George Leeporth? [Seeporth?] to be sent by mait to Land Office.

503   24 Dec 1811 A/4/306

LO Stu
Transmits patents

Amos Frost	Stu	-	4	15	24	SE
Thomas Poe	Stu	-	3	14	33	NE

James Sinclair	Stu	–	5	7	18	–
Jacob Shorb	Stu	–	9	10	26	SE
Jacob Shorb	Stu	–	9	9	1	SW
Jonathan Warrall	Stu	–	6	18	14	NW
Joseph Blackledge	Stu	–	1	7	19	NE
Alexander Johnston	Stu	–	3	11	32	NW

504   28 Dec 1811   A/4/307
LO Stu
Transmits patents

Joseph Smith	Stu	–	7	10	1	SW
Christian Wyman	Stu	–	5	7	30	NW
John Bashford	Stu	–	3	10	30	SW
Conrod Reber	Stu	–	8	12	20	SE
Andrew Whisler	Stu	–	9	10	35	NW
Anselm Patterson	Stu	–	6	8	31	NW
Jesse Brock	Stu	–	5	9	27	NW
Abner Murphy	Stu	–	5	8	32	NE
Peter Markly	Stu	–	4	10	29	NW
John Huff	Stu	–	7	12	14	NW
Robert Graham	Stu	–	7	9	30	SE
Robert George	Stu	–	4	13	32	SE
William McGaughey	Stu	–	4	6	10	SE

505   31 Dec 1811   A/4/307
Jesse Spencer, [Reg Chl]
Payment deficiency

-- Thrift & -- Downs	Chl	–*	12	7	14	S

*[Perhaps U.S. Military District].

506   31 Dec 1811   A/4/307
David Hoge, [Reg Stu]
Patent "urgently pressed for by Mr. Hyneman, a member of Congress"

Mordecai Lee	Stu	–	6	18	8	NE

507   31 Dec 1811   A/4/308
Daniel Symmes, [Reg Cin]
Transmits Treasury receipts

Martin Baum	Cin	Pre	8	3	1	NW
Martin Baum	Cin	Pre	7	3	27	+
Martin Baum	Cin	Pre	7	3	23	NE

508   2 Jan 1812   A/4/308
Hon. -- Hyneman
Transmits patents

Samuel Lewis	Chl	MS	21	10	31	SE
Samuel Lewis	Chl	MS	21	10	31	NE

509   2 Jan 1812   A/4/308
Charles Bohn
Defective assignment of Jacob Newman

[Charles Bohn?]	Zan	Mil	3	10	12	SE

510   2 Jan 1812   A/4/308
Thomas Gibson, [Reg Can]
Transmits Treasury receipt

John Zent*	Can	–	18	19	9	NW

*Assignee of John Williamson.

511   2 Jan 1812   A/4/308
Daniel Symmes, [Reg Cin]
Transmits Treasury receipt

John Warder? [Warden?]	Cin	Pre	5	3	14	SW

*Assignee of Ruth Mason.

512   4 Jan 1812   A/4/309
John Sloane, [Rec Can]
Transmits Treasury receipt

Abraham Hetrick? [Ketrick?]	Can	–	19	19	8	NE
Abraham Hetrick? [Ketrick?]	Can	–	19	19	10	NW
Abraham Hetrick? [Ketrick?]	Can	–	19	19	10	NE
John Shauck	Can	–	19	19	5	NE
John Shauck	Can	–	19	19	5	NW
John Shauck	Can	–	19	19	5	SW
John Shauck	Can	–	19	19	5	SE

513   4 Jan 1812   A/4/309
Samuel Gwathmey, [Reg Jef]
Transmits certificate

William West	Jef	–	9	3	2	NE

514   6 Jan 1812   A/4/309
LO Chl
Transmits patents

Jacob Brobst	Chl	–	20	14	30	SW
Michael Kraner	Chl	–	20	15	14	NE
Charles Rairy	Chl	MS	21	10	4	N
Daniel Finkhauser	Chl	–	19	16	10	SW
Isaac Kemper	Chl	–	17	18	10	SW
Felty Brats	Chl	–	18	14	14	NW
George Koshar? [Hoshar?]	Chl	–	20	14	3	NW
John Binheimer	Chl	–	20	12	7	N
Conrad Brougher	Chl	MS	21	10	24	SW

515   8 Jan 1812   A/4/310
Hon. Gen. [Thomas] Worthington
Encloses lists of lands in the Military and Refugee districts located subsequent to 14 Feb 1811 and prior to 9 Jan 1812, as required by Mr. [William] Hough.

516   8 Jan 1812   A/4/310
Isaac Kershner, Hagarstown
Returns defective assignment to Philip Kershner

Isaac Kershner	[Cin?]	Pre	9	4	1	SW

517   8 Jan 1812   A/4/310
LO Chl
Transmits patents

Thomas Armstrong	Chl	–	19	11	23	NW
John Christ	Chl	–	20	12	10	NW
William Philips	Chl	–	17	14	9	SE
Theodorus Williamson	Chl	–	20	14	35	SE
Daniel May	Chl	–	19	16	26	SW

518   8 Jan 1812   A/4/310
Daniel Symmes, [Reg Cin]
Transmits Treasury receipts

Martin Baum*	Cin	Pre	9	4	1	NE
Martin Baum*	Cin	Pre	9	4	1	NW
Martin Baum**	Cin	Pre	9	4	1	SW
Isaac Kershner***	Cin	Pre	9	4	1	SE
Martin Stickler	Cin	Pre	11	4	17	SW
Martin Stickler	Cin	Pre	11	4	23	W

*Transferred to Jacob Kershner.
**Transferred to Isaac Kershner.
***[There appears to be some confusion herein, as Isaac Kershner is also shown as having paid for all four quarters of Cin Pre 9 4 1 –.]

519   9 Jan 1812   A/4/311
David Hoge, [Reg Stu]
Transmits an assignment from Joshua Budd to Simon
    Martin & William Rinaman

Joshua Budd	Stu	–	1	9	3	–

520   9 Jan 1812   A/4/311
Daniel Symmes, [Reg Cin]
Returns defective documents for correction

Jacob Kesling	Cin	EML	1	13	27	SW
Jacob Kesling	Cin	WML*	1	13	27	SW
Daniel Richardson	Cin	–	5	2	27	W**
Thomas Hatfield***	Cin	–	5	3	28	NW
Ralph Phillips#	Cin	Pre	8	3	32	NE

*Correct designation.
**North end of West half. Assigned by Richardson to
    Arthur Vandever; reassigned to Daniel McDonald and
    then back to Vandever; mentions deposition of Wil-
    liam C. Shenk before Griffith Yeatman, magistrate.
***Assigned to Samuel Brodaway.
#Originally entered by Jesse Hunt; assigned to Ralph
    Phillips, who then assigned to John A. Tingley.

521   11 Jan 1812   A/4/312
LO Cin
Transmits patents

Christopher Hayden	Cin	EML	2	3	6	SE
Joseph Ulrick	Cin	EML	4	5	2	SE
Abraham Miller	Cin	EML	5	7	5	SW
John Ramsey	Cin	EML	1	6	24	NW
James Crawford	Cin	EML	2	7	14	SW
John Day & Robert Day	Cin	EML	2	8	24	SE
John Railsback	Cin	EML	2	7	18	NW
John Burke	Cin	EML	1	4	22	NE
Joseph Harris	Cin	EML	4	3	33	E
William Cooley	Cin	EML	2	4	9	NW
David Kimmel	Cin	EML	5	5	30	SW
Cornelius Vorhis	Cin	EML	6	4	30	NE
Jacob Rhendy	Cin	MR	9	2	28	NE

522   11 Jan 1812   A/4/312
LO Stu
Transmits patents

Presley Trumbo	Stu	–	7	14	25	NE
John Kennedy	Stu	–	6	10	6	NW
Jacob Albert	Stu	–	6	13	2	SE
Horton Howard	Stu	–	5	7	9	NW
John Freed	Stu	–	5	6	14	NW

523   14 Jan 1812   A/4/313
Hon. [Thomas] Worthington
Transmits patent

James McCleery	Chl	–	18	16	14	NW

524   15 Jan 1812   A/4/313
LO Stu
Transmits patents

Baltzer Hilbert	Stu	–	8	11	5	SE
Jesse White	Stu	–	5	7	20	SW
Ob[adiah?] Crew	Stu	–	5	17	3	SE
John Kennon	Stu	–	7	9	5	SE
Joseph Elliott	Stu	–	6	19	20	NW
Rudolph Bair	Stu	–	7	18	11	NE
George Fisher	Stu	–	5	11	10	NW
John Ebi	Stu	–	8	11	24	SE
George Carothers	Stu	–	6	11	8	SW
William McCaughan	Stu	–	9	10	14	SE
James Fisher	Stu	–	5	11	4	SW
John Nafe	Stu	–	9	10	7	SE
Christ. Briel	Stu	–	7	9	32	NW
George Row	Stu	–	10	2	26	SW
George Row	Stu	–	10	2	27	SE
John Hare	Stu	–	5	18	6	SW
Henry Hare	Stu	–	5	18	19	NE

525   15 Jan 1812   A/4/313
Wyllys Silliman, [Reg Zan]
Asks for patent to be issued

William Foy	Zan	Mil	2	2	20	NE

526   15 Jan 1812   A/4/313
Michael Foy, Waynesburg, Franklin County, Pennsyl-
    vania
Acknowledges receipt of "your letter enquiring for
    your father's patent;" will expedite [see entry
    525].

527   16 Jan 1812   A/4/314
Wyllys Silliman, [Reg Zan]
Returns defective documents brought to [GLO] by
    Peter Mills

William Melick	Zan	–	14	13	3	NE
--	Zan	Mil	1	2	24	SW
William Organ*	Zan	–	14	16	15	SE
David Beckwith	Zan	–	13	12	15	E+
J.? [T.?] Brown, Junior	Zan	–	10	6	31	+
J.? [T.?] Brown, Junior	Zan	–	10	6	32	+
Joseph Evans	Zan	–	12	12	17	E+
Joseph Evans	Zan	–	12	12	20	E+

*Assigned to Roggers Green? [Gumo?]; Levi Whipple,
    magistrate.

528   18 Jan 1812   A/4/314
David Hoge, [Reg Stu]
Requests final certificates, at prompting of member
    of Congress

George Clark	Stu	–	3	12	4	NE
Richard Vaughan	Stu	–	16	16	10	SW

529   18 Jan 1812   A/4/315
Daniel Symmes, [Reg Cin]
Requests final certificate, at prompting of member
    of Congress; mentions John Andrews

William S. Kyles	Cin	Pre	9	4	2	NE

530   18 Jan 1812   A/4/315
Wyllys Silliman, [Reg Zan]
Final certificate for William Foy has now been found
    among papers brought here by -- Mills.

531   20 Jan 1812   A/4/315
LO Stu
Transmits patents

John Nichols	Stu	–	3	5	29	NE
Daniel Merkley	Stu	–	7	20	11	NE
Daniel Merkley	Stu	–	7	20	10	SE
Peter Power	Stu	–	7	20	11	NW
John Reley? [Raley?]	Stu	–	7	20	1	NW
Jane Milligan	Stu	–	4	10	15	SW
Abraham Scott	Stu	–	2	5	29	NW
Stacy Shriver	Stu	–	4	17	19	SW
Joseph Spencer	Stu	–	4	7	26	NW

John Gams	Stu	–	7	19	10	N
Daniel Merkley	Stu	–	7	20	2	S
Peter Power	Stu	–	7	20	10	NE
John Reley	Stu	–	6	18	13	NW

532 20 Jan 1812 A/4/316
LO Cin
Transmits patents

Peter A. Banton	Cin EML	3	5	14	NE
Samuel Coat	Cin EML	5	6	5	NW
Charles Patty	Cin EML	5	8	19	NW
Adam Nelson	Cin EML	1	4	20	NW
Richard Sloan	Cin EML	1	6	14	SE
John Yount	Cin EML	5	6	36	SW
Jacob Lash	Cin EML	3	5	25	NW
Benjamin Owens	Cin EML	6	2	6	NE
-- Hall & -- Moses	Cin EML	2	4	23	SW
Nathan Sellers	Cin EML	2	7	9	SE
Ephraim Owen	Cin EML	5	4	1	SW
Robert Hays	Cin EML	1	6	19	SW
Thomas Smith	Cin EML	4	4	17	SW
William Newman	Cin EML	5	5	13	NE
John Maroney	Cin EML	2	8	34	NW
Thomas C. Wade	Cin EML	1	8	18	W
Silas Dooley	Cin EML	2	7	18	NE
Richard Brown	Cin EML	4	3	19	NW
Richard Brown	Cin EML	4	3	18	SW
Azarias Thorn	Cin EML	2	4	24	SW
Moses Coat? [Coal?]	Cin EML	5	6	5	SW
William Ramsey	Cin EML	2	6	31	NE
John Quin	Cin EML	3	6	30	SW
William Stewart	Cin EML	6	7	10	SW
Isaac Cooper	Cin EML	6	3	32	SW
James Brown	Cin EML	3	2	18	NW
James Brown	Cin EML	1	4	1	NE
John Hart	Cin EML	3	6	17	NW
Abijah Jones	Cin EML	6	3	30	SE
James Brown	Cin EML	1	6	23	SE
Thomas Marshel	Cin EML	1	7	24	SE
Benjamin Hawkins	Cin EML	3	3	8	NE
Robert Boyse	Cin EML	1	6	9	SE
George Branner	Cin EML	4	5	12	SE
-- Patterson & -- Clark	Cin EML	3	3	26	W
-- Cappock & -- Perry	Cin EML	5	11	6	SW
-- Bachtel & -- Taylor	Cin EML	2	4	10	E
William Fincher	Cin EML	5	6	27	SE
John Purviance	Cin EML	1	9	4	SW
James Port	Cin EML	1	4	17	SE
Richard Winans	Cin EML	5	8	1	SE
Jacob Spitler	Cin EML	5	5	29	SW
Peter Fleming	Cin EML	1	9	30	W
Robert Harding	Cin EML	4	4	7	–
Robert Parks	Cin EML	6	2	8	SE
Isaac Hartin	Cin EML	2	6	29	NE
John Pharis, Senior	Cin EML	1	2	20	NE
Alexander Tilford	Cin EML	6	5	19	NW
Isaac Paine	Cin EML	1	8	33	SW
Mortin Irwin	Cin EML	2	5	19	NE
John Biers	Cin EML	3	5	25	NE
Robert Bishop	Cin EML	1	6	5	NE
Henry Paddock	Cin EML	1	8	32	NW
Aaron Biggs	Cin EML	2	6	32	SW
John Hoover	Cin EML	5	6	35	SW

533 21 Jan 1812 A/4/317
LO Stu
Transmits patents

David Craig	Stu	–	3	9	15	NE
John Riley	Stu	–	6	19	12	SW
Martin Houser	Stu	–	7	7	1	–

Jacob Burgey	Stu	–	1	9	22	SW
John Jarvis	Stu	–	6	9	34	NE
James Woodburn	Stu	–	7	15	6	NW
Nicholas Kurtz	Stu	–	3	14	15	SW
Jonas Harris	Stu	–	2	12	22	NW

534 23 Jan 1812 A/4/317
James P. Stewart, Parkinsons Ferry
Transmits patents

James P. Stewart	Stu	–	5	18	27	SW
James P. Stewart	Stu	–	5	17	10	NE

535 23 Jan 1812 A/4/317
LO Cin
Transmits patents

Zach[ariah?] Selby	Cin EML	4	2	10	NE
Smith Charles	Cin EML	1	7	28	SW
Jesse Gough	Cin EML	2	6	30	SE
Joseph Harris	Cin EML	4	3	26	SW
William Ellerman	Cin EML	5	6	7	SW
William Robbins	Cin MR	9	3	5	SW

536 23 Jan 1812 A/4/318
LO Stu
Transmits patents

Henry Wolf	Stu	–	4	16	19	–
Samuel Talbot	Stu	–	6	18	24	N
John Cannon	Stu	–	2	11	26	SE
Michael? Boyer	Stu	–	7	17	3	E
P. Miller & F. Miller	Stu	–	9	10	33	NE
John Shepherd	Stu	–	6	13	34	E
Walter Bell	Stu	–	5	14	2	SE
Christ. Yoder	Stu	–	8	10	31	S
George Leporth	Stu	–	6	12	14	NE
Thomas Ramsey	Stu	–	6	19	23	S

537 24 Jan 1812 A/4/318
LO Stu
Transmits patents

Enos West	Stu	–	6	10	7	NW
Jacob McCay	Stu	–	6	9	6	NE
George Neas	Stu	–	7	20	31	SW
Peter Wise	Stu	–	7	19	30	SE
Francis McBean	Stu	–	2	10	34	NW
Frederick Stump	Stu	–	9	10	28	SE
Frederick Stump	Stu	–	9	10	27	SW
Michael Boyer	Stu	–	7	17	3	NW
James Ball	Stu	–	3	10	14	SE
William Sharrard	Stu	–	5	7	19	NW
Andrew Andsley	Stu	–	5	11	5	SE
George Albaugh	Stu	–	4	12	7	SW
Cyrus Boyd	Stu	–	5	7	20	NW
John James	Stu	–	4	15	28	NE

538 25 Jan 1812 A/4/318
David Hoge, [Reg Stu]
Transmits certificates; member of Congress interested

Abraham Wilhalm	Stu	–	9	12	27	NE
Conrad Deelman	Stu	–	9	12	22	NE

539 27 Jan 1812 A/4/319
Hon. J. Morrow
Transmits patents

Samuel Scholl	Mil	–	3	8	4	15
James Parkhill	Mil	–	4	10	3	18

540   27 Jan 1812   A/4/319
Daniel Symmes, [Reg Cin]
Transmits certificate; mentions John Warder

Henry Cadbury	Cin Pre	9	2	18	-

541   27 Jan 1812   A/4/319
Jesse Spencer, [Reg Chl]
Inquires whether tracts were offered for public sale

--	Chl -	17	1	3	+
--	Chl -	17	1	4	+
--	Chl -	17	1	6	+
--	Chl -	17	1	7	+

542   27 Jan 1812   A/4/319
Charles Roberts, Zanesville
Transmits patent

Mesheck Walker	Zan Mil	5	3	3	18

543   27 Jan 1812   A/4/319
LO Chl
Transmits patents

John Hammond & Thomas Hammond	Chl -	16	16	11	N
Billingslea Bull	Chl -	20	15	8	SW
Jesse D. Courtright	Chl MS	21	11	2	NW
John Defert	Chl -	20	14	4	SW
John Kerr	Chl -	17	16	17	NE
Moses Dawson	Chl -	20	11	28	SW

544   29 Jan 1812   A/4/319
Daniel Thuun
Answers query

Philip Gunckle	Cin EML	5	2	7	-

545   29 Jan 1812   A/4/320
LO Cin
Transmits patents

James McDonnel	Cin MR	9	6	21	SE
John Riddle	Cin MR	1	3	11	NW
David Munger	Cin Pre	4	4	13	SE+
John Downery	Cin MR	7	3	11	SE
David Huston	Cin MR	8	2	26	SE
John Riddle	Cin MR	1	3	11	SW
Philip Kiser	Cin MR	10	4	36	NE
Joseph Hill	Cin MR	12	4	8	SE
Richard Robenson*	Cin MR	10	5	2	SE
James Stewart	Cin MR	8	5	6	SW
James Alexander	Cin WML	1	14	36	NW
Charles Hunt	Cin WML	2	12	12	SE
Charles Hunt	Cin WML	2	12	13	NE
Benjamin Hill	Cin WML	1	14	26	SE
Thomas Skinner	Cin WML	1	7	15	NE
Jacob Keplinger	Cin MR	10	3	1	NW
Samuel Mitchell	Cin MR	12	4	10	SE

*So spelled.

546   30 Jan 1812   A/4/320
LO Cin
Transmits patents

Andrew Hodges	Cin MR	10	5	26	S
Nathan Paddock	Cin MR	9	2	7	S
James Wright	Cin MR	9	6	10	NE
George Petty	Cin MR	12	5	30	SE
Elnathan Cary	Cin MR	10	2	23	SW
Jacob Powers	Cin MR	2	2	26	SE
Thomas Sayres	Cin MR	11	6	34	NE
William C. Schenk	Cin MR	5	2	26	SW
George Petty	Cin MR	12	5	30	NE
John Slagle	Cin MR	8	2	6	NW
John Ireland	Cin MR	1	14	36	SW
Joseph McKinney	Cin MR	9	3	8	E
Jonathan Harshman	Cin MR	9	2	18	SE
Daniel Fouts	Cin WML	1	12	18	NW
George Troutman	Cin MR	3	2	8	NE
John Pence	Cin MR	9	4	18	SE
David Huston	Cin MR	8	2	26	NE
Archarry Berry	Cin MR	12	3	1	NE
George Troutman	Cin MR	3	2	8	SW
David Huston	Cin MR	11	2	30	NE
Joel Fuson	Cin MR	12	4	24	NW
James Wright	Cin MR	10	5	1	SE
Joseph Gaston	Cin MR	2	2	26	NE
David Peterbaugh	Cin MR	8	2	23	NE
David Peterbaugh	Cin MR	8	2	24	SE
William Bacome	Cin MR	11	4	17	NW
Andrew Wood	Cin MR	13	2	14	-

547   31 Jan 1812   A/4/321
Daniel Symmes, [Reg Cin]
Transmits certificate

Martin Baum	Cin Pre	9	4	1	SW

548   1 Feb 1812   A/4/321
Hon. Andrew Gregg
Transmits patent

Ulrick Longnecker	Stu -	9	9	2	NW

549   1 Feb 1812   A/4/321
LO Stu
Transmits patents

Joseph Johnson	Stu -	6	12	28	NW
John Miller	Stu -	8	11	36	NW
Absalom Kent	Stu -	6	12	9	SE
Henry Everhard	Stu -	8	11	20	NW
Frederick Oberlin	Stu -	8	11	20	SE
Michael Reed	Stu -	7	18	11	NW
Michael Reed	Stu -	8	10	30	SE
David Fancett	Stu -	5	7	19	SE
George Neas	Stu -	8	10	30	SW
Henry Springer	Stu -	2	10	5	NW
Thomas McPherrin	Stu -	7	15	23	SE

550   1 Feb 1812   A/4/322
LO Jef
Transmits patents

John Taylor	Jef 2M	10E	4N	32	SW
Jesse Henley	Jef 2M	8E	3N	33	NE
John Copple, Senior	Jef 2M	9E	2N	32	NE
Joseph Ryman	Jef 2M	4E	2N	5	SE
John Stucker	Jef 2M	10E	2N	6	SW
John Taylor	Jef 2M	10E	3N	4	+
John Taylor	Jef 2M	10E	3N	5	+
Jacob Shreader, Junior	Jef 2M	4E	3N	32	SW
Jacob Copple	Jef 2M	9E	2N	32	SE

551   1 Feb 1812   A/4/322
Frederick Stump, Postoffice, Chambersburg, Pennsylvania
Transmits patent

Frederick Stump	Can -	10	12	33	NW

552		4 Feb 1812				A/4/322
LO Zan						
Transmits patents						
Josiah Robe	Zan	Mil	1	1	23	NE
-- Ward & -- Burges	Zan	-	15	17	7	SE
William Hamilton	Zan	Mil	10	1	21	SW
Philip Kuhn	Zan	Mil	2	8	16	SE
Casper Cramer	Zan	Mil	10	7	25	W
Henry Dusinberry	Zan	-	15	17	32	SE
John Walters	Zan	Mil	7	1	2	SW
Nicholas Border	Zan	-	13	12	1	SW
John Kepler	Zan	-	13	12	1	NW
John Nicolls	Zan	Mil	7	5	2	SE
Charles Bennet	Zan	-	14	16	17	NE
Charles Hummel	Zan	-	15	17	23	SW
John Wartembe	Zan	Mil	6	1	22	SW
John Willson	Zan	-	15	17	30	NW
Mary Home? [Kome?]	Zan	-	15	17	25	SE
John Walters	Zan	Mil	7	1	9	NW
James Jeffries	Zan	-	4	15	11	NE
Samuel McCann	Zan	Mil	8	2	7	NW
Jacob Gombar?	Zan	Mil	3	2	8	SE
Alexander Culbertson	Zan	Mil	7	1	2	NE
Thomas King	Zan	Mil	15	16	4	SE
Isaac Vanhorne	Zan	-	14	16	11	SE
Stephen Ballard	Zan	Mil	1	1	9	SW
Mathias Croy	Zan	Mil	8	4	21	SW
John Hanna	Zan	Mil	1	3	25	SW
Jacob Sherg	Zan	-	15	17	30	SE
James Larron	Zan	Mil	1	1	8	NE
Isaac Congill*	Zan	Mil	4	4	22	NE
James Miskimen	Zan	Mil	4	4	8	NW
George Border	Zan	Mil	6	1	6	NE
Samuel Taylor	Zan	Mil	8	2	21	SW
Obed[iah] Meredith	Zan	Mil	9	6	21	SE
John Eseland	Zan	-	12	11	28	W
Edward Milner	Zan	Mil	1	2	16	SE
*So spelled.						

553		4 Feb 1812				A/4/323
LO Cin						
Transmits patents						
-- Welsh, -- Reed, & -- Parker	Cin	EML	6	21?	27	+
-- Welsh, -- Reed, & -- Parker	Cin	EML	6	21?	28	+
-- Welsh, -- Reed, & -- Parker	Cin	EML	6	21?	29	+
Samuel Black	Cin	MR	10	3	19	SW
Benjamin Vancleve	Cin	MR	8	2	30	SE
Joseph Reynolds	Cin	MR	11	4	31	SW
David Huston	Cin	MR	11	2	24	SE

554		5 Feb 1812				A/4/323
Hon. Thomas Worthington						
Transmits patents						
S? [L?] Conaway*	Zan	-	6	1	4	NW
J. Robinson*	Zan	-	12	10	24	W+
R. McConnel	Zan	-	12	10	10	+
R. McConnel	Zan	-	12	10	11	+
R. McConnel	Zan	-	7	1	8	SE
R. McConnel	Zan	-	7	1	8	SW
*Assignees of -- McConnell.						

555		5 Feb 1812				A/4/323
LO Stu						
Transmits patents						
Joseph Earl	Stu	-	4	17	30	NE
Leonard Richards	Stu	-	8	10	32	NW
Isaac Cadwalader	Stu	-	7	11	6	NE

556		5 Feb 1812				A/4/324
LO Cin						
Transmits patents						
Simon Bruner	Cin	MR	8	2	17	NW
Simon Bruner	Cin	MR	8	2	12	NE
Daniel Leffel	Cin	MR	9	4	24	SW
Joseph Reynolds	Cin	MR	11	4	31	NE
Samuel Black	Cin	MR	10	3	25	NE
Samuel Stewart & John Stewart	Cin	MR	8	5	15	+
Joseph Hewlings	Cin	MR	13	4	7	NW

557		5 Feb 1812				A/4/324
LO Zan						
Transmits patents						
Jacob Walters? [Wallers?]	Zan	Mil	4	9	12	SE
John Willy? [Wilty?]	Zan	-	13	12	7	SE
William Cunningham	Zan	Mil	1	2	25	SE
William McLean	Zan	-	12	13	17	SW
Nicholas Border	Zan	-	13	12	1	SE
Abraham Deaver	Zan	-	14	15	1	NW
Ezekiel Rose	Zan	-	14	14	3	SW
Samuel Ream	Zan	-	15	17	31	SE
Adam Fraunce	Zan	-	14	16	15	NW
Thomas Butler	Zan	Mil	8	6	6	SW
John Lanison	Zan	-	12	11	5	NW+
Henry Hanna	Zan	Mil	2	3	1	SE
Mathias Niddy, Senior	Zan	-	15	17	5	NW
William Dusinberry	Zan	-	15	17	28	NW
Thomas Clayton	Zan	-	15	16	18	NE
James Hastings	Zan	-	12	13	1	NW
John Bowers	Zan	Mil	7	1	11	NE
William Bigham	Zan	Mil	2	2	21	SW
John Adams	Zan	Mil	8	4	12	NE
Richard Lane	Zan	Mil	8	2	12	SW
Isaac Oldham	Zan	Mil	3	2	3	NW
Benjamin Resener	Zan	Mil	5	1	11	NE
John Buckhelder	Zan	Mil	3	9	22	SE
John Jacob Spangler	Zan	Mil	5	8	19	SE
John Kline	Zan	Mil	1	10	15	NW
George Adams	Zan	Mil	10	3	18	NE
John Williams	Zan	Mil	1	2	17	NW
David Frame	Zan	Mil	1	2	23	SW
David Fielas? [Fields?]	Zan	Mil	8	3	8	NW
Thomas Drennon	Zan	-	12	13	2	NE

558		6 Feb 1812				A/4/325
David Hoge, [Reg Stu]						
Inquires regarding patent, requested by member of Congress						
Peter Walter	Stu	-	5	17	26	N

559		7 Feb 1812				A/4/325
Hon. Thomas Worthington						
Transmits patents						
James Fullerton	Chl	-	16	17	13	SE
Winn Winship	Chl	-	20	11	17	SW
William Rogers	Chl	-	20	11	30	NW
Frederick Pontius	Chl	WS	21	11	5	SE

560		7 Feb 1812				A/4/325
Hon. Andrew Gregg						
Transmits patent						
Jacob Albright	Zan	Mil	4	8	6	NW

561		7 Feb 1812				A/4/325
LO Stu						
Transmits patents						

Isaiah Myers   Stu -   4 15 19 NW
Jacob Leffler   Stu -   6   9 19 NE
Joseph Lindesmith   Stu -   4 15 25 SE
Nathan Hole   Stu -   1   7 18 NE
John Aylimer? [Aytimer?] Stu -   4 15 25 SE
Samuel Heavilin   Stu -   5 10 30 NE
William Andrews   Stu -   9 10 14 NW
Nathaniel Haines   Stu -   5 18 25 SW
Joseph Gundy   Stu -   6 13 14 NE
James McKenzie   Stu -   2 10 31 SE
Matthew Cannon   Stu -   2 11 29 SE
Robert Patterson   Stu -   8   9   9 NE
Jacob Shaffer   Stu -   7 15   6 NE

562   8 Feb 1812   A/4/326
David Hoge, [Reg Stu]
Transmits certificate
Morris Albaugh   Stu -   5 12 17   E

563   8 Feb 1812   A/4/326
Wyllys Silliman, [Reg Zan]
Requests final certificate
John Lock   Zan Mil 1   8   8 SE

564   8 Feb 1812   A/4/326
Daniel Symmes, [Reg Cin]
Transmits Treasury receipts
John Lock   Cin EML 3   7 22 SW
John Lock   Cin EML 3   7 26 SW

565   8 Feb 1812   A/4/326
Thomas Gibson, [Reg Can]
Returns defective assignment of unnamed tract from
   John Bever to John Christmass

566   10 Feb 1812   A/4/326
Isaac Clendennon, St. Clairsville, Belmont County,
   Ohio
Transmits patent
Isaac Clendennon   Stu -   5   7 33 NE

567   10 Feb 1812   A/4/327
Morris Albaugh, Steubenville
Transmits patent
Morris Albaugh   Stu -   5 12 17   E

568   10 Feb 1812   A/4/327
Hon. Thomas Worthington
Transmits patent
John Carlisle   [Chl] WS 21   9 22 NW

569   10 Feb 1812   A/4/327
LO Stu
Transmits patents
Jacob Vanfossan   Stu -   2 10 23 NW
Amos Preston   Stu -   5 16 26 SE
Joseph Hayes   Stu -   7 15 36 SW
Joshua Dixon   Stu -   5 18 29 SE
Frederick Horn   Stu - 20 12 32 SE
Richard Ewers   Stu -   5   7 13 NW
Abraham Galladay   Stu -   9   9   3 NE
James Shepherd   Stu -   6   9 23 SE
Douglas Wilson   Stu -   7 18 32 SE
James Marques   Stu -   4 12   9 NE
Peter Maston, Junior   Stu -   4 17 17 SW

570   10 Feb 1812   A/4/327
LO Chl
Transmits patents
John Harnan*   Chl WS 21 11 25   W
John Milhorne   Chl -   6   9   6 NW
Samuel Meek   Chl -   7 16 36 SW
Philip Cherry   Chl MS 22   2   2 SW
John Ford   Chl - 20 15   1 NE
George H. Tong   Chl - 20 15   7 SE
John Harman*   Chl - 20 11   5 SE
David Aurand   Chl MS 21   9 36 NW
Andrew Barr   Chl MS 22   4   1 SE
John Ratcliff   Chl - 19 10 29 SE
George Hammel   Chl - 20 12   9 SW
William Bail   Chl - 16 16   3 SW
*So spelled.

571   13 Feb 1812   A/4/328
David Hoge, [Reg Stu]
Requests final certificate
Peter Walter   Stu -   5 17 26   N

572   13 Feb 1812   A/4/328
George Harness, Moorfield, Hardy County, Virginia
Transmits patents
George Harness   Chl LS 21   2 17   -
George Harness   Chl LS 21   2 18   +

573   13 Feb 1812   A/4/328
Hon. Thomas Worthington
Transmits patents
Joseph Farmer &
   James McClintock   Chl - 21   8 32 SE

574   13 Feb 1812   A/4/328
Hon. -- Condet
Transmits patents
Eli Hull*   [Mil?] - 15   8   3 16
Josiah B. Day **   [Mil?] - 15   8   3 14
*". . . late a soldier."
**Assignee of H. Rick.

575   13 Feb 1812   A/4/328
Hon. -- Jennings
Transmits patents & certificate
Aaron Keeler*   [Mil?] -   8   9   1 27
William Liggins**   [Mil?] -   1 10   1 14
*". . . late an ensign."
**Soldier.

576   13 Feb 1812   A/4/328
Robert Mitchell, Postoffice, Lewistown, Mifflin
   County, Pennsylvania
Transmits patent
Robert Mitchell   Chl - 16 15 31 SW

577   13 Feb 1812   A/4/328
Hon. William Piper
Transmits patent
Frederick Divert   Chl - 20 11   1 SW

578   13 Feb 1812   A/4/328
Hon. -- Laycock
Transmits patent
Thomas Henry   Can - 10 12   9 SE

579   14 Feb 1812   A/4/329
Hon. -- Morrow
Transmits patents

David Longhead	Cin EML	6	1	19	+
David Longhead	Cin EML	6	1	20	+
David Longhead	Cin EML	6	1	29	+
David Longhead	Cin EML	6	1	30	+
David Longhead	Cin EML	5	3	23	-
David Longhead	Cin EML	5	3	24	+

580   14 Feb 1812   A/4/329
Hon. -- Gregg

Isaiah Willis	Ch1 MS	21	9	19	NE
Isaiah Willis	Ch1 MS	21	9	19	SE

581   14 Feb 1812   A/4/329
LO Jef
Transmits patents

Christopher Fifer	Jef -	9E	1N	28	+
Jacob Trumbo	Jef -	8E	4N	8	NE

582   14 Feb 1812   A/4/329
LO Ch1
Transmits patents

Thomas Patton & Robert Patton	Ch1 -	19	11	10	SW
Adam Turner	Ch1 -	20	9	4	SW
Alexander Chambers	Ch1 -	19	13	31	SE
Alexander Chambers	Ch1 -	19	13	31	SW
Michael Blank	Ch1 -	17	14	6	NE

583   14 Feb 1812   A/4/329
J. H. Brinton, Philadelphia
Returns defective assignments; mentions -- Tilghman, judge.

584   14 Feb 1812   A/4/329
J. W. Condy
Returns defective assignments; mentions -- Tilghman, judge.

585   15 Feb 1812   A/4/329
Hon. -- Jennings
Transmits patents

James Bruce	Jef -	4E	4S	2	NW
William Provine	Jef -	4E	5N	31	SW

586   18 Feb 1812   A/4/330
LO Jef
Transmits patents

Richard Ruynolds*	Jef -	3E	4N	29	NE
Jacob Rhodes	Jef -	9E	1N	9	NW
George Kindle	Jef -	11E	5N	19	NE
Philbert Wright	Jef -	4E	2N	31	NE

*So spelled.

587   15 Feb 1812   A/4/330
Daniel Symmes, [Reg Cin]
Asks for final certificate

Daniel C. Cooper	Cin -	7	1	4	+

588   15 Feb 1812   A/4/330
Richard Forrest, [U.S. Department of State]

Inquires regarding patent at Gen. Thomas Worthington's request

Noah Zane	Ch1 -	17	17	23	-

589   17 Feb 1812   A/4/330
LO Stu
Transmits patents

David Edwards	Stu -	7	18	31	SW
William Kelly	Stu -	4	10	23	SE
Robert Johnson	Stu -	5	18	19	SE
Peter Flack	Stu -	1	9	21	SE

590   17 Feb 1812   A/4/330
Daniel Symmes, [Reg Cin]
Transmits certificate & Treasury receipt

Joseph P. Brown	Cin EML	5	4	21	SE

591   17 Feb 1812   A/4/330
Hon. Thomas Worthington
Transmits patent

Noah Zane	Ch1 -	17	17	23	-

592   18 Feb 1812   A/4/331
LO Stu
Transmits patents

William Johnson	Stu -	6	12	34	SE
Peter Nava	Stu -	9	10	28	NE
Hugh Orr	Stu -	5	11	24	NW
Conrad Smith	Stu -	9	12	17	NW
John King	Stu -	3	5	29	NW
Jacob Coleman	Stu -	9	12	10	SE
Philip Shultz	Stu -	7	17	10	SE
Joshua Whitaker	Stu -	4	15	11	-
John Beht	Stu -	1	9	22	NE
John Riley	Stu -	6	11	27	SW
David Robb	Stu -	2	8	27	NW
William Foutt	Stu -	2	11	28	SE
Nicholas Stump	Stu -	9	9	10	NW
Moses Gilson	Stu -	5	17	30	NW
Henry March	Stu -	2	10	12	SE
Aaron Brooks	Stu -	1	6	7	-
Wybrants Beatty	Stu -	4	12	33	SE
Parnel Hall	Stu -	8	11	19	SE
John McFadon	Stu -	7	9	28	NW
John N. Brock	Stu -	5	8	30	SE
Waddy Cobbs	Stu -	5	18	35	NE
Nancy Forney	Stu -	6	13	7	NW
Abraham Betz	Stu -	1	3	26	+
Benjamin Anderson	Stu -	7	19	12	SE
Benjamin Anderson	Stu -	5	17	30	SE

593   18 Feb 1812   A/4/331
LO Zan
Transmits patents

Isaac Hill	Zan -	9	6	2	NE
Caleb Dunn	Zan -	12	13	6	NE
Joseph Reeve	Zan -	8	8	10	NE
John Williams	Zan -	14	15	3	NE
John Colvin	Zan -	15	18	9	NE

594   18 Feb 1812   A/4/331
LO Ch1
Transmits patents

George Bontius*	Ch1 -	20	11	4	NE
Henry Liteanaker	Ch1 -	19	16	35	NE
David Brumback	Ch1 -	19	16	21	NW

* So spelled.

595 18 Feb 1812 A/4/331
LO Can
Transmits patents

| Philip Slusher | Can | - | 10 | 12 | 11 | SE |
| Philip Slusher | Can | - | 10 | 12 | 8 | SW |

596 18 Feb 1812 A/4/332
Hon. -- Jennings
Transmits patent

| Daniel Stout | Vin | - | 5E | 2S | 21 | NE |

597 18 Feb 1812 A/4/332
Hon. Thomas Worthington
Transmits patents

| Jacob Burnet | Cin | Pre | 9 | 4 | 20 | - |
| William Wells | Cin | MR | 5 | 4 | 29 | - |

598 18 Feb 1812 A/4/332
LO Chl
Transmits patents

Aaron Donaldson	Chl	-	20	15	28	SW
William D. Hendren? [Kendren?]	Chl	MS	21	11	20	NE
Samuel Lybrand	Chl	-	20	11	4	NW
Thomas Ijams	Chl	-	17	17	34	N
Elizabeth Rogers	Chl	-	21	5	17	+
Robert Winegardner	Chl	Mil	14	8	18	E
William Brundage	Chl	Mil	19	7	23	NE
Henry Keller	Chl	-	18	15	15	SE
Joseph McKee	Chl	-	3	8	21	SE

599 19 Feb 1812 A/4/332
LO Stu
Transmits patents

William Davis	Stu	-	6	14	24	SW
Alexander Cameron	Stu	-	7	18	34	SE
John Warnock	Stu	-	4	6	11	NE
James Cocker	Stu	-	2	10	12	NW
Henry Stanton	Stu	-	6	8	7	NW
Stephen Ford	Stu	-	3	9	15	SW
John Howell	Stu	-	5	9	25	SE
John Pennock	Stu	-	6	19	24	SW
Arthur Barrett, Senior	Stu	-	5	10	33	NW
John Winance	Stu	-	4	11	21	SE
Joseph Grimes	Stu	-	6	10	9	NE
Adam Knouff	Stu	-	4	14	11	NE
James Hewitt	Stu	-	7	17	23	NE
Michael Reed	Stu	-	8	10	30	NW
Martin Houser	Stu	-	7	19	1	-
Elijah French	Stu	-	4	17	31	NW
Jesse Milner	Stu	-	4	15	29	SW
Richard Carle	Stu	-	4	6	10	NE
George Thomas	Stu	-	6	17	10	NW
Absalom Kent	Stu	-	6	12	7	NE
Jacob Shively	Stu	-	6	18	30	SE
Daniel Johnson	Stu	-	3	10	13	SW
John Gouldin	Stu	-	3	14	20	NW
Stephen McBride	Stu	-	4	15	30	SE
John Worley	Stu	-	8	9	5	NE
Stephen Kinsey	Stu	-	5	9	33	NE
John Coffee	Stu	-	5	7	3	NE
James Chapman	Stu	-	9	9	11	NW
William Hutchison	Stu	-	4	8	3	SW
Nathaniel Thomas	Stu	-	4	15	4	-
Martin Boghart	Stu	-	6	13	9	SW
Asa Holloway, Senior	Stu	-	5	9	27	NE
John Grant	Stu	-	6	19	26	SE
Philip Creplever	Stu	-	6	13	8	SW
William Milton	Stu	-	7	11	18	NE
James Hazlett	Stu	-	4	10	18	NW
Amasa Lysy	Stu	-	6	13	34	SW
Hugh Cunningham	Stu	-	8	11	27	SE
Christian Yoder	Stu	-	8	10	31	N
Jacob Wright	Stu	-	2	8	34	SW
Samuel Sluts	Stu	-	7	15	36	NW
John Shay	Stu	-	6	9	34	SE
Tobias White	Stu	-	8	11	12	SW
Thomas Brooks	Stu	-	2	3	26	NE
Charles Blackmore	Stu	-	1	7	34	SE
Enos Ellis	Stu	-	4	15	32	NE
Henry Bough	Stu	-	2	10	13	SE

600 20 Feb 1812 A/4/334
Peter Ingleman, Postoffice, Staunton, Augusta County, Virginia
Transmits patent

| Peter Ingleman | [Cin] | EML | 3 | 4 | 12 | NW |

601 20 Feb 1812 A/4/334
Thomas Moffett, Postoffice, Abington, Washington County [state not given]
Transmits patent

| Thomas Moffett | [Cin] | WML | 2 | 12 | 10 | + |

602 20 Feb 1812 A/4/334
Daniel Symmes, [Reg Cin]
Transmits Treasury receipt

| William Cummins* | Cin | EML | 2 | 5 | 1 | SW |

*Tract purchased by son [whose name is not given].

603 20 Feb 1812 A/4/334
Hon. J. Morrow
Transmits patent

| Eli Baldwin | Mil | - | 4 | 10 | 1 | 5 |

604 20 Feb 1812 A/4/334
Hon. -- Jennings
Transmits patents

J. I.? Kelly & S. Kelly	Jef	-	9E	2N	35	SW
George Shannon	Jef	-	9E	3N	12	NE
Solomon Bower	Jef	-	4E	2N	2	NE

605 20 Feb 1812 A/4/334
LO Jef
Transmits patents

Abraham Giltner? [Gittner?]	Jef	-	9E	2N	36	SW
John Taylor	Jef	-	11E	3N	1	+
John Taylor	Jef	-	11E	3N	2	+
John Taylor	Jef	-	11E	3N	12	+
Joseph Willson	Jef	-	10E	4N	14	SE
John Abbett*	Jef	-	9E	1N	13	NE
Isaac Kenall*	Jef	-	3E	5N	25	+
Isaac Kenall*	Jef	-	3E	5N	36	+
Dennis Fitzpatrick	Jef	-	9E	1N	14	NW
Adam Kellar*	Jef	-	9E	1N	4	NW
Jonathan Lindly	Jef	-	1W	1N	2	NW
Jonathan Lindly	Jef	-	1W	1N	2	NE
Robert Field	Jef	-	2E	1N	23	NE
Joseph Farlow	Jef	-	1W	1N	11	SE
Robert Marshall	Jef	-	9E	4N	29	SW

*So spelled.

606		20 Feb 1812		A/4/335			

LO Cin
Transmits patents

John Harris	Cin	MR	5	3	29	NE
Peter Dill	Cin	EML	4	3	30	NW
William Brumbaugh	Cin	EML	5	4	30	NW
Jonathan Ballinger	Cin	EML	5	6	4	SE
Robert Marshall	Cin	EML	6	5	7	NE
John Jay	Cin	EML	5	6	25	SW
Charles Testan	Cin	EML	1	2	13	NW
Jonathan Mote	Cin	EML	5	6	20	NW
John Mast	Cin	EML	5	6	28	NW
Elijah Mendenhall	Cin	EML	3	4	34	SE
Joseph Smith	Cin	EML	3	3	6	E
Andrew Sheetz	Cin	EML	5	6	23	NE
Henry Hoover	Cin	WML	1	12	28	NE
William Ward	Cin	Pre	10	4	2	+
-- Vance & -- Clensey	Cin	Pre	6	3	30	+?
William Buckles	Cin	Pre	5	4	34	+
William Ward	Cin	Pre	10	5	31	W
Daniel Wilson	Cin	Pre	5	3	10	W
Arthur Johnston	Cin	Pre	8	3	4	SE

607		20 Feb 1812		A/4/335			

Hon. Thomas Worthington
Transmits patents

-- Phillips & -- Pierce	[Cin]	EML	2	12	36	NE
-- Phillips & -- Pierce	[Cin]	EML	2	12	36	SW

608	20 Feb 1812	A/4/335

Peter Audrain, [Reg Det]
Returns certificates for private claims ". . . which
had been patented previous to their arrival here";
mentions the following persons:

Joseph Bissonet	David McComb
Hubert Lacroix	Ichabod Leech
Joseph Bellair	Col. George Cotterall
Amable Bellair	George Cotterall
Henry Cunner	Henry Cotterall
Jaques Lasselle	James Cotterall
Elijah Brush	David Cotterall
John McComb	Victor Moriceau, widow
William McComb	& heirs of

Also returns surveys of -- Hull made for Alexis
Labadie and Dominique Labrose.

609		21 Feb 1812		A/4/336			

LO Cin
Transmits patents

Absalom Chenoweth	Cin	MR	10	5	10	SW
James Small	Cin	EML	2	8	32	SE
Lewis Dewis	Cin	WML	2	8	4	NE
Andrew Woods	Cin	WML	1	13	1	SE
Aaron Martin	Cin	WML	2	12	12	NE
James L. Chamberlain	Cin	EML	2	4	9	SW
John Stewart &						
James Stewart	Cin	MR	1	4	8	NE
Lewis Boyer	Cin	MR	12	1	15	NW
Peter Sintz	Cin	MR	9	4	24	SE
Jacob Keplinger, Senior	Cin	MR	10	4	8	NE

610	22 Feb 1812	A/4/336

-- Colvin, [U.S. Department of State]*
Transmits letter from Hon. Thomas Wilson for patent
in Virginia [Military District of Ohio]
*See entry 612 below.

611	22 Feb 1812	A/4/336

Hon. Samuel L. Mitchell
Transmits authenticated statement of facts which appear in the records in the case of the military
land warrant granted for the services of Amos
Kniffen and returns -- Buxton's letter & enclo-
sures.

612	22 Feb 1812	A/4/336

Hon. Thomas Wilson
Reports on warrant for land in Virginia [Military
District of Ohio] in name of John Hardiman, with
assignemtn to Zadock Walker; forwarded to -- Colvin, U.S. Department of State, for patenting.

613		22 Feb 1812		A/4/337			

Hon. Thomas Worthington
Transmits patents

Jacob Burnet	Cin	Pre	9	3	7	+
William Wells	Cin	Pre	5	3	17	-
William Wells	Cin	Pre	5	3	35	-

614		24 Feb 1812		A/4/337			

Thomas Gibson, [Reg Can]
Inquires regarding transfer

Alexander McMullen*	Can	-	13	15	4	SW

*Assignee of George Slidger?

615		24 Feb 1812		A/4/337			

Hon. Samuel L. Mitchell
Returns documents of Garret Sickles. Lots still remaining vacant are

--	Mil	-	1	6	11	1
--	Mil	-	1	6	11	2
--	Mil	-	1	6	11	3
--	Mil	-	1	6	11	4
--	Mil	-	1	6	11	5
--	Mil	-	1	6	11	6
--	Mil	-	1	6	11	7
--	Mil	-	1	6	11	8
--	Mil	-	1	6	11	13
--	Mil	-	1	6	11	14
--	Mil	-	1	6	11	15
--	Mil	-	1	6	11	16
--	Mil	-	1	6	11	17
--	Mil	-	1	6	11	18
--	Mil	-	1	6	11	19
--	Mil	-	1	6	11	20
--	Mil	-	1	6	11	21
--	Mil	-	1	6	11	28
--	Mil	-	1	6	11	29
--	Mil	-	1	6	11	31
--	Mil	-	1	6	11	40
--	Mil	-	2	7	18	9
--	Mil	-	2	7	18	13
--	Mil	-	2	7	18	14
--	Mil	-	2	7	18	15
--	Mil	-	2	7	18	16
--	Mil	-	1	7	19	None
--	Mil	-	2	7	19	None
--	Mil	-	2	7	17	24
--	Mil	-	2	7	17	25
--	Mil	-	2	7	17	26
--	Mil	-	2	7	17	27
--	Mil	-	2	7	17	28
--	Mil	-	2	7	17	29

```
--                      Mil  -   3   8  16   1          --                      Cin WML  1  14  12  NW
--                      Mil  -   3   8  16   6          --                      Cin WML  3   4   9  SE
--                      Mil  -   3   8  16   7          --                      Cin MR   8   4   8  SE
--                      Mil  -   4   7  16  None        --                      Cin WML  1  14  12  NE
                                                        --                      Cin MR   8   4   8  NE
                                                        --                      Cin EML  2   1  18  SE
616                     24 Feb 1812    A/4/337          --                      Cin EML  2   5  18  SE
Daniel Symmes, [Reg Cin]                                --                      Cin WML  2   8  13  NE
Returns defective transfer                              --                      Cin EML  2   8  13  NE
John McCormick*         Cin Pre  5   2  25   +          --                      Cin WML  1   9  32  NW
*Assigned to Joseph Sawyer.                             --                      Cin WML  1   9  32  SW
                                                        --                      Cin EML  1   4   8  SE
                                                        --                      Cin EML  1   4  18  SE
617                     24 Feb 1812    A/4/337          --                      Cin WML  1  15  17  NE
LO Chl                                                  --                      Cin WML  1  11   4  SW
Transmits patents                                       --                      Cin MR  10   5   4  NE
Jacob Levingood*        Chl  -   20  10  30  NW
Adam Martin             Chl Mil 21   9  35  SE
George Wolf             Chl  -   20  11  27  SW         624                     26 Feb 1812    A/4/339
Jacob Bumgarner         Chl  -   21   5  33  SW         Martin Bachtel, Postoffice, Hagarstown
Peter Row               Chl WS  21  11  22  NE          Transmits patent
Robert Shannon          Chl Mil 22   4   2  SW          Martin Bachtel          Can  -   10  12   7   +
Abraham Harris          Chl  -   20  14   5  NW
William Campbell        Chl WS  21  10  26  SW
William Jump            Chl WS  21  10   1  NW          625                     26 Feb 1812    A/4/339
Peter Hush              Chl  -   17  18   5  NE         LO Chl
David Spangler          Chl MS  22   4  28   S          Transmits patents
Henry Sackeiter         Chl WS  21  11   1  SE          Jacob Alspach, Junior   Chl  -   20  14  10  NE
                                                        Leonard Warner, Junior  Chl WS  21  11  14  NE
                                                        James Ritchie           Chl WS  21   9   4   -
618                     24 Feb 1812    A/4/338          Samuel Wilson           Chl Mil 14   8  20  SW
Hon. -- Morrow                                          William Keith           Chl  -   17  18  28  NE
Transmits patent                                        -- Morris & -- Hardesty Chl  -   20  13  13  NW
William Parkhill        Stu  -   3   9  29  NW          Samuel Willets          Chl  -   20  11  11  SW


619                     24 Feb 1812    A/4/338          626                     27 Feb 1812    A/4/340
Hon. S. B. Ormsby                                       Hon. Thomas Worthington
Transmits patent                                        Transmits patents
Patrick McFarlan        Vin  -   4E  2S   2  SW         William Wells           Cin Pre  5   3  36   S
                                                        William Wells           Cin Pre  5   4  17   +
                                                        William Wells           Cin Pre  5   4  23  -?
620                     24 Feb 1812    A/4/338
Hon. -- Jenkins
Delay in patenting due to faulty assignment             627                     27 Feb 1812    A/4/340
Park Campbell*          Stu  -   6  18   1  SW          Hon. Alexander Campbell
*Assignee of Isaac Jenkinson.                           Transmits patent
                                                        Henry Bedinger          Mil  -   7   9   2  30


621                     25 Feb 1812    A/4/338          628                     27 Feb 1812    A/4/340
David Hoge, [Reg Stu]                                   LO Cin
Transmits certificate                                   Transmits patents
Benjamin Knight         Stu  -   6  13  34  NW          Aaron Tullus            Cin EML  6   5  19  SW
                                                        Jacob Deel              Cin EML  4   5  35  SE
                                                        -- Hinds & -- Brown     Cin EML  3   3   3  SE
622                     26 Feb 1812    A/4/338          Abraham Demott          Cin EML  3   6   5  SW
Peter Audrain, [Reg Det]                                Moses Campbell          Cin EML  2   5  15  NE
Asks for Receiver's receipts corresponding to final    Abraham Fey             Cin EML  4   3  14  NW
certificate issued to Medard Labady* "for a tract      David Slutsman          Cin EML  5   4  19  SW
of land at la Grande Coulée, to which he was con-       Jacob Shively           Cin EML  5   4  19  NW
firmed in his right of pre-emption."                    Ephraim Smith           Cin EML  3   4  33  SW
*Also spelled Labadi herein.                            Jacob Smith             Cin EML  5   5  19  NE
                                                        -- Schnibely & -- Miller Cin EML 4   2   9  SW
                                                        -- Murphy & -- Ratliff  Cin WML  1  14  29  NW
623                     26 Feb 1812    A/4/339          --Trusdle & -- Moss     Cin WML  1   2  34   +
Daniel Symmes, [Reg Cin]                                Samuel Gripe            Cin EML  5   5  31  NW
Transmits certificates for correction                   Samuel Gripe            Cin EML  4   5  24   E
[names not given]       Cin EML  4   6  14  NE          Ann Russell             Cin EML  6   4  20  SE
--                      Cin MR   6   3  26   +          Isaac Russell           Cin EML  6   4   9  NW
--                      Cin MR   6   3  32   +          Robert Rosebrough       Cin EML  2   4   9  NE
--                      Cin MR   8   6  36  SW          Jacob Blusdel           Cin WML  1   6  28  NE
--                      Cin MR   8   4   8  NW
```

David Rees	Cin	WML	1	6 14	NE
Christian Miller	Cin	WML	2	12 24	NW
John Clark	Cin	EML	1	9 32	SW
-- Sutherland & -- Brown	Cin	EML	6	2 17	SE
Amos Hawkins	Cin	WML	1	14 27	SE
George Smith	Cin	WML	1	14 30	SW
James Cloyd	Cin	EML	4	4 6	NW
Robert McCleary	Cin	EML	6	2 17	NE
William Brown	Cin	EML	2	8 29	NW
Jacob Neff	Cin	EML	3	5 36	NW
Robert Gilchrist	Cin	Pre	5	2 10	W
William Hamar	Cin	Pre	7	2 23	+
William Hamar	Cin	Pre	7	2 24	-
George Shoup	Cin	Pre	6	3 35	SW
George Shoup	Cin	Pre	6	3 36	W
Richard Watts	Cin	Pre	4	2 22	S
Abner Crane	Cin	Pre	4	3 15	SE
Nicholas Horner	Cin	Pre	5	2 20	NE
-- Bigger & -- White	Cin	Pre	6	2 21	E
-- Bigger & -- White	Cin	Pre	6	2 21	NW*
John Cramer	Cin	Pre	6	3 31	+
Alexander Berryhill	Cin	Pre	5	3 5	-
John Humphries	Cin	Pre	9	4 6	+

*North one-half thereof.

629   27 Feb 1812   A/4/341
Daniel Symmes, [Reg Cin]
Asks for survey plat of tract

John Daniels*	Cin	Pre	5	3 19	+

*Assigned to John Keever.

630   27 Feb 1812   A/4/341
Hon. -- Jennings
Transmits patents

David Fouts	Jef	-	9E	1N	5	SE
Robert L. Plaskett	Jef	-	9E	1N	14	SW
George Shannon	Jef	-	10E	3N	18	+
George Shannon	Jef	-	9E	3N	24	SE
M. Robertson	Jef	-	8E	4N	17	NE
Eli Wright	Jef	-	3E	5S	7	SE
George Shannon	Jef	-	9E	3N	12	SE
James Bruce	Jef	-	3E	4S	28	NE
Samuel Jack	Jef	-	4E	1S	14	SW
Levi Burton	Jef	-	5E	2S?	30	NE

631   28 Feb 1812   A/4/341
LO Jef
Transmits patents

Henry Rats	Jef	-	4E	1N	6	SW
Henry Rats	Jef	-	4E	1N	6	SE
Jonathan Lindley	Jef	-	1E	1N	8	SE
Thomas Carr	Jef	-	4E	2N	12	SE
Charles Bucy	Jef	-	4E	1S	10	SE
Joseph McIntosh	Jef	-	11E	6N	35	SE
Joseph Jones	Jef	-	9E	1N	11	NE
John Gullion	Jef	-	11E	5N	3	NW

632   28 Feb 1812   A/4/342
LO Cin
Transmits patents

John Vaniman	Cin	EML	4	5 36	SW
John Holderman	Cin	EML	3	5 32	W
Abraham Demott	Cin	EML	3	6 6	SE
Rice Price	Cin	EML	1	8 17	NW
Adam Stever	Cin	EML	3	5 24	SE
Finney Hart	Cin	EML	1	7 3	SE
James Ireland	Cin	EML	1	9 29	SW
Robert Abernathy	Cin	WML	2	11 28	SW

Robert Hayse	Cin	EML	1	6 3	SE
John Sailor & Christian? Sailor	Cin	EML	3	4 1	SW
Joseph Millenger	Cin	EML	6	7 30	NE
David Miller	Cin	EML	5	4 13	NE
Simon Schafer	Cin	MR	9	2 25	SW
Zadock Cramer	Cin	MR	9	3 10	SW
George Beard	Cin	EML	5	5 8	SW
Jacob Palmer	Cin	MR	9	2 7	N
John Black	Cin	MR	10	3 19	NW
John Carlough	Cin	MR	8	5 18	SE
Abner Enoch	Cin	MR	4	2 29	+
William Gray	Cin	MR	9	6 33	SE
Philip Kiser	Cin	MR	10	4 29	NE
Peter Brunner	Cin	MR	10	4 23	SE
John Flinn	Cin	MR	10	2 17	SE
Samuel Black	Cin	MR	13	4 35	NE
Thomas Hamilton	Cin	MR	11	1 2	NW
Samuel McBeth	Cin	MR	8	3 12	SE
Joel Harbour	Cin	MR	12	3 6	SE
Zadock Cramer	Cin	WML	2	13 36	SE
Seymore Cobb	Cin	WML	2	12 11	SW
William Lewis	Cin	WML	2	12 15	+
James Baxter	Cin	Pre	7	2 25	N
Christian Holderman	Cin	EML	3	5 34	W
John Carlough	Cin	MR	8	5 18	NE
David Bonner	Cin	WML	1	11 34	SE
Thomas Baird	Cin	MR	13	5 33	SE
Wright Lancaster	Cin	WML	1	13 20	SE
Simon Ely	Cin	WML	2	11 32	+
-- Abernathy & -- Russing	Cin	WML	2	10 21	SW
James Stewart	Cin	MR	1	4 8	SE
Peter Bruner	Cin	MR	10	4 22	NE
Joseph Charles	Cin	WML	1	13 9	NW
-- Morgan & -- Mandlin	Cin	WML	1	14 34	SE
John Jefferies	Cin	EML	5	6 35	NW
Henry Young	Cin	EML	3	5 33	SE
Ob[ediah?] Harrell	Cin	EML	3	4 8	NW
David Attick	Cin	EML	2	7 26	SE
John Millenger	Cin	EML	6	7 30	SE
Michael Crowell	Cin	EML	1	8 20	NW
Robert Marshall	Cin	EML	6	5 29	NW

633   28 Feb 1812   A/4/343
LO Chl
Transmits patents

Andrew Black	Chl	Mil	18	7	12	SW
Thomas Cowen	Chl	-	16	17	26	NW
Bazil Meeks	Chl	MS	22	3	36	NW
Jacob Strouse	Chl	-	19	12	31	SE

634   29 Feb 1812   A/4/343
Daniel Symmes, [Reg Cin]
Asks for duplicate certificate & final certificate

John Vannice	Cin	EML	3	2 11	-
James Gillespie	Cin	Pre	9	2 28	NE

635   2 Mar 1812   A/4/343
Abraham Hetrick, Manchester, Maryland
Returns defective certificates from Can LO.

636   3 Mar 1812   A/4/343
Edmund H. Taylor, Esq.
Transmits Treasury receipts in favor of Thomas Lindly,
    Samuel Lindly, & Jonathan Lindly, paid for by Hon.
    -- Stanford.

637   3 Mar 1812   A/4/343
Peter Walter, Gettystown, Adams County, Pennsylvania
Transmits patent
Peter Walter   Stu - 5 17 26   N

638   4 Mar 1812   A/4/344
William Cummins, Lewistown, Mifflin County, Pennsyl-
   vania
Transmits patent
James Cummins*   [Cin] EML 2 6 36 SW
*See also entry 647.

639   4 Mar 1812   A/4/344
LO Cin
Transmits patents
John Aukerman? [Ankerman?] Cin EML 2 8 35 SW
Christian Brower   Cin EML 2 8 29 NE
Samuel Jay   Cin EML 6 4 30 SW
William Oliver   Cin EML 6 5 28 SE

640   4 Mar 1812   A/4/344
Mahlon Smith, St. Clairsville, Ohio
Transmits patent
Mahlon Smith   Stu - 5 8 10   -

641   4 Mar 1812   A/4/344
Hon. Gen. [Thomas] Worthington*
Transmits patents
Robert Clendenin   Chl - 20 11 5 SW
Philip Hoy   Chl - 20 14 18 NE
*Note states that patents were returned, ". . . they
   not having been [remainder of sentence illegible]."

642   5 Mar 1812   A/4/344
J. Jones, c/o W. Ritchie, Fredericktown, Maryland*
Transmits patent
Simon Martin &
   William Peneman   Stu - 1 9 3   -
*"This letter was returned as a dead one by the Gen-
   eral Post Office, 13 Aug 1812 & called for by Mr.
   Jones on 4 Nov 1812."

643   5 Mar 1812   A/4/344
Hon. Thomas Worthington
Transmits patents
Richard Vaughan   Stu - 6 16 10 SW
George Clark   Stu - 3 12 4   NE

644   5 Nov 1812   A/4/344
Hon. J. Morrow
Transmits patent
Jesse Winteringer &
   Nathan Winteringer   Zan Mil 10 7 13 SW

645   5 Mar 1812   A/4/344
Hon. William Findley
Transmits patent
David Findley   Zan - 12 13 10 SE

646   5 Mar 1812   A/4/345
LO Stu
Transmits patents
Abner Parson   Stu - 6 18 23 NW

James Davis   Stu - 6 14 30 SE
Jacob Painter   Stu - 7 19 36 SE
Philip Knight   Stu - 7 13 19 NE
John Reed   Stu - 6 8   31 SW

647   6 Mar 1812   A/4/345
William Cummins
"The patent for your son's* land having been sent to
   you in my absence, I have to request, if the Court
   shall give you the authority to hold it in trust,
   that you will return it to this Office with the
   decree."
*See entry 638.

648   7 Mar 1812   A/4/345
John Sevier, Hagarstown
Transmits patent
John Sevier   Chl - 19 15 31 SW

649   7 Mar 1812   A/4/345
J. W. Condy, Esq.
Transmits patents
J. W. Condy   Stu - 6 15 13 SW
J. W. Condy   Stu - 6 14 30 SW
J. W. Condy   Stu - 6 16 2   E
J. W. Condy   Stu - 6 16 1   W

650   7 Mar 1812   A/4/345
John H. Brinton, Esq., Philadelphia
Transmits patents
John H. Brinton   Stu - 7 18 24 N
John H. Brinton   Stu - 6 16 19 SW
John H. Brinton   Stu - 6 16 12 E
John H. Brinton   Stu - 7 17 23 NW
John H. Brinton   Stu - 6 16 12 SW
John H. Brinton   Stu - 7 15 12 SW

651   9 Mar 1812   A/4/346
Hon. -- Morrow
Transmits patent
C. Schenck   [Cin?] Pre 5 2 20 -

652   9 Mar 1812   A/4/346
James Findlay, [Rec Cin]
Inquires regarding accounts not having tract designa-
   tions, as follows:
   John Hanna   John Brownson
   Abraham Hackleman   John Ramsey
   Matthew Caldwell   -- Young & -- Christy
   William C. Schenk   Frederick Miller
   Joseph Stubbs   William McCreary
   William Cunningham   Christian Schively
   Robert Gilchrist   John Simmons

653   9 Mar 1812   A/4/346
William Dickson, [Reg Nas]
Returns defective documents

654   9 Mar 1812   A/4/347
LO Cin
Transmits patents
John Shenep   Cin EML 4 4 25 NW
Samuel Mitchell   Cin EML 2 7 25 NE
Henry Boysworth   Cin EML 1 8 19 W

John Pottinger	Cin EML	2	6	10	NE
Garret Rittenhouse	Cin EML	5	4	4	NE
Joel Williams	Cin EML	2	4	20	SE
David Tetter? [Fetter?]	Cin EML	4	4	31	SE
-- Pottinger & -- Railsback	Cin EML	2	7	34	SE
Isaac Esteb	Cin WML	1	12	10	NE
William Hunt	Cin WML	1	12	17	NW
Daniel Reed	Cin WML	1	9	7	NE
Abraham Lee	Cin WML	1	10	36	SE
Peter Smith	Cin WML	2	12	1	NE
Solomon Tyner	Cin WML	2	9	27	NW
John Humphries	Cin Pre	9	4	6	+
Alexander Wood	Cin Pre	5	2	22	SE
Christian Null	Cin Pre	4	3	12	W

655   10 Mar 1812   A/4/347
Hon. J. Morrow
Transmits patent

Obadiah Wells	Mil	-	7	4	2	1

656   11 Mar 1812   A/4/347
Daniel Symmes, [Reg Cin]
Transmits patent

Daniel Symmes	[Cin] MR	6	2	22	NE

657   11 Mar 1812   A/4/347
Robert Barnhill, Monmouth Court House, New Jersey*
Transmits patent

Robert Barnhill	[Cin] EML	2	5	11	SE

*"This patent was returned, as a dead letter, to
   this office on [8 Apr 1813]."

658   11 Mar 1812   A/4/348
Daniel Symmes, [Reg Cin]
Transmits patents & certificate

Daniel Symmes	Cin MR	6	2	22	NE*
Daniel Symmes	Cin MR	6	2	22	NW
Jacob Humbert	Cin -	5	4	15	-

*See also entry 656.

659   11 Mar 1812   A/4/348
LO Cin
Transmits patents

Samuel Deter	Cin EML	5	5	17	NW
Peter Smith	Cin WML	1	12	6	NW
Thomas Miller	Cin WML	1	6	13	SW
Isaac Esteb	Cin WML	1	12	4	NW
Thomas Nowman*	Cin MR	12	2	6	NE
Jacob Hollingsworth	Cin WML	2	11	23	NE
George Martin	Cin WML	2	11	9	+
John A. Ward	Cin MR	11	5	29	NE
Simon Schefer	Cin MR	9	2	25	SE
James Black	Cin MR	11	3	3	NE
Abraham Garr	Cin WML	1	13	30	NW
Philip Long	Cin MR	12	3	2	SE
Charles Hefly	Cin MR	7	3	12	NW
Edmund Hartin	Cin MR	8	5	35	SW
John Richardson	Cin EML	5	6	5	NE
Jacob Nave	Cin EML	1	8	20	SE
Jacob Nave	Cin EML	1	8	36	SW
Peyton Short	Cin MR	8	2	21	W
John Edwards	Cin MR	9	6	23	N
Philip Morningstar	Cin MR	7	3	9	NW
Griffith Foose	Cin MR	9	5	10	NE
Benjamin Wallingsford	Cin MR	9	6	24	SE
Benjamin Wallingsford	Cin MR	9	6	2	NE
James Johnston, Junior	Cin MR	9	3	12	NE

Benjamin Morris	Cin MR	10	4	25	SW
James H. Robinson	Cin EML	1	6	6	SE
Nicholas Coleman	Cin EML	3	6	4	SE
Robert Parks	Cin EML	6	2	17	NW
George Kelly	Cin EML	3	4	9	NW
Robert Gibson	Cin EML	7	1	30	+
Andrew Hood	Cin EML	5	4	3	SE
Frederick Smyer	Cin EML	2	5	13	NE
John Gamble	Cin EML	1	6	3	NE
David Birket	Cin EML	5	6	14	SE
Isaac Pedrick	Cin EML	5	6	30	N

*So spelled.

660   12 Mar 1812   A/4/349
David Hoge, [Reg Stu]
Tract may have reverted to the United States, due to
   "failure in payment in fifth year"

Conrad Dudderer*	Stu	-	2	13	15	SW

*"I have therefore written to the son (the father
   being dead) on the subject."

661   12 Mar 1812   A/4/349
John Dudderer, Petersburg, Adams County, Pennsylvania
Asks that Treasury receipts be sent to Peter Wilson,
   Rec Stu; Conrad Dudderer mentioned

662   16 Mar 1812   A/4/349
Transmits certificate & Treasury receipt

Henry Bonebreak	Can	-	10	11	12	SW

663   16 Mar 1812   A/4/349
LO Cin
Transmits patents

John Gregg	Cin MR	9	4	34	NE
Thomas Hill, heirs of	Cin WML	1	13	2	SE
Levi Jennings	Cin Pre	9	3	31	NW
John Terril	Cin Pre	5	3	19	+
Philip Siler	Cin Pre	9	2	18	+

664   18 Mar 1812   A/4/350
Daniel Symmes, [Reg Cin]
Inquires regarding account

Thomas Clawson	Cin Pre	6	2	31	SW

665   20 Mar 1812   A/4/350
John Welty, near Hagarstown, Maryland
Answers letter of inquiry

[John Welty?]	Stu	-	8	10	11	NE
[John Welty?]	Stu	-	8	12	30	NW

666   20 Mar 1812   A/4/350
Nathaniel Cutting, Esq., War Department
Writes "to obtain redress in the case of a lost Land
   Warrant.

667   21 Mar 1812   A/4/350
Daniel Symmes, [Reg Cin]
Returns defective documents

Samuel Freeman*	Cin Pre	6	2	6	SE+
Willis Nothcut**	Cin Pre	5	3	4	W+
John Rogers***	Cin Pre	6	2	28	+

*Mentions John Smith & Griffin Yeatman, magistrates.
**Mentions William Buckles, magistrate.
***Mentions John Vansil.

668   21 Mar 1812   A/4/351
John Badollet
Returns defective document; mentions Jacob Warnick,
   assignee of John Hamilton; sheriff of Knox County.

669   21 Mar 1812   A/4/351
James Findlay, [Rec Cin]
Explanations required; mentions Thomas R. Smith,
   Joseph McMaken, John Smith, Peyton Short.

670   21 Mar 1812   A/4/351
Hon. Jonathan Roberts
Transmits patent

Matthew Knox	Mil	-	3	7	1	4
Matthew Knox	Mil	-	3	7	1	5

671   24 Mar 1812   A/4/351
LO Cin
Transmits patents

Robert Buckles	Cin Pre	5	4	28	+
William Ward	Cin Pre	10	5	32	W
Joseph Sawyer	Cin Pre	5	2	25	+
Henry Seaman	Cin Pre	5	3	1	+
Arthur Johnston	Cin Pre	8	3	4	SW
Charles Morgan	Cin Pre	6	2	18	E
William Anderson	Cin Pre	8	4	31	-
Aaron Hartin	Cin Pre	5	3	31	+
John Judah	Cin Pre	8	3	13	+
Joel Vanmetre	Cin Pre	8	4	17	SW
Nathan Talbert	Cin Pre	6	2	27	NE
Richard Watts	Cin Pre	4	2	28	+
Richard Watts	Cin Pre	4	2	34	-?
Joseph Layton	Cin Pre	9	4	32	+
Samuel Irwin	Cin Pre	6	2	21	+
Francis Sunderland	Cin Pre	10	2	1	SE

672   24 Mar 1812   A/4/352
Izah? [Izak?] Procter, Baltimore
Returns papers relative to loss of Jonathan White's
   military land warrant.

673   25 Mar 1812   A/4/352
Hon. Thomas Worthington
Please give directions to [Thomas] Gibson, "as I
   much fear that when we send to his Office at Canton, he does not see our letters requesting him
   to state that Mr. Ruynolds* is authorized to sign
   certificates in his name."
*So spelled.

674   25 Mar 1812   A/4/352
William Broderick
Facts relative to the military land warrant issued
   for your services in the revolutionary war could
   not be sooner ascertained. "I now enclose an
   official certificate. . . ."

675   25 Mar 1812   A/4/352
Hon. -- Findley
Transmits patent

William Breading	Vin	- 11W	1S	13	S

676   25 Mar 1812   A/4/352
LO Mad

Transmits patents

Rudolph Boshart	Mad	- 1E	3	1	NE
Richard Harris	Mad	- 1W	3	14	NE
Richard Harris	Mad	- 1W	3	13	NW
James Walker	Mad	- 2E	1	15	+
Samuel Davis	Mad	- 2E	1	17	SE

677   26 Mar 1812   A/4/353
LO Cin
Transmits patents

William Holeman	Cin WML	1	13	34	SE
William Euker	Cin EML	6	5	29	SE
James Fleming	Cin EML	1	9	20	SW
Daniel Trimble	Cin EML	1	4	14	SE
William Mitchell	Cin EML	5	8	25	NE
Joseph Cooper	Cin EML	5	5	23	NW
Jonas Crane	Cin EML	1	2	18	SW
Adam Lee	Cin EML	1	2	9	NW
Azeriah Julien	Cin EML	5	9	3	SE
Elijah Mitchell	Cin EML	1	9	10	SW
James Fleming	Cin EML	1	9	20	SE
Robert Douglass	Cin EML	2	6	31	NW
Thomas Conaree	Cin EML	2	5	1	NE
Daniel Ullery	Cin EML	5	3	15	SE
John McClure	Cin EML	2	6	20	NW
Daniel Crissman	Cin EML	2	8	28	SE
Jacob Sinks	Cin EML	4	4	31	NE
Robert Douglass	Cin EML	1	6	36	NE
John Shewman	Cin EML	2	7	25	SW
John Millinger	Cin EML	6	7	29	SW
Joseph Pearson	Cin EML	5	5	1	SE
James Brown	Cin EML	6	6	31	E
David Jinkins	Cin EML	6	4	4	SW
Alexander McNutt? [McNull?]	Cin EML	3	7	26	NW
John Holderman	Cin EML	3	5	20	SW
Henry Rapp	Cin EML	4	4	25	NE
Aaron Powers	Cin EML	1	4	35	SW
Thomas Morgan	Cin WML	1	9	24	SE
Tabitha White	Cin WML	1	14	11	SW
John Smith	Cin WML	1	14	32	NW
John Drake	Cin WML	1	14	25	SE
John Smith	Cin WML	1	14	33	SE
Jacob Fouts	Cin WML	1	13	12	SW
John Harvey	Cin WML	1	13	3	W
Thomas Reeds	Cin WML	1	10	18	NW
John Pool	Cin WML	1	13	2	NW
John Wetter	Cin WML	1	11	24	SW
Tabitha White	Cin WML	1	14	11	SE
Richard Miner	Cin WML	1	11	4	NE
Jacob Kingery, Senior	Cin WML	1	11	34	NE
Abraham Hollingsworth	Cin WML	1	11	30	NE
John Levell?	Cin EML	5	8	24	NW
Jacob Skillman	Cin WML	1	11	5	NE
Henry Hoover	Cin WML	1	12	9	SE
John Burges	Cin WML	1	13	5	S
Ob[adiah?] Estes	Cin WML	2	10	33	SW
Samuel Ratter	Cin WML	1	11	12	SW
James Taylor	Cin WML	2	10	9	SW
John Roberts	Cin WML	2	11	26	SE
Samuel Tappin	Cin WML	1	11	8	NW
Charles Hunt	Cin WML	2	12	1	W
J. Bruce & A. Bruce	Cin WML	2	5	23	SW
Samuel Howell	Cin WML	1	10	18	NE
James Crooks	Cin WML	1	10	24	SE
Samuel McKenley	Cin WML	1	13	6	SE
Richard Maxwell	Cin WML	1	14	36	SE
Daniel Trimble	Cin WML	1	13	8	SE
Matthew Brown	Cin WML	2	11	35	NW
Jesse Davenport	Cin WML	1	13	11	SW
Mary Cook & Charity Cook	Cin WML	1	14	31	NW

William Logan	Cin WML	2	11	22	NE
Abraham Buckles	Cin Pre	5	3	15	NW
John Perrin	Cin Pre	9	4	3	-
John Riddle	Cin Pre	11	1	10	-
Daniel Funderburgh	Cin Pre	8	3	13	NE
Jacob Price	Cin Pre	9	2	17	NW
William Wells	Cin Pre	10	2	17	NE
David Harlis	Cin Pre	9	2	12	NE
Felix Hoover	Cin Pre	7	3	21	N
Thomas Thomas	Cin Pre	5	3	9	+

678   26 Mar 1812   A/4/354
David Hoge, [Reg Stu]
Transmits corrected patent

Joseph McKee	Stu	-	3	8	21	SE

679   27 Mar 1812   A/4/355
LO Mad
Transmits patents

John P. Steger	Mad	-	1E	3	17	SW
John P. Steger	Mad	-	1E	3	13	SW
John P. Steger	Mad	-	1E	3	13	NE
Nicholas Couch	Mad	-	2E	1	28	NE
James Vaulx	Mad	-	1E	3	15	SE
James Vaulx	Mad	-	1E	3	15	NE
Leven Gray	Mad	-	1E	2	28	NE
Rowland Cornelius	Mad	-	1W	2	33	NW
Richard Harris	Mad	-	1W	2	32	SE

680   27 Mar 1812   A/4/355
LO Cin
Transmits patents

Amos Hawkins	Cin WML	1	14	34	NE
Joseph Holeman	Cin WML	1	13	34	SW
Benjamin Flood	Cin WML	1	10	19	NW
David Ireland	Cin EML	1	9	17	SE
Henry Hapner	Cin EML	4	4	12	NE
Benjamin Pike	Cin EML	5	6	27	NW
William Nail, Senior	Cin EML	5	6	35	NE
John North	Cin EML	5	6	36	NW
Leonard Eller	Cin EML	5	6	35	SE
Alexander Rogers	Cin EML	2	7	22	NW
Thomas Fleming	Cin EML	1	4	34	SE
William Pearson	Cin EML	5	8	18	NW
Joseph Cappock*	Cin EML	5	6	4	SW
James Taylor	Cin WML	2	9	9	S
Jacob Little, Senior	Cin WML	1	12	5	SW
William Crawford	Cin WML	1	10	13	NW
Jacob Skillman	Cin WML	1	12	32	S
John Smith	Cin WML	1	13	2	SW
John Smith	Cin WML	1	12	7	NW
Thomas Skinner	Cin WML	2	9	7	+
George Keffer	Cin WML	1	11	26	SW
George Keffer	Cin WML	1	11	35	NW
John Meck	Cin WML	1	13	6	SW
Hugh Cull	Cin WML	1	13	29	NE
Joseph Woodcuck*	Cin WML	1	13	7	NE
Daniel Feather	Cin EML	5	5	20	SW
Talbert Iddings	Cin EML	5	6	27	SW
Samuel Jones	Cin EML	5	6	9	S
Gotham Lyon	Cin EML	2	5	7	NE
Andrew Brown	Cin EML	2	5	12	SW
Elisha Bassett	Cin EML	1	4	6	NW
John Hardin	Cin EML	1	8	18	NE
John Zimmerman	Cin EML	2	6	19	SW

*So spelled.

681   27 Mar 1812   A/4/356

Wyllys Silliman, [Reg Zan]
Returns defective certificates

John McIntire*	Zan	-	16	14	13	NW
John McIntire*	Zan	-	15	14	13	NE

*Assignee of Henry Crooks; [one of the two tract descriptions may be wrong].

682   28 Mar 1812   A/4/356
Thomas Gibson, [Reg Can]
A great number of final certificates cannot be acted
   upon because signed by -- Raynolds*, for whom we
   have received no authorization from you.
*So spelled; elsewhere spelled Ruynolds.

683   30 Mar 1812   A/4/356
John Badollet, [Reg Vin]
Transfer missing

Thomas Jones*	Vin	-	2E 4S?	7	+
Thomas Jones*	Vin	-	2E 4S?	8	+?
Thomas Jones*	Vin	-	2E 4S?	17	+?

*Assignee of Walter Taylor.

684   30 Mar 1812   A/4/356
Jesse Spencer, [Reg Chl]
Returns defective documents

David Shallenberger*	Chl	-	19	13	6	-
David Shallenberger*	Chl	-	19	13	7	-

*Transferred to Martin Landis by Henry Shallenberger
& Emanuel Carpenter, as administrators of the
estate of David Shallenberger; William Trimble, magistrate. "The above documents are accompanied by a
release of both sections to Martin Landis, in which
it is stated, that by the laws of Ohio the lands
above mentioned had descended to the undernamed persons, the only brothers and sisters of the Intestate,
each of whom had respectively attained the full age
of 21 years, viz.:
Michael Shallenberger)
Henry **Shallenberger**) brothers of the Intestate
Samuel Shallenberger)

Nancy Loveland, wife)
  of Joseph Loveland)
Barbary Landis, wife)
  of Martin Landis   ) sisters of the Intestate"
Mary Salome Carpenter,)
  wife of Emanuel Car-)
  penter   )

685   31 Mar 1812   A/4/357
Joseph Wood, [Reg Mar]
Transmits certificate

Thomas Dickenson	Mar	-	5	1	27	+

686   31 Mar 1812   A/4/357
Jesse Spencer, [Reg Chl]
Further complications in the transfer of tracts be-
  longing to David Shallenberger arise, because Henry
  Shallenberger was, in his own right, a part owner
  of the land. Discusses percentages of ownership
  due Henry Shallenberger and the other heirs.

687   1 Apr 1812   A/4/358
William R. Hynes, Baird's Town, Nelson County, Ken-
  tucky
Patent sent to LO Vin on 12 Dec 1811

William Gamble	Vin	-	4E	2S	1	NW

---

688   2 Apr 1812   A/4/358
Wyllys Silliman, [Reg Zan]
Transmits certificate
Nicholas? Titerick*   Zan - 15 16 11 SW
Nicholas? Titerick*   Zan - 14 16 11 SW
*Assignee of Bal[thasar?] Titerick. The latter
   tract designation appears to be the correct one.

689   2 Apr 1812   A/4/358
Jesse Spencer, [Reg Chl]
Tract of land appears to be incorrect, as it was
   patented to Jacob Rush
Peter Schreiner   Chl - 11 16 2 NE

690   3 Apr 1812   A/4/358
Hon. Thomas Worthington
Transmits patents
John Zane   Zan Mil 13 12 15 W+
Robert Speer   Zan Mil   4   2 21 NE
William Speer   Zan Mil   5   1   2 SE

691   3 Apr 1812   A/4/358
Hon. -- Jennings
Transmits patents
Thomas Morton   Stu   - 2   7 26 NE
William R. Dickinson   [Stu?] - 8 10 34 NW

692   3 Apr 1812   A/4/358
Hon. -- Laycock
Transmits patent
Moses Mendenhall   Stu   - 4 17 31 NW

693   4 Apr 1812   A/4/359
Charles Bohn, Baltimore
Transmits patent
Charles Bohn   Zan   - 3 10 12 SE

694   4 Apr 1812   A/4/359
William Foy, Senior, Postoffice, Waynesburg, Frank-
   lin County, Pennsylvania
Transmits patent
William Foy, Senior   Zan Mil 2 2 20 NE

695   4 Apr 1812   A/4/359
David Baker, Postoffice, Hagarstown, Maryland
Transmits patent
David Baker   Zan Mil 5 8 20 NE

696   7 Apr 1812   A/4/359
Samuel Gwathmey, [Reg Jef]
Returns defective certificate; mentions -- Rats.

697   8 Apr 1812   A/4/359
David Hoge, [Reg Stu]
Transmits patent
Thomas McPherrin   Stu   - 7 15 23 SE

698   8 Apr 1812   A/4/359
Hon. Thomas Worthington
Transmits patent
Joseph Farmer &
   James McClintock   Chl - 20 9 31 SW

699   8 Apr 1812   A/4/359
Hon. John Hyneman
Transmits patents
Mordecai Lee   Stu - 6 18 9 NW
Mordecai Lee   Stu - 6 18 8 NE

700   8 Apr 1812   A/4/359
Hon. -- Jennings
Transmits patent
Parker Campbell   Stu - 6 18 1 SW

701   9 Apr 1812   A/4/360
Nehemiah Tilton, [Reg Was]
Returns defective documents; mentions transfer of
   lands (Buffaloe Creek & Amite River) from Sylvester
   Stoats to Joseph Johnson; -- Williams; transfer of
   land from James Owens to Bartlett Owens; transfer
   of land from Henry Ratcliff to James Ratcliff.

702   11 Apr 1812   A/4/360
William Cook, Warren, Ohio
Discusses military land warrant 5558, issued to William Cook, and its conditional sale, on Cook's be-
   half by -- Williams, to Jackson.

703   13 Apr 1812   A/4/361
N[ehemiah] Tilton, [Reg Was]
Reports on unnamed final certificates.

704   14 Apr 1812   A/4/361
John Mathews, Springfield, Ohio
[Military land] warrant of Seely Scofield withdrawn
   by -- Davenport; mentions the following lots:
Previously located   Mil - 5 3 3   3
Vacant   Mil - 5 3 3   5
Vacant   Mil - 5 3 3   6
Vacant   Mil - 5 3 3   7
Vacant   Mil - 5 3 3   8
Vacant   Mil - 5 3 3   9
Vacant   Mil - 5 3 3 10
Vacant   Mil - 5 3 3 11
Vacant   Mil - 5 3 3 12
Vacant   Mil - 5 3 3 14
Vacant   Mil - 5 3 3 19
Vacant   Mil - 5 3 3 20
Vacant   Mil - 5 3 3 21
Vacant   Mil - 5 3 3 22
Vacant   Mil - 5 3 3 23
Vacant   Mil - 5 3 3 24
Vacant   Mil - 5 3 3 25
Vacant   Mil - 5 3 3 26
Vacant   Mil - 5 3 3 27
Vacant   Mil - 5 3 3 28
Vacant   Mil - 5 3 3 29
Vacant   Mil - 5 3 3 30
Vacant   Mil - 5 3 3 31
Vacant   Mil - 5 3 3 32
Vacant   Mil - 5 3 3 37
Vacant   Mil - 5 3 3 38
Vacant   Mil - 5 3 3 39
Vacant   Mil - 5 3 3 40

705   14 Apr 1812   A/4/361
Hon. John Davenport
Discusses military land warrant of Seely Scofield,
   withdrawn by Davenport. Letter from John Mathews,

surveyor at Springfield, Ohio, states that Scofield's
   son had called on him requesting a location under
   the warrant.

---

706   14 Apr 1812   A/4/361
Hon. William Findley
Acknowledges receipt of documents from Findley; men-
   tions Peter Mills

William Sloan	Zan Mil	5	1	10	SW
David Findlay*	Zan -	5	1	1	NW
David Findlay*	Zan -	12	13	10	SW

*So spelled. Assignee of James Findlay.

---

707   14 Apr 1812   A/4/362
Hon. J. Morrow
Reports on application

Richard Gray & Robert Gray [Cin]	MR	7	2	26	NW

---

708   14 Apr 1812   A/4/362
Hon. John Smith
Transmits patent

John Kirlin	Chl -	17	17	21	NE

---

709   14 Apr 1812   A/4/362
Daniel Bussard, Georgetown Ca.[?]*
Transmits patent

Daniel Bussard	Zan -	16	7	4	NE

*Possibly District of Columbia is meant.

---

710   14 Apr 1812   A/4/362
LO Cin
Transmits patents

Isaac Waldron	Cin EML	1	4	24	NW
Thomas B. Kyle	Cin EML	6	5	31	N
Samuel Teague	Cin EML	5	7	28	E
Robert Templeton	Cin WML	2	10	28	NW
George Hollingsworth	Cin WML	2	10	9	SE
Weire Cassady	Cin EML	3	5	23	SE
Samuel Heistand	Cin EML	4	5	35	NE
Robert Templeton	Cin WML	2	9	4	NW
George Hollingsworth	Cin WML	2	10	10	NW
Joseph Hollingsworth	Cin WML	2	11	27	SE
David Hollingsworth	Cin WML	1	11	7	SE
Levi Hollingsworth	Cin WML	2	11	22	SE

---

711   15 Apr 1812   A/4/362
LO Zan
Transmits patents

James Frame	Zan Mil	3	3	8	NE
Philip Baker	Zan -	15	17	7	W
Henry Pringle	Zan -	13	12	2	SE
Lewis Kems	Zan -	13	12	1	NE
Henry Clabaugh	Zan -	15	18	7	E
Garrett McCann	Zan -	14	15	20	NW

---

712   15 Apr 1812   A/4/362
Hon. William Findley
Transmits patent.

David Findley	Zan -	12	13	10	SW

---

713   16 Apr 1812   A/4/363
Hon. Asa Fitch
Transmits patents

Sally Ann Faulkner	Mil -	2	10	2	12
Sally Ann Faulkner	Mil -	2	10	2	18

---

714   16 Apr 1812   A/4/363
Daniel Symmes, [Reg Cin]
Transmits certificate

Abraham Holderman*	Cin EML	3	5	17	W

*Transferred to Laurence Shell.

---

715   17 Apr 1812   A/4/363
David Hoge, [Reg Stu]
Transmits patents

Jordan Jones	Stu -	3	15	29	NW
Abner Parson	Stu -	6	18	25	NE

---

716   17 Apr 1812   A/4/363
John Mathews
[Hon. John] Davenport has returned the military land
   warrant of Seely Scoffield* to us "to await your
   location [of the corresponding land] for it."

*So spelled herein.

---

717   17 Apr 1812   A/4/363
Jesse Spencer, [Reg Chl]
Transmits Treasury receipts, "the former receipts
   are stated to have been lost."

Christian Cagy	Chl -	19	16	25	NE
Jonathan Lee	Chl MS	21	11	36	NE

---

718   18 Apr 1812   A/4/363
LO Cin
Transmits patents

Jonathan Roberts	Cin WML	1	14	31	SE
Andrew Hoover	Cin WML	1	14	14	SW
John Addington	Cin WML	1	14	8	SE
John Addington	Cin WML	1	14	17	NE
Robert Templeton	Cin WML	2	9	4	SE
William Fouts	Cin WML	1	12	3	NW
Agnes Tayler*	Cin WML	2	9	3	NW
Esther Pemberton	Cin EML	4	7	12	NE
Casper Bottorf	Cin EML	2	7	34	NE
John Neff	Cin EML	3	5	19	SE
Nathan Hollingsworth	Cin EML	5	6	9	NE
Rebecca Compton	Cin EML	3	4	30	NW

---

719   18 Apr 1812   A/4/364
LO Vin
Transmits patents

John Swank	Vin -	4E	3S	25	SW
Squire Boone	Vin -	3E	5S	24	NE
James Lett	Vin -	7W	2N	20	SE
Jonathan Latham	Vin -	10W	2S	6	SE
John Adams	Vin -	11W	1S	14	SW
Valentine Shirley	Vin -	1W	2N	7	SW
Jacob Funk	Vin -	2E	5S	2	+

---

720   20 Apr 1812   A/4/364
Hon. John Smith
Transmits patent

Richard Carr	Cin Pre	10	1	18	2

---

721   22 Apr 1812   A/4/364
LO Jef
Transmits patents

John Kelly	Jef -	10E	1N	6	SE
Francis Giltner	Jef -	9E	1N	10	NW
Abraham McKay	Jef -	11E	4N	23	NE
George Henton	Jef -	3E	1S	14	NW

722		22 Apr 1812		A/4/364		
LO Cin						
Transmits patents						
Daniel Snider	Cin EML	4	4	20	SE	
David Railsback	Cin WML	2	13	35	SW	
-- McCutchin & -- Nickles	Cin WML	2	11	21	E	
Thomas Roberts	Cin WML	1	13	4	NW	
James Nickles	Cin WML	2	11	28	NW	
Henry Snider	Cin EML	4	4	18	E	
Henry Snider	Cin EML	5	5	28	SW	
David Snider	Cin EML	5	5	20	NE	
Thomas Roberts	Cin EML	3	3	8	SE	
Abraham Richardt	Cin EML	5	4	7	NW	
David Burntrager	Cin EML	5	7	6	SE	
Philip Swartzell	Cin EML	4	9	12	SW	
Jacob Deihe? [Deche?]	Cin EML	5	4	30	SW	
Abraham Richardt	Cin EML	5	4	6	SW	
Christopher Witter	Cin EML	1	6	32	SE	
Adam Harter	Cin EML	3	5	13	NW	
Isaac Embree	Cin EML	5	6	10	SW	

723		23 Apr 1812		A/4/365	
LO Cin					
Transmits patents					
Daniel Reed	Cin WML	1	9	6	SE
Lewis Little	Cin WML	1	12	6	NE
Martin Baum	Cin EML	1	4	27	SW
Jacob Bowman	Cin EML	5	4	13	SE
David Miller	Cin EML	5	5	17	SW
Martin Cable?	Cin EML	4	5	26	SE
Henry Null	Cin WML	1	14	11	NE

724		23 Apr 1812		A/4/365	
LO Stu					
Transmits patents					
John Richards	Stu	-	9	12	14	-
Henry Creaton	Stu	-	1	6	22	NW
W. S. Dodds & E. Dodds	Stu	-	3	9	15	SE
Jacob Bachtel	Stu	-	9	11	6	S
James Andrews	Stu	-	2	8	28	-
George Macenterfer	Stu	-	6	17	20	NW
Robert Orr	Stu	-	4	10	28	SE
Finley Blackburn	Stu	-	3	9	23	SW
James Johnson, Senior	Stu	-	7	12	23	SW
Benjamin Anderson	Stu	-	5	17	30	NE
Benjamin Anderson	Stu	-	7	19	12	NE
John Ruff	Stu	-	5	16	3	NE
Benjamin Masters	Stu	-	7	10	31	NW
Christopher Markley	Stu	-	8	12	36	NE
Christopher Markley	Stu	-	8	12	25	W
Daniel Stranghan [Straughan?]	Stu	-	4	17	7	NW
William Sinclair	Stu	-	4	7	8	SE

725		23 Apr 1812		A/4/365	
David Butt? [Bull?], Harper's Ferry, Maryland					
Transmits patent					
David Butt? [Bull?]	Zan	-	13	11	14	SW

726		23 Apr 1812		A/4/365	
Hon. William Findley					
Transmits patent					
William Sloan	Zan Mil	5	10	10	SW

727		23 Apr 1812		A/4/365	
Hon. Joseph Lewis					
Transmits patents					
Anne James	Mil	-	9	5	12	SE
Anne James	Mil	-	9	5	20	NE
Thomas James	Mil	-	8	5	16	SW

728		23 Apr 1812		A/4/366	
Isaac Van Horne, [Rec Zan]					
Transmits patents					
John Slack	Zan Mil	7	1	12	NW
Sarah Vanhorne	Zan Mil	14	16	8	SE

729		23 Apr 1812		A/4/366	
Hon. -- Jennings					
Transmits patent					
Henry Brown	Stu	-	7	19	11	NE

730		23 Apr 1812		A/4/366	
LO Vin					
Transmits patents					
George Hoke	Vin	-	5E	5S	24	+
George Hoke	Vin	-	5E	5S	25	-?
George Hoke	Vin	-	5E	5S	26	NE
John Brindley	Vin	-	5E	5S	12	+
Thomas Rogers	Vin	-	5E	5S	6	NE
Frederick Geiger	Vin	-	6E	3S	28	+

731		25 Apr 1812		A/4/366	
LO Cin					
Transmits patents					
Sebastian Stonebrecker	Cin EML	2	3	2	NW
Henry Oltfather	Cin EML	4	3	4	NE
David Bower	Cin EML	5	4	29	NE?
Garret Rittenhouse	Cin EML	5	5	27	SW
Samuel Henderson	Cin WML	1	14	1	E
Cornelius Ratliff	Cin WML	1	14	29	NW
James Jones	Cin WML	1	8	35	NW
Anthony Halberstudt*	Cin WML	2	8	10	NE
William Nicholas	Cin WML	2	11	28	NE
William Whitehead	Cin WML	2	13	36	SW
Patrick McCarty	Cin WML	3	10	25	+
Samuel Charles	Cin WML	1	14	32	SW
*So spelled.					

732		25 Apr 1812		A/4/367	
LO Zan					
Transmits patents					
William McConnell	Zan Mil	1	1	3	SE
John Wylie	Zan Mil	5	1	2	SW
John Wylie	Zan Mil	5	1	14	NW
John Wylie	Zan Mil	5	1	15	NE
Samuel Wylie	Zan	-	5	1	2	NW
John Crider	Zan Mil	1	9	10	SW
Joseph Vernon & Samuel Vernon	Zan Mil	7	1	8	NE
Frederick Schleiff	Zan Mil	4	9	22	SW
Frederick Schleiff	Zan Mil	4	9	20	SW
Moses Vanwinkle	Zan Mil	8	2	3	NW
Joel Zane & Silas Zane	Zan Mil	8	2	21	NW
Robert Brown	Zan Mil	4	2	23	NE
William J. Brown & A. Brown	Zan Mil	4	2	18	SE
Philip Shutt	Zan Mil	4	8	12	NE
Nathan Baker	Zan Mil	9	3	23	NW
David Ayres	Zan Mil	11	6	14	SW
Jacob Bower	Zan Mil	6	1	8	SW
Jacob Bower	Zan Mil	6	1	8	SE
Joseph Sprott	Zan Mil	1	2	25	W
John Blizzard	Zan Mil	10	3	23	SW
Reuben Blizzard	Zan Mil	9	3	18	SW

William Wolf	Zan Mil	3?	9	11	SW
David Evans	Zan Mil	9	3	4	SE
George Bollman	Zan Mil	4	8	10	SE
Levi Harrod	Zan Mil	11	5	3	SW
William Addy	Zan Mil	4	4	4	SW
John Benser	Zan Mil	2	7	11	NW
Michael Horne	Zan Mil	9	7	34	SE
David Fields	Zan Mil	8	3	8	SW
Adain? [Adair?] Brown, Junior	Zan Mil	11	1	12	SE
Joseph Satterthwaith	Zan Mil	1	1	9	NE

733   27 Apr 1812   A/4/367
LO Zan
Transmits patents

Archibald Boal	Zan	–	11	12	29	SW
Archibald Boal	Zan	–	11	12	32	NW
Allen McClain	Zan	–	13	12	9	NE
John King	Zan	–	15	16	7	SW
Edward Harris	Zan	–	15	18	7	SW
Samuel McCune	Zan	–	12	10	3	SW+
Joel Williams	Zan	–	8	8	4	NW
Barrick Brashear	Zan	–	14	15	2	NW
Joseph Montanya	Zan	–	13	2	3	NW
Joseph Robinson	Zan	–	15	18	9	SE

734   27 Apr 1812   A/4/368
LO Stu
Transmits patents

George Ramsey	Stu	–	7	17	10	SW
Samuel King	Stu	–	4	6	9	SE
Benjamin Waggoner	Stu	–	7	14	25	SW
William Hutchison	Stu	–	4	8	3	NE
Eli Nichols	Stu	–	4	7	29	NW
Martin Wingart	Stu	–	7	18	6	SE
Samuel Marsh	Stu	–	2	10	3	SE
Daniel Longenecker	Stu	–	8	9	17	SW
George Starr	Stu	–	3	9	18	NW
William Castleman	Stu	–	6	15	23	SW
Henry Hilterbrant	Stu	–	7	19	34	NE

735   27 Apr 1812   A/4/368
Robert Hanna, New Lisbon, Ohio
Transmits patent

Robert Hanna	Stu	–	1	7	30	SE

736   28 Apr 1812   A/4/368
Jesse Spencer, [Reg Chl]
Asks for speedy transmittal of certifice for J. W. Plummer & correction of land description for Shaffer

Joseph West Plummer*	Chl Mil	14	8	12	SW
E. Carpenter**	Chl	–	19	14	13	–

*Assignee of Nathan Wood.
**Patented to Carpenter in 1801, but reported by LO Chl as forfeited by Samuel Shaffer; this in error.

737   30 Apr 1812   A/4/368
LO Zan
Transmits patents

John Hanna	Zan Mil	1	2	5	NW
John Hanna	Zan Mil	1	2	4	SE
John Adams	Zan Mil	8	4	12	NE
Joseph McCoy	Zan Mil	7	4	25	SW
Richard Lane	Zan Mil	8	2	22	NW
John Brown	Zan Mil	6	1	6	SE
Thomas Blizzard	Zan Mil	9	3	23	SW

Jacob Levingood	Zan Mil	6	1	12	SE
Alexander Culbertson	Zan Mil	7	1	1	NW
Alexander Culbertson	Zan Mil	7	1	3	NE

738   30 Apr 1812   A/4/368
LO Stu

James Gordon	Stu	–	2	3	31	NW
John Henny	Stu	–	6	9	1	NW
Abraham Warner	Stu	–	6	13	33	SE
Thomas Kells	Stu	–	2	8	32	NE
Adam Creplever	Stu	–	6	13	2	SW
Samuel Smith	Stu	–	5	11	2	NW

739   30 Apr 1812   A/4/369
Hon. Thomas Worthington
"When the Warrant of Survey No. 5846, issued by Charles Blagrove, Esq., Register of the Land Office at Richmond, to the children & heirs of Charles Stockley, deceased, was presented to the War Office for patenting, it was found that the original claimant is therein stated to have been a Lieutenant. Under these circumstances it has been deemed necessary to obtain from Mr. Blagrove a certificate . . . as to the fact."

740   30 Apr 1812   A/4/369
Daniel Symmes, [Reg Cin]
Returns defective documents; mentions Spencer Freeman, -- Spencer, Spencer Free, assignee of Peter Demerce

William Henderson	Cin WML	2	9	8	SW
Solomon Stansbury*	Cin	–	5	3	7	E
Samuel Beck, Senior	Cin Pre	6	2	13	NE
John Smith**	Cin Pre	10	1	2	+
John Smith**	Cin Pre	11	6	31	NE
John Smith**	Cin Pre	11	6	31	NW

*Also spelled Stabrough, Standbrough; land transferred to David Linton.
**Transferred by his attorney, Fielding Lowry, to Christian Lefaver & Daniel Lefaver.

741   2 May 1812   A/4/370
Jesse Spencer, [Reg Chl]
Transmits certificate & discusses payments

William Thrift	Chl	–	12	7	14	S

742   2 May 1812   A/4/370
James Gordon, St. Clairsville, Ohio
Transmits patent

James Gordon	Unk	–	2	3	31	NW

743   4 May 1812   A/4/370
Hon. Dr. -- Mitchell
"I have not yet obtained the patent of Mr. Garret Sickles for military Bounty land; under present circumstances cannot presume to say when I probably shall obtain it. Mr. Sickles may however be informed that no objection lies against the claim, & that the land selected by him is secure to him."

744   4 May 1812   A/4/371
Samuel Smith, of Jefferson County, Ohio, to be left at the Postoffice, Steubenville
Patent sent to LO Stu

Samuel Smith	Stu	–	5	11	2	NW

745		4 May 1812		A/4/371		

William Raynolds, Esq., at LO Can
Transmits patent; asks for Thomas Gibson to author-
  ize Raynold's signature

William Barnhart	Can	–	8	11	25	SW
William Barnhart	Can	–	8	11	25	SE
Daniel Mosser*	Stu	–	8	11	25	NE

*This patent sent to LO Stu, from which it may be
  obtained.

746		4 May 1812		A/4/371		

Daniel Symmes, [Reg Cin]
Transmits certificates & Treasury receipts

[Robert Donovan]	Cin	MR	11	5	29	SE
[Robert Donovan[	Cin	MR	11	5	26	NE
James Smith	Cin	MR	11	4	17	SE
James Smith	Cin	MR	11	5	29	NW
James Smith	Cin	MR	11	5	36	SE

747		6 May 1812		A/4/372		

LO Chl
Transmits patents

Adam Cover	Chl	–	21	4	3	NE
John Zehring	Chl	–	20	11	17	NE
David List	Chl	WS	21	11	22	SW
Thomas Reber	Chl	MS	21	10	33	NE
James Ferguson	Chl	WS	21	10	28	W
Valentine Keffer	Chl	MS	21	11	18	SW
Abraham Boughman	Chl	–	18	16	7	SE
Jacob Corfman	Chl	–	17	16	11	NW
John Kile	Chl	MS	21	11	17	NE
John Skinner	Chl	–	16	17	36	SW
William Carson	Chl	MS	21	11	4	W
Valentine Reber	Chl	MS	21	11	12	SE
Patrick Owings	Chl	–	17	17	4	SW
Philip Helsel	Chl	MS	22	4	13	NW
Philip Helsel	Chl	MS	22	4	12	SW
William Martin	Chl	–	19	16	13	NW
William Snider	Chl	–	20	2	18	SW
John Moore	Chl	–	20	2	4	NW
Daniel Hall	Chl	–	18	16	5	NW
J. Williamson	Chl	MS	21	9	8	SW
Valentine Wolf	Chl	–	19	13	21	SW
Daniel Hoy	Chl	MS	21	11	2	NE
Mathias Barnhart	Chl	–	21	8	2	SE
William Stump	Chl	MS	21	10	35	SE
Ezekiel Groom	Chl	MS	[21]	10	9	SW
John McCrory	Chl	–	17	16	17	SE
Jeremiah Wright	Chl	MS	22	2	12	SE
John Cook	Chl	MS	19	16	36	NW
Isaac Coons	Chl	–	20	14	33	SE
Joseph Lambert	Chl	–	18	1	31	SW
Philip Crist	Chl	–	17	18	24	NE
Peter Fairchild	Chl	–	19	16	32	SW
John Gehr	Chl	–	19	11	9	S
John Bell	Chl	–	21	9	23	SE
John Swinehart	Chl	–	16	17	2	SE
Samuel Noble	Chl	–	20	11	2	NW
Henry Solliday	Chl	–	19	16	19	SE
Jacob Langenbock	Chl	MS	21	9	1	SW
Jacob Harman	Chl	–	20	13	11	NW
James Ramsey	Chl	–	21	11	18	SW
William Wilson	Chl	–	16	17	26	NE
Philip Crist	Chl	–	17	18	18	NE
Jacob Seneff	Chl	–	17	17	35	NE
George Sanderson	Chl	–	16	16	20	NE
Daniel Stevenson	Chl	–	20	13	15	NE
Mark McDowell	Chl	MS	22	4	35	SE
Owen Russell	Chl	–	16	2	19	SE
William Wiley	Chl	–	19	13	29	NE
Alexander McDonald	Chl	–	20	15	35	NE
George Harrison	Chl	–	20	14	35	SW
Joseph Bogle	Chl	–	16	17	10	NW
Thomas Green	Chl	–	16	16	14	NE
George Valentine	Chl	–	17	18	31	W
James Daniel	Chl	–	20	14	22	SW
Adam Haller	Chl	–	20	11	21	SE
John Rees	Chl	–	20	13	13	SE
John Wright	Chl	WS	21	11	30	NE
Bazel Meeks	Chl	MS	22	3	36	NE
-- Buzzard & -- Friend	Chl	–	19	13	32	NE
Isaac Terboss	Chl	Mil	19	7	19	SE
Thomas Townsend	Chl	Mil	14	8	21	NW
Joseph Hiestand	Chl	–	19	16	36	E
Anthony Weaver	Chl	WS	21	11	30	SW
Michael Tress	Chl	WS	21	11	18	SE
Michael Alspach	Chl	–	20	14	14	SW
Adam Weaver	Chl	–	14	16	5	NE
Isaac Blosser	Chl	–	17	16	23	SE
John M. Fulkamare	Chl	–	21	5	5	+
John M. Fulkamare	Chl	–	21	5	16	-?
Anne Rickabaugh	Chl	–	20	11	21	SW
L. Barnhart & M. Barnhart	Chl	WS	21	9	36	SW
Peter Whitmer	Chl	–	17	17	13	NE
Christian Hover	Chl	–	17	18	3	SW
John Shoemaker	Chl	–	20	15	20	NE
Silas Warren & B. Warren	Chl	MS	21	9	13	SW
Thomas Warner	Chl	–	18	16	18	NW
-- Weaver & -- Nevel	Chl	WS	21	11	18	NE
Michael Boyer	Chl	–	17	18	28	NW
Jacob Coffelt	Chl	–	20	15	17	SE
Matthew Taylor	Chl	MS	21	11	8	SW
Robert Clendenin	Chl	–	20	11	5	SW
Philip Hoy	Chl	–	20	14	18	NE
Peter Miller	Chl	WS	21	10	36	SE
David Swope	Chl	MS	21	9	7	SW
Jacob Bower	Chl	–	16	17	28	SW
Abraham Miller	Chl	–	18	16	18	S
George Ogg	Chl	–	16	16	24	NE
George Stout	Chl	–	20	12	17	NW
Frederick Pontius	Chl	–	20	10	15	SW
Leonard Warner, Senior	Chl	WS	21	11	13	N
Henry Alspach	Chl	–	19	15	2	SW
James McClelland	Chl	–	19	12	9	SW
William Skinner	Chl	–	16	17	36	NW
Joseph Hardesty	Chl	–	20	13	12	SE
John Argebright	Chl	–	21	8	26	NE
John Ramsey	Chl	–	16	17	14	NE
Jacob Kestler	Chl	WS	21	9	3	SE
William Organ	Chl	–	17	16	3	SW
Edward Young	Chl	–	17	16	14	SW
Joseph Fickle	Chl	–	16	17	36	NE
George Ritchey	Chl	MS	21	10	31	NW
Andrew Glaze	Chl	LS	22	3	5	+
Andrew Glaze	Chl	LS	22	3	6	+
Christopher Huston	Chl	–	17	16	13	SE
Philip Swisher	Chl	MS	21	11	23	SW
Henry Sellers	Chl	–	16	17	35	NE
Demil? [Demit?] Cole	Chl	MS	22	4	36	NW
John Wilson	Chl	MS	21	11	30	SE
George Rouch	Chl	–	19	16	32	NW
John Stuckey, Junior	Chl	–	19	14	33	SW
Edward Ricketts	Chl	–	20	15	23	SE
Abraham Drisbach	Chl	–	20	12	33	SW
Elihu McCracken	Chl	–	20	15	6	SW
John McNeal	Chl	WS	21	11	7	SW
William Stockham	Chl	–	20	4	34	NW
James Wallace	Chl	–	21	8	14	SE
Nicholas Tussing	Chl	MS	21	11	23	SE
Michael Trash	Chl	MS	21	11	14	SW
Matthew Taylor	Chl	MS	21	11	17	NW
Thomas Cole	Chl	–	20	14	21	NE

Name	Loc	Code				Dir
John U. Gesey	Chl	-	19	16	14	NW
Henry Humburger	Chl	-	17	18	33	NE
Ludwick Ridinghour	Chl	-	16	17	20	S
-- Mayer & -- Shock	Chl	WS	21	10	2	W
John Schoonhover	Chl	MS	21	11	25	SW
Christian King	Chl	-	16	16	17	NE
Samuel Hanson	Chl	-	20	9	20	SW
Christian Fagler	Chl	-	20	11	12	NE
James Mitchell	Chl	WS	21	9	33	NE
John Brewer	Chl	-	21	3	33	SW
Isaac Huffhines	Chl	MS	21	10	29	SE
Charles Rary	Chl	MS	21	11	28	NE
Matthias Kesler	Chl	-	20	13	32	SE
Matthias Kesler	Chl	-	20	13	35	SE
Matthias Kesler	Chl	-	20	13	35	NW
Matthias Kesler	Chl	-	20	13	35	NE
John Taylor	Chl	-	20	15	12	NW
Andrew Smith	Chl	-	16	17	4	SW
William Smith	Chl	MS	21	11	25	NW
James Willets	Chl	-	20	11	15	NE
Henry Kranwell	Chl	-	19	16	23	SW
George Wagnar*	Chl	-	18	14	25	SW
Samuel Nichols	Chl	-	20	9	30	SW
John Hampson	Chl	-	20	8	29	SW
Alexander Berry	Chl	-	20	11	28	NW
Joseph Bogle	Chl	-	16	17	13	NE
James Neely	Chl	-	16	15	6	NE
Jacob Pickle	Chl	-	19	12	6	SE
George White	Chl	-	19	12	29	NW
George Glaze	Chl	-	20	10	27	S
Henry Halten	Chl	-	20	10	24	SW

*So spelled.

748   7 May 1812   A/4/375
LO Stu
Transmits patents

Name	Loc	Code				Dir
Jesse Brock	Stu	-	5	9	28	SW
Samuel Dunn	Stu	-	6	9	26	SW
Edward Carpenter	Stu	-	7	11	26	NE
Simon Shuck	Stu	-	7	17	14	NW
Frederick Reed	Stu	-	7	14	13	SE
Timothy Grewell	Stu	-	7	20	25	NW
John Roller?	Stu	-	8	9	3	NE

749   7 May 1812   A/4/375
James Findlay, Esq.
Transmits Treasury receipt

Name	Loc	Code				Dir
William McClellan	Unk	-	6	2	11	NW

750   7 May 1812   A/4/376
LO Zan
Transmits patents

Name	Loc	Code				Dir
Edward Wiggins	Zan	Mil	5	4	11	NE
Isaac Taylor	Zan	Mil	8	2	19	NE
John Shott? [Sholl?]	Zan	Mil	2	8	16	NE
Philip Baker	Zan	Mil	6	1	9	SE
William Wartenby	Zan	Mil	6	1	23	SE
Jacob Horne	Zan	Mil	10	6	20	NE
John Hadden	Zan	Mil	5	1	8	SW

751   7 May 1812   A/4/376
LO Cin
Transmits patents

Name	Loc	Code				Dir
Jacob Froman	Cin	WML	1	6	34	NE
Matthew McClucken?	Cin	WML	1	10	3	NE
Adam Flack	Cin	WML	2	5	35	SE
Robert Hill	Cin	WML	1	14	35	SE
John Cartwright	Cin	WML	1	12	34	SW
William Cotton	Cin	WML	3	3	34	SE
Joseph Wasson	Cin	WML	1	14	25	SW
John Beard	Cin	WML	1	12	18	SE
John Smith	Cin	WML	1	13	5	NE
Moses Vail	Cin	EML	4	2	10	SE
James Marshall	Cin	EML	6	5	32	NE
John Jiams [Ijams?]	Cin	EML	1	7	3	NE
Henry Flory	Cin	EML	5	4	21	NW
John Olinger	Cin	EML	5	4	22	SW
John Cook	Cin	EML	6	2	4	NE
Eli Dixon	Cin	EML	1	7	11	NW
Joel Williams	Cin	EML	2	3	5	NE
Nathan Goodwin	Cin	EML	3	4	17	SW
Samuel McClure	Cin	EML	5	9	2	SW
Peter Owens	Cin	EML	1	2	4	NE
James Ireland	Cin	EML	1	9	30	SE
Robert Moore	Cin	EML	2	4	8	SW
William Wells	Cin	EML	6	7	14	+
William Wells	Cin	EML	6	7	15	+
Joseph Newman	Cin	EML	5	6	25	NW
William Ross	Cin	EML	2	3	6	NE
James Ball	Cin	EML	1	2	14	NE
Jacob Specht	Cin	EML	2	8	17	SW
Jesse Taney	Cin	EML	1	7	24	SE
Adam Andrew	Cin	EML	3	3	23	NW
Simon Ely	Cin	WML	2	10	5	+
John Harper	Cin	WML	1	10	25	SW
Isaac Less Masters	Cin	WML	1	6	34	SE
Beal Butler	Cin	WML	2	13	23	+
Thomas Bulla	Cin	WML	1	13	13	SW
Robert Gibson	Cin	EML	6	8	25	NE
John Harrison	Cin	EML	4	9	23	NE
Edward Thomas	Cin	EML	5	5	12	SW
John Morris	Cin	MR	9	4	18	NW
James Stafford	Cin	MR	10	2	24	SE
William Campbell	Cin	MR	9	6	19	SE
John Townsend	Cin	WML	1	13	4	SW
Henry Miller	Cin	WML	2	12	24	SE

752   7 May 1812   A/4/377
LO Cin
Transmits patents

Name	Loc	Code				Dir
John Allen	Cin	WML	1	7	25	NE
John Dawson	Cin	WML	1	6	20	SW
Henry Hormall	Cin	EML	1	3	1	SW+
Tobias Tillman	Cin	EML	3	7	20?	NW
Andrew Endsley	Cin	WML	2	13	25	S
Abraham Hamman	Cin	WML	1	10	13	SE
Isaac Beesar? [Beesan?]	Cin	WML	1	13	29	SW
Jeremiah Cox	Cin	WML	1	14	33	NW

753   9 May 1812   A/4/377
Daniel Symmes, [Reg Cin]
Urgently requests final certificate for Daniel C.
Cooper for lots in town of Dayton, Ohio.

754   9 May 1812   A/4/377
LO Stu
Transmits patents

Name	Loc	Code				Dir
William Henderson	Stu	-	5	10	17	NE
Jacob Hoover	Stu	-	8	11	8	NW
James Starr	Stu	-	4	6	35	NW
Andrew Whiteleather	Stu	-	5	17	23	NE
John Walker	Stu	-	2	8	34	SE
Andrew Kepler	Stu	-	9	12	4	W
Samuel Hicklen	Stu	-	6	19	4	SE
Abraham Galladay	Stu	-	9	10	35	SE
Joseph Strahl	Stu	-	5	7	27	SW
John Dunlap	Stu	-	5	9	23	NW

Name	Office	Type				
John Willitz	Stu	-	3	14	31	NW
Christopher Henny	Stu	-	9	12	9	NW
Conrad Reber	Stu	-	9	12	24	NE
John Dougherty	Stu	-	6	8	18	NE

755   11 May 1812   A/4/378
Joseph Wood, [Reg Mar]
Discusses account

-- Dickenson	Mar	-	5	1	27	+

756   12 May 1812   A/4/378
Hon. -- Findley
Transmits patent

Joh[n?] Nichols, Senior	Zan Mil	8	2	22	SW	

757   12 May 1812   A/4/378
-- Heckewelder, Zanesville
Transmits patent

Henry Davy	Zan Mil	1	9	2	NW	

758   16 May 1812   A/4/378
LO Zan
Transmits patent

Name	Office	Type				
James Johnson	Zan	-	10	9	14	NE
Samuel Wylie	Zan	-	10	9	31	NE
Thomas McKee	Zan	-	11	13	12	SE
James Glen	Zan	-	13	12	14?	NE
William Bicker	Zan Mil	3	10	21	SW	
Peter Fanley? [Farley?]	Zan	-	15	16	11	SE
Joseph W. Satterthwaite	Zan	-	9	8	4?	SE
Joshua W. Satterthwaite	Zan	-	9	8	2	NW
William Woodbridge	Zan Mil	3?	4	18	NE	
William Langly? [Longly?]	Zan	-	13	12	3	SE
Joel Williams	Zan	-	8	8	4	SE
Gabriel Cockrel	Zan	-	13	12	3	NE
William Clayton	Zan	-	15	16	7	SE
John Vansant	Zan	-	14	16	7	-
Jacob Titereck	Zan Mil	1	3	15	SW	
John Pritchard	Zan Mil	9	6	22	SE	
John Franz	Zan Mil	4	8	8	SE	
John Barton	Zan Mil	2	2	20	SW	
John Parkhill	Zan Mil	4	2	25	SE	
Samuel Stires?	Zan Mil	1	1	10	SW	
John Wilie	Zan Mil	5	1	2	NE	
Abraham Williams	Zan Mil	1	2	21	NW	
Christian Laragood?	Zan Mil	4	8	11	NW	
John Altomano	Zan Mil	3	8	6	W	
Abraham Clements	Zan Mil	2	2	8	SE	
John Paxton	Zan Mil	2	3	1	SW	
Abraham Thompson	Zan Mil	6	4	18	SE	
Jacob Bowers	Zan Mil	6	1	7	SE	
David Calhoon	Zan Mil	5	1	23	NW	
Daniel Wilkins	Zan Mil	11	3	16	NW	
John Bower? [Bowers?]	Zan Mil	6	1	6	SW	
John Lomiller	Zan Mil	4	8	13	NE	
Anthony Miller	Zan Mil	11	3	17	SW	
Alexander Culbertson	Zan Mil	7	1	2	NW	
William Woodbridge	Zan Mil	8	4	13	SE	
Peter Folk	Zan Mil	1	10	6	SW	
William Brown	Zan Mil	7	1	1	SE	

759   16 May 1812   A/4/379
Daniel Symmes, [Reg Cin]
Complains of errors in accounts; transmits Treasury receipts

Christian Bleakenstaff	Cin	-	6	4	27	SE
Reuben Ryan*	Cin EML	2	6	7	SE	

Name	Office	Type				
William C. Schenck	Cin MR	5	2	20	-	
--	Cin WML	2	3	2	NE	
--**	Cin EML	2	3	2	NE	
--	Cin MR	10	3	1	NW	
--	Cin MR	10	3	1	NE	
--	Cin WML	1	11	17	NE	
--	Cin WML	1	11	17	SE	
-- Hunt***	Cin Pre	7	2	9	W	
--	Cin EML	1	4	19	NW	
--	Cin EML	1	4	19	SW	
--	Cin MR	8	3	10	SE	
--	Cin MR	8	3	10	NE	
H. Vanmetre	Cin MR	10	6	23	SW	
--	Cin MR	14#	6	23	SW	
-- Arnold##	Cin	-	7	3	22	SW

*Tract already assigned to William Low.
**Previously sold.
***Assigned to H. Staley.
#Tract does not exist.
##Receipt states -- Shingletaker, assignee of Stude-
  baker. Asks whether Studebaker bought land from
  Arnold, who is the owner of record.

760   18 May 1812   A/4/380
Jesse Spencer, [Reg Chl]
Transmits patent

Daniel Aurand	Chl Mil	21?	9	36	NW	

761   18 May 1812   A/4/380
Hon. -- Jennings
Transmits patents

Peter Covert	Vin	-	9E	1N	3	SW
Moses Hoggatt	Vin	-	4E	2N	10	NE
Moses Hoggatt	Vin	-	4E	2N	10	NW
Lewis Fouts	Vin	-	9E	1N	6	+

762   18 May 1812   A/4/380
LO Jef
Transmits patents

Joseph Stanley	Jef	-	9E	1N	1	SE
Henry Towall	Jef	-	1W	2N	34	+
Jacob Fouts	Jef	-	8E	2N	24	SW

763   18 May 1812   A/4/381
LO Vin
Transmits patents

Daniel Grass	Vin	-	6W	7S	26	+
William McFaden	Vin	-	13W	7S	18	+
William McFaden	Vin	-	13W	7S	19	+
John Sprinkle	Vin	-	9W	7S	3	+
G. W. Johnston	Vin	-	4W	3S	32	+
John? Frank	Vin	-	3E	5S	30	+
John Reed	Vin	-	5E	6S	3	+
Peter Jones	Vin	-	11W	6S	25	+

764   18 May 1812   A/4/381
LO Chl
Transmits patents

Joseph Hedge	Chl	-	19	13	28	NW
John? Smith	Chl MS	21	10	13	SW	
Thomas Strawn	Chl	-	16	17	35	SW
Robert Skinner	Chl	-	16	16	2	NE
William Landerson	Chl	-	16	16	18	NW
Nicholas Young	Chl MS	22	4	12	NW	
Mark McDowell	Chl MS	22	4	35	NE	
Adam Plank	Chl	-	16	17	12	NE
William Wilson	Chl	-	20	15	12	SE

Henry Haimbough	Ch1	–	19	16	24	NW
William Grubb	Ch1	–	19	2	8	SW
John Brown	Ch1	MS	22	4	11	NE
James Gallaher	Ch1	–	16	1	29	SE

765   19 May 1812   A/4/381

Peter Audrain, [Reg Det]

"When an examination of the Certificates issued by
you for the private claims in your District was
had in this Department, much trouble arose from
the disagreement of the surveys with the decisions
of the Commissioners. The same may take place in
Certificates . . . for the second concessions to
claimants on the river Detroit. . . ."

766   20 May 1812   A/4/381

LO Vin

Transmits patents

Jesse Purcell	Vin	–	7W	2N	5	SE
William Purcell	Vin	–	7W	2N	8	NW
Henry Brenton? [Brinton?]	Vin	–	8W	1N	19	SE
Moses Boone	Vin	–	4E	5S	21	NW
Thomas Givens	Vin	–	13W	7S	6	SE
John Bates	Vin	–	4E	4S	4	NW
Abraham Rodarmel	Vin	–	7W	2N	5	SW
James Brenton	Vin	–	8W	1N	28	NW
Friend Spears	Vin	–	7W	2N	3	SW
Paul Tislow	Vin	–	8W	1N	29	NE
Levi Compton	Vin	–	12W	1N	11	NE
William Purcell	Vin	–	7W	2N	8	NE
James Emison	Vin	–	12W	2S	34	SE
James Emison	Vin	–	12W	3S	3	SE
James Emison	Vin	–	12W	2S	35	SW

767   20 May 1812   A/4/382

Wyllys Silliman, [Reg Zan]

Transmits patents & certificates

John Adams	Zan Mil	8?	4	4	SW	
William Wynn	Zan	–	6	1	9	SW

768   20 May 1812   A/4/382

Joseph Vance

Acknowledges receipt of military land warrants; mentions John Richmond Stokes, John Swinorton.

769   21 May 1812   A/4/382

R[ichard] Forrest, [U.S. Department of State]

Patent to Will not received; –– Piper of House of
Representatives inquires

Daniel Will?*	Cin EML	4	3	6	SE	

*Assignee of Henry Yount.

770   23 May 1812   A/4/383

Jesse Spencer, [Reg Ch1]

Transmits certificate; –– Smilie, member of Congress,
interested

Martin Landis	Ch1	–	19	13	6	–
Martin Landis	Ch1	–	19	13	7	–

771   23 May 1812   A/4/383

Daniel Symmes, [Reg Cin]

Erroneous tract description*

Samuel Holliday	Cin EML	16	17	32	NE	

*"There are only 15 ranges laid off to the Eastward
of the 2nd principal meridian."

772   25 May 1812   A/4/383

Hon. J. Morrow

Transmits patent

John? Vannice	[Cin] EML	3	2	11	–	

773   25 May 1812   A/4/383

John H. Brinton, Esq.

Transmits corrected patents

John H. Brinton	Stu	–	7	15	12	SW
John H. Brinton	Stu	–	7	18	24	N

774   25 May 1812   A/4/383

Wyllys Silliman, [Reg Zan]

Transmits patent

Barbara Prior	Zan Mil	8	2	15	NE	

775   25 May 1812   A/4/383

LO Stu

Transmits patents

Charles Miller	Stu	–	5	13	23	SW
Nathan Johnson	Stu	–	4	10	11	NW
Philip Jervis	Stu	–	6	9	26	NE
Isaac Votaw	Stu	–	4	17	7	NE
William Howard	Stu	–	1	6	18	NE
Jesse Felts	Stu	–	6	19	10	SE
John Cook	Stu	–	2	10	14	NW
William Chambers	Stu	–	4	11	35	NW
Thomas Hurford	Stu	–	8	11	20	NE
Alexander Calderhead	Stu	–	4	8	3	SE
Joel Johnson	Stu	–	6	12	28	SW
James McCoy	Stu	–	7	10	17	SE
John Newman	Stu	–	8	10	19	SE
Peter Boghart	Stu	–	5	14	31	NW
Samuel Martin	Stu	–	2	10	9	NE
Peter Miller	Stu	–	9	10	28	SW
Andrew Ferrier	Stu	–	5	11	23	–

776   25 May 1812   A/4/384

LO Jef

Transmits patents

Enoch Parr	Jef	–	5E	2N	18	SW
Rich Gilstrap	Jef	–	3E	1N	12	NE
James Mundell	Jef	–	5E	2S	6	NE
John Fleener	Jef	–	4E	2N	4	NE
Joseph Maxwell	Jef	–	1E	2N	2	NE
Lewis Woody	Jef	–	4E	2N	10	SW
Michael Burger	Jef	–	5E	3S	4	NW
George Bowman	Jef	–	5E	2S	32	SE
Jacob Fouts	Jef	–	8E	2N	23	SE
Abraham Connan	Jef	–	10E	1N	7	SE
Andrew Pitt	Jef	–	4E	2N	17	SE
Philberd Wright	Jef	–	4E	2N	32	SE
William Davenport	Jef	–	4E	5N	20	+
William Davenport	Jef	–	4E	5N	21	+
George Doup	Jef	–	6E	3S	20	+
George Doup	Jef	–	6E	3S	21	+
Daniel Robins	Jef	–	9E	3N	5	NE
James Blair	Jef	–	4E	2N	2	SW
Thomas Roseberry	Jef	–	8E	4N	14	SE

777   26 May 1812   A/4/385

Abraham Hetrick, Baltimore County, Maryland

Your patent delayed at LO Can due to illness of the
Register.

778   26 May 1812   A/4/385
Jesse Spencer, [Reg Chl]
Returns defective documents; will of John Graham on
    file in the Department
John Graham &
    Elijah Friend*   Chl – 20   12   33   NW
*Assigned to Peter Wolf by -- Earnest.

779   27 May 1812   A/4/386
LO Jef
Transmits patents

William Wells	Jef	–	5E	2S	1	SW
Asa Burt	Jef	–	1E	1N	2	SE
George Beck	Jef	–	3E	1N	11	NW
John Buchanan	Jef	–	11E	6N	35	SW
Bernard Giltner	Jef	–	9E	2N	31	SE
Jacob Persinger	Jef	–	4E	5N	22	NE
Jeremiah Sage	Jef	–	9E	2N	36	NE
Philberd Wright	Jef	–	4E	2N	33	SW
Philip Shuck	Jef	–	3E	5S	23	SE
Andrew Pitts	Jef	–	4E	2N	29	NW
Thomas Roseberry	Jef	–	8E	4N	13	SW
David Colclazer	Jef	–	3E	2N	27	SE

780   27 May 1812   A/4/386
LO Stu
Transmits patents

Thomas Werley	Stu	–	8	10	33	SE
Leonard Willaman	Stu	–	8	11	17	NE
Samuel Grey	Stu	–	4	15	14	SW
Isaac Thomas	Stu	–	4	9	21	SE

781   27 May 1812   A/4/386
Jonathan Sutton, Steubenville, [Ohio]
Transmits patent
Jonathan Sutton   Stu – 3   6   32   –

782   27 May 1812   A/4/386
LO Jef
Transmits patents

John Chenoweth	Jef	–	2E	1S	4	SW
Jacob Copple	Jef	–	9E	1N	3	NW
Henry Wyman	Jef	–	4E	1N	34	SE
Middleton Robertson	Jef	–	8E	4N	8	SE

783   28 May 1812   A/4/387
Jesse Spencer, [Reg Chl]
Transmits Treasury receipt
Jacob Hendricks   Chl – 19   16   7   SE

784   28 May 1812   A/4/387
Daniel Symmes, [Reg Cin]
Returns documents for correction; mentions Robert
    Scott
Jonathan Tullis*   Cin –** 4   3   13   –
*Assignee of William C. Shenk.
**"North of Judge Symmes' patent;" [probably MR is
    meant].

785   30 May 1812   A/4/387
David Hoge, [Reg Stu]
Transmits certificate & Treasury receipt in favor of
    Martin Wingar.

786   2 Jun 1812   A/4/387
LO Jef
Transmits patents

Adam Wyble	Jef	–	2E	1N	5	NE
Zeph. Blackford	Jef	–	9E	3N	35	SW
Peter Hubbard	Jef	–	4E	2N	8	SW
Samuel Arnett	Jef	–	10E	2N	7	NE
Robert Russell	Jef	–	8E	5N	15	NE
Leonard Sroutman? [Troutman?]	Jef	–	9E	1N	27	SE
Robert Field	Jef	–	2E	1N	13	NW
John? Giltner	Jef	–	9E	1N	23	SE

787   2 Jun 1812   A/4/387
LO Stu
Transmits patents

Benjamin Johnson	Stu	–	6	12	27	NW
Thomas Wilson	Stu	–	6	9	18	SE
Thomas Ligget	Stu	–	4	6	17	SW
John Ekey	Stu	–	2	6	15	NE
William Gibson	Stu	–	7	9	6	SW
Joseph? Roush	Stu	–	5	11	12	SE
Peter Shepherd	Stu	–	4	12	26	SE
Jacob Champer	Stu	–	4	11	22	SE

788   3 Jun 1812   A/4/388
Jesse Spencer, [Reg Chl]
Transmits certificate
Conrad Heyl*   Chl – 9   16   25   NE
*Transferred to Gerard Topkin; retransferred by Top-
    kin to Heyl.

789   3 Jun 1812   A/4/388
David Hoge, [Reg Stu]
Transmits certificate & Treasury receipt
Robert Andrews*   Stu – 8   9   8   N
*Assigned to John Shut & George Shut.

790   --   A/4/388
"June 5th 1812. Edward Tiffin, Esq., Commissioner
    of the General Land Office, entered on the duties
    of his Office."

791   6 Jun 1812   A/4/389
-- Patterson, Director of the Mint, Philadelphia
Requests a new seal for the General Land Office.

792   8 Jun 1812   A/4/389
Hon. Secretary of War
Requests that records, books, & papers remaining in
    the War Department touching or concerning the pub-
    lic lands of the United States be delivered to the
    General Land Office.

793   8 Jun 1812   A/4/389
Hon. Secretary of State
Requests that records, books, & papers remaining in
    the State Department touching or concerning the
    public lands of the United States be delivered to
    the General Land Office.

794   8 Jun 1812   A/4/390
Daniel Symmes, [Reg Cin]

Returns defective documents

Jacob Leichleder &						
Conrad Leichleder*	Cin	MR	6	2	29	–
William Jennings**	Cin	WML	4	1	2	+
Barnabas Blue	Cin	Pre	10	1	12	SW+
George Gephart***	Cin	Pre	6	1	19	SW
Ann Sparks#	Cin	Pre	6	3	34	+
Walter S. Burgess##	Cin	WML	1	12	8	NE
Thomas Cartmill &						
William Cartmill###	Cin	Pre	10	6	24	+
George Delong	Cin	MR	8	2	30	NW

*Assignees of Timothy Green.
**Assignee of Thomas Thompson.
***Assignee of David Blackburn.
#Assignee of John Irwin.
##Assignee of Joseph Powers.
###Assignees of Nathaniel Cartmill.

795   8 Jun 1812   A/4/391
Isaac Clendenon, St. Clairsville, Ohio
Answers letter regarding patent issuance.

796   8 Jun 1812   A/4/391
LO Stu
Transmits patents

Thomas Fanley	Stu	–	5	16	24	SE
Thomas Fanley	Stu	–	4	15	19	SW
James Stewart	Stu	–	5	10	27	SW
Matthias Lower? [Sower?]	Stu	–	1	9	21	SW

797   9 Jun 1812   A/4/392
Charles Wilson, Steubenville, Ohio
Answers inquiry regarding patent issuance.

798   10 Jun 1812   A/4/392
Wyllys Silliman, [Reg Zan]
Transmits certificate

Richard Burrell	Zan	Mil	3	10	25	–
Richard Burrell	Zan	Mil	3	10	16	–
John Wade*	Zan	Mil	3	10	18	–

*Assignee of Richard Burrell.

799   10 Jun 1812   A/4/393
David Hoge, [Reg Stu]
Certificates lost or mislaid; a duplicate requested

John Johnson	Stu	–	1	4	27	+
John Johnson	Stu	–	1	4	33	+

800   11 Jun 1812   A/4/393
Hon. R. Patterson, U.S. Mint, [Philadelphia]
Agrees to modification of seal design for General
   Land Office.

801   12 Jun 1812   A/4/393
Daniel Symmes, [Reg Cin]
Documents returned for correction

Jacob Prilliman?						
[Billiman?]*	Cin	Pre	10	2	7	N
William Smith	Cin	EML	2	3	15	SE
David Mount**	Cin	EML	12	12	36	SW
John Thain? [Kain?]	Cin	MR	11	3	2	S
Thomas Kelsey	Cin	–	5	3	27	N

*Assignee of Lewis Winters.
**"It is presumed that this land lies east of the
   second principal meridian."

802   12 Jun 1812   A/4/394
John Deford, Uniontown, Fayette County, Pennsylvania
Answers letter of inquiry regarding patent

John Deford	Unk	–	5	15	24	SW

803   16 Jun 1812   A/4/394
Daniel Symmes, [Reg Cin]
Transmits certificate

Ann Westfall	Cin	MR	7	3	36	NW

804   17 Jun 1812   A/4/394
Jesse Spencer, [Reg Chl]
Answers query regarding computation of interest.

805   17 Jun 1812   A/4/395
Daniel Symmes, [Reg Cin]
Transmits certificate

William McClelland	Cin	MR	6	2	11	NW

806   23 Jun 1812   A/4/395
Hon. Jeremiah Morrow, Chairman of the Land Committee,
   U.S. House of Representatives
Transmits copy of a report of the Land Commissioners
   at St. Louis.

807   23 Jun 1812   A/4/395
Hon. Thomas Worthington, Chairman of the Land Commission, U.S. Senate
Transmits copy of a report of the Land Commissioners
   at St. Louis.

808   24 Jun 1812   A/4/395
Jesse Spencer, [Reg Chl]
Transmits patents

John Shoemaker	Chl	–	20	15	20	NW
Adam Weaver	Chl	–	16	16	5	NE

809   25 Jun 1812   A/4/396
Speaker of the U.S. House of Representatives
President of the U.S. Senate
Transmits copies of a report of the commissioners
   for the District of Vincennes.

810   25 Jun 1812   A/4/396
David Hoge, [Reg Stu]
Transmits patent

George Starr	Stu	–	3	9	18	NW

811   25 Jun 1812   A/4/396
John Badollet, [Reg Vin]
Explains extension of law.

812   25 Jun 1812   A/4/396
Jesse Spencer, [Reg Chl]
Transmits patent

James Gallaher	Chl	–	16	1	29	SE

813   26 Jun 1812   A/4/397
David Hoge, [Reg Stu]
Transmits patent of Samuel Martin [no tract descrip-
   tion given].

814 26 Jun 1812 A/4/397
Thomas Gibson, Reg Can
Transmits certificate

George Clark	Can	–	10	12	26	S

815 27 Jun 1812 A/4/397
Jesse Spencer, [Reg Chl]
Documents returned for correction

Thomas Orr*	Chl	–	21	8	14	NW
George Dove**	Chl	–	20	15	6	NW
James Rose***	Chl	–	19	16	35?	W
-- Bowman#	Chl	–	18	16	8	N
-- Washburne##	Chl	–	19	8	7	N

*"This tract appears to have been purchased by A.
 McClintock, and his account is closed."
**Assignee of J. Lambert. "This appears to have
 been closed in the name of -- Dove & -- Shoemaker."
***Assignee of J. Nave.
#Assignee of -- Heise.
##Assignee of -- Westfall.

816 27 Jun 1812 A/4/398
Daniel Symmes, [Reg Cin]
Transmits certificate; mentions -- Cooper

Michael Ba--?	Cin EML	4	6	26	+	

817 30 Jun 1812 A/4/398
Robert Patterson, [U.S. Mint, Philadelphia]
Acknowledges receipt of seal for the General Land
 Office.

818 30 Jun 1812 A/4/398
Daniel Symmes, [Reg Cin]
Inquires regarding certificates

Felix Welton*	Cin MR	10	5	9	SE	
Felix Welton*	Cin MR	10	5	17?	NE	

*Assignee of John Foley.

819 30 Jun 1812 A/4/398
Hon. William Findley
Transmits patent of Peter Eckhart [not tract descrip-
 tion given].

820 30 Jun 1812 A/4/398
Hon. Gen. -- Lacock, U.S. House of Representatives
Transmits patents

Robert Moone	Can	–	13	15	6	SE
Robert Moone	Can	–	13	15	5	SW
Robert Moone	Can	–	11	16	11	SE
Joseph Hibbs	Can	–	13	15	3	NE
Joseph Hibbs	Can	–	13	15	10	NE

821 30 Jun 1812 A/4/399
Charles Wilson, Steubenville
Transmits patent

Charles Wilson	Stu	–	4	14	10	SE

822 30 Jun 1812 A/4/399
Hon. -- Anderson, U.S. House of Representatives
Transmits patent

James Bratton	Can	–	10	12	5	NE

823 1 Jul 1812 A/4/399
LO Can
Transmits patents

Robert Moone? [Moore?]	Can	–	10	12	15	NW
John? Christmass	Can	–	13	15	10	SW

824 1 Jul 1812 A/4/399
LO Vin
Transmits patents

John Adams	Vin	–	11W	1S	14	SW
Valentine Shirly	Vin	–	1W	2N	7	SW
Jacob Funk	Vin	–	2E	5S	2	+
James Lett	Vin	–	7W	2N	20	SE
Squire Boone	Vin	–	3E	5S	24	NE
Jonathan Latham	Vin	–	10W	2S	6	SE

825 1 Jul 1812 A/4/399
Frederick Bates, Esq., Recorder of land titles, St.
 Louis, Missouri
Transmits copy of new Act requiring investigation of
 land claims.

826 1 Jul 1812 A/4/399
Abraham Hetrick, Manchester, Baltimore County, Mary-
 land
Transmits patents

Abraham Hetrick	Can	–	19	19	8	NE
Abraham Hetrick	Can	–	19	19	10	SW

827 1 Jul 1812 A/4/399
Hon. -- Piper, U.S. House of Representatives
Transmits patent

William Lavering	Can	–	19	18	5	NW

828 1 Jul 1812 A/4/400
LO Stu
Transmits patents

David Larkin	Stu	–	6	10	14	NW
J. R. Dean	Stu	–	5	15	1	NW
Nathan Galbreath	Stu	–	4	16	29	E
Henry Doudna	Stu	–	5	7	32	NW
Samuel Woodmany	Stu	–	3	7	22	SW
Anthony Miller	Stu	–	5	16	1	–
Christopher McCraren?	Stu	–	7	9	11	SW
Peter Heffelly? [Hiffelly?]	Stu	–	1	9	21	NW
George Brokaw	Stu	–	5	9	15	NE
Robert Morrison	Stu	–	3	14	25	NE
Zaccheus Biggs	Stu	–	3	5	27	SE
Noah Zane	Stu	–	3	5	13	SE
John? McCorkle? [McConkle?]	Stu	–	6	11	3	SE
Jonathan Reed	Stu	–	5	9	29	NE
Peregrine Watkins	Stu	–	3	6	25	NE
George Leporth	Stu	–	6	12	14	NE
Adam Ross	Stu	–	5	10	24	SE
Zaccheus Biggs	Stu	–	7	9	35	NE
John? Firebaugh	Stu	–	6	13	14	SE
Daniel Bear	Stu	–	5	11	5	NE
Henry Johnson	Stu	–	6	10	24	NE
Charles Henderson	Stu	–	6	10	10	SE
Alexander Smith	Stu	–	11	9	29	NW
Samuel Bosserman? [Basserman?]	Stu	–	6	17	4	SE
Isaac Votaw, Senior	Stu	–	4	17	7	SE
Joseph McClain	Stu	–	5	11	17	NE
Sterling Johnston	Stu	–	4	7	7	NW
Samuel Boyd	Stu	–	5	11	7	SW
Michael Reed	Stu	–	7	18	11	SW
John Brill	Stu	–	7	9	33	SE

Thomas Major	Stu	–	3	7	21	SW
George Snillinghberger	Stu	–	3	14	29	SW
William R. Dickinson	Stu	–	8	10	34	NW
Philip Hammon	Stu	–	8	11	19	NE
Bezaleel Wells	Stu	–	8	10	9	SW
Adam Cnosser	Stu	–	2	11	31	NE

829   1 Jul 1812   A/4/400
LO Cin
Transmits patents

John Purviance	Cin EML	1	9	5	SE
Samuel Brier? [Brien?]	Cin EML	6	2	8	SW
William Low	Cin EML	6	3	19	SW
Joseph McMaken	Cin EML	2	4	26	SE
Joseph Cooper	Cin EML	5	5	36	NE
Samuel Dick	Cin EML	2	4	28	SE
Amos Butler	Cin EML	1	1	18	NE
David P. Purviance	Cin EML	1	9	20	NW
John Moore	Cin EML	2	4	7	SW
Joseph Miller & Jesse Miller	Cin EML	6	4	8	NW
John Vannice	Cin EML	3	2	11	–
Robert Glidwell	Cin WML	2	10	34	SW
Jesse Gerrard	Cin EML	6	4	5	NE
Asa Inman	Cin EML	5	7	30	NW
Aaron Hougham	Cin EML	2	8	30	NE
Henry Gephart	Cin EML	5	3	22	NW
David Railsback	Cin WML	2	12	2	NE
Robert Irwin	Cin EML	3	2	7	–
Aaron Sackett	Cin EML	2	4	23	NW
Abraham White	Cin EML	2	5	17	NW
Robert Comer	Cin WML	1	14	35	NE
Elizabeth Lydick	Cin EML	2	8	26	SE

830   1 Jul 1812   A/4/401
LO Zan
Transmits patents

John Walters	Zan –	17	1	11	NW
George Messer	Zan –	12	13	6	SE
C. Meyers & N. Kems	Zan –	13	11	7	N+
C. Meyers & N. Kems	Zan –	13	11	8	–
James Oldham	Zan Mil	3	3	18	SW
Samuel Ream & Jacob Ream	Zan –	14	15	27	SW
Christian Keasbear	Zan Mil	3	9	21	SE
J. Gaddis & L. Springer	Zan –	13	12	8	SW
John Johnston*	Zan –	10	7	5	NW
Magdalena? Mosser	Zan Mil	1	9	10	SE
David Miller	Zan Mil	1	9	12	NW
Abraham Gerber	Zan Mil	4	9	17	SW
Caleb Dunn	Zan –	12	13	6	NW
Samuel Thralls	Zan –	15	16	34	SW
Jonas Miller	Zan Mil	4	9	16	SW
Jacob Spring	Zan –	15	17	25	NE
James Wilson	Zan –	15	16	8	SW
Ezra May	Zan –	10	9	32	SW

*Sent separately to Mr. Johnston by post.

831   2 Jul 1812   A/4/402
Levin Wailes, Esq., Register of the land office,
    Opelousas, Louisiana
A lengthy letter explaining that patents for private
    claims cannot be issued, because land descriptions
    are imprecise & survey plats have not been pro-
    vided.

832   2 Jul 1812   A/4/403
Parke Walton, [Reg Was]
Accounts not correct; mentions -- Henderson.

833   7 Jul 1812   A/4/403
William Wynne, Leesburgh, Virginia
Transmits patent

William Wynne	Zan Mil	6	1	10	NW

834   7 Jul 1812   A/4/403
Henry Honebreake?, Chambs.? Franklin County, Pennsyl-
    vania
Transmits patent

Henry Honebreake?	Can	–	10	11	12	SW

835   7 Jul 1812   A/4/404
Circular letter to all Receivers
States that books are to be audited.

836   8 Jul 1812   A/4/404
John Johnston, Faucett's Town, Columbia County, Ohio
Transmits patent

John Johnston	Zan Mil?	10	7	5	NW

837   9 Jul 1812   A/4/405
[Persons named in entry 845]
Letter of instructions to auditors of the books of
    the district land offices.

838   9 Jul 1812   A/4/406
James O. Cosby, Western District
William Crawford, Eastern District
Transmits commissions appointing you commissioners
    for ascertaining land claims ". . . of that part
    of Louisiana which lies East of the river Miss-
    issippi & Island of New Orleans."

839   9 Jul 1812   A/4/406
Daniel Symmes, [Reg Cin]
Transmits certificate of John Wandner?

840   14 Jul 1812   A/4/407
Frederick Bates, [Recorder of land titles, St. Louis]
U.S. President approves of the lease of lead mines to
    Messrs. -- Dodge, -- Craighead, & -- Wilson.

841   14 Jul 1812   A/4/407
William Crawford, Esq., Warrenton, North Carolina
James O. Cosby, Esq., [no address given]
Additonal instructions regarding their duties as land
    commissioners in Mississippi Territory.

842   14 Jul 1812   A/4/408
Isaac Van Horn, Rec Zan
Acknowledges receipt of surety bond.

843   15 Jul 1812   A/4/409
"Sent to LO Stu 36 patents
Sent to LO Cin 22 patents"
[patents & descriptions not given].

844   15 Jul 1812   A/4/409
Captain Jonathan Walton, Schenectady, New York
Transmits patents for claimants in LO Det district.

Claimant	Acres	Location
Samuel Egnew	47.51	on River Raisin
Pierre Yax	416.14	on Lake St. Clair
William Walker	600.00	on River Detroit
Dominique Drouillard	122.91	on La Riviere aux Loutres
-- Meldrum & -- Park	300.00	on River St. Clair
Jean Baptiste Susor, widow & heirs of	402.18	on River Raisin
Thomas Menard, heirs of	101.55	on River Raisin
Whitemore Knaggs? [Knagge?]	270.80	on River Raisin
François Cattin	135.26	on River Raisin
Jacques Lasselle & François Lasselle	236.66	on River Raisin
Jacques Lasselle	253.60	on River Raisin
Hyacinte Leduc	101.47	on La grande Coulés
Etienne Couture?	92.00	on La grande Coulés
Antoine Benard dit Lafontaine	146.64	on La Riviere aux Loutres

845   15 Jul 1812 A/4/410

[Notation in register:]
"See pages 404 & 406 [entries 835, 837]. The blanks to be filled in as follows:

[Land Office]	[Appointed Auditor]
Chillicothe	Joseph Kerr, Esq.
Steubenville	James Pritchard, Esq.
Marietta	Joseph Wilcox, Esq.
Zanesville	William Wells, Esq.
Cincinnati	John McClean, Esq., Lebanon
Vincennes	Benjamin Parke, Esq.
Washington, Mississippi Territory	Henry Dangerfield, Esq.
St. Stephens	George S. Gains, Esq.
Canton	John Crumbacker, Esq.
Jeffersonville	Richard Ferguson, Esq.
Huntsville	John Childress, Junior, Esq.

846   15 Jul 1812 A/4/410

Parke Walton; Lemuel Henry; Nehemiah Tilton; Lavin Sewall
Transmits act of Congress regarding confirmation of claims to land in Mississippi Territory founded on warrants of survey granted by the British or Spanish governments.

847   15 Jul 1812 A/4/410

Levin Wailes, [Reg Opel]
Transmits newspaper clipping reporting upon an "Act giving further time for registering claims to land in the Western District of the territory of Orleans."

848   16 Jul 1812 A/4/411

Nehemiah Tilton, Reg WPL
Lewis Sewall, Reg EPL
Transmits an Act "confirming Grants of Land in the Mississippi Territory derived from the british Government of West Florida, not subsequently re-granted by the Government of Spain or of the United States."

849   17 Jul 1812 A/4/411

Captain Jonathan Walton, Schenectady, New York
Transmits patents for private claims in LO Det district

Claimant	Acres	Location
Joseph Campeau	121.94	on River Huron of Lake Erie
Joseph Campeau	104.22	on River Detroit
Antoine Riopell	203.11	on Mason's run
Pierre Lacroix	--*	at Michillimackinac
-- Rousseau & -- Bailly	--**	at Michillimackinac
Toussaint Pothier	--***	at Michillimackinac
Joseph Bourdeaux	89.09	on River Raisin
Jacob Dicks, widow & admin. of	219.78	on fork of River Rouge
William Cissne, widow of	270.81	on River Rouge
François Durocher	112.36	on River Rouge
Maurice Moran	170.00	on Detroit River
Antoine Beaubien	336.83	on Detroit River

*5,351 square feet.
**21,415 square feet.
***33,395 square feet.

850   16 Jul 1812 A/4/411

Hon. Thomas R. Gold, Whitestown, New York
Transmits three patents for the heirs of Edward Antill, "for lands appropriated for satisfying the claims of the Refugees from the British provinces of Canada & Nova Scotia."
Returns documents regarding curatorship & tutorship of the children of Colonel E. Antill; also power of attorney from J. Antill & William Hall to Garnet Lansing?; [copies retained in government file on the case].

851   17 Jul 1812 A/4/412

Garret Sickles, New York
Transmits patent by direction of Dr. -- Mitchell

Garret Sickles	Mil	- 11	6	1	21

852   17 Jul 1812 A/4/412

William McClelland, care of Nicholas Gorsuch, innkeeper, old town, Baltimore
Transmits patent

William McClelland	Cin MR	6	2	11	NW

853   17 Jul 1812 A/4/412

Captain Jonathan Walton, Schenectady
Transmits patents for private claims in LO Det district

Claimant	Acres	Location
Elijah Brush	134.18	on River Detroit
Etienne Lebeau	187.39	on river of Sables
James McGill	294.14	on north border of river Huron
James Conner	617.28	on river Huron
The widow Tucker* in trust for her sons	622.08	on river Huron of Lake St. Clair
Charles Tuckar* & Jacob Tuckar*	477.37	on river Huron of Lake St. Clair
John Tuckar*	639.00	on river Huron of Lake St. Clair
Edward Tuckar*	640.00	on river Huron of Lake St. Clair
Martin Nadault	253.44	on river aux Sables

Claimant	Acres	Location
Phillis Pattier?		
[Pettier?]	126.90	on Lake St. Clair
Laurent Griffard	103.84	on Lake St. Clair
Antoine Rivard	145.35	on Detroit River

*So spelled.

---

854   17 Jul 1812   A/4/413

Messrs. John & George Shutt, Postoffice, Boonsbor-
  ough, Washington County, Maryland

John Shutt &					
George Shutt	Stu	–	8	9 8	N

---

855   18 Jul 1812   A/4/414*

All Receivers

Requests reports to be sent to the General Land Office, rather than to Treasury Department, as previously was the case.

*[Letter out of sequence in register.]

---

856   20 Jul 1812   A/4/413

John Deford? [Defond?], Uniontown, Fayette County,
  Pennsylvania

Transmits patent

John Deford? [Defond?]	Stu	–	5	15 24	SW

---

857   20 Jul 1812   A/4/413

Frederick Baker, Postoffice, Hagarstown, Maryland

Transmits patent

Frederick Baker	Cin EML	5	3	30	SW

---

858   20 Jul 1812   A/4/413

-- Annin, Harper's Ferry, Maryland

Transmits patents

Joseph Hoffman	Chl MS	22	2	34	+
Joseph Hoffman	Chl MS	22	2	35	+

---

859   20 Jul 1812   A/4/414

Thomas Freeman, Esq.

Discusses claim & agrees that it is such a hard one
  to decide that Hook should apply to Congress for
  relief

-- Hook	WPL?	–	3	1	– –

---

860   20 Jul 1812   A/4/415

Samuel Smith, Esq., Capitol Hill

Transmits commission from U.S. President appointing
  Smith to be Receiver at Washington, Mississippi
  Territory "for lands of the United States East of
  Pearl River."

---

861   20 Jul 1812   A/4/415

LO Jef

Transmits patents

Henry Wyman	Jef	–	4E	1S	2	NW
James Arbuckle	Jef	–	9E	3N	19	SW
Henry Wyman	Jef	–	4E	1S	3	NE
Jonathan Lyon	Jef	–	10E	4N	27	SE
William Kelly	Jef	–	10E	1N	7	NE

---

862   20 Jul 1812   A/4/415

Jacob Tent, Chambs., Franklin County, Pennsylvania

Transmits patent

Jacob Tent	Can	–	18	19	9	NW

---

863   20 Jul 1812   A/4/416

LO Stu

Transmits patents

Aaron Brooks	Stu	–	1	6	9	NW
Aaron Brooks	Stu	–	1	6	5	SW
William Reed	Stu	–	2	10	18	NE
Robert Reley	Stu	–	4	15	21	NE
Thomas Wilson	Stu	–	5	10	17	NW
George Winrod?	Stu	–	6	10	14	NE
Evan Jeffreys	Stu	–	4	15	20	SW

---

864   20 Jul 1812   A/4/416

LO Can

Transmits patents

John Ockerman?	Can	–	19	18	4	SW
Robert Newell	Can	–	16	22	25	NW
Jacob Newman	Can	–	18	21	36	NE
John Leedy	Can	–	18	19	35	SW
David Lane	Can	–	17	23	31	NW
Thomas Newman	Can	–	15	21	23	NW
Joseph Friend	Can	–	17	21	3	NE
Henry Crites	Can	–	10	1	28	SE
Frederick Stump	Can	–	10	12	34	SW

---

865   20 Jul 1812   A/4/416

LO Cin

Transmits patents

William Carton	Cin WML	2	10	3	SW
John Kemp	Cin EML	4	2	4	SE
William Marks & M. Crume?	Cin EML	3	3	34	W
Caleb Lewis	Cin EML	4	7	11	NW
David Long	Cin EML	4	2	20	–
J. Miller & S. Clarke	Cin EML	3	3	26	NE
John Davison	Cin WML	1	13	8	N
William Miles, heirs of	Cin EML	5	7	31	SE
Andrew Zeller	Cin EML	4	3	25	–
Henry Hapner	Cin EML	3	6	4	NE
Jacob Delader	Cin EML	4	4	34	–?
Nathan Porter	Cin WML	1	8	19	SE?
Abraham Wimmer	Cin EML	3	4	3	NW
Martin Baum	Cin EML	2	5	26	NW
Ralph Brown	Cin EML	2	5	26	NE
R. Ewing & William Carrick	Cin EML	5	5	9	E
William Jay	Cin EML	5	6	6	SE
Abel Pearson	Cin EML	6	4	9	SW
Sarah Jennings	Cin EML	6	4	17	NW
Abraham Studebaker	Cin EML	5	8	31	SE
Stephen Wood	Cin EML	1	1	2	–?
Stephen Wood	Cin EML	1	1	11	+?
Samuel Patterson	Cin EML	1	6	30	E
Henry Garner	Cin EML	1	3	2	NE
Francis Ott	Cin EML	3	7	19	NW

---

866   20 Jul 1812   A/4/417

Levin Wailes, [Reg Opel]

Transmits Act of Congress "giving validity to the
  sale of certain tracts of public lands sold in the
  Western district of the territory of Orleans."

---

867   20 Jul 1812   A/4/417

William R. Johns, Georgetown

Transmits patent

Dennis Lockland	Mil	–	4	10	3	15

868   20 Jul 1812   A/4/417
James Kilburn, Esq., Worthington, Ohio
Transmits commission from the U.S. President appoint-
    ing ". . . yourself, William Ludlow, & Samuel Her-
    rick commissioners . . . for the purpose of ascer-
    taining, surveying, & marking the western boundary
    of the [Virginia Military District of Ohio]. The
    commissioners appointed [by] the State of Virginia
    are Generals Abraham Trigg, Robert Porterfield, &
    J. G. Jackson. . . ."

869   20 Jul 1812   A/4/418
William Ludlow, Esq., Oxford, Butler County, Ohio
Transmits commissions [with same text as in entry
    868]; a similar letter sent to Samuel Herrick, Esq.

870   20 Jul 1812   A/4/418
Charles Roberts, Zanesville
Transmits patents

Nathan Roberts*	Mil	-	5	3	3	21
Elias Green**	Mil	-	5	3	3	28
Elias Green***	Mil	-	5	3	3	27
Abner Wade#	Mil	-	6	2	1	3
Abner Wade#	Mil	-	6	2	1	4
Abner Wade#	Mil	-	6	2	1	5

*Assignee of William A. George.
**Assignee of John Cary.
***Assignee of David Brown.
#Assignee of Robert Durkee.

871   20 Jul 1812   A/4/418
Hon. John Smilie, Connelsville, Pennsylvania
Transmits patents

| John Mossman | Zan | - | 8 | 4 | 21 | NE |
| John Mossman | Zan | - | 8 | 4 | 24 | SE |

872   21 Jul 1812   A/4/419
Captain Jonathan Walton
Transmits patents for private claims in LO Det dis-
    trict

Claimant	Acres	Location
David Mitchell	--*	at Michillimackinac
-- Murdock &		
-- Cameron	--**	at Michillimackinac
Toussaint Pothier	--***	at Michillimackinac
François Magnen de Servieres?	207.17	on river Raisin
Oliver Ricard	146.54	on river St. Clair
François Chartier	108.57	on river St. Clair
Joseph Ricard	118.87	on river St. Clair
Isaac Ganier, heirs of	80.00	on river Rouge
Nicholas Patenode? Senior	96.57	on lake St. Clair
François Bonome	583.00	on river a Dube?
Louis Chapoton	134.59	on river Huron of Lake Erie
Alexander Grant, Esq.	255.85	on lake St. Clair
Christian Clemens, Esq.	235.66	on river Huron of Lake Erie
Pierre Grifford?	105.88	on river Detroit
Antoine Nicholas Petit	180.76	on river St. Clair
James Baby, Esq.	364.20	about a fork of river Rouge
George McDougal, Esq.	--#	on river Raisin
Robert Robertson?	54.72	on river Huron of Lake St. Clair

Josiah Bleakley	--##	at Michillimackinac
Jacques Giasson, heirs of	--###	at Michillimackinac
Charles Chandonet	--§	at Michillimackinac
John Campbell, heirs of	--§§	at Michillimackinac

*31,395 square feet.
**34,790 square feet.
***72,177 square feet.
#416/11,000 of an acre.
##36,230 square feet.
###19,945 square feet.
§91,200 square feet.
§§21,280 square feet.

873   21 Jul 1812   A/4/419
Daniel C. Cooper, Esq., care of Abraham Beadley, Esq.
Transmits patents

| Daniel C. Cooper | [Cin] Pre | 7 | 1 | 4 | + |

874   21 Jul 1812   A/4/420
Daniel Symmes, [Reg Cin]
Transmits certificate

| Charles Rector | Cin Pre | 10 | 4 | 12 | E |

875   23 Jul 1812   A/4/420
Captain Jonathan Walton, Schenectady
Transmits patents for private claims in LO Det dis-
    trict

Claimant	Acres	Location
Joseph Livernois, Junior	135.00	on River Rouge
Pierre Mini	207.60	on River Huron of St. Clair
Alexander Harrow, heirs of	640.00	on River Huron of St. Clair
George Cotterall) Henry Cotterall) John Cotterall)- James Cotterall) David Cotterall)	430.47	on River Huron of St. Clair
George Cotterall	319.82	on River Huron of St. Clair
Lewis Moran	76.12	on Detroit River
Ichabod Leech	540.70	on River Raisin
Antoine Lasselle, Junior	110.00	on River Raisin
Pierre Tessier, widow & heirs of	159.37	on River Raisin
Dr. Joseph Dozet	35.90	on River Raisin
Alexis Corrait dit Coquillard	105.54	on River Rouge
Wardens of the Church of St. Antoine	56.50	on River Raisin
Jean Baptiste Chovin, widow & heirs of	118.88	on Detroit River

876   23 Jul 1812   A/4/421
-- [not given]
Transmits patents for private claims in LO Det dis-
    trict. [This entire entry cancelled in register
    as erroneous.]

Claimant	Acres	Location
Samuel Lashley	--*	on Island of Michilli- mackinac
Ann Coates	507.26	on River Rouge
Richard Conner, widow & heirs of	640.00	on south border of river Huron of St. Clair

Claimant	Acres	Location
Francis Denoyer	63.12	on south side of River aux Sables
Christian Clemings, Esq.	-	

*24,400 square feet.

877   23 Jul 1812   A/4/421
LO Jef
Transmits patents

Alexander McKay	Jef	-	9E	4N	3	SW
James Stark	Jef	-	9E	1N	14	SE
Richard Giltner	Jef	-	9E	2N	36	NW
Abraham Wiseman	Jef	-	3E	5S	35	NW
John Kester	Jef	-	9E	1N	2	SW
Samuel Ledgerwood	Jef	-	11E	4N	19	SW
James Arbuckle	Jef	-	9E	3N	19	SE
Robert Marshall	Jef	-	8E	3N	20	NE
Henry Resline	Jef	-	10E	4N	35	NW
John Taylor	Jef	-	11E	4N	36	SE
John Taylor	Jef	-	10E	4N	32	SE
Alexander Persinger	Jef	-	4E	4N	6	NW
Robert Marshall	Jef	-	8E	3N	15	SW
Adam Bower	Jef	-	9E	1N	8	SE
Peter Hubbard	Jef	-	4E	2N	8	SE

878   23 Jul 1812   A/4/421
Felix Welton, Moorfields, Virginia
Transmits patent

Felix Welton	Cin	MR	10	5	17	NE

879   23 Jul 1812   A/4/421
David Osborn
Transmits patent

David Osborn	Cin	MR	12	5	9	SW

880   23 Jul 1812   A/4/422
William Penquite
Transmits patent

William Penquite	[Stu?]	-	2	11	17	NE
William Penquite	[Stu?]	-	2	11	17	NW

881   23 Jul 1812   A/4/422
John Pigott
Transmits patent

John Pigott	Stu	-	6	10	2	SE

882   23 Jul 1812   A/4/422
George Prince
Transmits patent

George Prince	Stu	-	8	10	15	NE

883   23 Jul 1812   A/4/422
Benjamin Knight
Transmits patent

Benjamin Knight	Stu	-	6	13	34	NW

884   23 Jul 1812   A/4/422
Captain Jonathan Walton, Schenectady
Transmits patents for private claims in LO Det district

Claimant	Acres	Location
Samuel Lashley	--*	on island of Michillimackinac
Ann Coates	507.26	on River Rouge

Claimant	Acres	Location
Richard Conner, widow & heirs of	507.26	on south bank of river Huron of Lake St. Clair
François Desnoyer	63.12	on south bank of River aux Sables
Christian Clemens, Esq.	256.41	on River Huron of Lake St. Clair
Nicholas Campeau	314.20	on River Huron of Lake St. Clair
Julian Campeau	108.88	on Lake St. Clair
Whitmore Knaggs**	600.00	on Miami River
William Brown, Esq.	600.80	on Miami River
Whitmore Knaggs	600.00	on Miami River
Charles Rouleau?	129.79	on River Rouge
Christian Clemens & James Conner	606.81	on River Huron of Lake St. Clair
Colonel Gabriel Godfrey	103.60	on River Raisin

*24,400 square feet.
**Assignee of Archibald Lyons.

885   23 Jul 1812   A/4/423
P[eter] Mills, Zanesville
Transmits patents for refugees, which have been delayed. Patents for heirs of Edward Antill were forwarded to -- Gold; those for Charlotte Hazen will be sent to -- Bleecker
3 patents for Elijah Ayer
1 patent for Elijah Ayer, Junior
2 patents for John Fulton
1 patent for the heirs of Gilbert Seamans
2 patents for Joshua Sprague.

886   23 Jul 1812   A/4/423
Hon. Harmanns Bleecker, Albany [New York]
Transmits three patents for Charlotte Hazen for lands in the Refugee Tract [of Ohio].

887   25 Jul 1812   A/4/424
Jacob Henderlick, Postoffice, Baltimore
Transmits patent

Jacob Henderlick	Chl	-	19	16	18	NE

888   25 Jul 1812   A/4/424
Jeremiah Topkin, Postoffice, Baltimore
Transmits patent

Jeremiah Topkin	Zan Mil	5	1	9	NW

889   25 Jul 1812   A/4/424
-- Bachtel, Hagarstown? Maryland
Transmits patent

-- Bachtell	Stu	-	8	10	21	SE

890   25 Jul 1812   A/4/424
LO Can
Transmits patents

Philip Slusher	Can	-	10	12	14	NE
Zephaniah Beale	Can	-	10	1	27	SE
John Smith	Can	-	10	11	4	-
Jacob Newman	Can	-	19	21	25	SE

891   25 Jul 1812   A/4/425
Dennis Boyse, Mercersburgh, Pennsylvania
Transmits patent

Dennis Boyse	Cin EML	2	5	18	SE

892   25 Jul 1812   A/4/425
Laurence Shell, Postoffice, Libertytown, Frederick
  County, Maryland
Transmits patent

| Laurence Shell | Cin EML | 3 | 5 | 17 | W |

893   25 Jul 1812   A/4/425
Messrs. -- Henderson & -- Calhoon, Baltimore
Transmits patent

| -- Henderson & -- Calhoon | Chl | - | 21 | 2 | 6 | + |

894   25 Jul 1812   A/4/425
Thomas Herty, Pen[nsylvania] Avenue, [Washington,
  D.C.]
Transmits patents

Thomas Jones*	Vin	- 13W	7S	7	+
Thomas Jones	Vin	- 2E	4S	7	+
Thomas Jones	Vin	- 2E	4S	8	+
Thomas Jones	Vin	- 2E	4S	17	+

*"Whose address is not known to this office."

895   25 Jul 1812   A/4/425
Isaac Van Horn, Esq., Zanesville
Transmits patents

| Isaac Van Horn | Zan Mil | 2 | 1 | 21 | NE |
| Isaac Van Horn | Zan Mil | 2 | 1 | 21 | SE |

896   25 Jul 1812   A/4/426
LO Chl
Transmits patents

Abraham Peters	Chl	-	20	12	10	SE
George Glaze	Chl	MS	21	9	10	NW
George Nigh	Chl	-	20	12	10	NE
Emanuel Carpenter	Chl	-	19	13	9	-
William Rollins	Chl	-	20	2	18	NW
George Walters	Chl	-	20	13	9	NE
Anthony Rapeholts	Chl	-	20	9	31	NW
Jacob Cagy	Chl	-	18	16	26	NE

897   25 Jul 1812   A/4/426
John W. Plummer, New Market, Frederick County, Mary-
  land
Transmits patent

| John W. Plummer | Chl Mil | 14 | 8 | 12 | SW |

898   25 Jul 1812   A/4/426
LO Jef
Transmits patents

David Lindley	Jef	- 1E	1N	21	NW
Thomas Lindley	Jef	- 1E	1N	20	NE
George Brook	Jef	- 4E	2N	8	NE
George Brook	Jef	- 4E	2N	8	NW
David Findly	Jef	- 1E	3N	34	NE
Linsfield Barnham	Jef	- 10E	4S	28	SE
Jacob Dean	Jef	- 2E	1S	4	NE
Owen Lindley	Jef	- 1E	1N	17	NE
Owen Lindley	Jef	- 1E	1N	17	SE
Jacob Molsenger	Jef	- 4E	1N	2	SE
George Summers	Jef	- 3E	4N	1	+
John Pittman	Jef	- 3E	4S	9	SE

899   24 Jul 1812*   A/4/426
David Moody
"You should shortly receive the following patent"

| Sterling Johnson** | Stu | - | 4 | 7 | 7 | NW |

*Out of sequence in register.
**Assignee of Adam Walter.

900   24 Jul 1812   A/4/427
Abraham Taylor, Franklinton, Ohio
General -- Worthington deposited papers relative to
  the claims of certain of the refugees from Canada
  & Nova Scotia. "In your capacity as agent appointed
  by the parties, [the following patents are trans-
  mitted]. . . . For the claim of John Taylor, no
  location was made by you. . . ." Also encloses
  documents deposited ". . . to facilitate confirmation of the claims of the heirs of -- Raynolds;"
  mentions Benjamin Raynolds; Hon. Jeremiah Morrow.
  [The General Land Office retained true copies of
  the documents returned.]

Robert Sharp	Ref	-	21	12	8	W
Robert Sharp	Ref	-	21	12	8	E
Nathaniel Reynolds, heirs of	Ref	-	18	17	26	E
Nathaniel Reynolds, heirs of	Ref	-	18	17	29	E
Nathaniel Reynolds, heirs of	Ref	-	18	17	29	W
John Morrison	Ref	-	17	19	7	E
John Morrison	Ref	-	21	12	26	E
David Dickey	Ref	-	21	12	20	E

901   24 Jul 1812   A/4/428
Captain Jonathan Walton, Schenectady
Transmits patents for private claims in LO Det dis-
  trict

Claimant	Acres	Location
Michael Tremble	244.96	on river Huron of Lake St. Clair
George Shindler	75.65	on Lake Huron
John Meldrum	422.17	on Lake St. Clair
Louis Griffard	217.59	on river Detroit
Michael Daussman	640.00	on island of Bois Blanc
David Beard, Esq.	334.96	on river Rouge
Louis Monmini	195.70	on La riviere aux Loutres?
Solomon Sibley	385.18	on La riviere aux Loutres?
Col. Gabriel Godfrey	449.42	on River Raisin
Jean Baptiste Petit	91.43	on Lake St. Clair
Jacques Lasselle	101.94	on River Raisin
Solomon Sibley	387.70	on River aux Loutres
Jean Duseau	99.88	on River aux Loutres
Jean Baptiste Lapointe	187.77	on River aux Loutres
François Nalliquet? [Valliquet?]	95.96	on River aux Loutres
François Nalliquet? [Valliquet?]	185.47	on River aux Loutres
Jacques Lasselle & François Lasselle	252.47	on River aux Loutres
Jean Baptiste Lasselle	193.38	on River aux Loutres
Charles Gouin, Senior	107.30	on Lake St. Clair
Ambroise Langlois dit Traversis?	361.55	on River Raisin
Jacques Lasselle & François Lasselle	304.34	on River Raisin
Pierre Fourcreaux?	73.76	on La grandes Coulés
-- Meldrum & -- Park	600.00	on River St. Clair
William Griffith, Junior	409.82	on River Raisin
Michael Daussman	--*	on Lake Huron
Jean Baptiste Faillon? [Taillon?]	197.26	on La riviere aux Loutres
Nicholas Drouillard, heirs of	111.14	on La riviere aux Loutres

*25,501 square feet.

902		27 Jul 1812			A/4/429

Isaac Clendenon, Belmont County, Ohio
Cancels original patent & transmits corrected one

Isaac Clendenon	Stu	–	5	7	33	NE

903		27 Jul 1812			A/4/429

LO Cin
Transmits patents

Abraham Studebaker	Cin	EML	4	9	30	SW
Spencer (a free man of color)	Cin	WML	1	13	34	NW
John Lennon	Cin	MR	11	2	19	NE
Isaac Darnell	Cin	MR	11	4	33	SW
Abraham Friend	Cin	MR	9	2	27	NW
George Buffinburgher	Cin	MR	8	6	35	+
Samuel Black	Cin	MR	13	3	3	NE
John Adney	Cin	MR	12	2	31	SW
John Knight	Cin	MR	11	2	13	SW
Daniel Keplinger	Cin	MR	10	4	2	NW
John Holderman	Cin	MR	9	2	32	SW
Richard Gray & Robert Gray	Cin	MR	7	2	26	NW
James Irwin	Cin	MR	9	2	15	NE
George Croft	Cin	MR	9	3	8	W
Andrew Redenbaugh	Cin	MR	11	1	23	NE
John Enoch	Cin	MR	9	4	34	S
Nathan Fitch	Cin	MR	11	5	35	SE
William Beard	Cin	MR	9	6	30	SE
James Turner	Cin	MR	12	5	17	NW
Jesse? Harbour	Cin	MR	12	4	29	NW
John Millhouse	Cin	MR	12	1	21	SW
Jacob Treber & Joseph Treber	Cin	MR	9	3	27	SE
A. Richards & E. Richards	Cin	MR	12	3	2	SW
Lewis Drake	Cin	MR	4	3	8	NW
Anthony Logan	Cin	MR	6	2	26	NE
James Irwin	Cin	MR	9	2	15	NW

904		27 Jul 1812			A/4/430

Benjamin Van Cleve, Dayton, Ohio
Transmits patent

Benjamin Van Cleve	Cin	MR	8	2	27	SE

905		27 Jul 1812			A/4/430

LO Chl
Transmits patents

Andrew Peck	Chl	–	20	15	5	NW
Christian Whiteman	Chl	MS	21	9	26	NW
Joshua Hedges, heirs of	Chl	MS	22	2	13	SE
Thomas Emmerson	Chl	MS	21	10	18	W
John McNeal	Chl	WS	21	11	18	NW

906		29 Jul 1812			A/4/430

James Davidson, Esq., F Street [Washington, D.C.?]
Transmits patent

John Wander	Cin	Pre	5	3	14	SW

907		29 Jul 1812			A/4/431

Martin Strickler, New Market, Sh [Shenandoah?]
County, Virginia
Transmits patents

Martin Strickler	Cin	Pre	11	4	23	W
Martin Strickler	Cin	Pre	11	4	17	SW

908		29 Jul 1812			A/4/431

Isaac Kershner, Hagerstown, Maryland
Transmits patents

Isaac Kershner	Cin	Pre	9	4	1	SW
Isaac Kershner	Cin	Pre	9	4	1	SE

909		29 Jul 1812			A/4/431

Hon. Samuel Ringold
Transmits patents

Martin Kershner	Cin	Pre?	8	3	1	NW
Martin Kershner	Cin	Pre?	7	3	27	3
Martin Kershner	Cin	Pre?	7	3	27	NE

910		29 Jul 1812			A/4/431

Andrew Reed, Xenia, Ohio
Transmits patent

Andrew Reed	Cin	Pre	8	3	14	2

911		29 Jul 1812			A/4/431

Joseph Pentecost, Washington, Pennsylvania
Transmits patent

Joseph Pentecost	Stu	–	7	9	28	NE

912		29 Jul 1812			A/4/431

Hon. John Pope, Lexington, Kentucky
Transmits patents

Thomas Helm	[Cin]	Pre	8	3	34	+
Thomas Helm	[Cin]	Pre	8	3	35	–

913		29 Jul 1812			A/4/432

Jacob Kershner, Hagerstown, Maryland
Transmits patents

Jacob Kershner	Cin	Pre	9	4	1	NW
Jacob Kershner	Cin	Pre	9	4	1	NE

914		29 Jul 1812			A/4/432

Joseph Copp, New York
Transmits patent; mentions military land warrant 569.

Joseph Copp	[Mil]	–	3	8	4	33

915		30 Jul 1812			A/4/432

James Kilbourn, Esq., Ohio
Delays until 5 October the date on which the commission was to have convened. Similar letters sent to -- Herrick, -- Ludlow, Generals -- Porterfield, -- Trigg, & -- Jackson.

916		31 Jul 1812			A/4/433

Philip Grymes, Reg No1
"If, in the course of your investigations whilst commissioner, any necessity arose for using compulsory measures for obtaining the attendance of witnesses, I wish thank you to inform me what they were. . . . Taking it for granted that the compulsory means used, if any, were such as bore with the smallest possible pressure upon the people, consistent with the object in view, . . . I wish to . . . learn whether any correct precedent has been established on the principle. . . ."

917		31 Jul 1812			A/4/434

William Crawford, Esq., Commissioner of the District East of the Island of Orleans, Warrenton, North Carolina
Discusses the taking of testimony under oath having

to do with settlements not made under any formal grant from French, British, or Spanish sovereigns.

application by Isaac Pence for tract probably meant for that purchased by Benjamin Simontt?

918   31 Jul 1812 A/4/434
George Dove, Harrisburgh, Buckingham County, Virginia
Transmits patent

George Dove	Chl	–	20	15	6	NE

919   31 Jul 1812 A/4/435
LO Chl
Transmits patents

Benjamin Bowman	Chl	–	18	16	8	NE
James Rose	Chl	–	19	16	35	W
Thomas Orr	Chl	–	21	8	14	NE
Isaac Washburn	Chl	–	19	8	7	NW
David Garinger	Chl	–	17	14	4	SW

920   31 Jul 1812 A/4/435
Joseph Wood, Reg Mar
Transmits patent

Philander B. Stewart	Mar	–	4	2	2	+

921   31 Jul 1812 A/4/435
John Laucks, Little York, Pennsylvania
Transmits patent

John Laucks	Chl	–	20	15	33	W

922   31 Jul 1812 A/4/435
William Raynolds, Canton, Ohio
Transmits patents

William Raynolds	[Can?]	–	9	11	19	NE
William Raynolds	[Can?]	–	9	11	19	SE

923   31 Jul 1812 A/4/435
LO Cin
Transmits patents

John Pence	Cin Pre	9	4	12	+
Isaac John	Cin Pre	4	4	9	+
John Gilliand	Cin Pre	9	4	28	SE
Daniel Wilson	Cin Pre	6	2	20	+?
Alexander Huey	Cin Pre	7?	2	14	+
Isaac Clyne?	Cin Pre	10	2	23	NW
William Low	Cin Pre	8	3	31	+
David Archer	Cin Pre	6	2	19	+
Moses Winters	Cin Pre	10	2	13	SW
John McDye	Cin Pre	10	2	34	NE
John Mench? [Rench?]	Cin Pre	7	2	23	+
John Mench? [Rench?]	Cin Pre	7	2	24	+
Colin Campbell	Cin Pre	4	2	6	W
John Bigger	Cin Pre	4	3	25	NE
Edward Ralston	Cin Pre	4	3	31	–
Isaac Shingledecker	Cin Pre	7	3	27	NE
Thomas Clawson	Cin Pre	6	2	31	SW
Thomas Wallace*	Cin Pre	9	3	34	E

*This entry entirely crossed out.

924   1 Aug 1812 A/4/436
Daniel Symmes, [Reg Cin]
Comments on discrepancies noted

John Stoneberger*	Cin MR	12	4	31	SE
James Galloway	Cin Pre	7	3	5	E
John Jackson	Cin Pre	9	3	16	N

*Patented to Stoneberger. Report that land had reverted to the United States must be in error;

925   1 Aug 1812 A/4/436
G. Bomford, New York
Discrepancy noted in military land warrant 1654, issued to William Price, late a lieutenant in the revolutionary army.

926   3 Aug 1812 A/4/437
John McLean, near Dayton, Ohio
Transmits patent

John McLean	Cin Pre	6	2	10	W

927   3 Aug 1812 A/4/437
LO Cin
Transmits patents

George Patty	Cin MR	12	5	30	SW
Thomas Wallace	Cin Pre	9	3	34	E
Samuel Logan	Cin MR	10	5	32	SE
John Thomas	Cin MR	11	5	26	NW
Peter Weaver	Cin MR	9	2	27	SE
John Clark	Cin MR	1	4	26	SW
Samuel Line	Cin MR	12	1	15	SE
Joel Harbour	Cin MR	12	3	6	SW
William Wilson	Cin MR	10	5	3	SE
Abraham B. Roll	Cin MR	9	3	33	NW
Abraham Snider	Cin MR	9	6	30	NW
John Carbley	Cin MR	11	1	23	SE
John Ross	Cin MR	9	2	27	SW
William Hall	Cin MR	9	5	4	S

928   4 Aug 1812 A/4/437
-- Knoblauch, Glasshouse, Washington
Transmits patent "for your friend"

Conrad Heyle	Chl	–	19	16	25	NE

929   4 Aug 1812 A/4/438
Peter Audrain, [Reg Det]
Discusses legal question arising from a conveyance by Francis Paul Malcher (private claimant to 347.12 acres on river Detroit) to Lewis Bienfait?, Joseph Serre *dit* St. Jean, Benoit Chapoton, Charles Rivard, & François Rivard for life annuity & payment to the son of Hypolite A. Bernard?.

930   4 Aug 1812 A/4/438
Richard Forrest, [U.S. Department of State]
Asks for a speedy return of records.

931   6 Aug 1812 A/4/439
LO Cin
Transmits patents

Abraham Vaneaton?	Cin WML	2	11	14	NW
Francis Jones	Cin EML	5	6	29	SE
John Hoover	Cin EML	5	6	29	NE
Thomas Harper	Cin WML	1	10	3	S
David Patty	Cin EML	4	9	33	NW
Joseph Idings	Cin EML	5	7	34	SW
Abraham Holderman	Cin EML	3	5	7	SE
Henry Knull	Cin EML	6	2	18	NW
Daniel Rex	Cin EML	3	7	33	SW
Samuel Ward	Cin EML	2	7	12	NW
William Murray	Cin EML	2	4	35	NW
William Murray	Cin EML	2	4	28	NE

James Sutton	Cin EML	2	6	3	E
Timothy Marsh	Cin EML	2	6	3	SW
William Murray	Cin EML	2	4	26	W
Samuel Robinson	Cin EML	1	7	4	SE
E. Farr & children	Cin EML	6	4	27	SW
William Duboise	Cin WML	1	10	30	SE
David Bradberry	Cin EML	3	6	36	SE
John McClellan	Cin EML	2	5	12	NE
Adam Reed	Cin WML	1	9	5	SW
John Ehrstine	Cin EML	5	4	2	–
William Long	Cin EML	5	7	17	SW
John Rench	Cin WML	5	5	28	NE
William Long	Cin EML	5	7	18	SE
Amos Hawkins	Cin EML	2	6	25	SE
James Willson	Cin EML	1	9	11	NW
Daniel Leare? [Leave?]	Cin EML	3	7	28	SW
Peter Keen	Cin EML	2	5	13	NW
Thomas Harper	Cin WML	1	10	11	N
William Miles, heirs of	Cin EML	5	6	6	NE
Samuel Nixon	Cin EML	1	4	30	SE
John Musselman	Cin EML	5	4	31	NW
Samuel Shannon	Cin WML	1	10	6	SW
John Waggoner & P. Waggoner	Cin EML	5	4	36	–
Samuel Patterson	Cin EML	1	6	19	SE
Gideon Wilkinson	Cin WML	1	9	9	NW
William King	Cin EML	5	5	34	SW
Matthew Huston	Cin EML	2	5	35	W
John Waggoner	Cin EML	5	5	8	SE
John James	Cin WML	1	5	3	–
Benjamin Byram	Cin EML	1	9	32	SE
Isaac Swearingen	Cin EML	6	7	10	SE
James McDill	Cin EML	1	6	28	NE
Barnabas Niles	Cin EML	6	5	20	SW

932   6 Aug 1812   A/4/440
Hon. William Crawford, Gettysburgh, Pennsylvania
Hon. Joseph Lefevre, Strasburg, Franklin County,
    Pennsylvania
Samuel Smith, Esq., "late a representative from your
    state, having been appointed receiver . . . for
    lands sold east of Pearl river, has given his bond
    . . . with the following sureties: David McKinney,
    Jacob Smith, Thomas McClelland, James Smith, &
    John M. Maclay."

933   6 Aug 1812   A/4/440
Hon. A. Gallatin
Transmits letter from applicants. Is leaving for
    Ohio with his family.

934   6 Aug 1812   A/4/441
Captain Jonathan Walton, Schenectady
Transmits patents for private claims in LO Det dis-
    trict

Claimant	Acres	Location
Joseph Guy	--*	at Michillimackinac
Adhemar St. Martin, heirs of	--**	at Michillimackinac
-- Trotier & -- Lapointe	--***	at Michillimackinac
Jean Baptiste Carow	--#	at Michillimackinac
Etienne Laviolette	96.22	on la Riviere aux Loutres
McTavish, Frobisher & Company	100.27	on River Rouge
Gabriel Godfroy, Senior	80.00	on River Rouge
Joseph Serre dit St. Jean	199.92	on river Detroit

Claimant	Acres	Location
Hubert Lacroix	106.20	on River Raisin

*6,888 square feet.
**15,873 square feet.
***37,029 square feet.
#2,544 square feet.

935   6 Aug 1812   A/4/442
LO Cin
Transmits patents

Ichabod Corwin	Cin Pre	4	3	20	S
Thomas C. Wade	Cin Pre	4	2	22	NE
James McCleary	Cin Pre	4	3	7	NW
Joseph Vence? [Vance?]	Cin Pre	11	5	27	SW
Daniel Yount	Cin Pre	4	4	14	NW
Thomas Sayers	Cin Pre	10	2	35	NW
Henry Steddam	Cin Pre	4	4	14	NE
David Stinchcomb	Cin Pre	10	1	12	+
William Freeman	Cin Pre	6	2	5	E
William Freeman	Cin Pre	6	2	6	NE
David Curry	Cin Pre	5	4	36	NW
Jacob Saum	Cin Pre	7	3	20	S
Moses Hopping	Cin Pre	7	4	18	+
Edward Covington	Cin Pre	10	5	13	–
Michael Auld	Cin Pre	4	3	6	+
Christian Null	Cin Pre	5	2	1	NE
William Tyler	Cin Pre	10	2	1	NW
James Johnston	Cin Pre	5	2	14	NE
John McDye	Cin Pre	10	1	3	NW
James Hole	Cin Pre	6	2	32	–
Daniel Knoops	Cin Pre	10	2	28	S
Jacob Long	Cin Pre	5	2	18	E
Aaron Nutt	Cin Pre	6	2	25	E
John Ewing	Cin Pre	6	2	33	NE
Thomas Kenton	Cin Pre	11	4	12	S
Alexander Hewston*	Cin Pre	6	2	30	W
Abijah Ward	Cin Pre	11	6	31	SE
Abijah Ward	Cin Pre	11	6	31	SW
John Gordon? [Gondon?]	Cin Pre	5	2	1	NW

*So spelled.

936   6 Aug 1812   A/4/442
Frederick Bates, [Commissioner, St. Louis]
Asks whether transcripts of hearings before Board of
    Land Commissioners, St. Louis, have been sent to
    U.S. Treasury Department, Washington, D.C.

937   7 Aug 1812   A/4/443
John Brahan, Esq., [Rec Hun]
Transmits draft drawn by Lieutenant Alpha Kingsley
    district paymaster, on Robert Brent, Esq., Pay-
    master of the Army of the United States.

938   7 Aug 1812   A/4/443
David Hoge, [Reg Stu]
Transmits corrected patent

Alexander Smith	Stu –	2	9	29	NW

939   7 Aug 1812   A/4/443
Lemuel Henry, late Receiver at St. Stephens [Rec EPR]
    or person authorized to transact his business in
    his absence
The U.S. President has appointed Samuel Smith to suc-
    ceed you as Receiver at Fort St. Stephen's; you
    will turn over all monies, records, etc.

940   7 Aug 1812   A/4/444
Samuel Smith, Receiver St Stephen's [Rec EPR]
Encloses letter [entry 939] to Lemuel Henry & issues
   further instructions.

941   8 Aug 1812   A/4/444
Lewis Sewall, Reg EPR
Payments made for tracts which have never been re-
   ported in the accounts of lands entered
Samuel Coleman   EPR   -   10   3 15   +
Robert McLaughlin   EPR   -   4 10 18   NW
Robert McLaughlin   EPR   -   4 10   7   SE
William Henry &
   James Walsh*   EPR   -   3   8 26   NE
Benjamin Jones   EPR   -   18   3 34   NW
*This might read William Henry Walsh & James Walsh.

942   8 Aug 1812   A/4/445
LO Cin
Transmits patents
Thomas Macy   Cin EML 6   4 31   NW
Jacob Bake   Cin WML 1 10 13   SW
John Mote   Cin EML 5   6 32   SE
Alexander Russell   Cin EML 5   9 35   NW
Frederick Steenberger   Cin EML 6   7 17   SW
Samuel Freeman   Cin EML 6   4 35   -
Samuel Freeman   Cin EML 6   4 36   -
William Campbell   Cin EML 1 10 28   SE
Jacob Rohrar*   Cin EML 5   3 15   SW
David Landies? [Sandies?] Cin WML 1 11   1   SW
Peter Wile   Cin EML 5   5 30   NE
David Fouts   Cin EML 4   3   6   NW
David Fouts   Cin EML 3   5   5   E
George Hollingsworth   Cin EML 5   5 27   SE
Elijah Teague   Cin EML 5   7 28   NW
James David   Cin WML 1 10   6   NE
George Stump   Cin EML 4   3 35   SE
John Jonsten*   Cin EML 6   3 10   NE
William Bruce   Cin EML 2   7   4   NE
Smith Hunt   Cin WML 2 12 12   NW
Jacob Blasdell   Cin EML 1   6 29   NE
Noadiah Potter   Cin EML 2 12 28   SW
John Pool   Cin WML 1 14 35   SW
Ezekiel Ross   Cin EML 1   4 26   NW
Evan Thomas   Cin EML 5   5 34   NE
John Kinnaird   Cin EML 6   8 31   SE
James Bear   Cin EML 4   3   6   NE
Michael Baker   Cin EML 4   6 26   -
William Robeson   Cin EML 2   5 11   NE
Michael Emrick   Cin EML 3   5   5   SW
Samuel Brown   Cin EML 5   8 19   NE
George Holler   Cin EML 4   5 35   NW
John Emrick   Cin EML 2   4 29   SW
Leonard Eller   Cin EML 5   6 26   SE
William Goodwin   Cin EML 3   4 17   NW
Daniel Wilkins   Cin EML 2   2   6   SE
Joel Williams   Cin EML 2   4 34   NE
John S. Riggs   Cin EML 6   2 10   SE
Robert McCormick   Cin EML 1   8 32   SE
Andrew Shirk   Cin WML 1   9 13   SW
William Fouts   Cin WML 1 13 13   NW
William Deniston   Cin WML 1 10 14   SE
Michael Snider   Cin WML 1 12 24   SW
David Mount   [Jef?**] -12E 12N 36   SW
Jacob Grewell   Cin EML 4   4 19   NW
Conrad Darr   Cin EML 2   4   5   NE
John Harney   Cin EML 1   9   9   NW
*So spelled.
**[This is not a normal land description in the LO
   Cin district; it probably refers to land in Indi-
   ana normally sold through LO Jef or LO Vin.

943   10 Aug 1812   A/4/447
Thomas Slooj, Esq., for Daniel Symmes, [Reg Cin]
Statement of account for land originally sold to
   Consley, now to be resold
Thomas Consley   Cin WML 1 13 19   NE

944   12 Aug 1812   A/4/448
James Galloway, Junior, Esq., Xenia, Ohio
Transmits ten pagents [without giving land descrip-
   tions].

945   12 Aug 1812   A/4/448
James Galloway, Junior, Esq., Xenia, Ohio
Transmits nine patents [without giving land descrip-
   tions]; two of these patents for John Galloway,
   [Senior?].

946   12 Aug 1812   A/4/449
G. Bomford, New York
Transmits patents
Henry R. Price*   [Mil] - 11   6   1 28
Henry R. Price*   [Mil] - 11   6   1 29
*"Heir of William Price, late a Lieutenant in Colonel
   Crame's? regiment of artillery."

947   14 Aug 1812   A/4/449
Lewis Sewall, [Reg EPR]
"The location of Jefferson College about to be made,
   it is deemed proper to apprize you what sections
   have ultimately been selected for that purpose in
   order to prevent the sale of any of them in the
   meanwhile."
Jefferson College   EPR   - 2W 10   1   -
Jefferson College   EPR   - 2W 10   2   -
Jefferson College   EPR   - 2W 10   3   -
Jefferson College   EPR   - 2W 10   4   -
Jefferson College   EPR   - 2W 10   5   -
Jefferson College   EPR   - 2W 10   6   -
Jefferson College   EPR   - 2W 10   7   -
Jefferson College   EPR   - 2W 10   8   -
Jefferson College   EPR   - 2W 10   9   -
Jefferson College   EPR   - 2W 10 10   -
Jefferson College   EPR   - 2W 10 11   -
Jefferson College   EPR   - 2W 10 12   -
Jefferson College   EPR   - 2W 10 13   -
Jefferson College   EPR   - 2W 10 14   -
Jefferson College   EPR   - 2W 10 15   -
Jefferson College   EPR   - 2W 10 16   -
Jefferson College   EPR   - 2W 10 17   -
Jefferson College   EPR   - 2W 10 18   -
Jefferson College   EPR   - 2W 10 19   -
Jefferson College   EPR   - 2W 10 20   -
Jefferson College   EPR   - 2W 10 21   -
Jefferson College   EPR   - 2W 10 22   -
Jefferson College   EPR   - 2W 10 23   -
Jefferson College   EPR   - 2W 10 24   -
Jefferson College   EPR   - 2W 10 25   -
Jefferson College   EPR   - 2W 10 26   -
Jefferson College   EPR   - 2W 10 27   -
Jefferson College   EPR   - 2W 10 28   -
Jefferson College   EPR   - 2W 10 29   -
Jefferson College   EPR   - 2W 10 30   -
Jefferson College   EPR   - 2W 10 31   -
Jefferson College   EPR   - 2W 10 32   -
Jefferson College   EPR   - 2W 10 33   -
Indian Reserve, Fuketchoo-
   ponta   EPR   - 2W 10 34   -
Indian Reserve, Fuketchoo-
   ponta   EPR   - 2W 10 35   -

Jefferson College	EPR	–	2W	10	36	–
Jefferson College*	EPR	–	1W	10	30	–
Jefferson College*	EPR	–	1W	10	31	–

*These two sections in lieu of the Indian Reserve
 sections above.

948   14 Aug 1812   A/4/450

William Taylor, Esq., Staunton, Virginia

Transmits patent issued to Anderson Wallace [no land
 description given] "for 580 acres of land in consideration of [his] services for three years as a
 Captain in the Virginia Line on Continental estab-
 lishment. . . ."*

*[A curious transaction, inasmuch as nearly all
 veterans from Virginia took land in the Virginia
 Military District of Ohio, which was not under
 Federal control or supervision.]

949   14 Aug 1812   A/4/450

LO Cin

Transmits patents

Ezekiel Arrowsmith	Cin Pre	11	4	12	N
John Knoops	Cin Pre	10	1	4	+
John Craft	Cin Pre	5	3	21	SE
Ludwick Kemp	Cin Pre	7	2	22	SW+
Joseph Martin	Cin Pre	10	2	17	NW
Abner Gerrard*	Cin Pre	5	3	34	N
George Slip	Cin Pre	5	3	10	E+
John Hershman	Cin Pre	7	2	3	SW
John Huston	Cin Pre	6	2	23	NE
Moses Miller	Cin Pre	8	4	30	–
Jacob Garard*	Cin Pre	5	4	21	+
John McKnight	Cin Pre	6	3	31	+
Zadock Street	Cin Pre	5	3	21	SW
Jeremiah Priest	Cin Pre	10	2	13	SE
John Kent	Cin Pre	7	3	22	SE
Andrew Karr	Cin Pre	4	2	9	S
John Carson	Cin Pre	4	2	25	+
Daniel Kelsey	Cin Pre	5	3	33	+
Aaron Hunt	Cin Pre	4	3	14	W+
Isaac Evans	Cin Pre	11	5	17	N
Samuel Caper? [Cuper?]	Cin Pre	10	2	17	SW
Christian Stephens	Cin Pre	11	4	17	NE
Andrew Stewart	Cin Pre	6	2	12	W+
James Russell	Cin Pre	6	2	31	SE
Daniel Kelsey	Cin Pre	5	2	3	+
Levi Martin	Cin Pre	10	1	3	E
Matthias Pearson	Cin Pre	6	1	9	SE
Robert T. James	Cin Pre	5	3	25	W+
Peter Smith	Cin Pre	11	4	22	NE
Philip Kizer	Cin Pre	11	4	7	E
Henry Pence	Cin Pre	11	4	10	NE
Henry Pence	Cin Pre	11	4	10	SE
Henry Pence	Cin Pre	11	4	10	NW
Henry Pence	Cin Pre	11	4	10	SW+
Lemuel? [Guniel?] Thomas	Cin Pre	5	4	34	+
Ebenezer Heaton?	Cin Pre	4	3	28	N
John Bigger	Cin Pre	4	3	31	+
William James, heirs of	Cin Pre	5	3	3	N
Peter Keslinger	Cin Pre	5	2	15	E
Zadock Street	Cin Pre	5	3	21	NE
Joseph Hanesck?	Cin Pre	5	3	24	W
Sampson Talbert	Cin Pre	12	4	1	SW
Robert Snodgrass	Cin Pre	6	2	2	SW
Uriah Blue	Cin Pre	10	1	18	+
Uriah Blue	Cin Pre	11	1	13	+
John Pence	Cin Pre	10	4	9	S
Stephen Gard? [Garet?]	Cin Pre	7	2	31	SE
John Enock*	Cin Pre	9	4	33	+
William Sweeny	Cin Pre	4	3	3	–

George Lawman	Cin Pre	9	3	23	E
Jonathan Munger	Cin Pre	5	2	4	+
John Enoch*	Cin Pre	9	4	27	+
John Wade	Cin Pre	6	2	24	+
Abel Crawford**	Cin Pre	9	4	27	+
Abel Crawford**	Cin Pre	9	4	27	+
Charles Stewart	Cin Pre	11	5	18	W
Ralph Stafford	Cin Pre	9	2	12	NW
Nathaniel Blackford	Cin Pre	4	4	36	W

*So spelled.

**[Apparently two distinct tracts within the same
 section.]

950   14 Aug 1812   A/4/452

LO Cin

Transmits patents

James Bennett	Cin WML	1	6	23	SE
William Searse?	Cin WML	1	13	9	SE
Nicholas Druly	Cin WML	1	12	10	SE
Stephen Kennedy	Cin EML	5	5	26	NW
Jacob Brower?	Cin EML	4	3	12	SW
Robert McElhany?	Cin EML	6	2	17	SW
Henry Aikenberry	Cin EML	3	5	29	NW
Hugh McDonald	Cin EML	2	7	19	SW
Moses Dooley	Cin EML	2	7	18	SW
Christian Harter*	Cin EML	3	5	27	W
John Bishop	Cin EML	1	6	4	NW
J. Treber & H. Treber	Cin EML	2	5	35	SE
J. S. Mow	Cin EML	4	4	20	NW
David Paesley*	Cin EML	1	6	3	SW
Alexander McBeth	Cin MR	10	5	23	SE
J. Williamson & W. Williamson	Cin MR	8	3	33	NE
J. Williamson & W. Williamson	Cin MR	8	3	33	NW
Edward Evans	Cin MR	10	5	25?	NW
Peter Merrick	Cin MR	9	4	30	NE
Enos Matson	Cin MR	8	2	26	SW
David Price	Cin MR	9	6	2	NW
Jacob Frantz	Cin MR	9	4	17	NE
Jacob Swisher	Cin MR	10	6	25	NW
William Luce	Cin MR	5	3	29	NW
Michael Enotrrie? [Eustrrie?]	Cin MR	12	5	20	NW
Samuel Harlin	Cin MR	5	3	26	NE
William Hamar	Cin MR	7	2	29	NE
Ezekiel Matson	Cin MR	6	2	2	NW
-- Ray & -- Cowan	Cin MR	9	5	9	NW
-- Ray & -- Cowan	Cin MR	9	5	15	NE
Joshua Baldwin	Cin MR	10	5	5	NE
John Davis	Cin MR	12	5	27	SE
Uriah Blue	Cin MR	11	1	23	SW
Henry Snider	Cin MR	8	2	23	SE
James Patterson	Cin MR	10	2	10?	SE
John Keller	Cin MR	1	4	8	SW
Isaac Evans	Cin MR	11	5	1	NE
Michael Fogel	Cin MR	7	3	11	NE
Peter Banta	Cin MR	6	1	20	SE
John Reynolds	Cin MR	11	4	20	NE
David Kizer	Cin MR	12	3	9	SE
Isaac Reynolds	Cin MR	11	5	10	S
Peter Dewitt	Cin MR	8	5	23	SE
John Brownson	Cin MR	11	1	4	SW
-- Thomas & -- Winn	Cin MR	11	5	7	SE
David Williams	Cin MR	4	4	26	NE
Nathaniel Bond	Cin MR	8?	2	24	NW
Michael Wilson	Cin MR	9	2	21	S
Daniel Jones	Cin MR	11	6	28	+

*So spelled.

951
LO WPR 14 Aug 1812 A/5/001
Transmits patents

John Davis	WPR	EML*	2	3	25	-
Hiram Singleton	WPR	WML*	1	1	9	-
Hiram Singleton	WPR	WML*	1	1	2	-
Hiram Singleton	WPR	WML*	1	2	37	-
William Hickman	WPR	EML*	1	2	14	-
Thomas Shropshire	WPR	EML*	8	2	11	-
Samuel Bridges	WPR	EML*	2	11	26	-
Peter Robert	WPR	WML*	2	1	11	-
Daniel Leatherman	WPR	WML*	2	1	7	-
Samuel Lacy	WPR	EML*	1	1	33	-
William Curtis	WPR	EML*	3	1	41	-
William Burd	WPR	EML*	3	1	47	-
John Kneeland	WPR	EML*	3	1	7	-
Francis Graves	WPR	EML*	2	1	9	-
William Cain	WPR	EML*	1	1	12	-
Jonathan Jones	WPR	EML*	1	9	4	-
John Tomlinson	WPR	EML*	1	1	2	-
Samuel Stockett	WPR	WML*	2	1	40	-
Sarah Blanton	WPR	WML*	2	10	9	-
James Dixon	WPR	WML*	1	1	20	-
Josias Gray	WPR	WML*	1	1	44	-
Henry Quine	WPR	WML*	3	2	24	-
John Courtney	WPR	EML*	3	1	30	-
William Lewis	WPR	EML*	3	15	30	-
Duncan Stewart	WPR	EML*	1	1	25	-
Reuben White	WPR	EML*	2	11	17	-
Leonard Hornsby	WPR	EML*	2	3	24	-
William Whitehead	WPR	EML*	1#	6	36	-
William Whitehead	WPR	EML*	1#	7	16	-
William Whitehead	WPR	EML*	1#	7	24	-

*Pre-emption.
#This could read Range 11.

952 17 Aug 1812 A/5/002
Captain Jonathan Walton, Schenectady, N. Y.
Transmits patents for private claims in Detroit district

Claimant	Acres	Location
Col. Gabriel Godfroy	229.69	on River Raisin
-- Godfroy & -- Beaugrand	640.00	on Miami River
Medard Labadi*	83.42	at Lagrande Coulée
John Whipple*	2.00	Northwest side of Miami River
Robert Forsyth	367.50	on Lake St. Clair
William Robison	20.23	on Lake St. Clair
Richard Pattinson	640.00	on North branch of River Huron of St. Clair
Richard Pattinson	640.00	on North branch of River Huron of St. Clair
Joseph Morrisseau	50.25	on Sandy Creek
George Meldrum, in trust	500.00	on River St. Clair
Francis Leonard	614.05	on Riviere aux Loutres
William Cissone, widow and heirs of	262.30	on River Rouge
John Askin	68.36	on River Rouge
Ignace Bouchard	283.97	on River Raisin
-- McDougall & -- Jereaume	269.18	on River Raisin
Nicholas Rivard	166.75	on Lake St. Clair
Frederick Grueter?	--**	at Michillimackinac
Jacob Franks	--***	at Michillimackinac
Prospert Thibault	91.70	on Riviere aux Loutres

Claimant	Acres	Location
John Askin, Junior	622.18	on River Huron of St. Clair

*Pre-emption.
**8,033 square feet.
***32,346.5 square feet.

953
LO Cin 18 Aug 1812 A/5/003
Transmits patents

Thomas Addington	Cin	WML	1	14	8	NE
Allen Ramsey	Cin	WML	2	8	14	SE
Gideon Wilkinson	Cin	WML	1	9	4	SW
William Swaford	Cin	WML	1	11	4	SE
Jacob Kesling	Cin	WML	1	13	28	SE
Jacob Kesling	Cin	WML	1	13	26	SE
John Clarke	Cin	WML	1	13	26	N
John Wilson	Cin	EML	6	2	4	SW
Abraham Myer	Cin	WML	1	11	23	SW
John Pentecost	Cin	WML	1	11	1	NW
Nathan Hawkins	Cin	EML	2	6	36	NW
James Willson	Cin	EML	6	2	9	-
Ms. Roll	Cin	EML	1	4	13	NE
Ms. Roll	Cin	EML	4	17	18	NE
John McLelland	Cin	EML	2	5	19	NE
Joseph Lamb	Cin	EML	5	5	12	SE
Isaac Reynolds	Cin	MR	11	4	21	NE
J. H. Robinson	Cin	EML	2	6	30*	NE
W. Carrington	Cin	EML	4	2	5	NE
Adam Deem	Cin	EML	4	2	5	SE
Jacob Mast?	Cin	EML	5	5	14	W
John Buchanan	Cin	EML	5	6	14	NW
Samuel Pearson	Cin	EML	5	6	3	SE
Jabez Bennet	Cin	EML	1	6	26	NW
Isaac Hart	Cin	EML	3	4	30	NE
John Bridge	Cin	EML	2	7	1	SE
Jacob Embree	Cin	EML	5	7	29	SE
James Youert	Cin	EML	6	4	4	E
Thomas Newman	Cin	EML	5	5	11	NE
John Philips	Cin	EML	1	3	17	NW
Joseph Hazlett	Cin	EML	3	2	17	SE
Othniel Looker	Cin	EML	2	2	18	SE
Joseph Harris	Cin	EML	4	3	26	SE
George Hurlass? [Harlass?]	Cin	EML	3	7	12	SW
S. Broadberry	Cin	EML	2	5	27	NW
Abraham Neaf? [Neal?]	Cin	EML	4	4	35	-
Joseph Rozer	Cin	EML	4	6	24	NW
Alexander Moore	Cin	EML	2	5	8	NE
Jacob Hansell	Cin	EML	1	4	8	NE
H. Whitenger	Cin	EML	1	3	6	SW
Isaac Bear	Cin	EML	4	3	7	SW
Ann Wilson	Cin	EML	3	3	29	W
John Smith	Cin	WML	1	14	32	NE
James Moore	Cin	WML	2	9	30	NE
James Frel	Cin	WML	1	9	3	NW
William Ross	Cin	WML	2	4	30	SE
Samuel Williams	Cin	WML	1	11	1	NE
William Torrence	Cin	WML	1	6	13	SE
David Bell	Cin	WML	2	9	8	NW
Abraham Myers	Cin	WML	1	11	23	SE
J. McDonnell	Cin	EML	5	6	18	NE
Ebenezer Paddock	Cin	EML	1	8	20	SW
J. Coleman	Cin	EML	4	4	19	SW
Jacob Kesling	Cin	EML	1	13	27	SW
L. Shell**	Cin	EML	3	5	17	W

*May read Section 33.
**Previously sent to Libertytown, Maryland, but returned as a dead letter, "he being removed to Ohio."

[77]

954   18 Aug 1812   A/5/004
George Clarke, Shippenburgh, Cumberland County, Pennsylvania
Transmits patent

George Clarke	Can	–	10	12	26	S

955   18 Aug 1812   A/5/004
Joseph Nourse, Esq., Register, U.S. Treasury
Transmits patents

Jacob Humbert	Cin EML	5	3	22	SW

956   19 Aug 1812   A/5/005
John Wade, Sharpsburgh [state not given]
Replies to inquiry regarding "two quarter sections of land for Richard Burch and one quarter for yourself;" final certificates have not yet arrived from LO Zan.

957   19 Aug 1812   A/5/005
Jesse Spencer, [Reg Chl]
Transmits patents; mentions patent of John Senior, sent to Hagarstown, Maryland

George Dilshaser	Chl	–	20	12	17	SE
Hugh O'Hara	Chl	MS	21	9	35	NW

958   21 Aug 1812   A/5/006
James Galloway, Junior, Esq., Xenia, Ohio
Transmits patents [locations not given]

	Acres	Warrant Number
James Galloway, Junior	40	5793
James Galloway, Junior	50	5864
James Galloway, Junior	120	5875
James Galloway, Junior	60	5875
James Galloway, Junior	150	5875
James Galloway, Junior	55	5875
James Galloway, Junior	140	5874
James Galloway, Junior	600	5874
James Galloway, Junior	100	5874

959   21 Aug 1812   A/5/007
LO Vin
Transmits patents

Thomas Pulliam	Vin	–	12W	1N	24	SE
Thomas Hoppore? [Hoppon?]	Vin	–	9W	1N	1	W
John Pitman	Vin	–	3E	3S	31	SW
John Snyder	Vin	–	2E	3S	36	NE
Thomas Casselberry	Vin	–	12W	7S	11	NW
Hosea Smith	Vin	–	8W	1N	28	NE
James Smith	Vin	–	12W	2S	34	NE
Lewis Allen	Vin	–	13W	4S	32	NW
William Bellers	Vin	–	7W	2N	9	NW
Samuel Gill	Vin	–	13W	6S	31	NW
Andrew Johnson	Vin	–	3E	5S	7	NW
Lemuel Baldwin	Vin	–	8W	1N	34	NW
Jacob Luts	Vin	–	5E	5S	1	+
George Humphreys	Vin	–	11W	1S	13	NE
Jesse Emmerson	Vin	–	12W	3S	25	NW
Thomas Tuggle	Vin	–	13W	5S	18	NW
Amos Robinson	Vin	–	13W	6S	17	SE
George Humphreys	Vin	–	11W	1S	35	NW
Joseph Wood	Vin	–	12W	1N	23	SW
John Flickner	Vin	–	5E	2S	26	SW
William Anthony	Vin	–	11W	8S	1	+
William Anthony	Vin	–	11W	8S	12	+
James Murphy	Vin	–	12W	4S	19	NW
John James & Jesse McGary	Vin	–	12W	3S	2	NW
J. C. Veale	Vin	–	7W	2N	17	NW

960   21 Aug 1812   A/5/008
LO Stu
Transmits patents

Joseph Fisher	Stu	–	2	11	24	NW
Thomas McCauslin	Stu	–	3	10	11*	–
Henry Gregory	Stu	–	6	9	28	NE
Many Charles	Stu	–	1	6	19	NW
James Shore	Stu	–	4	15	28	SE
John Slates?	Stu	–	4	11	34	NE
John Richards	Stu	–	9	12	13	SW
Samuel Garby	Stu	–	1	7	3	NE
Abraham Reem	Stu	–	12	1	27	S
William Bailey	Stu	–	6	8	7	SW
Jessee Foster	Stu	–	7	14	31	NE
Thomas Cannon	Stu	–	1	7	30	SE
Horace Potter	Stu	–	3	14	15	SE
Robert Maxwell	Stu	–	3	9	15	NW
W. Johnston (of James)	Stu	–	7	12	23	NE
Peter Leatherman	Stu	–	6	17	17	NW
John Maholm? [Malcolm?]	Stu	–	5	10	31	N
Peter Leatherman	Stu	–	6	17	8	SE
Leonard Roberts	Stu	–	7	15	29	SE
John Cadwallader	Stu	–	6	11	1	SW
James Rogers	Stu	–	3	14	20	SW
Ichabod Davis	Stu	–	3	13	12	SW
Benjamin Wells	Stu	–	8	10	6	SE
Benjamin Wells	Stu	–	8	11	17	NW
Benjamin Wells	Stu	–	5	7	11	SE
William Orr	Stu	–	10	4	38	NE
Samuel Ferguson	Stu	–	5	13	11	SE
William Fife	Stu	–	2	10	8	SW
Christian Carver	Stu	–	8	9	17	NE
Benjamin Wells	Stu	–	3	9	6	SE
John Loney? [Laney?]	Stu	–	5	9	30	NE
Matthias Glass	Stu	–	2	13	22	NW
Thomas Burkhead	Stu	–	5	10	17	NW
Bernard Bower	Stu	–	6	13	27	SE
William Pennock	Stu	–	7	20	14	NW
Samuel Colain? [Coloin?]	Stu	–	7	11	18	NW
James Caldwell	Stu	–	3	6	25	W
Bezaleel Wells	Stu	–	5	11	2	SW
Bezaleel Wells	Stu	–	5	11	2	SE
M. Schwitzer	Stu	–	8	10	12	NW
Mary Charles	Stu	–	2	10	29	SE
William Calahan	Stu	–	4	17	8	NE
Benjamin Miller	Stu	–	9	8	7	NE
John Meason? [Mason?]	Stu	–	9	11	9	W
William Knotts	Stu	–	7	17	30	SW
William McEnterfer	Stu	–	8	18	1	SE
Joshua Reeve	Stu	–	4	17	30	SE
Elisha Teelers	Stu	–	4	17	3	NE
James McCreary	Stu	–	7	16	32	SE
John McWilliams	Stu	–	5	8	23	SW
Andrew McIntosh**	Stu	–	2	9	36	NE
David Bowman	Stu	–	2	13	21	NW
William Crawford	Stu	–	2	10	1	SE
William Smith	Stu	–	4	8	22	W
John Johnston	Stu	–	2	8	15	SE
Joseph Holmes	Stu	–	4	6	5	NW
George Barricklow	Stu	–	5	10	15	SW
Ns. Tipton	Stu	–	6	15	1	NW
George Christy	Stu	–	5	11	19	SW
Samuel McWilliams	Stu	–	5	8	29	SE
Michael Jenkins	Stu	–	5	9	19	–
William Pumphrey	Stu	–	2	5	26	NW
William Pumphrey	Stu	–	3	7	21	NW
-- Forqueher & -- Shaw	Stu	–	2	10	26	NE
John Turnpaugh	Stu	–	5	10	32	SW
Richard Andrews	Stu	–	9	10	17	+
Richard Andrews	Stu	–	9	10	18	+
Samuel Bachtel	Stu	–	9	11	7	NE
Jacob Beckley	Stu	–	4	11	15	NE

Samuel Bosserman	Stu	–	6	17	4	NE
Daniel Easley	Stu	–	6	10	20	–
James Galloway	Stu	–	6	8	35	SW
J. H. Elson	Stu	–	6	14	18	NW
Abraham Craft	Stu	–	8	11	4	E
Bezaleel Wells	Stu	–	5	11	7	NE
Bezaleel Wells	Stu	–	3	15	28	SE
Bezaleel Wells	Stu	–	4	10	34	–
John Riddle	Stu	–	4	10	23	SW
Charles Porter	Stu	–	2	6	13	SW
Josias Reeves	Stu	–	5	8	33	NW
Isaac Haines	Stu	–	6	11	4	SE
Conrad Stinger	Stu	–	9	10	26	NW
Thomas Coney	Stu	–	4	14	11	SW
George Atkinson	Stu	–	3	7	15	SW
George Fetter	Stu	–	8	9	29	SE
Daniel Shuster	Stu	–	7	15	6	SW
Daniel Shuster	Stu	–	7	15	12	SE
John Hergus? [Hugus?]	Stu	–	7	18	11	SE
John Dodds	Stu	–	3	9	21	SE
Jacob Gaunt	Stu	–	4	16	3	–
W. Jarvis	Stu	–	6	9	27	NE
Thomas Griffiths	Stu	–	6	8	24	NW
Moses Hogeland	Stu	–	7	14	31	NW
Thomas Bay	Stu	–	3	11	3	N
Thomas Hale	Stu	–	3	10	15	SE
Enos Ellis	Stu	–	6	16	2	W
Camm Thomas	Stu	–	6	8	7	SE
David Moore	Stu	–	3	14	30	SE
George Holmes	Stu	–	4	6	11	E
J. McLaughlin	Stu	–	2	10	6	NW
Samuel Crawford	Stu	–	1	6	4	NE
J. Bottenburgh	Stu	–	1	4	27	+
J. Bottenburgh	Stu	–	1	4	33	E
-- Whitaker, heirs of	Stu	–	4	15	14	NW

*May read section 14.
**Returned from Land Office and altered in favor of
  Andrew McIntosh from Adam McIntosh.

961   21 Aug 1812 A/5/010
LO Cin
Transmits patents

Robert Grant	Cin	MR	14	4	27	+
Robert Grant	Cin	MR	14	4	28	+
George Leonard & J. Leonard	Cin	MR	12	5	18	SW
William McDonnell	Cin	MR	13	5	22	NE
Henry Robinson	Cin	MR	10	2	33	SW
Samuel Shields	Cin	MR	13	5	33	NW
James McBride	Cin	MR	8	5	28	SE
-- Bumberger, -- Brown, & -- Calhoon	Cin	MR	9	2	31	+
John Cox	Cin	MR	8	3	23	SW

962   24 Aug 1812 A/5/011
Edward Tiffin, Esq., Chillicothe
Discusses a letter from Reg EPR; much land will not
  sell for $2 per acre; ". . . the part of the reg-
  ister's letter which is least understood is that
  concerning the occupancy of the public lands, which
  increases to such a degree on the East side of the
  Tombigbee [River], as to amount to a powerful combination to awe down competition at the public
  sales which may take place;" discusses legal settlement of the area and intruders.

963   24 Aug 1812 A/5/012
Lewis Sewall, Reg EPR
"That part of your letter . . . where you intimate
  that the claimants and occupiers of land east of
Tombigbee [River] have formed a combination to over
  awe competition when the public sales shall take
  place, is not well understood. Be pleased to explain what kind of claimants and occupiers are
  meant. . . ."

964   24 Aug 1812 A/5/013
David Hoge, [Reg Stu]
Instruction to forward patent to Mr. Sutton at St.
  Clairsville, [Ohio]

Jonathan Sutton	Stu	–	3	6	32	–

965   24 Aug 1812 A/5/013
Jonathan Sutton, St. Clairsville, Ohio
Your patent will be forwarded to you by LO Stu

Jonathan Sutton	Stu	–	3	6	32	–

966   24 Aug 1812 A/5/014
Captain Jonathan Walton, [Schenectady, New York]
Transmits patents for private claims in Detroit LO
  district

Claimant	Acres	Location
James McGill	420.60	on Prairie ronde
William Conner	600.00	on River Huron of Lake St. Clair
Richard Pattinson	481.50	on River Huron of Lake St. Clair
Gabriel Godfroy	562.00	on River Huron of Lake Erie
Louis Beufait & Nicholas Loson	207.03	on River Detroit
Joseph Laderout	133.90	on River Detroit
Jonathan Nelson	467.08	on River Rouge
	Square Feet	
Joseph Lafamboise* heirs of	75,566	at Michillimackinac
Joseph Lafamboise* heirs of	22,328	at Michillimackinac
Alexis Laframboise*	16,402	at Michillimackinac
Jacques Giosson	10,227	at Michillimackinac
Dr. David Mitchell	6,177	at Michillimackinac
Daniel Bourasa	112,168	at Michillimackinac
George Shindler	72,883	at Michillimackinac
Simon Champagne	3,563	at Michillimackinac
André Sarrere	3,518	at Michillimackinac
-- Buisson & -- Laroche	9,485	at Michillimackinac
Ignace Petit	2,703	at Michillimackinac
Dr. David Mitchell, in trust	42,592	at Michillimackinac

*So spelled; no doubt Laframboise is correct.

967   27 Aug 1812 A/5/015
John Hepner, Mifflintown, Mifflin County, Pennsyl-
vania
Transmits patents

John Hepner	Can	–	17	22	11	NW
John Hepner	Can	–	16	18	21	–
John Hepner	Can	–	17	22	10	SW
John Metozan	Can	–	17	22	11	NE
John Metozan	Can	–	17	22	2	NE

968   27 Aug 1812 A/5/015
LO Can
Transmits patents

William Hough	Can	–	16	21	25	NW
William Hough	Can	–	16	21	26	SW

William Hough	Can	-	16	21	26	SE
William Hough	Can	-	16	21	26	NE
William Hough	Can	-	16	21	24	SW

969   27 Aug 1812   A/5/015

LO Mar
Transmits patents

Jacob Barker	Mar	-	7	17	11	NE
John Bennett	Mar	-	9	1	26	SE
Allen Cook	Mar	-	7	8	24	NW
D. McKibben? [McThibben?]	Mar	-	7	2	35	NE
Samuel Buskirk	Mar	-	4	3	6	SW
Samuel Dye	Mar	-	7	3	26	SW
John Dye	Mar	-	7	3	26	SE
John Cline	Mar	-	5	3	25	NE
Jane Ward	Mar	-	4	5	10	NW
Ambrose Danford	Mar	-	5	6	4	NE
Levin O'Key	Mar	-	3	4	21	SE
William Hodgin	Mar	-	5	6	33	SW
William Hodgin	Mar	-	5	6	29	NE
John Brown	Mar	-	4	3	24	NW
John Dye	Mar	-	7	3	31	SE
Cornelius Bryan	Mar	-	7	7	30	NE
Isaac Crew	Mar	-	6	7	12	SE
Hulings Ball	Mar	-	7	8	33	NW

970   28 Aug 1812   A/5/016

James Taylor, Esq., Campbell Courthouse, Campbell
County, Kentucky
Transmits four patents in the names of -- Buford &
-- Taylor for Virginia Military Bounty Land lying
between the Little Miami and Scioto Rivers; men-
tions military warrant 988 in favor of William
Musgrove with a chain of assignments containing
the following names: John Gunes, Edmund Baxter,
Edward Patchel, William Cooper, Jacob Smith, Ben-
jamin Rano, John Butler, Joseph Higgins, L. M.
Stockdell; also mentions warrant 108 in favor of
William Green.

971   28 Aug 1812   A/5/017

Shadrack Dial? [Deal?], Union Township, Clermont
County, Ohio
Transmits patent for 388.5 acres of land situated
between the Little Miami and Scioto rivers [Vir-
ginia Military District of Ohio?]

972   31 Aug 1812   A/5/017

Captain Jonathan Walton, Schenectady, New York
Transmits patent for private claim in Detroit LO
district
René Marsac for 70.61 acres on Lake St. Clair

973   31 Aug 1812   A/5/017

Daniel Symmes, [Reg Cin]
Transmits U.S. Treasury receipt; mentions certificate
in favor of George Morningstar and assigned to
David Halberstadt

Alexander Taylor	Cin	-	13	3	9	N
Alexander Taylor	Cin	-	12	4	24	SW

974   31 Aug 1812   A/5/017

Wyllys Silliman, [Reg Zan]
Transmits first certificate

-- Kent & -- Abbot*	Zan	-	14	13	12	NW

*Assigned to Eli House.

975   5 Sep 1812   A/5/018

John A. Fulton, Chillicothe
Transmits "six patents for lands lying between the
little Miami and the Sciota rivers" [Virginia Military District of Ohio]

976   5 Sep 1812   A/5/018

James Craig, New Lisbon, Ohio
Transmits patent

Isaac Craig	Stu	-	6	16	11	N

977   6 Sep 1812   A/5/019

Captain Jonathan Walton, Schenectady, New York
Transmits patents for private claims in Detroit LO
district

Claimant	Acres	Location
André Lamarre	126.58	on Miami Bay
John Askin	400.00	at the foot of the rapids of Miami River

978   7 Sep 1812   A/5/019

Jesse McCay, Chillicothe
Transmits "two patents in your name and one in the
name of George Aske? [Alkier?] for lands lying
between the Little Miami and Scioto rivers;"
[Virginia Military District of Ohio]; mentions an
assignment to John Vanbuskirk

979   10 Sep 1812   A/5/019

Thomas Gibson, [Reg Can]
Requests return of patents, "the owner having appointed an agent to receive them"

William Hough	Can	-	16	21	25	NW
William Hough	Can	-	16	21	26	SW
William Hough	Can	-	16	21	26	SE
William Hough	Can	-	16	21	26	NE
William Hough	Can	-	16	21	24	SW

980   10 Sep 1812   A/5/019

John Johnson, Piquatown, Ohio
Transmits corrected patent of David Clark [land description not given]

981   10 Sep 1812   A/5/020

S. Pleasonton, U.S. Department of State
GLO has made a thorough search for patent certificates
618-622 and 625-630 authorizing issuance of 41 patents in the Symmes purchase [LO Cin district]; "the
omission to record would not have been discovered,
at this time, were it not that one of the said patents came back for correction."

982   15 Sep 1812   A/5/020

Cadwallader Wallace, Esq., Chillicothe
Assignments of warrants improper; mentions patent
issuing in the name of Nathan Reid.

983   15 Sep 1812   A/5/021

LO Jef
Transmits patents

John Royse	Jef	-	3E	1S	15	NW
Christ. Harrison	Jef	-	9E	3N	13	NE
Benjamin Freeman	Jef	-	1E	2N	8	NE
William Lee	Jef	-	1E	2N	3	NE

James B. Mitchell	Jef	-	11E	4N	18	SE
Robert Field	Jef	-	1E	2N	7	SW
Jacob Fouts	Jef	-	8E	2N	23	NE
Henry H. Jones	Jef	-	2E	1S	29	SW
Philip Bowyer	Jef	-	10E	1N	6	NE
Hyram Speer	Jef	-	10E	2N	6	SE
D. Lattimore	Jef	-	9E	4N	30	NE
John Bowyer	Jef	-	10E	2N	31	SE
Amos Chetwood	Jef	-	9E	3N	8	NE
J. Clark, heirs & repre- sentatives of	Jef	-	10E	1N	18	+
J. Clark, heirs & repre- sentatives of	Jef	-	10E	1N	19	+
Robert Lott	Jef	-	11E	5N	28?	NW
Robert London, Senior	Jef	-	10E	2N	19	SW
George Ashe	Jef	-	12E	3N	16	SW
George Ashe	Jef	-	12E	3N	17	SE
George Ashe	Jef	-	12E	3N	20	+
George Ashe	Jef	-	12E	3N	21	+
Peter Mahan	Jef	-	1E	2N	35	SW
William Royse	Jef	-	3E	1S	9	SE
John Miller	Jef	-	4E	1N	31	SE
Gerardus Ryker	Jef	-	11E	4N	20	SW
D. H. Maxwell	Jef	-	9E	3N	13	NW
Thomas Copeland	Jef	-	2E	1N	18	SW
John Vancleave	Jef	-	11E	4N	9	NE
D. H. Maxwell	Jef	-	9E	3N	13	SW
John Giltner	Jef	-	9E	2N	26	NW
M. J. Pullian	Jef	-	11E	5N	2	SE?
Uriah Glover	Jef	-	2E	2N	7	NW
Archibald Dunwiddie	Jef	-	10E	4N	7	NE
James Blankenship	Jef	-	9E	4N	32	SE
Isaac Kindley	Jef	-	5E	2S	36	SE
George Eveleezar?	Jef	-	4E	3S	2	NE
Isaac Harrall	Jef	-	3E	4N	13	SE
Ezekiel Harrison	Jef	-	4E	3S?	2	SW
Jonathan Peter	Jef	-	11E	4N	31	SW
Daniel Eddleman	Jef	-	9E	4N	22	NW
Jacob Young	Jef	-	5E	2S	35	NW
David Finley	Jef	-	1E	2N	2	SW
William Lewis	Jef	-	2E	1N	24	NW
Valentine Coonrad	Jef	-	5E	2S	33	SW
Samuel Bowman	Jef	-	8E	2N	13	SW
David Finley	Jef	-	1E	2N	2	SE
Edward Cooley	Jef	-	4E	2N	28	NW
Josiah Johnston	Jef	-	4E	2N	30	SW
Abraham Bowman	Jef	-	10E	2N	31	SW
Jacob Stark	Jef	-	9E	1N	11	SE
Benjamin Freeman	Jef	-	1E	2N	4	SW
William Lindley	Jef	-	4E	2N	3	SE
William Lindley	Jef	-	4E	2N	11	NW
Benjamin Freeman	Jef	-	1E	2N	7	SE
-- Paul & -- Lyon	Jef	-	10E	4N	35	SE
-- Paul & -- Lyon	Jef	-	10E	4N	35	SW
-- Paul & -- Lyon	Jef	-	10E	3N	2	+
-- Paul & -- Lyon	Jef	-	10E	3N	3	+
William Lindley	Jef	-	4E	2N	2	NW

---

984   17 Sep 1812   A/5/022

James Galloway, Junior, Esq., Xenia, Ohio
Transmits nineteen patents for lands lying between
  the Little Miami and Scioto Rivers [Virginia Military District of Ohio]

---

985   18 Sep 1812   A/5/022

David Hoge, Reg Stu
Transmits corrected patents

William Orr	Stu	-	4	10	28	NE
-- Forquehar & -- Shaw	Stu	-	2	10	26	NE

---

986   21 Sep 1812   A/5/022

Andrew Ellison, Esq., West Union, Ohio
Transmits three patents for lands lying between the
  Little Miami and Scioto rivers [Virginia Military
  District of Ohio]

---

987   21 Sep 1812   A/5/022

James Davidson, Esq., F Street [Washington, D.C.?]
Transmits patents

John Warder*	Cin Pre	9	5	24	+
John Warder*	Cin Pre	9	5	17	-
John Warder*	Cin Pre	9	5	23	-

*Assignee of H. Cadbury.

---

988   22 Sep 1812   A/5/023

John Badollet, Reg Vin; N. Ewing, Rec Vin
Lengthy letter of "rules" implementing Acts of Congress of 23 Apr 1812 and 6 Jul 1812; methods of
  payment for land; forfeitures; publication of lands
  for sale; duties of Register and Receiver; copy of
  "rules" also sent to LO Jef.

---

989   22 Sep 1812   A/5/026

Lewis Sewall, Reg EPR
Inquires whether following tracts are vacant, as
  they have been selected by the trustees of Jefferson College "in lieu of the two sections covered
  by the Reserve of Futcheeponta [see entry 947]

Jefferson College	EPR	-	1W	10	30	-
Jefferson College	EPR	-	1W	10	31	-

---

990   22 Sep 1812   A/5/026

William Pelham, Esq., Falls of Schylkill near Philadelphia, Pennsylvania
Transmits four patents "in your favor . . . for lands
  lying between the Little Miami and Scioto rivers"
  [Virginia Military District of Ohio]

---

991   23 Sep 1812   A/5/026

LO Chl
Transmits patents

Thomas Herbert	Chl	-	21	10	26	SE
James Stanley	Chl	WS	21	9	9	NW
Charles Clymer	Chl	-	20	15	32	SE
Jacob Kester	Chl	-	19	16	9	NW
Robert Hunter	Chl	-	20	13	32	NW
Joseph Petty	Chl	-	16	16	30	SE
George Bower	Chl	-	21	2	33	NW
Risder* Beauchamp	Chl	WS	21	10	17	SW
J. Spangler & G. Spangler	Chl	-	20	11	9	E
Isaac Wheeler	Chl	-	20	11	11	NW
Samuel Ramsey	Chl	MS	21	11	7	W
John Hunser?	Chl	MS	21	9	8	SE
Abner Essery	Chl	-	20	9	18	NW
John Ritter	Chl	MS	21	10	13	NW
Jacob Fast	Chl	-	17	16	25	NW
William Murphy, Junior	Chl	-	18	16	3	NW
John Creviston	Chl	WS	21	10	30	SW
Thomas Watson	Chl	-	18	16	2	NE
Martin Corfman	Chl	-	19	16	20	N
William Law? [Daw?]	Chl	-	16	15	8	SW
James Hardy	Chl	-	21	10	34	SW
John Getz	Chl	-	21	8	24	NE
Abraham Hammasfar?	Chl	-	16	17	24	SE
George Heise	Chl	-	18	16	9	SE
George Heise	Chl	-	18	16	9	NW

Ludwick Kreamer	Ch1	–	20	15	31	SW
David Paine	Ch1	–	17	10	31	SW
-- Strohl, -- Amick, & -- Kesler	Ch1	–	16	16	33	NW
Frederick Besore	Ch1	–	17	17	34	SW
Jonathan Looker	Ch1	–	20	15	5	SE
Francis Kreamer	Ch1	–	11	8	23	NW
George Bolander	Ch1	WS	21	9	2	NW
Joseph Boiler	Ch1	–	21	5	26	NE
Abraham Miller	Ch1	LS	21	3	19	+
Abraham Miller	Ch1	LS	22	3	7	+
Elizabeth Saylor	Ch1	–	21	10	25	NE
John Mooney	Ch1	–	20	10	19	W
Joseph Custard	Ch1	–	17	17	10	NE
David Swayze	Ch1	–	17	17	8	SE
Abraham Pitcher	Ch1	–	17	15	31	SW
John Vanatta	Ch1	–	16	16	32	SW
Stephen Holcomb	Ch1	–	16	7	27	SE
Thomas Whealer*	Ch1	WS	21	9	35?	NE
Henry Strawser	Ch1	–	20	10	12	NE
John Mooney	Ch1	–	20	8	36	NW
John Mooney	Ch1	–	20	8	25	NE
-- Piper & -- Frederick	Ch1	WS	21	9	2	SE
J. Beavelhimer	Ch1	–	20	14	14	NW
Peter Reber	Ch1	MS	21	10	33	SW
Peter Reber	Ch1	MS	21	10	33	SE
Peter Reber	Ch1	MS	21	10	33	NW
Henry Alspach	Ch1	–	20	15	10	SE
Aaron Kinney	Ch1	–	21	1	7	+
Aaron Kinney	Ch1	–	21	1	8	+
William Caldwell	Ch1	WS	21	11	15	N
George Dreshback	Ch1	–	20	12	19	SW
Robert Hampton	Ch1	–	21	6	2	+
Robert Hampton	Ch1	–	21	6	3	+
William Gregg	Ch1	–	19	9	6	NW
Jacob Duflinger	Ch1	–	17	16	11	NE
G. Wilbahan*	Ch1	WS	21	10	34	NW
Robert Dunlop	Ch1	–	21	8	8	NW
James Ballack	Ch1	MS	22	3	13	NW
Darby Kolly? [Holly?]	Ch1	–	20	5	2	SW
John Steely	Ch1	WS	21	10	20	NE
Andrew Friend	Ch1	–	16	5	24	SE
Gabriel Steely	Ch1	WS	21	10	20	SW
Samuel Durben	Ch1	Mil	13	7	2	NE
Caleb Bennett	Ch1	–	20	6	20	SW
Elias Bixler	Ch1	–	19	12	23	SE
John Trimble	Ch1	Mil	13	7	2	SE
Abednoga* Davidson	Ch1	MS	21	11	27	SE
John Good, Senior	Ch1	–	17	18	12	NE
William McIntosh	Ch1	–	20	15	29	NE
Jacob Walters	Ch1	–	16	17	3	SW
John Reed	Ch1	WS	21	10	10	E
John Reed	Ch1	–	17	18	32	NW
Thomas Goldsgher? [Gallegher?]	Ch1	–	20	13	21	NE
William Talbot	Ch1	–	21	5	29	NW
Thomas Evans	Ch1	Mil	21	9	11	SW
Adam Altman	Ch1	Mil	21	9	11	NW
Jane Laverly	Ch1	Mil	22	3	23	NW
John Woodruff	Ch1	Mil	21	10	30	NW
Chris. Rockey	Ch1	Mil	21	10	12	SW
George Ritchey	Ch1	–	20	12	21	SW
Isaac Whitsel	Ch1	WS	21	10	14	SW
Andrew Wilson	Ch1	MS	21	10	7	NW
Andrew Thompson, Senior	Ch1	–	20	15	12	SW
John Heath	Ch1	–	20	7	9	NE
Emanuel Ruffner	Ch1	–	20	13	22	NW
Samuel Dreshback	Ch1	WS	21	11	35	SE
Robert Buckler	Ch1	–	21	3	33	NW
Henry Brown	Ch1	–	21	5	18	+
Hugh Wiley	Ch1	Mil	13	7	9	NE
Daniel Hollingshead	Ch1	–	17	10	20	NW

William Odle, Senior	Ch1	–	21	7	8	NE
J. Alexander	Ch1	–	21	7	8	SE
Henry Ritter	Ch1	–	20	14	5	SE
George Auker*	Ch1	–	16	15	2	SW
*So spelled.						

992		23 Sep 1812			A/5/028	
LO Cin						
Transmits patents						
Calbert Watson	Cin Pre	5	4	33	NE	
William Reeder	Cin Pre	6	2	13	SW	
Noah Tibbals	Cin Pre	5	2	5	+	
John Ewing	Cin Pre	6	2	33	+	
John Larew	Cin Pre	6	2	31	+	
Philip Jarber	Cin Pre	10	5	33	SE	
William Milligan	Cin Pre	4	4	7	–	
Isaac Ely	Cin Pre	7	2	10	SE	
James Galloway	Cin Pre	7	3	5	E	
Joseph Layton	Cin Pre	9	4	32	+	
Samuel Ward	Cin Pre	4	3	24	S	
Henry Creager	Cin Pre	6	2	28	W	
Solomon Stansborough	Cin Pre	5	3	15	SW	
Diana Evans	Cin Pre	4	4	22	+	
Thomas Renton	Cin Pre	11	4	18	SE	
W. C. Schenck	Cin Pre	4	3	17	–	
Jacob Darst	Cin Pre	6	2	12	+	
Jacob Coy	Cin Pre	7	3	25	+	
John A? Fingley? [Tingley?]	Cin Pre	8	2	33	NE	
Parker Adkins	Cin Pre	9	2	3	NW	
Jacob Smith	Cin Pre	7	3	19	SW	
Jacob Smith	Cin Pre	7	3	25	NE	
Jacob Kesling	Cin Pre	5	2	2	SW	
Elizabeth Johnston	Cin Pre	6	1	4	+	
George Gordon	Cin Pre	4	3	21	SE	
Arthur Saylor	Cin Pre	9	3	15	SE	
John Weaver	Cin Pre	7	1	7	+	
John Weaver	Cin Pre	7	1	13	N	
Joseph Evans	Cin Pre	4	4	15	W	
David Worman	Cin Pre	7	1	1	+	
James Breathers	Cin Pre	5	2	23	NE	
Peter Layman	Cin Pre	10	2	31	–	
William Holmes	Cin Pre	9	3	22	NE	
Samuel Winans?	Cin Pre	11	1	14	SW	
John Larew	Cin Pre	6	2	31	+	
John Keever? [Heever?]	Cin Pre	5	3	19	+	
Jesse Edwards	Cin Pre	9	2	9	NE	
Tobias Retter	Cin Pre	7	2	10	W	
William Paul	Cin Pre	9	3	23	W	
Cyrus Osborn	Cin Pre	4	2	27	+	
Cyrus Osborn	Cin Pre	4	2	33	+	
Joseph Williamson	Cin Pre	4	2	15	N	
Thomas Kelsey	Cin Pre	5	3	27	N	
Abraham Inlow	Cin Pre	8	4	6	SW	
Abraham Inlow	Cin Pre	8	4	6	NW	
Francis Sunderland	Cin Pre	10	2	1	NE	
Absalom Westfall & Jacob Westfall	Cin Pre	6	1	17	+	
William Knights	Cin Pre	11	2	31	SE	
John Goodwin	Cin Pre	5	4	33	SW	
Jeremiah Hopping	Cin Pre	8	4	19	SE	
John Winn	Cin Pre	10	5	12	–	
Daniel H. Reeder	Cin Pre	6	2	13	NW	
William Hunter	Cin Pre	4	3	33	NE	
Joel Westfall	Cin Pre	7	1	13	+	
John Vaugne? [Vaugrie?]	Cin Pre	6	2	7	SE	
Abner Cain	Cin Pre	5	4	33	NW	
James Kelsey	Cin Pre	4	3	32	SW	
James Gillespie	Cin Pre	7	2	28	NE	
Noah Tibbals	Cin Pre	5	2	6	SE	
Zadok Street	Cin Pre	5	3	21	NW	
James Long	Cin Pre	4	3	32	NE	

Michael Blue	Cin Pre	11	1	7	SE
Henry Price	Cin Pre	11	4	4	NW
William Skyles*	Cin Pre	9	4	2	NE
Joseph Cram	Cin Pre	5	2	28	N
Edward Wyatt	Cin Pre	9	2	1	NW
Shoble* Veal	Cin Pre	4	2	28	+
Jonathan Crispin	Cin Pre	5	3	14	NE
Ethel Kellog	Cin Pre	5	2	6	W
Elisha Webb	Cin Pre	11	2	25	SW

*So spelled.

993   23 Sep 1812   A/5/030
LO Can
Transmits patents

John Morgan	Can	–	18	22	3	NW
William Gass	Can	–	19	20	12	NW
Charles McKee	Can	–	17	23	31	SE
Henry Clapper	Can	–	10	1	35	NW
Henry Keith	Can	–	18	22	4	NW
Benjamin Fulton	Can	–	10	12	4	NE
Thomas Chapman	Can	–	10	1	35	SW
George Allen	Can	–	11	16	8	NE
Joseph Stibbs? [Hibbs?]	Can	–	13	15	2	NW
Jacob McEnterfer	Can	–	13	16	22	NE
Jacob McEnterfer	Can	–	13	16	23	NW
Joseph Stibbs	Can	–	13	15	3	SE
Ms. Murrow? [Marrow?]	Can	–	11	16	9	N
Joseph Stibbs	Can	–	13	16	34	NE
Thomas Cox	Can	–	13	16	35	SW
Daniel Kilgore	Can	–	10	11	3	NW
Zephaniah Beall	Can	–	10	1	22	SE
Valentine Smith	Can	–	3	15	12	SE
Zephaniah Beale	Can	–	10	1	23	+
Zephaniah Beale	Can	–	10	1	26	+
Henry Clapper	Can	–	10	1	34	SE
Thomas Mullen	Can	–	12	16	20	SE
William Wilson	Can	–	11	17	29	SE
Philip Slusher	Can	–	10	12	13	NW
Peter Ambrose	Can	–	14	19	20	NW
Thomas Drake	Can	–	15	19	4	SW
William Willson	Can	–	11	17	28	SE
Aquilla Hatton	Can	–	10	12	18	–
Thomas Mullen	Can	–	12	16	21	SW
Henry Amaine	Can	–	16	21	24	NE
John Smith	Can	–	17	23	27	SW
John Smith	Can	–	17	22	2	SW
John Yeaman	Can	–	17	23	22	SE
John Yeaman	Can	–	17	23	22	SW
Benjamin Murphy	Can	–	17	24	32	SE
Thomas Carr	Can	–	10	11	21	NW
Nicholas Smith	Can	–	12	16	29	SW
Charles McKee	Can	–	17	23	32	NW

994   23 Sep 1812   A/5/031
LO Stu
Transmits patents

Alexander McBratney	Stu	–	6	9	29	SW
William Addair	Stu	–	2	6	25	SW
Robert Duncan	Stu	–	4	7	1	NW
Jacob Adrian	Stu	–	3	10	19	NE
Henry Carver	Stu	–	7	12	14	SE
A. Burrell	Stu	–	5	10	33	NE
Aaron Brooks	Stu	–	2	11	36	SW
J. Johnson & L. Johnson	Stu	–	6	10	24	SE
William Stoukes?	Stu	–	2	8	21	SE
Adam Yurrack	Stu	–	9	12	23	NE
Daniel Drake	Stu	–	4	7	29	NE
Daniel Shaver?	Stu	–	4	11	35	SW
John Pugh	Stu	–	6	11	33	SW
Reuben Mills	Stu	–	6	8	2	SE

Leonard Hart	Stu	–	4	6	6	SW
Rachel Titus	Stu	–	6	11	1	SE
Thomas Crabtree	Stu	–	6	11	19	SW
John Votaw	Stu	–	3	14	7	SW
John Votaw	Stu	–	3	14	7	NW
Alexander Moore	Stu	–	3	10	17	SE
James Mahan?	Stu	–	5	10	17	SE
Daniel Shuster	Stu	–	7	15	36	NE
George Miller	Stu	–	6	9	28	NW

995   24 Sep 1812   A/5/031
LO Jef
Transmits patents

John Pettit	Jef	–	10E	1N	7	NW
Josiah Johnston	Jef	–	4E	2N	3	NW
Jacob Giltner	Jef	–	10E	1N	6	NW
Jesse Connell	Jef	–	10E	2N	5	+
Jesse Connell	Jef	–	10E	2N	8	+
Jesse Gray	Jef	–	10E	4N	26	NW
Aaron Hegeman	Jef	–	5E	1S	33	SE
James Stark	Jef	–	9E	1N	23	NE
Joseph Scott	Jef	–	2E	1N	10	SE
William Brown	Jef	–	10E	3N	19	+
John Windell	Jef	–	3E	5S	4	NW
Thomas Hodges	Jef	–	5E	2N	19	NW
Amos Wright	Jef	–	3E	2N	25	SE
Joshua Thompson	Jef	–	4E	2N	3	NE
Thomas Ewing	Jef	–	4E	5N	31	NW
Arthur Parr	Jef	–	4E	2N	12	SW
Val Coonrad	Jef	–	5E	2S	29	NE
William Applegate	Jef	–	3E	5S	4	SE
Andrew Mundle	Jef	–	5E	1S	32	SW
Ignatius? Thompson	Jef	–	1E	5S	17	+
Enoch Robnett?	Jef	–	9E	2N	33	NE

996   25 Sep 1812   A/5/032
LO Zan
Transmits patents

William Frame	Zan Mil	1	2	24	SE
Ns. Titerack	Zan	–	14	16	11	SW
Peter Umstol	Zan Mil	2	2	18	SE
David Vandeberg	Zan Mil	8	2	6	NE
Andrew Lantz	Zan Mil	2	3	23	NW
Joseph Keifer	Zan Mil	3	10	16	SE
Henry Freidline	Zan Mil	3	9	22	SW
Josiah Adams	Zan Mil	10	3	10	NE
Josiah Adams	Zan Mil	10	4	21	NE
John Altman	Zan Mil	4	8	10	NE
Michael Flickenger	Zan Mil	1	10	6	NE
Thomas Blizzard	Zan Mil	10	3	12	SE
-- Munroe & -- Converse	Zan Mil	8	6	15	NE
John Cummins	Zan Mil	7	1	10	NW
Thomas Milner	Zan Mil	5	1	12	NW
Jacob Thomas	Zan Mil	2	1	1	NW
Lewis Cass	Zan Mil	7	4	16	SE
James Williams	Zan Mil	8	4	10	NW
Elijah Hart	Zan Mil	7	1	10	NE
Henry Miller	Zan Mil	4	9	22	SE
Thomas Frame	Zan Mil	1	2	18	SE
Henry Myers	Zan Mil	5	1	7	NW
John Lambrecht	Zan Mil	1	6	2	NE
William Caples	Zan Mil	1	6	1	NE
Peter Saltsgiver	Zan Mil	2	2	11	SW
Jacob Miller	Zan Mil	4	9	21	SW
-- Bohn, -- Slingluff, & -- Deardorf	Zan Mil	3	8	1	NW
Thomas Frame	Zan Mil	1	2	19	SW
George Clarke	Zan Mil	11	1	22	NW
Robert Walker	Zan Mil	5	1	13	NW
James McCune	Zan Mil	4	4	4	SE

[83]

Henry Haines	Zan	Mil	8	5	18	NW
John McCune	Zan	Mil	4	4	3	NW
James Rightmire	Zan	Mil	10	7	24	SW
Jacob Mack	Zan	Mil	15	18	11	NE
John Bell	Zan	-	14	15	33	NW
Peter Fry	Zan	Mil	1	2	4	SW
Jacob Ebert	Zan	-	14	14	10	SW
John Melick? [Ahelick?]	Zan	-	14	14	17	SE
Isaac Cooper	Zan	-	15	6	8	NW
Henry Shipler	Zan	-	11	13	14	SE
Timothy Wheeler	Zan	-	15	16	14	NW
Isaac Zane	Zan	-	14	6	2	SE
Isaac Zane	Zan	-	14	6	2	NE
Alexander Marks	Zan	-	14	15	35	NW
Jacob Cooper	Zan	-	15	6	1	NE
Henry Shipler	Zan	-	11	13	13	SW

997   26 Sep 1812   A/5/033
LO Jef
Transmits patents

-- Paul, -- Davis, & -- Lyon	Jef	-	10E	3N	1	+
John Thomas	Jef	-	11E	4N	31	NE
William Kelly	Jef	-	10E	1N	8	NW
Samuel Plaskett	Jef	-	9E	1N	10	SE
William Kelly	Jef	-	10E	1N	17	+
-- Armstrong & -- Plaskett	Jef	-	10E	1N	4	+
-- Armstrong & -- Plaskett	Jef	-	10E	1N	9	+
Lewis Blankenship	Jef	-	9E	3N	5	SE
William Lockhart	Jef	-	10E	1N	7	SW
Samuel Maxwell	Jef	-	9E	3N	9	SE
Robert Simmington	Jef	-	9E	3N	9	NW
Joshua Wilkinson	Jef	-	10E	4N	34	NW
John Ryker	Jef	-	11E	4N	30	SW
John Henderson	Jef	-	9E	3N	14	NE
John Covert	Jef	-	9E	2N	35	NW
David Findley	Jef	-	1E	2N	3	SW
David Findley	Jef	-	1E	2N	3	NW
John K. Graham	Jef	-	8E	5N	10	SE

998   29 Sep 1812   A/5/034
LO Cin
Transmits patents

Jacob Gerrard	Cin	MR	9	6	1	NW
Thomas Chenowith	Cin	MR	9	7	32	+
James Sargent	Cin	MR	12	4	12	NE
John Winn	Cin	MR	11	5	14	NE
Joseph Reynolds	Cin	MR	11	5	12	SW
Peter Christ	Cin	MR	5	2	26	NE
Levi Jennings	Cin	MR	8	2	6	SW
John Swope	Cin	MR	11	2	1	NE
John Swope	Cin	MR	11	2	2	SE
John Mallory	Cin	MR	11	2	9	SW
Owen Morris	Cin	MR	11	2	13	NE
Philip Mathews	Cin	MR	14	2	2	SW
Samuel Stites	Cin	MR	8	3	31	N+
William Gowdy	Cin	MR	8	5	23	NE
Henry Deem	Cin	MR	8	2	36	+
Richard Robinson	Cin	MR	10	5	1	NE
William Curl	Cin	MR	10	6	25	NE
William Curl	Cin	MR	10	6	19	NW
James Lockridge	Cin	MR	13	3	15	NW
Michael Sills	Cin	MR	11	3	32	NW
Joseph Terrell	Cin	MR	13	4	32	SE
John Paul	Cin	MR	9	3	30	SE
Jacob Funderbaugh	Cin	MR	9	3	9	NE
Ezekiel Patty	Cin	MR	12	5	20	NE
David Gerrard	Cin	MR	11	1	3	NW
William Birt? [Bert?]	Cin	MR	9	6	2	SW
John Grover	Cin	MR	10	4	15	SE

George Logan	Cin	MR	7	4	24	+
John Freeman	Cin	MR	4	2	26	NE
David McConneighy	Cin	MR	9	2	13	SW
Jacob Coy	Cin	MR	6	2	11	NE
Peter Christ	Cin	MR	5	2	26	SE
Thomas Babcock	Cin	MR	8	3	23	+
John Reed	Cin	MR	12	5	19	SE
James Miller	Cin	MR	8	4	8	NW
Jacob Arnold	Cin	MR	8	2	18	NW
Justice Jones	Cin	MR	11	6	34	SE

Name	Town Lot	Square
Edward Dodson	18	1*
Edward Dodson	17	1*
Henry Craven	13	2*
James Armstrong	21	2*
Francis Martin	8	2*
-- Canes? & -- Reilly	29	2*
Griffin Yeatman	8	3*
Jacob Broadwell	10	2*
Jacob Broadwell	9	2*
Jacob Broadwell	18	2*

*Probably in Cincinnati.

999   29 Sep 1812   A/5/036
General [Thomas] Worthington
Transmits patent

John Kerr	Mil	-	19	7	2	1
--*	Unk	-	1	8	2	-
--**	Unk	-	17	7	1	-

*Suggested substitute location; "adjoining old Schoenbrun."
**Suggested substitute location; "on the waters of Allum Creek near the Indian Boundary."

1000   29 Sep 1812   A/5/036
R. Gilmore, Rutland, Vermont
Transmits patent in Refugee Lands granted to Chloe Shannon [description not given].

1001   2 Oct 1812   A/5/036
Abiathar V. Taylor, Franklinton, Ohio
Answers letter of inquiry; "the locations for Robert Sharp having been fairly made, and patents issued thereon, cannot be legally altered."

1002   2 Oct 1812   A/5/037
LO Cin
Transmits patents

-- Piper & -- Williams	Cin	WML	2	10	13	S
Richard Sedgewick	Cin	WML	1	12	11	SW
Benjamin Harris	Cin	WML	1	14	4	NE
Nathan Hill	Cin	WML	1	13	3	SE
Robert Morrison	Cin	WML	1	14	1	NW
Benjamin Cox	Cin	WML	1	14	5	SE
Jeremiah Cox	Cin	WML	1	14	12	NW
William Young	Cin	WML	1	14	30	NE
William Helm	Cin	WML	2	8	13	NE
Nathan Small	Cin	WML	1	13	11	NE
Amos Higgins	Cin	WML	1	13	12	NW
John Collins	Cin	WML	1	13	19	SE
Nathaniel McClure	Cin	WML	1	13	10	SE
Peter Weaver	Cin	EML	5	3	18	-
George Ward	Cin	MR	11	4	22	SW
Abraham Campbell	Cin	MR	11	4	34	NW
Thomas Chenowith	Cin	MR	9	6	7	SW
R. Gill & B. Gill	Cin	MR	10	1	6	SW
John Carmany	Cin	MR	5	3	29	SW
David Askren? [Ackrer?]	Cin	MR	13	4	23	SE

Thomas Vail	Cin	MR	13	4	13	SE
Daniel Valentin	Cin	MR	12	1	22	NE
Abraham Smith	Cin	MR	12	5	24	SE
Jonah Farquhar	Cin	MR	8	3	2	NW
Jonah Farquhar	Cin	MR	8	3	2	NE
John Taylor	Cin	MR	11	4	29	NE
John Mallory	Cin	MR	11	2	9	SE
Richard James	Cin	MR	9	6	1	SE
Justice Jones	Cin	MR	11	6	32	SE
Samuel Shields	Cin	MR	13	5	34	SE
Gasper* Melford	Cin	MR	10	6	31	SW
Stephen Jones	Cin	MR	9	6	7	NW
John Carlough	Cin	MR	8	5	18	NW
St. Leger Neal	Cin	MR	12	5	13	NE
William Hall	Cin	MR	2**	2	6	NW
Elijah Harnell? [Harnett?]	Cin	MR	9	5	27	NW
Frederick Fox	Cin	MR	5	2	22	SW
Richard James	Cin	MR	9	6	2	SE
W. Glenn & J. Glenn	Cin	MR	11	5	17	SE
William Copse	Cin	MR	12	5	22	NW
Henry Baker	Cin	MR	10	4	20	NE
Aaron Spencer	Cin	MR	9	6	30	NE
William Hicks	Cin	MR	9	3	12	SW

*So spelled.
**"Entire;" [the meaning of which is unknown].

<u>1003</u>   3 Oct 1812   A/5/038
David Hoge, Reg Stu
Transmits patent which had been "suspended in the expectation that the assignments might be found, but though they have not yet been discovered, the patent has been issued because your letter of 13 Jan 1812 asserts they were forwarded"

Samuel Doran	Stu	-	4	12	4	-

<u>1004</u>   5 Oct 1812   A/5/038
James O. Cosby, Esq., Commissioner of Land Claims in the Western District, East of the River Mississippi and Island of New Orleans, Elbert Court House, George
Forwards copies of recent land laws enacted by Congress

<u>1005</u>   5 Oct 1812   A/5/038
William Crawford, Esq., Commissioner of Land Claims in the Eastern District, East of the Mississippi River and Island of New Orleans, Warrenton, North Carolina
Forwards copies of recent land laws enacted by Congress

<u>1006</u>   5 Oct 1812   A/5/039
List of district land office officials

Joseph Wood	Reg Mar	Levi Barber	Rec Mar
Wyllys Silliman	Reg Zan	Isaac Vanhorne	Rec Zan
David Hoge	Reg Stu	John Sloane	Rec Can
Jesse Spencer	Reg Chl	Peter Wilson	Rec Stu
Daniel Symmes	Reg Cin	Samuel Finley	Rec Chl
Samuel Gwathmey	Reg Jef	James Findlay	Rec Cin
John Badollet	Reg Vin	Edmund H. Tay-	
William Dickson	Reg Hun	lor	Rec Jef
Nehemiah Tilton	Reg WPR	Nathaniel	
Lewis Sewall	Reg EPR	Ewing	Rec Vin
Philip Grymes	Reg Nol	John Brahan	Rec Hun
Levin Wailes	Reg Opl	Parke Walton	Rec WPR
John Caldwell	Reg Kas	Samuel Smith	Rec EPR

Frederick Bates, Recorder of Land Titles, St. Louis
Thomas Sloo, Commissioner of Land Claims, Kaskaskia

<u>1007</u>   6 Oct 1812   A/5/039
Thomas Gibson, Reg Can
Transmits certificates; mentions Alexander McMullen, assignee of George Stidger?

Frederick Slump? [Stump?]	Can	-	10	12	34	SE
Joseph Hoslar	Can	-	10	12	27	E

<u>1008</u>   6 Oct 1812   A/5/040
Jesse Spencer, Reg Chl
Patent appears to have been issued--"what became of it is unknown"

John Harman	Chl	-	20	11	5	NE

<u>1009</u>   5 Oct 1812   A/5/041
John Badollet, [Reg Vin]
Re-entries shall be made at the office where the original purchases were made, according to the law of 6 Jul 1812

<u>1010</u>   8 Oct 1812   A/5/041
David Holmes, Esq., President of the Board of Trustees of Jefferson College
Lewis Sewall, Reg EPR
Transmits act of the Secretary of the Treasury locating the 36 sections granted by law for the use of Jefferson College

<u>1011</u>   8 Oct 1812   A/5/041
Thomas Gibson, Reg CAn
Quantity of land expressed in certificate disagrees with the return of the Surveyor General (3 acres less)

William McMonigal	Can	-	14	19	6	NW

<u>1012</u>   12 Oct 1812   A/5/041
LO Cin
Transmits patents

Andrew Morrison	Cin	EML	1	9	9	SE
John Hudlow [Hudlors?]	Cin	EML	2	8	1	NW
Gabriel McCoole	Cin	EML	4	7	3	SW
Mathew Morehead	Cin	EML	1	3	2	NW
-- Devor & -- Armstrong	Cin	EML	2	12	35	NW
David Miles	Cin	EML	5	7	30	NE
Robert Boyse	Cin	EML	1	6	3	NE
J. Saylor & E. Saylor	Cin	EML	3	5	25	SW
Joseph McCorkle	Cin	EML	6	6	19	SW
-- Lower & -- Shooer	Cin	EML	4	4	2	SE
Susanna Miller	Cin	EML	5	8	30	SW
Susanna Miller	Cin	EML	4	9	36	NW
Barbary Soyr? [Soy?]	Cin	EML	3	6	13	SE
Nathan Horniday	Cin	EML	3	4	18	NE
Elijah Mendenhall	Cin	EML	2	6	6	SW
David Kinsey	Cin	EML	3	5	20	NW
George Shidler	Cin	EML	2	8	17	NW
Jacob Chribe?	Cin	EML	5	4	7	SW
Isaac Enoch	Cin	EML	3	6	17	NE
Rice Swailes	Cin	EML	6	4	6	SE
Levi Jones	Cin	EML	2	7	31	NE
Levi Jones	Cin	EML	2	7	30	SE
Jacob Wireck	Cin	EML	4	4	10	NW
William Swisher	Cin	EML	4	6	7	SW
John Belt	Cin	EML	1	3	11	NW
-- Stubbs & -- Guest	Cin	EML	2	6	35	SE
Samuel Marshall	Cin	EML	6	7	6	NE
Elias Spinage	Cin	EML	5	7	1	SW
Jacob Wyrick	Cin	EML	4	4	14	NE
Thomas Boone	Cin	EML	1	4	4	SE

Weire Cassady	Cin EML	3	5	26	NE	
Jacob Frantz	Cin EML	4	3	10	SW	
James Haworth	Cin EML	5	7	29	SW	
George Worthington	Cin EML	2	8	33	SW	
Sampson Haworth	Cin EML	5	7	31	NE	

1013   12 Oct 1812   A/5/042
Rufus Seth Reed, Esq., Erie Town, Erie County, Pennsylvania
Transmits patent

Rufus Seth Reed	[Cin] MR	14	3	6	SW

1014   13 Oct 1812   A/5/043
Joseph Vance, Franklinton, Ohio
Returns military land warrant 542 for signature of
   all the heirs of Adam Wallace; warrent was held
   jointly by Adam Wallace and Andrew Wallace; also
   transmits patents

Reuben Carpenter	[Mil]	–	16	6	1	37*
Jacob Poe	[Mil]	–	16	6	1	15*
Jacob Poe	[Mil]	–	17	7	1	W*

*First two patents for 100 acres each; last patent
  for 50 acres.

1015   14 Oct 1812   A/5/043
Jesse Spencer, Reg Chl
Transmits Treasury receipt

John Gochnour	Chl	–	19	16	8	N

1016   16 Oct 1812   A/5/043
Daniel Poorman, Post Office, Chambersburgh, Pennsylvania
Transmits patent

Daniel Poorman	Chl	–	16	16	29	NW

1017   16 Oct 1812   A/5/043
Isaac Claughburgh, Little York, Pennsylvania
Transmits patent

Isaac Claughburgh	Chl WS	21	11	11	E	

1018   20 Oct 1812   A/5/044
Samuel Gwathmey, Reg Jef
Corrected patent transmitted

Jacob Miller	Jef	–	4E	1N	31	SE

1019   21 Oct 1812   A/5/043
David Hoge, Reg Stu
Inquiry has been made at GLO regarding patents; sent
   to you in May 1811

Samuel Hicklen	Stu	–	6	19	4	SW
Samuel Hicklen	Stu	–	6	19	4	SE

1020   21 Oct 1812   A/5/044
Nathaniel Ewing, Rec Vin
Directs repayment to be made in the case of John
   Paul [land description not given]

1021   21 Oct 1812   A/5/045
John Badollet, Reg Vin
Explains handling of the case of John Paul; trans-
   mits corrected patents

Thomas Jones	Vin	–	2E	4S	7	+
Thomas Jones	Vin	–	2E	4S	8	+
Thomas Jones	Vin	–	2E	4S	17	+

1022   22 Oct 1812   A/5/046
Lewis Sewall, Reg EPR
Your return of Feb 1812 shows tract for $2 per acre
   sold to Daniel Dupre; the same tract was bidden
   for at public sale on 3 Sep 1811 by James Welch
   at the price of $5 per acre; if it has been for-
   feited by Welch, it could not legally be resold
   for less than $5 per acre

Daniel Dupre	EPR	–	1	11	21	+

1023   24 Oct 1812   A/5/046
Jesse Spencer, Reg Chl
Gairy's patents were sent to you on 22 Aug 1810

Gideon Gairy	Chl	–	18	16	6	E
Gideon Gairy	Chl	–	18	16	6	NW

1024   26 Oct 1812   A/5/046
David Hoge, Reg Stu
Transmits corrected patent

David Drake	Stu	–	4	7	29	NE

1025   27 Oct 1812   A/5/046
Lewis Sewall, Reg EPR
"It has been stated to this office that a patent was
   granted by the British government to Elias Vanderhorst for 3000 acres of land about 12 miles above
   the junction of the Tombigby and Alibamo rivers.
   The patent is said to have been granted dated 3 Apr
   1770, and to have been recorded at Pensacola in
   Book E, Folio 9, on 10th April in the same year.
   No mention of this claim appearing in the returns
   made to the Secretary of the Treasury by the late
   Board of Commissioners, and it being confidently
   asserted, that it was presented to them, I have
   been led to suppose that the land in question is
   not comprised within your district but may be eastward of it among lands to which the Indian title
   has not been extinguished. Should such be the
   case, the Commissioners must of course have de-
   clined to take the subject under consideration.
   But will not the record of their proceedings throw
   some light on the business?"

1026   28 Oct 1812   A/5/047
Wyllys Silliman, Reg Zan
Notes discrepancies in certificates

Sarah Baird	Zan Pre	15	18	3	NW	
G. C. Spangler	Zan Mil	4	8	16	NW	
Henry Leear? [Seear?]	Zan	–	4	16	8	NW

1027   28 Oct 1812   A/5/047
Samuel Gwathmey, Reg Jef
Notes discrepancies in certificates; mentions William
   West; M. Maurice, assignee of James Maxwell

-- Coffin*	Jef	–	4E	2N	9	NE

*Assignee of -- Hogatt, but mentions another assignee,
  -- Darrock.

1028   30 Oct 1812   A/5/048
Wyllys Silliman, Reg Zan
Transmits certificate and Treasury receipt

Patrick Johnson	Zan	–	13	12	8	SE

1029   2 Nov 1812   A/5/048
LO Cin
Transmits patents

George Wolf	Cin	Pre	7	3	18	+
Jesse Wilson	Cin	-	5	3	33	+
John McCabe	Cin	-	4	2	9	N
Michael Confer	Cin	-	7	4	30	-
Joseph Manderhall	Cin	EML	5	6	29	SW
Henry Lybrook	Cin	EML	1	7	19	SW
Daniel Ullery	Cin	EML	5	8	29	SW
Matthias Penter	Cin	EML	4	4	11	SE
Samuel Freeman	Cin	EML	6	3	3	NE
Jonathan Higgans?	Cin	EML	2	4	7	E
Jacob Vance	Cin	EML	3	7	32	SE
John Ruby	Cin	EML	4	4	10	SE
Jacob Rape	Cin	EML	3	6	23	NW
Albert Banta? [Bonta?]	Cin	EML	3	6	30	SE
Joseph Defrees	Cin	EML	6	7	11	+
Elijah Mendenhall	Cin	EML	3	4	27	SE
Matthew Quinn	Cin	Pre	7	3	5	SW
D. Puterbaugh, heirs of	Cin	Pre	4	3	35	E
D. Puterbaugh, heirs of	Cin	Pre	4	3	35	NW
John Smith	Cin	EML	1	4	8	SE
C. Fogalgasang, heirs of	Cin	EML	4	4	24	NW
William Swisher	Cin	EML	3	4	2	-
Henry Seiler	Cin	EML	4	4	14	SW
Jacob Haller	Cin	EML	4	5	33	SE
John Freeman	Cin	EML	6	4	34	-
Henry Heistand	Cin	EML	4	4	12	SE
David Shraider? [Kraider?]	Cin	EML	4	6	36	W
Henry Hall	Cin	EML	1	1	1	NW
Andrew Surface	Cin	EML	2	8	10	SE
Christopher Mason	Cin	EML	4	4	1	NE
Martin Baum	Cin	EML	5	2	30	+

1030   2 Nov 1812   A/5/049
LO Stu
Transmits patents

John Boyer	Stu	-	8	9	2	NW
Jacob Brown	Stu	-	5	15	16?	SE
John Brown	Stu	-	4	15	21	NW
Edward Crawford	Stu	-	5	11	13	NW
Henry Friday	Stu	-	9	11	18	NE
Alexander Russell	Stu	-	6	14	36	NW
John Smith	Stu	-	5	7	8	NW
James Wheeler	Stu	-	3	8	15	NE
Smith Bell	Stu	-	2	11	23	NE
John Honnold	Stu	-	6	9	5	SE
Henry Smith	Stu	-	3	8	22	NW
Anthony Ruff	Stu	-	8	11	5	N
Philip Slusser	Stu	-	8	10	8	NW
Joseph Lindersmith	Stu	-	4	14	2	NE
Bez[aleel] Wells	Stu	-	5	11	8	SE
Bez[aleel] Wells	Stu	-	5	11	8	SW
Adam Reed	Stu	-	8	10	22	NW
Andrew Shorb	Stu	-	9	10	34	NW
Anthony Ruff	Stu	-	8	9	12	NE
John Yant	Stu	-	7	15	11	NW
John Yant	Stu	-	7	15	12	NW
Francis Gilmore	Stu	-	5	10	25	NE
James Laughlin	Stu	-	7	16	24	NE
Bez[aleel] Wells	Stu	-	4	10	32	SE
Robert Russel	Stu	-	6	14	36	NE
William Davis	Stu	-	6	14	29	SE
John Johnston	Stu	-	1	4	27	+*
John Johnston	Stu	-	1	4	33	+*
Jesse Stewart	Stu	-	6	15	26	SE
John Hollinger	Stu	-	2	11	35	SE
Margaret Tagart	Stu	-	4	17	14	NE
Andrew Boyer	Stu	-	8	10	35	SW
Thomas Rowland	Stu	-	3	9	18	NE
Andrew Shorb	Stu	-	9	10	34	NE
Philip Finebaugh? [Firebaugh?]	Stu	-	5	12	33	SW**

Andrew Boyer	Stu	-	8	10	5	NE
Thomas Armstrong	Stu	-	2	10	14	SW

*Patents were returned and cancelled; one had previously been issued in favor of -- Bottenberg, the assignee of Johnson [so spelled here].
**Returned from district land office and altered in favor of the heirs of P. Firebaugh.

1031   3 Nov 1812   A/5/049
LO Cin
Transmits patents

David Puterbaugh, heirs of	Cin	MR	8	2	23	W
James Jones	Cin	WML	1	8	29	S
Vincent Cromwell	Cin	WML	2	12	36	SW
Thomas Robert	Cin	-	14E 17N	27		SW
John McKee	Cin	-	13E 16N	18		SE
John Bell	Cin	-	12E 16N	34		NE
Thomas Simons	Cin	-	12E 16N	35		NW
John Scott	Cin	-	13E 17N	32		SE
Benjamin McCarty	Cin	-	14E 14N	4		+
Benjamin McCarty	Cin	-	14E 14N	5		+
Benjamin Evans	Cin	-	14E 17N	33		NE
Zadock Smith	Cin	-	13E 14N	18		NE
Thomas McCoy	Cin	-	13E 16N	35		SE
William Hoozier	Cin	-	14E 16N	19		NW
William Lyttle	Town lot 19, Square 2*					
William Lyttle**	Town lot 7, Square 1*					
John Runyon	Cin	MR?	10	6	32	SW
Aaron Shrader***	Cin	MR	3	2	26	NW
William Reed	Cin	MR?	9	6	21	SW
Jonathan Page	Cin	MR?	10	6	33	SE
Charles Hillier	Cin	MR?	12	1	21	SE
Jacob Beal	Cin	MR?	8	3	2	S
John Harvey	Cin	-	13E 16N	35		NE
Samuel English	Cin	-	13E	2	24	-
Jacob Harris	Cin	-	7	3	9	NE
Elizabeth Robinson	Cin	MR	13	4	25	NE
Richard Hopkins	Cin	MR?	9	5	6	NE
Andrew Davis	Cin	MR?	11	4	32	SW
Andrew Davis	Cin	MR?	11	4	2	NW

*In Cincinnati.
**Place of this entry in the original register is jumbled and ambiguous.
***Also states "entire" which, in context, is ambiguous.

1032   3 Nov 1812   A/5/050
James Smith, Shippensburgh, Pennsylvania
Transmits patents

James Smith	Cin	MR	11	4	17	SE
James Smith	Cin	MR	11	5	29	NW

1033   3 Nov 1812   A/5/050
Robert Donovan, Shippensburgh, Pennsylvania
Transmits patents

Robert Donovan	Cin	MR	11	5	26	NE
Robert Donovan	Cin	MR	11	5	29	SE
Robert Donovan	Cin	MR	11	5	36	SE

1034   3 Nov 1812   A/5/050
Daniel Symmes, Reg Cin
Please return patent, forwarded to you on 18 Jan 1812, so "that it may be given to Mr. Marshall"

Thomas Marshall	Cin	EML	1	7	24	SE

1035   4 Nov 1812   A/5/050
LO Cin

Transmits patents

Christian Bleakenstaff	Cin EML	6	4	27	SE
Daniel Bailey	Cin EML	1	2	8	SE
John Mendenhall	Cin EML	2	6	8	SW
John Neff, Senior	Cin EML	3	4	5	SW
James Quinn	Cin EML	3	6	7	SE
Robert Scott	Cin EML	2	5	26	SE
Andrew Morrow	Cin EML	1	8	9	-
Peter Owens	Cin EML	1	1	2	SE

1036   4 Nov 1812   A/5/051
LO Can
Transmits patents

William Henry	Can	- 10	12	12	SE
William Caywood	Can	- 19	18	12	+
William Caywood	Can	- 19	18	1	S
Philip Zimmer? [Timmer?]	Can	- 17	23	25	NW
Luke Ingman	Can	- 15	21	10	SE
Luke Ingman	Can	- 16	22	24	SE
William McMomjak?	Can	- 15	21	1	SE
William McMomjak?	Can	- 15	21	3	S
William McMomjak?	Can	- 15	21	3	NW
William McMomjak?	Can	- 14	19	1	SE
John Bower	Can	- 13	16	8	SW
William Garrell	Can	- 13	15	2	SW
Jacob Bachman	Can	- 17	23	33	SE
Martin Ruffner	Can	- 17	23	14	SW
David Graham	Can	- 13	15	17	NE
David Ewers	Can	- 18	18	6	SW
Robert Barr	Can	- 12*	12	25	SE
Isaac Osburn	Can	- 18	22	36	SE
Isaac Osburn	Can	- 17	24	31	SW
Jacob Abert, Junior**	Can	- 17	21	2	NE
John Smith	Can	- 17	24	34	NW
John Smith	Can	- 17	23	34	E
John Smith	Can	- 17	22	4	NE
Henry Gaddis	Can	- 10	12	11	NW
Robert Warden? [Wanden?]	Can	- 10	12	11	SW
John Lowry	Can	- 10	12	3	NE
Zephaniah Beale	Can	- 14	8	15	S
Zephaniah Beale	Can	- 14	18	14	NW
William Henry	Can	- 13	15	9	SE
Zephaniah Beale	Can	- 14	18	15	NE
James Mussellman	Can	- 17	22	2	NW
Charles Kelly	Can	- 12	16	5	SW
John Dice	Can	- 18	24	21	NW
John Bower	Can	- 13	16	8	SW
John Bower	Can	- 13	16	9	SW
Samuel Morrison	Can	- 10	1	29	SW
Andrew Newman	Can	- 17	23	32	SW
James Hedges	Can	- 18	21	22	SW
James Hedges	Can	- 18	21	21	SE
James Hedges	Can	- 18	21	22	SE
James Hedges	Can	- 18	21	22	NW
John Coon	Can	- 19	19	12	SE
Fred Ault	Can	- 10	1	22	SW
Conrad Neighstadt	Can	- 10	12	11	NE
Conrad Ruffner	Can	- 10	12	13	SW
Conrad Ruffner	Can	- 10	12	13	NW
John Fisk	Can	- 12	12	36	NE
John Vannordstandt?	Can	- 13	16	26	NW
Isaac Vannordstandt?	Can	- 13	16	5	NW
Joseph Mann	Can	- 19	18	8	NW
Adam Nimmon?	Can	- 10	12	25	N
Alexander Johnston	Can	- 9	10	18	+

*May read range 10.
**Could also read "Senior."

1037   4 Nov 1812   A/5/051
Jesse Spencer, Reg Chl

Transmits certificates & Treasury receipts

Robert Dickson	Chl	- 22	4	1	SW
Robert Dickson	Chl	- 22	4	1	SE

1038   4 Nov 1812   A/5/052
David Hoge, Reg Stu
Transmits certificates & Treasury receipt; Will-
helm's patent to be handed to Senator -- Gregg

Abraham Willhelm	Stu	- 9	12	22	SE
George Bair	Stu	- 9	9	12	SW
Peter Nees? [Ness?]	Stu	- 10	2	14	SE
Robert Watson	Stu	- 6	8	21	SW

1039   4 Nov 1812   A/5/052
Hon. Jeremiah Morrow
Transmits patent; "three years ago, a patent certificate was sent to the Department of State . . .
but as it does not appear by the records of that
department, which were transferred to this office,
that a patent issued on the said certificate, . . .
the enclosed patent is granted."

John Kitchell, heirs of	Cin Pre	4	2	17	+

1040   5 Nov 1812   A/5/053
John Braham, Rec Hun
Interest should not be charged in this case; men-
tions Col. Return J. Meigs

George Smith	Hun	- 2E	1	33	+
George Smith	Hun	- 2E	1	34	+

1041   5 Nov 1812   A/5/053
LO Cin
Transmits patents

Christopher Smith	Cin WML	1	10	23	NW
John Allen	Cin WML	1	8	1	SW
John Allen	Cin WML	1	8	2	NW
Amariah Elwell	Cin WML	2	10	12	NW
Thomas Clarke	Cin WML	1	13	33	SE
Henry Miller	Cin WML	2	12	25	SW
Lemuel Lemmon	Cin WML	1	9	4	NE
John Henderson	Cin WML	2	11	3	NW
Mary Miner	Cin WML	1	12	33	NE
James Lamb	Cin WML	1	13	19	SW
William Thorn	Cin	- 13E	16N	30	NW
Joseph Evans	Cin	- 12E	16N	11	SE
William Thorn	Cin	- 13E	16N	18	SW
Elijah Lympus	Cin	- 12E	13N	34	NE
Henry Yount	Cin	- 12E	15N	2	NE
Henry Yount	Cin	- 12E	16N	35	SE
William Helm	Cin	- 12E	13N	23	NW
William Sparks	Cin	- 12E	14N	36	SE
James Stanton	Cin EML	1	11	17	NE
George Dike	Cin EML	1	11	7	NE
John Penwell	Cin EML	2	9	34	NW
William Farlow? [Tarlow?]	Cin EML	1	12	19	SE
John Norris	Cin EML	2	9	19	NW
Todd McNutt	Cin EML	1	9	13	SE
Samuel Gregg	Cin EML	5	2	8	SW
William Bond	Cin EML	1	14	14	NW
William Ardney	Cin EML	1	9	14	SW
-- Scott & -- Russell	Cin	- 13E	13N	28	SW
Henry Bowsman	Cin	- 13E	14N	5	NW
James Brown	Cin	- 13E	16N	8	NW
James Morrison	Cin	- 14E	18N	32	SW
Michael Manan	Cin	- 12E	12N	28	NE
William Arndt	Cin	- 13E	11N	5	NW
David Mount	Cin	- 13E	12N	31	SE
Peter Quakinbush	Cin	- 13E	17N	35	NW

J. B. Vanmetre	Cin	–	12E	15N	15	SW
Nimrod Ferguson	Cin	–	12E	15N	25	NW
Henry Hoover	Cin	–	13E	16N	10	SW
Henry Hoover	Cin	–	13E	16N	3	SE
Jehos[apha]t Morris	Cin	–	13E	16N	19	NE
Thomas Galyean	Cin	–	13E	17N	20	SW
Henry Hoover	Cin	–	13E	16N	3	NW
Nathan Richardson	Cin	–	12E	16N	36	SE
Jacob Galyean	Cin	–	13E	17N	20	NW
John Patterson	Cin	–	13E	15N	3	SE
Joseph Miner	Cin	–	12E	14N	35	SE
Thomas Simons	Cin	–	12E	16N	22	+
Robert Russell	Cin	–	12E	12N	9	SW
James O'Dell [or O. Dell]	Cin	–	13E	17N	24	SW
Isaac Wilson	Cin	–	13E	11N	5	NE
Joseph Evans	Cin	–	14E	17N	18	SE
Samuel Bond	Cin	WML	1	5	19	SW
Samuel Bond	Cin	WML	1	5	9	SE
Samuel Bond	Cin	WML	1	5	5	SE
John Whitehead	Cin	WML	1	13	31	SW
Christian Petafish?	Cin	WML	1	14	12	NE
Thomas Osborne	Cin	WML	2	10	21	NE
-- Gilligan & -- Champion	Cin	WML	1	10	30	NW
John Dickerson	Cin	WML	2	10	11	SE
Dennis Dusky	Cin	WML	1	9	29	NW
Dele Elder	Cin	WML	1	5	9	NW
John Short	Cin	WML	1	11	27	SE
Caleb Pugh	Cin	WML	1	5	8	NE
John Miller	Cin	WML	1	10	14	NE
Samuel Beiler? [Beeler?]	Cin	–	12E	16N	36	NW
Thomas Reed	Cin	–	12E	14N	34	SW
Joseph Evans	Cin	–	14E	17N	29	NE
Joseph Evans	Cin	–	13E	16N	15	NW
Jehos[apha]t Morris	Cin	–	12E	16N	13	NW
George Glaze?	Cin	–	12E	16N	36	SW
Jonathan Mevine?	Cin	–	14E	17N	14	NE
Jacob Case	Cin	–	12E	14N	24	SE
John Harvey	Cin	–	13E	16N	24	NE
Edward Drury	Cin	–	13E	16N	28	SW
John Beck	Cin	–	13E	16N	22	NW
William Wilson	Cin	–	12E	13N	11	NE
Jacob Hackelman	Cin	–	12E	14N	24	NW
John Hawkins	Cin	–	12E	16N	27	+
John Hawkins	Cin	–	12E	16N	28	+
James Hartap	Cin	WML	1	13	23	SE
Tobias Miller	Cin	WML	1	10	13	NE
John Whiteman	Cin	WML	2	12	25	SE
Abraham Lewis	Cin	WML	1	12	4	SE
Abraham Lewis	Cin	WML	1	12	9	NE
Abraham Lewis	Cin	WML	1	12	11	NW
Zach[ariah?] Stanley? [Hanley?]	Cin	WML	1	12	10	SW
John Caldwell	Cin	WML	1	8	1	SE
James Baxter	Cin	WML	1	10	23	SE
John Plummer	Cin	WML	1	12	28	SW
William Ardery	Cin	WML	1	9	23	NW
John Flint, Senior	Cin	WML	1	10	20	SW
Samuel Bond	Cin	WML	1	5	9	SW

1042   9 Nov 1812   A/5/055

Samuel H. Smith, Clinton, Knox County, Ohio

"The lot which you have pointed you, viz. [Mil] –
16 7 4 5, for the location of William Cook's
military land warrant, was located some time ago."

1043   9 Nov 1812   A/5/055

Thomas Gibson, Reg Can
Transfer defective

| Alexander McMullen* | Can | – | 13 | 15 | 4 | SW |

*Assignee of George Stidger.

1044   10 Nov 1812   A/5/056

Jesse Spencer, Reg Chl
Returns corrected patent for Samuel Ramsey [description not given]; comments on others enclosed

| Henry Ingman* | Chl | – | 20 | 13 | 12 | NE |
| Daniel Deffenbaugh** | Chl | – | 19 | 12 | 17 | SE |

*Received [for correction?].
**Copy of patent sent; "it does not appear by the
records in this office, that the original patent
in favor of Deffenbaugh . . . was ever sent to
this office from the Department of State."

1045   11 Nov 1812   A/5/056

Hon. Aaron Lyle, House of Representatives
Transmits patent

| David Campbell | Stu | – | 4 | 8 | 21 | SW |

1046   11 Nov 1812   A/5/056

Hon. -- Jennings
Transmits patent

| Samuel Black | Vin | – | 3E | 4S | 13 | NE |

1047   11 Nov 1812   A/5/056

Hon. Abner Lacok*, House of Representatives
Transmits patent

| James Dennis | Stu | – | 3 | 13 | 12 | NE |

*So spelled.

1048   11 Nov 1812   A/5/056

Samuel Gwathmey, Reg Jef
Transmits certificate & Treasury receipt

| Jacob Persinger | Jef | – | 4E | 5N | 22 | SW |

1049   12 Nov 1812   A/5/057

LO Stu
Transmits patents

Abraham Kraft	Stu	–	8	10	24	E
Robert Moore	Stu	–	3	7	21	SE
Levi Jennings	Stu	–	6	19	23	NE
John Kepler	Stu	–	9	12	5	W
Rowland Coleman	Stu	–	9	11	34	NE
John Rife	Stu	–	9	9	2	SW
Emmanuel Custer	Stu	–	5	12	14	NE
Joseph Moore	Stu	–	8	12	21	SW
Hugh Gaston	Stu	–	1	7	32	SE
Conrad Shively	Stu	–	1	7	34	NW
Conrad Brandenberry	Stu	–	5	15	24	NW
Val[enti]n? Somerlaird	Stu	–	2	8	21	SW
William McFarland	Stu	–	2	7	8	NW
Ebenezer Martin	Stu	–	2	10	4	NW
Christian Garver	Stu	–	8	9	17	NW
Daniel Longenecker	Stu	–	7	19	30	SW
Ellis Hoopes	Stu	–	4	9	15	SE
John Nichol	Stu	–	3	5	23	NW
John Graham	Stu	–	3	13	13	NE
James Wilson	Stu	–	6	10	12	NW
Abel Johnson*	Stu	–	6	12	34	NW
Richard Nicholson	Stu	–	5	16	36	SW
David Brady	Stu	–	8	11	21	SE
Jordan Jones	Stu	–	3	15	29	SW
Philip Arnold	Stu	–	8	10	23	NE
John Forcenight	Stu	–	2	13	22	NE
John Knight	Stu	–	6	10	18	NE
John Shorb	Stu	–	9	10	25	SW
John Gardner	Stu	–	4	10	22	SE
Richard Spencer	Stu	–	7	9	28	SW
Henry Sower?	Stu	–	10	2	26	NE

George Myers	Stu	-	9	12	10	NE
Daniel Creamer	Stu	-	9	12	11	NW
John Baghtel	Stu	-	8	9	28	NE
William Hopkins	Stu	-	3	7	22	SE
Daniel Shuster	Stu	-	7	15	27	NW
Michael Hols	Stu	-	8	11	25	NW
John Brinton	Stu	-	6	17	26	E
Chris. Kenney? [Henney?]	Stu	-	8	11	3	W
John Rice	Stu	-	8	11	30	SW
Jacob Bower	Stu	-	8	12	8	SW
David Reed	Stu	-	4	7	1	SW
Jesse Underwood	Stu	-	1	7	17	SE
Peter Smith	Stu	-	6	13	2	NW
George Macenterfer	Stu	-	6	17	18	NW
Benjamin Williams	Stu	-	4	12	13	SW
George Macenterfer	Stu	-	6	17	19	SE
Michael Snider	Stu	-	1	9	15	SE
Stephen Ogden	Stu	-	5	16	35	NE
Samuel McFadin	Stu	-	5	10	25	SE
Benjamin Helwig	Stu	-	7	15	9	SE
James Milleson	Stu	-	6	18	14	NE
Benjamin Haston	Stu	-	1	7	28	SE
Joseph Gladden	Stu	-	2	7	26	SE
James Blackburne	Stu	-	3	9	23	NE
John Smith	Stu	-	1	6	19	NE
George Gregory	Stu	-	7	18	9	NW
David Miller	Stu	-	4	11	8	SE

*"Returned from Land Office and altered in favor of Isaac Johnson, assignee of Abel [Johnson]."

1050   12 Nov 1812   A/5/057
LO Can
Transmits patents

Hugh Culbertson	Can	-	13	16	31	SW
Charles Rose	Can	-	13	16	6	NE
John Rose	Can	-	13	16	8	NW
Abraham Cuppey	Can	-	16	22	5	NW
John Ferguson	Can	-	18	22	25	SW
Aquilla Hatton	Can	-	11	16	12	SE
Robert Newell	Can	-	16	22	26	NE
William Ewing	Can	-	13	17	30	SW
William Ewing	Can	-	14	21	25	NW
Joseph Friend	Can	-	17	21	2	NW
Samuel Funk	Can	-	10	12	9	NE
Benjamin Emmins	Can	-	15	22	22	NE
Nicholas? Smith	Can	-	13	15	12	SW

1051   12 Nov 1812   A/5/058
LO Jef
Transmits patents

Thomas Nicholson	Jef	-	10E	2N	6	NW
Brazilla Baker	Jef	-	9E	1N	13	SE
Phileman Vawter	Jef	-	10E	4N	34	SE
Williamson Dunn	Jef	-	9E	3N	12	SW
William Logan	Jef	-	4E	3N	17	NW
William Jennings	Jef	-	12E	3N	7	+
William Jennings	Jef	-	12E	3N	18	+
John Paul	Jef	-	10E	4N	29	NW
John Paul	Jef	-	10E	4N	25	SW
John Barnes	Jef	-	9E	3N	36	SE
John Paul	Jef	-	10E	4N	24	SE
Zach[eu]s? Lindley	Jef	-	1E	1N	9	SW
John Paul (of Peter)	Jef	-	11E	4N	19	NW
William Lindley	Jef	-	1E	1N	8	SW
John Vawter	Jef	-	10E	4N	27	SW
Daniel Robbins	Jef	-	9E	3N	15	SW
Jonathan Lindley*	Vin	-	1W	1N	3	+

*"[Forwarded to you] by your desire."

1052   12 Nov 1812   A/5/058
Martin Wingar, Post Office, Hagerstown, Maryland
Transmits patents

Martin Wingar	Stu	-	9	11	10	SW
Martin Wingar	Stu	-	9	11	14	NW
Martin Wingar	Stu	-	9	11	9	SE

1053   12 Nov 1812   A/5/058
John Sloan, Rec Can
Transmits Treasury receipt

John Stump	Can	-	10	12	28	N

1054   13 Nov 1812   A/5/058
Peter Wilson, Rec Stu
Transmits Treasury receipt

Joseph Hoge	Stu	-	6	14	28	SE

1055   13 Nov 1812   A/5/059
Hon. John Smilie, House of Representatives
Transmits patent

Benjamin Ragers*	Can	-	13	15	4	NW

*So spelled.

1056   13 Nov 1812   A/5/059
Jesse Spencer, [Reg Chl]
Notes discrepancies

Isaac Kline*	Chl	MS	21	10	26	NE
--Grumrine**	Chl	-	6	16	34	SW

*Assignee of R. F. Slaughter; might read township 11.
**Assignee of -- Tortman?

1057   14 Nov 1812   A/5/059
Samuel Gwathmey, Reg Jef
Discrepancy in transfer from Jacob Keller to -- Conrad and -- Butt [land description not given]

1058   15 Nov 1812   A/5/059
David Hoge, Reg Stu
On 21 Aug [1812] "a patent was transmitted to you in favor of J. Bottenburgh, assignee of John Johnston . . . On 2 Nov [1812] a patent was transmitted for the same tract in favor of John Johnston. This error arose from there being duplicate final certificates in this office, one of them accompanied by a transfer. Be pleased to return the last named patent, that it may be cancelled."

J. Bottenburgh	Stu	-	1	4	27	+
J. Bottenburgh	Stu	-	1	4	33	+

1059   19 Nov 1812   A/5/060
James O. Cosby, Esq., Commissioner of Land Claims, Western District (East of the River Mississippi & Island of New Orleans), Wilkinson Court House, Mississippi Territory
Discusses assignment of one clerk to office; compelling witnesses to give testimony regarding land claims; preparation of a list of settlers already on the land

1060   20 Nov 1812   A/5/061
Daniel Symmes, Reg Cin
Requests final certificate be forwarded

Samuel Haines	Cin	EML	5	6	31	-

1061   20 Nov 1812   A/5/061

James O. Cosby, [Commissioner of Land Claims in the
    Western District, East of the River Mississippi &
    Island of New Orleans], Wilkinson Court House,
    Mississippi Territory
Writes regarding compensation for Cosby and his
    clerk

1062   20 Nov 1812   A/5/062

Stephen Ogden, Rebecca Furnace, near New Lisbon,
    Ohio
Your patent sent to LO Stu

Stephen Ogden	Stu	-	5	16	35	NE

1063   20 Nov 1812   A/5/062

Jesse Spencer, Reg Chl
Transmits certificate & Treasury receipt for Joel
    Posey [land description not given]

1064   20 Nov 1812   A/5/062

Peter Wilson, Rec Stu
Transmits Treasury receipt

John Branson	Stu	-	5	9	15	SW

1065   21 Nov 1812   A/5/063

Jesse Spencer, Reg Chl
Corrected patent cannot be found; sends duplicate
    for Gairy; Dickson's payments incomplete

Gideon Gairy	Chl	-	18	16	6	+
Robert Dickson	Chl	-	22	4	2	SE
Robert Dickson	Chl	-	22	4	1	SW

1066   22 Nov 1812   A/5/063

[Samuel] Gwathmey [Reg Jef] & [Edmund H.] Taylor
    [Rec Jef]
Acknowledges receipt of their letter regarding pro-
    visions for offering forfeited lands for sale at
    land offices not the seats of justice; to be for-
    warded to Congress

1067   22 Nov 1812   A/5/063

Hon. Jeremiah Morrow, Chairman, Land Committee
Transmits communication from Reg Jef & Rec Jef

1068   24 Nov 1812   A/5/064

Isaac Van Horne, Rec Zan
Transmits Treasury receipt

William Wilson	Zan	-	11	3	17	NW

1069   24 Nov 1812   A/5/064

James Pritchard, Steubenville, [Ohio]
Transmits patent

James Pritchard	Stu	-	2	8	21	NE

1070   24 Nov 1812   A/5/064

LO Vin
Transmits patents

W. C. Montgomery	Vin	- 12W	3S	13	SE
Josiah Culbertson	Vin	- 7W	2N	5	NW
Henry Cosenberry	Vin	- 5E	6S	7	+
Samuel Montgomery	Vin	- 12W	3S	24	NE
Jacob Warrick, heirs of	Vin	- 12W	3S	11	SE

1071   24 Nov 1812   A/5/064

LO Chl
Transmits patents

William Forster	Chl	-	17	18	20	SE
William Forster	Chl	-	17	18	20	NW
Andrew Forster	Chl	-	17	18	9	SW

1072   24 Nov 1812   A/5/064

LO Zan
Transmits patents

Samuel Herrick	Zan	-	13	12	14	SE
William Raynolds*	Zan	-	10	9	18	SE
Daniel Horton	Zan	-	12	13	4	NW
Edward Smith	Zan	-	13	12	10	SE
William Dodds	Zan	-	14	15	27	NE
Samuel Gist	Zan Mil	8	2	5	NE
David Staten	Zan Mil	1	2	14	SW
John Tilton	Zan Mil	11	5	4	SE
George Lapp	Zan Mil	10	7	6	NW
James Chalfant	Zan Mil	7	4	15	SE
George Stringer	Zan Mil	5	4	1	NW
Warne Hughes	Zan Mil	2	3	23	SW
John McCrary	Zan Mil	1	9	3	NW
James Chilcote	Zan	-	15	17	33	NW
Jonathan Lefferts	Zan	-	14	16	6	SW
William Thompson	Zan	-	14	15	11	SW
James Abin*	Zan	-	9	8	5	SE
William Organ	Zan	-	13	15	2	SE
Ezra Horton	Zan Mil	8	5	6	SW
Reson Baker	Zan Mil	4	4	5	SE
Jack Black	Zan Mil	10	7	4	SE
Benjamin Hosteller	Zan Mil	4	8	2	NE
-- Kelly & -- Zanes	Zan Mil	8	2	5	SE
John Frame	Zan Mil	2	1	19	SE
Abel Williams	Zan Mil	1	9	10	NE

*So spelled.

1073   24 Nov 1812   A/5/065

LO Cin
Transmits patents

John Clendening	Cin WML	1	9	33	NW
Daniel Feather	Cin EML	5	5	29	NE
Moses Rush	Cin EML	3	3	12	NW
David John	Cin EML	5	4	22	NW
Abraham Stoner	Cin EML	4	3	4	SE
Isaac Harvey	Cin	- 13E	17N	17	SW
William Short	Cin MR	10	3	7	SE
William Short	Cin MR	7	2	18	+
William Jones	Cin EML	3	3	21	SW
John Sloan	Cin EML	6	3	28	SW
Charles Sterrett	Cin EML	6	8	36	+
William Kennedy	Cin EML	6	3	28	NE
Hazzard Stephens	Cin WML	2	7	4	SW
Peter Warren	Cin EML	3	6	8	SW
Culbertson Park	Cin EML	6	7	18	NE
Jesse Jay	Cin EML	5	6	25	SW
Charles Stewart	Cin EML	1	3	3	NE
Benjamin Iddings	Cin EML	5	7	33	SE
Joseph Coppock	Cin EML	5	6	8	NW
Emmanuel Florey	Cin EML	5	4	18	SE
-- Bond & -- Kees	Cin EML	1	1	8	-
Jacob Michael	Cin EML	4	6	25	-
Jacob Worman?	Cin EML	4	6	24	SE
Peter Aikenberry	Cin EML	3	5	31	E
Alexander Russell	Cin EML	5	9	34	NE
Alexis Burke	Cin EML	1	4	22	NW
John Anderson	Cin EML	1	2	1	SE
Aaron Bonnell	Cin EML	1	2	18	NW
Jacob Kautz? [Hautz?]	Cin EML	6	3	34	NE
Barnett Starr	Cin EML	1	8	13	SW

Jonathan Page	Cin MR	10	6	33	SW
John Crowell	Cin WML	1	9	32	NW
Benjamin Hill	Cin WML	1	13	1	NW
John Hawkins	Cin WML	1	14	33	NE
Benjamin Pearson	Cin WML	1	14	20	SW
Amos Butler	Cin WML	2	9	20	NW
Amos Butler	Cin WML	2	9	20	NE
John Harvey	Cin EML	2	7	7	SW
James Currie	Cin EML	1	4	2	NW
Abraham Shower	Cin EML	4	6	24	SW
Jacob Uby? [Ulry?]	Cin EML	5	8	30	SE
Joseph Rhorer? [Koner?]	Cin EML	4	6	14	NE
James Taylor	Cin EML	2	7	2	NE
Benjamin Hutchins	Cin EML	6	3	29	SW
James Bays	Cin EML	1	6	5	SW
James Bays	Cin EML	1	6	29	NW
Cornelius Voley? [Viley?]	Cin WML	1	9	10	NE
-- Compton & -- Sunderland	Cin EML	6	3	13	+
-- Compton & -- Sunderland	Cin EML	6	3	14	+
James Westerfield	Cin EML	2	7	7	SE
James Hollenshead	Cin EML	2	8	8	NE
Moses Campbell	Cin EML	2	5	15	SW
James McFadden	Cin EML	6	6	30	SW
James White	Cin EML	2	7	18	SE
Peter Weaver	Cin EML	4	5	36	NW
John Jones	Cin EML	1	2	30	-
Benjamin Wharton	Cin EML	6	5	30	SE
Thomas Stephens & Rich-ard Stephens	Cin EML	2	4	12	E
John Buchannon	Cin EML	1	4	9	NW
Joseph P. Bowen	Cin EML	5	4	21	SE
Henry Butt	Cin EML	4	4	17	NE
Jonathan Beale? [Beak?]	Cin EML	2	3	2	SE
William Reed	Cin EML	4	2	5	SW
J. Fenton & R. Fenton	Cin EML	1	3	36	W
Samuel Martindell	Cin EML	5	5	1	NE
Thomas Coppock	Cin EML	5	6	4	NW
Devault Bonbrake	Cin EML	2	8	18	SE
Joseph Stowder?	Cin EML	4	5	25	NE
Abraham Thomas	Cin EML	6	5	33	SW
Finehas? [Finchas?] Hart	Cin EML	3	4	30	SW
Silvanus Swallow	Cin EML	6	3	29	NE
William Mason	Cin EML	6	3	33	SE
Christ[opher?] Reed	Cin EML	4	2	4	NW
Samuel G. Mitchell	Cin EML	2	8	27	SE
Reuben Holstead	Cin EML	1	4	17	SW
-- Long & -- Leslie	Cin EML	3	4	36	-
Jacob Blekinstafer	Cin EML	6	4	28	NE
Charles Hilliar	Cin MR	11	1	36	+
Susannah Butler	Cin WML	2	13	12	NE
Thomas Purcell	Cin WML	2	4	31	NE
Isaac Swaford	Cin WML	1	11	4	NW
Samuel G. Mitchell	Cin WML	1	15	36	SE
John Shaw	Cin WML	1	9	28	SW
Amos Butler	Cin WML	1	6	35	SE
J. Woollery, assignee of J? [G?] Pryer	Cin EML	1	2	9	SE
Philip Swartzell	Cin EML	4	4	29	NW
John Allen & James Allen	Cin EML	1	6	10	NE
Benjamin Shower	Cin EML	2	4	29	NW
John Murphy	Cin EML	4	4	6	SW
John Millenger	Cin EML	6	7	29	NW
Lewis Forrest	Cin EML	4	4	10	NE

1074   24 Nov 1812   A/5/066
Hon. Thomas Wilson, U.S. House of Representatives
[Replying to your inquiry] . . . "three patents issued in favor of Zadock Walker, assignee of David
  Scott, for one thousand acres and were forwarded
  to the Hon. John Smilie. . . . One patent, in
  favor of Z. Walker, assignee of John Hardiman,

was forwarded to Mr. Walker, 15 Aug last. . . ."

1075   24 Nov 1812   A/5/066
Hon. Thomas Worthington
Transmits three patents in favor of the heirs of Is-
  rael Ruland for lands in the Refugee Tract [of
  Ohio]

1076   24 Nov 1812   A/5/066
Ethan Stone, Esq., Cincinnati, Ohio
"The president of the United States having appointed
  Josiah Meigs of Georgia to be Surveyor-General of
  the United States, you will be pleased to deliver
  up to him all the books, papers, and other public
  property in any wise appertaining to the office,
  which the late Surveyor-General, Mr. Mansfield,
  left in your charge."

1077   24 Nov 1812   A/5/066
Hon. John Rhea, U.S. House of Representatives
"A final certificate of the register of the Land Office at Huntsville, in favor of the commissioners
  appointed to fix on a site for the town of Pulaski,
  has been lodged in this office, with instructions
  to send the patent for said site to Mr. Bumpass,
  Philadelphia. Mr. Moore . . . directed me to en-
  quire of you, whether there be any impropriety in
  sending said patent to Mr. Bumpass? . . ."

1078   24 Nov 1812   A/5/067
Joseph Nourse, Esq., Register of the [U.S.] Treasury
Discusses anticipated budget for the year 1813

1079   25 Nov 1812   A/5/067
David Hoge, Reg Stu
A patent forwarded to you on 15 Jan 1811 should be
  forwarded to Joseph Shields at Leesburgh, Loudon
  County, Virginia
Joseph Shields   Stu -   5 17 11 NE

1080   27 Nov 1812   A/5/068
Jesse Spencer, Reg Chl
Transmits patent; also returns erroneous certificates
  [not otherwise described]
James Lamb*   Chl - 20 12   4 W
*"Returned and corrected to be in favor of Peter
  Swineford."

1081   29 Nov 1812   A/5/069
David Hoge, [Reg Stu]
Transmits final certificate thought to be erroneous
-- Helavin?*   Stu -   8 10 27 SE
*Assignee of -- Nichols.

1082   29 Nov 1812   A/5/069
Hon. Philip Stewart, U.S. House of Representatives
Transmits patent
William Halinsdoff   Mil - 11   6   1   1

1083   2 Dec 1812   A/5/069
Hon. Speaker of the U.S. House of Representatives
Transmits report respecting claims to land in the
  territories of Orleans and Louisiana; and the

claims to land in the "Territory of Louisiana (near Missouri)"

1084 3 Dec 1812 A/5/070
LO Cin
Transmits patents

Abraham Miller	Cin	EML	4	5	35	SW
John Harvey	Cin	- 13E*	17N	29		SW
William Lamme?	Cin	- 13E	15N	18		SW
Leonard Schnep	Cin	MR	6	1	11	NW
Philip Hull	Cin	MR	9	2	32	NW
John Apple	Cin	MR	6	1	12	+
Martin Emmert	Cin	MR	5	2	11	SW
Martin Emmert	Cin	MR	5	2	11	SE
Job Martin	Cin	MR	12	5	28	NW
Nathaniel Hunter	Cin	MR	13	5	13	NW
Nathaniel Hunter	Cin	MR	13	5	13	NE
Henry Brandenburgh	Cin	MR	10	3	13	SW
Frederick Sumey? [Scimey?]	Cin	MR	1	12	33	NW
Elijah Piles	Cin	WML	2	5	1	NW
Philip Linch	Cin	WML	1	9	24	NW

*East of 2d meridian.

1085 3 Dec 1812 A/5/070
LO Zan
Transmits patents

John Yarger	Zan	-	15	16	31	NE
David Calhoon	Zan	-	11	13	3	SW
Peter Veatch	Zan	Mil	11	6	25	SW
Elizabeth Scholfield	Zan	-	15	17	24	SE
David Shrog	Zan	Mil	5	9	11	SW
James Officer	Zan	-	12	13	1	NE
James Blake	Zan	Mil	9	5	3	NW
Peter Miller	Zan	Mil	5	9	33	NE
Benjamin Hull	Zan	-	15	16	5	SE
Edward Ward	Zan	-	15	17	7	NE
Martin Higer	Zan	Mil	4	4	5	NW
Michael Kidwilder	Zan	Mil	4	4	7	NW
William McDonald	Zan	Mil	5	1	9	NE
James Henthorn	Zan	-	15	18	5	NE
John Flemens?	Zan	-	11	13	12	NW
John Davy	Zan	Mil	1	9	1	SE
Benjamin Fickle	Zan	-	14	15	17	NW
William Coffman	Zan	-	15	18	15	SW
Job Lewis	Zan	Mil	10	6	21	NE
George Jackson	Zan	Mil	9	3	22	NW
Galbraith Stewart	Zan	Mil	1	2	23	NE
James Cummins	Zan	Mil	5	1	9	SW
William McConnel	Zan	Mil	7	1	2	SE
Jonathan Stiles	Zan	Mil	2	3	17	SE

1086 3 Dec 1812 A/5/071
LO Jef
Transmits patents

John T. Little	Jef	-	6E	1S	5	SE
Archibald Dunwiddie	Jef	-	9E	3N	2	SE
Philip Copple	Jef	-	9E	2N	32	SW
Henry Green	Jef	-	2E	2S	34	SE
Isaac Hall	Jef	-	8E	5N	21	NE
Joseph Kleiser	Jef	-	9E	1N	15	NW
Joseph Kleiser	Jef	-	9E	1N	10	SW
John Henderson	Jef	-	9E	1N	15	SW
Matthew Coffin	Jef	-	4E	2N	4	SE
Joseph Eckert	Jef	-	4E	5S	4	NW
Thomas Scott	Jef	-	2E	2N	32	NE
James Underwood	Jef	-	10E	4N	23	NE
M. Hillis & E. Hillis	Jef	-	11E	4N	20	NW
Samuel Dumorey? [Deamorey?]	Jef	-	11E	4N	24	SW
John Brightman	Jef	-	5E	5S	13	+

1087 3 Dec 1812 A/5/071
Joseph Wood, Reg Mar
Transmits patent

Jacob Roush	Mar	-	14	5	8	SE

1088 3 Dec 1812 A/5/071
John Badollet, [Reg Vin]
Transmits patent

William Bateman	Vin	-	5E	2S	21	NW

1089 3 Dec 1812 A/5/072
LO Can
Transmits patents

William Koller? [Roller?]	Can	-	16	22	26	SW
William Irwin	Can	-	10	12	3	SW
William Koller? [Roller?]	Can	-	16	22	27	SE
William Koller? [Roller?]	Can	-	16	22	21	NW
Philip Smith	Can	-	13	15	13	SE
Jacob Sailor	Can	-	10	12	12	SW
James Morgan	Can	-	13	13	3	NW
William Ewing	Can	-	13	17	30	NW
John Gallaher	Can	-	11	17	25	NW
John Gilchrist	Can	-	11	16	13	SE
Jo[seph] Christmass	Can	-	13	15	9	NW
Jo[seph] Christmass	Can	-	10	12	2	SW
George Stinger	Can	-	10	1	33	NW
Philip Slusher	Can	-	10	12	5	SE
Matthew Patton	Can	-	11	17	36	NE
William McMonigal	Can	-	14	19	6	NW

1090 3 Dec 1812 A/5/072
LO Stu
Transmits patents

William Rhodes	Stu	-	4	15	28	SW
William Rhodes	Stu	-	4	15	18	NE
William Smith	Stu	-	7	12	3	NW
Samuel Jumpes	Stu	-	5	9	24	SW
Christopher Weaver	Stu	-	8	11	28	NE
Robert Young	Stu	-	4	12	1	NW
Jacob Nessley	Stu	-	2	10	8	SE
James Rutledge	Stu	-	4	12	2	SE
Thomas Copperthwait	Stu	-	4	17	13	N
John Taggart	Stu	-	1	8	36	NW
John Roth	Stu	-	3	16	3	-
Jo[seph] Huff	Stu	-	7	12	20	NE
Philip Firebaugh	Stu	-	6	13	14	NW
Thomas Williams	Stu	-	5	11	14	SW
Jacob Maples	Stu	-	5	14	7	NW
Hugh McDonough	Stu	-	6	12	4	NE
Hugh Davidson	Stu	-	9	9	14	S
Obadiah Campbell	Stu	-	3	14	50	SW
Philip Seefort? [Leefort?]	Stu	-	8	9	7	NW
Fielder Richardson	Stu	-	3	14	18	SE
Robert Meeks, Senior	Stu	-	5	11	9	SW
William Whinery	Stu	-	4	16	31	SW
Daniel Morgan	Stu	-	1	6	21	SE
Israel Wilson	Stu	-	7	11	5	NE
Robert Innis	Stu	-	5	9	28	SE
Jo[seph] Farmer	Stu	-	4	16	29	SW
Jo[seph] Snider	Stu	-	8	11	26	SW
William Holsinger	Stu	-	8	12	18	SE
John Tate	Stu	-	10	1	12	SW
Jacob Wyant	Stu	-	7	15	17	SW
Jacob Loutsenheiser	Stu	-	7	19	18	NW
Henry Holmes	Stu	-	7	9	6	SE
Nathan Shepherd	Stu	-	4	8	21	NW
George Davis	Stu	-	6	14	28	NW
James Blair	Stu	-	3	10	23	NE
Isaac Brown	Stu	-	6	8	19	NW

Jacob Hersh	Stu	–	9	11	1	SE
Joseph Rippey	Stu	–	3	10	23	SW
Thomas Fernley	Stu	–	4	15	31	SE
Robert McClelland	Stu	–	2	8	31	SW
George Hartford	Stu	–	4	11	4	SE
Lodowick Welsh	Stu	–	2	10	13	SW
Daniel Van Horne	Stu	–	5	13	17	SW
David Kinney	Stu	–	1	6	23	NW
Valentine Greer	Stu	–	5	13	11	NW
Andrew Dougherty	Stu	–	6	8	23	NW
Thomas Rogers	Stu	–	1	7	3	SW
Thomas George	Stu	–	5	13	6	NW
Robert Smith	Stu	–	3	9	18	SE
Daniel McCurdy	Stu	–	5	9	33	SE
Henry Mayer	Stu	–	8	11	5	SW
Philip Andre	Stu	–	4	15	26	NW
George Hartford	Stu	–	3	10	13	SE
John Shorb	Stu	–	9	10	25	NW

__1091__ 3 Dec 1812 A/5/074
Benjamin Hough, Chillicothe, Ohio
"The Secretary of the Treasury has referred your several letters to him and general Worthington, on the subject of obtaining copies of the locations and surveys, and running lines through in order to make a general and connected plat of the Virginia military reservation [for] this office. . . . If you will undertake to furnish copies of all the locations and surveys which have been made and monthly, or quarterly furnish all such as may be made, and run three lines as laid down in the birds-eye map of that district (now enclosed), and furnish two accurate, general connected plats, agreeably to the true intent and meaning of the act of Congress, on the terms specified in your letter . . . I am authorized . . . to agree thereto, and will enter into a contract accordingly."

__1092__ 4 Dec 1812 A/5/074
F. Freeman, Esq., Principal Surveyor
Discusses plan of the land district, East of Pearl River; includes list of townships between the Chickasha and Tombigbee rivers.

__1093__ 7 Dec 1812 A/5/075
Hon. Andrew Gregg, U.S. Senate
Transmits patent
Abraham Willhelm   Stu – 9 12 22 SE

__1094__ 7 Dec 1812 A/5/075
Thomas Marshall, Post Office, Baltimore
Transmits patent obtained from LO Cin
Thomas Marshall   Cin EML 1 7 24 SE

__1095__ 8 Dec 1812 A/5/075
David Hoge, Reg Stu
Transmits corrected patents
Isaac Johnson*   Stu – 6 4 12 NW
Philip Firebaugh, heirs of Stu – 5 12 33 SW
*Assignee of Abel Johnson.

__1096__ 8 Dec 1812 A/5/075
Daniel Symmes, Reg Cin
Transmits patents
-- Patterson & -- Lindlay   Cin EML 6 1 3 +

-- Patterson & -- Lindlay   Cin EML 6 1 4 +
-- Patterson & -- Lindlay   Cin EML 6 1 5 +
-- Patterson & -- Lindlay   Cin EML 6 1 9 +
-- Patterson & -- Lindlay   Cin EML 6 1 10 +
-- Patterson & -- Lindlay   Cin EML 6 1 6 -

__1097__ 11 Dec 1812 A/5/076
Nathaniel Ewing, Rec Vin
Transmits Treasury receipt
Joseph Brownley   Vin – 3 5 31 +
Joseph Brownley   Vin – 3 5 32 +

__1098__ 11 Dec 1812 A/5/076
David Hoge, Reg Stu
Transmits corrected patent
Andrew McIntosh   Stu – 2 9 36 NE

__1099__ 11 Dec 1812 A/5/076
James Barnes, St. Clairsville, Ohio
Transmits patents
James Barnes   Stu – 6 8 15 SW
James Barnes   Stu – 6 8 15 NE
James Barnes   Stu – 6 8 15 NW
James Barnes   Stu – 6 8 21 SE
James Barnes   Stu – 6 8 21 NE

__1100__ 11 Dec 1812 A/5/076
Benjamin Van Cleve, Dayton, Ohio
Transmits patent
J. W. Van Cleve   [Cin?] Pre 7 2 33 NE

__1101__ 14 Dec 1812 A/5/077
Daniel Symmes, Reg Cin
Transmits Treasury receipt in favor of William McNair [land description not given]

__1102__ 15 Dec 1812 A/5/077
Hon. President of the U.S. Senate
Transmits copy of "a report from the Commissioners in the Western land district of the Territory of Orleans (now State of Louisiana) [and a list] of such claims as have not been confirmed by them. . . ."

__1103__ 15 Dec 1812 A/5/077
Speaker of the U.S. House of Representatives
Submits copy of "a report from the Commissioners in the Western land district of the Territory of Orleans (now State of Louisiana) of such claims as have not been confirmed by them and reported on. . . ."

__1104__ 15 Dec 1812 A/5/077
Wyllys Silliman, Reg Zan
Encloses final certificate for correction; mentions John Reagh, assignee of Nathan Conrel, which should read Conard [land description not given].

__1105__ 17 Dec 1812 A/5/078
Nehemiah Tilton, Reg WPR
Returns document for emendation and correction; mentions Joseph Dunham and Daniel Williams, Senior, assignee, signed by heirs of Dunham; also transmits

patents

S. Middleton	WPR	–	3E	5	14	–
J. Randell	WPR	–	2E	11	28	–
S. Middleton	WPR	–	3E	5	5	–
M. McCullen	WPR	–	2E	3	28	–
J. Winburn	WPR	–	4E	2	1	SW

1106   17 Dec 1812   A/5/078
William Dickson, Reg Hun
Transmits patents

Silas Fuqua	Hun	–	1W	4	11	SW
Johnson Hodges	Hun	–	1E	3	7	SE

1107   18 Dec 1812   A/5/078
Thomas Gibson, Reg Can
Transmits certificate & Treasury receipts for forfeited lands

Abraham Hetrick	Can	–	19	19	10	NE
John Shauck	Can	–	19	19	5	NE
John Shauck	Can	–	19	19	5	NW
John Shauck	Can	–	19	19	5	SW
John Shauck	Can	–	19	19	5	SE

1108   18 Dec 1812   A/5/079
LO Zan
Transmits patents

Magdalene Levengood	Zan Mil	6	1	2	SW
James Frame	Zan Mil	3	4	23	NW
Jacob Land	Zan Mil	2	8	17	NW
James Gordon	Zan Mil	2	1	20	SE
George McCune	Zan Mil	4	4	3	SW
Daniel Whetstone	Zan Mil	1	2	22	NE
Michael Domer? [Dorner?]	Zan Mil	4	8	14	NE
Peter Folk	Zan Mil	1	10	5	SE
Isaac Draper	Zan Mil	9	7	15	NW
Philip Waggoner	Zan Mil	4	5	11	SW
Thomas Fuller	Zan Mil	4	4	18	NE
Peter Miller	Zan Mil	4	9	25	NW
John Yarger	Zan Mil	15	16	30	SE
Henry Miller	Zan Mil	11	13	11	SE
Hugh Addy	Zan Mil	4	4	4	NW
Jacob Bouzer	Zan Mil	8	5	17	NW
John Dorsey	Zan Mil	8	2	4	W
Andrew Zeigler? [Leigler?]	Zan –	14	15	23	NW
Joseph Torrence	Zan –	9	8	13	NW
Thomas Butler	Zan Mil	8	6	15	NW
Samuel Farquhar	Zan Mil	10	6	21	SE
Gideon Jennings	Zan Mil	1	9	5	SE
Jonathan Wood	Zan Mil	9	3	25	SE
David Hay	Zan Mil	5	6	24	SW
Richard Doughty	Zan Mil	7	3	20	NW
John Beiver? [Bewer?]	Zan Mil	6	2	25	NE
Thomas Richards	Zan Mil	9	1	20	SW
Simon Dudgeon	Zan Mil	11	6	18	NW
Henry Kretzer	Zan Mil	3	8	8	NE
George C. Spangler	Zan Mil	5	8	19	NE
Abraham Miller	Zan –	11	13	2	NE
Ezekiel Spurgin	Zan –	14	14	4	SE
Benjamin Heckley	Zan –	9	8	9	NE
Daniel Herne	Zan –	15	17	36	NW
Henry Davis	Zan –	10	9	6	SW
John Harbaugh	Zan Mil	1	10	7	SE
Richard Stronge	Zan Mil	6	1	9	NE

1109   18 Dec 1812   A/5/080
LO Chl
Transmits patents

Andrew Smith	Chl	–	17	17	9	SE
Conrad Reighle	Chl	–	16	17	2	NE
James Crosen	Chl	–	16	15	20	NW
John Ashbaugh	Chl	–	17	16	14	SE
Elnathan Schofield	Chl	–	14	19	23	SW
Jacob Dittoe	Chl	–	16	16	22	NE
Joel Bacon	Chl	WS	21	10	27	SE
John Mitten & Joshua Mitten	Chl	WS	21	11	17	NW
Christian Kromley	Chl	–	20	14	27	W
James Tobert	Chl	WS	21	10	22	NE
Jacob Fourman	Chl	–	18	14	13	NW
Abraham Doll	Chl	–	21	8	32	NW
Nathaniel Wilson	Chl	–	19	14	15	NE
Frederick Raver	Chl	–	20	15	28	SE
Joseph Ferguson	Chl	–	16	17	28	SE
Adam Pontieus	Chl	MS	21	11	32	SE
James Taylor	Chl	–	16	15	17	NW
John Teller	Chl	–	17	14	5	SW
Lewis Friedley	Chl	MS	21	10	35	SE
Abraham Huffort	Chl	–	17	16	23	SW
John Ritter	Chl	MS	21	10	23	–
Walter Hews	Chl	MS	21	11	24	SE
-- Reed & -- Emrick	Chl	–	16	15	2	NW
Charles Hanger	Chl	–	20	9	9	NW
Jacob Hautz	Chl	–	16	16	33	SW
David Crull, Senior	Chl	–	21	3	34	SW
Christian Deal	Chl	–	16	16	4	NW
Daniel Ludwig	Chl	WS	21	11	21	E
David Hess	Chl	–	16	16	11	SE
John Christy	Chl	–	20	12	10	SW
John Brooks	Chl	–	17	18	1	NW
John Stoker	Chl	–	17	17	35	SW
Jacob Dittoe	Chl	–	16	16	21	NE
Samuel Tallman	Chl	MS	21	11	2	SE
Zacheriah Welch	Chl	–	21	8	25	SW
Samuel Tallman	Chl	MS	21	11	1	SW
Henry Hall	Chl	MS	21	10	13	NE

1110   18 Dec 1812   A/5/081
LO Cin
Transmits patents

Robert Templeton	Cin	WML	2	9	4	SW
Robert Carr	Cin	WML	1	11	35	SW
Samuel Landers? [Sanders?]	Cin	–	12E*	15N	27	NW
-- Drake & -- Ross	Cin	WML	2	3	2	NE
Walter Tucker	Cin	WML	1	9	18	SE
David Prestley	Cin	WML	1	11	27	SW
Elijah Wade	Cin	WML	1	13	13	SE
Abraham Miller	Cin	EML	4	2	8	NE
Isaac Lirman? [Sirman?]	Cin	WML	2	10	24	NE
David Bell	Cin	EML	1	3	10	SE
David Prestley	Cin	EML	1	6	32	SW
William Rittenhouse	Cin	MR	2**	1	26	SE
Christopher Canaga	Cin	MR	11	5	18	SE
Micah French	Cin	MR	9	5	21	NW
William Jones, John Jones, & Jacob Jones	Cin	MR	8	5	27	NE
David Mount	Cin	–	12E*	12N	35	SE
Solomon Horney	Cin	–	12E*	15N	34	SE
John Nixon	Cin	–	12E*	16N	23	NE
John Cromwell	Cin	WML	1	11	4	SW
Joseph Addington	Cin	WML	1	14	17	NW
John Winn	Cin	MR	11	5	7	SW
Henry Phoutz	Cin	EML	5	6	23	NW
-- Sutherland & -- Brown	Cin	EML	6	2	3	NW
Christian Hosteller	Cin	EML	4	6	36	E
John Goldsmith	Cin	EML	2	7	4	NW

*East of second meridian.
**Fractional.

1111   18 Dec 1812   A/5/081

David Halverstadt, New Lisbon, Columbiana County,
  Ohio
Transmits patent
David Halverstadt   Cin MR 7   3   9 SW

1112   18 Dec 1812   A/5/081
Alexander Taylor, Warm Springs, Bath County, Vir-
  ginia
Transmits patents
Alexander Taylor   Cin MR 13   3   9 N
Alexander Taylor   Cin MR 12   4 24 SW

1113   18 Dec 1812   A/5/082
Parke Walton, Rec WPR
Transmits Treasury receipt; mentions J. Archer,
  assignee of Robert Moore [land description not
  given]

1114   18 Dec 1812   A/5/082
Wyllys Silliman, Reg Zan
Returns certificate for correction
[Patentee not named]   Zan - 10   7   5 SW

1115   18 Dec 1812   A/5/081
John Badollet, Reg Vin
Returns certificate for correction
[Patentee not given]   Vin - 12W 1N 1 SW
[Patentee not given]   Vin - 12W 1N 1 SE
[Patentee not given]   Vin - 6E 3S 2 +

1116   19 Dec 1812   A/5/081
Thomas Gibson, Reg Can
Transmits patent
John Smith   Can - 17 24 34 NW

1117   19 Dec 1812   A/5/082
Jesse Spencer, Reg Chl
Transmits corrected patent for Daniel Aquabrough
  [land description not given]

1118   21 Dec 1812   A/5/083
David Hoge, Reg Stu
Transmits patent
Isaiah Burson [Burton]* Stu -   4 15 14 SE
*Spelled both ways in letter; assignee of T. M.
  Gilton.

1119   22 Dec 1812   A/5/083
Jesse Spencer, Reg Chl
Transmits corrected patent
Peter Swineford   Chl - 20 12   4 W

1120   22 Dec 1812   A/5/083
Samuel Gwathmey, Reg Jef
"In the case of -- Davidson, . . ., who purchased a
  tract which had been previously sold at Vincennes,
  he must certainly be permitted to transfer his
  entry to another tract."

1121   22 Dec 1812   A/5/084

Wyllys Silliman, Reg Zan
Slight deficiency in payment noted
[Patentee not given]   Zan - 14 13 12 NW

1122   28 Dec 1812   A/5/084
Hon. Aaron Lysle*
Transmits patent
David Craig   Stu -   2   5 26 SE
*So spelled; probably Lytle is meant.

1123   28 Dec 1812   A/5/084
John McDonald, Scotch Settlement, care of James Camp-
  bell, Esq., Baltimore
Patent in your favor sent to LO Stu; if lost, copy
  can be provided
John McDonald   Stu -   2 10 27 SE

1124   28 Dec 1812   A/5/085
Jacob Claypool, near Lancaster, Ohio
Transmits patent
Jacob Claypool   Chl - 19 15 21 NE

1125   28 Dec 1812   A/5/085
John Badollet, [Reg Vin]
Returns certificate for correction; mentions John
  Trueblood

1126   28 Dec 1812   A/5/085
Jesse Spencer, [Reg Chl]
Serjeant's patent, which you inquire about, was de-
  livered to -- Tiffin on 15 Feb 1809 "and he directs
  me to inform you that he recollects perfectly well
  that he gave it on his return to Mr. Serjeant."
  Shock's patent not forthcoming because assignment
  did not accompany it
Snowden Serjeant   Chl - 21   5 28 +
Henry Shock*   Chl WS 21 11 35 NE
*Assignee of Jesse Spencer.

1127   29 Dec 1812   A/5/086
Lt. Col. James Morrison, Lexington, Kentucky
Land Warrant No. 564 [warrantee's name not given]
  transferred to John Johnson, per instruction of
  -- Nourse, Register of the U.S. Treasury

1128   29 Dec 1812   A/5/086
Hon. Alexander Campbell, U.S. Senate
Transmits patent
George Schultz   Chl - 21   1   9 NW

1129   31 Dec 1812   A/5/087
Frederick Hoover, Bedford, Pennsylvania
Transmits patent
Frederick Hoover   Stu -   7 20 34 NE

1130   31 Dec 1812   A/5/087
LO Stu
Transmits patents
Peter Lance & John Lance Stu -   6 10 24 NW
Peter Dickerhuff   Stu -   8 12 30 SE
Jacob Nessley   Stu -   2 10   9 SW
Andrew Hendricks   Stu -   4 10 35 NE
Jacob Holtz   Stu -   5   8 15 NW

Jacob Speelman	Stu	–	8	11	9	SE
Matthew Picken	Stu	–	7	14	26	SW
Jacob Parker	Stu	–	6	8	21	NW
Nathan Shepherd	Stu	–	4	8	22	SE
Thomas Oliver	Stu	–	2	9	25	SE
Jacob Styres? [Stynes?]	Stu	–	4	8	22	NE
William Holmes	Stu	–	2	6	22	NE
James Alexander	Stu	–	2	8	15	SW
John Winance	Stu	–	4	11	21	SW
Daniel McCurdy	Stu	–	2	5	29	NE
Henry Stanton	Stu	–	5	7	33	SE
James Lyle	Stu	–	3	9	21	NE
Jacob Stees	Stu	–	4	11	15	SW
John Tester	Stu	–	9	11	1	SW
Charles McDevit	Stu	–	2	11	31	SE
Christian Shell? [Sholl?]	Stu	–	5	17	23	SW
William Young	Stu	–	3	14	31	SW
Melcher Tester	Stu	–	8	12	30	NE
John H. Johnson	Stu	–	7	20	11	SW

1131 31 Dec 1812 A/5/087
Joseph Wood, Reg Mar
Transmits patent

[Patentee not given]	Mar	–	7	8	27	SE

1132 31 Dec 1812 A/5/088
LO Zan
Transmits patents

Philip Waggoner	Zan	Mil	4	4	6	NW
Joseph Bland	Zan	Mil	8	2	6	SE
James Deprew	Zan	Mil	1	1	21	NW
Joseph Moore & James Moore	Zan	–	11	13	5	SE
Joseph Moore & James Moore	Zan	–	11	13	8	NE
William Robertson*	Zan	Mil	5	1	16	NE
William Robinson*	Zan	Mil	5	1	16	NW
James Delong	Zan	Mil	1	1	22	SW
George Delong	Zan	Mil	1	1	11	NW
Ebenezer Ryan	Zan	Mil	8	2	19	SW
George Gimlens	Zan	Mil	2	8	15	SE
John Kinesly	Zan	Mil	3	9	19	NE
Anthony Miller	Zan	Mil	11	3	16	SE
Martin Higer	Zan	Mil	4	4	5	NE
Thomas Milner	Zan	Mil	1	2	16	NE
George Gimlens	Zan	Mil	2	8	14	SW
James Thompson	Zan	Mil	8	4	8	SW
Christian Winkelblech	Zan	Mil	4	9	21	NW
Edward Ward	Zan	–	8	8	3	NE
George Fluckey	Zan	–	15	16	6	SW
Levi Lewis	Zan	–	19	9	28	SW
Benjamin Coddington	Zan	–	15	15	3	SE
Henry Sellers	Zan	–	15	16	8	NE
Joseph Sellers	Zan	–	15	16	3	SW
William Smith	Zan	–	13	12	11	SE
George Hanimet	Zan	–	15	17	3	SW
James Officer	Zan	–	11	13	6	NW
Daniel Converse	Zan	–	13	12	10	SW
William Smith	Zan	–	12	13	18	SW
James Reed*	Zan	–	9	7	28	SW
Joseph Reid*	Zan	–	9	7	29	NE
Robert McIntire	Zan	–	11	13	17	NW
James Smith	Zan	–	15	18	18	SW
Charles Henderson	Zan	Mil	6	1	11	NW
Joseph Reid	Zan	–	9	7	20	NW
James Leeper	Zan	Mil	3	8	8	SE
Lewis Nye	Zan	–	14	15	8	SE
James Bratton	Zan	Mil	1	3	15	SE
Philip Ports	Zan	Mil	1	9	13	NE
Thomas Johnson	Zan	Mil	5	4	10	NE
Richard Tilton	Zan	Mil	7	4	16	NE
Daniel Van Voorhies	Zan	Mil	5	1	17	NE

*So spelled.

1133 31 Dec 1812 A/5/089
LO Cin
Transmits patents

-- Reeder & -- Wood	Cin	Pre	5	3	18	NW
Jonathan Crespin	Cin	Pre	5	3	9	+
Levi Jennings	Cin	Pre	8	2	6	SE
Samuel Broadaway	Cin	Pre	5	3	28	NW
C. Lefevre & D. Lefevre	Cin	Pre	10	1	2	+
William Ward	Cin	Pre	12	5	19	SW
William Ward	Cin	Pre	11	5	24	SW
William Ward	Cin	Pre	12	5	25	SE
Samuel Stitt?	Cin	Pre	4	3	32	–*
James Tatman? [Latman?]	Cin	Pre	8	3	22	SW
W. Thenton? & M. Thenton? [Kenton?]	Cin	Pre	11	4	6	W
James Stafford	Cin	Pre	9	2	6	SW
James Stafford	Cin	Pre	9	2	6	NW
Samuel Logan	Cin	Pre	11	5	21	NE
Peter Smith	Cin	Pre	9	3	10	SE
Peyton Short	Cin	Pre	7	2	34	+
Peyton Short	Cin	Pre	8	2	34	+
Peyton Short	Cin	Pre	8	2	7	+
William Short	Cin	Pre	8	2	19	+
William Short	Cin	Pre	8	2	13	+
Peyton Short	Cin	Pre	8	2	25	+
Peyton Short	Cin	Pre	8	2	31	+
Arthur Brown	Cin	Pre	5	3	20	+
Jacob Tremble	Cin	Pre	4	4	19	N
Peyton Short	Cin	Pre	8	2	10	–
Henry Clark	Cin	Pre	7	1	13	+
J. Retter & J. Retter	Cin	Pre	1	11	13	NW

*Three-fourths of section.

1134 31 Dec 1812 A/5/089
LO Chl
Transmits patents

George Wells	Chl	–	20	15	17	SW
James Martin	Chl	MS	21	9	31	NE
John Shoup	Chl	MS	21	9	26	SW
Jesse Mounts	Chl	–	20	5	8	NE
Josiah Shackford	Chl	–	21	2	32	NW
John Hoover	Chl	–	20	13	3	SW
Philip King	Chl	MS	21	11	1	NW
Peter Lertman?	Chl	–	17	18	24	SE
John Wright	Chl	–	20	15	25	NE
Jacob Delong	Chl	–	20	10	11	NE
John Rockey	Chl	–	20	14	10	NW
Jacob Hautz	Chl	–	16	16	30	SW
David Hamilton	Chl	–	19	12	9	NE
Daniel Ludwig	Chl	WS	21	11	21	W
Daniel Baum	Chl	WS	21	10	34	SW

1135 31 Dec 1812 A/5/090
LO Vin
Transmits patents

William Robinson	Vin	–	14W*	7S	10	SE
George Walls	Vin	–	5E*	2S	32	NE
William Lindley	Vin	–	1W*	1N	13	NW
-- Jones & -- Snyder	Vin	–	6W*	8S	15	+
Hosea Smith	Vin	–	8W*	1N	28	SE
Samuel McConnell	Vin	–	5W*	1N	35	SW
James Montgomery	Vin	–	12W*	3S	24	NE
George Charley	Vin	–	4E*	3S	19	NE
Daniel Comer	Vin	–	7W*	2N	4	SE
Isaac White, heirs of	Vin	–	14W*	8S	35	+
Isaac White, heirs of	Vin	–	14W*	9S	2	+

Isaac White, heirs of	Vin	– 13W*	4S	34	NW
Jeremiah Harrison	Vin	– 11W*	1S	36	SE
William H. Harrison	Vin	– 3E*	3S	19	SW
John Paul	Vin	– 6E*	3S	3	+
Henry Funk	Vin	– 2E*	4S	35	+
Samuel Gordon**	Vin	– 13W*	7S	18	+
William H. Harrison	Vin	– 13W*	7S	8	+
Eli Hawkins**	Vin	– 8W*	2N	6	+
Eli Hawkins**	Vin	– 8W*	2N	1	+

*West of second principal meridian.
**Land description partially blotted and may be wrong.

1136   2 Jan 1813 A/5/090
Daniel Symmes, Reg Cin
Transmits Treasury receipt

Martin Kershner	Cin	Pre 7	3	23	SW
Martin Kershner	Cin	Pre 7	3	23	NW
Martin Kershner	Cin	Pre 7	3	23	SE
Martin Kershner	Cin	Pre 8	3	1	NE

1137   2 Jan 1813* A/5/091
David Hoge, Reg Stu
Returns corrected patents

Isaac Johnson**	Stu	– 6	4	12	NW
Philip Firebaugh	Stu	– 5	12	33	SW

*"Should have been recorded under date of 18 Dec 1812."
**Assignee of Abel Johnson.

1138   4 Jan 1813 A/5/092
Hon. the President of the U.S. Senate
Transmits a statement showing amount of land sold prior to the opening of the several land offices [statement not included on microfilm]

1139   6 Jan 1813 A/5/092
Daniel Symmes, Reg Cin
Requests final certificate

Felix Walton*	Cin	MR 10	5	9	SE

*Assignee of J? Baldwin.

1140   6 Jan 1813 A/5/092
Wyllys Silliman, Reg Zan
Requests return of patent "or to be sent by you to him at Urbana, Ohio"

Joseph Sheefer	Zan	– 3	10	16	SE
Joseph Sheefer	Zan	– 3	10	24	SE

1141   7 Jan 1813 A/5/093
Peter Wilson, Rec Stu
Transmits Treasury receipt

John Piggott	Stu	– 7	11	9	NE

1142   7 Jan 1813 A/5/093
John Badollet, Reg Vin
Transmits final receipt

Josiah Trueblood	Vin	– 6E	2S	35	+

1143   9 Jan 1813 A/5/093
Hon. Jeremiah Morrow, Chairman, Land Committee
Services of translator still required by board of commissioners, Western Land District, Orleans Territory (now State of Louisiana).

1144   9 Jan 1813 A/5/094
Benjamin Hough, Chl
Terms of agreement for survey line through Virginia Military District of Ohio.

1145   9 Jan 1813 A/5/096
Wyllys Silliman, Reg Zan
Transmits Treasury receipt

Benjamin Rutter	Zan	– 15	17	26	SW

1146   11 Jan 1813 A/5/096
John Carter, St. Clairsville, Ohio
Transmits patent

John Carter	Stu	– 5	8	15	SW

1147   11 Jan 1813 A/5/096
Daniel Symmes, Reg Cin
Trequests final certificate

Hon. Jeremiah Morrow*	Cin	Pre 7	2	13	NE

*Paid in full by William Stewart, 10 Apr 1811.

1148   11 Jan 1813 A/5/096
S. H. Smith, New Ark [Newark?] [state not given]
To send list of lots still vacant in U.S. Military District of Ohio. "You will receive a patent for [–] Cooke's military warrant when it is located. . . ."

1149   11 Jan 1813 A/5/097
Lewis Sewall, Reg St. Stephan's [EPR]
Answers query: "Whether a claimant under a pre-emption title, who clearly and evidently loses by the interference of donations, a part of the tract granted him by the Commissioners, can pay for remains only, and obtain a patent for that alone?" Cites first section of Act of 21 Apr 1806 (Land Laws, p. 295); also section 3 of Act of 3 Mar 1803 (Land Laws, p. 284).

1150   12 Jan 1813 A/5/097
Reg Cin
Gives status of account

James McKinney	Cin	MR 12	1	32	+

1151   12 Jan 1813 A/5/098
LO Jef
Transmits patents

William Davis	Jef	2	5E	2S	4	SW
John Ritchie	Jef	2	9E	4N	33	SW
Jonathan Mauck	Jef	2	3E	4S	17	NW
William Thompson	Jef	2	9E	1N	2	SE
Thomas Braxton	Jef	2	1E	1N	5	NW
Philip Copple	Jef	2	9E	2N	34	SW
John Maxwell	Jef	2	9E	3N	15	NW
William Anderson	Jef	2	9E	3N	4	SW
Jesse Lowell? [Towall?]	Jef	2	1W	1N	1	SE
William West	Jef	2	9E	3N	2	NE
Zachariah Nixon	Jef	2	4E	2N	17	NW
William Wiseman	Jef	2	3E	5S	27	NW
Robert Gilcrease	Jef	2	4E	3N	33	NE
William Brooks	Jef	2	1E	2N	25	SE
David Parr	Jef	2	4E	2N	24	NE
Jacob Persinger	Jef	2	4E	5N	22	SW
James Young	Jef	2	4E	2N	4	NW
Jonathan Lindley	Jef	2	1E	2N	29	NW
George Wilson	Jef	2	9E	4N	33	NW

1152				12 Jan 1813		A/5/098

Wyllys Silliman, Reg Zan
Transmits patents

John Mathew, Richard						
McBride, Andrew McBride	Zan	–	14	15	1	NE
John Reah	Zan	–	11	5	7	SW

1153				12 Jan 1813		A/5/099

LO Vin
Transmits patents

John Tuggle	Vin	–	13W	5S	18	SW
Thomas Stone	Vin	–	12W	3S	13	NW
Peter Brinton	Vin	–	8W	1N	27	NE
Richard Steen	Vin	–	7W	2N	4	SW
John Hurst	Vin	–	4E	3S	19	SW
James Patton	Vin	–	12W	3S	27	NE
James Patton	Vin	–	12W	3S	22	SE
James Patton	Vin	–	12W	3S	15	NE
James Patton	Vin	–	12W	3S	14	NW
Daniel Baldwins	Vin	–	6W	8S	28	+
Vatchel Hancock	Vin	–	6E	3S	32	+
Edward Stappleton	Vin	–	12W	3S	2	NE
Thomas Cummings	Vin	–	1W	6S	9	+
Samuel Conner	Vin	–	1W	7S	3	+
Samuel Conner	Vin	–	1W	7S	10	+
George Boone	Vin	–	4E	5S	28	NW
John Stroud	Vin	–	5E	2S	20	NE

1154				12 Jan 1813		A/5/099

LO Stu
Transmits patents

Martin Helman	Stu	–	8	10	27	SE
Amasa Lipsey	Stu	–	7	11	12	SW
John Carns	Stu	–	8	9	21	NE
Robert Baxter	Stu	–	6	10	6	SE
John Baxter	Stu	–	5	10	28	NE
James McCreary	Stu	–	7	16	31	NE
John Yant	Stu	–	7	15	12	NE
Daniel McConochy	Stu	–	6	17	23	NE
Christopher Markley	Stu	–	8	12	26	SE
James McCraron?	Stu	–	6	8	35	NW
Benjamin Kirk	Stu	–	5	9	15	SE
Philip Hewit	Stu	–	8	12	20	NE
Adam Bain? [Bair?]	Stu	–	6	17	17	NE
Abraham Yandt?	Stu	–	9	9	24	SE
George Barkhurst	Stu	–	3	6	19	NE
John Shannon	Stu	–	6	8	30	SE
John Apple	Stu	–	3	10	23	SW
John McMaster	Stu	–	4	13	32	NE
Michael King	Stu	–	7	9	20	SW
Joshua Cooper	Stu	–	4	14	4	SW
John Cranston	Stu	–	7	9	11	NE
Nathan Pim	Stu	–	5	16	34	NE
Adam Bair	Stu	–	6	17	7	NE
Zaccheus Biggs	Stu	–	7	19	35	NW

1155				12 Jan 1813		A/5/100

LO Chl
Transmits patents

Isaac Kline	Chl	MS	21	11	26	NE
Michael Grimrine	Chl	–	16	16	34	SW
Jacob Bumgarner	Chl	–	21	5	33	SE
William Williamson	Chl	MS	21	9	29	SE
Peter Cronninger	Chl	–	21	10	34	NE
William Moore *et al*	Chl	–	20	2	15	SW
Abraham Myers	Chl	–	20	13	22	NE
Henry Holler	Chl	–	20	11	19	NE
David Wiley	Chl	–	19	13	28	NE
John Ely	Chl	–	20	12	17	NE

1156				12 Jan 1813		A/5/100

LO Cin
Transmits patents

David Thimmet? [Kimmet?]	Cin	EML	5	4	35	–
Zebulon Barkalow	Cin	EML	5	2	31	–
John Miller	Cin	WML	1	10	1	E
John Eickman	Cin	EML	3	7	23	SW
Jacob Fenton?	Cin	EML	1	1	9	NW

1157				18 Jan 1813		A/5/100

Speaker, U.S. House of Representatives
Transmits report of commissioners who surveyed the
western boundary of the Virginia Miliary District
of Ohio.

1158				18 Jan 1813		A/5/101

Hon. J. Morrow, U.S. House of Representatives
Transmits patent

George P. Torrence	[Cin?]	EML	3	6	18	S

1159				20 Jan 1813		A/5/101

Hon. -- Hempstead, U.S. House of Representatives
Papers regarding Auguste Chouteau's claim have discrepancies and have to be returned to LO.

1160				20 Jan 1813		A/5/101

Daniel Symmes, Reg Cin
Transmits patents

Jonah Emyert*	Cin	EML	2	4	13	NW
Margaret McCoy	Cin	WML	1	13	18	SE

*Assignee of James Brown, to whom original patent
was erroneously made out.

1161				23 Jan 1813		A/5/102

LO Cin
Transmits patents

Peter Karan?	Cin	EML	6	4	6	NW
Matthias Parson	Cin	*	13	15	29	SW
Samuel Harlan	Cin	*	13	13N	6	NW
William Lee	Cin	MR	13	3	3	NW
William McBeth	Cin	MR	13	5	34	NE
Conrad Kaster	Cin	EML	2	7	5	NE
Abiah Hays	Cin	WML	1	6	22	SE
Thomas Herron	Cin	EML	2	5	17	SW
Samuel Hunt	Cin	EML	3	3	2	NE
Hiram Martin	Cin	EML	2	4	13	NE
Balser Snider	Cin	EML	3	6	4	NW
James Johnson	Cin	EML	2	4	10	NW
John Flint	Cin	WML	2	10	24	NW
John Flint	Cin	WML	1	10	20	NW
Enoch Limpus	Cin	*	12	13N	34	NW
Benjamin Woods	Cin	MR	2	2	26	SW
Benjamin Bayles	Cin	MR	13	2	20	–
Peter Karan	Cin	EML	6	5	32	SW
William Clark	Cin	EML	1	2	23	W
Jacob Kingery	Cin	WML	1	12	25	SW
Isaac Cooper	Cin	EML	5	5	34	NW
-- Brandons & -- Parks	Cin	EML	6	7	1	+
Philip Lybrook	Cin	WML	1	12	25	NW
William Moss	Cin	WML	1	12	25	SE
John Kinney	Cin	MR	7	3	10	SW
William Lytle	Cin	Town, Sq. 1, lot				1
William Lytle	Cin	Town, Sq. 1, lot				2
William Lytle	Cin	Town, Sq. 1, lot				3
William Lytle	Cin	Town, Sq. 1, lot				4
John P. Fingle	Cin	Pre	4	2	7	E
Matthew Hueston	Cin	Pre	10	1	10	+
James Dearth	Cin	Pre	4	3	36	S
Archibald Mercer	Cin	Pre	4	4	6	+

*East of Second Principal Meridian Line.

1162   23 Jan 1813 A/5/103
LO Chl*
Transmits patents

William Wilmuth	Chl	MS	22	2	25	SE
Robert Dickson	Chl	MS	22	4	2	SE
Robert Dickson	Chl	MS	22	4	1	SW

*This entire entry crossed out--"erroneous."

1163   23 Jan 1813 A/5/103
LO Can
Transmits patents

Philip Slusher	Can	-	10	12	8	SE
William Houston	Can	-	18	21	24	SE
Peter Weygandt	Can	-	10	1	34	NW
Christian Smith	Can	-	13	15	9	SW
Jacob Newman	Can	-	18	21?	35	SE
Stephen Harris	Can	-	10	1	28	SW
Philip Deywalt	Can	-	10	12	35	NE
Daniel Moore? [Moone?]	Can	-	10	1	20	NE
Stephen Harris	Can	-	10	1	29	SE
David Morrow	Can	-	11	16	5	NW
John Richey	Can	-	11	16	26	NW
James Kidoo	Can	-	12	17	36	NE
Jacob Bossert	Can	-	18	19	10	SE
John Cook	Can	-	19	18	5	SE
John Cook, Junior	Can	-	19	19	31	NW
William Blair	Can	-	19	18	6	NE
Robert Lytle	Can	-	10	1	27	SW
Henry Timmer? [Zimmer?]	Can	-	17	20	32	SE
Frederick Brown	Can	-	13	15	24	SE
Henry Smith	Can	-	13	15	12	N
Henry Kampf	Can	-	11	17	23	NE
James Kidoo	Can	-	11	17	30	SE
George Wyrick	Can	-	18	19	10	NW
John Young, Junior	Can	-	19	20	25	NE
John Richey	Can	-	10	1	32	NE
John Richey	Can	-	10	1	31	S
Joseph Hoslar	Can	-	10	12	27	E
Peter Weygandt	Can	-	10	1	35	NE
Frederick Stump	Can	-	10	12	34	SE
Philip Slusher	Can	-	10	12	8	NE

1164   23 Jan 1813 A/5/104
Jesse Spencer, Reg Chl
Transmits patent

William Wilmoth	Chl	MS	22	2	5	SE

1165   26 Jan 1813 A/5/104
John Kerr, Esq., Chl
Transmits patents

Joseph Kerr*	Mil	-	-	-	-	-
John Kerr**	Mil	-	-	-	-	-

*100 acres, based on military land warrant 482.
**50 acres, based on military land warrant 589, in
 part.

1166   26 Jan 1813 A/5/104
Hon. Peter Little
Transmits patents

-- Slingluff & -- Fahnestock	Mil	-	-	-	-	-
Christian Deardorff	Mil	-	-	-	-	-

1167   26 Jan 1813 A/5/104
Hon. T. Worthington
Transmits patent

-- Ijams & -- Sunderland	Chl	-	17	16	4	NW

1168   27 Jan 1813 A/5/104
Hon. Jeremiah Morrow, U.S. House of Representatives
Transmits patents and letter from Mr. -- Schenck

--	[Cin?]	MR	5	2	28	NW
--*	[Cin?]	Pre	4	3	17	-
--**	[Cin?]	-	4	3	19	-
Thomas Wintwringer	[Cin?]	-	7	8	9	NE

 *Patent sent to LO in Sep 1812.
**Final certificate not yet received.

1169   28 Jan 1813 A/5/105
LO Hun
Transmits patents

William O. Murrey	Hun	-	1	3	23	NW
William O. Murrey	Hun	-	1	3	22	NE
William O. Murrey	Hun	-	1	3	23	SE
William O. Murrey	Hun	-	1	3	22	SE

1170   28 Jan 1813 A/5/105
LO WPR
Transmits patents

David Batson	WPR	WML	1	1	28	-
William Whitehead	WPR	EML	11	6	35	SE

1171   28 Jan 1813 A/5/105
Samuel Gwathmey, Reg Jef
Please return patent*

Jacob Persinger	Jef	-	4E	5N	22	SW

*"It should have been handed to Hon. -- Breckenridge
 of Virginia to had to the patentee. . . ."

1172   28 Jan 1813 A/5/105
Hon. -- Poindexter
Encloses abstract of Mr. -- Pollock's claim, as re-
 ported by the commissioners.

1173   30 Jan 1813 A/5/105
Eli House, Postoffice, Traptown, Frederick County,
 Maryland
Transmits patent

Eli House	Zan	-	14	13	12	NW

1174   30 Jan 1813 A/5/105
Joseph Wood, Reg Mar
Transmits patent

Samuel Edgerton	Mar	-	5	6	34	NE

1175   30 Jan 1813 A/5/106
Patrick Johnson, Bedford, Chster County, Pennsylvania
Transmits patent

Patrick Johnson	Zan	-	13	12	8	SE

1176   1 Feb 1813 A/5/106
Wyllys Silliman, [Reg] Zan
Errors in computation of interest periods

Henry Weller	Zan	-	15	14	26	SW
Benjamin Leverage	Mil	-	1	2*	21	SW

*Two or five.

1177   1 Feb 1813 A/5/106
Christian Eby, Postoffice, Baltimore
Three patents for you sent to postoffice on 22 Mar
 1810. "If you are entitled to more, please describe
 tracts. . . ."

1178   2 Feb 1813   A/5/107
Alexander Macomb, New York
Letter regarding John Ramsey's claim, under British
   grant, to land on the bank of the Mississippi
   River at Pointe Coupée. Details should be for-
   warded to Commissioner James O. Cosby.

1179   3 Feb 1813   A/5/108
Parke Walton, Rec Wsh
Enquiry received regarding claim of Elias Vanderhorst
   to 3,000 acres, under British grant, in EPR district. His name appears in schedule of 16 Dec 1808
   but no further information available.

1180   4 Feb 1813   A/5/108
John Stine, Reading, Berks County, Pennsylvania
Does not know why final certificate for lands in
   Ch1 LO district have been delayed so long. Will
   inquire.

1181   4 Feb 1813   A/5/109
Jesse Spencer, Reg Ch1
Inquires regarding final certificates
John Stine   Ch1 - 21 11 9 NW
John Stine   Ch1 - 21 11 9 SW
John Stine   Ch1 - 21 11 9 SE
John Stine   Ch1 - 21 11 8 SE

1182   5 Feb 1813   A/5/109
Christian Eby, care of John Seely, Innkeeper, Old
   Town, Baltimore
Transmits patents; they had been forwarded to you
   care of postoffice, Baltimore, on 22 Mar 1810 and
   returned to this office as dead letter.

1183   5 Feb 1813   A/5/109
Lewis Sewall, Reg St. Stephens [EPR]
Corrects Reg LO regarding the down payment to be
   made for lands sold at public auction.

1184   6 Feb 1813   A/5/110
Fredrick Bates, Recorder of Land Titles, St. Louis,
   Missouri Territory
Returns defective documents. Mentions 1,036 acres
   of land claimed by Auguste Chouteau on Mill Creek
   and a town lot; 1,031 acres by Chouteau under
   Leclede Legast, the original claimant. Mentions
   partial land descriptions "N57 45W and S57 45E,
   instead of N75 45W and N75 45E."

1185   8 Feb 1813   A/5/112
Columbus Lawson, Reg ELA
Letter of appointment.

1186   8 Feb 1813   A/9/112
Lloyd Posey, Rec ELA
Letter of appointment.

1187   8 Feb 1813   A/5/112
William Garrard
Letter of appointment. Postscript mentions open
   letter to Philip Grymes, former Reg, directing him
   to deliver books, etc., of office.

1188   8 Feb 1813   A/9/113
Philip Grymes, former Reg, New Orleans
Letter directing him to turn over books of office
   for LO ELA to Columbus Lawson.

1189   10 Feb 1813   A/5/113
Benjamin Hough, Ch1
Contracts executed; cannot forward a copy of the
   land laws.

1190   12 Feb 1813   A/5/114
Isaiah Burson, New Lisbon, Ohio
Patent you have inquired about was sent to Reg Stu
   on 21 Dec 1812.

1191   12 Feb 1813   A/5/114
Jacob Bower, Hagerstown, Maryland
Patent you have inquired about was sent to LO Ch1 on
   10 May 1812.

1192   12 Feb 1813   A/5/114
Hon. Thomas Worthington, U.S. Senate
Forwards list of all locations made in U.S. Military
   District and Refugee Lands from 4 Jan 1812 to pres-
   ent, to be forwarded to [Benjamin] Hough, Auditor
   of the State of Ohio.

1193   13 Feb 1813   A/5/115
William Crawford, Commissioner, in the Eastern District and at Ft. Stoddard, Mississippi Territory
Gives directions as to accounting entries and regarding translation of French and Spanish documents.

1194   15 Feb 1813   A/5/115
Hon. James Monroe, Secretary of State
James Abbott, Rec Det, submits accounts; appointment
   date requested.

1195   18 Feb 1813   A/5/116
LO Cin
Transmits patents
Abraham Lewis   Cin WML 1 12   9 SW
William Armstrong   Cin WML 1   9   9 SE
Alexander Telfer   Cin WML 1   9   2 SW
Silas Gregg   Cin * 13E 14N   7 NE
James Furgus   Cin MR   9   2 32 SE
Abraham Vaneaton   Cin * 13E 14N 22 NE
Absalom Thomas   Cin MR   8   6 12 NE
Lewis Circle   Cin EML 4   6 23 SE
Philip Long   Cin EML 4   3 28 NE
Christian Waldsmith   Cin EML 2   3 15 NE
Andrew Hodges, deceased** Cin MR 9 5 20 NE
William Gaston   Cin MR   2   3   8 S
Joseph Meeker   Cin EML 6   2 10 SW
Jacob Wheeler   Cin Town, Sq. 3, lot 15
Nathan Sellers   Cin EML 2   8 35 NW
John James   Cin WML 2   9 17 NW
Eli Johnston   Cin EML 2   3   2 NE
John Stansbury   Cin WML 1   8 23 NE
Ezekiel French   Cin MR 11   1 26 +
Mahlon Brown   Cin WML 1   6 23 NE
John Pursel   Cin WML 1   7   9 NW
Daniel Kemp   Cin EML 3   5 30 -
Henry Sater   Cin WML 1   8 14 NE
Henry Sater   Cin WML 1   8 24 NW

Owen Sensy	Cin	WML	1	12	3	SW
Isaac Willetts	Cin	*	13E	16N	21	NW
George Death	Cin	*	13E	14N	20	NE
Jabes Winship	Cin	WML	2	8	13	SE
John Tharp	Cin	WML	2	9	8	NE
Jacob Wilson	Cin	MR	9	2	15	SW
Michael Olson	Cin	EML	1	4	36	SW
Jacob Wheeler	Cin	MR	2	3	8	+
Jacob Wheeler	Cin	Town, Sq. 3, lot 14				
Jacob Hultsz	Cin	MR	9	6	5	+
Jacob Hultsz	Cin	MR	9	6	6	+
Jacob Juoy	Cin	MR	12	3	1	SW
Jacob Deibert	Cin	MR	10	4	29	SE
Daniel Miller	Cin	MR	2	2	26	+
Thomas Tipton	Cin	MR	12	5	32	SE
John Aikman	Cin	EML	3	7	23	NE
James McDaniel	Cin	MR	9	6	20	NE
Peter Slutman	Cin	EML	3	5	21	SE
Henry Biear?	Cin	EML	3	6	22	SW
Daniel Wilkins	Cin	EML	2	2	6	SW
Reuben Slatton? [Hatton?]	Cin	EML	1	4	18	SW
Levi Gard	Cin	EML	1	7	31	SE
Samuel Walker	Cin	WML	1	13	12	NE
Samuel Rodehaffar	Cin	EML	4	4	11	NW
John Pence	Cin	EML	4	4	11	SW
David Miles	Cin	EML	5	7	30	SE
James Cloud	Cin	WML	1	7	27	SW
John McCormick	Cin	MR	2	2	8	SE
John McCormick	Cin	MR	2	2	8	SW
John A. Penn	Cin	MR	12	1	17	SE
George Bort	Cin	EML	3	7	20	NW
Philip Swartzley	Cin	EML	4	3	3	W
John Sater? [Later?]	Cin	WML	1	8	13	NW
William McCampbell	Cin	MR	11	1	22	NE
James Dittis	Cin	MR	11	5	26	SW
Peter Williamson	Cin	MR	3	3	11	SE
Aaron Sibbett	Cin	MR	2	3	26	NE
Patrick Long	Cin	MR	1	4	26	SE
Joseph James	Cin	MR	3	4	11	SW
Rachel Thatcher? [Hatcher?]	Cin	MR	9	6	24	NE
Thomas Stone	Cin	MR	3	2	26	SE
Samuel Harlan	Cin	*	13E	14N	31	NW
James Johnston	Cin	EML	6	7	19	NW
Gaspar Koons	Cin	WML	1	13	10	SW
Samuel Harlan	Cin	**	13E	14N	31	SW
John Nixon	Cin	**	12E	16N	23	NW
James Caldwell	Cin	EML	1	6	9	NW
Henry Kroll	Cin	EML	5	4	10	SE
Samuel Burck	Cin	EML	6	3	7	SW
James Reed	Cin	EML	6	4	33	SE
John Hendershot	Cin	EML	6	7	29	NE
Christopher Miller	Cin	EML	2	2	26	NE
Abner Dooley	Cin	-	2	7	6	SE
John Norris	Cin	*	14E	14N	19	SE
Abraham Powell	Cin	MR	11	5	29	SW

*Second Principal Meridian.
**Shown as EML, but almost certainly Second Principal Meridian is meant.

1196 18 Feb 1813 A/5/118
LO Zan
Transmits patents

Lewis Pierce	Zan	-	11	13	20	NE
Joseph Vernon	Zan	Mil	6	1	5	NE
Ezra? May	Zan	-	10	9	32	NW
John Vernon	Zan	Mil	6	1	3	SW
Robert McMillan	Zan	Mil	10	7	14	NE
James Richardson	Zan	Mil	4	9	23	SE
Philip Winklebleck	Zan	Mil	4	9	18	NE
Henry Miller	Zan	Mil	4	9	23	SW
James Richardson	Zan	Mil	4	9	23	NE

Adam Smith	Zan	-	15	18	6	NE
Charles Uhl	Zan	Mil	7	9	23	E
Joseph Fickle	Zan	-	15	17	28	SE
Robert Latta	Zan	-	10	9	32	SE
Philip Howell	Zan	-	11	13	9	NW
Richard Dickerson	Zan	Mil	3	1	20	SW
Samuel Farquahar*	Zan	Mil	9	5	4	NE
John Ebey	Zan	-	15	17	20	SE
Christ[ophe]r Lenhart	Zan	-	15	17	9	NE
Joseph Evans	Zan	-	12	12	17	+
Joseph Evans	Zan	-	12	12	20	+
David Beckwith	Zan	-	13	12	15	+
James Bratton	Zan	Mil	2	2	5	NE
Samuel Newell	Zan	Mil	3	3	13	NE
John Sell	Zan	Mil	1	9	2	NE
Samuel Farquhar*	Zan	Mil	9	5	5	NE
-- Leon & -- Stump	Zan	Mil	9	3	19	NE
-- Leon & -- Stump	Zan	Mil	9	3	4	SW
Charles Uhl	Zan	Mil	7	9	19	W
Hugh Graham	Zan	Mil	2	1	2	SW
David Robe	Zan	Mil	2	2	19	NE
Nathaniel Spurgeon	Zan	Mil	10	6	3	NW
Nathan Wilson	Zan	-	9	1	8	NW
Samuel Sprague	Zan	-	10	7	5	SW
Henry Hummel	Zan	-	15	17	24	NW
Ephraim Sayers	Zan	-	11	10	30	+
John Thompson	Zan	-	14	15	10	NW
Stephen Butler	Zan	Mil	10	9	22	SE
John Butler	Zan	Mil	10	7	20	SE
Joseph Hanger	Zan	Mil	10	7	13	NW
Robert Warrick	Zan	Mil	2	4	21	NW
James Foreacre	Zan	Mil	1	1	2	NW
John Butler	Zan	Mil	10	9	19	SE
Joseph Turner	Zan	-	14	16	14	NE

*So spelled.

1197 18 Feb 1813 A/5/119
LO Stu
Transmits patents

Charles Porter	Stu	-	5	11?	27?	SE
John Eysennoggle	Stu	-	6	14	33	SE
Thomas Short	Stu	-	4	6	34	SE
George Fetter	Stu	-	8	9	24	SW
John Cameron	Stu	-	4	14	19	SW
George Miller	Stu	-	9	10	13	SW
Christopher Bair	Stu	-	7	18	35	W
Henry Neff, Junior	Stu	-	3	5	30	-
Henry Blythe	Stu	-	4	11	12	SE
Adam Warner	Stu	-	8	11	22	SW
John Shaw	Stu	-	7	18	12	SW
Henry Sidwell	Stu	-	3	7	21	NE
Martin Funk	Stu	-	8	11	28	SW
Hardick Warren	Stu	-	3	6	19	SE
John Coope	Stu	-	4	9	21	NE
John Henderson, Junior	Stu	-	7	9	17	-

1198 18 Feb 1813 A/5/119
LO Can
Transmits patents

George Boylestone	Can	-	10	11	17	SE
Elijah Stansberry	Can	-	10	12	35	NW
Michael Bosse	Can	-	10	11	36	SW
Joseph Colker	Can	-	10	12	33	NE
Samuel McWilliams	Can	-	19	20	28	SE
Michael Bosse	Can	-	10	11	36	SE
William Alban	Can	-	10	1	17	NW
Zephaniah Beale	Can	-	14	21	14	SE
Zephaniah Beale	Can	-	14	21	3	SE
Zephaniah Beale	Can	-	14	21	25	NE
Zephaniah Beale	Can	-	14	21	24	SE

1199   22 Feb 1813   A/5/120
Hon. E. Hempstead
Reports on Auguste Chouteau's land claim; mentions
   -- Morales.

1200   22 Feb 1813   A/5/120
Daniel Symmes, Reg Cin
Encloses final certificates for Jacob Burnet; in-
   quires regarding discrepancies, as per below

Not sold, per books	Cin Pre	7	2	14	S
Sold, but not to -- Stinson	Cin Pre	8	2	22	+
Sold, but not to -- Stinson	Cin Pre	8	2	23	+
Sold to another person	Cin Pre	10	2	23	NE
Incorrect description?	Cin WML	2?	4	29	NW
Correct description?	Cin WML	2?	4	29	SE
Whole section already sold	Cin EML	5	2	8	-
Sold to others in quarter sections	Cin Pre	5	3	30	-
Alexander Dearmond, entered 2 Nov 1812	Cin EML	1	3	22	NW
L. Sawyers paid first instal- ment	Cin EML	1	3	22	NW

1201   23 Feb 1813   A/5/121
Hon. Jeremiah Morrow
Transmits patents

Jacob Burnet	Cin Pre	7	3	15	NW
Jacob Burnet	Cin Pre	7	3	15	SE
Jacob Burnet	Cin Pre	7	3	15	NE
Jacob Burnet	Cin Pre	9	2	6	SE

1202   24 Feb 1813   A/5/121
Thomas Freeman, Surveyor General
Answers letter regarding salaries of Ward Graham,
   -- Winton.

1203   24 Feb 1813   A/5/122
Daniel Symmes, Reg Cin
Transmits final certificates for correction (short
   payments)

--	Cin EML	6	5	34	+
--	Cin MR	11	4	11	SE
--	Cin MR	11	4	11	NW
--	Cin EML	5	4	21	NE
--	Cin EML	2	5	1	NE
--	Cin EML	2	5	1	SE
--	Cin WML	2	4	22	SW
--	Cin MR	11	1	7	NW
--	Cin EML	1	7	25	NE
--	Cin EML	1	10	27	NE
--	Cin MR	10	5	6	SW
--	Cin EML	1	10	23	SW
--	Cin EML	4	6	18	NW
--	Cin *	13E	14	22	SW
--	Cin EML	6	4	17	SW
--	Cin EML	5	2	31	-

*Second Principal Meridian.

1204   25 Feb 1813   A/5/122
Abiathar V. Taylor, Franklinton, Ohio
Does not have papers, said to have been given to
   General [Thomas] Worthington, regarding location
   of John Taylor's lands in the Refugee Tract.

1205   27 Feb 1813   A/5/123
Nathaniel Frye, Esq.
Transmits military patent in favor of John Wilkins.

1206   27 Feb 1813   A/5/123
Thomas Gibson, Reg Can
Transmits final certificates and patents

John Christmas*	Can	- 9	10	17	+
John Christmas*	Can	- 9	10	20	+
Henry Dimmer? [Timmer?]	Can	- 17	23	24	SE
William Kerr	Can	- 13	13	10	NW
Abraham Timmer	Can	- 17	23	31	NE
Daniel Carter	Can	- 16	22	9	W
Daniel Carter	Can	- 17	23	10	NE
Philip Tolman	Can	- 18	18	6	NE
Amos Farquhar	Can	- 18	18	6	SE
Daniel Carter	Can	- 17	23	22	NW

*Returned for correction of certificates.

1207   27 Feb 1813   A/5/123
Samuel Gwathmey, Reg Jef
Transmits final certificate for correction; also
   transmits patents

--*	Jef	- 1E	2N	31	SE
Michael Munroe	Jef	- 9E	3N	19	NE
Thomas Draper	Jef	- 4E	2N	21	NE
Samuel Arnett	Jef	- 10E	2N	7	SE
Thomas McCay	Jef	- 9E	4N	10?	NW
George Beck	Jef	- 3E	1N	11	SW
Isaiah Spurgeon	Jef	- 4E	2N	14	SE
John Vancleve	Jef	- 2E	2N	33	SW
William Holliday	Jef	- 1E	1N	9	NE
John Royse	Jef	- 3E	1S	15	SW
Jacob Persinger**	Jef	- 4	5	22	SW

*Final certificate returned for correction.
**Again requests return of patent.

1208   27 Feb 1813   A/5/124
James O. Cosby, Land Commissioner, Wilkinson Court-
   house, Mississippi Territory
Transmits written notice of the claim of John Ramsay
   to 1,000 acres of land in your district; an original
   British patent for the same land, granted to John
   Elliott, Esq., Captain General and governor in chief
   in and over the province of West Florida, to John
   Walker, dated at Pensacola, 24 Apr 1769, and there
   recorded in book E, folio 1, and a deed of convey-
   ance from John Walker and Hannah, his wife, to John
   Ramsay.

1209   27 Feb 1813   A/5/124
John Badollet, Reg Vin
Whether lands now in LO Jef district, but originally
   sold by LO Vin, which have reverted to the United
   States, can be resold through LO Vin.

1210   27 Feb 1813   A/5/125
Nathaniel Ewing, Rec Vin
Samuel Gwathmey, Reg Jef
Edmund H. Taylor, Rec Jef
Transmits copies of letter to LO Vin above.

1211   1 Mar 1813   A/5/126
John Reed, Reg Hun; John Brahan, Rec Hun
Transmits letters of appointment.

1212   1 Mar 1813   A/5/126
William Dickson, former Reg Hun [Madison County]
Letter directing him to turn over books to his suc-
   cessor.

1213   1 Mar 1813   A/5/127
David Hoge, Reg Stu
Transmits receipts

Peter Nees	Stu	–	10?	2	14 SE
George Bair	Stu	–	9	9	12 SW

1214   1 Mar 1813   A/5/127
Daniel Symmes, Reg Cin
Returns final certificate containing discrepancies;
   mentions Peyton Short

--	Cin	–	12	1	32 +

1215   2 Mar 1813   A/5/127
John Stine, Reading, Berks County, Pennsylvania
Upon resurveying the land you bought, it was found
   to be larger than originally thought, and you
   must pay additional amount.

1216   3 Mar 1813   A/5/128
Samuel Gwathmey, Reg Jef
Patent in favor of Jacob Persinger, who you were requested to return, for the Hon. -- Breckenridge,
   was transmitted to your office 27 May 1812, rather
   than the date previously stated in my letter of
   28 Jan 1813.

1217   6 Mar 1813   A/5/129
Hon. H. Clay, Lexington, Kentucky
As requested by John Graham, of the U.S. Department
   of State, I forward a certified copy of a patent
   issued 6 May 1805 in favor of George Rice for 300
   acres in the U.S. Military District.

1218   8 Mar 1813   A/5/130
Hon. Abner Laycock, Beavertown, Pennsylvania
Upon examination of papers relative to tract pur-
   chased by Joseph Sheerer, deceased, I find the
   affidavit names his heirs Agness and four others;
   transfer is signed by Nancy and four others.
   Therefore, patent herewith issued in favor of the
   heirs of [Joseph] Sheerer who can transfer it to
   -- Alexander, and he to William Wray and Joseph
   Wray.

1219   8 Mar 1813   A/5/130
John Reed, Reg Hun, Mississippi Territory
Transmits patent

Benjamin Murnell? [Murinell?]	Hun WML	3	1	26 SE

1220   9 Mar 1813   A/5/130
John Badollet, Reg Vin
Returns erroneous final certificate; tranmits pat-
   ents

Jonathan Mock*	Vin	–	2E	3S	26	SE
Jacob Weatherhalt	Vin	–	2W	8S	3	+
Jacob Weatherhalt	Vin	–	2W	8S	4	+
Thomas Horral	Vin	–	7W	2N	9	SE
James McClure	Vin	–	10W	2S	18	NW
Daniel Darrock	Vin	–	1W	2N	13	NW
Thomas Braxton	Vin	–	1W	2N	24	NE
Jonathan Lindley	Vin	–	1W	2N	13	S
Henry Hopkins	Vin	–	10W	2S	7	SW
Adam Davis	Vin	–	1W	2N	36	NW
George Humphreys	Vin	–	11W	1S	25	NW
William Applegate	Vin	–	3E	5S	3	SW

J. Warrick, heirs of	Vin	– 12W	3S	10	SE
John Wood	Vin	– 13W	1N	36	NE
Jonas Fleshman	Vin	– 2E	5S	13	N
Hervey Heth	Vin	– 3E	3S	36	NE
William Berry	Vin	– 6W	8S	2	+
William Berry	Vin	– 6W	8S	11	+
Thomas Lindley	Vin	– 1W	2N	13	NE
Henry Edwards	Vin	– 7W	2N	20	NW
Samuel Kimmel	Vin	– 14W	7S	9	SE
Samuel Kimmel	Vin	– 14W	7S	15	NE
James Stewart	Vin	– 12W	3S	1	NW
Jesse Hollowell	Vin	– 1W	1N	11	NW
Spencer Wood	Vin	– 12W	1N	1	SE
John Hurst	Vin	– 4E	3S	8	NW
William Wright	Vin	– 5E	3S	15	SW
Edward Wells	Vin	– 12W	3S	17	NE
John Lopp? [Lapp?]	Vin	– 3E	5S	22	SW
John Lopp? [Lapp?]	Vin	– 3E	5S	34	SE

1221   9 Mar 1813   A/5/131
Lewis Sewall, Reg Fort Stephens, Mississippi Territory; Samuel Smith, Rec Fort Stephens
Answers query regarding occupancy and settlement and
   the need to give a donation [tract], having been
   presented a valid pre-emption certificate.

1222   10 Mar 1813   A/5/132
Comptroller of the U.S. Treasury
The former Rec EPR [Lemuel Henry] rendered no accounting reports since 1811 and "the United States are in
   danger of losing a considerable sum of money, due
   from the late receiver at that place, unless immediately attended to." Balance due the United States
   estimated to be $12,251.67, less salaries and con-
   tingent expenses he may have paid out.

1223   10 Mar 1813   A/5/132
Hon. Edward Hempstead, St. Louis, Missouri Territory
Returns instructions regarding Louisiana lands, given
   to -- Morales.

1224   11 Mar 1813   A/5/133
Daniel Symmes, Reg Cin
Again requests final certificate

Samuel Haines	[Cin?]	–	5	6	31 –

1225   13 Mar 1813   A/5/133
Jesse Spencer, Reg Chl
Transmits patents

Caleb Evans*	Chl	–	21	10	5 SE
Samuel Edwards*	Chl	–	21	10	5 NE

*Assignees of James Stewart.

1226   13 Mar 1813   A/5/134
Nehemiah Tilton, Reg Wsh
Returns final certificate for short payment

William Neatans	Wsh	–	1W	1	7 +

1227   15 Mar 1813   A/5/134
Wyllys Silliman, Reg Zan
Returns final certificate (overpayment)

Peter Smith	Zan Mil	3	9	12 SE

1228   15 Mar 1813 A/5/135
Hon. Edward Hempstead, St. Louis, Missouri Territory
Transmits translated instructions for -- Morales.

1229   16 Mar 1813 A/5/135
Samuel Smith, Rec St Stephens [EPR]
Since predecessor Lemuel Henry is dead, you are instructed to post books and render his quarterly accounts from 1 Jan 1812 to date.

1230   17 Mar 1813 A/5/135
Nehemiah Tilton, Reg Wsh [WPR]
Returns final certificate (underpayment); mentions John Purvis, who assigns to Silas Dinsmore. Also transmits patents, as follows

William Downs	WPR	-	3E	15	29	-
David Montgomery	WPR	-	4E	3	30	NW
Frederick Newsom	WPR	-	5E	2	28	NW
William Jones	WPR	-	4E	2	4	SW

1231   17 Mar 1813 A/5/136
Hon. William Findley, Westmoreland County, Pennsylvania
Transmits patent

David Findley	Zan Mil	4	2	22	SW

1232   22 Mar 1813 A/5/137
John Reed, Reg Hun
Answers letter, signed by Hugh Kerr for Reg Hun, stating that several patents sent from this office are missing; mentions Samuel Davis; James Walker; -- Harris, assignee of -- Freeman. Transmits patent

Allen Christian	Hun	-	1E	3	30	NE

1233   22 Mar 1813 A/5/137
Jesse Spencer, Reg Chl
Returns final certificate for correction

Thomas Worthington	Chl	-	17	14	15	NE

1234   22 Mar 1813 A/5/137
David Hoge, Reg Stu
Failed to enclose first certificate

--	Stu	-	1	7	32	NW

1235   23 Mar 1813 A/5/138
Daniel Symmes, Reg Cin
Patent returned for signature; mentions Jesse Harbour.

1236   25 Mar 1813 A/5/138
Daniel Symmes, Reg Cin
Returns final certificate (short payment); mentions G? P. Torrence.

1237   29 Mar 1813 A/5/139
John Reed, Reg Hun
Transmits patent

Nathan Strong	Hun EML	1	3	8	SW

1238   30 Mar 1813 A/5/139
John Matthews, Springfield, Muskingum County, Ohio
Transmits patent

Seely Schoffield	Mil	-	5	3	3	12

1239   30 Mar 1813 A/5/140
Isaac Van Horne, Rec Zan
Transmits duplicate receipts

John Lock	Zan Mil	1	8	8	SE

1240   30 Mar 1813 A/5/140
John Wade, Postoffice, Sharpsburg, Washington County, Pennsylvania
Transmits patent

John Wade	Zan Mil	3	10	18	SE

1241   30 Mar 1813 A/5/140
Daniel Symmes, Reg Cin
Your returns show the following errors:

-- Ennis[1]	Cin Pre	5	3	12	SW
-- Wheeler[2]	Cin Pre	8	3	17	NE
--	Cin	-	1	?	3	-
--[3]	Cin	*	4E	16	24	SW
John Lock[4]	Cin EML	3	7	22	SW
John Lock[4]	Cin EML	3	7	26	SW

*Second Principal Meridian.
[1]Assignee of John Smith; Smith is not charged with that tract on our books.
[2]Assignee of Jesse Hunt; this land was purchased by Thomas Hunter.
[3]There is no such tract on the books for the Second Principal Meridian; name of Henry Krown, original purchaser, is not found.
[4]Please send final certificates or state reason why they should not issue. Error noted in payments for first tract.

1242   1 Apr 1813 A/5/141
LO Zan
Transmits patents

Michael Stonehocker	Zan Mil	5	6	16	SW
Levi Dean	Zan	-	8	5	17	SE
Jeremiah Reed	Zan	-	14	14	32	NE
Isaac Sparks	Zan Mil	1	9	1	W
John Robinson	Zan Mil	6	1	5	SW
James Richardson	Zan Mil	4	8	3	NW
James Brown, Junior	Zan	-	10	6	31	+
James Brown, Junior	Zan	-	10	6	32	+
James Officer	Zan	-	11	13	6	SW
Thomas Satterthwaite	Zan Mil	2	1	11	SE
Yost Miller	Zan Mil	4	9	25	SE
Peter Saltsgiver?	Zan Mil	1	2	4	NW
Peter Lepley	Zan Mil	10	6	24	NE
George Kollar	Zan Mil	1	9	9	NE
Matthew Mitchell	Zan Mil	5	1	1	NE
John M. Stonehocker	Zan Mil	7	4	2	NE
Thomas Harris	Zan	-	15	18	7	NW
Thomas Hummel	Zan Mil	10	1	22	NW
Stephen Shock	Zan Mil	6	1	9	NW
William Bay	Zan	-	10	9	28	NE
William Hamilton	Zan	-	15	18	15	NE
Abraham Carver	Zan Mil	3	8	4	NE
Robert McIntire	Zan	-	15	16	2	NW
Richard Burrell	Zan Mil	3	10	25	NW
William Wynn	Zan Mil	6	1	9	SW
John Butler	Zan Mil	10	9	22	NE
John Wade	Zan Mil	3	10	16	SW
William George, Senior	Zan	-	15	18	12	SW
John Porter	Zan	-	15	16	1	SE

William Sellers & Isaac Sellers	Zan	–	15	16	5	SW
John Gardner	Zan	–	15	16	34	NW
Joseph Wiley	Zan	–	14	15	32	SE
Joseph Burges	Zan	–	15	17	18	NW
Henry Flowers	Zan	–	15	17	28	SW
James Dye	Zan	–	9	7	2	SE
Abraham Umstot	Zan	Mil	1	2	5	NE
James Warrack	Zan	Mil	1	3	14	SW
Joseph Passmore	Zan	Mil	6	1	10	SE
Zachariah Philips	Zan	–	14	15	22	NW
John Matthews	Zan	–	14	15	12	NW
George Clapper	Zan	–	12	13	5	SW
Johnson Brewster	Zan	–	12	13	9	SE
John Flemons? [Hemens?]	Zan	–	11	13	12	NE

1243   1 Apr 1813   A/5/142
LO Cin
Transmits patents

Jacob Wheeler	Cin	Pre	8	4	18	–
Jacob Wheeler	Cin	Pre	9	4	19	–
David Huston	Cin	Pre	7	2	2	SW
Garret Vannest	Cin	Pre	4	2	18	+
John Jay	Cin	Pre	5	4	33	SE
William Tanner	Cin	Pre	5	4	30	+
Sylvanus Daniel, Junior	Cin	Pre	5	3	25	SW
William Wilkins[1]	Cin	Pre	4	4	22	NW
John Enoch	Cin	Pre	13	5	20	–
John Kiszer? [Kizer?]	Cin	Pre	7	2	7	NW
Owen Davis[2]	Cin	Pre	8	5	32	+
John Enoch	Cin	Pre	13	5	21	–
William C. Schenck	Cin	Pre	4	3	19	–
Martin Keever, Junior	Cin	Pre	4	4	24	N
Martin Keever, Junior	Cin	Pre	4	4	24	SE
Martin Keever, Junior	Cin	Pre	4	4	24	+?
Daniel Broadstreet[3]	Cin	Pre	5	3	33	–
William Stewart	Cin	Pre	7	2	13	NE
Samuel Brown	Cin	Pre	8	3	21	NE
Caleb Harvey	Cin	WML	2	13	12	W
Caleb Harvey	Cin	WML	2	13	11	+
Benjamin Hutchins	Cin	* 14E	18N	28	NW	
John Turner	Cin	WML	1	15	32	SE
George Glaze	Cin	* 12E	14N	1	NE	
William Cox	Cin	WML	2	14	24	+
William Cox	Cin	WML	2	14	13	+
Samuel Stewart	Cin	MR	3	3	8	NE
Joseph Harris	Cin	MR	1	3	11	SE
James McClure	Cin	MR	9	2	9	SW
Pierson Layne? [Sayne?]	Cin	MR	3	3	11	NW
Samuel Stewart	Cin	MR	8	5	12	SW
St. Leager Neal	Cin	MR	12	5	7	NW
Hezekiah Mount	Cin	* 12E	14N	31	+	
Hezekiah Mount	Cin	* 13E	12N	32	NW	
John Conner	Cin	WML	2	8	13	NW
John Conner	Cin	WML	2	8	11	SW
John Brown, Senior	Cin	EML	2	3	21	SW
Joseph Cooper	Cin	EML	5	5	14	SE
Adam Deem	Cin	EML	3	5	11	SE
Nicholas Keese	Cin	EML	4	5	11	NW
Joseph Coppock	Cin	EML	4	7	1	SW
Jesse Kenworthy	Cin	EML	3	3	6	NW
John Conner	Cin	WML	2	8	14	NE
David Mount	Cin	* 12E	12N	34	NE	
Hezekiah Mount	Cin	* 13E	12N	32	SW	
Jacob Blacklige	Cin	* 13E	12N	19	NE	
Richard Kolb	Cin	* 13E	15N	28	SE	

*Second Principal Meridian.
[1]"Corner."   [2]"Survey 1."   [3]"274 a[cre]s."

1244   1 Apr 1813   A/5/143

Wyllys Silliman, Reg Zan
Returns certificate for correction

--		Zan	–	10	9	31 SE

1245   2 Apr 1813   A/5/143
David Hoge, Reg Stu
Encloses first certificate forwarded by Senator --
    Gregg

George Bair*	Stu	–	9	9	12	SW

*Transferred to John Willeman.

1246   2 Apr 1813   A/5/144
Jesse Spencer, Reg Chl
Returns defective certificates

C. Rokohl*	Chl	–	19	14	15	NW
George Steely**		[not described]				

*Transferred to John Shurr.
**Transferred to J. Brown & G. Brown.

1247   5 Apr 1813   A/5/144
Nehemiah Tilton, Reg WPR, Washington, Mississippi
    Territory
Returns defective certificates; mentions Landlot
    [Lancelot?] Porter; John Porter's land on the Homo-
    chitto [River?]; John Reynolds, or his assignee;
    Abel Eastman, deceased.

1248   6 Apr 1813   A/5/145
Hon. Thomas Robertson, Richmond [Virginia?]
"I . . . have not found in the records of this office
    anything relative to the grant of land you mention."

1249   7 Apr 1813   A/5/145
Daniel Symmes, Reg Cin
Returns defective certificates and patent

William Short	Cin	Pre	8	2	3	+
-- McCleary*		[not described]				

*Assignee of Robert Park? [Parks?]

1250   9 Apr 1813   A/5/146
John Piggott, Postoffice, Leesburgh, Virginia
Transmits patent

John Piggott	Stu	–	7	11	9	NE

1251   10 Apr 1813   A/5/147
LO Cin
Transmits patents

William Watkins, Senior	Cin	Pre	5	3	18	S
Jacob White	Cin	Pre	4	3	2	SW
Jacob White	Cin	Pre	4	3	14	E
Christopher Knoops	Cin	Pre	10	2	33	NE
Christopher Knoops	Cin	Pre	10	2	34	SE
Lewis Lechlider & Joseph Coleman	Cin	Pre	6	2	35	E
William Short	Cin	Pre	8	2	9	W
William Short	Cin	Pre	8	2	15	NE
William Short	Cin	Pre	7	1	6	+
William Short	Cin	Pre	9	2	1	SW
William Short	Cin	Pre	9	2	12	SW
William Short	Cin	Pre	9	3	32	S
William Short	Cin	Pre	9	3	35	N
William Short	Cin	Pre	9	3	35	SW
William Short	Cin	Pre	9	3	3	–
William Short (Survey 1)	Cin	Pre	9	3	19	–
William Short	Cin	Pre	8	3	30*	NW

William Short		Cin	Pre	8	3	36	E
William Short		Cin	Pre	9	3	20	-
William Short		Cin	Pre	7	2	24*	NW
William Short		Cin	Pre	7	1	4*	N
William Short	(Survey 3)	Cin	Pre	8	3	24*	N
William Short		Cin	Pre	8	1	3	+
William Short		Cin	Pre	8	2	33	+
John Lock, Junior		Cin	EML	3	7	21	SE
William Gifford		Cin	EML	3	4	28	SE
James Jones		Cin	WML	1	7	4	NW
James Baxter		Cin	WML	1	10	25	NW
Isaac Lindley		Cin	WML	1	4	12	NE
James Baxter		Cin	WML	1	10	26	SE
William McKinney		Cin	MR	12	1	1	SW
James Alexander Warwick		Cin	MR	2	2	8	NE

*All north of Mad River.

1252 10 Apr 1813 A/5/148

LO Zan

Transmits patents

Daniel McComas	Zan	-	11	13	14	SW
John Bush	Zan	-	15	16	10	SE
Philip Munch	Zan	-	15	18	10	NW
William Conwell	Zan	-	13	10	5	SE
Thomas Lanfesty	Zan	-	9	8	8	NW
Isaac Miller	Zan	Mil	5	9	12	SE
Amelia Platt	Zan	-	11	5	25	NW
Jacob Miller	Zan	Mil	4	9	22	NE
Jacob Levengood	Zan	Mil	6	1	12	SW
Lewis Nye	Zan	-	9	3	19	SE
William Norris	Zan	-	7	4	14	SE
Lewis Nye	Zan	-	9	3	19	SW
William Blunt	Zan	-	8	2	4	SE
Asa B. Snider & John Snider	Zan	-	9	3	23	NE
Andrew Thompson	Zan	-	6	1	20	SE
Philip Barrack	Zan	-	10	3	25	NW
Levi Harrod	Zan	-	11	6	23	SE
Jacob Stutzman	Zan	-	5	9	21	NE

1253 10 Apr 1813 A/5/148

LO Stu

Transmits patents

Charles Irvin? [Irwin?]	Stu	-	7	10	27	NW
Abner Wells	Stu	-	3	7	15	NW
Joseph Hendricks	Stu	-	5	12	20	NE
William Birney	Stu	-	4	10	22	NE
George Snider	Stu	-	4	7	26	SW
Robert Billingsley	Stu	-	1	7	10	S
Jesse Miller	Stu	-	5	18	23	NW
Jesse Miller	Stu	-	5	18	24	SW
William Foulks	Stu	-	1	6	22	SW
Alexander McKitrick	Stu	-	5	11	15	SW
Michael Miller	Stu	-	6	18	32?	NE
Isaac Craig	Stu	-	6	17	36	SW
John Hendricks	Stu	-	4	11	21	NE
Isaac Lemasters	Stu	-	5	11	11	SE
John Reeves	Stu	-	7	12	7	SE
John Cooper	Stu	-	7	12	14	SW
John Shaw	Stu	-	5	15	1	SW
Alexander Moore	Stu	-	5	10	31	SW
William Crafford	Stu	-	3	13	12	SE
James Alexander	Stu	-	3	6	19	NE
Jonathan Taylor	Stu	-	4	9	15	NE

1254 12 Apr 1813 A/5/149

John Steen, Postoffice, Reading, Pennsylvania

Transmits patents

John Steen	Chl	-	21	11	9	NW
John Steen	Chl	-	21	11	9	SE
John Steen	Chl	[WS?]	21	11	8	SE

[107]

1255 12 Apr 1813 A/5/149

Jesse Spencer, Reg Chl

Transmits U.S. Treasury receipts

John Steen	Chl	WS	21	11	8	SE
John Steen	Chl	-	21	11	9	NW
John Steen	Chl	-	21	11	9	SE

1256 12 Apr 1813 A/5/149

Secretary of War

Requests furlough for Jared Mansfield, former Surveyor General, to enable him to return to Cincinnati to help J. Meigs, the present Surveyor General, for about four weeks.

1257 14 Apr 1813 A/5/150

Archibald McIntire, Comptroller, Albany [New York?]

Stephen Thorn granted the following patents in 1810

Stephen Thorn	Mil	-	2	5	2	25
Stephen Thorn	Mil	-	2	10	2	15
Stephen Thorn	Mil	-	3	7	1	7
Stephen Thorn	Mil	-	3	7	1	10
Stephen Thorn	Mil	-	2	7	4	15
Stephen Thorn	Mil	-	2	7	4	8
Stephen Thorn	Mil	-	2	7	4	9
Stephen Thorn	Mil	-	3	8	4	4
Stephen Thorn	Mil	-	3	8	4	5
Stephen Thorn	Mil	-	3	8	4	6
Stephen Thorn	Mil	-	1	6	2	14

1258 14 Apr 1813 A/5/150

David Hoge, Reg Stu

Transmits first certificates

Henry Markey	Stu	-	8	11	21	SW
Henry Markey	Stu	-	8	11	30	NE

1259 15 Apr 1813 A/5/151

Andrew Gregg, Potter's Mills, Centre County, Pennsylvania

Transmits patent

Peter Nees	Stu	-	10	2	14	SE

1260 17 Apr 1813 A/5/151

Jared Mansfield, New Haven or West Point

Transmits furlough for four weeks to go to Cincinnati to help J. Meigs, Surveyor General.

1261 20 Apr 1813 A/5/151

John Reed, Reg Hun, Mississippi Territory

Transmits patents

Bennet Wood	[not described*]					
D. Thompson	Hun	-	1E	3	19	NW

*Seven patents.

1262 20 Apr 1813 A/5/152

Daniel Symmes, Reg Cin

Transmits defective certificates; mentions Benjamin Whiteman, assignee of John Davis

-- Enstine [also Eustine]	Cin	MR	12	5	20	NW
--	Cin	Pre	10	3	32	SW
John Lock	Cin	?	3E	7	22	SE

1263 21 Apr 1813 A/5/152

Jesse Spencer [Reg Chl]

Please return final certificate of Gen. [Thomas] Worthington, which had been sent back as incorrect; to be reconsidered.

1264   22 Apr 1813   A/5/152
Gilman Bryant, Mount Vernon, Knox County, Ohio
Tomlinson has paid only first instalment

John Tomlinson	Mil	-	12	7	16	-

1265   22 Apr 1813   A/5/153
LO Cin
Transmits patents

John Bayley	Cin Pre	6	2	25	NW
Richard Sinnip	Cin Pre	7	2	4	-
James Stephenson	Cin Pre	4	3	4	SW
William Ward	Cin Pre	11	5	25	S
William Ward	Cin Pre	11	5	25	NW
William Reeder	Cin Pre	5	3	18	NE
Jonathan Dound	Cin Pre	9	2	35	+
William Ward	Cin Pre	11	5	23	-
William Ward	Cin Pre	10	5	30	N
Samuel Everman	Cin Pre	5	2	27	+
Isaac Spinning	Cin Pre	7	2	17	-
Isaac Spinning	Cin Pre	7	2	18	+
Joseph Chenoweth	Cin Pre	5	4	28	+
John Williams	Cin Pre	10	2	1	SW
Josiah Dungan	Cin Pre	4	2	7	+
Henry Williams	Cin Pre	9	3	30	SW
John Rogers	Cin Pre	11	2	32	-
John Lingle *et al*	Cin Pre	9	5	35	-
David Garrison	Cin Pre	8	4	17	NE
James Blackburn	Cin Pre	4	3	7	SW
Benjamin Dye	Cin Pre	10	2	32	SW
Samuel McCord	Cin Pre	10	5	33	W
Joseph Reynolds	Cin Pre	11	4	3	-
Henry Opdycke	Cin Pre	6	2	7	SW
Jacob Burnet	Cin Pre	8	5	34	SW
Jacob Burnet	Cin Pre	8	5	34	SE
Jacob Burnet	Cin Pre	8	5	34	NW
Jacob Burnet	Cin Pre	9	2	6	NE
Isaac Wood	Cin Pre	6	2	4	-
James Lenon	Cin Pre	10	2	28	NE
John Duncan	Cin Pre	6	2	20	NW
Thomas Moore	Cin Pre	11	5	25	NE
Jesse Bracken	Cin Pre	9	3	7	E*
James Atkins	Cin Pre	5	2	12	NE
John Shindledecker	Cin Pre	7	3	22	SW
Anthony Logan	Cin Pre	6	2	27	SE
Richard Mills	Cin Pre	6	2	13	SE
Richard Lackey (Survey 4)	Cin Pre	4	4	24	-

*"All NW of Mad River."

1266   23 Apr 1813   A/5/154
Daniel Symmes, Reg Cin
Returns erroneous certificate*

Solomon Miller	Cin Pre	3	2	26	NE

*States "should be 13," without indicating whether range, township, or section is meant.

1267   27 Apr 1813   A/5/154
Joseph Nourse, Reg U.S. Treasury
Since Rec Cin claims a large amount for stationery expense over last 12 years, please inform me (for purposes of comparison) how much has been expended by Rec Stu and Rec Chl during similar period.

1268   30 Apr 1813   A/5/155
Daniel Symmes [Reg Cin]
Returns defective certificates
-- Cutler, assignee of

-- Chambers[1]	Cin Pre	8	2	7	SE
--	Cin EML	4	5	5	SE
(Survey 1)	Cin Pre	8	3	5	-

-- Wilson, assignee of

-- Blackburne	Cin Pre	5	3	14	NW
--	Cin Pre	10	2	28	N
--	Cin Pre	11	1	13	N

[1]This section sold as follows, according to Gen LO books: in 1804 to A. Glasmore, 200 acres (reverted); in 1801 to P[eyton] Short, 205 acres, patented; in 1810 to J. Clayton, 270 acres (first instalment only).

1269   3 May 1813   A/5/156
Ninian Edwards, Governor of the Illinois Territory, Kaskaskia
Requests that the lease on the Wabash saline deposit be renewed for one year. [This letter not sent.]

1270   4 May 1813   A/5/156
David Hoge, Reg Stu
Transmits first certificate

Obed Pierpont	Stu	-	6	14	18	SW

1271   5 May 1813   A/5/156
Wyllys Silliman, Reg Zan
Transmits first certificate

John Hammock	Zan	-	2	8	28	SE

1272   5 May 1813   A/5/157
Samuel Gwathmey, Reg Jef
Transmits first certificate

John Evans	Jef	-	4E	2N	10	SE

1273   6 May 1813   A/5/157
Benjamin Hough, Auditor of the State of Ohio, Chl
Authorizes payment of $1000 for surveys and locations in Virginia Military District of Ohio; mentions Col. [Richard Clough] Anderson.

1274   6 May 1813   A/5/158
Thomas Gibson, Reg Can
Transmits certificates

Andrew Craig*	Can	-	17	21	1	NW
Samuel Lewis**	Can	-	17	21	1	NE

*Assigned to Samuel Lewis and reassigned (by Lewis) to Robert Darling.
**Assigned to Robert Darling.

1275   6 May 1813   A/5/158
President of the United States
Discusses renewal of lease on the Wabash saline deposits; mentions Albert Gallatin, Ninian Edwards.

1276   7 May 1813   A/5/159
Samuel Gwathmey, Reg Jef
Discusses laws regarding time given for payments of land; mentions Jonathan Clark.

1277   7 May 1813   A/5/159
Abraham Bradley, Junior, Deputy Postmaster General
Asks for return of surveying equipment used by -- Pease during survey of Northern Road.

1278   10 May 1813   A/5/160
Thomas Freeman, Esq., Washington, Mississippi Terri-
    tory
Final certificate to Francis E. Harris cannot issue
    until we have your power of attorney to Lewis Win-
    ston
Francis E. Harris*   Mad - 1E   3 21 NW
*Assignee of Thomas Freeman.

1279   10 May 1813   A/5/160
John Reed, Reg Hun
Following patents were transmitted 25 Mar 1812; also
    mentions [Thomas] Freeman
Rudolph Bashart   Hun EML   1   3   1 NE
R. Harris   Hun WML   1   3 14 NE
R. Harris   Hun WML   1   3 13   -
James Walker   Hun EML   2   1 15   +
Samuel Davis   Hun EML   2   1 17 SE

1280   10 May 1813   A/5/161
Governor [Ninian[Edwards, [Illinois Territory, Kas-
    kaskia]
Acknowledges agreement regarding Wabash saline depos-
    its; mentions [Albert[Gallatin, now on mission to
    Russia.

1281   12 May 1813   A/5/161
Daniel Symmes, Reg Cin
Returns defective certificates [several without names
    or land descriptions being given]
William Ward   Cin Pre 10   5 30   S

1282   12 May 1813   A/5/162
Gilman Bryant, Mount Vernon, Knox County, Ohio
Tomlinson has paid only first instalment
John Tomlinson   Chl Mil 12   7 16   -

1283   12 May 1813   A/5/162
John Gibson, Esq., acting as Governor of Indiana
    Territory, Vin
Discusses lease of silver and lead mines solicited
    by -- Paddock and associates, who wish to coin any
    silver found. General terms of lease set forth.
    Also mentions salt royalties.

1284   13 May 1813   A/5/163
Jesse Spencer, Reg Chl
Transmits patent
Isaac Decker*   Chl Mil 21 10   1 NW
*Assignee of George Sharp.

1285   14 May 1813   A/5/163
Isaac Van Horne, Rec Zan
Transmits U.S. Treasury receipt
Benjamin Rutter*   Zan - 15 17 26 SW
*Assignee of Adam Starret.

1286   14 May 1813   A/5/164
Nehemiah Tilton, Reg Wsh, Mississippi Territory
Calculates payments for -- Nealaris; mentions Wil-
    liam Dinsmore.

1287   17 May 1813   A/5/165

Isaac Van Horne, Rec Zan
Acknowledges receipt of $5 to be paid to John Lock.

1288   17 May 1813   A/5/165
John Lock, Frederick Town, Maryland
Transmits patents and explains $5 overpayment in LO
    Zan district
John Lock   Cin EML   3   7 26 SW
John Lock   Cin EML   3   7 22 SW

1289   17 May 1813   A/5/165
Isaac Van Horne, Rec Zan
Again acknowledges receipt of $5 for John Lock.

1290   22 May 1813   A/5/166
Daniel Symmes, Reg Cin
Transmits first certificate
William Wason   Cin EML   6   4   3 NE

1291   22 May 1813   A/5/166
Columbus Lawson, Reg New Orleans [ELA]
Acknowledges letter reporting receipt of records from
    Ferdinand Ybanez, acting as deputy to Philip Grymes;
    asks for copy of Bayou La Fourche plat prepared by
    Walter Gilbert.

1292   24 May 1813   A/5/167
Hon. -- Robertson, U.S. House of Representatives
Columbus Lawson has given appropriate sureties of
    office; mentions Joshua Lewis and Martin Gordon,
    both of the City of New Orleans.

1293   24 May 1813   A/5/167
Hon. -- Tait, U.S. Senate
It is not known if [James O.] Cosby, Commissioner in
    LO WPR district, has ever gone to his post. Con-
    gressmen ". . . and the people are quite out of
    patience at his delay or neglect. Will you be so
    good as to inform me, if you have any information
    relative to him, or of his intentions."

1294   26 May 1813   A/5/167
William Crawford, Commissioner of Land Claims, Fort
    Stoddert, Mississippi Territory
-- Acre, clerk in LO St. Stephens, will be paid by
    this office upon receipt of information from you.

1295   27 May 1813   A/5/168
Richard Rush, Esq., Comptroller of the U.S. Treasury
Transmits oaths of office for John Reed, Reg Hun,
    Madison County, Mississippi Territory, and for
    Columbus Lawson, Reg ELA.

1296   29 May 1813   A/5/168
President of U.S. Senate
Speaker of U.S. House of Representatives
Transmits report of land commissioners in Kaskaskia
    district; discusses classes of claims rejected;
    mentions -- Boynton.

1297   29 May 1813   A/5/170
President of U.S. Senate

Speaker of U.S. House of Representatives
Transmits letter from Reg Kas regarding claims
  granted under special circumstances.

1298   31 May 1813   A/5/170
President of the United States
Reports the fact that James O. Cosby has never
  entered upon his office of commissioner in WPR
  district of Louisiana. -- Magruder, former Senator from Louisiana and -- Robertson, Representative from Louisiana, have both urged appointment
  of a replacement for Cosby.

1299   2 Jun 1813   A/5/171
John Sloane, Rec Can
Transmits U.S. Treasury receipt
John Stump   Can   - 10 12 28 SW

1300   4 Jun 1813   A/5/172
John Badollet, Reg Vin
Transmits patent and notes slight difference in in-
  terest due
Henry Heth   Vin   -   4 3 31 NW

1301   5 Jun 1813   A/5/172
Daniel Symmes, Reg Cin
Transmits first certificate and U.S. Treasury re-
  ceipt
--   Cin MR   3 3 26 SW

1302   5 Jun 1813   A/5/172
L. Wailes, Reg Opl
-- Garrard, Rec Opl, has named Will Turner & L.
  Charliere? [Chachere?] as sureties. Since these
  men are unknown to the representative from your
  state, you are requested to procure testimonials
  as to their standing and property.

1303   7 Jun 1813   A/5/173
David Hoge, Reg Stu
Transmits U.S. Treasury receipt
Frederick States*   Stu   -   4 11 34 SE
*Assignee of James Chambers.

1304   7 Jun 1813   A/5/173
Daniel Symmes, Reg Cin
Hon -- McClean has applied for two patents; Hon. --
  Alexander has applied for one patent
Charles Brown   Cin Pre   4 3 24 N
Charles Null*   Cin Pre   4 3 12 +
John Edgar   Cin EML   7 2 26 NE
*Assignee of the administrators of Henry Null.

1305   7 Jun 1813   A/5/173
Thomas Gibson, Reg Can
Requests first certificate
Jacob Bowman*   Can   - 12 16 18 NE
*Assignee of William Henry.

1306   7 Jun 1813   A/5/174
Wyllys Silliman, Reg Zan
Requests first certificate for Wolford; Hon. --
  Griffin requests Miller's patent

Frederick Wolford*   Zan   -   5 1 6 NE
David Miller   Zan Mil 1 9 20 NE
*Transferred to William Self and further transferred
  to John Self.

1307   8 Jun 1813   A/5/174
James Findlay, Rec Cin
Transmits U.S. Treasury receipt
James Smith   Cin MR   12 4 22 NE
James Smith   Cin MR   12 4 22 SE

1308   12 Jun 1813   A/5/175
Joseph Wood, Reg Mar
Transmits patent
Isaac Loun? & John Loun?   Mar - 5 3 13 NE

1309   12 Jun 1813   A/5/175
Excellency N[inian] Edwards, Governor of Illinois
  Territory, Kaskaskia, via Russellville
Sends copies of letters previously sent.

1310   12 Jun 1813   A/5/175
John Mauck, Junior, Manchester, Baltimore County,
  Maryland
Transmits patents
John Mauck, Junior   Can   - 19 19 5 SE
John Mauck, Junior   Can   - 19 19 5 NE
John Mauck, Junior   Can   - 19 19 5 NW
John Mauck, Junior   Can   - 19 19 5 SW

1311   12 Jun 1813   A/5/175
Abraham Hetrick, Manchester, Baltimore County, Mary-
  land
Transmits patent
Abraham Hetrick   Can   - 19 19 10 NE

1312   12 Jun 1813   A/5/175
Joel Pusey, Tawney Town, Frederick County, Maryland
Transmits patent
Joel Pusey   Chl Mil 14 8 19 NW

1313   12 Jun 1813   A/5/176
LO Cin
Transmits patents
William McNair   Cin MR   8 2 11 NE
James Remy   Cin WML   1 8 25 NW
Felix Welton   Cin MR   10 5 9 SE
Jacob White   Survey 2   Cin MR 8 2 8 -
Daniel Strader   Cin EML   2 8 18 W
Cephas Carey   Cin EML   6 8 30 SE
Joseph Evans   Cin EML   5 6 21 NW
John Snell   Cin MR   11 5 28 NW
William Jenkins   Cin EML   1 3 21 NE
Nimrod Ferguson   Cin   * 12E 15N 25 NE
Isaac Bear   Cin EML   4 3 5 NW
Esther Green   Cin EML   3 4 30 SE
David Pressly   Cin EML   1 6 17 NW
John Woods   Cin EML   6 3 29 SE
Abel Stout   Cin EML   2 5 21 NW
Robert Taylor   Cin EML   2 6 21 NE
David Pressly   Cin EML   1 6 20 NE
James C. Morris &
  William Barr   Cin, Square 2, lot 15
Henry Steddom   Cin   * 13E 17- 34 SE
Phinchas McCray   Cin EML   4 3 36 SW

Name	Code					Dir
William Jones	Cin	EML	3	3	17	NE
William Evans	Cin	EML	1	3	28	NE
Joseph Pottorf	Cin	EML	3	5	8	NW
William Custar	Cin	MR	11	4	5	NW
James Leviston	Cin	* 14E	14-		19	NE
Samuel Harlin	Cin	* 13E	14-		31	SE
Benjamin Evans	Cin	* 14E	17-		22	SW
David Mount	Cin	* 13E	11-		5	SE
William Farmer	Cin	EML	5	5	26	SW
John Stockdale	Cin	WML	2	9	21	SE
Aaron Vanchoyk	Cin	EML	5	4	10	NW
John Pentz, Senior	Cin	MR	12	3	1	NW
William Mitchell	Cin	MR	10	2	3	SE
William Arnett	Cin	* 13E	11-		4	NW
William Hastings	Cin	* 14E	16-		7	SE
Obadiah Harris	Cin	* 14E	17-		11	SE
John Richardson	Cin	* 13E	13N		20	SE
Ralph Wildridge & William Smith	Cin	WML	1	7	5	E
George Gresmer	Cin	MR	1	4	26	NE
William Crawford	Cin	* 13E	16-		26	SE
William Crawford	Cin	* 13E	16N		25	SW
George Frazer	Cin	* 13E	14-		30	NW
John Baldwin	Cin	* 14E	17-		14	SW
Noah Beauchamp	Cin	* 12E	14-		24	NE
Henry Paddock	Cin	EML	1	7	4	NE
Samuel Kyle	Cin	EML	6	5	31	SE
Daniel Wilson	Cin	WML	2	10	12	NE
Simeon Wilson, of D.G.[?]	Cin	WML	1	10	14	SW
Charles Stuart	Cin	MR	8	6	36	SW
Peter Emmard	Cin	WML	2	12	26	NE
Jackson Rambo	Cin	WML	1	13	31	NE
Daniel Miller	Cin	WML	1	12	30	NW
John Judy	Cin	EML	3	7	31	SE
John Hardin	Cin	WML	1	13	24	NE
John Miller	Cin	WML	1	10	1	SW
William White	Cin	WML	2	2	25	SE
James Johnston	Cin	EML	6	7	30	NW
Henry Paddock	Cin	EML	1	8	29	SE
George M. Caven	Cin	MR	12	1	1	NW
Philip Wheard	Cin	EML	3	6	32	NE
Samuel Kyle	Cin	WML	5	7	36	E
Andrew Turner	Cin	EML	1	4	24	SW
Jesse Devenport**	Cin	WML	1	13	22	NW
Moses De Camp	Cin	EML	1	4	14	NE
William Cox	Cin	MR	12	5	13	NW
John Aip? [Stip?], Junior	Cin	MR	13	5	26	NE
Daniel McDonald	Cin	MR	4	3	11	SE
Daniel McDonald	Cin	MR	4	3	11	SW
Daniel McDonnel**	Cin	EML	4	3	35	SW
William Stuart	Cin	EML	1	4	36	NE
William Miller	Cin	MR	8	5	30	SE
Michael Wolf	Cin	EML	2	4	10	SW
George Wilson	Cin	* 12E	12-		26	SW
Samuel McCray	Cin	WML	1	9	10	SE
Philip Wickle	Cin	EML	3	6	15	NW
John Ross	Cin	MR	10	6	32	NW
John Starr	Cin	* 14E	14-		6	SE
Hezekiah Broadbury	Cin	EML	2	5	34	-
Joseph Rorer	Cin	EML	4	6	13	SE
Joseph Rorer	Cin	EML	4	6	14	SE
Samuel Huston	Cin	EML	2	11	28	SE
Joseph Reid	Cin	MR	9	5	14	SE
William Bouge? [Bonge?]	Cin	EML	2	6	18	NW
John Peck	Cin	EML	6	4	4	NW

*Second Principal Meridian.
**So spelled.

Name	Code					Dir
Benjamin Wallam	Chl	-	18	14	26	SW
George Richards	Chl	-	16	16	10	NE
Michael Anspacher	Chl	-	19	16	10	SE
Joseph Shoots	Chl	-	20	11	33	NW
Adam Kreamer	Chl	-	20	15	8	SE
Henry Holler	Chl	-	20	12	28	NE
David Ridgeway	Chl	-	16	6	22	NW
Jacob Culp	Chl	-	18	16	12	SW
Jacob Spade	Chl	MS	21	9	36	SE
Archibald Campbell	Chl	MS	21	10	8	NE
Jacob Saltsgaver	Chl	-	21	9	9	SE
John Shurr	Chl	-	19	14	15	NW
William Dorm	Chl	WS	21	9	6	SW
Willis Speakman	Chl	-	14	8	12	SE
William Moore & J. Norris	Chl	-	20	2	5	NE
Ephraim Trumbo	Chl	-	18	2	18	NE
Matthew Ferguson	Chl	WS	21	10	15	NE
Matthew Ferguson	Chl	WS	21	10	15	SE
George Long	Chl	-	17	18	26	SE
Benjamin Kerns	Chl	-	20	2	8	+
William Caldwell	Chl	WS	21	10	15	NW
William Caldwell	Chl	WS	21	10	15	SW
Joseph? Brown & George Brown	Chl	WS	21	10	17	NE
Solomon Wilkinson	Chl	-	19	10	28	NE
John Williamson	Chl	-	19	15	15	NW
Barnet Vankirk	Chl	MS	21	9	32	NW
James Blue	Chl	-	20	10	21	NE
James Baugher	Chl	-	20	14	7	SE
George Ritchey	Chl	-	20	12	21	NW
Benjamin Boman	Chl	-	20	13	22	SW
John Abbernarthy	Chl	-	20	10	11	NW
Jesse Stoneman	Chl	-	17	18	3	N
John Swinehart	Chl	-	16	17	9	SW
William Hinton	Chl	Mil	19	6	24	SE
Peter Dun? [Dwin? Dum?]	Chl	-	20	10	12	SE
Frederick Waiser & J. Roads	Chl	-	20	11	28	SE
James Loveridge	Chl	Mil	13	7	20	SW
Caspar Eckelberger	Chl	Mil	12	7	25	NE
Emmanuel Traxler	Chl	-	20	3	34	NW
William Grubb	Chl	-	19	2	8	NE
Daniel Bench	Chl	-	19	10	23	NW
William Fulton	Chl	-	16	17	1	NE
John Irwin	Chl	Mil	13	7	21	SE
George Green	Chl	Mil	15	3	7	SE
Michael Van Grundy	Chl	-	21	8	15	SE
Adam Devenbaugh	Chl	-	19	13	14	NW
Alexander Chambers	Chl	WS	21	11	13	S
Jacob Ensley	Chl	-	21	10	3	NE
James Diggens	Chl	-	21	8	23	SW
John Saylor? [Taylor?]	Chl	-	20	12	32	NE
John Hornbaker	Chl	MS	22	4	36	SE
Adam Strayer	Chl	MS	21	9	34	SW
David Layman	Chl	-	16	15	6	SE
John Courtright	Chl	-	20	15	23	SW
Adam Housholder	Chl	-	17	17	36	NW
David Kemren? [Themren?]	Chl	-	19	16	26	SE
Adam Stewart	Chl	-	20	18	15	NE
Philip Pontius	Chl	MS	21	10	9	NW
Joshua Horner	Chl	-	18	2	17	NE
Joshua Horner	Chl	-	19	2	15	NW
Edward Crosby	Chl	-	16	17	10	NE
Charles Decker	Chl	-	21	11	36	SE
Jonathan Hays	Chl	Mil	15	3	24	NE
Aaron Donaldson	Chl	-	20	15	29	SE
Anthony Boucher	Chl	WS	22	4	1	+
Anthony Boucher	Chl	WS	22	4	2	+

1314   12 Jun 1813   A/5/178
LO Chl
Transmits patents

1315   12 Jun 1813   A/5/179
LO Stu
Transmits patents

Matthew Lyons	Stu	–	1	7	32	NW
George Fresh	Stu	–	4	8	21	SE
Adam Kimmel	Stu	–	5	12	2	SE
Jacob Glass	Stu	–	7	14	17	SE
Jonathan Grable	Stu	–	4	11	4	NW
Miles Hart	Stu	–	4	6	33	NE
Rudolph Bair	Stu	–	6	17	17	SE
Adam Bair	Stu	–	6	17	18	NE
Robert Lattimore	Stu	–	7	18	18	NW
Aaron Brooks	Stu	–	1	7	33	SW

1316   12 Jun 1813   A/5/180
LO Zan
Transmits patents

David James	Zan	–	11	12	1	SE
George Mitchell	Zan	Mil	4	4	19	NW

1317   12 Jun 1813   A/5/180
LO Can
Transmits patents

Daniel Cook	Can	–	18	20	5	NW
Francis Mitchell	Can	–	19	20	11	SW
James Miller	Can	–	13	13	17	S
Vacheal Metcalf	Can	–	15	21	22	NE
Nathan Fidler	Can	–	19	18	10	NE

1318   14 Jun 1813   A/5/180
William Garrard, Rec WLA
Your sureties, William Turner and L. Chachere, are
   insufficient and you should give others.

1319   14 Jun 1813   A/5/181
David Hoge, Reg Stu
Transmits final certificates and U.S. Treasury re-
   ceipts

Peter Troxel	Stu	–	8	11	22	NW
Jacob Rouland	Stu	–	9	11	33	SW

1320   15 Jun 1813   A/5/181
On.? B. Green, Trenton, New Jersey
Certificate to Margaret Uri represents complete title to land [not otherwise described]; certificates to Palser Shilling cannot be patented until
   boundaries of tracts are described; likewise,
   certificate to James Cole, for a lot in the City
   of Natchez, cannot be patented until surveyed.

1321   15 Jun 1813   A/5/181
Gilman Bryant, Mount Vernon, Ohio
John Tumbleston [elsewhere Tomlinson] has paid for
   Ch1 Mil 12 7 15 SE and SW but neglected to
   send receipts to LO Ch1 for final patenting.
   Since the land remains his, as original purchaser,
   your subsequent payments for it are null and void
   and will be refunded.

1322   15 Jun 1813   A/5/182
Samuel Finley, Rec Ch1
Directs him to refund payments to Gilmant [so
   spelled] Bryant et al; mentions [John] Tomlinson.

1323   15 Jun 1813   A/5/182
David Hoge, Reg Stu
Transmits final certificate

John Davis*	Stu	–	1	6	5	NE
John Davis*	Stu	–	1	7	30	NW

*Assignee of -- Henry.

1324   16 Jun 1813   A/5/182
Daniel Morgan, Washington, Mason County, Kentucky
Your patent was sent to LO Stu [land description not
   given].

1325   16 Jun 1813   A/5/183
LO Jef
Transmits patents

John Cline	Jef	–	11E	5N	32	NE
Zacheriah Nixon	Jef	–	4E	2N	17	NE
James Smith	Jef	–	9E	2N	30	NW
William Nichols? [Nicholas?]	Jef	–	8E	3N	28	SW
Thomas Thompson, Senior	Jef	–	5E	2N	7	SE
William Lindley	Jef	–	1E	2N	31	SW
Jesse Howell	Jef	–	1E	1N	6	SW
John Rogers	Jef	–	9E	1N	12	NE
John Woodfill	Jef	–	10E	4N	13	SE
William McKnight	Jef	–	5E	2N	8	NW
John McPheters	Jef	–	3E	1S	14	NE
Francis Fresh	Jef	–	11E	6N	26	SE
John Hobson	Jef	–	4E	1S	9	NE
James Wildman	Jef	–	10E	4N	1	NW
Francis Sanders	Jef	–	10E	4N	26	SW
Abraham Fleener? [Flesner?]	Jef	–	4E	3N	32	SE
John Fleener	Jef	–	4E	3N	35	NW
John Paul	Jef	–	10E	4N	33	W
Edward Hensley	Jef	–	4E	2N	13	SE
Benjamin Brewer, Senior	Jef	–	4E	2N	17	SW
William Whitesell	Jef	–	8E	4N	10	SE
Daniel Woodfill	Jef	–	11E	4N	18	SW
Jacob Coldzer	Jef	–	2E	1N	4	NW
Thomas Cooley	Jef	–	4E	2N	28	NE
Gersham Lee	Jef	–	11E	4N	23	NW
John Giltner	Jef	–	9E	2N	26	NE
Thomas Thompson, Junior	Jef	–	5E	2N	7	NE
James Edwards	Jef	–	10E	4N	20	SE
Samuel Ryker	Jef	–	11E	5N	9	W
Thomas Henderson	Jef	–	10E	2N	31	NW
Amos Thornburgh	Jef	–	4E	2N	19	NW
-- Sebre? & -- Trotter	Jef	–	10E	4N	32	NE

1326   17 Jun 1813   A/5/184
John Mitchell, St. Clairsville, Belmont County, Ohio
Transmits patents

John Mitchell	Stu	–	5	7	14	W
John Mitchell	Stu	–	5	16	25	NE

1327   17 Jun 1813   A/5/184
LO Hun
Transmits patents

Charles Burrus	Hun	WML	2	2	19	SE
Abraham Perkins	Hun	WML	3	2	24	NE
Charles Burrus	Hun	WML	2	2	19	NE
Abraham Perkins	Hun	WML	3	2	24	SE
Charles Burrus	Hun	WML	2	2	19	SW
Francis E. Harris	Hun	EML	1	3	17	SE
Charles Burrus	Hun	WML	2	2	19	NW
Hezekiah Bayles	Hun	EML	2	2	5	+
James Mahan	Hun	EML	2	3	34	SW
Dr. James Maning	Hun	WML	1	2	25	SE
Moses Poor	Hun	EML	2	1	28	SW
William Hogan	Hun	EML	1	4	18	NW
Samuel Fulton	Hun	WML	1	3	24	NE

1328		17 Jun 1813			A/5/185	

LO Cin
Transmits patents

James Benson (Survey 2)	Cin Pre	5	4	24	+
James Benson (Survey 2)	Cin Pre	5	4	18	+
Othniel Huron	Cin Pre	4	3	22	SW
John Ennis	Cin Pre	5	3	12	NW
John Ennis	Cin Pre	5	3	12	SE
John Robinson	Cin Pre	5	2	21	-
-- Kirby & -- Ferguson	Cin Pre	4	4	21	S
Daniel G. Howell	Cin Pre	2	1	26	NW
Israel Harris	Cin Pre	5	3	23	-
George Shoup, heirs of	Cin Pre	7	2	21	NE
-- Steele & -- Pierce, &					
D. Lindsey*	Cin Town of Dayton, lt 6				
Martin Kershner	Cin Pre	7	3	23	NW
Samuel McKinney	Cin Pre	9	3	15	SW
James Lamme	Cin Pre	9	3	14	-
David Pugh	Cin Pre	4	4	12	-
Peter Sellers, heirs of	Cin **	4	3	21	+
Laurence Shell	Cin Pre	7	2	19	SE
George Fryberger, heirs of	Cin Pre	7	2	21	SW
Stephen Dye	Cin Pre	10	1	9	+
Martin Kershner	Cin Pre	7	3	23	SE
Martin Kershner	Cin Pre	7	3	23	SW
William Ward	Cin Pre	11	5	27	SE
William Ward	Cin Pre	11	5	21	SE
William Ward	Cin Pre	11	5	21	SW
Joseph Coe Survey 2	Cin Pre	11	1	19	+
Daniel McDonald Survey 2	Cin Pre	5	2	28	+
Daniel McDonald Survey 2	Cin Pre	5	2	34	+
John Paul	Cin Pre	9	3	30	SW
William Ward	Cin Pre	12	4	3	-
William Ward	Cin Pre	11	5	31	-
William Ward	Cin Pre	11	5	22	-
John Paul	Cin Pre	9	3	28	NW
William Ward	Cin Pre	10	5	30	S
Isaac Vannest Survey 2	Cin Pre	4	2	18	+
-- Kirby & -- Carter					
Survey 1	Cin Pre	4	4	34	W
George Fryberger, heirs of	Cin Pre	7	2	6	NE?
William McDonald Survey 6	Cin Pre	5	3	25	SE
Jacob Hufford	Cin Pre	6	2	3	E
William Martindale	Cin Pre	5	4	32	-
John Taylor	Cin Pre	6	1	22	+
John Fisher	Cin Pre	4	2	9	NW
Eleanor Buchannon	Cin Pre	4	3	31	1
Jabish Phillips	Cin Pre	4	4	28	NW
Benjamin Knoops	Cin Pre	10	2	33	NW
Benjamin Knoops	Cin Pre	10	2	34	SW
James Lennon (2 parcels)	Cin Pre	10	2	28	NE
-- Reed & -- Carrick	Cin **	4	2	19	-
William Maxwell, heirs of	Cin Pre	6	3	18	-
William Maxwell, heirs of	Cin Pre	6	3	18	-
William Maxwell, heirs of	Cin Pre	6	3	24	-
William Maxwell, heirs of	Cin Pre	6	3	30	-
William Maxwell, heirs of	Cin Pre	7	3	13	1
William Maxwell, heirs of	Cin Pre	7	3	19	4
John Long	Cin MR	12	3	2	NW
-- Moore & -- Dixon	Cin MR	14	2	14	+
-- Moore & -- Dixon	Cin MR	14	2	15	+
James Patterson	Cin EML	3	4	5	NW
Richard H. Hunt	Cin MR	8	4	24	SE
Joseph Butcher	Cin MR	9	3	17	SW
John Heighway	Cin MR	8	4	8	SW
James Bennent	Cin EML	1	6	10	SE
Charles Hillierd	Cin MR	12	1	28	+
Stephen Bouge? [Bonge?]	Cin EML	2	6	17	NW
William Jones	Cin EML	3	3	21	NW

*10.5 acres "in and out of lot 6."
**"North of John C. Symmes patent [tract]."

1329		18 Jun 1813	A/5/186

Nehemiah Tilton, Reg Wsh
-- Dinsmore [now in Washington, D.C.] has convinced
   me that he has paid in full for his lands; please
   return final certificates.

1330		18 Jun 1813	A/5/187

Lewis Sewall, Reg Fort St. Stephen [EPR]
Several persons holding pre-emption certificates in
   LO EPR district wish to purchase in the ordinary
   manner; how many cases are there?

1331		18 Jun 1813	A/5/187

John Shorb, Canton, Ohio
Transmits patents

Christopher Pollmer*	Stu	-	9	10	35	NE
Conrad Speilman*	Stu	-	8	11	26	NE

*Assignee of John Shorb.

1332		19 Jun 1813	A/5/187

Daniel Symmes, Reg Cin
Transmits final certificate

Nicholas Coleman	Cin EML	3	6	15	SW

1333		21 Jun 1813	A/5/188

Speaker of U.S. House of Representatives
President of U.S. Senate
Transmits report of land commissioners for Louisiana;
   important summary of claims allowed, requiring Con-
   gressional action, or disallowed; mentions claims
   of Baron -- de Bastrop, François de Castro, Joseph
   Gilliard from Pascagoula Indians, -- Miller & --
   Fulton from Choctaw Indians and from Appalache and
   Tensaw Indians, Manuel de Salcedo (Spanish gover-
   nor).

1334		21 Jun 1813	A/5/190

Michael Jones, Reg Kas
John Caldwell, Rec Kas
Acknowledges receipt of plat for lands in LO Kas district; believes law does not allow pre-emption
   right therein to cultivators previously settled.

1335		22 Jun 1813	A/5/191

Daniel Symmes, Reg Cin
Disputed land title; mentions -- Ensey, -- Piatt, --
   Andrews

John Smith of Hamilton County	Cin MR	6	2	23	NW

1336		22 Jun 1813	A/5/191

Jesse Spencer, Reg Chl
Transmits patent; originally sent to Hon. -- Smith
   of Virginia, who did not know patentee

John Kirlin	Chl -	17	17	21	NE

1337		23 Jun 1813	A/5/191

Hon. -- Piper, U.S. House of Representatives
The original patent was sent to Alexander Ogle, Esq.,
   Somerset, Pennsylvania, in 1810 at Mr. Will's re-
   quest

Daniel Will	Cin ?	4	3	6	SE

1338 24 Jun 1813 A/5/192
David Hoge, Reg Stu
Please return patent as Hon. -- Rhea, Member of Congress from Pennsylvania, has applied for it

John Rife	Stu	-	9	9	2 SW

1339 24 Jun 1813 A/5/192
Thomas Cooper Vanderhorst, Charleston, South Carolina
Transmits letter from Parke Walton, Rec WPR, showing that claim of Elias Vanderhorst was presented to land commissioners for EPR district.

1340 26 Jun 1813 A/5/194
David Hoge, Reg Stu
Transmits first certificate

Thomas Curtis	Stu	-	5	7	30 SE

1341 29 Jun 1813 A/5/195
Edward McDermott, Zenia [Xenia], Ohio
Transmits patent

Edward McDermott	Cin	MR	8	2	15	SW

1342 30 Jun 1813 A/5/195
Morris Miller, Esq., Savannah, Georgia
"Your friend Dr. [--] White, called at this office to make enquiries . . . respecting the lands of Benjamin and Daniel Ward, on the Iberville, in West Florida. The only records at the seat of government respecting lands in West Florida, are deposited at the office of the secretary of state. . . . There is not found the copy of any deed of grant . . . either to Mrs. [--] Orgam, or to Benjamin, Daniel, or John Ward, for land in that, or any other part of Florida."

1343 6 Jul 1813 A/5/195
Jesse Spencer, Reg Chl
Transmits patent

Isaac Hutton	Chl	-	19	15	22	SW

1344 6 Jul 1813 A/5/196
Daniel Symmes, Reg Cin
Transmits duplicate receipt

John Lock	Cin	?	3	7	22	SE

1345 6 Jul 1813 A/5/196
James O. Cosby, Commissioner, WPR
Acknowledges list of the actual settlers in district who have no claims derived from the French, British, or Spanish governments. "I am really glad to find that you have been at your post and attending to your official duties. . . ."

1346 6 Jul 1813 A/5/196
Joseph Curtis, Postoffice, Baltimore
Transmits patent

Joseph Curtis	[Cin]	MR	3	3	26	SW

1347 6 Jul 1813 A/5/197
John Badollet, Reg Vin
Notes discrepancies

--	Vin	-	4E	3S	31	NW

1348 7 Jul 1813 A/5/197
David Hoge, Reg Stu
Requests duplicate certificates

--	Stu	-	6	9	11	-
--	Stu	-	5	10	34	SW
Jacob Nessley	Stu	-	2	9	8	+
Jacob Nessley	Stu	-	2	9	14	+
Joshua Cecil*	Stu	-	5	10	20	SW

*Assignee of John McMillan.

1349 8 Jul 1813 A/5/198
Lewis Sewall, Reg EPR, Fort St. Stephens, Mississippi Territory
Explains eligibility for land purchase in district.

1350 9 Jul 1813 A/5/199
Daniel Symmes, Reg Cin
Calls attention to errors in calculations

--	Cin	Pre	4	3	10	NW
--	Cin	MR	7	3	29	NW
--	Cin	?	6	4	25	+
--	Cin	?	6	4	26	-
--	Cin	?	7	3	6	SE
--	Cin	?	13	5	15	+
--	Cin	?	5	4	30	SE
-- Surveys 3 & 5	Cin	?	4	4	24	-

1351 10 Jul 1813 A/5/199
Daniel Symmes, Reg Cin
Transmits patents

William Owens	Cin	Pre	11	4	9	+
William Owens	Cin	Pre	11	4	10	+
William Owens	Cin	Pre	11	4	15	+

1352 13 Jul 1813 A/5/200
Hon. John Rhea, U.S. Representative from Pennsylvania
Has written to LO Stu to retrieve patent

John Rife	Stu	-	9	9	2 SW

1353 13 Jul 1813 A/5/200
Daniel Symmes, Reg Cin
Returns certificates for correction

--	Cin	Pre	11	1	13	+
--	Cin	EML	1	2	1	SW
--	Cin	Pre	11	4	30	+
--	Cin	Pre	11	1	20	+
--	Cin	Pre	9	4	21	+
--	Cin	?	1	4	30	+
--	Cin	?	6	1	9	+
--	Cin	?	6	1	10	+
--	Cin	?	6	1	26	+
--	Cin	?	6	2	33	+
--	Cin	?	4	2	1	W

1354 14 Jul 1813 A/5/202
Nehemiah Tilton, Reg Wsh, Mississippi Territory
Transmits patents; mentions Gray Briggs, magistrate in Franklin County, Mississippi [Territory]; L. Porter, John Porter

John Thompson	Wsh	-	4	3	32	SW
Jacob Fudge	Wsh	-	5	2	8	SW
-- Kinsler & -- Barrett	Wsh	-	5	2	15	SW
John Thompson	Wsh	-	4	2	6	NE

1355   14 Jul 1813   A/5/202
Wyllys Silliman, Reg Zan
Encloses certificate for correction; mentions Charles
    Sullivan, Military district lands.

1356   17 Jul 1813   A/5/203
John Evans, c/o B. Ragsdale, Raleigh, North Carolina
Transmits patent

John Evans	Jef	–	4E	2N	10 SW

1357   20 Jul 1813   A/5/203
S. Smith, now in Washington, [D.C.]
Relief for Francis Stringer must be by act of Con-
    gress.

1358   22 Jul 1813   A/5/204
Daniel Symmes, Reg Cin
Money still due; mention Jesse Hunt pre-emption.

1359   23 Jul 1813   A/5/204
Hon. John McLean
Transmits patents

Jesse Hunt	[Cin]	MR	9	4	15	S
Jesse Hunt	[Cin]	MR	10	2	15	–
Jesse Hunt	[Cin]	MR	10	2	5	–
Jesse Hunt	[Cin]	MR	7	3	6	S
Jesse Hunt	[Cin]	MR	7	3	6	NE
Jesse Hunt	[Cin]	MR	9	4	9	W
Jesse Hunt	[Cin]	MR	9	4	9	SE
Jesse Hunt	[Cin]	MR	8	5	33	–
Jesse Hunt	[Cin]	Pre	7	1	2	+

1360   24 Jul 1813   A/5/204
John Shorb, Canton, Ohio
Corrected patents issued with appropriate assign-
    ments.

1361   26 Jul 1813   A/5/204
Columbus Lawson, Reg [ELA]
Discusses the composite system--combining old and
    new land descriptions--and the reasons for it.

1362   27 Jul 1813   A/5/205
Lewis Winston, Huntsville, Madison County, Missis-
    ippi Territory
Requests copy of power of attorney whereby Winston
    represents Thomas Freeman in the sale of land to
    -- Harris

Thomas Freeman	[Hun]	–	1E	3	21	NW

1363   27 Jul 1813   A/5/206
Gilman Bryant, Mount Vernon, Ohio
Original purchaser is entitled to patent. "It is
    not in my power to afford you any relief."

1364   27 Jul 1813   A/5/206
Jesse Spencer, Reg Chl
Transmits patent

John Hunter	Chl	WS	21	11	24	SW

1365   27 Jul 1813   A/5/206
Hon. -- Lacock

Transmits military patents for John Lawrence and the
    heirs of Michael Brannon.

1366   28 Jul 1813   A/5/206
Hon. Richard Rush, Comptroller of the U.S. Treasury
Transmits sureties for Isaac Van Horn, Rec Zan;
    mentions Lewis Cass, marshall; Samuel Herrick,
    district attorney; Samuel Sullivan, associate
    judge of the court of common pleas for Muskingum
    County [Ohio].

1367   28 Jul 1813   A/5/206
James Lawson, Andersonville, South Carolina
Has written to Reg EPR for list of persons having
    paid first instalments in a timely manner.

1368   28 Jul 1813   A/5/207
Thomas Gibson, Reg Can
Transmits first certificate

Henry Brumbach	Can	–	18	22	22	NE

1369   28 Jul 1813   A/5/207
LO Cin
Transmits patents

Hugh McSherry	Cin	MR	11	4	4	NE
Joseph Longfellow	Cin	MR	12	4	15	SE
Samuel Blue	Cin	MR	12	4	23	SE
Thomas Patton	Cin	MR	9	5	14	NW
Benjamin Foos	Cin	MR	9	5	4	NW
Benjamin Foos	Cin	MR	9	5	4	NE
Thomas Davis	Cin	MR	12	5	1	NW
Abraham Yeazel	Cin	MR	10	5	2	SW
Daniel Moore	Cin	MR	8	4	24	NW
William Sparks	Cin	WML	1	11	20	SW
Andrew Cornelison	Cin	EML	3	3	24	W
William Sutherland White	Cin	* 12E	12–	3	SE
Abijah O'Neall	Cin	EML	5	5	5	SW
Smith Gregg	Cin	EML	6	3	32	NE
Thomas J. Worman	Cin	* 13E	16–	17	NW
James Tyner	Cin	* 12E	14–	22	NE
Francis Thomas	Cin	* 14E	17–	12	+
Charles Moffit	Cin	* 14E	18–	32	SE
Jesse Johnston	Cin	EML	6	3	3	SW

*Second Principal Meridian.

1370   29 Jul 1813   A/5/207
John Badollet, Reg Vin
Returns defective final certificates

Jacob Warrick, heirs of	Vin	–	12W	3S	12	NW
--	Vin	–	11W	1S	25	NW
--	Vin	–	13W	4S	31	SW
--	Vin	–	3E	6S	2	+
--	Vin	–	3E	6S	11	+

1371   29 Jul 1813   A/5/208
LO Cin
Transmits patents

James Wills Surveys 4 & 5	Cin	Pre	4	4	28	–
James Frazee	Cin	Pre	10	2	28	N
William Short	Cin	Pre	8	2	3	+
Jacob Cutler	Cin	Pre	8	2	7	SE
John Davis	Cin	Pre	8	4	20	W
George Shoup, heirs of	Cin	Pre	7	3	32	S
Martin Kershner	Cin	Pre	8	3	1	NE
John Sutherland & Abraham Huff	Cin	Pre	4	1	2	+

John Sutherland &						
Abraham Huff	Cin	Pre	4	2	32	+
Charles Null	Cin	Pre	4	3	12	−
Jonah Farquhar	Cin	Pre	9	4	2	NW
James Chatham	Cin	Pre	6	1	2	S
Joseph Vandola	Cin	Pre	5	4	36	SW
John McDye	Cin	Pre	10	2	35	SE
Stephen Vineyard	Cin	Pre	4	4	22	+
Philip Harshman	Cin	Pre	7	3	32	NW
Paul Lewis	Cin	Pre	4	4	21	NE
Joseph Stafford	Cin	Pre	9	2	17	S
Jonathan Donnell	Cin	Pre	9	4	17	SW
John Reynolds	Cin	Pre	11	4	9	+
Nathaniel Garrard	Cin	Pre	11	1	19	+
John Bradford	Cin	Pre	7	2	15	NW
William Gaudy, J. B. [Gaudy?], & J. S? [Gaudy?]	Cin	Pre	5	4	36	SE
William Wason	Cin	EML	6	4	33	NE
John Wolf	Cin	MR	8	3	15	S*
Benjamin Purcel	Cin	WML	3	5	36	NE
Elijah Bell	Cin	MR	11	4	14	SW
Conrad Huffman	Cin	WML	1	5	30	SW
Frederick Miller	Cin	EML	3	7	11	NW
William Anthony	Cin	EML	1	4	18	NW
Peter Hann	Cin	WML	1	8	14	SE
William B. Allen & J. S? Allen	Cin	WML	1	8	11	NW
Ewel Kindell & J. Turner	Cin	** 14E	16−	21		NE
Ithamar White	Cin	WML	1	9	26	NE
Ezra Kellog	Cin	EML	2	4	18	SE
Jesse Swisher	Cin	EML	3	7	15	NE
Charles Dawson	Cin	WML	2	5	1	SW
John K. Steel	Cin	EML	2	6	18	SE
Ninian Nichells	Cin	MR	10	6	13	SW
Jacob Kuntz	Cin	EML	5	5	4	SW
Jacob Little	Cin	** 13E	15N	10		SW
James Miller	Cin	MR	8	4	8	NE
William R. [McConnels], James L. [McConnels], & Alexander McConnels	Cin	EML	6	2	31	−
James Miller	Cin	MR	8	4	8	SE
John Swallow	Cin	EML	6	3	19	SE
Elisha Taber	Cin	MR	11	5	20	SE
John Stout	Cin	WML	1	9	18	NE
Jesse Hunt	Cin	MR	10	2	36	NW
Samuel Woods	Cin	WML	1	14	26	SW
John McIntire	Cin	MR	13	4	20	SW
John H. Piatt	Cin	Square	3, lot	10		
John H. Piatt	Cin	Square	3, lot	11		
John H. Piatt	Cin	Square	3, lot	6		
George P. Torrence	Cin	MR	12	1	32	+
Thomas Stafford	Cin	** 12E	16−	34		NW
Daniel Ross	Cin	EML	1	4	10	NW
John Shaw	Cin	** 12E	15−	11		SE
Robert Brown	Cin	** 13E	14−	30		NE
Robert Brown	Cin	** 13E	14−	19		SE
Robertson Jones & James Jones	Cin	WML	1	8	30	NE
Henry Royer	Cin	EML	4	5	11	SW
James McAlexander	Cin	MR	12	4	36	SW
Thomas Daniel	Cin	MR	13	4	19	SW
Devault Crowell	Cin	EML	1	8	12	NE
Thomas Elliott	Cin	EML	1	3	33	E
Thomas Babcock	Cin	MR	8	3	30	+
Abel Crawford	Cin	MR	10	4	32	NW
James Wall	Cin	MR	13	4	4	NE
Robert Morris	Cin	EML	2	5	21	NE
John Reed	Cin	EML	9	5	10	SW
Moses Conger	Cin	WML	2	8	12	SE
Jacob Elsworth	Cin	MR	10	6	19	NE
John Port	Cin	** 13	15	15		SW

John Port	Cin	** 13E	15−	15		NW
William Kirkpatrick	Cin	** 13E	13−	12		SE
Thomas Gilliland	Cin	MR	9	4	22	NE
John Wall	Cin	?	13	4	4	SW

*"Except 50 acres in SE corner."
**Second Principal Meridian.

1372   30 Jul 1813   A/5/209
John Lock, Frederick Town, Maryland
Transmits patent

John Lock	Cin	EML	3	7	22	SE

1373   30 Jul 1813   A/5/210
Richard Rush, Comptroller of the U.S. Treasury
Transmits bond for Lloyd Posey, Rec ELA.

1374   30 Jul 1813   A/5/210
His excellency Thomas Posey, Governor of the Indiana
   Territory
Acknowledges bond for Lloyd Posey, Rec ELA.

1375   30 Jul 1813   A/5/210
Daniel Symmes, Reg Cin
Mentions John Lock; does not favor repayment to --
   Boyce for overpayment, as patent already issued

-- Boyce	[Cin?]	−? 1E	6	3		NW

1376   31 Jul 1813   A/5/210
LO Jef
Transmits patents

Samuel McKinley	Jef	* 10E	2N	18	NE
Robert Hollowell	Jef	* 2E	1S	3	NE
Zachariah Lindley	Jef	* 2E	1N	33	SW
Zacheriah Nixon	Jef	* 4E	2N	5	SW
John Boggs	Jef	* 1E	2N	8	NW
John Saffers	Jef	* 5E	5S	5	SW
William Lindley	Jef	* 4E	2N	20	NW
Samuel McKinley	Jef	* 10E	2N	19	NE
Samuel McKinley	Jef	* 10E	2N	18	NW
Samuel McKinley	Jef	* 9E	2N	13	NE
John Boggs	Jef	* 1E	3N	31	NE
Thomas Carr	Jef	* 4E	2N	5	NE
Jacob Young	Jef	* 4E	1S	2	NE
William Lindley	Jef	* 1E	1N	21	SW
John Pittman	Jef	* 3E	4S	8	SW
John West	Jef	* 11E	4N	15	NW
Mason Watts	Jef	* 10E	5N	13	NE
William Edwards	Jef	* 10E	4N	28	SW
William Edwards	Jef	* 10E	3N	6	NE
J. Armstrong & William Plaskett	Jef	* 10E	1N	8	SE
John McMillan	Jef	* 9E	3N	23	NE
Robert Hollowell	Jef	* 1E	1N	11	SE
Benjamin Ramsay	Jef	* 9E	3N	4	NW
Samuel Blankenbaker	Jef	* 3E	2N	13	SE
James Wright	Jef	* 4E	2N	18	NE
Samuel Ewing	Jef	* 4E	5N	30	+

*Second Principal Meridian.

1377   31 Jul 1813   A/5/211
LO Stu
Transmits patents

Robert Wood	Stu	−	6	14	33	NE
Lodowick Sharrards	Stu	−	6	17	2	NE
Joseph Eichar	Stu	−	8	10	15	SE
John Spahr	Stu	−	3	9	21	NW

Henry Markey	Stu	–	8	11	30	NE
John Crawford	Stu	–	2	11	35	SW
Christian Hoover	Stu	–	7	20	35	S
Elias Yeagley	Stu	–	2	8	22	NW
Jacob Shenenberger	Stu	–	8	11	15	SE
George Abel	Stu	–	4	11	15	SE
Henry Markey	Stu	–	8	11	21	SW
Simon Essig	Stu	–	8	11	22	NE
Simon Essig	Stu	–	8	11	21	NE
John Henderson	Stu	–	3	11	9	SE
Mahlon Wileman	Stu	–	7	20	23	SW
Thomas Shepherd	Stu	–	3	11	8	NE
Thomas Stanley, Junior	Stu	–	4	17	18	SW
Joseph Burt	Stu	–	1	7	1	NE
Jonathan Wright	Stu	–	6	10	11	SE
John Montgomery	Stu	–	4	12	14	SE
John Long	Stu	–	5	15	26	SW
Charles Brown	Stu	–	5	15	27	NE
Jacob Baghtel	Stu	–	8	9	10	NW
David Moody	Stu	–	5	11	9	NW
Jonas Fagley	Stu	–	5	9	28	NW

1378   31 Jul 1813   A/5/211
LO Can
Transmits patents

John Bever et al	Can	–	13	15	3	NW
Daniel A? Byles	Can	–	10	1	20	NW
Joseph H. Larwill?	Can	–	13	15	4	SE
Samuel Hays	Can	–	11	16	12	NE
John Knight	Can	–	12	16	28	NE
Valentine Smith	Can	–	12	16	19	NE
William McMonigal	Can	–	12	15	17	SE
William McMonigal	Can	–	15	22	36	SE
Valentine Smith	Can	–	12	16	7	SE
Valentine Smith	Can	–	13	15	13	N
Henry Smith	Can	–	13	15	24	NE
John Bever	Can	–	13	15	14	–
Nicholas Stump	Can	–	9	19?	19	NE
Benjamin Bunn	Can	–	15	21	15	SE
Aaron Young	Can	–	18	20	30	NW
Joseph Mitchell	Can	–	19	18	4	NE
Harry Hammon	Can	–	10	1	8	SE
John Lowry	Can	–	10	12	3	NW
Archibald Steel	Can	–	10	12	22	NE
Richard Hardgrove	Can	–	10	1	27	NE
John Bever	Can	–	10	12	10	NW
John Bever	Can	–	10	12	10	SW
John Bever	Can	–	13	13	2	NW
John Bever	Can	–	10	12	2	SE
John Bever	Can	–	11	16	12	NW
Thomas Moore	Can	–	11	16	12	SW
John Bever	Can	–	10	12	9	SW
John Bever	Can	–	10	12	10	NE
John Bever	Can	–	10	12	10	SE

1379   31 Jul 1813   A/5/213
LO Zan
Transmits patents

Jacob Stutsman	Zan	Mil	5	9	20	SW
Bennett Suttles	Zan	–	14	15	8?	NW
Thomas Hanna	Zan	Mil	1	2	15	SW
John Stowner	Zan	Mil	7	3	23	SE
Isaac Deardorff	Zan	Mil	3	10	19	NW
George Skinner	Zan	–	15	16	19	SW
Nicholas Fitarick? [Titarick?]	Zan	–	13	11	17	SE
William Gibson	Zan	Mil	3	4	23	SE
Joseph Derroh	Zan	–	14	15	3	SE
Adam Mosholder	Zan	Mil	10	5	3	NW
Samuel Vernon	Zan	Mil	6	2	25	NW

Elijah Stephens	Zan	–	10	9	33	NW
Abraham Welker	Zan	Mil	10	7	16	NE
Barbara Prior	Zan	Mil	8	2	15	NW
Samuel Newell	Zan	Mil	3	3	13	NE
Sarah Clarkson	Zan	–	13	12	13	NW
James Sinclair	Zan	–	11	13	23	NE
Adam Miller	Zan	–	15	18	18	SE
Nicholas Kime	Zan	Mil	5	9	20	SE
John Erlewine	Zan	Mil	10	5	3	SW
Wentworth Riker	Zan	–	8	5	7	SE
Jonas Stutsman	Zan	Mil	5	9	21	NW
Archibald Campbell	Zan	Mil	5	1	24	SE
Daniel Patterson	Zan	Mil	2	2	4	SE
Isaac Van Horn	Zan	–	14	16	2	SW
Jacob Hains	Zan	Mil	6	1	20	NW

1380   7 Aug 1813   A/5/213
Samuel Smith, Esq., St. Stephens, now in Washington
    City [D.C.]
Your statement relative to conflicting claims at
    Fort St. Stephens must be determined by law and
    not by the Commissioner of the GLO.

1381   7 Aug 1813   A/5/214
Levi Barber, Rec Mar
Instructions on payment to Joseph Willcox for audit
    of LO Mar books.

1382   7 Aug 1813   A/5/214
James O. Cosby, Commissioner, Western District of
    Louisiana East of the Mississippi River and the
    Island of New Orleans
William Crawford, Commissioner, Eastern District of
    Louisiana East of the Mississippi River and the
    Island of New Orleans
Lengthy set of instructions as to reporting of claims.

1383   10 Aug 1813   A/5/216
Samuel Finley, Rec Chl
Instructions on payment to Isaac Davis [near Chilli-
    cothe] for audit of LO Chl books.

1384   10 Aug 1813   A/5/217
Daniel Symmes, Reg Cin
Transmits patents; mentions letter from J[ohn]
    C[leves] Short

William Short	Cin	Pre	9	3	31	E
William Short	Cin	Pre	9	3	25	–
William Short	Cin	Pre	9	3	36	N
William Short	Cin	Pre	9	3	36	SE

1385   11 Aug 1813   A/5/217
John Cleves Short, Cincinnati
Mentions necessary corrections in land descriptions.

1386   12 Aug 1813   A/5/217
Thomas McCune, Steubenville
Acknowledges receipt of his audit of LO Stu accounts.

1387   13 Aug 1813   A/5/218
Daniel Symmes, Reg Cin
Discrepancies noted in the following certificates

--	Cin	Pre	9	3	32	+
--	Cin	EML	3	4	9	NE
--	Cin	MR	13	5	27	–

--	Cin	Pre	8	2	32	+
--	Cin	-	1	14	5	NE
--	Cin	-	1	12	5	NW
--	Cin	Pre	9	2	17	NE
--	Cin	WML	1	12	4	NE

1388   16 Aug 1813   A/5/219
Nehemiah Tilton, Reg Wsh, Mississippi Territory
Land description too vague; mentions John Henderson
   "on the waters of Thompson creek."

1389   17 Aug 1813   A/5/220
President of the United States
Register of Fort St. Stephens [Lewis Sewall] having
   recommended removal of public records to safer
   place, due to Indian warfare, question submitted
   to you for decision. [Also discusses sending
   Federal troops as an alternative.]

1390   18 Aug 1813   A/5/220
Daniel Symmes, Reg Cin
Discrepancies noted

--*	Cin	-	2E	4	4	NW
--**	Cin	EML	1	4	34	NW
--***	Cin	MR	11	3	17	SE

*Previously sold to Catherine Boyse.
**Previously sold and patented to Lucy Ramsey.
***Previously entered by Coats Thornton.

1391   19 Aug 1813   A/5/221
LO Vin
Transmits patents

Joseph English	Vin	*	8W	5S	26	SE
Adam Glaze	Vin	*	2W	7S	7	+
David Young	Vin	*	4E	5S	25	NW
John Dawson	Vin	*	3E	4S	32	SW
William Bateman	Vin	*	5E	2S	15	NE
Joseph Burton	Vin	*	5E	2S	36	SW
Abraham Reed	Vin	*	5E	5S	35	+
Samuel Aldridge	Vin	*	13W	7S	6	NW
Thomas Rogers	Vin	*	14W	5S	1	NW
Thomas Montgomery	Vin	*	12W	2S	26	NW
Joseph Farlow	Vin	*	1W	1N	14	NE
Jacob Warrick, heirs of	Vin	*	12W	3S	23	NW
Joseph Farlow	Vin	*	1W	1N	11	SW
Abraham Walk	Vin	*	4E	2S	27	SE
Henry Reis	Vin	*	4E	4S	1	NE
John Stephens	Vin	*	4E	4S	35	SE
William Lathom	Vin	*	11W	1S	25	SE

*Second Principal Meridian.

1392   19 Aug 1813   A/5/222
LO Cin
Transmits patents

Daniel Deardorff	Cin	Pre	4	3	33	NW
Arthur Vandavier	Cin	Pre	6	1	19	NW
Henry Staley	Cin	Pre	7	2	9	W
Henry Strader	Cin	Pre	6	1	7	SW
Jonathan Donnell	Cin	Pre	9	4	23	SE
Mary M. Young	Cin	Pre	4	2	5	S
Thomas Wilson	Cin	Pre	5	4	20	+
Daniel Doty	Cin	Pre	4	2	4	S
George Adams	Cin	Pre	6	1	21	+
George Adams	Cin	Pre	6	1	27	+
George Adams	Cin	Pre	6	1	28	-
Noah Tibbles	Cin	Pre	5	2	5	+
James Clensy Survey 1	Cin	MR	6	3	26	+
James Clensy Survey 1	Cin	MR	6	3	32	+
John Hall	Cin	EML	2	4	14	SE
George Shoup, heirs of	Cin	Pre	8	2	2	+
David Sutton	Cin	Pre	4	3	35	SW
James Frazee	Cin	Pre	10	2	30	NE
Richard Mason	Cin	Pre	6	1	7	E
Samuel Still? [Hill?] Survey 3	Cin	Pre	7	3	13	+
David Fox	Cin	Pre	4	3	10	S

1393   19 Aug 1813   A/5/222
LO Stu
Transmits patents

Archibald Fletcher	Stu	-	4	10	21	SW
Jacob Nessley	Stu	-	2	9	8	+
Jacob Nessley	Stu	-	2	9	14	-
John Richardson	Stu	-	6	11	8	NE
John Meyner	Stu	-	5	16	15	NE
John Bushong	Stu	-	8	12	6	W
Joseph Snively	Stu	-	9	10	36	SW
Joseph Snively	Stu	-	9	10	36	NE
John Stewart	Stu	-	7	10	17	NW
Robert Partridge	Stu	-	3	13	1	SE
John Fishel	Stu	-	3	12	17	SE
Obed Pierpoint	Stu	-	6	18	14	SW
John Shearman	Stu	-	9	9	13	NE
Joseph Fife	Stu	-	2	10	8	NW
Joshua Cecil	Stu	-	5	10	20	SW
Joseph Snively	Stu	-	8	9	19	NW
Michael Miller	Stu	-	6	18	10	SW
William Grimes	Stu	-	5	10	15	NW
John Shorb	Stu	-	9	10	25	E
John Wynants	Stu	-	5	12	8	SW
James Gray	Stu	-	7	14	20	SE
Peter Shorb	Stu	-	9	10	26	NE
Reason Pumphrey	Stu	-	6	9	11	-
John Perry	Stu	-	5	10	34	SW
Frederick States? [Slates?]	Stu	-	4	11	34	SE
Anthony Housel	Stu	-	6	17	3	NE
Henry Bard	Stu	-	1	7	26	SW
Jacob Brown	Stu	-	5	15	23	NW
John Summer	Stu	-	1	9	15	NE
John Fry	Stu	-	6	13	20	NW
George Helwig	Stu	-	7	15	9	SW
Thomas Williams	Stu	-	6	8	2	SW
Henry Barriger	Stu	-	4	10	21	NW
Peter Ebi	Stu	-	8	11	12	SE
Jesse Underwood	Stu	-	1	7	17	NW
William Disart	Stu	-	4	8	15	SE
Adam McGowen	Stu	-	5	18	4	NE
George Frank	Stu	-	8	12	28	SW
John McGirr	Stu	-	7	20	26	SW
Jacob Welday	Stu	-	2	6	15	SW
Rudolph Bair	Stu	-	6	17	17	SW
Martin Houser	Stu	-	7	20	27	SE
Martin Houser	Stu	-	7	20	34	NW
Andrew Smith	Stu	-	3	12	5	SW
Peter Troxel	Stu	-	8	11	22	NW
John Raber*	Stu	-	8	12	8	NE
John Davis	Stu	-	1	7	30	NW
Thomas Rankin	Stu	-	5	10	31	SE
Jacob Harter	Stu	-	8	11	9	SW
John Reber*	Stu	-	8	12	9	NW
Isaac Dwire	Stu	-	5	14	32	SW
Nathaniel Harpley	Stu	-	7	20	26	NW
John Street	Stu	-	5	16	21	NE
Morris Dunlevy	Stu	-	3	9	21	SW
Adam Smith	Stu	-	8	10	15	SW
John Crawford	Stu	-	5	15	14	SW
Jacob Rowland	Stu	-	9	11	33	SW
Henry Beamer	Stu	-	7	15	10	NW

Bezaleel Wells	Stu	-	8	10	4	NW
Bezaleel Wells	Stu	-	8	11	20	SW
Bezaleel Wells	Stu	-	8	10	5	SW
Bezaleel Wells	Stu	-	8	10	9	NW
Bezaleel Wells	Stu	-	8	10	9	SE
Bezaleel Wells	Stu	-	8	11	32	SW
Bezaleel Wells	Stu	-	8	11	32	NW
Thomas Campbell	Stu	-	2	8	22	NE
Valentine Berger	Stu	-	5	10	21	SE
Hugh Gwyn	Stu	-	4	9	22	SW
Horace Potter	Stu	-	3	14	22	SE
Bezaleel Wells	Stu	-	5	11	5	NW

*So spelled.

1394   19 Aug 1813   A/5/224
John Crumbacker, near Canton, [Ohio]
Acknowledges receipt of audit of LO Can books.

1395   19 Aug 1813   A/5/224
Jesse Spencer, Reg Chl
Transmits first certificate

James Buchannon	Chl	-	17	8	2	W

1396   20 Aug 1813   A/5/225
Edmund H. Taylor, Rec Jef
Instructs him to pay Richard Ferguson [of Louis-
   ville, Kentucky] for audit of LO Jef books.

1397   23 Aug 1813   A/5/225
Daniel Symmes, Reg Cin
Transmits patent; calls attention to discrepancies

Sylvester Thompson	Cin	EML	5	8	38	W
John Smith, assignee of*	Cin	MR	6	2	23	NW
-- Worman**	Cin	MR	7	3	29	SE

*Land appears to have reverted and to have been
   entered by J. H. Pratt.
**Appears to have been entered by C. Stephenson.

1398   23 Aug 1813   A/5/225
John Hamm, Zanesville
Acknowledges receipt of his audit of LO Zan books.

1399   23 Aug 1813   A/5/226
Nehemiah Tilton, Reg Wsh, Mississippi Territory
Transmits patents; mentions document from orphan's
   court relative to the estate of Abel Eastman
   [which may have been sent to GLO by mistake]

Silas Dinsmore	Wsh	-	4W	5	3	E
Silas Dinsmore	Wsh	-	4W	5	8	E
Silas Dinsmore	Wsh	-	4W	5	3	W
Silas Dinsmore	Wsh	-	4W	5	8	W

1400   24 Aug 1813   A/5/227
John Johnson, Vincennes
Acknowledges receipt of his audit of LO Vin books.

1401   24 Aug 1813   A/5/227
Daniel Symmes [Reg Cin]
"The late chief clerk of this office having departed
   this life, . . . the following suspended" matters
   have been found in his desk

N. Williams[1]	Cin	MR	9	4	35	NW
J. Henderson & W. Henderson[2]	Cin	Pre	9	3	15	N
Jonathan Hunter[3]	Cin	Pre	10	6	22	-
George Stafford[4]	Cin	MR	10	3	31	SW
-- Studebaker[5]	Cin	-	9	2	22	SE
-- Spinning & -- Garbuck[6]	Cin	MR	7	2	11	NW
B. Whiteman[7]	Cin	Pre	8	5	20	+
B. Whiteman[7]	Cin	Pre	8	5	21	+
--[8]	Cin	Pre	5	3	4	+
--[8]	Cin	Pre	6	2	6	+
--[8]	Cin	Pre	6	2	28	+
--[9]	Cin	-	5	2	12	SE
--[9]	Cin	-	5	2	12	W
--[10]	Cin	EML	6	7	18	SE
Arthur Vandeveer[11]	Cin	Pre	5	2	27	+
--[12]	Cin	EML	4	4	29	NE
--[13]	Cin	MR	5	2	30	NW
Joseph Sawyer[14]	Cin	Pre	5	2	25	+
Jesse Bond[15]	Cin	WML	1	13	6	NE
William Rhode[16]	Cin	-	2	13	26	SE
--[17]	Cin	-	11	6	31	NE
--[17]	Cin	-	11	6	31	NW
Thomas Henderson[18]	Cin	-	2	9	8	SW
-- Craig[19]	Cin	MR	10	5	4	NE
John Bigger[20]	Cin	MR	4	3	25	+
--[21]	Cin	EML	4	4	13	-
Joseph Parkes, Junior[22]	Cin	[no description]				

1. Assignee of John Rue. The power of attorney
   from Rue to Samuel Smith is conditional and a
   proper sale is not made.
2. Assignees of John Jackson. Another survey is
   required.
3. Documentation incomplete.
4. Assignee of Adam Verdier. No first certificate
   found.
5. Assignee of John Mills and Seth Mills. Transfer
   incomplete; see letter dated 14 Mar 1811.
6. Assignees of D. C. Cooper. Secretary Gallatin
   has endorsed as follows: "Telford has only
   assigned his right to south 1/2 of 1/4 section,
   and has retained his right to north half of it,
   the assignment of Cooper being for the said quarter section undivided to Telford and Spinning."
7. Assignee of Arthur St. Clair. No certificate or
   assignment found.
8. Certificates returned to you 21 Mar 1812 to perfect the transfers.
9. Certificates returned to you 14 Dec 1811 to perfect the transfers.
10. Transfer returned to you on 6 Feb 1810 for correction.
11. Assignee of Daniel Richardson. Transfer defective.
12. Defective transfer sent to you 9 Dec 1811.
13. Suspended for want of power of attorney.
14. Assignee of John McCormick. Defective transfer
   returned 24 Feb 1812.
15. Assignee of James Randall. "Inadmissible without Meeks' release or some proof of erasure being with his consent."
16. Assignee of Lazarus Whitehead. "To get over the
   difficulty, John Rhode may assign to William
   Rhode."
17. Defective transfers returned 30 Apr 1812.
18. Assignee of William Henderson. "The assignment,
   alias affidavit, does not name the range."
19. Assignee of -- Sinks? [Links?]. "A certificate
   that Baldwin is a magistrate [is required]."
20. Description appears to be erroneous, as stated in
   our letter to you of 12 May 1809.
21. We wrote on 17 Dec 1811 asking for proof that the
   persons named in the final certificate were the
   heirs of C[hristia]n Fogalgasang."
22. Assignee of Jacob White. Transfer deficient.

1402   24 Aug 1813   A/5/229
Jesse Spencer, Reg Chl
"In the desk of the late J.J. Moore the following
   suspended documents have been found. I will thank
   you to enable me (so far as may be in your power)
   finally to dispose of them, by issuing patents"

Christopher Creamer[1]	Chl	–	21	11	24	NW
-- Shock[2]	Chl	–	21	11	35	NE
-- Lively[3]	Chl	–	17	16	13	NE
P. Needless[4]	Chl	–	20	15	32	NW
-- Wolf[5]	Chl	–	20	12	33	NW
--[6]	Chl	–	21	9	34	NW
--[7]	Chl	–	18	14	20	–
--[8]	Chl	–	16	17	10	NE
--[9]	Chl	–	17	16	10	W
--[10]	Chl	WS	21	11	17	NW
--[10]	Chl	–	17	18	27	SE
--[11]	Chl	–	21	10	14	SW
--[11]	Chl	–	20	14	31	NW
--[12]	Chl	–	17	16	2	NW
--[13]	Chl	–	21	10	14	SE
--[14]	Chl	–	19	13	6	–
--[14]	Chl	–	19	13	7	–
--[15]	Chl	–	17	14	5	NW
--[15]	Chl	–	19	15	15	NE

1. Assignee of George Ankany. The assignment is
    defective.
2. Assignee of -- Mace, assignee of Jesse Spencer.
    No transfer found.
3. Assignee of -- Crosen. No assignment found.
4. Assignee of T. Fayette and G. Fayette. No
    assignment found.
5. Assignee of -- Graham and -- Friend. Defective
    transfer forwarded to you on 26 May 1812.
6. Defective transfer forwarded to you 18 Jun 1810.
7. Defective transfer forwarded to you 31 Mar 1812.
8. Defective transfer.
9. "No proof of administration or power of attorney
    from one administration to the other."
10. Transfers were returned, at least one of them on
    14 Nov 1811.
11. Transfers now returned. Proof of magistracy
    wanting.
12. First assignments not acknowledged.
13. "One of the assignments attached by wafers."
14. Transfers returned 30 Mar 1812.
15. Transfers returned 18 Sep 1811.

1403   25 Aug 1813   A/5/230
David Hoge, Reg Stu
On examining papers in the desk of the late Mr. Moore
   [Chief Clerk, GLO] final certificate in favor of
   Kail was found. Apparently the land was first
   entered by Isaac Wood. In your letter of 14 Oct
   1808 you request return of certificate to you, as
   Kail is willing to take other land.

Peter Kail	Stu	–	5	11	18	SE
J. McCleary*	Stu	–	4	10	21	SE

*Assignee of Isaac Osburn. Defective transfer re-
turned to you on 29 Nov 1811.

1404   25 Aug 1813   A/5/230
Philemon Beecher, New Lancaster, Ohio
Transmits patent

Philemon Beecher	Chl	–	19	15	11	NE

1405   27 Aug 1813   A/5/230
Daniel Symmes, Reg Cin
Discrepancies noted as follows

--	Survey 1 or 2	Cin	MR?	9	4	21	+
--[1]		Cin	Pre	7	3	20	+
--[2]		Cin	EML	3	5	1	SE
--[3]		Cin	–	8	2	29	SW?
--[4]		Cin	MR	5	6	34	–
--[5]		Cin	Pre	8	3	21	SE
--[6]		Cin	MR 2?	2	34		E
--[7]		Cin	EML	1	1	30	–
--[7]		Cin	EML	1	1	31	–
--[7]		Cin	EML	1	1	island	
--[8]		Cin	WML	1	7	4	E
--[8]		Cin	MR 12	4	17		SE
--[9]		Cin	MR 13	5	26		NE
--[10]		Cin	MR	9	3	17	NE

1. Power of attorney needed to complete transfer.
2. Payment not found.
3. Should it be SE quarter?
4. Transfer attached with wafers and does not de-
    scribe tract.
5. How many acres in tract--100 or 150? "Do you
    have the transfer from Cossard to Mercer?"
6. "Should not this be range 13?"
7. A repayment does not appear in certificate.
8. Short payments.
9. Over payment.
10. A repayment does not appear.

1406   27 Aug 1813   A/5/231
Nehemiah Tilton, Reg Wsh, Mississippi Territory
In the desk of the late Mr. Moore [Chief Clerk, GLO]
   suspended documents were found

--[1]	Wsh	–	2W	2	31	–
--[1]	Wsh	–	2E	3	32	–
--[2]	Wsh	–	3E	2	41	–
--[1]	Wsh	–	3E	2	41	S
--[1]	Wsh	–	3E	1	6	S
Robert Montgomery[3]	Wsh	–	4E	2	34	–
Robert Montgomery[4]	Wsh	–	6-	2	34	–
Robert Montgomery[4]	Wsh	–	3-	2	29	–
Jacob Fudge[5]	Wsh	–	5-	2	8	SW
-- Barrett & -- Kinsler[6]	Wsh	–	5-	2	15	SW
George Sorrell[7]	Wsh	[not described]				
F. L. Claiborne[8]	Wsh	[not described]				

1. Assignments needed.
2. Correction of acreage.
3. Assigned to Sylvester Dunn.
4. So shown on GLO books.
5. First certificate assigned land to -- Barrett &
    -- Kinsler. Please return patent for correction.
6. Assignees of Thomas Gibson. Cannot determine
    whether patent is correct.
7. "On the waters of Big black [creek?]" Assigned
    to William Miller and by him to Ignatius Flowers.
    Certificate cannot be found.
8. In city of Natchez, but not otherwise described.

1407   26 Aug 1813   A/5/232
Joseph Wood, [Reg] Mar
Discrepancy in account

Joseph Holden*	Mar	–	6	2	7	+

*Assignee of Isaac Wilson, who purchased only the
west half section. The east half section was purchased by W. Skinner.

1408   27 Aug 1813   A/5/232
Adam Sighbert, Washington, Pennsylvania
Transmits patent

Adam Sighbert*	Stu	–	8	10	35	NW

*Assignee of Barnet Sickman.

1409   28 Aug 1813   A/5/232
John Reed, Reg Hun
The following incomplete transactions were found in
  the desk of the late chief clerk [of GLO]

--1	Hun	-	2E	1	15	+
--1	Hun	-	2E	1	17	SE
--1	Hun	-	1E	3	1	NE
--1	Hun	-	1W	3	14	NE
--1	Hun	-	1W	3	13	NW
--2	Hun	-	1W	4	22	NE

1. Duplicate final certificates issued for reasons
  unknown to GLO. Patents were forwarded to you
  on 25 Mar 1811.
2. Three years interest due on balance outstanding.

1410   28 Aug 1813   A/5/233
John Nichols, care of John Sloan, Canton [Ohio]
Transmits patent

John Nichols	Stu	-	8	10	25	NE

1411   28 Aug 1813   A/5/233
Samuel Gwathmey, Reg Jef
Transmits final certificate

Solomon Bowers*	Jef	-	9E	2N	19	SW

*Should it not be Range 5?

1412   28 Aug 1813   A/5/234
Robert Darling, Coshocton, Ohio
Transmits patents

Robert Darling	Can	-	17	21	1	NW
Robert Darling	Can	-	17	21	1	NE

1413   31 Aug 1813   A/5/234
Samuel Finley, Rec Chl
Since the death of Mr. Moore [chief clerk, GLO] an
  attempt is being made to regenerate this office.
  Please submit your quarterly reports and explain
  why you have not done so since 1810.

1414   31 Aug 1813   A/5/235
Oliver Spencer, Cincinnati
Acknowledges receipt of audit report on LO Cin books.

1415   1 Sep 1813   A/5/235
Joseph Wood, Reg Mar
Transmits patent

Barnard Eagan	Mar	-	7	8	27	NE

1416   1 Sep 1813   A/5/235
Daniel Symmes, Reg Cin
Encloses sundry documents "which have been laying
  by a long time suspended"

--1	Cin MR	7	2	3	SE
--2	Cin Pre	7	3	20	NE
--3	Cin Pre	7	3	21	S
--4	Cin -	5	5	25	-
--4	Cin -	5	5	31	-
--5	Cin MR	11	4	30	+
--6	Cin MR	7	2	26	SW
--7	Cin MR	4	3	29	SW
--7	Cin MR	4	2	26	SE
--8	Cin MR	3	2	21	NW
--7	Cin -	1W	14	36	+
--6	Cin Pre	8	2	22	-
--6	Cin Pre	11	5	34	NE
--5,7	Cin -	5	3	30	+
--5	Cin -	9	4	32	-
--5	Cin -	10	4	3	-
--5	Cin -	11	4	15	-

1. Needs acknowledgment before a magistrate.
2. Needs proof that Maherd? is a magistrate. Should
  this be NE or NW?
3. Needs proof that Maherd? is a magistrate.
4. Should read Township 4.
5. Description is too vague.
6. Overcharged.
7. Short charged.
8. Should be Range 9.

1417   2 Sep 1813   A/5/236
Wyllys Silliman, Reg Zan
Assignment returned to you for correction on 10 Jul
  1810

James Welch*	Zan	-	1	3	8	NW
-- Cloud	Zan	-	10	2	16	SW

*Assignee of William Welch.
**Assignment from -- Jenkins to -- Gardner to -- Cloud
  is missing.

1418   3 Sep 1813   A/5/236
John Read, Reg Hun, Mississippi Territory
Defective documents returned

John Binnion	Hun	-	8	3	34	NE

1419   3 Sep 1813   A/5/237
Daniel Symmes, Reg Cin
Returns defective documents

--1		Cin MR	12	1	7	SE
--1		Cin EML	1	6	28	NW
--2		Cin MR	7	4	35	NW
--1		Cin EML	2	11	20	NE
--1	Survey 2	Cin MR	8	3	34	-
--1		Cin Pre	7	3	2	+
--1		Cin Pre	8	3	20	-

1. Short payment.
2. Neither acreage nor payments agree with GLO books.

1420   6 Sep 1813   A/5/238
Richard Rush, Comptroller of U.S. Treasury
Forwards bond for William Garrard, Rec WLA.

1421   6 Sep 1813   A/5/238
Allan B. Magruder, Esq., Opelousas [Louisiana]
On the basis of information you have communicated to
  me, I have approved the bond of [William] Garrard,
  Rec WLA.

1422   6 Sep 1813   A/5/238
Samuel Gwathmey, Reg Jef
Transmits revised patent

Henry Rats	Jef	-	4E	1N	6	SW

1423   6 Sep 1813   A/5/238
John Sloan, Rec Can
Mentions interest due from John Stump. "I will thank
  you to state what are the perquisites taken from
  those who enter land. I apprehend . . . that they
  are unauthorized by law."

Horace Hill*	Can	-	14	18	11	SE

*Assigned to James Hendricks.

1424   8 Sep 1813   A/5/239
His Excellency Ninian Edwards, Governor of Illinois
    Territory, at Russelville, Logan County, Kentucky
Saline deposit lease to include clause requiring
    approval by the President of the United States;
    new lessees to pay for improvements of the old
    lessee.

1425   6 Sep 1813   A/5/239
William Crawford, Land Commissioner, Mobile [Ala-
    bama]
Acknowledges appointment of -- Acre as clerk; pay-
    ments can be made from Fort St. Stephens.

1426   10 Sep 1813   A/5/240
Daniel Symmes, Reg Cin
Lengthy discussion regarding computation of fraction-
    al sections; mentions computation in following
    transaction
-- Boyce   Cin   -   1E   6   3 NW

1427   11 Sep 1813   A/5/241
David Hoge, Reg Stu
Transmits patent
John Weller   Stu   -   7 19 30 NE

1428   11 Sep 1813   A/5/241
John Sloan, Rec Can
Since the death of the chief clerk [of GLO] it has
    been discovered that you have not forwarded quar-
    terly reports since 1810. Do so immediately.

1429   11 Sep 1813   A/5/242
Isaac Van Horn, Rec Zan
Since the death of the chief clerk [of GLO] it has
    been discovered that you have not forwarded quar-
    terly reports since 1811. Do so immediately.

1430   14 Sep 1813   A/5/242
David Hoge, Reg Stu
Joseph Reeves has asked for three patents. They
    were sent to you in September 1810; please re-
    turn them to GLO for forwarding to him.

1431   14 Sep 1813   A/5/242
Isaac Van Horn, Rec Zan
Transmits U.S. Treasury receipt
Andrew Carroll   Zan   - 15 18 17 NW

1432   15 Sep 1813   A/5/243
George F. Pope, Corydon, Indiana Territory
Transmits patent
Joseph Decker, Junior* Vin - 5E 3S 21 NE
*An assignee of a person unnamed in letter.

1433   16 Sep 1813   A/5/243
LO Hun
Transmits patents
Niel McCarn   Hun WML   1   2   30 NW
John Hughs   Hun WML   1   4   10 NE
George Dilworth   Hun WML   1   3   33 SW
Andrew Scioley   Hun WML   1   4   13 NW
Levi Hinds   Hun EML   2   3   7   NE
Levi Hinds   Hun EML   2   3   8   NW
James Manning   Hun EML   1   2   30 NW
John Loy   Hun EML   2   3   31 NE
William Gray   Hun WML   1   4   7   NE
John Reedy   Hun WML   1   4   10 SW
James Manning   Hun EML   1   2   30 SW
James Manning   Hun EML   1   2   31 NW
James Manning   Hun WML   1   2   25 SW
James Manning   Hun WML   1   2   25 NE
Reuben Stone   Hun EML   1   3   12 SW
John W. Hewlett   Hun EML   1   3   25 NE
George Smith   Hun EML   2   1   33 +
George Smith   Hun EML   2   1   34 +
James Woods   Hun EML   1   4   7   SW
John Connally   Hun EML   1   3   18 NW
Daniel Tilman   Hun WML   2   1   36 NW
James Scruggs   Hun WML   2   1   35 NW
Charles Toney   Hun WML   1   3   26 NE
Spencer Ball   Hun WML   1   4   15 NW

1434   16 Sep 1813   A/5/243
LO WPR
Transmits patents
Bartlett Ford*   WPR EML   3   5   13 -
James Ratcliff*   WPR EML   2   3   16 -
John Ford*   WPR EML   4   6   30? S
Joseph Lowry*   WPR EML   3   2   27 -
Joseph Lowry*   WPR EML   4   2   20 -
*Pre-emption claim.

1435   16 Sep 1813   A/5/244
Jesse Spencer, Reg Chl
Please forward final certificate, even though over-
    payment noted
Jacob Henderlick   Chl   - 19 16   7 SE

1436   16 Sep 1813   A/5/244
LO Cin
Transmits patents
Adam Kite   Cin Pre 11   4   30 +
Thomas Smith, heirs of Cin Pre 5   3   2   -
Thomas Smith, heirs of Cin Pre 5   3   3   -
Ezekiel French   Cin Pre 11   1   20 +
Charles Hilliard   Cin Pre 11   1   20 +
Aaron M. Crumley   Cin Pre   5   4   30 SE
John Osborn   Cin Pre   4   4   23 -
Henry Opdycke   Cin Pre   6   2   13 NE
Sylvanus Tuttle   Cin MR   10   5   1   SW
Benjamin Knoops   Cin MR   11   2   14 SW
Jacob Lechleider &
    Conrad Lechleider Cin MR   6   2   29 NE
John McCleary   Cin EML   6   2   4   NW
Demovil Talbott   Cin MR   13   1   4   +
James Johnston   Cin WML   1 13   4   NE
William Brier & David
    Brier   Cin MR   11   3   35 SE
David Bailey   Cin WML   1 13   23 NE
James Demint   Cin MR   9   4   5   E
Alexander Black   Cin MR   12   5   23 NW
Abraham Vanmeter   Cin * 12E 15N 27 NE
Frederick Blue   Cin MR   11   2   21 NE
Demovil Talbott   Cin MR   13   2   27 SE
Demovil Talbott   Cin MR   13   2   28 NW
Zacheriah Glover   Cin * 12E 14- 20? NW
James Humphries   Cin MR   12   4   30 SW
James Wetherow   Cin EML   2   4   30 SE
John Overpeck   Cin MR   10   3   4   NW
John Miller   Cin WML   1 10   12 NW
James Martindale   Cin * 13E 17- 26 SE

John Greener	Cin	WML	2	1	4	+
Joseph Florey	Cin	EML	5	4	20	SW
Henry Miller	Cin	WML	1	12	24	NE
John Smith	Cin	EML	1	4	20	SW
Isaac Sturgis	Cin	MR	1	3	8	NE
William Cummins	Cin	MR	13	4	32	NW
Rosetta Robinson, heirs of	Cin	MR	13	4	25	SW
Gabriel Cox	Cin	MR	9	6	35	SW
Samuel Stewart	Cin	MR	3	3	8	NW
Thomas Kersey	Cin	* 13E	17-	34		NE
Martin Judy	Cin	MR	9	5	13	SE
Willis Whiston	Cin	* 14E	17-	27		NW
James Wood	Cin	WML	1	9	5	SE
John McKee	Cin	* 13E	16N	18		NE
Andrew May	Cin	EML	1	7	12	SW
Joseph Hough & T. Blair	Cin	EML	2	4	14	SW
Abraham Clark	Cin	MR	1	3	8	NW
Jacob Neff	Cin	EML	3	4	10	NE
John H. Ratt & J. Andrews	Cin	MR	10	1	1	+
John H. Ratt & J. Andrews	Cin	MR	10	1	7	-
Stephen McFarland	Cin	Town, Sq. 3, lot 16				
John Taylor	Cin	MR	12	5	13	SE
James McIntire &						
John McIntire	Cin	MR	9	4	22	NW
Barnabas Niles	Cin	MR	2	4	26	SE
James Wethroe	Cin	EML	1	8	18	SE
William Snodgrass	Cin	MR	1	3	26	SE
William Wilson, Junior	Cin	EML	2	12	26	NW
Benjamin Schooler	Cin	MR	14	3	31	NW
Peter Bolsel	Cin	MR	12	1	14	NW
William Runyon	Cin	EML	1	7	24	NW
William Hetdrick &						
Abraham Hetdrick	Cin	WML	1	9	7	SE
Arthur Thomas	Cin	MR	12	5	32	NE
Rodham Talbott	Cin	EML	7	1	19	+
Michael Snider	Cin	WML	2	12	24	SW
Daniel Newcomb	Cin	MR	12	5	34	SE

*Second Principal Meridian.

1437   17 Sep 1813   A/5/245
John Brahan, Rec Hun
Having directed that quarterly reports be examined,
"I was much surprised to be informed that no quar-
terly reports have been received from you. Those
accounts must be forwarded immediately. . . ."

1438   17 Sep 1813   A/5/246
Peter Wilson, Rec Stu
Examination of your quarterly accounts has discovered
large amounts due the United States. Asks whether
the auditor's interpretation of Wilson's reports
are correct.

1439   17 Sep 1813   A/5/246
William Fullerton, Little York, Pennsylvania
Asks to have witness to transfer go before a magistrate to prove the transfer; mentions George Bu-
channon.

1440   17 Sep 1813   A/5/247
Peter Wilson, Rec Stu
Issues instructions as to how the deposits of persons excluded by lot from purchasing land are to
be repaid.

1441   18 Sep 1813   A/5/247
LO Can
Transmits patents

Jacob Bowman	Can	-	11	16	11	NE
Jacob Bowman	Can	-	10	1	32	SW
James Dennis	Can	-	10	12	12	NE

1442   20 Sep 1813   A/5/247
Henry Dangerfield, Washington, Mississippi Territory
Acknowledges receipt of his audit of LO Wsh books.

1443   20 Sep 1813   A/5/248
Parke Walton, Rec WPR
Criticizes the manner in which books have been kept
and requires a transcript of the entire register
of entries.

1444   20 Sep 1813   A/5/249
Peter Wilson, Rec Stu
The following errors noted in your accounts, beginning in 1808 and pertaining to the following transactions

N. Sidwell	Stu	-	6	8	5	-
G. Austine	Stu	-	5	16	18	SE
G. Austine	Stu	-	5	16	18	SW
B. Freezel	Stu	-	1	7	10	N

1445   20 Sep 1813   A/5/252
James Craig, New Lisbon, Ohio
Transmits patent

Robert Burton	Stu	-	4	15	20	NW

1446   22 Sep 1813   A/5/253
Daniel Symmes, Reg Cin
Transmits copy of act for relief of John James Dufour
and his associates; encloses following final certificates

--	Cin	Pre	10	4	1	+
--	Cin	Pre	9	3	32	+
--	Cin	Pre	8	4	13	+
--	Cin	-	8	2	6	NE
--	Cin	-	8	3	36	NW
--	Cin	-	4	3	22	NW
--	Cin	-	6	3	24	N
--	Cin	-	6	3	28	N

1447   22 Sep 1813   A/5/253
Jesse Spencer, Reg Chl
Following land said to have been forfeited; if so,
to what tract does the subsequent payment apply?

Siburn Hinton	Chl	-	19	6	24	NW

1448   24 Sep 1813   A/5/254
Robert Thompson, Canton, Ohio
Transmits patent

Robert Thompson	Can	-	12	17	31	SE

1449   24 Sep 1813   A/5/254
Samuel Gwathmey, Reg Jef
Mentions error in certificate for M. Maurice.

1450   27 Sep 1813   A/5/255
John Badollet, Reg Vin
Transmits patents

Josiah Trueblood	Vin	-	6E	2S	26	+
Josiah Trueblood	Vin	-	6E	2S	35	+

1451   27 Sep 1813   A/5/255
John Brahan, Rec Hun
Interest must be charged in following transactions

| Thomas Freeman | Hun | - | 1E | 3 | 15 | SW |
| Thomas Freeman | Hun | - | 1E | 3 | 15 | NW |

1452   28 Sep 1813   A/5/255
Edmund H. Taylor, Rec Jef
Transmits U.S. Treasury receipt

| Thomas M. Reed | Jef | - | 8E | 3N | 19 | SE |

1453   1 Oct 1813   A/5/256
Daniel Symmes, Reg Cin
Errors noted in following transactions

-- Lamme*	Cin Pre	6	1	9	-
-- Lamme*	Cin Pre	6	1	10	-
William Adams**	Cin EML	13	13	21	NW
--*	Cin EML	3	3	2	NW

*Short payment.
**Land sold to John Morrow in March 1812.

1454   2 Oct 1813   A/5/256
Jesse Spencer, Reg Chl
First certificate was returned to you on 28 May 1812

| -- | Chl | - | 19 | 16 | 7 | SE |

1455   2 Oct 1813   A/5/256
Joseph Reeves, Woodbury, West [New?] Jersey
Transmits patent

Joseph Reeves	Stu	-	3	15	15	SW
Joseph Reeves	Stu	-	3	15	22	NW
Joseph Reeves	Stu	-	3	15	15	SE

1456   7 Oct 1813   A/5/257
Jared Mansfield, New Haven [Connecticut]
I have been unable to obtain a furlough for you, so
that you may go to Cincinnati. Perhaps you should
write to the [Secretary of War], now in the neigh-
borhood of the [Great?] Lakes.

1457   7 Oct 1813   A/5/258
David Hoge, Reg Stu
Explanatory letter received regarding error in final
certificates

| Peter Kail | Stu | - | 5 | 11 | 18 | SE |
| Isaac Wood | Stu | - | 5 | 11 | 18 | SW |

1458   7 Oct 1813   A/5/258
J. Childress, Esq., Nashville, West Tennessee
Acknowledges receipt of his audit of LO Hun books.

1459   7 Oct 1813   A/5/259
Hon. Abner Lacock, Beaver, Pennsylvania
Patent for which you inquire was sent to LO Can

| James Dennis | Can | - | 10 | 12 | 12 | NE |

1460   8 Oct 1813   A/5/259
Levi Barber, Rec Mar
Edmund H. Taylor, Rec Jef
Samuel Smith, Rec St. Stephens, Mississippi Terri-
tory
Quarterly reports missing [for various periods].

1461   13 Oct 1813   A/5/261
Daniel Symmes, Reg Cin
Discrepancies noted in following final certificates

| --* | Cin EML | 1 | 4 | 23 | SE |
| --** | Cin MR | 1 | 1 | 10 | + |

*Overpaid.
**Cause of repayment not understood.

1462   18 Oct 1813   A/5/261
Hon. -- Rush, Comptroller of U.S. Treasury
Additional set of sureties for William Garrard [Rec
WLA] received.

1463   20 Oct 1813   A/5/263
Thomas Gibson, Reg Can
Transmits first certificates and U.S. Treasury re-
ceipt

| William Lavering | Can | - | 20 | 18 | 25 | SE |
| John Lavering | Can | - | 20 | 18 | 36 | NE |

1464   21 Oct 1813   A/5/264
Wyllys Silliman, Reg Zan
Transmits first certificate and U.S. Treasury receipt

| Elias Danhaver | Zan | - | 13 | 11 | 17 | NE |

1465   22 Oct 1813   A/5/265
John Sloan, Rec Can
Instructs him as to computation of commissions; mentions Joseph S. Collins, now a clerk in GLO and
formerly clerk at LO Can.

1466   23 Oct 1813   A/5/266
Levi Barber, Rec Mar
Gives instructions as to computations and reports;
mentions transaction of John Kerr in which there
appears to be an error.

1467   23 Oct 1813   A/5/267
Nehemiah Tilton, Reg WPR
Parke Walton, Rec WPR
Certificate of confirmation to John Henderson is
without adequate land description and has not been
surveyed. His remedy can only be by application
to Congress.

1468   23 Oct 1813   A/5/267
James Findlay, Rec Cin
If you have doubts about my instruction on calculating fractional acreage, you can hold transaction
with -- Lamme until Mr. Gallatin's return this
winter.

1469   23 Oct 1813   A/5/268
Peter Wilson, Rec Stu
You state your first quarterly report cannot be veri-
fied until the confused accounts of your predecessor have been audited. Instead, send me a list of
completed transactions with patents issued, and I
shall return a transcript of each account. Mentions following transaction

| Solomon Hoge | Stu | - | 5 | 8 | 8 | - |

1470   25 Oct 1813   A/5/269
Nehemiah Tilton, Reg Wsh, Mississippi Territory
Transmits patents

-- Barrett & -- Kinsler	Wsh EML	5	2	8	SW
Isaac Alexander	Wsh EML	2	3	32	-
Matthew Tool	Wsh EML	3	2	41	-
Matthew Tool	Wsh EML	3	1	6	-
Sylvester Dunn	Wsh EML	4	2	34	-
Sylvester Dunn	Wsh EML	3	2	29	-
Ignatius Flowers	Wsh EML	4	13	20	-
John Bisland	Wsh EML	2	5	27	+
John D. Wilds	Wsh WML	2	2	31	-

1471   26 Oct 1813   A/5/270
Andrew Gregg, Esq., Greencastle, Pennsylvania
Acknowledges receipt of payment*

Jacob Concer	Zan	-	4	7	5	NW

*In letter which follows, forwards U.S. Treasury receipt to Isaac Van Horn, Rec Zan.

1472   27 Oct 1813   A/5/270
Isaac Van Horn, Rec Zan
Requires vouchers for sums deposited in 1809 by John Comach? [Cormack?], George Jackson, and Benjamin Tupper.

1473   30 Oct 1813   A/5/271*
Richard Rush, Comptroller of U.S. Treasury
Public lands of LO Cin are partly in Ohio and partly in Indiana Territory, and it is difficult to determine from records of GLO the amount of money due the State of Ohio for roads. Suggests accounting method.
*Paginated as 272.

1474 .   30 Oct 1813   A/5/271*
Daniel Symmes, Reg Cin
Comments on monthly returns and returns patent for correction

--	Cin Pre	6	2	20	S

*Paginated as 272.

1475   1 Nov 1813   A/5/272
David Hoge, Reg Stu
Transmits first certificate and U.S. Treasury receipt

Michael Knave	Stu	-	9	10	22	SE

1476   3 Nov 1813   A/5/272
Wyllys Silliman, Reg Zan
Transmits first certificate and U.S. Treasury receipt

William Wilson, Junior	Zan	-	11	3	17	NW

1477   4 Nov 1813   A/5/272
LO Jef
Transmits patents

Thomas Conly	Jef	-	9E	2N	12	SE
Martin Pottorf	Jef	-	4E	3N	33	SW
David Barker	Jef	-	10E	4N	14	NE
James Allen	Jef	-	4E	2N	31	SE
John Field	Jef	-	8E	3N	25	NE
Valentine Coonrad	Jef	-	5E	2S	20	SE
Patrick Brown	Jef	-	10E	4N	36	NE
William Wood	Jef	-	8E	3N	26	NE
Joseph S. Hensley	Jef	-	10E	4N	20	NW
David Fouts	Jef	-	5E	2N	6	SW
Peter Tabler	Jef	-	5E	4S	10	NW
William Applegate	Jef	-	3E	5S	9	NE
William Bateman	Jef	-	5E	2S	10	SE
Peter Tabler	Jef	-	5E	4S	11	SW
Benjamin Van Cleave	Jef	-	2E	1N	5	SW
John Bush	Jef	-	4E	1S	2	SW
Nehemiah Hunt	Jef	-	8E	3N	33	SE
Patrick Welsh	Jef	-	9E	2N	35	NE
Jacob Fouts	Jef	-	8E	2N	24	NW
Christopher Schuch	Jef	-	3E	5S	19	NE
Osias Jennings	Jef	-	8E	3N	25	NW
Joseph Lewis	Jef	-	11E	5N	21	SW
David Sears	Jef	-	4E	2N	19	NE
Jacob Sears	Jef	-	4E	2N	19	SW
John Trueblood	Jef	-	6E	2S	20	NW
Robert Bratton	Jef	-	4E	2N	11	SE
Edmund Findley	Jef	-	2E	2N	10	SE
Joseph Maxwell	Jef	-	1E	2N	4	NW
David Findley	Jef	-	1E	2N	25	SW
John Paul	Jef	-	10E	4N	25	NE
John Paul	Jef	-	10E	4N	33	SE
Robert Denny	Jef	-	4E	3N	35	SW
William Wright	Jef	-	4E	2N	32	SW
Henry Robertson	Jef	-	9E	2N	28	SW
James Harberson	Jef	-	4E	2N	18	SE
David Irvin	Jef	-	5E	1S	34	SW
Richard Gilstrap	Jef	-	3E	1N	1	SE

1478   4 Nov 1813   A/5/273
LO Cin
Transmits patents

John Dawson	Cin MR	11	5	15	NW
William Newell	Cin MR	13	5	33	NE
Jacob Case	Cin WML	2	11	34	NE
James Harper	Cin EML	1	4	9	SE
Thomas Cook	Cin WML	2	11	13	SE
David Shearer	Cin EML	2	8	7	NE
John Hunt	Cin WML	1	12	6	SW
Joseph Smith	Cin MR	9	6	18	NW
John Leslie	Cin EML	3	4	35	NE
Henry Smith	Cin EML	6	4	19	SW
John Harvey	Cin WML	1	13	6	NW
David Truan	Cin EML	1	7	14	NW
Samuel Holmes	Cin WML	1	13	10	NE
David J. P. Fleming	Cin EML	1	9	20	NE
John Reininger	Cin EML	4	3	27	SE
Richard Parmer	Cin MR	11	2	28	SW
Peter F. Ireland	Cin EML	1	8	28	NW
William Johnston	Cin *	14E	17-	5	SW
Nathan Stubbs	Cin EML	2	7	30	NW
James Jameson	Cin WML	1	10	2	SE
John Stip, Junior	Cin MR	13	5	32	NE
William Nelson	Cin WML	1	9	5	NW
Thomas McCoy	Cin WML	2	13	25	NW
Henry Dillbone	Cin MR	12	1	1	NE
William Grimes & James Grimes	Cin WML	1	13	28	NW
James Tanner	Cin WML	2	11	2	SW
Wright Lancaster	Cin *	13E	15-	10	SE
Andrew Fouts	Cin WML	2	12	14	NW
John Wallace	Cin *	13E	15-	6	SW
Sarah Symons & Lydia Symons	Cin *	12E	16-	12	SW
John Miller	Cin WML	1	10	14	NW
George Galloway	Cin MR	7	4	36	NW
George Galloway	Cin MR	7	3	11	NW
John Haller	Cin MR	10	5	24	NE
Nicholas Coleman	Cin EML	3	6	15	SW
Joseph Caldwell	Cin *	12E	15-	33	SW
James Finney	Cin MR	1	4	11	S

James Dingman	Cin	MR	13	1	9	+
James Dingman	Cin	MR	13	1	10	−
Christopher Hausel? [Hansel?] & George Hausel? [Hansel?]	Cin	WML	1	10	27	NW
Henry Metzger	Cin	EML	5	4	22	SE
Rebecca Aerl	Cin	EML	6	7	7	SE
Benjamin Cilley	Cin	WML	1	9	23	SW
John Cory	Cin	MR	11	2	17	SW
Enos Terry	Cin	EML	2	12	26	SE
Joseph Lyon	Cin	WML	3	4	1	NW
Baylis Cloud	Cin	WML	1	7	28	NE
John McCord & Henry Potts?	Cin	EML	1	8	3	W
Isaac Martin	Cin	MR	11	3	31	SE
Joseph Bond	Cin	*	14E 17N	15		SE
Jacob Pottorf	Cin	EML	2	7	24	SW
Frederick Holsapple	Cin	EML	4	5	1	SE
George Galloway Survey 3	Cin	MR	6	2	1	−
Aaron Garrison	Cin	WML	1	6	1	SW
Edward Webb	Cin	*	12E 13−	22		NE
Jacob Stoner	Cin	EML	2	12	35	NE
William Arnett	Cin	*	13	11	6	NE
Benjamin Cilley	Cin	WML	1	9	26	NW
Benjamin Wood	Cin	WML	1	9	35	NW
Hugh Maxwell	Cin	WML	1	11	29	SW
Samuel Williamson	Cin	EML	5	5	35	SW
William Webb	Cin	*	12E 14−	12		NW
James Black, Senior	Cin	MR	10	3	32	NE
John Winn	Cin	MR	9	6	13	SE
James Barber	Cin	EML	1	4	19	NE
William Nicol	Cin	MR	4	2	11	NW
Ebenezer Wead, Junior, & Robert Wead	Cin	MR	7	2	26	SW
John Pence	Cin	−	10	4	3	S+
Jacob Huffman Survey 2	Cin	−	9	4	21	−
James Galloway	Cin	MR	8	3	5	1
John Nowman [Newman?]	Cin	MR	11	4	30	N
Joseph Reynolds	Cin	MR	11	4	15	E
Nicholas Douley	Cin	WML	1	12	11	NE
James Morrison	Cin	WML	1	14	5	NE
William Vandershee	Cin	MR	9	2	34	+
Samuel Harlan	Cin	*	13E 14−	31		NE
John Winn	Cin	MR	10	5	6	NW
Joseph Wagner	Cin	EML	2	7	1	NW
John Simmons	Cin	MR	11	2	34	W
Benjamin Bose? [Booe? Bore?]	Cin	*	12E 14−	21		SW
Jacob C. Cook	Cin	EML	2	9	35	SE
Jesse Bond	Cin	WML	1	14	31	SW
John Pippenger? [Peppinger?]	Cin	EML	4	6	35	NE
Isaac Henderson	Cin	WML	1	6	11	NE
James Coppock	Cin	EML	6	4	29	SW
Henry French	Cin	EML	3	5	1	SE
Demovil Talbott	Cin	MR	13	2	34	E

*Second Principal Meridian.

1479 5 Nov 1813 A/5/276
Wyllys Silliman, Reg Zan
Please send final certificate for John Hammock. Explain your statement that W. Hull land has been forfeited; it was patented

John Hammock	Zan	−	9	8	28	SE
W. Hull	Zan	Mil	10	1	19	SE

1480 5 Nov 1813 A/5/276
David Hoge, Reg Stu
Transmits first certificate and U.S. Treasury receipt

Robert Watson	Stu	−	6	8	21	SW

1481 6 Nov 1813 A/5/276
LO Cin
Transmits patents

John Heighway	Survey	Cin Pre	5	3	22	2
Archibald Loury, heirs of		Cin Pre	9	5	34	1
Daniel Deardorff		Cin Pre	4	3	34	2
George Wolf	Survey 1	Cin Pre	7	3	18	NW
George Wolf	Survey 4	Cin Pre	7	3	18	SE
Jacob White		Cin Pre	4	3	1	N
John D. Campbell Survey 2 & 3		Cin Pre	8	2	4	−
Nathaniel Cartmell		Cin Pre	10	6	28	−
Daniel McKinnon		Cin Pre	10	5	4	S
Daniel McKinnon		Cin Pre	10	5	10	SE
William Ward		Cin Pre	12	4	7	−
William Ward		Cin Pre	11	5	17	SW
David Loury		Cin Pre	9	3	9	S
James McClure		Cin Pre	9	2	9	NW
Michael Carver		Cin Pre	10	2	27	S
Michael Blue, Senior		Cin Pre	10	1	23	+
Michael Blue, Senior		Cin Pre	10	1	17	W+
Martin Hill & Samuel Hill		Cin Pre	11	5?	30	E
Rulif Peterson		Cin Pre	9	4	14	NE
Tobias Whitesill		Cin Pre	6	1	13	NW
John McGrew		Cin Pre	6	2	27	W
Samuel Kirkpatrick		Cin Pre	7	3	33	+
Jonathan Monger		Cin Pre	5	3	3	+
Arthur Vandeveer		Cin Pre	5	2	27	W+
John Heaton	Survey 2	Cin Pre	5	4	28	−
Joseph Crane		Cin Pre	5	2	28	+
Joseph Crane		Cin Pre	5	2	34	+
Samuel Coapstick Survey 1		Cin Pre	4	2	13	−
Jonathan Donnel Survey 2		Cin Pre	9	3	2	−
Lewis Bruner? [Braner?]		Cin Pre	8	2	28	−
Robert Moodie Survey 2		Cin Pre	8	4	13	NW+
John Wallace		Cin Pre	9	3	36	SE
Henry Jennings		Cin Pre	9	2	1	SE
Thomas Arnett		Cin Pre	5	3	19	SW
John Devor		Cin Pre	7	2	19	NE
James Snodgrass		Cin Pre	6	2	7	NE
Hugh Andrew		Cin Pre	8	2	15?	E
Hugh Andrew		Cin Pre	8	2	15?	SW

1482 6 Nov 1813 A/5/277
Thomas Gibson, Reg Can
Transmits corrected patent, now in the name of -- Aten, instead of -- Allen. Also transmits first certificate and U.S. Treasury receipt

John Stump	Can	−	10	12	28	N
John Stump	Can	−	10	12	28	SW

1483 8 Nov 1813 A/5/277
David Hoge, Reg Stu
Transmits first certificate and U.S. Treasury receipt

Joseph Hogue*	Stu	−	6	14	28	SE

*So spelled.

1484 9 Nov 1813 A/5/278
Thomas Gibson, Reg Can
Please correct final certificate

Samuel Osbun*	Can	−	18	22	26	NE

*So spelled.

1485 9 Nov 1813 A/5/278
LO Chl
Transmits patents

James Lambert	Chl	−	21	10	14	SW
Daniel Klick	Chl	−	20	14	31	NW

1486		9 Nov 1813			A/5/278		
LO Zan							
Transmits patents							
Andrew Bell	Zan	Mil	5	1	24	SW	
Thomas Dew, Junior	Zan	-	13	12	7	NW	
Charles Sullivan	Zan	-	10	8	6	NE	
George Olinger	Zan	-	15	17	17	SE	
Jacob Reece	Zan	-	14	16	15	NE	
John Frame	Zan	Mil	2	1	20	SW	
Edward Harris	Zan	Mil	11	1	19	NE	
Thomas Harris	Zan	-	15	18	18	NE	
John Waggoner	Zan	-	14	14	9	NW	
Solomon Robinson	Zan	Mil	10	7	6	NE	
Nathaniel Banning	Zan	-	14	15	7	SE	
Samuel Arbuckle	Zan	Mil	11	5	5	SW	
Israel Robinson	Zan	-	11	14	17	NE	
John Cress ("of William")	Zan	Mil	8	2	20	NW	
Joseph Williams	Zan	Mil	1	1	1	SW	
James Cunningham	Zan	Mil	2	2	20	NW	
Abraham Furney	Zan	-	3	4	14	SW	
Henry B. Goe	Zan	-	12	12	5	W+	
Henry B. Goe	Zan	-	12	12	8	-	

1487		9 Nov 1813			A/5/279		
LO Cin							
Transmits patents							
John Kain	Cin	MR	11	3	2	S	
William Short	Cin	MR	7	1	12	+	
James Black	Cin	MR	8	2	29	SE	
Robert Russell	Cin	MR	9	3	17	NE	
Jacob Wilson	Cin	MR	9	2	21	NW	
William Short	Cin	MR	8	2	9	E	
David Burnstager, heirs of	Cin	Pre	4	3	25	W+	
James Clensey Survey 5	Cin	Pre	6	3	31	-	
Jacob Snuff	Cin	Pre	4	3	20	N	
Jesse Hunt	Cin	Pre	9	4	15	N	
Aaron Cossard? [Copard?]	Cin	Pre	8	3	21	SE	
George Zimmerman	Cin	Pre	7	2	3	SE	
Jacob Herron	Cin	Pre	7	3	20	S	
Jacob Herron	Cin	Pre	7	3	21	N	
Lewis Braner	Cin	Pre	8	2	22	-	
David Linton	Cin	Pre	5	3	7	SE+	
William Short	Cin	Pre	9	3	36	SW+	
Barnabas Blue	Cin	Pre	10	1	12	SW+	
Owen Hatfield Survey 2	Cin	Pre	5	3	30	-	
James Henderson &							
William Henderson	Cin	Pre	9	3	15	N	

1488		9 Nov 1813			A/5/279		
LO Jef							
Transmits patents							
Philip Hoggatt	Jef	-	4E	2N	21	SE	
Francis Giltner	Jef	-	9E	1N	9	NE	
Elisha Denny	Jef	-	4E	3N	34	SW	
Jacob Motsinger	Jef	-	4E	1N	2	SW	
Thomas Evans	Jef	-	4E	2N	33	NW	
Jacob Copple	Jef	-	3E	1N	12	NW	
William Watson	Jef	-	3E	5S	9	NW	
Solomon Bower	Jef	-	5E	2N	19	SW	
Beverly Vawter	Jef	-	10E	4N	29	SE	
Jonathan Lindley	Jef	-	1E	2N	20	NW	
James Hutcherson*	Jef	-	4E	5N	22	NW	
Joseph Lame	Jef	-	10E	5N	36	NW	
Samuel Ewing	Jef	-	4E	5N	29	+	
Abraham Watson	Jef	-	3E	5S	10	NE	
John Stephenson	Jef	-	1E	5S	18	SE	
Zachariah Nixon	Jef	-	4E	2N	19	SE	
Thomas Lindley	Jef	-	1E	1N	9	SE	
*So spelled.							

1489		9 Nov 1813			A/5/280		
LO Can							
Transmits patents							
William Rambo	Can	-	19	18	4	NW	
James Fraer?	Can	-	18	18	4	SW	
Michael Oswalt	Can	-	9	10	30	+	
John Meason	Can	-	10	12	26	NE	
Jacob Bowman	Can	-	13	15	15	SE	
Jacob Bowman	Can	-	12	16	18	SE	
Jacob Bowman	Can	-	12	15	20	NE	
Daniel Harbaugh &							
Reasin Beall	Can	-	18	21	20	SE	
Thomas Oram	Can	-	15	21	22	SE	
Frederick Zimmer	Can	-	17	22	10	SE	
William Eagle	Can	-	15	21	26	NW	
Jeremiah Achison	Can	-	10	1	28	NE	
John Bever	Can	-	13	15	10	NW	
Noah Cook	Can	-	19	20	23	NE	
Noah Cook	Can	-	18	20	18	NW	
Alexander Findley	Can	-	15	21	26	NE	
William Scott	Can	-	16	22	7	NE	
Nathaniel McDowell	Can	-	10	12	5	SW	
George Snyder	Can	-	13	16	21	NE	
Benjamin Cuppy	Can	-	16	22	5	SE	
William Byal	Can	-	10	12	14	SW	
Reasin Beall	Can	-	18	21	20	NE	
John Christmass	Can	-	9	10	17	+	
John Christmass	Can	-	9	10	20	-	
Robert Newell	Can	-	16	22	26	SE	
Leonard Stands	Can	-	10	12	29	NE	
Alexander Cameron	Can	-	10	12	6	-	
John Mitchell	Can	-	19	18	3	NW	
John Mitchell	Can	-	19	18	3	SE	
James Morgan	Can	-	13	14	20	SE	
George Boydstone	Can	-	12	16	4	NE	
James Mitchell	Can	-	19	19	33	SE	
John Shenneberry	Can	-	15	21	23	SW	
Nathan Warner	Can	-	13	15	6	SW	
Aaron Beard	Can	-	15	21	13	SW	
Jonathan Butler	Can	-	13	14	33	NE	
Samuel Parry*	Can	-	17	21	18	SE	
John Evans	Can	-	18	19	13	NW	
*So spelled.							

1490		9 Nov 1813			A/5/281		
LO Stu							
Transmits patents							
Samuel Langstaff	Stu	-	4	17	18	NE	
Jacob Nessley	Stu	-	2	8	12	NE	
John Waggoner	Stu	-	7	14	19	SW	
Michael Castner	Stu	-	3	10	1	E	
Robert Wilkin	Stu	-	7	11	20	NW	
Daniel McPeek	Stu	-	7	10	33	NE	
Samuel Foster	Stu	-	5	9	29	SW	
Daniel McPeek	Stu	-	7	10	35	SW	
Daniel McPeek	Stu	-	7	10	34	NE	
Hugh McComb	Stu	-	7	10	23	NE	
Thomas Curtis	Stu	-	5	7	30	SE	
Joseph Keiser	Stu	-	6	13	2	NE	
Jonathan Hamilton	Stu	-	2	11	31	SW	
Jacob Nessley	Stu	-	2	12	9	-	
Jacob Nessley	Stu	-	2	12	11	-	
Aaron Bartholomew	Stu	-	2	8	12	SE	
Thomas Langstaff	Stu	-	4	17	18	NW	
Jacob Nessley	Stu	-	2	8	12	NW	
Robert Crawford	Stu	-	7	17	6	NE	
David Paisley	Stu	-	2	8	27	SE	
Alexander Moore	Stu	-	5	10	35	NE	
Thomas Hays	Stu	-	7	9	28	SE	
Peter Kail	Stu	-	5	11	18	SE	
Robert T. Wells	Stu	-	3	6	21	SW	

William Pumphrey	Stu	–	2	5	26	SW
Charles D. Wells	Stu	–	5	10	35	SW
Edmund Peale	Stu	–	3	7	22	NE
Abraham Pittenger	Stu	–	5	11	11	NE
John Patton	Stu	–	8	10	33	NE
Benjamin Pancake	Stu	–	1	7	27	SW

1491   9 Nov 1813   A/5/281
LO Mar
Transmits patents

Samuel Danford	Mar	–	4	5	22	SE
John Stanley	Mar	–	5	6	18	NW
Aaron W. Putnam	Mar	–	10	2	8	SW
Moses Ball	Mar	–	7	8	21	NW
Robert Safford	Mar	–	14	4	8	+
Daniel Dye	Mar	–	5	3	3	NW

1492   10 Nov 1813   A/5/282
Henry Brumbock, Mundlesville, Shenandoah County,
   Virginia
Transmits patent

Henry Brumbock	Can	–	18	22	22	NE

1493   10 Nov 1813   A/5/282
John Badollet, Reg Vin
Transmits patent

James Emison	Vin	–	12W	3S	3	NE

1494   11 Nov 1813   A/5/283
Jesse Spencer, Reg Chl
Applications for the same lands were made by these
   men in both July & August; please explain dupli-
   cation

George Lance	Chl	–	17	11	29	SW
John Kelso	Chl	–	17	11	12	SE

1495   12 Nov 1813   A/5/283
John Brahan, Rec Hun
Your letter states that you were ignorant of the re-
   quirement to file quarterly returns; see letter to
   Rec Zan of 16 Oct 1804, a copy of which was sent
   to you on 11 Jul 1809.

1496   15 Nov 1813   A/5/284
James Findley, Rec Cin
Transmits U.S. Treasury receipt

John Kirby	Cin	MR	2	2	8	NW

1497   15 Nov 1813   A/5/284
David Hoge, [Reg] Stu
Please return patent; it should have been sent to
   Leesburgh

Thomas Curtis	Stu	–	5	7	30	SE

1498   16 Nov 1813   A/5/286
Jesse Spencer, Reg Chl
Patent returned and corrected from SW to SE

Adam Strayer	Chl	MS	21	9	34	SE

1499   16 Nov 1813   A/5/286
Thomas Gibson, Reg Can
Where two or more persons apply for the same tract
   at the same time, their receipts must be registered
and decision made by lot; mentions Joab Garrett

Samuel Coulter	Can	–	15	19	13	SE

1500   19-20 Nov 1813   A/5/288
LO WPR
Transmits patents

Henry Hanna	WPR	EML	2	2	37	SE
John Porter	WPR	EML	3	5	1	–
John Porter	WPR	EML	4	5	37	–
John Porter	WPR	EML	3	6	45	–
John Porter	WPR	EML	4	6	37	–

1501   19 Nov 1813   A/5/288
LO Stu
Transmits patents

John Turner	Stu	–	10	1	14	NW
Thomas Johnston	Stu	–	10	2	34	NE
Nathan Baldwin	Stu	–	3	14	21	NW
Levi Williams	Stu	–	7	16	32	NW
John Morrison	Stu	–	2	8	1	SW
Zenas Kimberly	Stu	–	9	12	34	NE
George Grimes	Stu	–	5	15	23	NE
John Brausz	Stu	–	8	10	15	NW
Benjamin Price	Stu	–	8	9	26	SE
Joseph Pentecost	Stu	–	7	19	26	W
Preston Beck	Stu	–	4	16	31	NW

1502   19 Nov 1813   A/5/288
LO Cin
Transmits patents

John Lenox & Richard Lenox	Cin	EML	6	8	31	NE
James McClurken	Cin	WML	1	11	13	NE
Abraham Nave	Cin	EML	1	8	36	NW
Abraham Nave	Cin	EML	3	4	1	NW
John Bigger Survey 3	Cin	MR	4	3	25	–
Hugh Boyd	Cin	MR	4	3	29	SW
John Freeman	Cin	MR	4	2	26	SE
Isaac Spinning & Adam Garlough?	Cin	MR	7	2	11	NW
Joseph Leatherman	Cin	EML	4	4	29	NE
George Stafford	Cin	MR	10	3	31	SW
Jacob Dills	Cin	MR	12	1	26	W
John Jordan	Cin	WML	1	12	12	NE
Abner Denman	Cin	MR	11	1	12	NW
Anthony Halberstadt	Cin	WML	2	9	22	SW
John Galbreath	Cin	* 14E	16–		31	NW
John Bell	Cin	* 14E	16–		17	SE
William Low	Cin	EML	1	7	36	SW
James Young	Cin	EML	2	5	22	NE
John Bell	Cin	* 14E	16N		17	SW
Samuel Alexander	Cin	MR	10	3	21	SE
Michael Flake & William Flake	Cin	WML	2	5	35	SW
Robert Kennedy	Cin	EML	1	9	34	SE
William Norman	Cin	MR	7	3	29	SE
Chatfield Howell	Cin	WML	1	10	30	NE
James Wright	Cin	WML	1	14	27	NE
William Bruce	Cin	EML	4	3	23	–
John H. Ratt	Cin	Town,	Sq. 3,	lot	7	
Daniel Teagarden	Cin	* 13E	11–		3	NE
Robert Hanna, Junior	Cin	WML	2	10	33	NW
Abraham Nave	Cin	EML	1	8	25	SW
John H. Ratt	Cin	WML	1	4	4	+

*Second Principal Meridian.

1503   22 Nov 1813   A/5/289
David Hoge, Reg Stu
Transmits first certificate & Treasury receipt

Lambert Myers	Stu	–	5	15	27	SE

1504   23 Nov 1813   A/5/290
David Hoge, Reg Stu
Transmits first certificate & Treasury receipt
James Vale*   Stu   -   1   7   31   NW
John Vale   Stu   -   1   7   20   SW
*Assignee of John Vale.

1505   23 Nov 1813   A/5/290
John Badollet, Reg Vin
Sends instructions regarding handling of transaction
    with George Humphreys.

1506   25 Nov 1813   A/5/291
Wyllys Silliman, Reg Zan
Transmits U.S. Treasury receipt
Daniel Piper   Zan   -   3   10   14   SW
Daniel Piper   Zan   -   3   8   5   NE

1507   25 Nov 1813   A/5/291
LO Hun
Transmits patents
Benjamin Eddins   Hun WML   3   2   24   NW
Benjamin Eddins   Hun WML   3   2   23   +
Benjamin Eddins   Hun WML   3   2   26   -
David Dickey   Hun WML   1   3   20   NE
Henry King   Hun WML   1   1   15   NE
Charles King   Hun WML   1   1   10   NW
John Weaver   Hun EML   2   3   8   SW
Lewis Tillman   Hun WML   3   1   23   SE
Moses Jones   Hun EML   1   1   26   NW
David Harless   Hun EML   2   3   6   SW
William Bird   Hun WML   1   4   7   SE
Magness Teague   Hun EML   1   3   2   NW
Hugh McVay   Hun WML   1   3   25   SE
Jacob Prewett   Hun EML   1   2   20   NE
Jacob Prewett   Hun EML   1   2   21   SE
Hugh McVay   Hun WML   1   3   25   SW
Charles King   Hun WML   1   1   10   NE
Nathaniel Power   Hun EML   1   1   34   NE
George Dickey, Senior   Hun WML   1   3   32   SW
Charles Carrell   Hun WML   3   2   13   NW
Charles Kennedy   Hun EML   1   2   35   NE
Littleberry Adams   Hun WML   3   2   1   NE
Jesse Wilson   Hun EML   1   3   11   SE
John Lawler   Hun EML   2   3   19   SW
Nathaniel Power   Hun EML   1   1   35   NW
William Roundtree   Hun EML   1   3   21   SE
Isaac Stewart   Hun WML   1   1   12   SE
Isaac Stewart   Hun WML   1   1   12   SW
Robert Lanford   Hun WML   1   4   3   SW
Archibald M. Donnell   Hun WML   1   4   15   SE
Stephen Griffith   Hun EML   1   1   26   SW
Thomas Adams   Hun WML   3   1   14   SE
Bennet Wood   Hun EML   1   2   35   SE
James Walker   Hun EML   2   1   8   NE
William Hogan   Hun WML   1   4   13   NE
Daniel Tilman   Hun WML   2   2   4   SE
John Derrick   Hun EML   2   3   21   NW
James Christian   Hun EML   1   2   30   NE
Moses Vincent   Hun EML   1   3   30   SW
Stephen Kennermere?
  [Thennermere?]   Hun EML   2   3   6   NW
Stephen Jones   Hun WML   1   2   23   SW
John Murphy   Hun WML   1   1   24   NW
George Dilworth   Hun WML   1   3   33   SE
Rowland Cornelius   Hun WML   1   2   33   NE
Jarvis Milam   Hun EML   2   1   17   NE
John Brahan   Hun WML   1   3   36   NE
Peyton Cox   Hun WML   1   3   13   NE

Reuben Brock   Hun WML   1   2   24   SE
John Grayson   Hun EML   1   5   1   NW
John W. Howlett   Hun EML   1   3   25   SE
Charles Hedgpeth   Hun WML   1   2   36   NE
Ebenezer Byram   Hun EML   2   3   21   NE
Littleberry Adams   Hun WML   2   2   23   NE
William Roundtree   Hun EML   1   3   21   NE

1508   26 Nov 1813   A/5/292
Daniel Symmes, Reg Cin
Transmits first certificate and U.S. Treasury receipt;
    also states that Lock has surveyed the tract and
    finds it smaller than originally thought; a refund
    is possibly due him
John Lock   Cin EML   3   7   20   NE

1509   26 Nov 1813   A/5/293
Jesse Spencer, Reg Chl
Transmits first certificate & U.S. Treasury receipt
Aquilla Fishpaw   Chl   -   20   15   25   W

1510   27 Nov 1813   A/5/293
Peter Wilson, Rec Stu
Transmits U.S. Treasury receipt
Isaac Y. McFarland   Stu   -   5   7   8   SE

1511   27 Nov 1813   A/5/293
Jesse Spencer, [Reg] Chl
Transmits patent
James Pearse*   Chl [not described]
*Assignee of James Waddle.

1512   30 Nov 1813   A/5/293
Wyllys Silliman, [Reg] Zan
Welty's friend entered tract Zan   -   3   8   25   SW
    for him, instead of Zan   -   3   1   29   SW, which
    Welty had improved. Error can only be corrected
    by Congress, if application is made within three
    months.

1513   30 Nov 1813   A/5/294
David Hoge, Reg Stu
Transmits first certificate & U.S. Treasury receipt
George Able   Stu   -   4   11   22   NW
Jacob Floar   Stu   -   2   13   15   NE

1514   1 Dec 1813   A/5/294
David Hoge, [Reg] Stu
Please send patent, which was forwarded to you on 19
    Aug [1813] to Pierpoint at Waterford, Loudon County,
    Virginia
Obed Pierpoint   Stu   -   6   14   18   SW

1515   7 Dec 1813   A/5/294
John H. Brinton, Esq., Philadelphia, [Pennsylvania]
Transmits U.S. Treasury receipt [for undescribed
    tracts of land].

1516   7 Dec 1813   A/5/295
Jesse Spencer, [Reg Chl]
Since you had omitted to report that these two tracts
    had reverted to the United States, I assumed your
    description was in error; mentions -- Gallatin and

General -- Worthington
-- Lance	Chl	-	17	11	29	SW
-- Kelso	Chl	-	17	11	12	SE

1517   8 Dec 1813   A/5/296
John Sloan, Rec Can
Transmits U.S. Treasury receipt; assignment of land
   informal and has been returned to McCutcheon for
   correction
Alexander McCutcheon   Can   -   17   23   29   SW

1518   8 Dec 1813   A/5/296
James Findlay, Rec Cin
Objects to excessive charges for stationery over
   last 13-year period, as well as to a faulty precedent in calculating discounts.

1519   8 Dec 1813   A/5/297
Jesse Spencer, [Reg Chl]
Please send final certificate
Conrad Moots*   Chl WS?   21   11   7   NE
*Assignee of James Denny, the assignee of Peter
   Betzger. [This letter is unclear and transaction
   may be reversed.]

1520   8 Dec 1813   A/5/297
Wyllys Silliman, Reg Zan
Returns final certificate short paid
--   Zan   -   2   7   12   NE

1521   8 Dec 1813   A/5/297
Daniel Symmes, Reg Cin
Mr. -- Alexander wants a patent in following names;
   please forward final certificates. The following
   final certificates presented
Joseph McCune, John Irwin,
   & John Hunter   Cin Pre   8   4   32   -
--   Cin Pre   8   5   36   NE
--   Cin Pre   8   5   36   NW

1522   9 Dec 1813   A/5/298
David Hoge, Reg Stu
Transmits first certificate & U.S. Treasury receipt
James Caldwell*   Stu   -   3   6   19   SW
*Assignee of George Barkhurst.

1523   13 Dec 1813   A/5/298
Hon. Samuel McKee, Chairman of the Committee on the
   Public Lands
Transmits "an extract from the record of claims to
   land in the Territory of Missouri, relative to
   the case of col[onel] Daniel Boon. 'Colonel Daniel Boon, a claim for 1000 arpen[t]s of land situate in Femme Osage, district of St. Charles.
   Produces a concession from Dr. Zenon Trudeau,
   Lieut[enant] Governor, dated January 24th, 1798,
   and a certificate of Trudeau to him dated January
   9th, 1800; also, a letter from Dr. Zenon Trudeau
   to him dated in the year 1798, inviting him to
   remove with his family, to Louisiana, with the
   promise of a grant of land, and also a commission
   from Dr. Charles D. Delassus, lieutenant governor,
   to him said claimant, dated 11th July, 1800, appointing him commandant of the District of the
   Femme Osage.

'Colonel D. Boone stated to the board that on his
arrival in Louisiana, he took his residence, with
his lady, at his son's Daniel M. Boone, in the
said district of Femme Osage, and adjoining the
lands he now claims; that they remained there until about two years ago, when he moved to a younger
son's, Nathan Boone, where he now lives. It was
proved that the said claimant is of the age of
about 70 years, and his wife about 68. He further
stated, that having enquired of Charles D. Delassus,
as to the propriety of improving and settling his
land within a year and a day from the date of the
concession, as directed by the Spanish laws, he
was informed by said Delassus, that being commandant of the said district, he needed not trouble
himself about the cultivating of the same, as by
the commission he held (of commandant of said district) he was not considered as coming within the
meaning of said law.

'Testimony Taken: February 15th 1806: Jonathan
Bryan, being duly sworn, say that he knew colonel
Daniel Boon in this country in the year 1800.

'Opinion of the board [of land commissioners]:
December 1st 1809: Full board. It is the opinion
of the board, that this claim ought not to be confirmed.'"

1524   13 Dec 1813   A/5/299
Wyllys Silliman, [Reg] Zan
"Hon. -- Griffin has applied for a patent for [tract]
   Zan - 8 8 25 W. As that tract does not
   appear to have been purchased by him, I suppose
   the application should have been for [tract]
   Zan - 1 2 25 W, the patent for which was
   sent to you 24 Apr 1812. . . . Please return it,
   that it may be given [to him]."

1525   13 Dec 1813   A/5/299
Nathaniel Ewing, Rec Vin
Transmits U.S. Treasury receipt; Brownley "paid a
   like sum on 11 Dec 1812 and the receipt was for-
   warded to you--did it reach you? . . ."
Joseph Brownley   Vin   -   3S   5E   31   +
Joseph Brownley   Vin   -   3S   5E   32   -

1526   15 Dec 1813   A/5/300
Hon. Samuel McKee, Chairman of the Committee on the
   Public Lands
Answering your query whether GLO has any evidence to
   substantiate the facts in several petitions which
   you enclosed: I enclose [herewith] extracts of
   letters from land commissioners in WPR district.
   Some of the petitioners have had land allotted to
   them on the west side of the Tombigbee River.
   [Thereafter follow three abstracts; mentions claims
   of heirs of James McGrew (original claimant), John
   Flood McGrew (original claimant Julien de Castro),
   John F. McGrew and Cl. McGrew.]

1527   15 Dec 1813   A/5/303
J. H. Brinton, Esq., Philadelphia, [Pennsylvania]
Transmits U.S. Treasury receipt and corrects previ-
   ous one
J. H. Brinton   [?]   -   9   10   12   SW

1528   16 Dec 1813   A/5/303
Daniel Symmes, Reg Cin
Hon. -- Whitehill has presented a final certificate.
  Please forward first certificate & assignment, if
  they are in your office
William McKim*   Cin Pre 7 3 19 -
*Assignee of Ralph Philips.

1529   17 Dec 1813   A/5/303
John Patton, Canton, Stark County, Ohio
Your patent was sent to LO Stu on 9 Dec 1813
John Patton   Stu - 8 10 33 NE

1530   18 Dec 1813   A/5/304
LO Cin
Transmits patents

Name		Twp	Rng	Sec	Qtr
Allen Spencer & James Wiley	Cin WML	1	8	11	SE
Reuben Dooley	Cin EML	2	7	7	NW
John Garlaugh	Cin MR	8	5	24	SE
James Moorehouse	Cin MR	9	3	28	SW
Richard Robinson	Cin MR	10	5	1	NW
Adin Antram? [Autram?]	Cin EML	2	5	1	SW
Samuel Brandenburgh	Cin MR	10	3	22	NW
Jacob Lichty	Cin EML	5	3	22	NE
David Francis	Cin EML	1	2	1	NW
Jesse Farmer	Cin EML	5	5	27	NW
Lewis Johnston	Cin * 12E	14N	23	NW
Maurice Kain, heirs of	Cin MR	12	5	25	SW
Henry Leatherman	Cin MR	12	4	1	NE
Samuel Case	Cin WML	2	8	10	NW
Jacob Criss	Cin EML	5	5	12	NE
Amos White	Cin EML	2	5	8	NW
John McGriff	Cin EML	3	7	7	NW
Mercer Brown	Cin EML	3	4	11	SW
John Kesling	Cin WML	1	13	27	SE
Enoch Sutton	Cin MR	11	1	15	NW
David Fares	Cin EML	1	6	25	NW
Paul Huston	Cin EML	1	3	12	NW
Thomas Burk	Cin EML	1	4	26	SW
Robert Harvey	Cin WML	1	12	27	NE
Joseph Spitler	Cin EML	4	6	23	NW
John Fryback	Cin EML	6	3	23	+
John Fryback	Cin EML	6	3	24	-
Lemuel Lemmon	Cin WML	1	10	34	SE
Jacob Kesling	Cin WML	1	13	26	SW
James M. Galloway	Cin MR	7	4	35	NW
John D. Campbell Survey 2	Cin MR	8	3	34	-
Archibald Johnston	Cin * 12E	14-	12	SW
William Coats	Cin EML	5	8	30	NE
Benjamin Hinds	Cin WML	1	9	29	SW
Nehemiah Dunn	Cin EML	1	3	28	SW
Jacob Hell & J. Black	Cin EML	3	5	4	E
John Tillman	Cin EML	3	7	3	SW
Thomas Wilson	Cin MR	11	2	14	NE
Martin Baum	Cin MR	6	1	26	+
Jeremiah French	Cin EML	1	1	10	+
Jeremiah Reeder	Cin Town, Sq. 2, lot 23				
Ethan A. Brown	Cin WML	1	4	22	-
Ethan A. Brown	Cin WML	1	4	23	+
Joseph Vanmater	Cin * 13E	13-	3	NE
Joseph Vanmater	Cin * 13E	13-	2	NW
Colder Haymond	Cin WML	1	8	11	SW
Samuel Lee	Cin WML	1	9	23	SE
John Whitmar	Cin MR	11	4	24	SW
John Craig	Cin EML	3	3	11	SE
Mercer Brown	Cin EML	3	4	25	NW
Elnathan Kemper	Cin MR	2+	3	8	SE
Benjamin Brandon	Cin EML	5	8	13	NW
James Deneen	Cin EML	1	4	23	SW
Daniel Fetter	Cin EML	5	6	21	SW

Name		Twp	Rng	Sec	Qtr
John Brown	Cin MR	9	1	1	+
William McCreary	Cin EML	1	6	14	NE
William Phares	Cin EML	3	3	10	SW
Jacob Gripe & Catherine Jordie	Cin EML	4	5	2	SW
Benjamin Powell	Cin WML	2	5	24	SW
Samuel Stover	Cin * 14E	15-	32	SE
Joseph Green	Cin MR	12	1	12	NE
John Harrell	Cin * 12E	13-	28	SE
Joseph McIntire	Cin EML	5	8	2	SW
George Hollingsworth	Cin * 12E	14-	12	NE
James Vaughan	Cin WML	2	5	2	NE
Michael Yakely	Cin EML	2	4	35	SW
George Beam	Cin EML	4	6	35	NW
George Glaze	Cin * 12E	16-	35	NE
James Reed	Cin EML	6	3	3	SE
William Black	Cin MR	10	3	23	S
Frederick Black	Cin EML	3	7	19	SE
Frederick Black	Cin EML	3	7	18	NW
Peter Redenhour	Cin EML	1	6	33	SE
Samuel Littrell	Cin * 14E	14-	19	SW

*Second Principal Meridian.

1531   18 Dec 1813   A/5/306
LO Can
Transmits patents

Name		Twp	Rng	Sec	Qtr
David Zedeker	Can	-	17	22	6	NW
David Morrow	Can	-	11	16	5	NE
William Forbes	Can	-	11	17	34	SW
Henry Baughman	Can	-	16	22	5	SW
Hugh Cunningham	Can	-	17	23	31	SW
Samuel Hindman	Can	-	13	15	11	SE
Jacob Stall	Can	-	11	18	36	SW
Noah Cook	Can	-	18	21	32	SW
Joseph Kithcart	Can	-	11	16	14	NW
Joseph Kithcart	Can	-	11	16	11	SW
Joseph Kithcart	Can	-	11	16	15	NE
David Lilley	Can	-	14	19	1	NE
Noah Cook	Can	-	18	21	32	NE
Noah Cook	Can	-	18	21	34	NE
James Hindman	Can	-	13	15	23	NE
Massom Metcalf	Can	-	10	1	33	SW
Massom Metcalf	Can	-	10	1	33	SE
Jacob Smith	Can	-	12	16	19	NW
James Hendricks	Can	-	14	18	11	SE
Peter Weygandt	Can	-	10	1	36	NW

1532   18 Dec 1813   A/5/306
LO Zan
Transmits patents

Name		Twp	Rng	Sec	Qtr
Daniel Dyer	Zan Mil	5	1	3	NW
John Miller	Zan Mil	4	9	15	SE
Christian Yoller? [Yotter?]	Zan Mil	5	9	19	SW
Andrew Derner	Zan Mil	6	1	2	NE
Peter Baker	Zan Mil	10	7	14	NW
Peter Baker	Zan Mil	10	7	7	SW
Jacob Baughman	Zan Mil	10	7	14	SW
Abraham Harsberger	Zan Mil	4	9	15	SW
John Conner	Zan Mil	4	1	23	NE
John Hosack	Zan Mil	3	3	12	SW
Samuel Farquhar	Zan Mil	9	5	4	NW
John Williams	Zan	-	15	17	1	SE
William Robertson	Zan Mil	10	7	6	SE

1533   18 Dec 1813   A/5/307
LO Jef
Transmits patents

Name		Twp	Rng	Sec	Qtr
Bailey Johnson	Jef * 9E	1N	5	NE
Robert Armstrong	Jef * 3E	1S	1	SW

Thomas Russell	Jef	*	4E	3S	11	NW	
James McGrew	Jef	*	2E	1S	4	SE	
Luke Vaughan	Jef	*	4E	3S	12	NW	
Thomas Montgomery	Jef	*	9E	2N	6	NE	
William Montgomery	Jef	*	9E	2N	20	SE	
William Montgomery	Jef	*	9E	2N	28	NW	
Roger McNight	Jef	*	1E	2N	7	NW	
William Wright	Jef	*	2E	3N	5	NE	
Elijah Wright	Jef	*	4E	1N	6	NW	
Simon Denny	Jef	*	1E	2N	3	SE	
Nicholas Blankenbaker	Jef	*	5E	2N	19	SE	
Nicholas Blankenbaker	Jef	*	4E	2N	6	NE	
John Patterson	Jef	*	9E	1N	27	SW	
Samuel Ryker	Jef	*	11E	5N	21	SE	
William Gordon	Jef	*	4E	2N	9	NW	
Isaac Hohnan	Jef	*	4E	5N	12	+	
William McKnight	Jef	*	5E	2N	8	SW	
Robert Lott	Jef	*	11-	4N	17	SW	
John Paul	Jef	*	10-	4N	35	NE	

*Second Principal Meridian.

1534 18 Dec 1813 A/5/307
LO Stu
Transmits patents

William Nichols	Stu	-	4	11	8	NE
David Snyder	Stu	-	7	19	35	SW
Patrick Scott	Stu	-	3	14	28	NE
Thomas Price	Stu	-	7	20	2	NW
Abraham Holm	Stu	-	8	11	10	W
Peter Foulk	Stu	-	9	9	1	SE
George Seller	Stu	-	9	10	14	SW
Thomas Rotch	Stu	-	9	10	4	SW
Thomas Rotch	Stu	-	9	10	8	NE
George Love	Stu	-	4	8	15	SW
John Hendricks, Junior	Stu	-	5	12	20	SE
Edward McGuire	Stu	-	6	14	24	SE
William Smith	Stu	-	4	6	18	SE
Andrew Frank	Stu	-	7	15	30	SW
Nathan Shepherd	Stu	-	4	8	21	NE
Robert Griffin	Stu	-	6	10	25	SW
Adam Knouf	Stu	-	4	14	11	SE

1535 18 Dec 1813 A/5/308
Thomas Curtis, Leesburgh, Virginia
Transmits patent

Thomas Curtis	[?]	-	5	7	30	SE

1536 18 Dec 1813 A/5/309
Thomas Gibson, Reg Can
You must repay William & James Campbell on tract already sold to Key, or their payments may be transferred to another tract

John E. Key	Can	-	11	17	17	NW
John E. Key	Can	-	11	17	17	SW

1537 20 Dec 1813 A/5/309
Hon. Shadrach Bond, [U.S.] House of Representatives
". . . I am of the opinion that no persons are entitled to pre-emption rights in the districts of Kaskaskia and Shawneetown but those who have inhabited and cultivated a tract in one of those districts agreeably to the act of 5 Feb 1813."

1538 20 Dec 1813 A/5/310
Jesse Spencer, Reg Chl
Transmits patents

Michael Earnest	Chl	WS	21	10	1	SW

James Trimble	Chl	Mil	13	7	12	NE
William W. Farquhar	Chl	Mil	14	8	11	SE
William Kendall	Chl	-	19	4	14	NE
John Williamson*	Chl	-	20	12	19	SE

*Final certificate not found in GLO.

1539 22 Dec 1813 A/5/310
John Badollet, Reg Vin
Final certificate for John Paul was not enclosed in your letter.

1540 24 Dec 1813 A/5/311
Messrs. -- Brinton & -- Condy, Philadelphia, [Pennsylvania]
Transmits patents

-- Brinton & -- Condy	Stu	-	8	10	29	NW
-- Brinton & -- Condy	Stu	-	7	17	14	SW
J. W. Condy	Stu	-	8	10	20	NW
J. W. Condy	Stu	-	7	17	14	SE
J. H. Brinton	Stu	-	8	10	20	SW

1541 27 Dec 1813 A/5/312
Zaccheus Biggs, Ohio
". . . The United States is in want of all its funds, and if your convenience will permit you to make any payments . . . it will be highly pleasing. . . ."

1542 28 Dec 1813 A/5/313
David Hoge, Reg Stu
Transmits patents which had been issued previously, but not sent to us for transmittal to you

Jacob Neff	Stu	-	3	6	20	SW
Paul Fisher	Stu	-	1	6	21	NE
John Warnock*	Stu	-	4	6	11	NW

*This patent was sent to you on 19 Feb 1812. If the patent is erroneously written as NE quarter, it should be returned for correction.

1543 30 Dec 1813 A/5/314
Samuel Dick, Cincinnati, [Ohio]
Your final certificate presented by Mr. -- McClean; there appears to be a short payment

Samuel Dick	Cin	-	2	3	9	-

1544 30 Dec 1813 A/5/315
Hon. Speaker of U.S. House of Representatives
Hon. President of U.S. Senate
A lengthy and important annual report regarding the 400,000,000 acres of land still remaining to be distributed.

1545 30 Dec 1813 A/5/322
Hon. -- Creighton, U.S. House of Representatives
Transfer from -- Phillips to -- Starling & -- De Lashmut cannot be found by LO Cin.

1546 6 Jan 1814 A/5/324
LO Hun
Transmits patents

Edward Ward	Hun	WML	2	3	26	NE
Henry Hains	Hun	EML	1	4	32	NE
Archibald McDonnell	Hun	WML	1	4	22	NE

1547
LO Stu
Transmits patents

7 Jan 1814   A/5/325

John Brown	Stu	–	6	8	24	SW
Thomas Stewart	Stu	–	6	14	11	NW
George Brown	Stu	–	4	15	21	SE
Samuel Bachtel	Stu	–	8	12	5	S
Adam Yarrick	Stu	–	9	12	8	NE
Arthur Martin	Stu	–	5	10	24	SW
Henry Vantilburgh	Stu	–	2	8	23	SE
Matthew Law	Stu	–	7	10	17	SW
William Thompson & Adam Thompson	Stu	–	7	9	16	NW
Joseph McCasland	Stu	–	5	13	18	SE

1548
LO Cin
Transmits patents

7 Jan 1814   A/5/326

Joseph Stafford	Cin	Pre	9	2	17	NE
Joseph Parks, Junior	Cin	Pre	4	2	1	2
Daniel C. Cooper	Cin	Pre	7	2	31	NW
Daniel C. Cooper	Cin	Pre	7	2	31	NE
Daniel C. Cooper	Cin	Pre	7	2	33	W
Daniel C. Cooper	Cin	Pre	7	1	9	+
Daniel C. Cooper	Cin	Pre	7	2	35	+
Daniel C. Cooper	Cin	Pre	8	4	14	+
Daniel C. Cooper	Cin	Pre	7	1	3	+
Daniel C. Cooper	Cin	Pre	7	1	10	+
Daniel C. Cooper Survey 1	Cin	Pre	7	1	10	+
Samuel Schooley	Cin	Pre	5	4	34	NW
Ann Westfall	Cin	Pre	7	3	36	NW
George Shoup, heirs of	Cin	Pre	7	3	32	+
Abraham Cary	Cin	Pre	9	5	33	–
John Ensey	Cin	Pre	6	2	23	NW
George Shoup, heirs of, & George Fryberger	Cin	Pre	7	2	21	NW
James Galloway (Blacksmith)	Cin	Pre	8	3	5	+
Francis Sipe	Cin	Pre	8	4	34	–
John Geer	Cin	MR	9	5	3	SE
Deborah Ingham	Cin	EML	5	6	30	SE
Jacob Kesling	Cin	WML	1	13	27	NE
John D. Jenkins	Cin	MR	9	6	35	NW
Michael Baker	Cin	EML	4	6	27	NW
Juliana Frégin	Cin	EML	2	4	26	NE

1549
LO Chl
Transmits patents

7 Jan 1814   A/5/326

Jacob Henderlick	Chl	–	19	16	7	SE
John Overmire	Chl	–	16	16	4	SW
John Judy	Chl	–	20	11	12	SE
Smith Goodin	Chl	–	16	16	14	SW
Jacob Barnhart	Chl	–	20	13	7	NW
Abraham Mussey? [Miessy?]	Chl	–	19	16	10	NW
John Knight	Chl	MS	21	9	34?	NW
James Smith	Chl	–	17	7	32	NE
Solomon Munroe	Chl	–	20	3	3	NW
Leonard Wolf	Chl	–	20	11	21	NE
Jacob Switzer	Chl	–	19	15	15	NE
John Waggoner	Chl	–	16	16	29	SE
John Perkins	Chl	–	20	11	33	SW
William Lucas, Senior	Chl	LS	21	3	30	+
William Lucas, Senior	Chl	LS	22	3	8	+
Elizabeth Sackett	Chl	–	19	14	17	SE
John Waggoner	Chl	–	16	17	27	NW
Joseph Dixon	Chl	–	19	9	6	SE
Daniel Nuneemachar?	Chl	–	16	17	24	SW
George Trout	Chl	–	16	17	34	NE
Washington Evans	Chl	Mil	15	3	13	SW
Washington Evans	Chl	Mil	15	3	13	NW

Frederick Pontius	Chl	–	17	14	8	SW
Matthias Dege	Chl	Mil	16	2	9	SE
Abraham Green	Chl	Mil	15	3	23	NW
Joseph Dixon	Chl	–	20	8	13	NE
Elisha Rawles	Chl	–	20	8	7	S
John Weatherington	Chl	MS	22	4	14	NE
George Waller	Chl	–	20	14	14	SE
George Green	Chl	Mil	15	3	8	NW
Nathaniel Wyatt	Chl	Mil	19	7	22	SW
Herbert Winegardner	Chl	–	17	17	15	SW
Abraham Harnison? [Harrison?]	Chl	–	20	15	30	NW
James Robinson & George Robinson	Chl	–	16	7	13	NW
John McArthur	Chl	–	20	15	9	SE
Peter Klick	Chl	–	20	12	27	SW
John Fry, Senior	Chl	–	20	15	29	NW
Henry Roller	Chl	–	20	14	22	SE
Benjamin Williams	Chl	Mil	19	7	22	NE
Henry Imler	Chl	–	20	11	17	SE
Joseph Brown	Chl	MS	21	10	8	W
Isaac Dawson	Chl	–	20	10	4	NW
Philemon Beecher	Chl	–	19	15	11	SE
Abraham Van Courtright	Chl	–	20	14	23	NE
John Betty	Chl	–	20	12	14	SW
Isaac Larimer	Chl	–	17	16	36	NW
Isaac Larimer	Chl	–	17	16	26	SE
Ezekiel Slaughter	Chl	–	20	5	5	NW
John Klinger	Chl	–	18	13	25	SE
John Martin	Chl	–	22	3	23	NE
Joseph Cox	Chl	–	20	8	13	SE
Jacob Heistand	Chl	–	19	16	18	NW
Elnathan Scofield	Chl	–	19	14	23	SE
Elnathan Scofield	Chl	–	19	14	23	NW
Abraham Green	Chl	Mil	15	3	17	SE
Edmund Mace	Chl	WS	21	11	26	SW

1550
LO Can
Transmits patents

7 Jan 1814   A/5/328

Abraham Cuppy	Can	–	16	23	31	SE
John McBride	Can	–	13	15	11	NE
Philip Stiltz	Can	–	19	19	11	W
Philip Stiltz	Can	–	19	19	8	NW
William Harah	Can	–	15	22	10	NW
John Andrews	Can	–	17	22	27	SW
Jacob Roads	Can	–	11	16	10	SW
Philip Roads	Can	–	11	16	1	NE
Michael Bear	Can	–	11	18	34	SE
Barnhark* Sickman	Can	–	11	17	14	NW
Ephraim Young	Can	–	11	17	3	NW
Jacob Beam	Can	–	18	21	25	SW
Jacob Beam	Can	–	18	21	36	NW
Jacob Beam	Can	–	18	21	36	SE
Frederick Brown	Can	–	12	16	19	SW
Thomas Dean	Can	–	10	12	24	SE
Jacob Hay	Can	–	13	13	9	SW
William Hanger? [Hauger?]	Can	–	13	13	10	SW
Thomas Cameron	Can	–	15	22	6	NW
William Slater	Can	–	17	22	36	SW
Peter Kinney	Can	–	17	22	36	SE
Henry Naugle	Can	–	17	22	35	SW
John Palmer	Can	–	17	22	36	NW
John Edgington	Can	–	10	1	8	SW
David Custard	Can	–	13	16	33	NW
Stephen Henry	Can	–	13	15	11	NW

*So spelled.

1551
LO Jef
Transmits patents

7 Jan 1814   A/5/329

Name	LO		Twp	Rng	Sec	Part
Morris Maurice	Jef	–	5E	1S	31	SE
Jesse, William Junior? [or John?], & David Hillis, heirs of William [Senior?] Hillis	Jef	–	11E	5N	29	NE
James Rodman	Jef	–	5E	2N	18	SE
Samuel Ledgewood	Jef	–	11E	4N	19	SW
Alexander Little	Jef	–	4E	2N	11	NE
Andrew Fulton	Jef	–	10E	3N	30	+
Thorrias Gassaway	Jef	–	8E	4N	21	NW
Jesse Bogue	Jef	–	4E	3N	34	SE
Edward Millis	Jef	–	1E	2N	18	SW
Robert Field	Jef	–	1E	2N	18	NE
Adam Wyble	Jef	–	2E	1N	4	NW
John Ogle	Jef	–	9E	1N	5	SW
Reuben Wright	Jef	–	3E	5S	18	SE
Christian Shirley	Jef	–	5E	3S	1	NW
Samuel Gwathmey	Jef	–	6E	2S	6	NW
Samuel Gwathmey	Jef	–	1E	3N	19	–
Samuel Gwathmey	Jef	–	5E	2S	22	NW
Samuel Gwathmey	Jef	–	5E	2S	14	SW

1552   7 Jan 1814   A/5/329
LO Zan
Transmits patents

John Kelly	Zan Mil	8	2	5	NW
John Kelly	Zan Mil	8	2	21	SE
Andrew McBride	Zan –	15	17	27	NE
Ebenezer Finley	Zan –	8	8	7	NW

1553   8 Jan 1814   A/5/329
Nehemiah Tilton, Reg Wsh, Mississippi Territory
Transmits U.S. Treasury receipt

James Lea	Wsh EML	5	1	8	SW

1554   10 Jan 1814   A/5/330
Governor [Ninian] Edwards, Kaskaskia, Illinois Territory
Writes regarding royalties from saline deposit [on Wabash River]; instructs governor to release Pettway & Company from their bid.

1555   10 Jan 1814   A/5/331
Wyllys Silliman, Reg Zan
Transmits first certificate & U.S. Treasury receipt

Jonathan Carlisle, Junior	Zan –	13	11	14	NE

1556   19 Jan 1814   A/5/333
LO Jef
Transmits patents

William Watson	Jef	–	3E	5S	8	NE
Robert Robertson	Jef	–	5E	2N	7	SW
John Robinson	Jef	–	4E	2N	13	SW
Benjamin Hains	Jef	–	5E	2S	5	NW
Benjamin Hains	Jef	–	5E	2S	5	NE
Samuel Little	Jef	–	4E	3S	31	NE
John Robertson	Jef	–	5E	2N	18	NW
Peter Mikesell	Jef	–	10E	2N	31	NE

1557   19 Jan 1814   A/5/333*
LO Vin
Transmits patents

John Smith	Vin	–	5E	5S	26	SE
Peter McHintosh	Vin	–	4E	5S	24	NW
David Benson	Vin	–	12W	4S	11	SW
John Smiler	Vin	–	4E	3S	10	NE
Jonathan Hauser	Vin	–	3E	3S	36	NW
John Gray	Vin	–	14W	5S	1	NE
Joshua Everton	Vin	–	12W	4S	7	SE
David Groves	Vin	–	1W	6S	28	+
John Wood	Vin	–	12W	1N	32	NE
John Riggs & William Frymires? [Trymires?]	Vin	–	1W	7S	6	SW
Vatchel Hancock	Vin	–	6E	3S	31	+
Jonathan Lindley	Vin	–	1W	2N	14	+
Thomas Polke	Vin	–	2W	7S	21	NW
Jacob Taylor	Vin	–	13W	4S	17	NW
John D. Hays	Vin	–	5E	2S	34	SW
James Smith	Vin	–	2E	3S	13	NW
Peter Miller	Vin	–	4E	3S	22	NE
Robert Hollowell	Vin	–	1E	1S	2	SE
John Hollowell	Vin	–	1E	1S	11	SW
John Hollowell	Vin	–	1E	1S	11	NW

*[This page should have been numbered 334.]

1558   20 Jan 1814   A/5/333
James Findlay, Rec Cin
Transmits U.S. Treasury receipt

James Smith	Cin MR	12	4	22	SE
James Smith	Cin MR	12	4	22	NE

1559   21 Jan 1814   A/5/333
William Blackburn, Salem, Columbiana County, Ohio
Patent seems to have been sent to LO Stu in September 1807

--	Stu –	4	16	2	–

1560   21 Jan 1814   A/5/334
Thomas Gibson, Reg Can
Tract cannot be sold at private sale, as it contains a salt spring [reserved to United States government]

--	Can –	16	19	9	–

1561   22 Jan 1814   A/5/334
Daniel Symmes, Reg Cin
Transmits final certificates for correction (short & over payments)

--	Cin E*	3	4	3	NE
--	Cin E*	3	7	21	NW
--	Cin W*	1	11	26	NW
--	Cin **	12	16	13	SW
--	Cin E*	5	5	28	SE
--	Cin W*	1	11	2	SW
--	Cin MR	5	3	11	NW

*Perhaps EML and WML are meant.
**East of 3d [Meridian?].

1562   22 Jan 1814   A/5/335
Richard Rush, Comptroller of U.S. Treasury
Discusses need for a suit to recover $120,710.15 from the estate of Lemuel Henry, late Rec St Stephens; mentions [Thomas] Malone, executor of Henry's estate.

1563   25 Jan 1814   A/5/337
Daniel Symmes, Reg Cin
Calls attention to discrepancies

D. Symmes*	Cin MR	2	2	8	NW
George Dawson**	Cin ?	10	5	21	NE

*Record of purchase on 5 Nov 1808 cannot be found in GLO.

**Application recently by -- Anbogart? [Arbogast?]
& -- Easton needs explanation, as tract apparently
already sold to Dawson.

1564		29 Jan 1814		A/5/338

Robert Watson, Little York, Pennsylvania
Transmits patents

Robert Watson	Stu	-	6	8	21	SW

1565		29 Jan 1814		A/5/338

William Lavering, McConnelsburgh, Pennsylvania
Transmits patent

William Lavering	Can	-	20	18	25	SE

1566		29 Jan 1814		A/5/338

Michael Knaves, Post Office, Chambersburgh, Pennsylvania
Transmits patent

Michael Knaves	Stu	-	9	10	22	SE

1567		29 Jan 1814		A/5/338

John Carlisle, Chillicothe
Transmits patent

John Carlisle	Chl	-	21	9	22	NE

1568		25 Jan 1814		A/5/339

LO Jef
Transmits patents

William Moore	Jef	-	1E	2N	35	SE
Adam Glaze	Jef	-	5E	4S	36	+
Samuel Heron	Jef	-	5E	2N	18	NE
William McCarland	Jef	-	9E	3N	2	NW
William Pangburn	Jef	-	3E	5S	18	NW
George Hentor? [Hinton?]	Jef	-	2E	1N	5	SE
George Hentor? [Hinton?]	Jef	-	2E	1N	5	SE*

*[Duplicates above tract description and may be in-
correct.]

1569		29 Jan 1814		A/5/339

LO Stu
Transmits patents

Joseph McClean	Stu	-	5	12	25	SE
John Trumbo	Stu	-	7	14	25	NW
George Seghefsoot? [Seghefoost?]	Stu	-	17	17	7	NW
George Stenger	Stu	-	4	11	35	NE
David Kirkland	Stu	-	4	7	1	SE
James Porter	Stu	-	3	10	17	SW
Charles Porter	Stu	-	5	12	25	SW
Stephen Forst? [Ford?]	Stu	-	3	10	7	NW
Joseph Gotschall	Stu	-	5	12	12	NE
D. Wallace & A. Wallace	Stu	-	4	8	15	NE
Absalom Ridgely	Stu	-	4	6	4	NW
Joseph Hogue	Stu	-	6	14	25	SE
Stephen Ford	Stu	-	3	9	36	NW
Christian Spiker	Stu	-	6	12	20	NW
Valentine Creamer	Stu	-	7	12	31	NW
John Scott	Stu	-	3	14	20	SE
Jacob Houtz	Stu	-	3	16	12	SW
John Hawler? [Hausler?]	Stu	-	9	12	11	NE
Joseph McKeel	Stu	-	8	9	6	NW
Benjamin Todd	Stu	-	3	13	2	NW
William Siddell	Stu	-	1	7	29	NW
William Hoober	Stu	-	7	20	35	NW
John Hawler	Stu	-	9	12	12	W
Abraham Hupler	Stu	-	9	11	7	SW

Richard Gillson	Stu	-	1	6	17	SE
Michael Poweal?	Stu	-	5	16	14	SE
James Webb	Stu	-	3	16	5	SW
James Lowrey	Stu	-	2	11	34	SE
John Early	Stu	-	1	8	15	NW
Andrew Woodward	Stu	-	7	17	5	NE
John McCleary	Stu	-	4	10	21	SE
John Sapp	Stu	-	2	8	1	N
James Kelly	Stu	-	4	12	10	NE
Hugh Parks	Stu	-	3	6	15	NE
Nathan Shaw	Stu	-	2	8	17	NW
James? [Joseph?] Hutchinson	Stu	-	4	6	24	SW
George Wilson	Stu	-	3	10	1	SW
Joseph Maholin	Stu	-	5	10	28	SE
Stephen Workman	Stu	-	3	5	4	SE
Daniel Wise	Stu	-	9	12	24	SW
William Hollinger	Stu	-	8	12	18	SW
D. Creamer, heirs of	Stu	-	9	12	11	S
William Floyd? [Floyll?]	Stu	-	10	12	15	NW
Conrad Dudderer, heirs of	Stu	-	2	13	15	SW

1570		29 Jan 1814		A/5/340

A note stating that "several packages of patents
dated December & January recorded in volume 7,
pages 144 to 237, were sent to the respective
Land Offices without copying the Lists in this
book."

1571		29 Jan 1814		A/5/341

Nehemiah Tilton, Rec Wsh, Mississippi Territory
Instructions regarding arrears of interest.

1572		1 Feb 1814		A/5/342

Wyllys Silliman, Reg Zan
Advises him to obey summons to attend trial of General -- Hull and to find competent substitute as
temporary Reg Zan.

1573		2 Feb 1814		A/5/343

David Hoge, Reg Stu
Returns patent for correction [except last descrip-
tion]

-- Huston*	Stu	-	1	7	28	SE
Jacob Nessley**	Stu	-	2	9	8	+
Jacob Nessley**	Stu	-	2	9	14	-
--***	Stu	-	4	6	11	NW

*Spelling changed from "Haston."
**No transfer from Nessley, Senior, to Nessley, Jun-
ior, found.
***Patent you returned 4 Mar 1812 cannot be found.

1574		2 Feb 1814		A/5/343

Hon. Speaker of U.S. House of Representatives
Reg WPR believes a short extension of time needed,
without which "many of their most industrious &
worthy citizens must lose their lands."

1575		2 Feb 1814		A/5/344

Nehemiah Tilton, Reg WPR, Washington, Mississippi
Territory
Transmits an act passed 25 Jan 1814 "granting Moses
Hook the right of pre-emption."

1576		3 Feb 1814		A/5/344

Daniel Symmes, Reg Cin

". . . I am at a loss to know how it happens that
  payments on account of pre-emption lands are now
  received, how it happens that these tracts were
  not offered for sale in April last, on account of
  failure of payment within the time prescribed by
  law. . . ."

--*   Cin Pre   7   2   21 SE

*Purchased in December 1804.

| 1577 | | 4 Feb 1814 | | A/5/344 |

Hon. R. Beall, U.S. House of Representatives
Transmits patent for military land for Samuel H.
  Smith.

| 1578 | | 4 Feb 1814 | | A/5/345 |

David Hoge, Reg Stu
Requests final certificate

John Hendricks   Stu   -   12   5   20 SE

| 1579 | | 4 Feb 1814 | | A/5/345 |

Wyllys Silliman, Reg Zan
Transmits first certificate & U.S. Treasury receipt

Isaiah Frost   Zan Mil 11   8   11 SE
Isaiah Frost   Zan Mil 10   8   16 NW
Isaiah Frost   Zan Mil 11   8   20 NE
Isaiah Frost   Zan Mil 11   8   21 SE

| 1580 | | 5 Feb 1814 | | A/5/345 |

Hon. -- Jennings, U.S. House of Representatives
Transmits patent

Peter Coopers*   Vin   -   4E 2S   34 SW

*So spelled.

| 1581 | | 5 Feb 1814 | | A/5/345 |

Peter Lesourd, Post Office, Baltimore [Maryland?]
Transmits patent

Peter Lesourd   Cin MR   3   3   26 SE

| 1582 | | 5 Feb 1814 | | A/5/346 |

LO Cin
Transmits patents

Remember Blackman   Cin WML   1   8   19 NW
Philip Harwood   Cin WML   1   8   13 NE
Daniel Seward   Cin MR   2   1   11   +
Henry Lybrook   Cin WML   1 12   26 SE
Joel Ferguson   Cin * 12E 15- 11 NE
Jacob Line   Cin MR   3   2   16 SW
Daniel Vandamark   Cin MR   13   2   7 NE
J. E. Ferris & A. Ferris   Cin MR   2   4   8   +
John White   Cin * 12E 14-   2 SE
Henry Whitesell   Cin EML   1   8   12 SE
Luke Voorhis   Cin EML   1   7   12 SE
William Ogle   Cin WML   1 11   34 SW
James Rees   Cin WML   1   9   23 NE
James McGaw   Cin EML   1   7   33 SE
Ephraim Brown   Cin WML   1 10   19 SE
Joshua Howell   Cin MR   11   3   31 NW
Joseph Adams   Cin EML   5   9   35 SW
Stephen Corner   Cin * 14E 17- 27 NE
Joseph Bell   Cin * 13E 14- 33 NE
Peter Ambrose   Cin EML   1   4   29 SW
Peter Ambrose   Cin EML   1   4   33 NW
Owen Davis   Cin MR   9   6   36 NE
Owen Davis   Cin MR   10   6   31 SE
John White   Cin * 12E 14-   2 SW
Jacob Lesh   Cin EML   3   5   12 NW

Harman Wairam? [Wavram?]   Cin * 13E 16- 36 NE
William Thorn   Cin * 13E 16- 19 NW
George Kelly   Cin EML   4   3   32 NW
Francis Johnston   Cin EML   6   8   32 SW
William Butler   Cin MR   2+   4   26 NW
William Butler   Cin MR   2+   4   26 NE
Isaac Goble   Cin EML   1   7   28 NE
William Denman   Cin * 12E 14- 20 SW
John Watson   Cin ?   3   1   5   +
John Watson   Cin ?   3   1   6   +
David Odum   Cin * 12E 16- 12 NW
Jeremiah Sims   Cin MR   9   4   24 NE
William Wilson   Cin MR   13   4   19 SE
Moses Coppock   Cin EML   6   4   32 NW
William Fox   Cin * 13E 17- 23 SE
Benjamin Jones   Cin MR   9   5   2 SW
John Lybrook   Cin EML   1   7   19 NE
James Alexander   Cin EML   1 10   28 NE
James Johnston   Cin EML   5   9   24 NE
Peter Baysinger   Cin MR   10   3   1 NE
William Ogle   Cin WML   1 10   4 NE
Samuel Marshall   Cin EML   6   7   5 SW
A. Spencer & A. Small   Cin MR   11   1   15 NE
Samuel Patterson   Cin EML   2   6   21 SE
John Gibson   Cin EML   6   8   24 SE
Linus Basscam? [Bassam?]   Cin EML   6   2   3 NE
James Atwood   Cin EML   1   7   1 NW
John Baker   Cin * 12E 12N 33 SE
Samuel Bard   Cin EML   2   5   18 SW
Eli Stringer   Cin * 13E 13N 27 SE
James W. Bailey   Cin EML   1   3   7 NW
John Williams   Cin WML   1 12   7 SW
James Hollingsworth   Cin WML   1 11   20 NW
Thomas Hughes   Cin WML   2 12   22   +
William Pugh   Cin EML   1   7   35 SE
Johnathan** Higgins   Cin * 13E 15- 33 NE
S. Maze & D. Maze   Cin * 13E 13- 13 SE
Henry Bacome**   Cin MR   12   4   14 NW
Samuel Searey? [Searcy?]   Cin WML   1   2   11 SW
Henry Vail   Cin EML   2   7   14 SW
Christian [Christopher?]
  Cary   Cin MR   1   3   26   W
Jacob Miller   Cin EML   3   4   13 NE
Thomas Newell   Cin MR   13   5   28 NW
George Dick   Cin EML   2   3   12 NW
William Goff   Cin WML   1 10   34 SW

*Second Principal Meridian.
**So spelled.
+"Fractional."

| 1583 | | 8 Feb 1814 | | A/5/348 |

Isaac Van Horne, Rec Zan
Has no information regarding cash advance to Colonel
  -- Huntington.

| 1584 | | 10 Feb 1814 | | A/5/349 |

Daniel Symmes, Reg Cin
Member of Congress has applied for patent

--   Cin WML   2 10   33 NE

| 1585 | | 11 Feb 1814 | | A/5/349 |

Wyllys Silliman, Reg Zan
Inquires regarding transfers

John? Selp? [Self?]   Zan   -   5   1   6 NE

| 1586 | | 11 Feb 1814 | | A/5/349 |

Patrick Johnston, Oxford Post Office, Chester County,
  Pennsylvania
Transmits patent; it had been sent to Bedford and

returned as a dead letter
Patrick Johnston   Zan   - 13 12   8 SE

1587   16 Feb 1814   A/5/351
Hon. -- Piper, U.S. House of Representatives
Transmits corrected patent
Charles McLaughlin &
  Peter Smith   Mil   - 14   8   3 18

1588   16 Feb 1814   A/5/351
Joseph Wood, Reg Mar
Transmits patents
William Danford   Mar   -   4   5 22 NE
Jacob Moore   Mar   -   4   5 28 NW

1589   19 Feb 1814   A/5/353
Frederick Bates, Recorder of Land Titles, St. Louis,
  Missouri Territory
Transmits copy of act for the relief of Daniel Boone.

1590   19 Feb 1814   A/5/353
Jesse Spencer, Reg Chl
Transmits U.S. Treasury receipt
Henry Roberts*   Chl WS 21 10 14 NW
*Assignee of Samuel Roberts, assignee of Henry Hus-
  ton.

1591   22 Feb 1814   A/5/354
LO Cin
Transmits patents
James Black   Cin MR   8   2 24 SW
Edward Gallaghan   Cin EML 6   3   4 SE
Samuel Walker   Cin * 14E 16- 27   +
Robert Flack   Cin WML 1 10   5   W
Benjamin Beeson   Cin EML 12 15 24 NW
Joshua Howell   Cin MR 11   3 31 SW
Enoch Pearson   Cin EML 6   4 29 NE
Matthew Brown   Cin WML 2 11 29   +
William Leaper   Cin WML 1 10 10 NW
John Gullion   Cin WML 2   2 35 SW
Philip Jones   Cin WML 1   9   9 NE
Solomon Miller**   Cin   -   3   5 26 NE
*Second Principal Meridian.
**Wants patent to this description, or to tract
  Cin - 13   5 26 NE; Miller is not certain
  which.

1592   22 Feb 1814   A/5/354
LO Jef
Transmits patents
Samuel Gwathmey   Jef   - 4E 5S 29 NE
Samuel Gwathmey   Jef   - 4E 5S 17 SW
Adam Bower   Jef   - 3E 3N 24 NE
John Marton*   Jef   - 4E 1S 14 NW
Noel Fouts   Jef   - 4E 2N 30 NE
Michael Kennier   Jef   - 9E 4N 15 NE
Philip Copple   Jef   - 3E 2N 34 SE
James Robertson   Jef   - 9E 2N 30 NE
Robert Ellison   Jef   - 3E 3N 12 SE
Jacob Marts   Jef   - 1E 2N   2 NW
*So spelled.

1593   22 Feb 1814   A/5/355
Jesse Spencer, Reg Chl
Patent for Walter Dun to be forwarded when returns
  for month are received and posted.

1594   25 Feb 1814   A/5/356
Daniel Symmes, Reg Cin
Correction of your returns to be attended to "and a
  return obtained from the Surveyor General relative
  to your purchase of tract on 5 Nov 1808"
Daniel Symmes   [Cin?] -   2   2   8 NW

1595   26 Feb 1814   A/5/356
Peter Wilson, Rec Stu
Discrepancy noted in payments
John Robinson   [Stu] -   1   9 31   -

1596   2 Mar 1814   A/5/356
James Findlay, Rec Cin
Notes discrepancies in repayment for following trans-
  actions
John James Dufour [et al]   Cin WML 3   2 15   -
John James Dufour [et al]   Cin WML 3   2 22   +
John James Dufour [et al]   Cin WML 3   2 27   +

1597   5 Mar 1814   A/5/357
David Hoge, Reg Stu
Returns patent for John Hendricks; wants the one for
  Joseph Hendricks, which is erroneously described
John Hendricks   Stu   -   5 12 20 SE
Joseph Hendricks   Stu   -   5 12 20 NE

1598   5 Mar 1814   A/5/357
Wyllys Silliman, Reg Zan
Requests final certificate
Elias Danhaver   Zan   - 13 11 17 NE

1599   5 Mar 1814   A/5/358
Elias Danhaver, Philadelphia
Promises patent without delay
Elias Danhaver   Zan   - 13 11 17 NE

1600   5 Mar 1814   A/5/358
Samuel Finley, Rec Chl
Transmits U.S. Treasury receipt
John Tomlinson   Chl   - 12   7 15   S
John Tomlinson   Chl   - 12   7 16   -

1601   7 Mar 1814   A/5/358
LO Zan
Transmits patents
John Stires? [Hires? Slires?]Zan Mil 1   1 10 SE
Joseph Cheney   Zan Mil 9   4 22 SE
John Henderson, Senior &
  Junior   Zan Mil 9   3 16 SE
Daniel Sapp & John Grier   Zan Mil 10   7   4 SW
Nancy Dennison   Zan   -   6   2 15 NE
Andrew Hanna   Zan   -   3   1 20 NE
Abel Slack   Zan   -   6   2   8 NW
Conrad Emry   Zan   - 15 18 18 NW
Jacob Bouzer   Zan   -   8   5 18 NE
Andrew Cusac   Zan   - 15 16 14 NE
William Frazer   Zan   - 12 13 27 SE
Zachariah Chandler   Zan   - 12 13 11 SE

1602   7 Mar 1814   A/5/359
LO Jef
Transmits patents
Jacob Burkhart   Jef   - 5E 2S   8 NW

Henry Smith	Jef	–	9E	4N	24	NE
Henry Smith	Jef	–	9E	4N	13	SE
John Henderson	Jef	–	9E	3N	11	NW
Thomas Rand? [Brand? Prand?]	Jef	–	12E	6N	3	NW
Joseph Warnock	Jef	–	9E	1N	27	NW
Evan Hinton? [Henton?]	Jef	–	3E	1S	11	SE
Jacob Rice	Jef	–	2E	4S	29	+
Robert Simmington	Jef	–	10E	2N	32	+
Robert Simmington	Jef	–	10E	3N	33	+
William Bigham	Jef	–	10E	3N	31	+
William Bigham	Jef	–	10E	3N	32	–
John Wendell	Jef	–	2E	5S	4	NE
John Wendell	Jef	–	3E	4S	33	SE
Isaac V. Buskirk	Jef	–	5E	2S	26	SE
Jesse Spurgin	Jef	–	4E	2N	25	NE
George Hatabaugh	Jef	–	4E	3N	9	SW

1603   9 Mar 1814   A/5/359
Hon. James Kilbourn, U.S. House of Representatives
Comments on proposal to extend land sales to three
    territories west of Ohio. Sees strategic advan-
    tage and, if wagon road is opened, also a sales
    advantage. However, "as a public officer, I am
    sorry on deep reflection I cannot see the advan-
    tages I expected when you conversed with me on
    the subject."

1604   10 Mar 1814   A/5/360
Lewis Sewall, Reg St. Stephens
Asks for comments on T. C. vander Horst's claim to
    3,000 acres under British grant.

1605   10 Mar 1814   A/5/361
T. C. Vander Horst, Charleston, South Carolina
Have transmitted plat of Elias Vanderhorst's claim
    to 3,000 acres of land in Mississippi Territory
    to LO St. Stephens for comment.

1606   12 Mar 1814   A/5/362
David Hoge, Reg Stu
Peter Wilson, Rec Stu
Encloses act for relief of William Crawford.

1607   12 Mar 1814   A/5/363
J. H. Brinton, Esq., Philadelphia
Furnishes statement of amounts still owed on follow-
    ing tracts

--	Stu	–	8	10	18	SW
--	Stu	–	8	10	18	NE
--	Stu	–	8	10	18	NW
--	Stu	–	9	10	13	NE
--	Stu	–	9	10	13	SE
--	Stu	–	8	10	7	SE
--	Stu	–	8	10	7	SW
--	Stu	–	9	10	12	SE
--	Stu	–	9	10	12	NE
--	Stu	–	9	11	36	SE
--	Stu	–	9	10	3	SE
--	Stu	–	9	10	3	NE
--	Stu	–	9	10	2	NW
--	Stu	–	9	10	12	SW

1608   12 Mar 1814   A/5/363
Abiather S. Taylor, Franklinton, Ohio
Transmits patent, in response to your letter to

General [Thomas] Worthington

John Taylor	Ref	–	21	12	18	W

1609   14 Mar 1814   A/5/363
Hon. W. Wilson, U.S. House of Representatives
Act of 23 Apr 1812 imposed new duties on Land Commis-
    sioners at Detroit . . . "but it is not known at
    this office that they have been performed, or any
    part of them, as we have had no returns or reports
    of any kind since June 1811."

1610   16 Mar 1814   A/5/364
LO Can
Transmits patents

John Kinney	Can	–	18	22	10	NE
Adam Tener	Can	–	15	22	7	SW
Michael Grayham	Can	–	19	20	4	SW
John Edington	Can	–	10	1	18	N
John Edington	Can	–	10	1	8	NW
John Edington	Can	–	10	1	18	SE
George Miller	Can	–	13	13	10	NE
John Bowman	Can	–	17	22	11	SW
John Kinney	Can	–	11	16	5	SW
John Kinney	Can	–	11	16	5	SE
William Fulks	Can	–	18	23	33	SW
John Knight	Can	–	12	16	28	NW
Daniel Smith	Can	–	14	20	35	NE
Daniel Carter	Can	–	16	22	29	NE
Daniel Carter	Can	–	16	22	29	SE
Eli Booth	Can	–	15	19	4	SE
Andrew Proudfoot	Can	–	16	22	9	NE
Robert Grayham	Can	–	12	15	33	SW
David Boughman	Can	–	12	18	27	SE
David Drake	Can	–	15	19	8	NE
Isaac Bonnett	Can	–	15	20	26	SW
John Young	Can	–	19	20	4	SE
John Boughman	Can	–	11	17	24	SE

1611   16 Mar 1814   A/5/364
John Stump, Chambersburg, Pennsylvania
Transmits patents

John Stump	Can	–	10	12	28	N
John Stump	Can	–	10	12	28	SW

1612   16 Mar 1814   A/5/364
Jesse Spencer, Reg Chl
Transmits patent

Winn Winship	Chl	WS	21	10	13	SW

1613   17 Mar 1814   A/5/366
Hon. George M. Troup, U.S. House of Representatives
Reports total acres sold in Ohio and Mississippi Ter-
    ritory from 1810 to 1813 and estimates land still
    to be sold in Ohio and Indiana Territory.

1614   21 Mar 1814   A/5/367
William Crawford, Land Commissioner, EPR
". . . I have to observe, Sir, that no human eye has
    seen the communication you formerly sent me rela-
    tive to the frauds it is supposed Harry Toulmin, J.
    Smith, etc., are attempting to practice on the
    government. He must, as you surmise, have obtained
    the copy by basely opening the packet in the post
    office. . . ."

1615   21 Mar 1814   A/5/367
John Stein, Reading, Pennsylvania
GLO has written to LO Chl for final certificate.

1616   21 Mar 1814   A/5/368
Thomas Gibson, Reg Can
The following are reserved from public sale

Salt spring reservation	Can	–	16	19	4	–
Salt spring reservation	Can	–	16	19	8	–
Salt spring reservation	Can	–	16	19	9	–
Salt spring reservation	Can	–	16	19	10	–

1617   21 Mar 1814   A/5/368
Jesse Spencer, Reg Chl
Please transmit final certificates for

John Stein	Chl	–	21	11	9	NW
John Stein	Chl	–	21	11	9	SE
John Stein	Chl	–	21	11	8	SE

1618   22 Mar 1814   A/5/368
John H. Brinton, Philadelphia
Acknowledges receipt of U.S. Treasury receipts and
   asks for tract assignments.

1619   26 Mar 1814   A/5/370
Peter Wilson, Rec Stu
Transmits U.S. Treasury receipt

| William King | Stu | – | 4 | 16 | 31 | SE |

1620   30 Mar 1814   A/5/370
John Sloan, Rec Can
Despite your promise of punctuality, not one quar-
   terly return has yet arrived.

1621   30 Mar 1814   A/5/371
Hon. Adam Seybert, U.S. House of Representatives
No information is yet available regarding Walter
   Brasheur's claim to 8,000 acres of land on an is-
   land in the Gulf of Mexico.

1622   31 Mar 1814   A/5/371
Hon. –– Robertson, U.S. House of Representatives
Encloses map of the acres between the Tombigbee and
   Alabama rivers ceded by the Indians.

1623   1 Apr 1814   A/5/372
LO Zan
Transmits patents

Samuel Elliot	Zan	Mil	5	1	3	SW
John Wolford	Zan	Mil	8	5	18	SW
Nathan McGreer	Zan	Mil	1	9	2	SW
Nathaniel Spurgeon	Zan	Mil	10	7	7	NW
Philip Baker	Zan	Mil	6	1	2	SW
Samuel Christler	Zan	Mil	6	2	22	SE
Henry Stull	Zan	Mil	2	3	18	SW
Thomas Latta	Zan	Mil	5	1	8	SE

1624   1 Apr 1814   A/5/372
LO Jef
Transmits patents

David Finley	Jef	–	1E	3N	35	SW
Stephen Gudgell	Jef	–	9E	2N	3	NE
Jesse Vauster? [Veuster?]	Jef	–	10E	4N	34	NE

Joseph Echert? [Eckert?]	Jef	–	4E	2S	5	SE
James Hays	Jef	–	9E	5N	33	NE
Joshua Deputy? [Depuly?]	Jef	–	8E	4N	8	SW
Solomon Deputy? [Depuly?]	Jef	–	8E	5N	30	SE
Richard Slythe	Jef	–	6E	3S	18	SW
John W. Coffee	Jef	–	4E	2N	24	SE
Thomas Louden	Jef	–	9E	2N	24	SE
Jacob Garrett	Jef	–	5E	2N	19	NE
John Brower	Jef	–	4E	2N	28	SE
Martin Overturff	Jef	–	11E	6N	26	NE
Christopher Marro? [Marrs?]	Jef	–	4E	1N	2	NW
Henry Dewalt	Jef	–	4E	2N	14	NW
Philip Byerley	Jef	–	5E	2S	7	SE
George Capely	Jef	–	4E	2S	23	NE
Abraham Long	Jef	–	9E	4N	15	NW
Samuel Brown	Jef	–	3E	1N	26	SE
James Alexander	Jef	–	9E	5N	24	SE

1625   2 Apr 1814   A/5/373
LO Cin
Transmits patents

Abraham Frye? [Tye?]	Cin	E*	4	3	10	NE
William Fenton	Cin	MR	10	5	31	NE
Giles Mattin	Cin	**	3E 13–		2	SW
John Larrison?	Cin	W*	1	8	23	SE
William Baerlin?	Cin	**	14E 17–		18	NE
James Cloyd	Cin	E*	3	5	1	NE
Jacob? [Joab?] White	Cin	MR	1	3	8	SE
Amos Boardman & David G. Boardman	Cin	W*	2	5	25	–
Samuel Alexander	Cin	MR	10	3	21	NE
Israel Davis	Cin	W*	1	8	35	SE
Alexander Mills	Cin	E*	5	7	20	SE
John Morrow	Cin	W*	1	14	14	NE
James Gordon? [Gosden?]	Cin	E*	2	5	19	SW
William Dickey	Cin	**	12E 14–		5	+
George Price	Cin	E*	2	9	12	SW
David Hanna	Cin	MR	9	6	12	+
John Painter	Cin	E*	2	9	12	SE
John Howard	Cin	W*	1	5	4	NW
Julius Lane	Cin	E*	2	6	26	SW
John Stanley	Cin	W*	1	12	14	SE
Leonard Sayre? [Layn?]	Cin	E*	2	3	15	NW
John Nubel? [Niebel?]	Cin	MR	6	1	8	NE
William Thorn	Cin	**	13E 16–		21	SW
Joseph Williamson	Cin	E*	1	9	32	NE
John Lock	Cin	E*	3	7	20	NE
Leonard Sayre	Cin	E*	1	3	22	SW
William Henderson	Cin	MR	10	3	32	NW
John Hubbert, Senior	Cin	W*	2	4	10	SE
Jones? [Jonas?] Hanes	Cin	E*	1	4	27	NW
James Cloyd	Cin	E*	3	5	26	SE
Joseph Nelson	Cin	W*	1	12	28	SE
George Handley	Cin	E*	1	3	9	NW
George Stewart	Cin	MR	10	6	21	SE
John Hudlow	Cin	E*	2	8	11	NW
Samuel Morison	Cin	E*	2	4	14	NW
Joseph E. Milburn	Cin	W*	2	4	1	SE
William Sturgeon	Cin	E*	5	4	10	NE
Isaac Reynolds	Cin	MR	11	4	25	NE
Jacob Tartar? [Tartans?]	Cin	**	13E 13–		3	NW
James Tharp, Senior	Cin	E*	4	4	18	NW
Eliakim Hardin	Cin	**	13E 15–		31	SW
George Vincy? [Viney?]	Cin	MR	10	5	18	NW
Joseph Layton Survey 1 & 4	Cin	MR	9	4	32	–
Samuel Dinwidee	Cin	MR	5	3	11	NW
Elisha Adamson, heirs of	Cin	MR	11	5	32	SE
John Hainey? [Harney?]	Cin	E*	4	3	36	NW
Jacob Miller	Cin	E*	4	1	7	–
Obadiah Welliver	Cin	E*	1	4	23	SE

*Presumably EML, or WML, is meant.
**Second Principal Meridian.

[139]

1626   2 Apr 1814   A/5/374
LO Stu
Transmits patents

Edward Milner	Stu	–	6	16	3	E
Jesse Milner	Stu	–	6	16	10	NE
Jacob Munich? [Minnich?]	Stu	–	8	10	22	SW
Robert Andrews	Stu	–	8	9	5	S
John Kimel	Stu	–	5	12	20	SW
Thomas Mayes	Stu	–	4	12	13	NW
John George	Stu	–	2	6	19	SE
John Galbraith	Stu	–	6	18	13	NE
Alexander Rankin	Stu	–	3	8	15	SW
Hans Wilson	Stu	–	4	11	18	NE
James Biden? [Braden?]	Stu	–	3	11	32	SW
David Cunningham	Stu	–	6	10	5?	NE
Peter Springer	Stu	–	3	14	21	NE
John Cadwallader, Senior	Stu	–	7	11	12	SE
Thomas Adams	Stu	–	3	12	27	NE
John Cadwallader	Stu	–	7	11	12	NE
John Pollock	Stu	–	4	10	15	SE
Henry Armine	Stu	–	3	6	26	NE
Basil Ridgeway	Stu	–	6	9	29	NW
Christopher Dillon	Stu	–	7	10	3	NE
Matthew Adams	Stu	–	3	14	22	NE
Robert Manwell	Stu	–	2	11	29	NW
Thomas Clear?	Stu	–	2	8	22	SE
Peter Wise	Stu	–	8	9	26	NW
Lambert Myers	Stu	–	5	15	27	SE
Joseph Danal?	Stu	–	5	7	11	NW
Jacob Bachtel	Stu	–	8	12	17	N
Jacob Bachtel	Stu	–	8	12	19	E
Jesse Bates	Stu	–	6	9	20	SE
Samuel Kemble? [Kimble?]	Stu	–	2	11	27?	NE
Esau Powell & Jacob Powell	Stu	–	2	11	29	NE
John Porterfield	Stu	–	4	7	7	SW
Andrew Barngas?	Stu	–	2	11	28	NE
Angus McIntosh	Stu	–	2	10	23	NE
Benjamin Miller	Stu	–	7	17	19	SE
Isaac Clay	Stu	–	9	11	29	NE
Robert Williams	Stu	–	10	1	22	+
Joseph Day	Stu	–	3	9	22	SW
Abraham Yandt	Stu	–	9	9	24	NE
John Ogle	Stu	–	5	13	35	SE
Samuel Vale	Stu	–	1	7	31	NW
William McCloskey	Stu	–	1	8	22	SW
Joseph* Groninger	Stu	–	9	10	23	SE
Frederick Heron	Stu	–	8	10	34	NE
Peter Yeagley	Stu	–	2	8	23	NW
Jesse Calahan	Stu	–	3	16	21	SW
John Miller	Stu	–	3	14	35	NW
Samuel McCormick	Stu	–	2	10	19	SW
Peter Wise	Stu	–	8	9	26	NW
Robert Hall	Stu	–	7	10	2	NW
Thomas Rogers, Senior	Stu	–	1	7	4	NE
John Pollock	Stu	–	5	11	10	SE
Casparus Garretson	Stu	–	7	11	23	NE
James McC. Galbraith	Stu	–	4	10	23	NE
Derrick Johnson	Stu	–	6	11	31	SE
Thomas Williams	Stu	–	5	7	21	SW
Peter Lindesmith	Stu	–	4	15	34	SE

*Originally written as John, but perhaps crossed out.

1627   4 Apr 1814   A/5/376
Hon. E. Hempstead, St. Louis, [Missouri]
Patent will be issued to you as soon as report of
    Recorder of Land Titles at St. Louis has been re-
    ceived. Mentions Certificate 35 to John Graham
    for 471 arpents of land, plus two transfers of
    title.

1628   4 Apr 1814   A/5/376
George Abel, Hillsborough, Loudon County, Virginia
Transmits patent

George Abel	Stu	–	4	11	22	NW

1629   4 Apr 1814   A/5/376
John Vale, York Town, Pennsylvania
Transmits patent

John Vale	Stu	–	1	7	20	SW

1630   5 Apr 1814   A/5/377
Hon. Hugh Caperton, U.S. House of Representatives
Price of reserved sections in Ohio Company's land
    purchase, on sale at LO Mar, is $4.00 per acre.

1631   5 Apr 1814   A/5/377
Frederick Bates, Esq., St. Louis, Missouri Territory
The Shibboleth mine may again be leased to -- Dodge,
    -- Wilson, & -- Craighead for up to three years,
    if satisfactory terms can be arranged.

1632   7 Apr 1814   A/5/378
Jesse Spencer, Reg Chl
Transmits patents

John Moffitt	Chl	–	20	7	9	NW
Allen Scott	Chl	Mil	12	7	24	SW
J. Forsyth	Chl	Mil	12	7	24	NW

1633   7 Apr 1814   A/5/378
Hon. -- Jennings, U.S. House of Representatives
Transmits patent

John Lapp? [Lopp?]	Vin	–	4E	2S	14	NW

1634   7 Apr 1814   A/5/378
Thomas Gibson, Reg Can
Construes certain sections of the Act of 11 Feb 1805.

1635   8 Apr 1814   A/5/379
Hon. -- Jennings, U.S. House of Representatives
Transmits patent

C. L. Byrns	Vin	–	4E	2S	14	E

1636   9 Apr 1814   A/5/379
LO Cin
Transmits patents

Daniel Lowderback	Cin	MR	11	4	5	SW
John Colleson	Cin	MR	9	4	24	NE
John Widney	Cin	EML	6	7	6	SE
Leonard Sparks	Cin	WML	1	8	12	SW
Samuel Riker	Cin	MR	1	4	8	NW
John Moffett	Cin	EML	5	8	13	SE
William McLucas	Cin	*	13	15N	9	NE
William Thorn	Cin	*	13	16-	21	SE
Christian Waldsmith	Cin	MR	1	5	26	+
Samuel Charles	Cin	*	14	18-	28	SW
John Driscol	Cin	MR	7	3	12	SW
Peter Swinehart	Cin	EML	4	4	31	SW
Adam Swinehart	Cin	EML	4	4	30	SE
Jacob Swinehart	Cin	EML	4	4	18	NE
David Wason	Cin	EML	1	9	9	SW
John Addington	Cin	WML	1	14	9	SW
John Weathers & James Conway	Cin	WML	2	4	29	NW

Joseph Sills	Cin	MR	10	3	36	SW
Thomas Brown	Cin	EML	2	6	7	NW
John Fenton	Cin	WML	2	2	36	NE
Stephen Wood	Cin	MR	2	1	8	NE
Jacob Biblet? [Boblet?]	Cin	EML	3	5	12	NE
John Maxwell	Cin	*	14	16-	17	NE
Arthur Thomas, heirs of	Cin	MR	12	5	32	NW
James Johnston	Cin	MR	5	2	8	NW
Elizabeth McKee	Cin	MR	9	3	10	NE
Zebulon Baird	Cin	MR	9	4	18	SW
Moses McIlvain	Cin	MR	13	5	25	NE
Samuel Brown	Cin	EML	1	6	1	SE
John Merritt	Cin	MR	11	3	32	SW
Francis Humphreys	Cin	MR	7	4	36	SW
John Miller	Cin	WML	1	10	2	NW
Leonard Schnipe	Cin	MR	6	1	11	SW
Jacob Weybrecht	Cin	EML	5	5	15	NW
Thomas Townsend	Cin	WML	1	5	5	NW
Robert Burns	Cin	EML	6	6	31	SW
James Nichols, Senior	Cin	*	12	14-	12	SW
William Lease	Cin	EML	3	7	35	NW

*East of Second Principal Meridian.

1637   9 Apr 1814   A/5/380
Jesse Spencer, Reg Chl
Transmits corrected patent

--	Chl	-	20	10	19	W

1638   9 Apr 1814   A/5/381
Hon. M. S? Miller
Transmits transcript from records of West Florida
   containing deed in favor of Marg Orgam?; mentions
   letter from M. Miller.

1639   9 Apr 1814   A/5/381
Joseph Wood, Reg Mar
Transmits final certificate, presumably for tract
   described

--	Mar	-	5	5	32	NE

1640   9 Apr 1814   A/5/381
Wyllys Silliman, Reg Zan
Transmits U.S. Treasury receipt

John Horniringhaus? [Hamringhaus?]	Zan	-	2	8	25	SW

1641   11 Apr 1814   A/5/382
Ephraim Thayer, Co-assignee of B. Thayer, Zanesville
Transmits patent

Ephraim Thayer	Mil	-	6	2	1	36
Ephraim Thayer	Mil	-	6	2	1	39

1642   11 Apr 1814   A/5/382
Thomas Gibson, Reg Can
Transmits first certificate & U.S. Treasury receipt

James Nesbit	Can	-	19	20	14	SE

1643   12 Apr 1814   A/5/382
Benjamin Hough, Chillicothe [Ohio]
Answers inquiry regarding boundaries of Virginia
   Military District of Ohio [of which Hough was a
   surveyor]; mentions Round Head's Town at head-
   waters of Scioto River.

1644   12 Apr 1814   A/5/383
Hon. John Rhea of Tennessee, U.S. House of Representatives
Comments on letter from C. Royston, who served three
   years during the Revolution; his claim to land
   should be on the state of Virginia.

1645   14 Apr 1814   A/5/383
Jesse Spencer, Reg Chl
Transmits final certificate

John Stine	Chl	-	21	11	9	SE
John Stine	Chl	-	21	11	9	SW
John Stine	Chl	-	21	11	9	NW

1646   16 Apr 1814   A/5/383
C. Royston, Knoxville, Tennessee
"Your letter . . . has been referred to me. In it,
   you state that when you were a soldier, you were
   promised one hundred acres of land. If you served
   to the end of the war, and can send me your discharge or other sufficient proof of that fact, I
   will procure for you a warrant for 100 acres, if
   you have not (nor any agent for you) already obtained a warrant from the United States. If you
   served in the Virginia line, and have not received
   any land from that state, I believe it is not yet
   too late for an application, but the application
   must be made at the land office in Richmond."

1647   20 Apr 1814   A/5/386
Governor [Ninian] Edwards, Illinois Territory
The President [of the United States] approves of the
   lease of the Saline near the Wabash River to John
   Bates & Company.

1648   22 Apr 1814   A/5/387
Leonard White, Wyllis Hargraves, & Philip Trammel
Request that they examine the lands on and about the
   United States Saline in Illinois Territory and re-
   port regarding them to GLO.

1649   23 Apr 1814   A/5/388
Thomas Doigs? [Dorgs?], Albany, New York
The United States cannot pay a fee for your plan to
   distribute its lands to agriculturists without
   first examining it.

1650   23 Apr 1814   A/5/389
John Read, Reg Hun
Transmits patent

John Binnion	Hun	EML	2	3	34*	NE

*Might read 24.

1651   25 Apr 1814   A/5/390
LO WPR
Transmits patents

Nathaniel Scudder	WPR	EML	1	1	11	SE
John Brent	WPR	EML	9	3	3	SW
John Brent	WPR	EML	9	3	10	NW
Duncan Stewart	WPR	EML	1	1	24	+
John Travis	WPR	EML	5	2	33	NW
John Dixson	WPR	EML	2	2	41	NE
David Lea	WPR	EML	4	1	12	NE
John Germany	WPR	EML	1	2	27	SE
John Germany	WPR	EML	2	2	36	SW

1652   25 Apr 1814 A/5/391
Samuel Gwathmey, Reg Jef, & Edmund H. Taylor, Rec
 Jef
Directs sale of fractional sections lying around
 Clark's Grant.

1653   25 Apr 1814 A/5/391
Daniel Symmes, Reg Cin
Notes discrepancies
Jacob Stover*   Cin EML 5 4 7 NE
--**   Cin MR 9 4 7 SW
--***   Cin - 1 15 29 NW
*Entry by G. P. Torrence is in error; Stover paid
 in full.
**Entry by L. Davis is in error; tract previously
 sold.
***First instalment paid, but tract does not appear
 to have been applied for.

1654   27 Apr 1814 A/5/391
Nehemiah Tilton, Reg Wsh, Mississippi Territory
Interest payments due
William Lattimore   Wsh - 5 1 8 NW
James Lea   Wsh - 5 1 8 SW

1655   27 Apr 1814 A/5/392
Samuel Smith, Rec EPR, St. Stephens, Mississippi
 Territory
Expenses allowed for moving LO at St. Stephens to
 Fort Stoddard.

1656   30 Apr 1814 A/5/393
Thomas Sloo? Cincinnati
Appointment as Reg Shw.

1657   30 Apr 1814 A/5/393
Shadrach Bond
Appointment as Rec Kas replacing John Caldwell, who
 has been appointed Rec Shw.

1658   30 Apr 1814 A/5/393
John Caldwell, Kaskaskia [Illinois Territory]
Appointed Rec Shw.

1659   30 Apr 1814 A/5/394
Daniel Symmes, Reg Cin; James Findlay, Rec Cin
Transmits Act for the relief of Dennis Clark, passed
 18 Apr 1814, to be acted upon.

1660   2 May 1814 A/5/394
Thomas Gibson, Reg Can
Requests final certificate
Alexander McCutcheon* Can - 17 23 29 SW
*Assignee of Stephen D. Minton, assignee of Hugh
 Wiley.

1661   2 May 1814 A/5/394
John Sloane, Rec Can
Transmits patents
Hugh McCullough   Can - 13 13 1 SW
Hugh McCullough   Can - 13 13 12 NE

1662   2 May 1814 A/5/395
Samuel Finley, Rec Chl
Duplicate receipts requested on transactions with
 the following purchasers [and year of purchase]
Henry Markle, 1804   -- Harmon, 1808
Andrew Barr, 1807   John McNaughten, 1808
Samuel Arrowsmith, 1807 Elizabeth Russell, 1808
Noah Zane, 1807   Jacob Coffelt, 1808
John Huber, 1807   John Webster, 1808
John Shiplor, 1807   Thomas Worthington, 1809
G. Shuster, 1808   Alexander McClintock, 1809
Ns. Delong, 1808   John Waggoner, 1809
William Stump, 1808   William Irwin, 1809
William McFarland, 1808

1663   3 May 1814 A/5/396
Benjamin Hough, Chillicothe
Received four bound volumes & surveys of Virginia
 Military District of Ohio, delivered by wagoner
 Jonathan Anderson.

1664   5 May 1814 A/5/397
Thomas Doige, Albany, New York
Your plan for the disposal of public lands is returned herewith, there being numerous objections
 to it.

1665   5 May 1814 A/5/398
LO Jef
Transmits patents
Samuel Demaree   Jef - 11E 4N 5 SW
John Braselton   Jef - 4E 2N 23 SE
David Findley   Jef - 1E 2N 4 NE
John Smiley   Jef - 4E 2N 14 NE
James Crawford   Jef - 10E 4N 29 NE
Robert Long   Jef - 3E 5S 7 NE
James Wooley   Jef - 10E 7N 36 SW
Daniel Wooley   Jef - 10E 6N 3 NW
James Davis   Jef - 4E 3N 27 SE
Thomas Taylor   Jef - 9E 3N 15 SE
Henry Watson   Jef - 3E 5S 8 SE
Hezekiah Coates   Jef - 4E 3S 1 SW
John Jones   Jef - 8E 4N 3 SE

1666   5 May 1814 A/5/398
LO Can
Transmits patents
Samuel Hoffmire   Can - 19 18 11 NW
Nathan Fidler   Can - 20 18 25 SW
Adam Tiner   Can - 15 22 18 SE
David Ayers   Can - 14 18 14 NE
Thomas Mitchell   Can - 19 18 4 SE
George Boydstone   Can - 12 17 28 NW

1667   5 May 1814 A/5/399
LO Cin
Transmits patents
John Shellabarger &
 Martin Shellabarger Cin MR 8 4 29 SW
Joseph Reynolds   Cin MR 11 3 9 SW
Leonard Knaf, heirs of Cin MR 7 3 29 NW
David Blue   Cin MR 2 4 22 SW
Levi Hawkins   Cin EML? 2 5 1 SE
William Wells   Cin MR 10 1 8 +
Abiathar Hathaway Cin * 12 14- 26 SW

Joseph Stephenson	Cin	WML	1	13	20	NE
John Ross	Cin	MR	9	2	28	SW
Elijah F. Davis	Cin	MR	13	4	19	NW
Christopher Smith	Cin	WML	1	10	8	SE
William Stuart	Cin	EML	2	3	17	NE
Moses Reardon	Cin	WML	1	9	14	SE
Robert Dixon	Cin	EML	5	7	7	SE
Charles Collet	Cin	*	13	12-	34	SW
William Manson	Cin	MR	11	2	23	SW
Henry Coons	Cin	EML	1	4	11	SE
Conrad Critz	Cin	MR	8	6	17	SE
Phinehas Roberts	Cin	WML	1	14	20	NW
Henry Beck	Cin	WML	2	12	26	SW
Samuel Enyard	Cin	MR	3	2	8	SE
Amy Woods	Cin	EML	5	5	30	SE
Thomas Newell	Cin	MR	13	5	28	NE
Samuel Newell	Cin	MR	13	5	28	SW
Ebenezer Heaton, Senior	Cin	*	13	14-	21	NW
Daniel Heaton	Cin	*	13	14-	19	NW
Samuel Job	Cin	WML	1	12	4	SW
Josias Lambert	Cin	*	13	15-	27	NW
John Lower	Cin	EML	2	9	25	SE
Robert Hews	Cin	EML	2	3	22	NE
Peter Andrews	Cin	EML	4	4	9	NW
Peter Vanordsdal	Cin	EML	3	5	17	SE
Michael Flack &						
William Flack	Cin	WML	2	5	36	NW
Amer Bruce	Cin	WML	2	5	1	SE
Abraham Hosteller	Cin	EML	4	5	23	SE
William Conner	Cin	*	12	13-	4	SW
Marcus Clark	Cin	MR	12	4	35	NW
David Fudge	Cin	Pre	5	2	2	E
Jacob Cassart	Cin	Pre	8	3	20	-
Jesse Wilson	Cin	Pre	5	3	14	NW
John Sutherland	Cin	Pre	7	3	2	+
Lewis Dewees	Cin	Pre	11	1	7	NW
William Lamme	Cin	Pre	6	9	1	N
William Lamme	Cin	Pre	1	10	1	-
Jacob Prillaman? [Prellaman?]	Cin	Pre	10	2	7	N
J. McCasher? heirs of	Cin	Pre	5	2	25	E
Edward Newcom	Cin	Pre	7	2	13	SW
Thomas Corey	Cin	Pre	9	2	3	SW
Daniel Corey	Cin	Pre	4	3	7	SE+
Samuel Wharton	Cin	Pre	5	3	15	SE
John Holderman	Cin	Pre	9	1	2	+
Lemuel Hopkins	Cin	EML	2	7	9	NW
John Ebert	Cin	MR	11	3	5	NE
Solomon Beck	Cin	WML	2	12	36	E
James Marshal	Cin	EML	6	5	33	NW
Abraham Hess	Cin	EML	5	5	29	SE
Conrad Critz	Cin	MR	8	6	17	SW
Archibald Moore	Cin	MR	13	4	17	SW
John Bridges	Cin	*	12	13-	20	SE
James Vaughan	Cin	WML	2	6	35	SW
John Miller	Cin	WML	1	11	12	NW

*East of Second Principal Meridian.

1668   9 May 1814   A/5/402
Thomas Gibson, Reg Cin
Transmits U.S. Treasury receipt
| John Wade | Can | - | 9 | 9 | 31 | NW |

1669   9 May 1814   A/5/403
Wyllys Silliman, Reg Zan
Transmits U.S. Treasury receipt
| John Wade | Zan | - | 3 | 9 | 3 | NE |

1670   10 May 1814   A/5/403
John Badollet, Reg Vin
Your letter regarding suit against -- Posey in Kentucky will be laid before the President [of the United States].

1671   13 May 1814   A/5/403
Samuel Finley, Rec Chl
For audit of your accounts, please send vouchers for the following transactions [with year occurring]:
John Urrly, 1806   Martin Telkurr? [Zelkurr?] 1806
R. F. Slaughter, 1806   George Harness, 1806

1672   13 May 1814   A/5/404
Peter Wilson, Rec Stu
Was there not an error in the 1812 payment on this 1806 transaction?
| Conrad Dudderer | Stu | - | 2 | 13 | 15 | SW |

1673   14 May 1814   A/5/404
Alexander Ogle, Somerset, Pennsylvania
Land sales in Illinois Territory will begin on the first Monday in October [1814] at LO Shw.

1674   16 May 1814   A/5/405
Thomas Gibson, Reg Can
There is no redress available to purchaser. "The errors of surveyors will sometimes be in favor of purchasers--sometimes against them; each takes the error that falls to his lot."

1675   16 May 1814   A/5/405
Hon. Secretary of the U.S. Treasury
"I entirely agree with governor [--] Clark, that the public mineral lands situate in the Territory of Missouri, are worthy the consideration of government and that, if the rapacious speculations of individuals have progressed to the alarming extent he portrays, it is high time to check them. . . ."

1676   17 May 1814   A/5/406
Thomas Gibson, Reg Can
Returns corrected patent for Daniel Tilbrough [no tract description given].

1677   18 May 1814   A/5/406
Jesse Spencer, Reg Chl
Transmits patent
| John Stine? [Stone?] | Chl | WS | 21 | 11 | 8 | SE |

1678   18 May 1814   A/5/407
Joseph Wood, Reg Mar
Transmits patents
| Peter Bayles | Mar | - | 13 | 5 | 8 | NE |
| John Gray | Mar | - | 5 | 3 | 36 | NW |

1679   19 May 1814   A/5/407
Joseph C. Gist, Westminster, Frederick County, Maryland

"Annexed you have a copy of a Caveat filed in this office by James Taylor, agent for James Morrison, against a military land warrant in favor of Mordecai Gist. On examining the warrant which you left yesterday, I find on the back of it an assignment in favor of Morrison, although a paper is pasted over it, and the assignment crossed.

"I have directed that a patent shall not issue, at present, and that the lots you located shall be reserved until you have settled the claim of Mr. Morrison.

"[Caveat] I hereby enter a Caveat against No. 108, a Military land warrant, for eight hundred and fifty acres of land, in the name of William Calhoon, executor of the last will and testament of Mordecai Gist, in trust for the uses and purposes mentioned in his last will. He the said Gist, being a brigadier-general in the Maryland line--Because a warrant issued to the said Gist, in his life time, No. 850, for a similar quantity, which warrant was transferred to James Morrison, by the said Gist, as appears by an assignment on the original warrant, now presented for location. [signed] James Taylor, agent for James Morrison, Washington, March 29th 1810."

1680   20 May 1814   A/5/408
John Badollet, Reg Vin
Writes regarding claims of certain citizens of Kentucky to lands on islands in the Ohio River; may have to ask for a Supreme Court decision thereon.

Also instructs Reg Vin to select a particularly flagrant case of stripping bark [from trees on public land] for tanneries and to sue the miscreants as an example to others.

1681   20 May 1814   A/5/408
Robert Wickliffe, District Attorney, Lexington [Kentucky]
Asks him to consider case of *The Heirs of May* vs. *Francis Posey, in Ejectment*, filed in the circuit court at Frankfort, Kentucky. Encloses plats of land in question. Also mentions a similar case brought by a Mr. Henly.

1682   20 May 1814   A/5/409
Samuel Finley, Rec Chl
Transmits U.S. Treasury receipt
John Gachnour? [Gerchnour?] Chl - 19 16 8 N

1683   20 May 1814   A/5/409
Daniel Symmes, Reg Cin
Discrepancy noted; the land was entered by A. Lasen? Samuel Beaten? [Beater?] Cin * 12 14- 25 SE
*East of Second Principal Meridian.

1684   20 May 1814   A/5/410
Peter Wilson, Rec Stu
Transmits U.S. Treasury receipt
Daniel Hisey   Stu - 2 12 21 SW
Daniel Hisey   Stu - 2 12 21 NE

1685   20 May 1814   A/5/411
Lewis Sewell, Reg [EPR] St. Stephens, Mississippi Territory

Expects information shortly regarding -- Vanderhorst's claim.

1686   23 May 1814   A/5/411
Daniel Symmes, Reg Cin
Assignment of J. C. Boardman (a minor) to B. Squires was illegal.

1687   23 May 1814   A/5/412
Nehemiah Tilton, Reg Wsh, Mississippi Territory
Rec WPR states that Robert Montgomery purchased 200 acres of land on 1 Jan 1809, & that he has been ejected on the plea that the land was covered by a British patent confirmed by the U.S. Commissioners in 1803. Inquires as to the circumstances of the 1809 sale.

1688   23 May 1809   A/5/413
John Sloane, Rec Can
Transmits U.S. Treasury receipt
John Wright   Can - 7 9 18 SW

1689   24 May 1814   A/5/413
LO Hun
Transmits patents

Obadiah Jones	Hun	- 1E	2	28	SE
John Brahan	Hun	- 1E	3	13	NW
Charles Carrell	Hun	- 3W	2	14	NE
John Lamberton	Hun	- 2E	3	30	NW
John Couch	Hun	- 1W	4	22	SE
Matthew W. Weaver	Hun	- 1W	3	1	SW
James Roper	Hun	- 1E	3	9	NW
James McCrackin	Hun	- 2W	3	5	SW
John Nicholson	Hun	- 1W	3	29	NE
Robert Lankford	Hun	- 1W	4	3	SE
Thomas Miller	Hun	- 2E	1	9	SE
Robert Watson	Hun	- 1E	2	3	SW
Peter Bass	Hun	- 1W	4	2	SW
Joseph Adams	Hun	- 2W	1	27	SE
William Simpson	Hun	- 1E	5	17	NE
Thomas Strong	Hun	- 1E	3	7	NE
Elijah Hussey	Hun	- 1W	3	31	SE
John Grayson	Hun	- 1E	5	2	SE
Thomas Miller	Hun	- 2E	1	10	+
Jesse Wilson	Hun	- 1E	3	14	NW
Matthew W. Weaver	Hun	- 1W	3	11	NE
Laurence Carlile	Hun	- 1E	3	23	NE
Laurence Carlile	Hun	- 1E	3	23	NE
William McWilliams	Hun	- 1W	4	10	NW
James McGown	Hun	- 1E	1	26	SE
Hugh Rogers	Hun	- 1W	4	4	SE
William Helms	Hun	- 1E	2	28	NW
Richard Crowson	Hun	- 1E	3	24	NW
Jacob Prewett	Hun	- 1E	2	21	SW
James Douglass	Hun	- 1E	3	12	NE
James Douglass	Hun	- 1E	3	12	SE
S[olomo]n? Massingale	Hun	- 2E	3	30	SW
S[amue]l? Johnston	Hun	- 2W	3	24	SE
Henry Miller	Hun	- 1W	2	31	NE
David Cobb	Hun	- 2E	4	32	+
Samuel Acklin	Hun	- 1W	4	23	SE
Abel Hill	Hun	- 2E	3	27	SE
Stephen Smith	Hun	- 1E	4	28	SW
Wallis Estill	Hun	- 1W	1	13	NE
Joseph Matthews	Hun	- 1E	2	29	NW
Charles Carrell	Hun	- 3W	2	12	SW
Thomas McCrary	Hun	- 1E	2	23	SE

Obadiah Jones	Hun	-	2W	2	24	NW
Samuel Allen	Hun	-	1E	1	17	NW
Samuel Allen	Hun	-	1E	1	17	SW
Littleberry Adams	Hun	-	2W	1	29	SE
John Webster	Hun	-	1E	4	8	SW
Benjamin Wilson	Hun	-	1E	3	14	SE
Samuel Allen	Hun	-	1E	1	19	NW
Samuel Allen	Hun	-	1W	1	24	SE
Wallis Estill	Hun	-	1W	1	13	SW
William Hogan	Hun	-	1W	4	12	SE
John Johnston	Hun	-	2E	2	32	+
John Withers	Hun	-	2W	4	12	+
Woodliff Bevil	Hun	-	1E	3	8	SE
Samuel Allen	Hun	-	1E	1	20	NW
Samuel Allen	Hun	-	1E	1	19	SW
Samuel Allen	Hun	-	1E	1	20	NE
Samuel Allen	Hun	-	1E	1	19	NE
Samuel Allen	Hun	-	1E	1	19	SE
Obadiah Jones	Hun	-	2W	2	13	SW
John Fletcher	Hun	-	1W	3	3	SW
Solomon Massingale	Hun	-	2E	3	30	SE
Francis E. Harris	Hun	-	1E	3	21	NW
William Moseley	Hun	-	3W	1	36	NE
William Moseley	Hun	-	3W	1	36	NW
William Moseley	Hun	-	3W	1	36	SE
Caleb Owen	Hun	-	1E	3	3	NE
Jacob Prewett*	Hun	-	1E	2	21	NW
John Bridwell	Hun	-	1E	2	17	NW
Absalom Looney	Hun	-	1W	4	12	SW
Jacob Prewitt*	Hun	-	1E	2	17	SE
James Woods	Hun	-	2E	1	9	NW
Samuel Allen	Hun	-	1E	1	17	SE
D[anie]l? Tillman &						
James Scruggs	Hun	-	2W	2	2	NW
John Allison	Hun	-	1W	3	32	NE
John Lowry	Hun	-	1E	2	17	SW
Floode Mitchell	Hun	-	3W	1	25	NW
Flemming Hodges	Hun	-	2W	3	25	NW
Floode Mitchell	Hun	-	3W	1	26	NE
William Gray	Hun	-	1W	4	8	NW
Henry Harless	Hun	-	1E	3	14	SW
Samuel Allen	Hun	-	1W	1	24	NE

*So spelled.

1690   25 May 1814   A/5/415
LO Hun
Transmits patents

David Childress	Hun	-	1E	2	2	NW
America M. Allison	Hun	-	1E	2	34	SE
M[ichae]l? Montgomery	Hun	-	1W	3	35	SW
Daniel Wright	Hun	-	1E	2	26	NW
Daniel Wright	Hun	-	1E	2	26	NE
William Shackleford	Hun	-	1E	2	24	SW
Samuel Davis	Hun	-	2E?	1	29	SE
Samuel Moon & John Moon	Hun	-	2E?	3	31	SW
Elijah Franklin	Hun	-	2E?	1	4	SE
John Wright	Hun	-	-?	2	25	NW
Thomas McCrary	Hun	-	1E?	2	23	SW

Note: Ranges with question marks obscured in microfilm, but probably could be read on the original document.

1691   28 May 1814   A/5/416
Josiah Meigs, Surveyor General, Cincinnati, Ohio
Discusses best way to survey lands in Missouri Territory; mentions letters from -- Bates & -- Russell, & suggestions of -- Rector. Feels that surveys will have to be delayed, because of general Indian hostilities.

1692   2 Jun 1814   A/5/417
William Reynolds, Canton [Ohio]
Acknowledges letter reporting death of [Thomas] Gibson, Reg Can.

1693   2 Jun 1814   A/5/417
Peter Wilson, Rec Stu
Transmits U.S. Treasury receipt

Jacob Beard	Stu	-	8	11	21	NW

1694   4 Jun 1814   A/5/419
Daniel Symmes, Reg Cin
Requests final certificate; if there is any outstanding balance due, it will be paid by -- Baum of Cincinnati, according to Jennings

William Jennings*	Cin	WML	4	1	2	+

*Assignee of Thomas Thompson.

1695   6 Jun 1814   A/5/419
Maurice Moran, Detroit
No fee required for copy of patent.

1696   8 Jun 1814   A/5/419
Reasin Beall, Reg Can
Forwards appointment to office & instructions.

1697   8 Jun 1814   A/5/420
Wyllys Silliman, Reg Zan
Requests patent corrections

--	Zan	Mil	8	8	5	NE
--	Zan	-	9	8	25	SW

1698   8 Jun 1814   A/5/420
John Read, Reg Hun
Shortpayment on land described below; also requests final certificates for Thomas Freeman, whose Washington, D.C., agent is -- Bradley

--	Hun	-	1W	2	23	NE

1699   8 Jun 1814   A/5/420
Samuel Gwathmey, Reg Jef
Short payment & lacks assignment

--	Jef	-	3E	2N	24	SE

1700   8 Jun 1814   A/5/420
David Hoge, Reg Stu
Overpayment

--	Stu	-	7	10	36	NE

1701   8 Jun 1814   A/5/420
Daniel Symmes, Reg Cin
The following accounts show discrepancies, as noted

Arthur Dixon [assignment needed]	Cin	*	12	13-	2	NE
-- [short paid]	Cin	EML	1	2	33	NE
-- [over paid]	Cin	MR	8	5	6	NW
-- [short paid]	Cin	MR	9	6	33	NE
-- [over paid]	Cin	EML	4	6	13	SE
-- [short paid]	Cin	MR	9	2	22	NE
-- [over paid]	Cin	MR	11	5	12	NE
-- [short paid]	Cin	EML	3	4	8	NE

*East of Second Principal Meridian.

1702   10 Jun 1814   A/5/421
Frederick Bates, Recorder of Land Titles, St. Louis,
    Missouri Territory
Instructions regarding leasing of mineral rights by
    the United States government.

1703   10 Jun 1814   A/5/422
Lewis Sewall, Reg EPR, St. Stephens, Mississippi
    Territory
No evidence to support the claim of Elias Vander-
    horst, even though allowed in the investigation
    made by Parke Walton [former Reg EPR].
Has also received a certificate in favor of Joseph
    Campbell, representative of Augustin Rochon &
    Louisa Rochon, assigned by his administrator to
    Lemuel Henry, & by the executors of Lemuel Henry
    to George Fisher.

1704   13 Jun 1814   A/5/423
David Hoge, Reg Stu
Forwards corrected patent for James Vale [no tract
    description given].

1705   13 Jun 1814   A/5/423
John Badollet, Reg Vin
Transmits first certificate

Joseph Brownley	Vin	-	3E	5S 31	-
Joseph Brownley	Vin	-	3E	5S 32	-

1706   15 Jun 1814   A/5/424
Hon. Edward Hempstead, St. Louis, Missouri Territory
Transmits certificate from Recorder of Land Titles.
    Patents cannot issue, as land description is too
    vague. "Claimants had better wait till their
    tracts can be described with precision."

1707   16 Jun 1814   A/5/42?
Daniel Symmes, Reg Cin
Transmits U.S. Treasury receipt

Joseph Penn*	Cin	MR	8	3 17	SW

*Assignee of West Burgess.

1708   18 Jun 1814   A/5/425
Governor [Ninian] Edwards, Sydney Grove
Has received your recommendation of Col. Benjamin
    Stephenson for RecKas; however, Shadrach Bond was
    already appointed, when John Caldwell was trans-
    ferred to Rec Shw.

1709   18 Jun 1814   A/5/426
LO Zan
Transmits patents

Henry Miller	Zan Mil	4	9	19	SE
John Hanna	Zan Mil	3	3	5	NW
John Bryan & James Bryan	Zan Mil	9	4	12	NW
Timothy M. Gates	Zan	-	12	11 33	E+
Edward Miller	Zan	-	12	11 33	W+
Elias Danhaur	Zan	-	13	11 17	NE
George Kreager	Zan Mil	10	1	19	SW
Neale McNaughten	Zan	-	11	13 29	NE
Thomas Bickel, Senior	Zan Mil	4	8	7	SW
John Ramsay & James Ramsay	Zan	-	15	15 18	SE
Peter Lepley	Zan Mil	7	8	25	SW
Thomas Bickel, Senior	Zan Mil	4	8	7	SE
Elam McClain	Zan Mil	8	4	10	SW
Daniel Marriott	Zan Mil	3	1	21	SW
John Concal	Zan Mil	10	7	13	SE
Lewis Laughbaugh	Zan Mil	4	8	12	SW
Isaac Cowgill	Zan Mil	4	4	21	NE
John Fitz Morris	Zan	-	10	9 31	SE
John Calhoon	Zan Mil	10	1	20	NE
Philip Schoff	Zan Mil	4	4	19	SE

1710   18 Jun 1814   A/5/426
LO Cin
Transmits patents

Ephraim Brown	Cin WML	1	11	2	SW
Eli Butler	Cin *	14	16-	21	NW
John Hoover	Cin EML	5	6	34	-
William Harvey	Cin *	13	16-	24	SE
Daniel Seward	Cin EML	2	3	12	SE
David Gray	Cin WML	1	10	36	NE
John Sater	Cin WML	1	8	12	SE
Lemuel Lemmon	Cin WML	1	10	33	SW
Robert Gray	Cin MR	2	1	8	SE
David Carson	Cin WML	2	13	26	NE
Jacob Wolf	Cin EML	1	8	10	W
Michael Cullver	Cin WML	1	12	31	SE
Joseph Jones	Cin EML	6	4	22	SE
David Ewing	Cin *	13	12-	2	SE
William Coe	Cin WML	1	10	7	SW
Jeremiah Cox	Cin *	13	17-	29	SE
William Fincher	Cin *	13	16-	4	SE
John Smith	Cin MR	13	5	22	SE
John Hoover	Cin *	12	16-	23	SE
Felix Ashcroft	Cin EML	1	4	33	SW
Robert Rhea	Cin EML	2	7	7	NE
William Maddock	Cin EML	1	6	1	NE
Elijah Garrison	Cin WML	1	6	2	NW
Tobias Tillman	Cin EML	3	8	28	SW
Enoch D. John	Cin EML	1	4	19	SW
Jesse Jay	Cin EML	6	4	30	SE
William Short	Cin MR	8	1	4	+
Archibald McGrew	Cin MR	11	4	11	SE
Archibald McGrew	Cin MR	11	4	11	NW
John Winn	Cin MR	10	5	6	SW
William Taylor	Cin MR	10	6	15	-
William Taylor	Cin MR	10	6	9	+
John Daniel	Cin MR	12	4	17	SE
Andrew Noffsinger	Cin EML	2	11	20	NE
Peter Studebaker & David Studebaker	Cin EML	2	11	20	SE
David John & Benjamin John	Cin EML	5	4	21	NE

*East of Second Principal Meridian.

1711   20 Jun 1814   A/5/428
LO Chl
Transmits patents

Barnet Henry Bowman	Chl	-	16	16 29	NE
John Waggoner	Chl	-	16	15 4	SE
Andrew List	Chl WS	21	11	22	SE
John Elliott	Chl Mil	18	7	19	NW
Sarah Love	Chl	-	17	6 1	NE
Abraham Graffis	Chl	-	17	16 11	SE
Joseph Dittoe	Chl	-	16	16 28	NW
Peter Rosigh? [Rough?]	Chl	-	19	16 2	NW
Samuel Prough	Chl	-	19	13 32	NW
Jacob Clouse	Chl Mil	16	2	9	NE
William Rawlings	Chl	-	18	4 18	S
William Jones	Chl	-	18	2 9	SW
Henry Bowman	Chl	-	18	14 26	NE
John Barnes	Chl	-	21	5 29	SW
Daniel Smith	Chl Mil	16	2	10	NW
John Hodge	Chl	-	16	16 28	SW
John Hodge	Chl	-	16	16 20	SW

Michael Hinton	Chl	-	20	11	33	NE
John Williamson	Chl	-	19	16	27	SE
Kinnear Spencer &						
Jesse Spencer, Executors	Chl	-	20	14	5	SW
John Williamson	Chl	-	20	12	19	SE
William Edwards	Chl	WS	21	11	34	NE
George Fenstermacher	Chl	-	19	16	31	W
Samuel McWilliams	Chl	Mil	19	7	12	SW
Joash Miller	Chl	MS	21	9	4	SE
William Stump	Chl	WS	22	4	6	+

1712   20 Jun 1814   A/5/428
John Stine, Reading, Berks County, Pennsylvania
Transmits patents

John Stine	Chl	WS	21	11	9	NW
John Stine	Chl	WS	21	11	9	SE

1713   20 Jun 1814   A/5/429
James Crawford, Steubenville [Ohio]
Transmits patent

James Crawford	Stu	-	2	7	29	NE

1714   20 Jun 1814   A/5/429
John Deford, Union Town, Pennsylvania
Transmits patent

John Deford	Stu	-	5	15	14	SE

1715   20 Jun 1814   A/5/429
James Davison, Greencastle, Franklin County, Pennsylvania
Transmits patent

James Davison	Can	-	18	22	9	NE

1716   20 Jun 1814   A/5/429
Independence Gist, Esq., Emmitsburgh, Frederick County, Maryland
Transmits patent

M[ordecai?] Gist, heirs or legal representatives of	[tract description not given]

1717   20 Jun 1814   A/5/430
LO Stu
Transmits patents

Daniel Swearingen	Stu	-	2	9	22	NW
Eli Towne, Junior	Stu	-	7	12	31	SE
Thomas Booth	Stu	-	1	7	10	N
Michael Yutzey	Stu	-	8	10	19	SW
John Horseman	Stu	-	5	8	36	NE
Jacob Champer	Stu	-	6	14	6	NE
Michael Miller	Stu	-	6	17	3	SE
James Marsh	Stu	-	1	7	8	SW
Lewis Smith	Stu	-	1	6	19	SE
Jacob Champer	Stu	-	5	14	25	SW
Jacob Shover	Stu	-	4	11	34	NW
David Ebi	Stu	-	8	11	12	NE
Samuel Huston	Stu	-	1	6	21	SW
John Galbraith	Stu	-	6	18	12	SE
Isaac Wood	Stu	-	5	11	18	SW
Thomas Rotch	Stu	-	9	10	5	SW
Thomas Rotch	Stu	-	9	10	8	NW
Thomas Rotch	Stu	-	9	10	9	NW
Thomas Rotch	Stu	-	9	10	4	NE
Thomas Rotch	Stu	-	9	10	4	NW
Thomas Rotch	Stu	-	9	10	5	NE
Thomas Rotch	Stu	-	9	10	4	SE
Thomas Rotch	Stu	-	9	10	9	SW
Thomas Rotch	Stu	-	9	10	5	NW
Thomas Rotch	Stu	-	9	11	31	+
Thomas Rotch	Stu	-	9	11	32	SE
Thomas Rotch	Stu	-	9	11	32	NE
Thomas Rotch	Stu	-	9	10	5	SE
Edie Stewart, heirs of	Stu	-	4	7	29	SE
William Blackledge	Stu	-	6	17	33	NE
John Henry Gilbert	Stu	-	6	9	14	S
Joseph Cochran	Stu	-	1	4	31	NE
Samuel Jones	Stu	-	2	7	11	NE
Charles Hammond	Stu	-	3	6	21	NW
Charles Hammond	Stu	-	3	6	21	NE
James Armstrong	Stu	-	3	13	4	SW
John Nauftzger	Stu	-	5	12	31	SE

1718   21 Jun 1814   A/5/431
LO Jef
Transmits patents

William McKee	Jef	*	2	4S	20	+
John Saffer	Jef	*	5	5S	8	NW
William Stephens	Jef	*	3	2S	33	NW
James Hubbard	Jef	*	4	2S	32	SE
J. Brothers & John Ramsay	Jef	*	9	3N	4	SE
Jacob Short	Jef	*	11	4N	22	NE
William Allen	Jef	*	10	4N	11	NE
David Hillis	Jef	*	11	4N	29	NE
D. Hillis & James Hillis	Jef	*	11	4N	29	SE
William Rigney	Jef	*	2	1N	8	NW
James McCartney	Jef	*	8	4N	24	NW
Susannah Elliott	Jef	*	3	1N	14	NE
William McFarland	Jef	*	8	3N	34	SE
Jacob Coonrod & Israel Butts	Jef	*	3	4S	8	NW
John Beare?	Jef	*	11	4N	25	SE
James McGee	Jef	*	4	5N	31	NE
Rufus Gale	Jef	*	12	5N	17	SE
Jacob Coonrod	Jef	*	4	4S	5	NE
Thomas Poulson	Jef	*	3	1S	21	NW
Daniel Lattimore	Jef	*	9	4N	30	SE
Charles Bailey	Jef	*	1	2N	34	NE
Samuel Lewis	Jef	*	1	3N	30	SW
John Vancleave	Jef	*	2	2N	33	SE
John Lapp	Jef	*	3	2N	15	NW
John Ketcham	Jef	*	4	5N	13	NW
Robert Simmington	Jef	*	10	3N	6	SW
William McFarland &						
A. Steele	Jef	*	8	3N	34	NW
Philip Schultz	Jef	*	4	1S	1	SW
Rufus Gale	Jef	*	12?	5N	20	NE
Thomas Hughes	Jef	*	9	5N	33	SW
Joseph Allen	Jef	*	4	2N	22	NE
John Brown	Jef	*	5	2S	9	SE
David Colclazer	Jef	*	3	2N	34	NE
Robert Patterson	Jef	*	9	1N	24	+
Robert Patterson	Jef	*	9	1N	25	-
Hugh Snodgrass	Jef	*	9	2N	1	NW
John Barnes	Jef	*	9	3N	36	NE
Allen Kendall	Jef	*	5	2S	36	NW
Adam Davis	Jef	*	1	1N	7	NE
Zachariah Nixon	Jef	*	4	2N	9	NE
Thomas Thompson	Jef	*	5	3N	37	NW
William Lofton	Jef	*	3	1S	10	NW
Thomas Lamb	Jef	*	5	1S	26	NW
Uriah Glover	Jef	*	2	2N	8	SW
Uriah Glover	Jef	*	2	2N	8	NW
Matthew Cowley	Jef	*	9	3N	3	SW
John Sage	Jef	*	4	4N	8	SE

*Second Principal Meridian.

1719   21 Jun 1814   A/5/432
LO Can

Transmits patents

John Sorrels	Can	–	12	15	21	NE
Joseph Davison*	Can	–	18	21	26	SW
Moses Dunham	Can	–	12	15	15	NE
Moses Dunham	Can	–	12	15	10	SE
Christopher Majers? [Myers?]	Can	–	10	12	1	SW
Nottingham Houston	Can	–	17	24	23	SW
Jacob Roads	Can	–	11	16	9	SE
John Nailor	Can	–	15	21	5	NW
Stephen Harris	Can	–	12	18	36	SE
John Weygandt	Can	–	10	1	28	NW
William Kelley	Can	–	15	22	18	NE
John McCrory	Can	–	17	23	28	NE
Samuel Hill	Can	–	17	23	32	NE
Abraham Rowland	Can	–	9	9	7	SE
Stephen Morgan	Can	–	14	18	13	NE
Jacob Kinmerer	Can	–	14	18	13	SW
James Nesbit, Junior	Can	–	19	20	14	SE
John Reed	Can	–	16	23	36	SW
Michael Switzer	Can	–	11	16	10	NW
Michael Switzer	Can	–	11	16	3	SW
Vacheal Metcalf	Can	–	16	23	27	NW
Thomas Parkison	Can	–	12	17	1	NW
Alexander McKee	Can	–	18	23	32	NW
John C. Phipps	Can	–	16	23	28	NW
Isaac Phipps	Can	–	17	25	23	NW
Isaac Phipps	Can	–	17	25	22	NE
John Trusdall	Can	–	12	16	29	SE
Joseph Kerr	Can	–	15	22	26	W
William Thomas	Can	–	12	16	31	NE
Thomas Johnstone	Can	–	12	15	2	S
John Jacob Foot	Can	–	18	21	19	NE
Rosanna Raimer	Can	–	18	21	7	SW
Emmanuel Brown	Can	–	12	16	22	SW
Emmanuel Brown	Can	–	12	16	21	SE
John L. Dawson	Can	–	13	13	2	SE
Jesse Richards	Can	–	13	15	1	SE
Isaac Bonnet	Can	–	15	20	27	SE
Jacob Kintner	Can	–	12?	16	23	NE
John Wright	Can	–	12	15	11	NE
Aaron Beard	Can	–	14	19	19	SE
John Glasgow	Can	–	11	16	6	NE
Thomas Johnstone	Can	–	13	16	17	NE
David Drake	Can	–	15	19	15	NW
Jacob Singrey	Can	–	19	20	32	NW
Rees Pritchard	Can	–	15	22	17	NW
Lawrence Winkler	Can	–	12	17	22	SE
Jacob Brackbeal	Can	–	12	17	20	SW
Major Tyler	Can	–	14	19	30	SW
Charles Hoy	Can	–	20	12	15	SW
James Taggert	Can	–	11	17	30	SW
James Taggert	Can	–	11	17	30	NW
Joseph White	Can	–	9	9	25	+
Joseph White	Can	–	9	9	36	–
David Newell	Can	–	17	23	30	SW
William Ranfrew	Can	–	17	23	19	SE
Rachel Richardson	Can	–	18	18	5	NW
John Nafzer	Can	–	9	9	17	NE
Calvin Hebert	Can	–	15	20	33	NE

*This entry crossed out in the original document.

1720   21 Jun 1814   A/5/434
John Badollet, Reg Vin
Transmits patents

Tousaint Dubois	Vin	–	4E	6S	26	+
Tousaint Dubois	Vin	–	4E	6S	27	–

1721   21 Jun 1814   A/5/434
John Henderson, Natchez
Transmits patent based on confirmation certificate

John Henderson	WPR	–	1E	1	10	+

1722   21 Jun 1814   A/5/434
James Morrison or Charles Witkins, Lexington Kentucky
Your complaint that John Bates has not paid you for
    your improvements to the United States Saline on
    the Wabash River has been forwarded to the Governor
    of Illinois Territory for action.

1723   21 Jun 1814   A/5/434
Governor [Ninian] Edwards, Illinois Territory
Forwards complaint of previous lessees of United
    States Saline on the Wabash River regarding nonpay-
    ment by successor. [Similar letter to Leonard
    White, U.S. Agent, Shawneetown, Illinois].

1724   21 Jun 1814   A/5/435
Joseph Davison, Greencastle, Franklin County, Penn-
    sylvania
Transmits patent

Joseph Davison	Can	–	18	21	26	SW

1725   21 Jun 1814   A/5/435
Jesse Spencer, Reg Chl
Transmits patent

-- Williamson & -- Griffith	Chl	WS	21	18*	23	SE

*May read Township 10.

1726   24 Jun 1814   A/5/437
LO Cin
Transmits patents

John Wright	Cin	WML	1	11	9	NE
Benjamin Hill	Cin	WML	1	14	35	NW
David Bradbery	Cin	*	13	17	21	SW
John Flinn	Cin	MR	10	3	35	SW
Jesse Hunt	Cin	MR	10	2	24	SW
Jeremiah Priest	Cin	MR	10	3	27	NW
John Merritt	Cin	MR	10	3	35	NW
Jesse Hunt	Cin	MR	8	5	17	E
Robert Abernathy	Cin	*	13	14	35	NW
John Merritt	Cin	MR	11	3	32	SE
Frederick Miller	Cin	EML	3	7	11	SW
William Blunt	Cin	*	13	18	29	SW
George Adams	Cin	*	12	12	35	NW
John Simmons	Cin	MR	12	2	25	SW
Philip Wools	Cin	WML	1	12	17	NE
Daniel Kersner	Cin	MR	7	3	12	NE
Elisha Lesley	Cin	MR	8	5	27	NW
Benjamin McCartey	Cin	*	12	13	9	NE
William Thorn	Cin	*	12	16	24	SE
William Thorn	Cin	*	12	16	13	SE
Amos Davis	Cin	EML	4	3	28	NW
William Thorn	Cin	*	12	16	24	NE
William Thorn	Cin	*	13	16	19	SW
John Murphy & James Murphy	Cin	MR	14	2	7	+
James Stafford	Cin	MR	10	2	18	SW
Daniel Drake	Cin	Town, Square 2, #11				
Ruggles Winshall	Cin	WML	2	9	28	SE
Hugh Newell	Cin	MR	13	3	14	NW
Henry Bray	Cin	*	13	13	11	NW
John Dewitt	Cin	WML	2	3	24	NE
John Pentecost, Junior	Cin	EML	1	7	7	NW
John Collins	Cin	EML	2	7	13	SE
Jonas Haney	Cin	MR	11	1	24	SE

*East of Second Principal Meridian.

1727   24 Jun 1814   A/5/438
John Brahan, [Rec] Hun
Answers query regarding extension of payment; mentions a Col. -- Ward.

1728   24 Jun 1814   A/5/438
Hon. J. G. Jackson, Clarksburg, Virginia
Transmits patents
J. G. Jackson   [Mil?] - 8 4 3 26
J. G. Jackson   [Mil?] - 8 4 3 36

1729   27 Jun 1814   A/5/438
J. W. Condy, J. H. Brinton, Isaac Bonsall, Philadelphia, Pennsylvania
Transmits nineteen patents [tracts not described].

1730   27 Jun 1814   A/5/439
James O? Cosby, St. Helena*
Requests written report for submission to Congress.
*Query at foot of letter asks what is nearest post office to St. Helena. Also, a note to the postmaster at Woodville, Wilkinson County, Mississippi Territory, requesting his aid in getting letter to Cosby.

1731   29 Jun 1814   A/5/440
John Badollet, Reg Vin
Mentions case brought against Charles Carson to eject him from a tract of land he purchased from the United States.

1732   5 Jul 1814   A/5/441
Michael Jones, Reg Kas
Letter interprets Act of 16 Apr 1814 having to do with claims to land previous to commencement of American sovereignty. [Mentions numerous claims by number and, specifically, that of Nicholas Jarvis and his sons.]

1733   6 Jul 1814   A/5/442
Nehemiah Tilton, Reg Wsh, Mississippi Territory
Discusses various claims for certificates of confirmation; mentions that of David Ferguson.

1734   7 Jul 1814   A/5/443
Hon. E. Bacon, Comptroller of the United States Treasury
Again urges a suit against the estate of Lemuel Henry, former Rec EPR, St. Stephens, Mississippi Territory, and his sureties. Henry's executors are Thomas Malone & Benjamin S. Smoot.

1735   8 Jul 1814   A/5/443
David Hoge, Reg Stu
Directs him to lease saline spring with certain restrictions to
-- Peterson   Stu - 3 11 34 -

1736   8 Jul 1814   A/5/444
John Caldwell, Rec Shw
Interprets Act of 5 Feb 1813 "giving the right of pre-emption in the purchase of lands, to certain settlers in the Illinois Territory."

1737   11 Jul 1814   A/5/445
Ezekiel Bacon, Comptroller of the United States Treasury
Zaccheus Biggs, late Rec Stu, was dismissed for "having lent the public monies." His account still shows an amount outstanding for six years, and he will not pay until compelled to do so.

1738   11 Jul 1814   A/5/446
Secretary of the United States Treasury
Submits report from Frederick Bates, Recorder of Land Titles, St. Louis, regarding mineral rights in Missouri Territory. Mentions speculations of -- Scott, U.S. Attorney; Messrs. Dodge & Co., late lessees of the Shibboleth mine; claim of John Smith (of Tennessee) under grant to St. Vrain Lapus, made by the governor of Louisiana, Baron -- de Carondolet (1796).

1739   11 Jul 1814   A/5/447
John Sloane, Rec Can
Transmits U.S. Treasury receipt
C[hristian] West   [tract not described]
Francis Baughman   [tract not described]
Henry Shauck   [tract not described]
George Ruhlman   [tract not described]
John Edwards   [tract not described]

1740   11 Jul 1814   A/5/447
John Shauck, Junior, Manchester, Baltimore County, Maryland
Transmits duplicate U.S. Treasury receipt
Christian West   [tract not described]
Francis Baughman   [tract not described]
Henry Shauck   [tract not described]
George Ruhlman   [tract not described]
John Edwards   [tract not described]

1741   11 Jul 1814   A/5/448
Lewis Sewall, Reg [EPR], St. Stephens, Mississippi Territory
Mentions Lemuel Henry; deficiency in tract of Edward L. Wailes; asks whether justice was done regarding pre-emption claims thereon.

1742   14 Jul 1814   A/5/448
N. J. Roosevelt, Esq., New York
Answers his letter to -- Cutting; Reg Vin to forward final certificate for -- Fulton.

1743   14 Jul 1814   A/5/449
John Read, Reg Hun, Mississippi Territory
Reports on patents thought to be missing; mentions corrected patent for Thomas Bibb.

1744   15 Jul 1814   A/5/449
John Badollet, Reg Vin
[N. J.] Roosevelt of New York has written for patents of -- Fulton.

1745   15 Jul 1814   A/5/450
James O. Cosby, Land Commissioner, St. Helena, Louisiana
Directs him to make final report on land claims.

1746		15 Jul 1814			A/5/451		
Bezaleel Wells, Steubenville [Ohio]							
Transmits patents							
Bezaleel Wells	Stu	–	7	19	31	NE	
Bezaleel Wells	Stu	–	8	12	31	SW	
Bezaleel Wells	Stu	–	7	18	6	NW	
1747		20 Jul 1814			A/5/451		
John H. Brinton, Philadelphia							
Transmits patents							
John H. Brinton	Stu	–	9	10	13	SE	
John H. Brinton	Stu	–	8	10	7	SE	
John H. Brinton	Stu	–	8	10	7	SW	
John H. Brinton	Stu	–	9	10	12	NE	
John H. Brinton	Stu	–	9	10	12	SE	
John H. Brinton	Stu	–	9	10	3	SE	
John H. Brinton	Stu	–	9	11	36	SE	
John H. Brinton	Stu	–	9	10	3	NE	
John H. Brinton	Stu	–	6	16	7	NE	
John H. Brinton	Stu	–	7	17	13	SE	
John H. Brinton	Stu	–	5	16	20	N	
John H. Brinton	Stu	–	9	10	12	SE	
John H. Brinton	Stu	–	9	10	2	NW	
John H. Brinton	Stu	–	8	10	18	SE	
John H. Brinton	Stu	–	8	10	18	NW	
John H. Brinton	Stu	–	8	10	18	NE	
John H. Brinton	Stu	–	9	10	13	NE	
1748		20 Jul 1814			A/5/452		
LO Zan							
Transmits patents							
James Cunningham	Zan	Mil	1	2	20	SE	
Margaret Wilson	Zan	Mil	1	2	18	SW	
Isaac Freeman	Zan	–	12	13	2	SW	
Henry Richard	Zan	–	11	13	13	NE	
Barney Dewit	Zan	Mil	10	7	4	NW	
Joshua Lemert	Zan	Mil	9	4	12	NE	
Abraham Warne	Zan	–	11	13	19	NE	
Samuel Drum	Zan	Mil	9	1	15	NE	
Joseph Clark	Zan	–	12	13	5	NW	
John Bowers	Zan	Mil	6	1	8	NW	
1749		21 Jul 1814			A/5/452		
LO Cin							
Transmits patents							
George P. Torrence	Cin	EML	1	3	2	SW	
Abraham Clark	Cin	EML	2	5	18	NE	
John Perrin	Cin	MR	9	5	27	SE	
John Winn	Cin	MR	10	5	17	NW	
John Winn	Cin	MR	11	5	7	NE	
Thomas Henderson	Cin	*	13 13–	34	NW		
Thomas Henderson	Cin	*	13 13–	27	SW		
William Buster	Cin	WML	1	8	10	NW	
John Perrin	Cin	MR	9	5	27	SW	
Eliha Hopkins	Cin	EML	2	7	5	SE	
Ebenezer Heaton	Cin	*	13 14–	17	NW		
James Cownover & John Cownover	Cin	*	12 15–	1	SW		
David Purviance	Cin	EML	1	9	31	SE	
John Quick	Cin	WML	2	8	2	SW	
Samuel Ayres	Cin	EML	2	4	9	SE	
James Jacob	Cin	WML	1	13	11	NW	
Alexander Dearmond	Cin	EML	1	3	22	NW	
James Wall	Cin	MR	13	4	4	NW	
James Matson	Cin	EML	1	2	34	SE	
James Martin	Cin	WML	1	11	28	NE	
Valentine Sherer	Cin	MR	8	2	21	NE	
Joseph Lee	Cin	WML	1	10	23	NE	
Thomas Patton	Cin	MR	9	5	19	SW	

Paul Larsh	Cin	EML	1	7	10	SW	
Elijah Fox	Cin	*	13 16–	9	NE		
David Gard	Cin	WML	1	6	24	SW	
Jacob Stutzman	Cin	EML	5	4	15	SE	
Jacob Stutzman	Cin	EML	5	4	15	SW	
Isaac Miller	Cin	*	13 15–	19	SE		
Ziba Wingate	Cin	MR	8	3	10	NE	
Philip Marshall	Cin	EML	1	9	28	SE	
George Shugart	Cin	*	14 17–	1	+		
Samuel Mitchell	Cin	EML	3	6	21	SE	
Jacob Bonebrake	Cin	EML	2	8	19	NE	
George Miller	Cin	*	13 15–	19	NE		
Henry Woodhouse	Cin	EML	6	3	33	NW	
George Eaker	Cin	EML	6	5	29	SW	
George Croft	Cin	MR	9	3	7	W**	

*East of Second Principal Meridian.
**"Lot north of Mad River."

1750		21 Jul 1814			A/5/453		
LO Stu							
Transmits patents							
John Brinker	Stu	–	6	17	7	SW	
Andrew Boyer	Stu	–	8	11	31	SE	
Daniel Shuster	Stu	–	7	15	27	NE	
Nimrod Johnson	Stu	–	7	14	31	SW	
Matthias Shilds	Stu	–	6	13	33	SW	
Noah Zane	Stu	–	3	6	15	SE	
John Hart	Stu	–	6	9	12	SW	
John Freed	Stu	–	5	16	14	NE	
George Adam Rex	Stu	–	8	11	22	SE	
David Peck	Stu	–	2	5	8	SW	
Peter Stoner	Stu	–	7	17	6	NW	
William C. Anderson	Stu	–	6	8	34	NW	
William Porter	Stu	–	2	6	13	NW	
Duncan McGeehan	Stu	–	3	13	3	NE	
Valentine Rinehart	Stu	–	7	17	28	NE	
James McPherson	Stu	–	3	9	6	SW	
John Clark	Stu	–	4	8	15	NW	
Charles Wilson	Stu	–	8	9	1	NE	
Moses Gillaspy	Stu	–	4	14	1	NE	
Christian Flickener? [Flickever?]	Stu	–	8	9	27	SW	
Thomas Traul	Stu	–	9	9	24	NW	
Daniel Teterick	Stu	–	7	11	26	SW	
Peter Wise	Stu	–	8	11	1	NE	
Joseph Springer	Stu	–	2	10	5	SE	
Philip Yeant	Stu	–	8	9	20	SE	
John Bowman	Stu	–	8	11	1	NW	
Thomas Taggart	Stu	–	1	7	24	NE	
John McLaughlin	Stu	–	1	6	3	SW	
Abraham Rum? [Reem?]	Stu	–	8	12	17	S	
James Price	Stu	–	8	9	1	NW	
Andrew Smith	Stu	–	5	11	8	NE	
Isaac Wheldon	Stu	–	7	12	7	NE	
George Adams	Stu	–	3	12	9	NE	
Hugh Linn	Stu	–	4	14	2	NW	
Daniel McCallister	Stu	–	3	13	6	W	

1751		22 Jul 1814			A/5/455		
Reazin Beall, Reg Can							
The right to this quarter section must be decided by							
— Bose & — Croninger by lot							
—	Can	–	10	11	36	NW	
1752		22 Jul 1814			A/5/456		
Nehemiah Tilton, Reg Wsh, Mississippi Territory							
Transmits patents							
— Ratcliffe	Wsh	EML	2	7	41	–	
— Ratcliffe	Wsh	EML	2	6	6	–	
Micajah Frazer	Wsh	WML	2	2	21	–	

1753		23 Jul 1814		A/5/456		
LO Ch1						
Transmits patents						
David Evaris	Ch1	Mil	15	3	14	SE
Daniel Parkinson	Ch1	–	16	16	4	SE
John Ox	Ch1	–	17	16	5	SE
William Boman	Ch1	–	18	16	4	SE
John Coon? [Cron?]	Ch1	MS	21	11	26	SE
Henry Engle	Ch1	–	16	15	17	SW
John Snook	Ch1	–	17	10	8	NE
John Hixson	Ch1	–	20	8	21	NE
John Sturgeon	Ch1	–	16	17	23	SE
Daniel Snyder	Ch1	–	16	17	27	SW
David Weaver	Ch1	MS	21	11	28	NW
Andrew Wickiser	Ch1	–	19	15	22	NW
David Roberts	Ch1	–	17	17	9	NE
Frederick Gliner	Ch1	–	17	14	8	NW
Philip Miller	Ch1	–	17	18	26	NE
David Neely	Ch1	–	17	16	15	NW
Joseph Dittoe	Ch1	–	16	16	20	SE
John Lutz	Ch1	–	19	12	18	W
George Powel	Ch1	MS	21	11	5	NE
John Bennet	Ch1	–	20	4	33	NE
Joseph Crouch & John Crouch	Ch1	–	17	9	30	NE
Samuel Chany	Ch1	–	20	15	32	SE
Philemon Beecher	Ch1	–	18	16	8	SE
George Buzzard	Ch1	–	19	12	8	SE
Peter Starkey	Ch1	–	17	18	13	NW
Godfrey Weimer	Ch1	–	17	18	13	SE
John Smith & Andrew Dildine	Ch1	MS	21	10	14	SE
Philemon Needless	Ch1	–	20	15	32	NW
Jacob Graffis	Ch1	–	17	16	2	NW
Jacob Wiseman	Ch1	–	17	18	27	SE
Jacob Alspach, Senior	Ch1	–	19	15	3	SW
Samuel Drake	Ch1	–	20	14	20	NE
John Gundy	Ch1	–	21	8	11	SE
Adam Gates	Ch1	–	21	8	11	NW
Christopher Westenhaver	Ch1	–	17	14	12	SE
William Wilson	Ch1	–	16	17	23	SW
William Wilson	Ch1	–	16	17	25	SW
William Hamilton & John Williamson	Ch1	–	20	13	22	SE
Jacob Mechling	Ch1	–	16	17	18	NE
John Dunkle	Ch1	WS	21	11	8	NE
Jesse D. Courtright	Ch1	–	20	14	22	NW
Felix Renick & William Lewis	Ch1	–	21	7	8	SW
Samuel Zertman	Ch1	–	16	16	33	SE
John Daniels	Ch1	–	16	17	18	NW
Lewis Scothorn	Ch1	MS	21	9	1	SE
Abraham Baker	Ch1	–	18	6	34	NW
Christian Kaufman	Ch1	–	17	17	21	NW
Caleb Hedges	Ch1	–	19	13	33	SW
John Baker	Ch1	–	17	6	6	NE
Hester Ray, et al	Ch1	–	17	16	12	SE
Peter Hempy	Ch1	–	19	15	31	SE
George Stoltz	Ch1	–	17	17	21	SW

1754	25 Jul 1814	A/5/458

Thomas Bates, Recorder of Land Titles, St. Louis, Missouri Territory
If the United States has clear title to Shibboleth Mine, then rent should be recoverable at law from Messrs. -- Dodge, -- Wilson, & -- Craighead. Mentions claims of John Smith under a grant To St. Vrain Lassus; offer of -- Portenay.

1755	27 Jul 1814	A/5/460

LO Jef
Transmits patents

Stephen Gudgell	Jef	*	9	2N	11	NE

Daniel Gudgell	Jef	*	9	2N	3	NW
John Purkiser?	Jef	*	2	5S	13	SE
Jonathan Lindley	Jef	*	2	2N	32	SW
Jonathan Lindley	Jef	*	1	1N	8	NE
Jesper Wilson	Jef	*	2	1N	32	SE
Henry Lookingbell	Jef	*	4	1S	4	NW
Robert McKay, Junior	Jef	*	11	4N	25	NW
Leonard Carns	Jef	*	4	1S	2	SW
Henry Nyman	Jef	*	5	1N	20	NE
Henry Berkshire	Jef	*	5	2S	34	NE
Zachariah Nixon	Jef	*	4	2N	18	NW
John Zenor	Jef	*	5	4S	22	NE

*East of Second Principal Meridian.

1756		27 Jul 1814		A/5/460		
LO Ch1						
Transmits patents						
Dorsey Mason	Ch1	Mil	15	3	8	SW
George Long	Ch1	–	17	18	12	SW
James Holmes	Ch1	–	18	16	4	NE
John Stapleton*	Ch1	–	20	12	30	W
John Stebelton*	Ch1	–	20	12	30	SE
Jacob Kesler	Ch1	Mil	15	3	18	NW
David Swope	Ch1	MS	21	11	31	SW
Isaac Flemming	Ch1	–	20	2	15	SE
Walter Hews	Ch1	–	20	15	18	SW
Philip Ebright	Ch1	–	20	15	26	NW
John McCutchan	Ch1	WS	21	10	34	NW
Jacob Bachman	Ch1	–	17	17	22	SW
Thomas Saultz? [Santz?]	Ch1	–	19	9	20	NE
Jacob Buzzard	Ch1	–	19	12	8	SW
Daniel Funk & J. Philips	Ch1	–	17	14	8	NE
Joseph Wright	Ch1	–	21	11	24	NE
John Leather	Ch1	–	20	12	2	NE
John Ritter	Ch1	–	20	14	18	NW
Thomas Cherington & William Cherington	Ch1	–	16	6	29	NW
William Brown	Ch1	MS	21	9	23	SW
John Weatherington	Ch1	–	22	4	14	NW
James Baldwin	Ch1	–	20	14	32	NW
John Harrison	Ch1	–	20	14	32	SW
Jacob Kesler	Ch1	–	15	3	18	SW
Patrick Owings	Ch1	–	17	16	8	NE
Conrod* Stump	Ch1	–	20	14	17	SE
David Lyle	Ch1	–	18	16	10	S
Daniel Mier	Ch1	–	19	16	29	NW
Robert Black	Ch1	–	19	16	24	SW
Daniel McCallum	Ch1	–	20	15	5	NE
Jacob Beery	Ch1	–	20	13	6	NW
Robert McClung	Ch1	–	18	16	23	NW
Michael Wagoner	Ch1	–	19	15	15	SE
Robert Darlinton*	Ch1	–	1	3	28	SE
William Williamson	Ch1	MS	21	9	15	NW
Winn Winship	Ch1	WS	21	10	1	SE

*So spelled.

1757		27 Jul 1814			A/5/461		
LO Cin							
Transmits patents							
William Robinson	Survey 3	Cin	Pre	7	2	23	E*
William Robinson	Survey 3	Cin	Pre	7	2	24	–
Robert Renick		Cin	Pre	9	4	5	W
William Ward	Survey 1	Cin	Pre	10	4	1	+
George W. Green		Cin	Pre	11	2	31	NE
James Tatman, heirs of		Cin	Pre	8	3	21	NW
Robert C. Crawford		Cin	Pre	8	2	5	SE
Henry Harter & James? Weatherhead		Cin	Pre	11	2	34	SE
John Dodson		Cin	Pre	11	2	27	NW
John Hole, heirs of	Survey 2	Cin	Pre	6	1	3	SW+

Matthew Newcom, heirs of

Survey 2	Cin Pre	6	1	3	SE+
Robert Crawford	Cin Pre	9	2	4	NW
John McCabe Survey 2	Cin Pre	6	1	10	SW+
William Mullin	Cin Pre	5	2	2	NW

*West side of East half.

1758   28 Jul 1814   A/5/462
Reasin Beall, Reg Can
Agent, Captain -- Stuhl, has requested patent;
  please return it to GLO for transmittal to Stuhl

James Hendricks	Can	-	14	18	11	SE

1759   30 Jul 1814   A/5/462
Joseph Wood, Reg Mar
Transmits patent

James Collins	Mar	-	5	5	32	NE

1760   30 Jul 1814   A/5/463
LO Vin
Transmits patents

Name	Dist		Range	Twp	Sec	Qtr
James Shields	Vin	*	1W	3N	32	NW
John Cox	Vin	*	13W	4S	15	NW
George Boone	Vin	*	4E	5S	21	SE
James Moutray	Vin	*	12W	4S	8	NW
Thomas Shouse	Vin	*	13W	4S	9	SE
Smith Mounce	Vin	*	12W	3S	24	SE
William Smith	Vin	*	7W	2N	29	NW
Michael Cammack	Vin	*	11W	1S	14	NW
Ratliff Boone	Vin	*	8W	5S	29	SE
John Thompson	Vin	*	5W	1N	29	NE
Thomas Aikman	Vin	*	7W	2N	4	NE
John Gray	Vin	*	13W	5S	6	NW
Samuel Murphey	Vin	*	13W	4S	22	SW
James Lindsey	Vin	*	8W	1N	19	SW
John Hollowell	Vin	*	2E	3S	1	NW
Henry Hollowell	Vin	*	2E	2S	6	NW
Shubel York	Vin	*	14W	6S	28	NE
William Horrall	Vin	*	7W	2N	9	SW
William Wallis	Vin	*	7W	2N	17	NE
George Halbrooks	Vin	*	11W	3S	13	NE
George Humphreys	Vin	*	11W	1S	13	NW
Henry Hurst	Vin	*	4E	3S	3	NE
Thomas Clay	Vin	*	6W	8S	10	-
Adlai Campbell	Vin	*	1W	2N	30	SW
Daniel Grass	Vin	*	6W	7S	35	+
John Hurst	Vin	*	4E	3S	5	SW
James Smith	Vin	*	2E	3S	12	SW
Joseph Montgomery	Vin	*	12W	4S	18	NW
Jesse Lindley	Vin	*	4E	3S	5	NW
Joseph Case	Vin	*	6W	1N	7	N+
Benjamin Brown	Vin	*	4E	5S	22	SW
Joseph Johnson	Vin	*	12W	3S	34	NW
Benjamin Creble	Vin	*	3E	3S	29	SE
Nathan Dean	Vin	*	5E	2S	28	SE
George Snyder	Vin	*	4E	5S	17	NE
John Paul	Vin	*	6E	3S	2	+

*Second Principal Meridian.

1761   30 Jul 1814   A/5/464
LO Chl
Transmits patents

Edward Miller	Chl	-	17	2	36	SE
James Hews	Chl	MS	21	11	25	NE
Amos Livesey	Chl	-	17	17	9	SW
Moses Hail	Chl	-	17	8	29	SW
John Henthorne	Chl	-	17	18	22	NW
Conrad Brougher	Chl	-	19	12	27	NE
Samuel Work	Chl	-	17	16	24	SE
Elijah Austine	Chl	MS	21	10	11	SE
Elijah Scofield	Chl	-	16	17	1	SE
Samuel Orr	Chl	-	21	8	15	SW
Richard Wilson	Chl	-	17	16	24	NW

1762   3 Aug 1814   A/5/467
Daniel Symmes, Reg Cin
Transmits patent; mentions error in patent for --
  Keever

-- McDonal* Surveys 2 & 5	Cin Pre	4	4	24	+

*Assignee of -- Heighway.

1763   8 Aug 1814   A/5/468
Samuel Aore? late clerk at Mobile [Alabama]
Regarding his removal from office by -- Crawford
  [apparently to prevent him from receiving amount
  due him by law].

1764   8 Aug 1814   A/5/468
Michael Jones [Reg Kas] & Shadrach Bond [Rec Kas]
Discusses section 16 [of each township] as reserved
  for schools and cannot be sold as pre-emption
  right or located by holders of confirmed claims.

1765   8 Aug 1814   A/5/469
John Shauck, Manchester, Baltimore County, Maryland
Discusses his land transaction; mentions assignment
  of -- Edwards.

1766   8 Aug 1814   A/5/469
Benjamin Starritt, Carnesville, Franklin County,
  Georgia
Thomas Freeman, Surveyor-General, Washington, Miss-
  issippi Territory, is the officer who appoints sur-
  veyors south of the State of Tennessee.

1767   8 Aug 1814   A/5/469
Robert Babcock, Zanesville [Ohio]

Robert Babcock*	Mil?	-	7	9	2?	13

*[Presumably the patentee--the letter is ambiguous.]

1768   9 Aug 1814   A/5/469
Reasin Beall, Reg Can
Please return patent

James Nesbitt	Can	-	19	20	14	SE

1769   9 Aug 1814   A/5/470
James Nesbitt, Plymouth, Luzerne County, Pennsylvania
Will forward patent as soon as it is returned from
  LO Can

James Nesbitt	Can	-	19	20	14	SE

1770   9 Aug 1814   A/5/470
Thomas Sloo, Reg Shw
Requests larger plat of district; mentions [John]
  Caldwell, Rec Shw.

1771   10 Aug 1814   A/5/471
Michael Jones [Reg Kas] & Shadrach Bond [Rec Kas]
Asks how much land will remain in reserved tract for
  private distribution after land is allotted for
  seminary.

1772   12 Aug 1814   A/5/471
John Galbraith, Steubenville [Ohio]
Transmits patents
James Galbraith   Stu?   -   11   15   12   SE
James Galbraith   Stu?   -   11   15   22   NE
James Galbraith   Stu?   -   11   15   23   NW
James Galbraith   Stu?   -   11   15   21   -
John Galbraith   Stu?   -   11   15   15   SW
John Galbraith   Stu?   -   11   15   1   -
John Galbraith   Stu?   -   11   15   12   W
John Galbraith   Stu?   -   11   15   11   NW

1773   12 Aug 1814   A/5/472
Daniel Symmes, Reg Cin
Discrepancies noted
--   Cin   ?   9   3   34   W
--   Cin   ?   11   4   5   NE
Jacob Pence*   Cin   ?   11   5   34   NE
*Assignee of Thomas Cowhick [so spelled].

1774   15 Aug 1814   A/5/472
Jacob Beard? [Beart?] Post Office, Hagerstown, Mary-
   land
Transmits patent
Jacob Beard?   Stu   -   8   11   21   NW

1775   15 Aug 1814   A/5/472
Jonathan W. Condy, Philadelphia
Transmits patent
Jonathan W. Condy   Stu   -   6   16   17   SW

1776   15 Aug 1814   A/5/472
Daniel Chicken, Smyrna, Kent County, Delaware
Transmits patent
Daniel Chicken   Stu   -   7   11   24   NW

1777   15 Aug 1814   A/5/473
John Nichols, Canton, Ohio
Transmits patents
John Nichols   Stu   -   7   19   11   SE
John Nichols   Stu   -   6   19   26   SW
John Nichols   Stu   -   8   12   33   SW

1778   15 Aug 1814   A/5/473
Samuel Gwathmey, Reg Jef
Transmits patent
Michael Giltner?   Jef   *   9E   2N   26   SW
*Second Principal Meridian.

1779   16 Aug 1814   A/5/473
LO Cin
Transmits patents
Martin Weighbricht   Cin EML 5   4   8   S
Jesse Bond   Cin WML 1   13   6   NE
John Wolf   Cin MR   7   3   12   SE
John McCormick   Cin MR   8   3   10   SE
Samuel Halstead   Cin EML 1   2   9   NE
Adam Redenbaugh   Cin MR   1   4   26   NW
Josiah Conger   Cin EML 1   7   23   NE
John Creek   Cin WML 1   11   31   SE
John Creek   Cin WML 1   11   32   SW
John Hendershot   Cin MR 12   1   26   NE
George Giltner   Cin * 12   12   36   NE
Richard Colliser   Cin WML 1   9   10   NW
George Vanbuskirk   Cin * 12   16   23   SW

Moses Marsh   Cin EML 1   3   30   SE
David Klammar   Cin EML 4   5   29   SE
Jonas Pearson   Cin EML 6   4   28   SW
Cornelius McPhaill   Cin EML 1   3   7   NE
John Swank   Cin EML 4   5   4   SE
Emmanuel Miller   Cin EML 4   9   10   NE
John Pryer   Cin EML 1   3   31   NE
John Bonner   Cin MR   7   2   19   NW
Daniel Alexander   Cin MR   5   3   26   SW
Jehu John   Cin EML 1   4   19   SE
Peyton Short   Cin MR   7   1   5   +
William McChristy   Cin EML 3   4   8   NE
Nicholas Reagan   Cin * 12   13   2   NE
John Powers   Cin WML 1   10   31   SW
Hugh Bell   Cin * 13   14   36   SW
William Walter   Cin * 13   15   22   NW
John Clark   Cin EML 1   4   21   SE
Joel Hollinger   Cin MR 10   4   18   NW
William Townsley   Cin EML 6   8   25   NW
Joseph Gripe   Cin EML 4   4   11   NE
Daniel Shively   Cin EML 4   5   10   NE
Ephraim Bowen   Cin WML 1   16   28   NE
*East of the Second Principal Meridian.

1780   16 Aug 1814   A/5/474
LO Mar
Transmits patents
Richard Dille   Mar   -   3   4   30   NE
James Tice   Mar   -   6   3   20   SW
William Pool   Mar   -   5   6   7   NE
Henry Bailey   Mar   -   7   8   6   NE
-- Linn & -- Barrett   Mar   -   5   5   11   SE

1781   16 Aug 1814   A/5/475
LO Chl
Transmits patents
William Stright   Chl   -   16   16   25   SW
Archibald Bryson   Chl   -   16   16   25   SE
Elijah Glover   Chl   -   21   1   12   +
John Dunkle   Chl   -   20   14   21   SW
William Forster   Chl   -   17   18   29   E
William Forster   Chl   -   17   18   18   S
William Forster   Chl   -   17   18   28   SW
Henry Capill? [Cassill?] Chl   -   18   9   36   NE
Jeremiah Roach   Chl   -   17   7   32   NW
Daniel Ranier   Chl MS 21   10   14   NW
William Roberts   Chl MS 22   4   12   SE
George Taylor   Chl   -   16   7   36   NW
John Ritter   Chl   -   20   14   18   SE
John Manly   Chl   -   17   17   5   SW
Robert Work   Chl Mil 13   7   9   SE
Moses Swaine   Chl   -   17   12   33   NE
Jacob Bachman   Chl   -   17   17   22   NW
Edward Saltz & John Ortman Chl -   20   9   7   SE
John Wolf   Chl   -   16   15   10   NE
Andrew Kelly   Chl   -   20   8   9   SW
John Solt   Chl   -   20   14   21   SE
George Trout   Chl   -   16   17   14   SW
Andrew List, Senior   Chl   -   21   9   34   SW
George Sydenbender   Chl WS 21   9   33   SW
Thomas Greene   Chl   -   16   16   13   NW
Ludwick Bonsey   Chl   -   16   15   4   SW
Caleb Evans   Chl Mil 15   3   25   NW
Anthony Dittoe   Chl   -   16   15   13   NE
A. Ashbaugh & F. Ashbaugh Chl   -   17   16   12   SW
Lawrence Crisley   Chl   -   16   15   11   SE
William Copline   Chl   -   16   16   21   SE
Jacob Holsmer   Chl   -   19   11   12   NW
David Van Gundy   Chl WS 21   9   22   SW
Augustine Smith   Chl   -   16   1   26   +

Matthew Edmiston	Chl	-	16	7	14	SW
George Smith	Chl	MS	21	10	8	SE

1782 16 Aug 1814 A/5/476
LO Stu
Transmits patents

John Wendell	Stu	-	2	12	22	NE
Jacob Oberlin	Stu	-	10	2	27	NE
Joseph Hobson	Stu	-	10	1	13	SW
George Hetzler	Stu	-	8	12	20	W
Robert Gilmore	Stu	-	2	6	36	NE
John Nimmon	Stu	-	9	10	22	NE
John Shorb	Stu	-	8	10	8	NE
William Croxton	Stu	-	5	14	26	SW
William Croxton	Stu	-	5	14	26	NW
Christian Kinder	Stu	-	6	15	1	SE
John Cunningham	Stu	-	2	6	22	NW
Samuel Russell	Stu	-	6	14	29	NE
Jacob Smith	Stu	-	8	12	25	SE
William Doyle	Stu	-	10	2	24	NW
John Vale	Stu	-	1	7	21	SE
John Vale	Stu	-	1	7	21	SW
Joseph Hobson	Stu	-	10	1	24	NW
E. O. Bryan	Stu	-	6	10	28	NW
Mage Thompson	Stu	-	6	16	1	NW
E. O. Bryan	Stu	-	6	10	28	NE
Mary Metz	Stu	-	6	17	1	NE
John Knox	Stu	-	3	11	3	NE
Samuel Welsh	Stu	-	5	11	28	SE
Hugh Shotwell	Stu	-	7	12	14	NE
John Shotwell	Stu	-	7	12	21	SE

1783 17 Aug 1814 A/5/477
LO Cin
Transmits patents

Joseph Gripe	Cin	EML	4	5	34	SW
William Cooper	Cin	EML	2	6	35	NW
William Cooper	Cin	EML	1	7	4	SW
John Radley	Cin	WML	1	4	19	SE
John Rex	Cin	EML	3	6	5	NE
John Capehart	Cin	EML	4	2	9	NW
Abisha McCay	Cin	WML	3	2	31	SE
Edward Webb	Cin	*	12	13	33	NE
Felix Ashcroft	Cin	EML	1	3	4	NW
Isaac Aerl	Cin	EML	8	1	12	+
Peter Rifner	Cin	EML	1	2	7	SW
Henry Abfel	Cin	EML	4	4	15	SE
John Wolf	Cin	MR	8	3	8	SW
Joseph Siers	Cin	WML	1	8	4	NE
Archibald McGrew, Senior	Cin	MR	11	4	11	NW
William Steward	Cin	MR	11	1	29	+
James Martindale	Cin	*	13	17	35	NE
John Clark	Cin	EML	1	4	28	NW
David Nighswonger	Cin	EML	3	7	10	SE
John Willson, Junior	Cin	MR	11	2	26	SW
James Tanner	Cin	EML	2	9	1	NE
Samuel Trotter	Cin	EML	5	8	7	NE
John Musselman	Cin	EML	4	5	26	NE
Stephen Ulrich	Cin	EML	4	5	24	SW
Philip Doddridge	Cin	*	13	15	15	SE
John Doddridge	Cin	*	13	15	24	NW
Daniel Teagarden	Cin	*	13	12	5	NE
Oliver M. Spencer	Cin	MR	11	2	24	NE
Oliver M. Spencer	Cin	MR	11	2	12	-
John Smith	Cin	EML	1	4	29	NW
Moses Baker	Cin	*	12	13	12	NW
John S. Gano	Cin	MR	1	2	8	SE
Daniel Razor, Senior	Cin	EML	5	5	15	SE
James Cannon	Cin	EML	6	8	29	SE
Elijah Garrison	Cin	WML	1	7	28	SE

William Wilson	Cin	*	12	15	35	NW
Joseph Nelson & John Nelson	Cin	EML	1	7	31	W
Samuel Hogg	Cin	MR	10	5	23	NW
Thomas Cartmill	Cin	MR	10	6	23	NE
James Craig	Cin	WML	2	9	11	NW
John Knipe	Cin	*	12	15	12	NE
Moses Greer & Joshua Greer	Cin	EML	5	4	3	SW
James Knight, Junior	Cin	WML	2	9	17	NE
William Snodgrass	Cin	*	12	14	33	SW
Archibald Reed	Cin	*	13	14	18	SE
Archibald Reed	Cin	*	13	14	18	SW
Isaac Enoch	Cin	EML	3	6	8	NE
Oliver M. Spencer	Cin	MR	11	2	18	S
Oliver M. Spencer	Cin	MR	11	2	18	NE
William Sparks	Cin	*	12	14	19	+
William Sparks	Cin	*	12	14	30	-
John Doddridge	Cin	*	13	15	12	W
David Jenkins	Cin	*	13	15	22	E
Timothy Covalt	Cin	MR	6	1	14	SE
Joseph Rorer	Cin	EML	5	5	7	W
Frederick Steenbarger	Cin	MR	12	3	7	NE
Jane Johnston	Cin	EML	5	8	3	SE
William Siers	Cin	WML	1	8	10	SW
John Kenneday	Cin	EML	2	5	17	SE
Peter Demoss	Cin	EML	2	6	31	SE
Jacob Titus	Cin	EML	2	3	5	NW

*East of the Second Principal Meridian.

1784 17 Aug 1814 A/5/478
LO Stu
Transmits patents

Robert Hogue	Stu	-	5	8	29	NW
John Krydar	Stu	-	8	11	15	NW
John Brown, Senior	Stu	-	6	15	19	SW
John Brown, Senior	Stu	-	6	15	25	SW
Andrew Hendricks	Stu	-	5	12	3	NW
Jacob Hendricks	Stu	-	5	12	3	NE
Austin Allen	Stu	-	9	10	10	SW
Cornelius Baxter	Stu	-	6	15	27	NE
Jacob Kirk	Stu	-	10	1	14	SW
John Cadwallader, Junior	Stu	-	7	12	1	SW
Michael Ault	Stu	-	4	6	5	SE
Samuel Davidson	Stu	-	7	12	27	SE
Abraham Ackerson	Stu	-	5	7	35	SW
Samuel Douglass	Stu	-	6	8	34	SE
Samuel Wright	Stu	-	4	6	5	NW
William Whinery	Stu	-	4	16	32	NW
Valentine Barriger	Stu	-	5	10	21	NE
John Raber	Stu	-	8	12	8	SE
Michael Myer	Stu	-	9	12	1	-
Jacob Calvert	Stu	-	3	5	27	SW
George Frank	Stu	-	8	12	28	NE
Winans Clark	Stu	-	9	10	3	SW
Caleb Cooper & Imla? Cooper	Stu	-	7	12	8	NW
W. Cooper & John Cooper	Stu	-	7	12	9	SW
Robert Guttray	Stu	-	5	9	35	NW
Jacob Sagar	Stu	-	4	11	4	SW
Daniel Bair? [Baer?]	Stu	-	4	10	35	NW
John Archbold	Stu	-	5	11	17	NW
John Calvert	Stu	-	3	5	26	SW
Joseph McCaughey	Stu	-	10	1	13	NW
Peter Witteracht	Stu	-	1	9	22	NW
Thomas Blackledge	Stu	-	3	7	22	NW
David Parkhill	Stu	-	3	9	35	SW
James McConnell	Stu	-	7	10	35	NW
Thomas Herford	Stu	-	7	19	33	SW
John Zerbe	Stu	-	8	10	22	SE
Isaiah Swem	Stu	-	4	17	17	NE
Jolly Rutter	Stu	-	6	13	35	SE
Joseph? [James?] Cadwallader	Stu	-	7	12	2	NE

1785			17 Aug 1814		A/5/480	G. Vannest, heirs	Survey 1	Cin Pre?	4	2	12	W+
LO Cin						Barzil Meck? [Meek?]		Cin Pre?	9	2	30	NE
Transmits patents						Jesse Hunt		Cin Pre?	7	3	28	–
William Ward	Survey 2	Cin Pre?	9	5	24 SW+	John Ewing		Cin Pre?	6	2	33	+
V. Oilar? [Osler?] heirs of	Cin Pre?	7	2	21	SE	William Turnbull		Cin Pre?	5	3	30	NE
Thomas Irwin	Survey 3	Cin Pre?	4	2	10 SE+	Alexander Ross		Cin Pre?	4	3	28	SE+
William Stinson		Cin Pre?	8	3	22 E	Jonathan Crane		Cin Pre?	4	3	15	W
William Stinson		Cin Pre?	8	3	23 E+	Jesse Hunt		Cin Pre?	10	2	14	–
Jacob Cozard		Cin Pre?	8	3	15 SW+	V. Gebhart, heirs	Survey 2	Cin Pre?	6	1	25	S
Vanzandt Morgan		Cin Pre?	7	2	7 SW	V. Gebhart, heirs	Survey 2	Cin Pre?	6	1	31	S
William Cox		Cin Pre?	5	2	22 NW	Jesse Hunt		Cin Pre?	8	3	24	W*
Isaac Miller		Cin Pre?	8	3	17 NW	Jesse Hunt		Cin Pre?	7	3	34	–
John Williams		Cin Pre?	10	2	7 SE	*Lot 2.						

[End of source A]

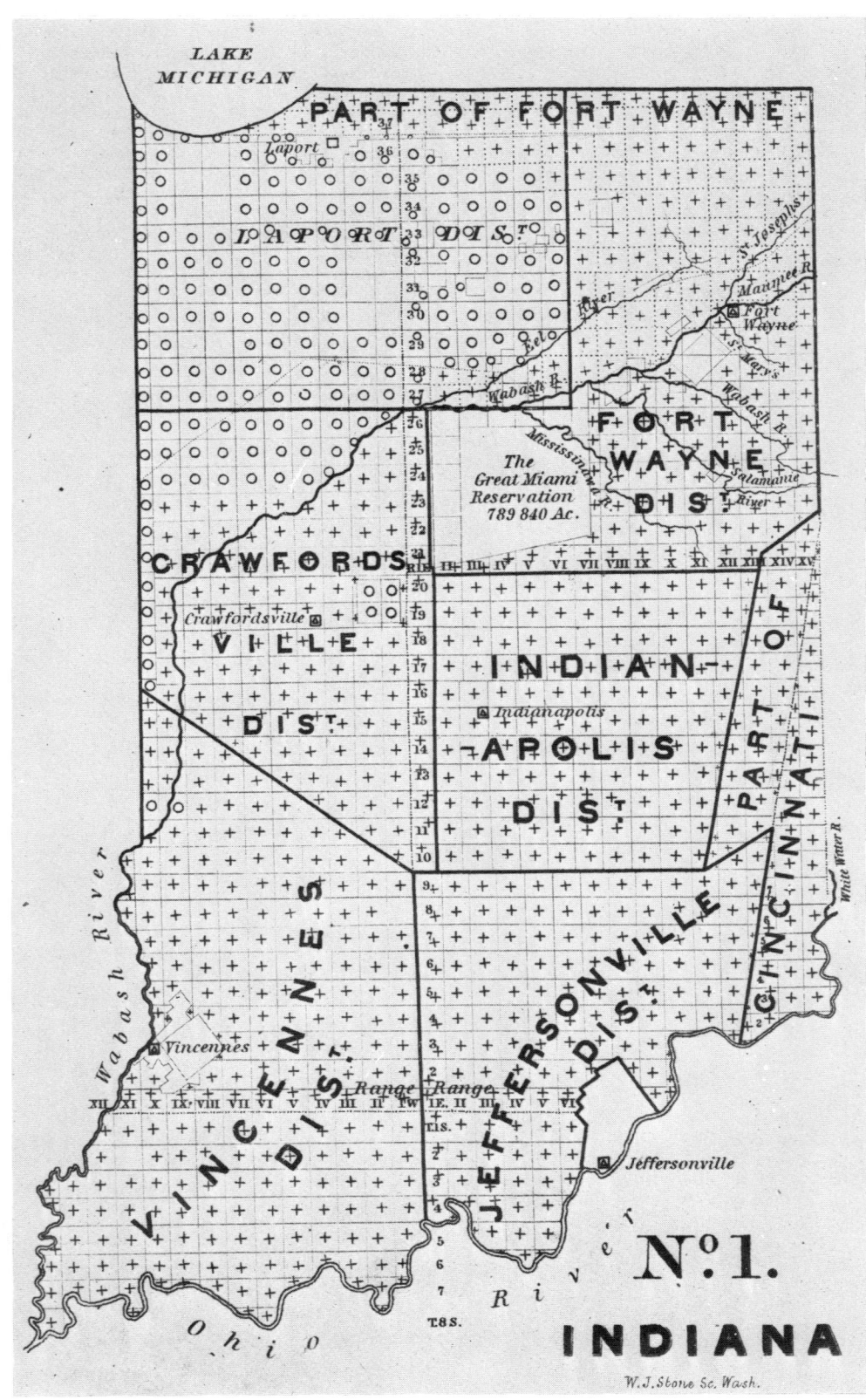

MAP 5. Tract map of Indiana showing land office districts

[156]

NAME INDEX

Abbernathy, John, 1314

Abbett, John, 605

Abbot, None, 974

Abbott, John, 605

Abel, George, 1377, 1628

Abel. *See also* Able

Abernathy, John, 1314

Abernathy, None, 632

Abernathy, Robert, 632, 1726

Abert, Jacob, Junior, 1036

Abert. *See also* Albert, Albrecht, Albright, Allbright, Ebert

Abfall, Henry, 10

Abfel, Henry, 1783

Abfel. *See also* Apfel, Obfal

Abin, James, 1072

Able, George, 1513

Able. *See also* Abel

Abrams, John, 489

Achison, Jeremiah, 1489

Ackerson, Abraham, 1784

Acklin, Samuel, 1689

Ackrer, David, 1002

Acre, None, 1294, 1425

Acre, Samuel, 1763

Adair, William, 994

Adams, Andrew, 373

Adams, George, 557, 1392, 1726, 1750

Adams, John, 283, 490, 557, 719, 737, 767, 824

Adams, Jonah, 4

Adams, Joseph, 1582, 1689

Adams, Josiah, 996

Adams, Littleberry, 1507, 1689

Adams, Matthew, 1626

Adams, Samuel, 284

Adams, Thomas, 1507, 1626

Adams, William, 4, 1453

Adamson, Elisha, 1625

Addair, William, 994

Addington, John, 718, 1636

Addington, Joseph, 1110

Addington, Thomas, 953

Addison, Jonathan, 132

Addy, Hugh, 1108

Addy, William, 732

Addy. *See also* Eddy

Adkins, Parker, 992

Adney, John, 903

Adrian, Jacob, 994

Aebi, Christian, 1177, 1182

Aebi, David, 1717

Aebi, John, 355, 524, 1196

Aebi, Peter, 1393

Aebi. *See also* Ebey, Ebi, Eby, Uby

Aerl, Isaac, 1783

Aerl, Rebecca, 1478

Aerl. *See also* Earl

Agnew, Samuel, 844

Agnew. *See also* Egnew

Aguabraugh, Daniel, 497

Ahelick, John, 996

Aikenberry, Henry, 950

Aikenberry, Peter, 1073

Aikman, John, 1195

Aikman, Thomas, 1760

Aikman. *See also* Eichmann, Eckman

Aip, John, Junior, 1313

Akert, George, Junior, 270, 442

Akert, Geroge, Senior, 270

Akert. *See also* Eckart

Akinson, W., 110

Alban, William, 1198

Albaugh, George, 537

Albaugh, Morris, 235, 244, 562, 567

Albaugh. *See also* Alspach

Albert, Jacob, 522

Albert. *See also* Abert, Albrecht, Albright, Allbright, Ebert

Albrecht, Jacob, 390, 478, 560

Albright, Jacob, 390, 560

Albrecht, Albright. *See also* Abert, Albert, Allbright, Ebert

Aldridge, Samuel, 500, 1391

Alecks, Bazil, 331

Alexander, Daniel, 1779

Alexander, Isaac, 1470

Alexander, J., 991

Alexander, James, 67, 545, 1130, 1582, 1624

Alexander, John, 1253

Alexander, None, 1218, 1521

Alexander, None, *Honorable*, 1304

Alexander, Samuel, 1502, 1625

Alexander, William, 332

Alkier, George, 978

Allbright, Jacob, 478

Allbright. *See also* Abert, Albrecht, Albright, Ebert

Allen, Austin, 1784

Allen, George, 993

Allen, J. S., 1371

Allen, James, 1073, 1477

Allen, John, 76, 752, 1041, 1073

Allen, Joseph, 1718

Allen, Lewis, 959

Allen, None, 1482

Allen, Samuel, 1689

Allen, William, 1718

Allen, William B., 1371

Allenworth, William, 6

Alliman, Henry, 370, 379

Alliman, John, 370, 379

Alliman. *See also* Alman

Allison, America M., 1690

Allison, Archibald, 271

Allison, John, 1689

Alman, James, 9

Alman. *See also* Alliman

Alsbach, Jacob, Junior, 85

Alspach, George, 537

Alspach, Henry, 747, 991

Alspach, Jacob, Junior, 625

Alspach, Jacob, Senior, 1753

Alspach, Michael, 747

Alspach, Morris, 235, 244, 562, 567

Alspack, Jacob, Junior, 85

Alspach, Alspack. *See also* Albaugh

Alt, Fred, 1036

Alt, Michael, 1784

Alt. *See also* Auld

Altman, Adam, 991

Altman, Ebenezer, 314

Altman, John, 996

Altomano, John, 758

Altvater, Henry, 731

Amaine, Henry, 993

Ambrose, Peter, 993, 1582

Amick, None, 991

Ammann, Henry, 993

Anbogart, None, 1563

Anderson, Benjamin, 592, 724

Anderson, Hugh, 305

Anderson, James, 391

Anderson, John, 252, 1073

Anderson, Jonathan, 1663

Anderson, None, 279

Anderson, None, *Honorable*, 822

Anderson, Richard Clough, 1273

Anderson, Robert, 284

Anderson, Wallace, 948

Anderson, William, 440, 671, 1151

Anderson, William C., 1750

André, Philip, 1090

Andrew, Adam, 751

Andrew, Hugh, 1481

Andrews, J., 1436

Andrews, James, 724

Andrews, John, 134, 529, 1550

Andrews, None, 1335

Andrews, Peter, 1667

Andrews, Richard, 960

Andrews, Robert, 789, 1626

Andrews, William, 561

Andsley, Andrew, 537

Andsley. *See also* Endsley, Ensley

Angle, Michael, 459

Angle, Nicholas, 347

Angle. *See also* Engel

Ankany, George, 1402

Ankerman, John, 639

Annin, None, 309, 451, 858

Annin, Samuel, 228

Ansbacher, Michael, 1314

Anspach, George, 24

Anspach, Jacob, 257

Anspach, John, 24

Anspach, Peter, 378

Anspacher, Michael, 1314

Anthony, George, 456

Anthony, William, 959, 1371

Antill, Edward, 850, 885

Antill, J., 850

Antram, Adin, 1530

Antrim, Joshua, 34

Aore, Samuel, 1763

Apfel, Henry, 1783

Apfel, Peter, 337

Apple, John, 1084, 1154

Apple, Peter, 327, 337

Apfel, Apple. *See also* Abfel, Obfal

Applegate, William, 995, 1220, 1477

Aquabrough, Daniel, 1117

Arbogast, None, 1563

Arbuckle, James, 861, 877

Arbuckle, Samuel, 1486

Archbold, John, 1784

Archer, David, 923

Archer, J., 1113

Ardery, William, 1041

Ardney, William, 1041

Argebright, John, 747

Arhart, Philip, 384

Arhart. *See also* Erhardt

Armine, Henry, 1626

Armstrong, Andrew, 362

Armstrong, J., 1376

Armstrong, James, 323, 998, 1717

Armstrong, None, 997, 1012

Armstrong, Robert, 1533

Armstrong, Thomas, 332, 517, 1030

Armstrong, William, 473, 1195

Arndt, William, 1041

Arndt. *See also* Arnst, Earnest, Ernest, Ernst

Arnett, Samuel, 786, 1207

Arnett, Thomas, 1481

Arnett, William, 1313, 1478

Arnold, Jacob, 998

Arnold, John, 101

Arnold, None, 759

Arnold, Philip, 1049

Arnst, William, 258

Arnst. *See also* Arndt, Earnest, Ernest, Ernst

Arrowsmith, Ezekiel, 949

Arrowsmith, Samuel, 1662

Aschbach, A., 1781

Aschbach, F., 1781

Aschbach, John, 1109

Ashbaugh, A., 1781

Ashbaugh, F., 1781

Ashbaugh, John, 1109

Ashcroft, Felix, 1710, 1783

Ashe, George, 983

Asher, William, 319

Aske, George, 978

Askin, John, 952, 977

Askin, John, Junior, 952

Askren, David, 1002

Atchison, Jeremiah, 1489

Aten, None, 1482

Atherton, Peter, 326, 436

Atkins, James, 1265

Atkinson, George, 960

Atkinson, W., 110

Atkinson, Watson, 447

Attick, David, 632

Atwood, James, 1582

Audrick, Jacob, 478

Augustus, David, 85

Auker, George, 991

Aukerman, John, 639

Auld, Michael, 935

Ault, Fred, 1036

Ault, Michael, 1784

Auld, Ault. *See also* Alt

Aurand, Daniel, 760

Aurand, David, 570

Austin, Jeremiah, 107

Austine, Elijah, 1761

Austine, G., 1444

Autram, Adin, 1530

Ayer, Elijah, 885

Ayer, Elijah, Junior, 885

Ayers, David, 1666

Ayers, Jacob, 237

Aylimer, John, 561

Ayres, David, 732

Ayres, Samuel, 1749

Aytimer, John, 561

Babcock, Robert, 1767

Babcock, Thomas, 998, 1371

Baby, James, 872

Bach. *See* Bake, Bough

Bachman, Jacob, 193, 290, 1036, 1756, 1781

Bachmann, Abraham, 337, 747

Bachmann, David, 1610

Bachmann, Francis, 1739, 1740

Bachmann, Henry, 1531

Bachmann, Jacob, 1532

Bachmann, John, 1610

Bachmann. *See also* Baughman, Baumann, Boman, Boughman, Bousman, Bowman

Bachtel, Isaac, 134, 455, 461

Bachtel, Jacob, 724, 1626

Bachtel, Martin, 624

Bachtel, None, 532, 889

Bachtel, Samuel, 960, 1547

Bachtel. *See also* Baghtel, Bechtel, Bughtel

Backhaus, Christian, 269

Backhaus, James, 269

Backhaus, John, 269

Bishop, Benjamin, 115

Bishop, James, 122

Bishop, John, 950

Bishop, Robert, 532

Bisland, John, 1470

Bissonet, Joseph, 608

Bixler, Elias, 991

Bizand, William, 132

Black, Alexander, 1436

Black, Andrew, 470, 633

Black, Frederick, 1530

Black, J., 1530

Black, Jack, 1072

Black, James, 659, 1487, 1591

Black, James, Senior, 1478

Black, John, 632

Black, Robert, 1756

Black, Samuel, 553, 632, 903, 1046

Black, William, 121, 194, 1530

Blackburn, David, 794

Blackburn, Finley, 724

Blackburn, James, 1265

Blackburn, Robert, 26, 357

Blackburn, William, 1559

Blackburne, James, 1049

Blackburne, None, 1268

Blackford, John, 324

Blackford, Nathaniel, 949

Blackford, Zeph., 786

Blackledge, Jacob, 1243

Blackledge, Joseph, 503

Blackledge, Thomas, 1784

Blackledge, William, 1717

Blacklige, Jacob, 1243

Blackman, Remember, 1582

Blackmore, Charles, 599

Blagrove, Charles, 739

Blair, Adam, 288

Blair, James, 488, 776, 1090

Blair, T., 1436

Blair, William, 1163

Blaisdell, Jacob, 942

Blake, James, 1085

Bland, Joseph, 1132

Blank, Michael, 582

Blankenbaker, Nicholas, 1533

Blankenbaker, Samuel, 1376

Blankenship, James, 983

Blankenship, Lewis, 997

Blanton, Sarah, 951

Blasdell, Jacob, 942

Blasdell. *See also* Blaisdell, Blusdell

Blau, Benjamin, 182

Blau. *See also* Blue

Bleakenstaff, Christian, 291, 759, 1035

Bleakenstaff, Jacob, 1073

Bleakenstaff. *See also* Blekinstafer, Blickenstab

Bleakley, Josiah, 872

Bledso, Abraham, 6

Bledsoe, Isaac, 351

Bledsoe, None, 333

Bleecker, Harmanns, *Honorable*, 886

Bleecker, None, 885

Blekinstafer, Jacob, 1073

Blickenstab, Christian, 759

Blekinstafer, Blickenstab. *See also* Bleakenstaff

Blizzard, John, 732

Blizzard, Reuben, 732

Blizzard, Thomas, 737, 996

Blocksom, Fisher A., 260

Blocksom, William, 151

Blosser, Isaac, 747

Blount, William, 1252, 1726

Blount. *See also* Blunt

Bloyd, Jacob, 234

Blue, Barnabas, 492, 794, 1487

Blue, Benjamin, 182

Blue, Cornelius, 465

Blue, David, 1667

Blue, Frederick, 1436

Blue, James, 1314

Blue, Michael, 992

Blue, Michael, Senior, 1481

Blue, Samuel, 1369

Blue, Uriah, 949, 950

Blue. *See also* Blau

Blunt, William, 1252, 1726

Blunt. *See also* Blount

Blusdel, Jacob, 628

Blusdel. *See also* Blaisdell, Blasdell

Blythe, Henry, 1197

Boal, Archibald, 733

Boardman, Amos, 1625

Boardman, David G., 1625

Boardman, J. C., 1686

Boblet, Jacob, 1636

Bockins, John, 5

Boehm, Peter, 355

Boehme, Henry, 1393

Boehme, Jacob, 1550

Boehme, Boehmer. *See also* Beam, Beamer

Boggs, John, 1376

Boggs, Moses, 339

Boghart, Martin, 599

Boghart, Peter, 268, 775

Bogle, Joseph, 456, 747

Bogle, William, 286, 327, 370, 376

Bogue, Jesse, 1551

Bohlaender, George, 991

Bohn, Charles, 297, 427, 509, 693

Bohn, None, 29, 138, 996

Boiler, Joseph, 991

Bolander, George, 991

Bollman, George, 732

Bolsel, Peter, 1436

Boman, Benjamin, 1314

Boman, William, 1753

Boman. *See also* Bachmann, Baumann, Boughman, Bousman, Bowman

Bomford, G., 925, 946

Bonbrake, Devault, 1073

Bond, Jesse, 1401, 1478, 1779

Bond, John P., 489

Bond, Joseph, 1478

Bond, Nathaniel, 950

Bond, None, 1073

Bond, Samuel, 67, 291, 463, 1041

Bond, Shadrach, 1537, 1657, 1708

Bond, William, 1041

Bonebrake, Devault, 1073

Bonebrake, Jacob, 1749

Bonebreak, Henry, 662

Bonebreak. *See also* Honebreake

Bonge, Stephen, 1328

Bonge, William, 1313

Bonhomme, François, 872

Bonnell, Aaron, 1073

Bonner, David, 632

Bonner, John, 1779

Bonnet, Isaac, 1719

Bonnett, Isaac, 1610

Bonome, François, 872

Bonsall, Isaac, 1729

Bonsey, Ludwick, 1781

Bonta, Albert, 6, 1029

Bonta. *See also* Banta

Bontius, George, 594

Bontius. *See also* Pontius

Boobs, Jacob, 253

Booe, Benjamin, 1478

Boogher, Samuel, 56

Boon, Daniel, *Colonel*, 1523

Boone, Daniel, 1589

Boone, Daniel M., Junior, 1523

Boone, Daniel, *Colonel*, 1523

Boone, George, 1153, 1760

Boone, Moses, 766

Boone, Nathan, 1523

Boone, Ratliff, 1760

Boone, Squire, 719, 824

Boone, Thomas, 1012

Boone. *See also* Bunn

Boos, Benjamin, 1478

Boos. *See also* Bose, Bosse

Bootes, Garret, 269

Bootes. *See also* Butts

Booth, Eli, 1610

Booth, Thomas, 1717

Border, George, 552

Border, Nicholas, 552, 557

Bore, Benjamin, 1478

Bort, George, 1195

Borton, Benjamin, 5

Bose, Benjamin, 1478

Bose, None, 1751

Bose. *See also* Boos, Bosse

Boshart, Rudolph, 676

Boshart. *See also* Bashart, Bossert, Bussard, Buzzard

Bosse, Michael, 1198

Bosse. *See also* Boos, Bose

Bosserman, Samuel, 828, 960

Bossert, Jacob, 1163

Bossert. *See also* Bashart, Boshart, Bussard, Buzzard

Bottenberg, None, 1030

Bottenburgh, J., 960, 1058

Bottorf, Caspar, 433, 718

Bouchard, Ignace, 952

Boucher, Anthony, 1314

Boucher. *See also* Baucher, Baugher

Bouge, Stephen, 1328

Bouge, William, 1313

Bough, Henry, 599

Bough. *See also* Bach, Bake

Boughman, Abraham, 337, 747

Boughman, David, 1610

Boughman, John, 1610

Boughman. *See also* Bachmann, Baumann, Bowman, Bousman, Bowsman

Bourasa, Daniel, 966

Bourdeaux, Joseph, 849

Bousman, Laurence, 196

Bousman. *See also* Bachmann, Baumann, Boughman, Bowman, Bowsman

Bouzer, Jacob, 1108, 1601

Bouzer. *See also* Bauzer, Bowser

Bowen, Ephraim, 1779

Bowen, Joseph P., 1073

Bower, Adam, 28, 877, 1592

Bower, Bernard, 960

Bower, David, 731

Bower, George, 991

Bower, Jacob, 732, 747, 1049, 1191

Bower, John, 758, 1036

Bower, Solomon, 387, 604, 1488

Bower. *See also* Bauer, Bowers

Bowers, Jacob, 318, 758

Bowers, John, 132, 557, 758, 1748

Bowers, Solomon, 1411

Bowers. *See also* Bauer, Bower

Bowie. *See* Booe

Bowland, James, 346

Bowman, Abraham, 983

Bowman, Barnet Henry, 1711

Bowman, Benjamin, 121, 919, 1314

Bowman, Christian, 305

Bowman, David, 960

Bowman, George, 776

Bowman, Henry, 141, 1711

Bowman, Jacob, 723, 1305, 1441, 1489

Bowman, John, 100, 1610, 1750

Bowman, None, 815

Bowman, Samuel, 983

Bowman. *See also* Bachmann, Baumann, Boughman, Bousman, Bowsman

Bowser, Daniel, 6

Bowser. *See also* Bauzer, Bouzer

Bowsman, Henry, 1041

Bowsman, Lawrence, 469

Bowyer, John, 983

Bowyer, Philip, 983

Bowyer. *See also* Boyer

Boyce, None, 1375, 1426

Boyce. *See also* Boyse

Boyd, Cyrus, 537

Boyd, Hugh, 1502

Boyd, Samuel, 828

Boydstone, George, 1489, 1666

Boydstone. *See also* Boylestone

Boyer, Andrew, 1030, 1750

Boyer, John, 983, 1030

Boyer, Lewis, 609

Boyer, Michael, 339, 536, 537, 747

Boyer, Philip, 983

Boyer. *See also* Bowyer

Boyle, Hugh, 75

Boylestone, George, 1198

Boylestone. *See also* Boydstone

Boynton, None, 1296

Boyse, Catherine, 1390

Boyse, Dennis, 48, 67, 291, 891

Boyse, James, 115, 459

Boyse, John, 486

Boyse, Robert, 532, 1012

Boyse. *See also* Boyce

Boysworth, Henry, 654

Brackbeal, Jacob, 1719

Brackbeal. *See also* Brechbeil

Bracken, Jesse, 1265

Bradberry, David, 931

Bradbery, David, 1726

Braden, James, 1626

Bradford, John, 288, 1371

Bradley, Abraham, Junior, 1277

Bradley, None, 1698

Bradstone, Martin, 131

Brady, David, 1049

Brahan, John, 1006, 1507, 1689

Brand, Ludwick, 364

Brand, Thomas, 1602

Brandenberg, Samuel, 1530

Brandenberry, Conrad, 1049

Brandenbourg, Henry, 316

Brandenburg, Conrad, 1049

Brandenburgh, Henry, 1084

Brandenburgh, Samuel, 1530

Brandon, Benjamin, 1530

Brandons, None, 1161

Braner, Lewis, 1487

Branner, George, 532

Brannon, Michael, 1365

Branson, John, 339, 1064

Braselton, John, 1665

Brashear, Barrick, 733

Brasheur, Walter, 1621

Brats, Felty, 514

Bratton, James, 822, 1132, 1196

Bratton, Robert, 1477

Braucher, Conrad, 514, 1761

Braucher, Jacob, 314

Brauer, Christian, 639

Brauer, Jacob, 950

Brauer, John, 6, 747, 1624

Brausz, John, 1501

Braxton, Thomas, 1151, 1220

Bray, Henry, 1726

Breading, William, 675

Breathers, James, 992

Brechbeil, Jacob, 1719

Brechbeil. *See also* Brackbeal

Breckenridge, None, *Honorable*, 1171, 1216

Breitstein, Martin, 131

Brenner, George, 67

Brent, John, 1651

Brent, Robert, 937

Brenton, Henry, 766

Brenton, James, 766

Brewer, Benjamin, Senior, 1325

Brewer, John, 747

Brewer, None, 338

Brewster, Johnson, 1242

Brickley, Paul, 402

Bridge, John, 953

Bridges, John, 1667

Bridges, Samuel, 951

Bridwell, John, 1689

Briel, Christ., 524

Brien, Andrew D., 142

Brien, Samuel, 829

Brier, David, 1436

Brier, Samuel, 829

Brier, William, 1436

Briggs, Gray, 1354

Briggs, William Smith, 329

Bright, David, 85

Bright, Nicholas, 283

Bright, Nimrod, 141

Brightman, John, 1086

Brill, John, 828

Brindley, John, 730

Brinker, George, 430

Brinker, John, 1750

Brinton, Henry, 766

Brinton, J. H., 8

Brinton, James, 766

Brinton, John, 1049

Brinton, John H., 11, 12, 31, 44, 58, 69, 583, 650, 773, 1515, 1527, 1540, 1607, 1618, 1729, 1747

Brinton, Peter, 1153

Broadaway, Samuel, 520, 1133

Broadberry, Hezekiah, 475

Broadberry, S., 953

Broadberry, Simeon, 475

Broadbury, Hezekiah, 1313

Broadstone, Martin, 131

Broadstreet, Daniel, 1243

Broadstreet, David, 475

Broadway, Samuel, 520, 1133

Broadwell, Jacob, 998

Brobs, Jacob, 337

Brobst, Jacob, 514

Brock, J. N., 387

Brock, Jesse, 504, 748

Brock, John N., 592

Brock, Reuben, 1507

Brodaway, Samuel, 520

Broderick, William, 674

Brokaw, Abraham, 134

Brokaw, George, 828

Brombaugh, Samuel, 371

Brombaugh. *See also* Broomback, Brumbach

Brook, Francis, 101

Brook, George, 898

Brooks, A., 387

Brooks, Aaron, 592, 863, 994, 1315

Brooks, John, 1109

Brooks, Thomas, 599

Brooks, William, 1151

Broomback, Jacob, 85

Broomback. *See also* Brombaugh, Brumbach

Broovoock, Henry B., 313

Brothers, J., 1718

Brothers, James, 992

Brougher, Conrad, 514, 1761

Brougher, Jacob, 314

Brower, Christian, 639

Brower, Jacob, 950

Bulla, Thomas, 751

Bumberger, None, 961

Bumberger, William, 372

Bumgarner, Jacob, 269, 319, 617, 1155

Bumgarner. *See also* Baumgaertner

Bumpass, None, 1077

Bunn, Benjamin, 1378

Bunn. *See also* Boon, Boone

Burbick, Arthur, 281

Burch, Henry, 182

Burch, Richard, 956

Burck, Samuel, 1195

Burd, William, 951

Burger, John, 280

Burger, Michael, 776

Burger. *See also* Berger

Burges, John, 677

Burges, Joseph, 1242

Burges, None, 552

Burgess, West, 1707

Burgess, Walter S., 794

Burgey, Jacob, 533

Burk, Thomas, 1530

Burke, Alexis, 1073

Burke, John, 521

Burke, Samuel, 1195

Burkel, Thomas, 372

Burkhart, Jacob, 1602

Burkhead, Thomas, 960

Burnet, George William, 62

Burnet, Isaac, 448

Burnet, Jacob, 306, 597, 613, 1200, 1201, 1265

Burnet, John, 62

Burns, Archibald, 101

Burns, James, 217

Burns, John, 101

Burns, Robert, 1636

Burnside, Alexander, 55

Burnsides, None, 456

Burnstager, David, 1487

Burntrager, David, 722

Burrel, Richard, 360

Burrell, A., 994

Burrell, Richard, 360, 798, 1242

Burres, John, 413

Burrowes, Joseph, 21

Burrus, Charles, 1327

Bursen, Joseph, 473

Burson, Isaiah, 1118, 1190

Burson, J., 110

Burt, Asa, 779

Burt, Joseph, 1377

Burt, William, 998

Burton, Isaiah, 1118

Burton, Joseph, 1391

Burton, Levi, 630

Burton, Robert, 1445

Bury, Isaac, 239

Busby, John, 159

Bush, James, 490

Bush, John, 132, 1252, 1477

Bush, Nicholas, 132

Bushong, John, 1393

Buskirk, Isaac V., 1602

Buskirk, Samuel, 969

Bussard, Daniel, 103, 325, 709

Bussard, David, 39, 419

Bussard. *See also* Bashart, Boshart, Bossert, Buzzard

Buster, William, 1749

Butcher, Joseph, 1328

Butler, Amos, 26, 115, 829, 1073

Butler, Beal, 67, 751

Butler, Eli, 1710

Butler, John, 970, 1196, 1242

Butler, Jonathan, 1489

Butler, Stephen, 1196

Butler, Susannah, 457, 1073

Butler, Thomas, 557, 1108

Butler, William, 1582

Butt, David, 725

Butt, Henry, 1073

Butt, None, 1057

Butts, Israel, 1718

Butts. *See also* Bootes

Buxton, None, 611

Buzzard, George, 1753

Buzzard, Henry, 332

Buzzard, Jacob, 1756

Buzzard, None, 747

Buzzard. *See also* Bashart, Boshart, Bossert, Bossard

Byal, William, 1489

Byerley, Philip, 1624

Byers, John, 532

Byles, Daniel A., 1378

Byram, Benjamin, 931

Byram, Ebenezer, 1507

Byrns, C. L., 1635

Cable, Martin, 723
Cadbury, H., 987
Cadbury, Henry, 540
Cadwalader, Isaac, 555
Cadwalader, Michael, 1085
Cadwallader, James, 1784
Cadwallader, John, 960, 1626
Cadwallader, John, Junior, 1784
Cadwallader, John, Senior, 1626
Cadwallader, Joseph, 1784
Cadwallader. *See also* Kidwilder
Cagey, Jacob, 331
Cagy, Christian, 478, 717
Cagy, Jacob, 331, 456, 896
Cain, Abner, 992
Cain, William, 951
Cain. *See also* Kain
Calahan, Jesse, 1626
Calahan, William, 960
Calahan. *See also* Gallaghan
Calderhead, Alexander, 775
Caldwell, James, 27, 100, 257, 960, 1195, 1522
Caldwell, John, 1006, 1041, 1657, 1658, 1708, 1770
Caldwell, Joseph, 1478
Caldwell, Matthew, 101, 652
Caldwell, Robert, 53
Caldwell, William, 153, 991, 1314
Calhoon, David, 318, 758, 1085
Calhoon, John, 1709
Calhoon, None, 893, 961
Calhoon, William, 1679
Calton, None, 279
Calvert, Jacob, 1784
Calvert, John, 1784
Calvin, John, 593
Cameron, Alexander, 599, 1489
Cameron, John, 1197
Cameron, None, 872
Cameron, Thomas, 1550
Cameron. *See also* Kemren
Cammack, Michael, 1760
Campbell, Abraham, 1002
Campbell, Adlai, 1760
Campbell, Alexander, 378
Campbell, Alexander, *Honorable*, 627, 1128

Campbell, Archibald, 1314, 1379
Campbell, Colin, 923
Campbell, David, 1045
Campbell, James, 1123, 1536
Campbell, John, 329, 872
Campbell, John D., 1481, 1530
Campbell, Joseph, 1703
Campbell, Moses, 323, 628, 1073
Campbell, None, *Honorable Doctor*, 172
Campbell, Obadiah, 1090
Campbell, Parker, 700
Campbell, Part, 620
Campbell, Thomas, 1393
Campbell, William, 617, 751, 942, 1536
Campeau, Joseph, 849
Campeau, Julian, 884
Campeau, Nicholas, 884
Canaga, Christopher, 1110
Candy, J. B., 110
Candy, None, 8, 12
Candy. *See also* Condy
Canes, None, 998
Cannon, James, 1783
Cannon, John, 536
Cannon, Lindley, 5
Cannon, Lindsey, 5
Cannon, Matthew, 561
Cannon, Thomas, 960
Capehart, John, 1783
Capely, George, 1624
Caper, Samuel, 949
Caper. *See also* Cooper, Cuper
Caperton, Hugh, *Honorable*, 1630
Capill, Henry, 1781
Caples, William, 996
Cappock, Joseph, 680
Cappock, None, 532
Carbley, John, 927
Carey, Cephas, 1313
Carl, William, 998
Carle, Richard, 57, 599
Carlile, Laurence, 1689
Carlisle, John, 184, 568, 1567
Carlisle, Jonathan, Junior, 145, 1555
Carlough, John, 448, 632, 1002
Carlough. *See also* Garloch
Carmany, John, 1002
Carne, Henry, 270

Carne, Jacob, 270

Carns, John, 1154

Carns, Leonard, 1755

Carondolet, None, *Baron de*, 1738

Carothers, George, 524

Carow, Jean Baptiste, 934

Carpenter, E., 736

Carpenter, Edward, 748

Carpenter, Emanuel, 684, 896

Carpenter, Emanuel, Junior, 332

Carpenter, Mary Salome, 684

Carpenter, Reuben, 1014

Carr, Andrew, 949

Carr, George, 261

Carr, Hugh, 10

Carr, Richard, 408, 720

Carr, Robert, 1110

Carr, Thomas, 276, 631, 993, 1376

Carrell, Charles, 1507, 1689

Carrick, None, 1328

Carrick, William, 865

Carrington, W., 953

Carroll, Andrew, 1431

Carson, Charles, 1731

Carson, David, 1710

Carson, John, 949

Carson, William, 747

Carter, Daniel, 1206, 1610

Carter, John, 1146

Carter, Joshua, 280

Carter, None, 1328

Cartmell, Nathaniel, 1481

Cartmill, Nathaniel, 794

Cartmill, Thomas, 794, 1783

Cartmill, William, 794

Carton, William, 865

Cartwright, John, 751

Carver, Abraham, 1242

Carver, Christian, 960

Carver, Henry, 27, 994

Carver, Michael, 1481

Carver. *See also* Garber, Garver, Gerber, Jarber

Cary, Abraham, 1548

Cary, Christian, 1582

Cary, Christopher, 1582

Cary, Elnathan, 546

Cary, John, 870

Case, Jacob, 1041, 1478

Case, Joseph, 1760

Case, Samuel, 1530

Casebier, Christian, 830

Casebier. *See also* Kaesebier, Keasbear

Cass, Lewis, 996, 1366

Cassady, Weire, 710, 1012

Cassart, Jacob, 1667

Casselberry, Thomas, 959

Cassill, Henry, 1781

Castleberry, Thomas, 959

Castleman, William, 734

Castner, Michael, 1490

Castro, François de, 1333

Castro, Julien de, 1526

Cathcart, Joseph, 1531

Cathcart. *See also* Kithcart

Cattin, François, 844

Caven, George M., 1313

Caywood, William, 1036

Cecil, Joshua, 1348, 1393

Chachere, L., 1318

Chalfant, James, 1072

Chalfant, Mordecai, 337

Chalfant, Robert, 331, 456

Chamberlain, James L., 609

Chambers, Alexander, 582, 1314

Chambers, James, 52, 1303

Chambers, None, 1268

Chambers, William, 775

Champagne, Simon, 966

Champer, Jacob, 787, 1717

Champion, None, 1041

Chandler, John, 89

Chandler, Martin, 132

Chandler, Zachariah, 1601

Chandonet, Charles, 872

Chany, Samuel, 1753

Chany. *See also* Cheney

Chapman, James, 599

Chapman, Thomas, 993

Chapman, William, 27

Chapoton, Benoit, 929

Chapoton, Louis, 872

Charles, Emanuel, 960

Charles, Joseph, 632

Charles, Many, 960

Charles, Mary, 960

Charles, Samuel, 731, 1636

Charles, Smith, 535

Charley, George, 1135

Charliere, L., 1302

Charlton, James, 91

Chartier, François, 872

Chatham, James, 1371

Cheney, Joseph, 1601

Cheney. *See also* Chany

Chenoweth, Absalom, 609

Chenoweth, John, 782

Chenoweth, Joseph, 1265

Chenowith, Thomas, 998, 1002

Cherington, Thomas, 1756

Cherington, William, 1756

Cherry, Philip, 570

Chetwood, Amos, 983

Chicken, Daniel, 1776

Chilcote, James, 1072

Childress, David, 1690

Childress, J., 1458

Childress, John, 837, 845

Chouteau, Auguste, 1159, 1184, 1199

Chovan, Baptiste, 313

Chovin, Jean Baptiste, 875

Chribe, Jacob, 1012

Chribe, John, 329

Chribe, Samuel, 329

Chribe. *See also* Cribbee, Kribe

Christ, John, 319, 517

Christ, Peter, 998

Christ, Philip, 414, 747

Christ, Simon, 263

Christ. *See also* Criss

Christian, Allen, 1232

Christian, James, 1507

Christler, Samuel, 1623

Christmas, John, 1206

Christmass, John, 491, 565, 823, 1489

Christmass, Joseph, 1089

Christy, George, 960

Christy, John, 270, 1109

Christy, None, 652

Cilley, Benjamin, 1478

Circle, Lewis, 1195

Cisne, William, 849

Cissone, William, 952

Clabaugh, Henry, 711

Claiborne, F. L., 1406

Clapper, George, 1242

Clapper, Henry, 993

Clark, Abraham, 1436, 1749

Clark, David, 980

Clark, Dennis, 1659

Clark, George, 528, 643, 814

Clark, Henry, 1133

Clark, Horatio, 263

Clark, J., 983

Clark, John, 67, 142, 329, 412, 628, 927, 1750, 1779, 1783

Clark, Jonathan, 1276

Clark, Joseph, 1748

Clark, Marcus, 1667

Clark, Ninian, *Governor [of Illinois]*, 1675

Clark, None, 532, 1652

Clark, William, 1161

Clark, Winans, 1784

Clarke, George, 954, 996

Clarke, John, 953

Clarke, S., 865

Clarke, Thomas, 1041

Clarkson, Sarah, 1379

Claughburgh, Isaac, 1017

Claughburgh. *See also* Clowburg, Klaburg

Clawson, Thomas, 664, 923

Clay, H., *Honorable*, 1217

Clay, Isaac, 257, 1626

Clay, James, 120

Clay, Thomas, 1760

Claypool, Jacob, 1124

Claypoole, Jacob, 39, 121

Claypoole, William, 325

Clayton, J., 1268

Clayton, Joseph C., 478

Clayton, Thomas, 557

Clayton, William, 758

Clear, Thomas, 1626

Cleck, Daniel, 240

Cleck, Philip, 240

Clem, John, 153

Clemens, Christian, 872, 884

Clemens, John, 1085

Clements, Abraham, 318, 758

Clemings, Christian, 876

Clemons, John, 1242

Clendenin, Robert, 641, 747

Clendening, John, 1073

Conaway, L., 554

Conaway, S., 554

Concal, John, 1709

Concal. *See also* Congill, Conkle, Konkle, Kunckel

Concannon, William, 470

Concer, Jacob, 1471

Condet, None, *Honorable*, 574

Condon, John, 271

Condon. *See also* Gondon

Condy, Jonathan W., 341, 353, 354, 441, 446, 460, 466, 584, 649, 1540, 1729, 1775

Condy, None, 12, 1540

Condy. *See also* Candy

Coney, Thomas, 960

Confer, Michael, 1029

Conger, Josiah, 1779

Conger, Moses, 1371

Congill, Isaac, 552

Conkle, Jacob, 294

Conkle. *See also* Concal, Congill, Konkle, Kunckel

Conkling, Joseph, 6

Conly, Thomas, 1477

Conn, Thomas, 51

Conn. *See also* Kahn

Connally, John, 1433

Connan, Abraham, 776

Connell, Jesse, 276, 995

Conner, James, 853, 884

Conner, John, 1243, 1532

Conner, Richard, 876, 884

Conner, Samuel, 1153

Conner, William, 966, 1667

Conrad, Daniel, 349

Conrad, Jacob, 185, 1718

Conrad, None, 1057

Conrad, Valentine, 983, 995, 1477

Conrad. *See also* Conrod, Coonrad

Conrel, Nathan, 1104

Conrod, Daniel, 349

Consley, Thomas, 943

Converse, Daniel, 47, 1132

Converse, James, 331

Converse, None, 996

Converse, Simon, 331

Conway, James, 1636

Conwell, William, 1252

Cook, Allen, 969

Cook, Charity, 677

Cook, Daniel, 1317

Cook, Eli, 91

Cook, Jacob C., 1478

Cook, John, 383, 747, 751, 775, 1163

Cook, John, Junior, 1163

Cook, Mary, 677

Cook, Noah, 1489, 1531

Cook, Peter, 134

Cook, Thomas, 1478

Cook, William, 355, 702, 1042

Cooke, John, 487

Cooke, None, 1148

Cooley, Edward, 983

Cooley, Thadeus, 130

Cooley, Thomas, 1325

Cooley, William, 521

Coon, George, 153

Coon, John, 1036, 1753

Coon. *See also* Kuhn

Coonrad, Val, 995

Coonrad, Valentine, 983, 1477

Coonrad. *See also* Conrad, Conrod

Coons, Henry, 1667

Coons, Isaac, 747

Coons. *See also* Kuhnz, Kuntz

Coope, John, 1197

Cooper, Caleb, 1784

Cooper, D. C., 1401

Cooper, Daniel C., 316, 449, 587, 753, 873, 1548

Cooper, Imla, 1784

Cooper, Isaac, 532, 996, 1161

Cooper, Jacob, 261, 996

Cooper, John, 1253, 1784

Cooper, Joseph, 677, 829, 1243

Cooper, Joshua, 1154

Cooper, Levi, 490

Cooper, W., 1784

Cooper, William, 135, 142, 153, 970, 1783

Cooper. *See also* Caper, Cuper

Coopers, Peter, 1580

Copeland, Thomas, 983

Copeland, William, 268

Copline, William, 1781

Copeland, Copline. *See also* Cowpland

Copp, Joseph, 914

Copperthwait, Thomas, 1090

Copple, Jacob, 317, 550, 782, 1488

Copple, John, Senior, 550

Copple, Philip, 1086, 1151, 1592

Copple. *See also* Kappel, Koppel

Crame, None, *Colonel*, 946

Cramer, Casper, 552

Cramer, John, 628

Cramer, Zadock, 632

Cramer. *See also* Creamer, Kraemer, Kreamer

Crane, Abner, 628

Crane, Amos, 142

Crane, Jonas, 677

Crane, Jonathan, 1785

Crane, Joseph, 1481

Cranston, John, 1154

Cranwell, Henry, 747

Craven, Henry, 998

Crawford, Abel, 949, 1371

Crawford, Daniel, 5

Crawford, Edward, 1030

Crawford, James, 521, 1665, 1713

Crawford, John, 57, 1377, 1393

Crawford, None, *Honorable Doctor*, 174

Crawford, Robert, 1490, 1757

Crawford, Robert C., 1757

Crawford, Samuel, 960

Crawford, William, 142, 680, 838, 841, 960, 1253,
            1313, 1382, 1425, 1606

Crawford, William, *Honorable*, 113, 932

Creager, Henry, 992

Creager. *See also* Kreager, Kreger, Krieger, Krueger

Creamer, Christopher, 1402

Creamer, D., 1569

Creamer, Daniel, 1049

Creamer, Valentine, 1569

Creamer. *See also* Cramer, Kraemer, Kreamer

Creaton, Henry, 724

Creble, Benjamin, 1760

Creble. *See also* Grable, Grayble, Kraehbuhl

Creegan, James, 220

Creek, John, 101, 1779

Creighton, None, *Honorable*, 1545

Creighton, Thomas, 355

Creplever, Adam, 738

Creplever, Philip, 599

Crespin, Jonathan, 1133

Cress, John, 1486

Cress, William, 1486

Creviston, John, 991

Crew, Isaac, 969

Crew, Obadiah, 524

Cribbee, John, 212

Cribbee. *See also* Chribe, Kribbe

Crider, John, 732

Crider. *See also* Kraider, Kreider, Krydar

Cripman, Daniel, 26

Crisley, Lawrence, 1781

Crisman, Benjamin, 121, 181

Crispin, Jonathan, 992

Criss, Jacob, 1530

Crissman, Daniel, 26, 350, 677

Crist, Philip, 747

Crist. *See also* Christ

Crites, Henry, 864

Critz, Conard, 1667

Croft, George, 903, 1749

Croll, John, 91

Croll. *See also* Crull, Kroll

Cromley, Christian, 1109

Cromley. *See also* Crumley, Kromlegh, Kromley

Cromwell, John, 1110

Cromwell, Vincent, 1031

Cron, John, 1753

Cron. *See also* Crown, Krohn, Krown

Croninger, None, 1751

Cronninger, Peter, 1155

Crooks, Henry, 681

Crooks, James, 677

Crosby, Edward, 1314

Crosen, James, 1109

Crosen, None, 1402

Crosin, William, 319

Crouch, John, 1753

Crouch, Joseph, 1753

Crouse, Daniel, 339

Crouse, Jacob, 232

Crouse. *See also* Kraus

Crow, Thomas, 52, 253

Crowell, Devault, 1371

Crowell, John, 1073

Crowell, Michael, 632

Crown, Henry, 1241

Crown. *See also* Cron, Krohn, Krown

Crowson, Richard, 1689

Croxton, William, 1782

Croy, Mathias, 552

Crull, David, Senior, 1109

Crull. *See also* Croll, Kroll

Crumbaker, John, 837, 845, 1394

Crumbaker. *See also* Krumbacher

Crume, M. 865

Crumbine. *See* Krumbein

Davis, Elijah F., 1667

Davis, Henry, 1108

Davis, Ichabod, 960

Davis, Isaac, 1383

Davis, Israel, 1625

Davis, James, 646, 1665

Davis, John, 94, 294, 440, 448, 950, 951, 1323, 1371, 1393

Davis, Joseph, 187

Davis, L., 1653

Davis, Lewis, 187

Davis, None, 997

Davis, Owen, 288, 1243, 1582

Davis, Samuel, 134, 474, 676, 1232, 1279, 1690

Davis, Thomas, 1369

Davis, William, 142, 599, 1030, 1151

Davison, Hugh, 10

Davison, James, 1715

Davison, John, 865

Davison, Joseph, 1719, 1724

Davy, Henry, 229, 757

Davy, John, 1085

Daw, William, 991

Dawson, Charles, 1371

Dawson, David, 430

Dawson, George, 1563

Dawson, Isaac, 1549

Dawson, John, 752, 1391, 1478

Dawson, John L., 1719

Dawson, Moses, 543

Day, John, 135, 521

Day, Joseph, 1626

Day, Josiah B., 574

Day, Robert, 521

Dayton, Jonathan, 161

De Bastrop, None, *Baron*, 1333

De Camp, Moses, 1313

De Carondolet, None, *Baron*, 1738

De Castro, François, 1333

De Castro, Julien, 1526

De La Fayette, G., 1402

De La Fayette, T., 1402

De Lashmut, None, 1545

De Salcedo, Manuel, 1333

De Servieres, François M., 872

Deal, Christian, 331, 1109

Deal. *See also* Deel, Dell, Dial, Diehl, Dill, Doll, Teal, Teil

Deamorey, Samuel, 1086

Dean, J. R., 828

Dean, Jacob, 898

Dean, James, 478

Dean, Levi, 1242

Dean, Mason, 270

Dean, Nathan, 1760

Dean, Thomas, 1550

Deardorf, None, 996

Deardorff, Christian, 297, 1166

Deardorff, Daniel, 1392, 1481

Deardorff, Isaac, 119, 1379

Deardorf, Deardorff. *See also* Dierdorff

Dearmond, Alexander, 1200, 1749

Dearth, James, 1161

Dearth. *See also* Darst, Duerst

Death, George, 1195

Deaver, Abraham, 557

Deaver, Levi, 54

Deche, Jacob, 722

Deche. *See also* Dege, Deihe

Decker, Charles, 1314

Decker, Elias, 430

Decker, Elisha, 52

Decker, Isaac, 1284

Decker, Joseph, Junior, 1432

Deel, Jacob, 628

Deel. *See also* Deal, Dell, Dial, Diehl, Dill, Doll, Teal, Teil

Deelman, Conrad, 538

Deelman. *See also* Diehlmann

Deem, Adam, 953, 1243

Deem, Henry, 998

Deem. *See also* Dehm

Defert, John, 543

Deffenbauch, Daniel, 332, 1044

Deffenbaugh, Mary, 452, 472

Deffenbauch, Deffenbaugh. *See also* Devenbaugh, Tiefenbach

Defond, John, 856

Deford, John, 802, 856, 1714

Defrees, Joseph, 1029

Dege, Matthias, 1549

Dege. *See also* Deche, Deihe

Dehm, Adam, 953, 1243

Dehm, Henry, 998

Dehm. *See also* Deem

Dehuff, Peter, 418

Deibert, Jacob, 1195

Deihe, Jacob, 722

Deihe. *See also* Deche, Dege

Delader, Jacob, 865

Delassus, Charles D., *Doctor*, 1523

Dell, James O., 1041

Delong, George, 794, 1132

Delong, Jacob, 1134

Delong, James, 1132

Delong, Ns., 1662

Demaree, Samuel, 1665

Demerce, Peter, 740

Demint, James, 1436

Demoss, Peter, 1783

Demott, Abraham, 628, 632

Deneen, James, 1530

Deniston, William, 942

Denman, Abner, 1502

Denman, William, 1582

Dennis, James, 1047, 1441, 1459

Dennison, Nancy, 1601

Dennison, William, 124

Denny, Elisha, 1488

Denny, James, 331, 467, 1519

Denny, Robert, 1477

Denny, Simon, 1533

Denoyer, Francis, 876, 884

Deprew, James, 1132

Depuly, Joshua, 1624

Depuly, Solomon, 1624

Deputy, Joshua, 1624

Deputy, Solomon, 1624

Derner, Andrew, 1532

Derner. *See also* Doerner, Dorner, Turner

Derrick, John, 1507

Derroh, Joseph, 156, 1379

Desnoyer, François, 876, 884

Deter, Abraham, 10

Deter, Samuel, 659

Deter. *See also* Dieter

Devenbaugh, Adam, 1314

Devenbaugh. *See also* Deffenbaugh, Tiefenbach

Devenport, Jesse, 1313

Devor, John, 1481

Devor, None, 1012

Devore, James, 305

Devries, Joseph, 1029

Dew, Thomas, Junior, 1486

Dewalt, Henry, 1624

Dewalt, Philip, 1163

Dewees, Lewis, 1667

Dewis, Lewis, 609

Dewit, Barney, 1748

Dewitt, John, 1726

Dewitt, Peter, 950

Deywalt, Philip, 1163

Dial, Shadrack, 971

Dial. *See also* Deal, Deel, Dell, Diehl, Dill, Doll, Teal, Teil

Dice, John, 1036

Dick, George, 1582

Dick, Samuel, 829, 1543

Dickenson, None, 755

Dickenson, Thomas, 685

Dickerhuff, Peter, 1130

Dickerson, John, 1041

Dickerson, Joshua, 134

Dickerson, Richard, 1196

Dickey, David, 900, 1507

Dickey, George, Senior, 1507

Dickey, William, 1625

Dickinson, William R., 373, 691, 828

Dicks, Jacob, 849

Dickson, Andrew, 410

Dickson, Robert, 1037, 1065, 1162

Dickson, William, 1006, 1212

Diddridge, John, 1783

Diddridge. *See also* Dietrich, Ditrick, Doddridge, Teterick, Titarick, Titerack

Diehl, Christian, 331, 1109

Diehl, Edward, 327

Diehl, Jacob, 628, 722

Diehl, Peter, 606

Diehl, Shadrack, 971

Diehl. *See also* Deal, Deel, Dell, Dial, Dill, Doll, Teal, Teil

Diehlmann, Conrad, 397, 538

Diem. *See* Deem, Dehm

Diener. *See* Tener, Tiner

Dierdorff, David, 116

Dierdorff. *See also* Deardorf, Deardorff

Dieter, Abraham, 10

Dieter. *See also* Deter

Dietrich, Batson, 490

Dietrich. *See also* Diddridge, Ditrick, Doddridge, Teterick, Titarick, Titerack

Diggens, James, 1314

Dike, George, 1041

Dildine, Andrew, 1753

Dill, Peter, 67, 606

Dill. *See also* Deal, Deel, Dell, Dial, Diehl, Doll, Teal, Teil

Dillbone, Henry, 1478

Dille, Richard, 1780

Dillon, Christopher, 1626

Dills, George, 283

Dills, Jacob, 1502

Dilshaser, George, 957

Dilts, George, 283

Dilts, Jacob, 10, 1502

Dilworth, George, 445, 1433, 1507

Dimmer, Henry, 1206

Dindore, John, 239

Dingman, James, 1478

Dinsmore, None, 1329

Dinsmore, Silas, 1230, 1399

Dinsmore, William, 1286

Dinwidee, Samuel, 1625

Dinwidee. *See also* Dunwiddie

Disart, William, 1393

Ditrick, Batson, 490

Ditrick. *See also* Diddridge, Dietrick, Doddridge, Teterick, Titarick, Titerack

Dittis, James, 1195

Dittoe, Anthony, 1781

Dittoe, Jacob, 1109

Dittoe, Joseph, 1711, 1753

Divert, Frederick, 406, 577

Dixon, Arthur, 1701

Dixon, Eli, 751

Dixon, James, 951

Dixon, John, 489

Dixon, Joseph, 1549

Dixon, Joshua, 569

Dixon, None, 1328

Dixon, Robert, 50, 1667

Dixon, Stephen, 356

Dixson, John, 1651

Doddridge, Philip, 1783

Doddridge. *See also* Diddridge, Dietrich, Ditrick, Teterick, Titarick, Titerack

Dodds, E., 724

Dodds, John, 960

Dodds, W. S., 724

Dodds, William, 1072

Dodge, None, 840, 1631, 1738, 1754

Dodson, Edward, 998

Dodson, John, 1757

Doernbach, John, 960

Doerner, Andrew, 1532

Doerner. *See also* Derner, Dorner, Turner

Doerr, Conrad, 942

Doherty, Andrew, 269

Doige, Thomas, 1664

Doigs, Thomas, 1649

Doll, Abraham, 1109

Doll. *See also* Deal, Deel, Dell, Dial, Diehl, Teal, Teil

Domer, Michael, 1108

Donaldson, Aaron, 598, 1314

Donnel, Jonathan, 1481

Donnell, Archibald M., 1507

Donnell, Jonathan, 1371, 1392

Donovan, Robert, 408, 746, 1033

Dooley, Abner, 1195

Dooley, Moses, 950

Dooley, Reuben, 1530

Dooley, Silas, 532

Doran, Samuel, 1003

Dorance, Samuel, 477

Dorans, Samuel, 477

Dorgs, Thomas, 1649, 1664

Dorm, William, 1314

Dorner, Michael, 1108

Dorner. *See also* Derner, Doerner, Turner

Dorsey, John, 1108

Doty, Daniel, 1392

Doudna, Henry, 828

Dougherty, Andrew, 1090

Dougherty, John, 754

Dougherty, Thomas, 221

Doughty, Richard, 1108

Douglass, James, 1689

Douglass, Robert, 677

Douglass, Samuel, 1784

Douley, Nicholas, 1478

Dound, Jonathan, 1265

Doup, George, 78, 79, 776

Douse, Henry, 430

Dove, G., 255

Dove, George, 70, 71, 78, 79, 815, 918

Dove, None, 815

Downery, John, 545

Downs, None, 505

Downs, William, 1230

Doyle, William, 1782

Dozet, Joseph, *Doctor*, 875

Drake, Daniel, 994, 1726

Drake, David, 1024, 1610, 1719

Drake, John, 677

Drake, Lewis, 903

Drake, None, 1110

Drake, Samuel, 319, 1753

Drake, Thomas, 993

Drake, Zephaniah, 240

Draper, Isaac, 1108

Draper, Thomas, 1207

Dreisbach, Abraham, 747

Dreisbach, H., 254

Drennon, Thomas, 557

Dreshback, Samuel, 991

Driesbach, Abraham, 747

Driesbach, George, 991

Driesbach, Samuel, 991

Drisbach, Abraham, 747

Driscol, John, 1636

Drouillard, Dominique, 844

Drouillard, Nicholas, 901

Druly, Nicholas, 950

Drum, Henry, 52

Drum, Samuel, 1748

Drury, Edward, 1041

Dubois, Tousaint, 284, 1720

Duboise, William, 931

Dudderer, Conrad, 660, 661, 1569, 1672

Dudderer, John, 661

Dudgeon, Simon, 1108

Duerst, Jacob, 992

Duerst. *See also* Darst, Dearth

Duflinger, Jacob, 991

Dufour, John James, 1446, 1596

Dulman, Conrad, 397

Dulman. *See also* Tolman, Toulmin

Dum, Peter, 1314

Dumbold, Abraham, 253

Dumorey, Samuel, 1086

Dun, Peter, 1314

Dun, Walter, 1593

Duncan, John, 14, 1265

Duncan, Robert, 994

Duncan, Samuel, 485

Duncan. *See also* Dunkin

Dunckall, John, 85

Dunckall. *See also* Dunkil, Dunkle

Dungan, Joseph, 357

Dungan, Josiah, 1265

Dungan. *See also* Duncan, Dunkin

Dunham, Eliazar, 224

Dunham, Joseph, 1105

Dunham, Moses, 1719

Dunkil, John, 239

Dunkil. *See also* Dunckall, Dunkle

Dunkin, John, 14

Dunkin. *See also* Duncan, Dungan

Dunkle, John, 96, 1753, 1781

Dunkle. *See also* Dunckall, Dunkil

Dunlap, John, 754

Dunlevy, Daniel, 9

Dunlevy, Morris, 1393

Dunlop, Robert, 991

Dunn, Caleb, 593, 830

Dunn, James, 101

Dunn, Nehemiah, 1530

Dunn, P., 414

Dunn, Samuel, 748

Dunn, Sylvester, 1406, 1470

Dunn, Thomas, 257

Dunn, Williamson, 1051

Dunwiddie, Archibald, 983, 1086

Dunwiddie. *See also* Dinwidee

Dupre, Daniel, 1022

Dupree, James, 1132

Durach, Amos, 329

Durach. *See also* Darrock, Durragh

Durben, Samuel, 991

Durkee, Robert, 870

Durocher, François, 849

Durragh, Amos, 329

Durragh. *See also* Darrock, Durach

Durst. *See* Darst, Dearth, Duerst

Duseau, Jean, 901

Dusinberry, Henry, 552

Dusinberry, William, 557

Dusky, Dennis, 1041

Duvall, John, 440

Dwin, Peter, 1314

Dwire, Isaac, 1393

Dwyer, Isaac, 1393

Dye, Benjamin, 1265

Dye, Daniel, 1491

Dye, James, 1242

Dye, John, 969

Ellison, Andrew, 986

Ellison, Robert, 1592

Elson, J. H., 960

Elsworth, Jacob, 1370

Elwell, Amariah, 1041

Ely, Isaac, 992

Ely, John, 254, 1155

Ely, Simon, 632, 751

Embree, Amos, 212, 234

Embree, Isaac, 722

Embree, Jacob, 953

Emerson, Jesse, 959

Emerson, Thomas, 905

Emison, James, 766, 1493

Emmard, Peter, 1313

Emmerich. *See* Emreg, Emrick

Emmerson, Jesse, 959

Emmerson, Thomas, 905

Emmert, Martin, 1084

Emmins, Benjamin, 1050

Emreg, John, 380

Emrey, John, 380

Emrick, Christopher, 135, 153, 224

Emrick, John, 942

Emrick, Michael, 942

Emrick, None, 1109

Emry, Conrad, 1601

Emyert, Jonah, 1160

Endsley, Andrew, 752

Endsley, John, 57, 115

Endsley. *See also* Andsley, Ensley

Engel. *See* Angle, Engle, Ingle

Engelmann. *See* Ingleman

Engle, Caleb, 493

Engle, Henry, 1753

Engle, Isaac, 411

Engle, Michael, 384, 459

Engle. *See also* Angle, Ingle

English, James, 434

English, Joseph, 1391

English, Samuel, 1031

Enlas, Jacob, 470

Ennis, John, 1328

Ennis, None, 1241

Enoch, Abner, 632

Enoch, Isaac, 1012, 1783

Enoch, John, 903, 949, 1243

Enock, John, 949

Enotrrie, Michael, 950

Ensey, John, 1548

Ensey, None, 1335

Ensley, Jacob, 1314

Ensley. *See also* Andsley, Endsley

Enstine, None, 1262

Enterken, William, 319

Enyard, Samuel, 1667

Erhardt, Philip, 384

Erhardt. *See also* Arhart

Erlewine, John, 1379

Erlewine. *See also* Earlywine, Fruehwein

Ernest, Michael, 412

Ernst, Michael, 1538

Ernst, None, 778

Ernst, William, 268

Ernest, Ernst. *See also* Arnst, Earnest

Esel. *See* Yeazel

Eseland, John, 352

Especk, Christian, 104

Essery, Abner, 991

Essig, Simon, 1377

Esteb, Isaac, 654, 659

Esterling, Caleb, 26

Estes, Obadiah, 677

Estill, Wallis, 1689

Euker, William, 677

Eulas, Jacob, 470

Eustine, None, 1262

Eustrrie, Michael, 950

Evans, Benjamin, 91, 1031, 1313

Evans, Caleb, 1225, 1781

Evans, David, 732

Evans, Diana, 992

Evans, Edward, 950

Evans, Isaac, 81, 949, 950

Evans, John, 402, 1272, 1356, 1489

Evans, Joseph, 527, 992, 1041, 1196, 1313

Evans, Thomas, 85, 991, 1488

Evans, Washington, 1549

Evans, William, 1313

Evansdant, John, 283

Evaris, David, 1753

Eveleezar, George, 983

Everhard, Henry, 549

Everman, Samuel, 1265

Everton, Joshua, 1557

Everton, Mary, 26

Flick. *See also* Flach, Fleck, Flake

Flickener, Christian, 1750

Flickenger, Michael, 996

Flickever, Christian, 1750

Flickner, John, 959

Flinn, John, 632, 1726

Flint, John, 1161

Flint, John, Senior, 1041

Floar, Jacob, 1513

Flood, Benjamin, 680

Florey, Emmanuel, 1073

Florey, Henry, 84

Florey, Joseph, 1436

Flory, Henry, 751

Flowers, Henry, 1242

Flowers, Ignatius, 1406, 1470

Flowers, R., 318

Flowers, Richard, 272, 290

Floyd, William, 1569

Floyll, William, 1569

Fluckey, George, 1132

Fluhr, Jacob, 1513

Flynn. *See* Flinn

Fogalgasang, C., 1029

Fogalgasang, Catharina, 495

Fogalgasang, Christian, 495, 1401

Fogalgasang, George, 495

Fogalgasang, Jacob, 495

Fogalgasang. *See also* Vogelgesang

Fogel, Michael, 950

Fogel. *See also* Vogel

Foht, John, 349

Foht, Jonas, 349

Foht. *See also* Fast, Faust, Fouts, Pfautz, Pfoutz, Phoutz

Foley, James, 369

Foley, John, 818

Folk, George, 114

Folk, Peter, 758, 1108

Folker, Christopher, 101

Foos, Benjamin, 1369

Foose, Griffith, 659

Foos, Foose. *See also* Fuss

Foot, John Jacob, 1719

Forbes, Arthur, 356

Forbes, William, 1531

Forcenight, John, 1049

Ford, Adam C., 337

Ford, Bartlett, 1434

Ford, John, 85, 570, 1434

Ford, Stephen, 380, 599, 1569

Ford, William, 53, 271

Foreacre, James, 1196

Forney, Nancy, 592

Fornig, Peter, 77

Forquehar, None, 960, 985

Forrest, Lewis, 1073

Forrest, Richard, 299, 322, 334, 340, 365, 370, 382, 387, 405, 409, 431, 588, 769, 930

Forst, Stephen, 1569

Forster, Andrew, 103, 1071

Forster, William, 103, 1071, 1781

Forsyth, J., 1632

Forsyth, Robert, 952

Fost, Adam, 57

Fost. *See also* Fast, Faust, Foht, Fouts, Pfautz, Pfoutz, Phoutz

Foster, Jessee, 960

Foster, Samuel, 1490

Foulk, Peter, 1534

Foulk. *See also* Folk

Foulks, William, 1253, 1610

Fourcreaux, Pierre, 901

Fourman, Jacob, 1109

Fouts, Andrew, 26, 1478

Fouts, Daniel, 163, 546

Fouts, David, 630, 942, 1477

Fouts, Henry, 1110

Fouts, Jacob, 335, 677, 762, 776, 983, 1477

Fouts, Lewis, 140, 761

Fouts, Noel, 1592

Fouts, William, 163, 592, 718, 942

Fouts. *See also* Fast, Faust, Foht, Fost, Pfautz, Pfoutz, Phoutz

Fowler, Samuel, 487

Fox, David, 1392

Fox, Elijah, 1749

Fox, Frederick, 484, 1002

Fox, William, 1582

Fox. *See also* Fuchs

Foy, Michael, 526

Foy, William, 525, 530

Foy, William, Senior, 245, 694

Fraer, James, 1489

Frame, David, 557

Frame, James, 711, 1108

Frame, John, 1072, 1486

Frame, Thomas, 996

Frame, William, 996

Francis, David, 1530

Frank, Andrew, 1534

Frank, George, 1393, 1784

Frank, John, 763

Franklin, Elijah, 1690

Franks, Jacob, 952

Frantz, Jacob, 950, 1012

Franz, John, 758

Fraunce, Adam, 557

Frazee, James, 1371, 1392

Frazer, George, 1313

Frazer, James, 1489

Frazer, Micajah, 1752

Frazer, William, 1601

Frech, Francis, 1325

Frech, George, 1315

Fredderolf, Frederick, 452

Fredderrolf, Frederick, 472

Fredderrolf. *See also* Fiederrolf

Frederick, None, 991

Free, Spencer, 740

Freed, John, 522, 1750

Freeman, Benjamin, 983

Freeman, F., 1092

Freeman, Henry, 212

Freeman, Isaac, 1748

Freeman, John, 329, 998, 1029, 1502

Freeman, None, 1232

Freeman, Samuel, 667, 942, 1029

Freeman, Spencer, 740

Freeman, Stephen, 402

Freeman, Thomas, 859, 1202, 1278, 1279, 1362, 1451, 1698, 1766

Freeman, William, 935

Freezel, B., 1444

Fregin, Juliana, 1548

Frei, John, Senior, 1549

Frei, Peter, 996

Freibach, John, 457, 1530

Freibach. *See also* Fryback

Freiberger, George, 1328, 1548

Freiberger. *See also* Fryberger

Freidline, Henry, 996

Freimeier, William, 1557

Freimeier. *See also* Frymires

Freitag, Henry, 1030

Frel, James, 953

French, Elijah, 599

French, Ezekiel, 1195, 1436

French, Henry, 475, 1478

French, Israel, 424

French, Jeremiah, 1530

French, Micah, 1110

French, Ralph, 91

Fresh, Francis, 1325

Fresh, George, 1315

Friday, Henry, 1030

Fried, John, 522

Friedlein, Henry, 996

Friedley, Lewis, 1109

Friedrich. *See* Frederick

Friend, Abraham, 903

Friend, Andrew, 337, 991

Friend, Augustine, 337

Friend, Elijah, 476, 778

Friend, Joseph, 296, 864, 1050

Friend, None, 747, 1402

Friend, Samuel, 332

Frobisher, None, 934

Frohmann, Jacob, 751

Froman, Jacob, 751

Frost, Amos, 503

Frost, Isaiah, 1579

Frost, William, 350

Frueher. *See* Fraer

Fruehwein, John, 1379

Fruehwein. *See also* Earlywine, Erlewine

Fry, John, 1393

Fry, John, Senior, 1549

Fry, Peter, 996

Fryback, John, 457, 1530

Fryback. *See also* Freibach

Fryberger, George, 1328, 1548

Frye, Abraham, 1625

Frye, Nathaniel, 1205

Frymires, William, 1557

Fuchs, Frederick, 484

Fuchs. *See also* Fox

Fudge, David, 1667

Fudge, Jacob, 1354, 1406

Fulkamare, John M., 747

Fulkamore, John Martin, 292

Fulks, William, 1253, 1610

Fuller, Thomas, 1108

Fullerton, James, 559

Fullerton, William, 1439

Fulton, Andrew, 1551

Fulton, Benjamin, 993

Fulton, John, 885

Fulton, John A., 975

Fulton, None, 1333, 1742, 1744

Fulton, Samuel, 1327

Fulton, William, 1314

Funderbaugh, Jacob, 998

Funderburgh, Daniel, 677

Funderbaugh, Funderburgh. *See also* Von Der Berg, Vonderbach

Funk, Daniel, 1756

Funk, Henry, 1135

Funk, Jacob, 43, 719, 824

Funk, Martin, 1197

Funk, Samuel, 1050

Funkhauser, Daniel, 337

Funkhauser. *See also* Finkhauser

Fuqua, Silas, 1106

Furgus, James, 1195

Furney, Abraham, 1486

Fuson, Joel, 546

Fuss, Griffith, 659

Fuss, John Jacob, 1719

Fuss. *See also* Foos

Gachnour, John, 1682

Gachnour. *See also* Gochnour

Gaddes, Jacob, 132

Gaddis, Henry, 1036

Gaddis, J., 830

Gaddis, None, 271

Gains, George S., 837, 845

Gairy, Gideon, 52, 1023, 1065

Galbraith, James, 1772

Galbraith, James McC., 1626

Galbraith, John, 1626, 1717, 1772

Galbraith, Nathan, 268

Galbreath, John, 1502

Galbreath, Nathan, 828

Gale, Rufus, 1718

Galladay, Abraham, 569, 754

Gallaghan, Edward, 1591

Gallaghan. *See also* Calahan

Gallaher, James, 764, 812

Gallaher, John, 1089

Gallaher. *See also* Gallegher

Gallaspy, None, 319

Gallatin, Albert, *Honorable*, 933, 1275, 1280, 1401, 1468, 1516

Gallaway, William, 459

Gallegher, Thomas, 991

Gallegher. *See also* Gallaher

Galloway, George, 1478

Galloway, James, 924, 960, 992, 1478, 1548

Galloway, James M., 1530

Galloway, James, Junior, 56, 944, 945, 958, 984

Galloway, John, Senior, 945

Galyean, Jacob, 1041

Galyean, Thomas, 1041

Gamble, John, 659

Gamble, William, 486, 496, 687

Gammler. *See* Gomlar

Gams, John, 531

Ganier, Isaac, 872

Gano, John S., 1783

Garard, Jacob, 949

Garard. *See also* Garrard, Gerrard

Garber, Philip, 992

Garber. *See also* Carver, Garver, Gerber, Jarber

Garbrick, Adam, 114

Garbuck, Adam, 316

Garbuck, None, 1401

Garby, Samuel, 960

Gard, David, 1749

Gard, Levi, 1195

Gard, Stephen, 465, 949

Gardiner, J., 24

Gardner, Jacob, 251

Gardner, John, 100, 116, 1049, 1242

Gardner, None, 1417

Gardner, William, 268

Garet, Stephen, 949

Garinger, David, 919

Garlach, Adam, 1502

Garlach, John, 1530

Garlach. *See also* Carlough, Garlaugh, Garlough

Garland, David, *Honorable*, 192

Garlaugh, John, 1530

Garlough, Adam, 1502

Garlough. *See also* Carlough, Garlach

Garner, Henry, 101, 865

Garr, Abraham, 659

Garrard, Abner, 949

Garrard, David, 998

Garrard, Jacob, 949, 998

Garrard, Nathaniel, 1371

Garrard, None, 1302

Garrard, William, 1318, 1420, 1421, 1462

Garrard. *See also* Garard, Gerrard

Garrell, William, 1036

Garretson, Casparus, 1626

Garrett, Jacob, 1624

Garrett, Joab, 1499

Garringer, David, 332

Garrison, Aaron, 1478

Garrison, Abraham, 426

Garrison, David, 1265

Garrison, Elijah, 1710, 1783

Garver, Christian, 1049

Garver. *See also* Carver, Garber, Gerber, Jarber

Gary, J. J., 486

Gary, J. M., 486

Gass, William, 133, 143, 993

Gassaway, Thorrias, 1551

Gaston, Hugh, 1049

Gaston, Joseph, 546

Gaston, William, 1195

Gates, Adam, 1753

Gates, Jacob, 449

Gates, Timothy M., 1709

Gaudy, J. B., 1371

Gaudy, J. S., 1371

Gaudy, William, 998, 1371

Gaudy. *See also* Gowdy

Gaul, George, 52

Gaunt, Jacob, 960

Gaunt. *See also* Yandt, Yant, Yount

Gause, Jesse, 70, 256

Gavel, None, 475

Gebhard, Valentin, 21

Gebhardt, Henry, 829

Gebhart, V., 1785

Geer, John, 1548

Gehr, John, 747

Gehringer. *See* Garinger

Geier, John, 1548

Geiger, Frederick, 160, 730

George, John, 1626

George, Robert, 504

George, Thomas, 1090

George, William A., 870

George, William, Senior, 1242

Gephart, George, 794

Gephart, Henry, 829

Gephart. *See also* Gebhardt

Gerber, Abraham, 830

Gerber, Philip, 992

Gerber. *See also* Carver, Garber, Garver, Jarber

Gerberich. *See* Garbrick, Garbuck

Gerchnour, John, 1682

Gerlach. *See* Carlough, Garlach, Garlaugh, Garlough

Germany, John, 1651

Gerrard, Abner, 949

Gerrard, David, 998

Gerrard, Jacob, 949, 998

Gerrard, Jesse, 115, 829

Gerrard, Lodowick, 1377

Gerrard. *See also* Garard, Garrard

Gesey, John U., 747

Gesey. *See also* Giese

Gesserman, William, 497

Getz, John, 991

Giasson, Jacques, 872

Gibson, John, 1582

Gibson, Robert, 659, 751

Gibson, Thomas, 134, 1406, 1692

Gibson, William, 787, 1379

Giese, John U., 747

Giese, Nicholas, 1243

Giese. *See also* Gesey

Gieseman, George, 470

Gifford, William, 1251

Gift, Nicholas, 212

Gilbert, John Henry, 1717

Gilbert, Walter, 1291

Gilchrist, John, 111, 1089

Gilchrist, Robert, 628, 652

Gilcrease, Robert, 1151

Gilham, Thomas, 131

Gill, B., 1002

Gill, R., 1002

Gill, Samuel, 959

Gillaspy, Moses, 1750

Gillespie, George, 56, 135, 142

Gillespie, James, 435, 634, 992

Gillespie, John M., 288

Gillespy, None, 319

Gilliand, John, 923

Gilliard, Joseph, 1333

Gilligan, None, 1041

Gilliland, Hugh, 474

Gilliland, John, 923

Gilliland, Thomas, 1371

Gillson, Richard, 1569

Gillstrape, Richard, 317

Gilman, Benjamin Ives, 202

Gilmore, Francis, 1030

Gilmore, Nathaniel, 131

Gilmore, R., 1000

Gilmore, Robert, 1782

Gilson, John, 131

Gilson, Moses, 378, 592

Gilstrap, Rich, 776

Gilstrap, Richard, 317, 1477

Giltner, Abraham, 605

Giltner, Bernard, 779

Giltner, Francis, 140, 721, 1488

Giltner, George, 1779

Giltner, Jacob, 995

Giltner, John, 786, 983, 1325

Giltner, Michael, 1778

Giltner, Richard, 877

Gilton, T. M., 1118

Gimlens, George, 1132

Giosson, Jacques, 966

Giphart, Valentin, 21

Giphart. *See also* Gebhard, Gebhardt, Gephart

Gison, Thomas, 1007

Gist, Independence, 1716

Gist, Joseph C., 1679

Gist, Mordecai, 1679, 1716

Gist, Samuel, 1072

Gittner, Abraham, 605

Givens, George, 262

Givens, Thomas, 766

Gladden, Joseph, 1049

Gladden, None, 119

Gladden, William, 106

Glasgow, John, 1719

Glasmore, A., 1268

Glass, David, 28

Glass, Jacob, 1315

Glass, John, 120

Glass, Matthias, 960

Glaze, Adam, 1391, 1568

Glaze, Andrew, 747

Glaze, George, 327, 747, 896, 1041, 1243, 1530

Glen, James, 758

Glen, John, 268

Glen, William, 269

Glenn, J., 1002

Glenn, W., 1002

Glick, Daniel, 240, 430

Glick, Jacob, 314

Glick, Peter, 339

Glick. *See also* Click

Glidwell, Robert, 829

Gliner, Frederick, 1753

Glover, Elijah, 1781

Glover, Uriah, 983, 1718

Glover, Zacheriah, 1436

Goble, Isaac, .1582

Gochnour, John, 99, 1015

Gochnour. *See also* Gachnour

Godfroy, Gabriel, 966

Godfroy, Gabriel, *Colonel*, 884, 901, 952

Godfroy, Gabriel, Senior, 934

Godfroy, None, 952

Goe, Henry B., 480, 481, 1486

Goetz, John, 991

Goff, William, 1582

Gold, None, 885

Gold, Thomas R., *Honorable*, 850

Goldsgher, Thomas, 991

Goldsmith, John, 1110

Goldthwait, John, 430

Golloday, Abraham, 219

Gombar, Jacob, 552

Gomlar, Jacob, 176

Gondon, John, 935

Gondon. *See also* Condon

Good, John, 430

Good, John, Senior, 94, 991

Goodin, Smith, 1549

Goodwin, John, 992

Goodwin, Nathan, 751

Goodwin, Richard, 153

Goodwin, William, 942

Goodwine, Seth, 101

Gordon, George, 470, 992

Gordon, James, 738, 742, 1108, 1625

Gordon, John, 935

Gordon, Martin, 1292

Gordon, Samuel, 1135

Gordon, Thomas, 384

Gordon, William, 1533

Gorsuch, Nicholas, 852

Gosden, James, 1625

Gotschall, Joseph, 1569

Gough, Jesse, 535

Gouin, Charles, Senior, 901

Gouldin, John, 599

Gowdy, William, 998

Grable, Benjamin, 1760

Grable, Jonathan, 1315

Grable. *See also* Creble, Grayble, Kraehbuhl

Graffis, Abraham, 1711

Graffis, Jacob, 332, 1753

Graham, David, 1036

Graham, Hugh, 1196

Graham, Jared, 52

Graham, John, 363, 412, 476, 778, 1049, 1217, 1627

Graham, John K., 997

Graham, None, 316, 1402

Graham, Robert, 504, 1610

Graham, Ward, 1202

Grant, Alexander, 313, 872

Grant, George, 119, 186

Grant, John, 599

Grant, Robert, 961

Grass, Daniel, 763, 1760

Grate, George, 355

Grauntz, Adam, 275

Graves, Francis, 951

Gray, David, 1710

Gray, James, 1393

Gray, Jesse, 995

Gray, John, 1557, 1678, 1760

Gray, Josias, 951

Gray, Leven, 679

Gray, Richard, 707, 903

Gray, Robert, 707, 903, 1710

Gray, Samuel, 780

Gray, Thomas, 269

Gray, William, 632, 1433, 1689

Grayble, Jonathan, 380

Grayble. *See also* Creble, Grable, Kraehbuhl

Grayham, Michael, 1610

Grayham, Robert, 1610

Grayson, John, 1507, 1689

Greave, Isaac, 478

Greave, John, 430

Green, Abraham, 1549

Green, Clemuel, 498

Green, Elias, 870

Green, Esther, 1313

Green, George, 1314, 1549

Green, George W., 1757

Green, Henry, 1086

Green, Joseph, 1530

Green, On. B., 1320

Green, Raynal, 188

Green, Regnal, 191

Green, Roggers, 527

Green, Thomas, 747

Green, Timothy, 794

Green, William, 970

Greene, Thomas, 1781

Greener, John, 1436

Greenewald, Abraham, 217

Greer, Joshua, 1783

Greer, Moses, 1783

Greer, Valentine, 1090

Gregg, Andrew, 1259, 1471

Gregg, Andrew, *Honorable*, 397, 548, 560, 580, 1038, 1093, 1245

Gregg, John, 663

Gregg, Samuel, 1041

Gregg, Silas, 10, 1195

Gregg, Smith, 1369

Gregg, William, 991

Gregory, George, 1049

Gregory, Henry, 960

Greip, John, 329

Greip, Samuel, 329

Greip. *See also* Grieb, Gripe

Grenwell, Jacob, 465

Gresmer, George, 1313

Grewell, Jacob, 942

Grewell, Timothy, 748

Grey, Samuel, 780

Grieb, Isaac, 478

Grier, John, 1601

Grier, Valentine, 1090

Griesemer. *See* Gresmer

Griffard, Laurent, 853

Griffard, Louis, 901

Griffard, Pierre, 872

Griffin, None, *Honorable*, 1306, 1524

Griffin, Robert, 1534

Griffith, None, 1725

Griffith, Stephen, 1507

Griffith, William, Junior, 901

Griffiths, Thomas, 960

Grifford, Pierre, 872

Grigg, Thomas, *Captain*, 246

Grimes, George, 1501

Grimes, James, 1478

Grimes, Joseph, 599

Grimes, William, 1393, 1478

Gripe, Jacob, 1530

Gripe, John, 135, 329

Gripe, Joseph, 1779, 1783

Gripe, Samuel, 329, 628

Gripe. *See also* Greip, Grieb

Groenewald, Abraham, 217

Groninger, John, 1626

Groninger, Joseph, 1626

Groom, Ezekiel, 747

Groundz, Adam, 275

Grous, George, 116

Grover, John, 998

Groves, David, 1557

Groves, John, 89

Grubb, William, 764, 1314

Gruber, Christian, 349

Gruber, John, 998

Grueter, Frederick, 952

Grumrine, Christian, 52

Grumrine, Michael, 1155

Grumrine, None, 1056

Grumrine, Peter, 135

Grymes, Philip, 1006, 1291

Gudgell, Daniel, 1755

Gudgell, Stephen, 1624, 1755

Guerke. *See* Pickle *(translation)*

Guest, None, 1012

Gullion, John, 631, 1591

Gumo, Roggers, 527

Gunckle, Philip, 544

Gunckle. *See also* Concal, Congill, Conkle, Konkle, Kunckel

Gundy, Christian, 239

Gundy, John, 1753

Gundy, Joseph, 561

Gunes, John, 970

Gustin, Jeremiah, 107

Guttray, Robert, 1784

Guy, Joseph, 934

Gwathmey, Samuel, 1006, 1551, 1592

Gwyn, Hugh, 1393

Hack, Peter, 27

Hackelman, Jacob, 1041

Hackleman, Abraham, 652

Hadden, John, 750

Haeusel, Anthony, 1393

Haeusle, Levi, 477

Haeusle, Samuel, 119

Haeusel, Haeusle. *See also* Hausel, Housel, Housley

Haeusler, John, 1569

Haeusler. *See also* Hoslar

Haffort, Solomon, 339

Hafner. *See also* Hapner, Hepner

Haggerty, Isabella, 257

Hahn, Daniel, 114

Hahn, Peter, 1371

Hail, Moses, 1761

Hailey, Thomas, 22

Haimbough, Henry, 764

Haines, Henry, 996

Haines, Isaac, 960

Haines, Leonard, 433

Haines, Nathaniel, 561

Haines, Samuel, 1060, 1224

Hainey, John, 1625

Hains, Benjamin, 1556

Hains, Henry, 1546

Hains, Jacob, 1379

Hains, Jesse, 474

Halberstadt, A., 387

Halberstadt, Anthony, 731, 1502

Halberstadt, David, 973, 1111

Halberstall, Michael, 10

Halberstudt, Anthony, 731

Halbrooks, George, 1760

Hale, Moses, 1761

Hale, Thomas, 960

Halinsdoff, William, 1082

Hall, Benjamin, 473

Hall, Daniel, 747

Hall, Henry, 1029, 1109

Hall, Isaac, 1086

Hall, John, 131, 212, 475, 1392

Hall, Nathan, 132

Hall, None, 532

Hall, Parnel, 592

Hall, Richard D., 350

Hall, Robert, 1626

Hall, William, 850, 927, 1002

Haller, Adam, 747

Haller, Henry, 337, 1314

Haller, Jacob, 1029

Haller, John, 1478

Haller. *See also* Holler

Halstead, Samuel, 1779
Halten, Henry, 747
Halverstadt, David, 1111
Hamar, William, 435, 628, 950
Hamburger, Henry, 747
Hamilton, David, 1134
Hamilton, John, 668
Hamilton, Jonathan, 1490
Hamilton, Thomas, 142, 632
Hamilton, William, 370, 378, 552, 1242, 1753
Hamlin, John, 493
Hamm, John, 1398
Hamman, Abraham, 752
Hammasfar, Abraham, 991
Hammel, George, 570
Hammer, Elisha, 459
Hammer, Jacob, 53
Hammet, James, 175
Hammock, John, 1271, 1479
Hammon, Harry, 1378
Hammon, John, 461
Hammon, Martin, 51
Hammon, Philip, 828
Hammond, Charles, 1717
Hammond, John, 543
Hammond, Thomas, 543
Hampson, Bryan, 255
Hampson, John, 476, 747
Hampton, Robert, 991
Hamringhaus, John, 1640
Hanaway, John, 478
Hancock, John, 56
Hancock, Vatchel, 1153, 1557
Handley, George, 1625
Hanes, Abraham, 329
Hanes, Jonas, 1625
Hanes, Jones, 1625
Hanesck, Joseph, 949
Haney, Jonas, 1726
Hanger, Charles, 1109
Hanger, Joseph, 1196
Hanger, William, 1550
Hanimet, George, 1132
Hanley, Zachariah, 1041
Hann, Peter, 1371
Hanna, Andrew, 1601
Hanna, David, 1625
Hanna, Henry, 557, 1500

Hanna, James, 27
Hanna, John, 552, 652, 737, 1709
Hanna, Robert, 362, 735
Hanna, Robert, Junior, 1502
Hanna, Thomas, 323, 1379
Hansel, Christopher, 298, 1478
Hansel, George, 1478
Hansell, Jacob, 953
Hanson, Samuel, 747
Hantz, George Adam, 57
Hapner, Abraham, 224
Hapner, Henry, 680, 865
Harah, William, 1550
Harah. *See also* O'Hara
Harbaugh, Daniel, 1489
Harbaugh, John, 1108
Harberson, James, 1477
Harberson, John, 403
Harbough, William, 323
Harbour, Elisha, 91
Harbour, Jesse, 903, 1235
Harbour, Joel, 632, 927
Harbour, William, 212
Hardesty, Joseph, 747
Hardesty, None, 625
Hardesty, William, 384
Hardgrove, Richard, 1378
Hardiman, John, 612, 1074
Hardiman. *See also* Hardman
Hardin, Eliakim, 1625
Hardin, Ignatius, 434
Hardin, John, 680, 1313
Harding, John, 169
Harding, Robert, 532
Hardisty, John, 394
Hardisty, Ralph, 394
Hardman, Daniel, 134, 268
Hardman. *See also* Hardiman
Hardy, James, 991
Hare, Henry, 268, 524
Hare, John, 134, 524
Hargraves, Wyllis, 1648
Hargrove, William, 486
Harlan, Samuel, 1161, 1195, 1478
Harlass, George, 475, 953
Harless, David, 1507
Harless, Henry, 1689
Harlin, George, Junior, 347

Harlin, Samuel, 950, 1313

Harlis, David, 677

Harman, Jacob, 747

Harman, John, 570, 1008

Harmon, None, 1662

Harnan, John, 570

Harnell, Elijah, 1002

Harner, Abraham, 459

Harner, George, 142

Harner, Michael, 168

Harness, George, 419, 572, 1671

Harness, Joseph, 159

Harnett, Elijah, 1002

Harney, John, 942, 1625

Harnison, Abraham, 1549

Harper, James, 1478

Harper, John, 751

Harper, Richard, 332

Harper, Thomas, 931

Harpley, Nathaniel, 1393

Harpur, Richard, 332

Harrall, Isaac, 983

Harrell, John, 1530

Harrell, Obediah, 632

Harris, Abraham, 617

Harris, Benjamin, 359, 1002

Harris, Edward, 733, 1486

Harris, Francis E., 1278, 1327, 1689

Harris, Israel, 1328

Harris, Jacob, 1031

Harris, John, 316, 606

Harris, Jonas, 533

Harris, Joseph, 521, 535, 953, 1243

Harris, None, 325, 1232, 1362

Harris, Obadiah, 1313

Harris, R., 1279

Harris, Richard, 676, 679

Harris, Stephen, 1163, 1719

Harris, Thomas, 1242, 1486

Harris, William, 236

Harrison, Abraham, 1549

Harrison, Bejamin, 134

Harrison, Christ., 983

Harrison, Ezekiel, 983

Harrison, George, 747

Harrison, Jeremiah, 1135

Harrison, John, 751, 1756

Harrison, William H., 1135

Harrod, Levi, 732, 1252

Harrow, Alexander, 313, 875

Harsberger, Abraham, 1532

Harschmann, John, 949

Harshman, Jonathan, 546

Harshman, Philip, 1371

Harshman. *See also* Hershman, Hirschmann, Horseman

Hart, Elijah, 996

Hart, Finehas, 1073

Hart, Finney, 632

Hart, Isaac, 953

Hart, John, 532, 1750

Hart, Leonard, 994

Hart, Miles, 1315

Hart, Richard, 384

Hartap, James, 1041

Harter, Adam, 722

Harter, Christian, 350, 386, 950

Harter, George, 459

Harter, Henry, 1757

Harter, Jacob, 474, 1393

Hartford, George, 1090

Hartford, Thomas, 268, 370

Hartin, Aaron, 671

Hartin, Edmund, 659

Hartin, Isaac, 532

Hartin, Joseph, 359

Hartman, David, 182

Hartman, John, 357

Hartzell, Abraham, 56

Harvey, Caleb, 1243

Harvey, David, 271

Harvey, Isaac, 1073

Harvey, John, 359, 677, 1031, 1041, 1073, 1084, 1478

Harvey, Robert, 1530

Harvey, William, 1710

Harwood, Philip, 1582

Hashman, Peter, 359

Hastings, James, 557

Hastings, William, 1313

Haston, Benjamin, 1049

Haston, None, 1573

Hatabaugh, George, 1602

Hatch, John, 55

Hatcher, Isaac, 118, 246

Hatcher, Rachel, 1195

Hatchinson, Samuel, 57

Hatfield, Levin, 289

Hatfield, Owen, 1487

Hatfield, Thomas, 520

Hathaway, Abiathar, 1667

Hathaway, Edward, 478

Hatton, Aquilla, 993, 1050

Hatton, Reuben, 1195

Haucher, Henry, 82

Hauger, Henry, 82

Hauger, William, 1550

Hausel, Christopher, 1478

Hausel, George, 1478

Hausel. *See also* Haeusel, Haeusle, Heuslie, Housel

Hauser, George, 478

Hauser, Jacob, 239

Hauser, John, 337

Hauser, Jonathan, 1557

Hauser, Martin, 5, 410, 533, 599, 1393

Hauser. *See also* Houser

Haushalter, Adam, 1314

Hausler, John, 1569

Hautz, Christian, 274, 292, 293, 372

Hautz, Jacob, 85, 1073, 1109, 1134, 1569

Hautz. *See also* Houtz

Hawkins, Amos, 628, 680, 931

Hawkins, Benjamin, 192, 532

Hawkins, Eli, 1135

Hawkins, John, 1041, 1073

Hawkins, Levi, 1667

Hawkins, Nathan, 953

Hawler, John, 1569

Hawn, Daniel, 114

Haworth, James, 1012

Haworth, Sampson, 1012

Hawthorne, Nathan, 53

Hay, Charles, 57

Hay, David, 1108

Hay, Jacob, 18, 1550

Hay. *See also* Heu, Hoy

Haycock, John, 100

Hayden, Christopher, 521

Hayes, Andrew, 434

Hayes, Joseph, 569

Haymond, Colder, 1530

Hays, Abiah, 1161

Hays, James, 1624

Hays, John D., 1557

Hays, Jonathan, 364, 1314

Hays, Robert, 532

Hays, Samuel, 1378

Hays, Thomas, 1490

Hays, William, 485

Hayse, Robert, 632

Hazen, Charlotte, 885, 886

Hazlett, James, 599

Hazlett, Joseph, 953

Heaston, Daniel, 135

Heaston, John, 135

Heath, John, 991

Heaton, Daniel, 1667

Heaton, Ebenezer, 949, 1749

Heaton, Ebenezer, Senior, 1667

Heaton, John, 1481

Heaton, None, *Doctor*, 49

Heavilin, Samuel, 561

Heckewelder, John, 210, 382, 393

Heckewelder, None, 757

Heckley, Benjamin, 1108

Hedge, Joseph, 764

Hedges, Caleb, 1753

Hedges, James, 1036

Hedges, Jesse, 337

Hedges, Joshua, 146, 905

Hedges, Mary, 146

Hedgpeth, Charles, 1507

Hedrick, Abraham, 1436

Hedrick, William, 1436

Heever, John, 992

Heever. *See also* Hoober, Hoover, Hover, Huber, Huver

Heffelly, Peter, 828

Hefly, Charles, 659

Hegeman, Aaron, 995

Heiger, Martin, 1085, 1132

Heighway, John, 1328, 1481

Heighway, None, 1762

Heil, Conrad, 788, 928

Heil, Moses, 1761

Heil. *See also* Heyl

Heimbach. *See* Haimbaugh

Heimleck, Andrew, 182

Heimlich, Andrew, 182

Heinemann. *See* Hyneman

Heinz. *See* Hynes

Heise, George, 991

Heise, None, 815

Heise. *See also* Hisey

Heistand, Henry, 1029

Herter, George, 459

Herter, Jacob, 474

Herty, Thomas, 894

Hess, Abraham, 1667

Hess, David, 1109

Hesser, Peter, 134

Heston, John, 1

Heth, Henry, 1300

Heth, Hervey, 1220

Hetrick, Abraham, 512, 635, 777, 826, 1107, 1311, 1436

Hetrick, William, 1436

Hetzler, George, 1782

Heu, Philip, 319

Heu. *See also* Hay, Hoy

Heuslie, Samuel, 119

Heuslie. *See also* Haeusel, Haeusle, Hausel, Housel

Hewit, Philip, 1154

Hewitt, James, 599

Hewitt, Russell, 185

Hewlett, John W., 1433, 1507

Hewlings, Joseph, 556

Hews, James, 1761

Hews, Robert, 1667

Hews, Walter, 337, 1109, 1756

Hews. *See also* Hughes

Hewston, Alexander, 935

Hewston. *See also* Houston, Hueston, Huston

Heyl, Conrad, 788

Heyle, Conrad, 928

Heyl, Heyle. *See also* Heil

Hibbs, Joseph, 820, 993

Hicklen, Samuel, 257, 754, 1019

Hickman, William, 951

Hicks, William, 1002

Hiestand, Joseph, 747

Hiestand. *See also* Heistand

Hiffelly, Peter, 828

Hiffelly. *See also* Heffely

Higer, Martin, 1085, 1132

Higgans, Jonathan, 1029

Higgens, Jonathan, 495

Higgins, Amos, 1002

Higgins, Jonathan, 1582

Higgins, Joseph, 970

Highway, John, 1328

Highway. *See also* Heighway

Hilbert, Baltzer, 524

Hildebrandt, Henry, 734

Hill, Abel, 1689

Hill, Benjamin, 545, 1073, 1726

Hill, George, 174

Hill, Horace, 1423

Hill, Isaac, 593

Hill, Joseph, 545

Hill, Martin, 1481

Hill, Nathan, 1002

Hill, None, 119

Hill, Robert, 751

Hill, Samuel, 17, 37, 38, 106, 144, 156, 1392, 1481, 1791

Hill, Thomas, 663

Hillard, Isaac, 440

Hilliar, Charles, 50, 1073

Hilliard, Charles, 1328, 1436

Hilliard, Isaac, 440

Hillier, Charles, 50, 1031

Hillierd, Charles, 1328

Hillis, D., 1718

Hillis, David, 1551, 1718

Hillis, E., 1086

Hillis, Edward, 1551

Hillis, James, 1718

Hillis, Jesse, 1551

Hillis, John, 1551

Hillis, M., 1086

Hillis, William, Junior, 1551

Hillis, William, Senior, 1551

Hilterbrant, Henry, 734

Hindman, James, 1531

Hindman, Samuel, 1531

Hinds, Benjamin, 1530

Hinds, Levi, 1433

Hinds, None, 628

Hinton, Evan, 1602

Hinton, George, 721, 1568

Hinton, Michael, 1711

Hinton, Siburn, 1447

Hinton, William, 1314

Hinton. *See also* Henton

Hires, John, 1601

Hirsch, Jacob, 1090

Hirschberger, Abraham, 1532

Hirschmann, John, 949

Hirschmann, Philip, 1371

Hirschmann. *See also* Harschman, Harshman, Hershman, Horseman

Hisey, Daniel, 1684

Hisey. *See also* Heise

Hite, Andrew, Senior, 400

Hite, Conrad, 263, 270

Hixson, John, 1753

Hobbs, Joshua, 240

Hoblet, Boston, 50

Hobson, John, 1325

Hobson, Joseph, 134, 1782

Hoch. *See* Hoke

Hochstraat, Hochstrasse, Hochweg. *See* Heighway

Hodge, John, 1711

Hodges, Andrew, 546, 1195

Hodges, Flemming, 1689

Hodges, Johnson, 1106

Hodges, Thomas, 995

Hodgin, William, 969

Hoeflich, Charles, 659

Hoeflich, Peter, 828

Hoesch, Peter, 617

Hoeschmann, Peter, 359

Hoffman, George, 451

Hoffman, Joseph, 309, 451, 858

Hoffmire, Samuel, 1666

Hofheinz, Isaac, 747

Hofmann, Conrad, 1371

Hofmann, Jacob, 1478

Hoffman, Hofmann. *See also* Huffman

Hofmeier, Samuel, 1666

Hogan, William, 1327, 1507, 1689

Hogatt, None, 1027

Hoge, David, 1006

Hoge, Joseph, 1054

Hoge, Solomon, 1469

Hogeland, James, 384

Hogeland, Moses, 960

Hogg, Samuel, 1783

Hoggatt, Moses, 761

Hoggatt, Philip, 1488

Hogue, Joseph, 1483, 1539

Hogue, Robert, 1784

Hohnan, Isaac, 1533

Hohner. *See* Honer

Hoke, George, 730

Holcomb, Samuel R., 269

Holcomb, Stephen, 991

Holden, Joseph, 1407

Holderman, Abraham, 101, 714, 931

Holderman, Christian, 632

Holderman, John, 632, 677, 903, 1667

Hole, James, 935

Hole, John, 1757

Hole, Nathan, 474, 561

Hole, Zachariah, 72, 115

Holeman, Joseph, 680

Holeman, William, 677

Hollenshead, James, 1073

Holler, George, 942

Holler, Henry, 1155, 1314

Holler. *See also* Haller

Holliday, Samuel, 771

Holliday, William, 1207

Hollinger, Joel, 1779

Hollinger, John, 1030

Hollinger, William, 1569

Hollingshead, Daniel, 991

Hollingsworth, Abraham, 677

Hollingsworth, David, 10, 710

Hollingsworth, George, 710, 942, 1530

Hollingsworth, Jacob, 659

Hollingsworth, James, 459, 1582

Hollingsworth, Joel, 372

Hollingsworth, Joseph, 91, 710

Hollingsworth, Levi, 710

Hollingsworth, Nathan, 718

Holloway, A., 489

Holloway, Asa, 384

Holloway, Asa, Senior, 599

Holloway, Ephraim, 27

Holloway, Joseph, 134

Hollowell, Henry, 1760

Hollowell, Jesse, 1220

Hollowell, John, 279, 1557, 1760

Hollowell, Robert, 1376, 1557

Holly, Darby, 991

Holm, Abraham, 1534

Holman, George, 50

Holmes, David, 1010

Holmes, Francis, 474

Holmes, George, 960

Holmes, Henry, 1090

Holmes, James, 1756

Holmes, Joseph, 960

Holmes, Samuel, 1478

Holmes, William, 289, 992, 1130

Hols, Michael, 1049

Holsapple, Frederick, 1478

Holse, Esther, 384

Holsinger, William, 1090

Holsmer, Jacob, 1781

Holstead, Reuben, 1073

Holtz, Jacob, 1130, 1195

Holz, Michael, 1049

Holzapfel, Frederick, 1478

Holze, Esther, 384

Holzer, John, 270

Home, Mary, 552

Honebreake, Henry, 834

Honebreake. *See also* Bonebreak

Honer, Jacob, 130

Honnold, John, 1030

Hoober, William, 1569

Hoober. *See also* Heever, Hoover, Hover, Huber, Huver

Hood, Andrew, 10, 659

Hoofnagle, George, 19

Hook, Moses, 1575

Hook, None, 859

Hooper, Jacob, 478

Hoopes, Ellis, 1049

Hoover, Andrew, 212, 718

Hoover, Christian, 337, 1377

Hover, David, 448

Hoover, Felix, 677

Hoover, Frederick, 1129

Hoover, Henry, 606, 677, 1041

Hoover, Jacob, 94, 754

Hoover, John, 532, 931, 992, 1134, 1710

Hoover, William, 1569

Hoover. *See also* Heever, Hoober, Hover, Huber, Huver

Hoozier, William, 1031

Hoozier. *See also* Hosier

Hopkins, Eliha, 1749

Hopkins, Henry, 1220

Hopkins, Lemuel, 1667

Hopkins, Richard, 1031

Hopkins, Tippits F., 297

Hopkins, William, 1049

Hopper, Thomas, 280

Hopping, Jeremiah, 992

Hopping, Moses, 935

Hoppon, Thomas, 959

Hoppore, Thomas, 959

Hormall, Henry, 752

Horn, Frederick, 569

Hornbaker, John, 1314

Horne, Daniel, 53

Horne, Jacob, 750

Horne, Michael, 732

Horner, George, 142

Horner, Joshua, 1314

Horner, Nicholas, 628

Horner, None, 316

Horney, Solomon, 1110

Horniday, Nathan, 1012

Horniringhaus, John, 1640

Hornsby, Leonard, 951

Horral, Thomas, 1220

Horrall, William, 1760

Horseman, John, 1717

Horseman. *See also* Harschmann, Hershman, Hirschmann

Horton, Daniel, 1072

Horton, Ezra, 1072

Horton, Howard, 522

Horton, Isaac, 532

Hosack, John, 1532

Hoshar, George, 514

Hosher, George, 478

Hosier, Isaac, 367

Hosier, Jacob, 114

Hosier. *See also* Hoozier

Hoslar, Joseph, 1007, 1163

Hoslar. *See also* Haeusler

Hosteller, Abraham, 1667

Hosteller, Benjamin, 1072

Hosteller, Christian, 1110

Hosteller, Jacob, 87, 113

Hostetler, Jacob, 87, 113

Hough, Benjamin, 1091, 1144, 1189, 1192, 1273, 1643, 1663

Hough, John, 35

Hough, Joseph, 1436

Hough, William, 97, 247, 383, 499, 515, 968, 979

Hougham, Aaron, 829

House, Eli, 974, 1173

Housel, Anthony, 1393

Housel. *See also* Haeusel, Hauesele, Hausel, Heuslie, Housley

Houser, Jacob, 239

Houser, John, 337

Houser, Jonathan, 1557

Houser, Martin, 5, 410, 533, 599, 1393

Houser. *See also* Hauser

Housholder, Adam, 1314

Housley, Levi, 477

Hunter, Jonathan, 1401

Hunter, Nathaniel, 1084

Hunter, Robert, 430, 991

Hunter, Thomas, 1241

Hunter, William, 992

Huntington, None, *Colonel*, 1583

Hunyard, Benjamin, 380

Hupler, Abraham, 1569

Hurford, Thomas, 378, 775

Hurford. *See also* Hereford, Herford

Hurlass, George, 953

Huron, Othniel, 1328

Hursey, Jane, 132

Hurst, Henry, 1760

Hurst, John, 1153, 1220, 1760

Hush, Peter, 327, 617

Hussey, Elijah, 1689

Huston, Alexander, 935

Huston, Benjamin, 1049

Huston, Christopher, 747

Huston, David, 291, 545, 546, 553, 1243

Huston, Ebenezer, 949

Huston, Henry, 1590

Huston, John, 949

Huston, Matthew, 931

Huston, None, 1573

Huston, Paul, 1530

Huston, Robert, 131, 305

Huston, Samuel, 135, 1313, 1717

Huston. *See also* Hewston, Houston, Hueston

Hutcherson, James, 1488

Hutchins, Benjamin, 1073, 1243

Hutchinson, James, 1488, 1569

Hutchinson, Joseph, 1569

Hutchinson, Samuel, 57

Hutchison, William, 599, 734

Hutchinson, Hutchison. *See also* Hatchinson

Hutton, Isaac, 1343

Huver, Jacob, 94

Huver. *See also* Heever, Hoober, Hoover, Hover, Huber

Hyneman, John, *Honorable*, 699

Hyneman, None, *Honorable*, 508

Hynes, William R., 687

Ibáñez, Ferdinand, 1291

Iddings, Benjamin, 1073

Iddings, Talbert, 680

Idings, Joseph, 931

Ier, Francis, 289

Igel. *See* Yeagel

Ijams, John, 751

Ijams, None, 1167

Ijams, Thomas, 16, 248, 598

Imler, Henry, 1549

Ingham, Deborah, 1548

Ingle, Isaac, 411

Ingleman, Peter, 18, 264, 266, 600

Ingman, Henry, 1044

Ingman, Luke, 1036

Inlow, Abraham, 992

Inman, Asa, 829

Innis, Robert, 1090

Inskeep, Abraham, 434

Ireland, David, 680

Ireland, James, 67, 632, 751

Ireland, John, 546

Ireland, Peter F., 1478

Irvin, Charles, 1253

Irvin, David, 1477

Irwin, Charles, 1253

Irwin, James, 903

Irwin, John, 492, 794, 1314, 1521

Irwin, Morton, 532

Irwin, Robert, 829

Irwin, Samuel, 671

Irwin, Thomas, 1785

Irwin, William, 56, 1089, 1662

Jack, Samuel, 630

Jackson, George, 1085, 1472

Jackson, J. G., 868

Jackson, J. G., *Honorable*, 1728

Jackson, John, 924, 1401

Jackson, John G., 63

Jackson, None, 702

Jackson, None, *General*, 915

Jacob, James, 1749

Jaeckli, Michael, 1530

Jaeckli. *See also* Yeagley

Jaeger, John, 1085, 1108

James, Anne, 727

James, David, 1316

James, John, 537, 931, 959, 1195

James, Joseph, 1195

James, Richard, 1002
James, Robert T., 949
James, Thomas, 727
James, William, 949
Jameson, James, 1478
Jandt. *See* Gaunt, Yandt, Yant, Yount
Janney, Amos, 474
Jarber, Philip, 992
Jarber. *See also* Carver, Garber, Garver, Gerber
Jarvis, John, 533
Jarvis, Nicholas, 1732
Jarvis, W., 960
Jauch, Michael, 473
Jaucke, Jacob, 126
Jauch, Jaucke. *See also* Yoke
Jaunt. *See* Gaunt, Jandt, Yandt, Yant, Yount
Jay, Jesse, 1073, 1710
Jay, John, 6, 372, 606, 1243
Jay, Samuel, 639
Jay, Thomas, 372
Jay, William, 865
Jefferies, John, 632
Jeffreys, Evan, 863
Jeffries, James, 552
Jenkins, David, 234, 677, 1783
Jenkins, Jesse, 153
Jenkins, John D., 1548
Jenkins, Michael, 455, 960
Jenkins, None, 1417
Jenkins, None, *Honorable*, 620
Jenkins, William, 153, 1313
Jenkinson, Isaac, 620
Jenkinson, J., 502
Jennings, Gideon, 1108
Jennings, Henry, 1481
Jennings, Jonathan, *Honorable*, 149
Jennings, Levi, 56, 663, 998, 1049, 1133
Jennings, None, *Honorable*, 176, 403, 421, 426, 575, 585, 596, 604, 630, 691, 700, 729, 761, 1046, 1580, 1633, 1635
Jennings, Obadiah, 35
Jennings, Osias, 1477
Jennings, Sarah, 865
Jennings, William, 794, 1051, 1694
Jennings, William, *Honorable*, 167
Jer, Francis, 289
Jereaume, None, 952
Jervis, Philip, 775
Jewel, John, 398

Jiams, John, 751
Jinkins, David, 677
Job, Samuel, 1667
Jocho. *See* Yoho
Joerg, Jacob, 552
Joerg, Johannes, 447
Joerg. *See also* Sherg, Shirk, Yarrick, Yerk, York, Yurrick
John, Benjamin, 1710
John, David, 1073, 1710
John, Enoch D., 1710
John, Isaac, 923
John, James, 537
John, Jehu, 1779
Johns, Charles, 335
Johns, Nathan, 384
Johns, William R., 867
Johnson, Abel, 1049, 1095, 1137
Johnson, Andrew, 959
Johnson, Bailey, 1533
Johnson, Benjamin, 787
Johnson, Daniel, 599
Johnson, DeMay, 259
Johnson, Derrick, 1626
Johnson, Henry, 828
Johnson, Isaac, 134, 1049, 1095, 1137
Johnson, J., 994
Johnson, James, 457, 758, 1161
Johnson, James, Senior, 724
Johnson, Joel, 775
Johnson, John, 9, 447, 799, 980, 1127, 1400
Johnson, John H., 1130
Johnson, Joseph, 549, 701, 1760
Johnson, L., 994
Johnson, Nathan, 775
Johnson, Nimrod, 1750
Johnson, None, 1030
Johnson, Patrick, 1028, 1175
Johnson, Robert, 9, 589
Johnson, Silas, 448
Johnson, Sterling, 438, 899
Johnson, Thomas, 1132
Johnson, William, 9, 592
Johnston, Alexander, 503, 1036
Johnston, Archibald, 1530
Johnston, Arthur, 288, 606, 671
Johnston, Bailey, 317
Johnston, Benjamin, 9
Johnston, Eli, 1195

Karan, Peter, 1161

Karr, Andrew, 949

Karr, Hugh, 10

Kaster, Conrad, 1161

Kaster. *See also* Custar, Custer, Kester, Koester

Kastner, Michael, 1490

Kaufman, Christian, 1753

Kaufmann, William, 1085

Kautz, Jacob, 6, 1073, 1134

Kaylor, John, 50

Kaylor. *See also* Koehler, Kohler, Kollar, Koller

Keasbear, Christian, 830

Keasbear. *See also* Casebier, Kaesebier

Keeler, Aaron, 575

Keen, Peter, 931

Kees, None, 1073

Keese, Nicholas, 1243

Keever, John, 10, 428, 629, 992

Keever, Martin, Junior, 1243

Keever, None, 1762

Keffer, George, 680

Keffer, Valentine, 337, 747

Keever, Keffer. *See also* Keifer, Kever, Kiefer

Kehl, Peter, 9, 1403, 1457, 1490

Keifer, Joseph, 399, 996

Keil, John, 269, 747

Keil. *See also* Kehl, Kile, Kyle

Keim, Nicholas, 1379

Keiser, Adam, 337

Keiser, Joseph, 1490

Keiser. *See also* Kaiser, Keyser, Kiser, Kizer

Keith, Henry, 993

Keith, Price, 199

Keith, William, 625

Kellar, Adam, 605

Keller, Henry, 293, 598

Keller, Jacob, 1057

Keller, John, 251, 950

Kelley, Nicholas, 269

Kelley, William, 1719

Kellog, Ethel, 992

Kellog, Ezra, 1371

Kells, Thomas, 738

Kelly, Andrew, 1781

Kelly, Charles, 1036

Kelly, George, 659, 1582

Kelly, J. I., 604

Kelly, James, 1569

Kelly, John, 721, 1552

Kelly, Martin, 52

Kelly, None, 1072

Kelly, Robert, 440

Kelly, S., 604

Kelly, Thomas, 258

Kelly, William, 589, 861, 997

Kelsey, Daniel, 475, 949

Kelsey, James, 992

Kelsey, Thomas, 801, 992

Kelso, John, 1494

Kelso, None, 1516

Kelton, Henry, 489

Kemble, Samuel, 1626

Kemp, Daniel, 1195

Kemp, Jacob, 21

Kemp, John, 115, 142, 865

Kemp, Ludwick, 291, 949

Kemp, Philip, 21

Kemp. *See also* Kaempf, Kampf

Kemper, D., 487

Kemper, Daniel, 337

Kemper, Elnathan, 1530

Kemper, Isaac, 337, 514

Kemper, J., 487

Kemper, Jacob, 337

Kemren, David, 1314

Kemren. *See also* Cameron

Kems, Lewis, 711

Kems, N., 830

Kenall, Isaac, 605

Kendall, Allen, 1718

Kendall, Isaac, 605

Kendall, James, 317

Kendall, William, 52, 240, 1538

Kendall. *See also* Kindell, Kindle

Kendren, William D., 598

Kenneday, John, 1783

Kennedy, Charles, 1507

Kennedy, John, 489, 522

Kennedy, Robert, 1502

Kennedy, Stephen, 950

Kennedy, William, 1073

Kennermere, Stephen, 1507

Kenney, Chris., 1049

Kennier, Michael, 1592

Kennon, John, 524

Kenny, Richard, 134

Kent, Absalom, 549, 599

Kent, Jacob, 247

Kent, John, 949

Kent, None, 974

Kenton, M., 1133

Kenton, Simon, 428

Kenton, Thomas, 935

Kenton, W., 1133

Kenworthy, David, 367

Kenworthy, Jesse, 76, 1243

Kepler, Andrew, 57, 754

Kepler, John, 57, 552, 1049

Keplinger, Daniel, 903

Keplinger, Jacob, 545

Keplinger, Jacob, Senior, 609

Kercher, Jacob, 50

Kercker, Jacob, 142

Kerlin, John, 87, 483

Kernes, George, 35

Kerns, Benjamin, 1314

Kerns, George, 5

Kernsby, Joshua, 486

Kerr, Hugh, 1232

Kerr, John, 332, 344, 543, 999, 1163, 1466

Kerr, Joseph, 837, 845, 1165, 1719

Kerr, William, 1206

Kersey, Thomas, 1436

Kershman, Jonathan, 347

Kershner, Isaac, 516, 518, 908

Kershner, Jacob, 518, 913

Kershner, John, 342

Kershner, Martin, 909, 1136, 1328, 1371

Kershner, Philip, 516

Kersner, Daniel, 1726

Kesler, Jacob, 1756

Kesler, Matthias, 747

Kesler, None, 991

Kesling, Jacob, 520, 953, 992, 1530, 1548

Kesling, John, 1530

Keslinger, Peter, 949

Kesser, Peter, 384

Kessler, Jacob, 747

Kessler, Matthias, 747

Kester, Jacob, 991

Kester, John, 877

Kester. *See also* Custar, Custer, Kaster, Koester

Kestler, Jacob, 747

Ketcham, John, 1718

Ketrick, Abraham, 512

Kettleborough, Jacob, 478

Kettry, Martin, 52

Kever, Peter, 316

Kever, Valentine, 430

Kever. *See also* Keever, Keffer, Keifer, Kiefer

Key, John E., 1536

Key. *See also* O'Key

Keyser, Daniel, 473

Keyser, David, 950

Keyser, Jacob, 410

Keyser, John, 1243

Keyser, Joseph, 1490

Keyser, Peter, 384

Keyser, Philip, 545, 632, 949

Keyser. *See also* Kaiser, Keiser, Kiser, Kizer

Kidoo, James, 1163

Kidwilder, Michael, 1085

Kidwilder. *See also* Cadwallader

Kiefer, George, 680

Kiefer, John, 10, 399, 428, 629, 992

Kiefer, Joseph, 399, 996

Kiefer, Martin, Junior, 1243

Kiefer, None, 1762

Kiefer, Peter, 316

Kiefer, Valentine, 337, 430, 747

Kiefer. *See also* Keever, Keffer, Keifer, Kever

Kieler, Aaron, 575

Keith, Price, 120

Kilbourn, James, 915

Kilbourne, James, *Honorable*, 1603

Kilburn, James, 868

Kile, John, 269, 747

Kile. *See also* Kehl, Keil, Kyle

Kilgore, Daniel, 993

Kimberly, Zenas, 1501

Kimble, Samuel, 1626

Kime, Nicholas, 1379

Kimel, John, 1626

Kimmel, Adam, 1315

Kimmel, David, 521

Kimmel, Samuel, 1220

Kimmerer, Jacob, 1719

Kimmerer. *See also* Kinmerer

Kimmet, David, 1156

Kindell, Ewel, 1371

Kindell. *See also* Kendall, Kindle

Kinder, Christian, 1782

Kindle, George, 276, 586

Kindle. *See also* Kendall, Kindell

Kindley, Isaac, 983

Kinesly, John, 1132

King, Charles, 1507

King, Christian, 747

King, Henry, 1507

King, John, 240, 592, 733

King, Michael, 1154

King, Philip, 1134

King, Samuel, 734

King, Thomas, 552

King, William, 931, 1619

Kingery, Jacob, 1161

Kingery, Jacob, Senior, 677

Kingery, Joseph, 10, 21

Kingsley, Alpha, 937

Kinmerer, Jacob, 1719

Kinmerer. *See also* Kimmerer

Kinnaird, John, 942

Kinney, Aaron, 991

Kinney, David, 1090

Kinney, John, 1161, 1610

Kinney, Peter, 1550

Kinser, Adam, 337

Kinsey, David, 1012

Kinsey, Stephen, 599

Kinsler, None, 1354, 1406, 1470

Kintner, Jacob, 1719

Kinzer. *See* Kinser

Kiplinger, Jacob, 545

Kiplinger. *See also* Keplinger

Kirby, John, 1496

Kirby, None, 1328

Kircher, Jacob, 142

Kirk, Benjamin, 1154

Kirk, Jacob, 1784

Kirkland, David, 1569

Kirkpatrick, Samuel, 1481

Kirkpatrick, William, 1371

Kirlin, John, 708, 1336

Kirschner, Daniel, 1726

Kirschner, Isaac, 516, 518, 908

Kirschner, Jacob, 50, 518, 913

Kirschner, John, 342, 1682

Kirschner, Martin, 909, 1136, 1328, 1371

Kirschner, Philip, 516

Kiser, Philip, 372, 545, 632

Kiszer, John, 1243

Kiser, Kiszer. *See also* Kaiser, Keiser, Keyser, Kizer

Kitchell, John, 1039

Kite, Adam, 1436

Kithcart, Joseph, 1531

Kithcart. *See also* Cathcart

Kizer, David, 950

Kizer, Philip, 949

Kizer. *See also* Kaiser, Keiser, Keyser, Kiser

Klaburg, Isaac, 292

Klaburg. *See also* Claughburgh, Clowburg

Klammar, David, 1779

Klar, Thomas, 1626

Klaus. *See also* Clouse

Kleck, Daniel, 240

Kleck, Philip, 240

Klein, Isaac, 923, 1155

Klein, John, 557, 969, 1325

Klein. *See also* Cline, Clyne, Kline

Kleiser, Joseph, 1086

Klick, Daniel, 1485

Klick, Peter, 1549

Kline, Isaac, 1056, 1155

Kline, John, 557

Kline. *See also* Cline, Clyne, Klein

Klinger, John, 1549

Knabe. *See* Knave, Nave

Knaegle. *See* Nagley

Knaf, Leonard, 1667

Knage, Christian, 355

Knage, Jacob, 384

Knagg, Christian, 355

Knagge, Whitemore, 844

Knaggs, Whitemore, 844

Knaggs, Whitmore, 884

Knaggy, Jacob, 384

Knappenberger, Conrad, 148

Knauff, Adam, 599, 1534

Knauff. *See also* Kneff, Knouf, Neff

Knave, Michael, 1475

Knaves, Michael, 1566

Knayer, Michael, 430

Kneeland, John, 951

Kneff, Jacob, 659

Kneff. *See also* Knauff, Knouf, Neff

Kneip. *See* Knipe

Knies. *See* Neas, Nees

Kniffen, Amos, 611

Knight, Benjamin, 621, 883

Knight, James, Junior, 1783

Knight, John, 903, 1049, 1378, 1549, 1610

Knights, William, 992

Knipe, John, 1783

Knoblauch, None, 928

Knoll, Charles, 1304, 1371

Knoll, Christian, 654, 935

Knoll, Henry, 723, 931, 1304

Knoll. *See also* Knull, Null

Knoop, John, 329

Knoops, Benjamin, 1328, 1436

Knoops, Christopher, 1251

Knoops, Daniel, 935

Knoops, John, 448, 949

Knotts, William, 960

Knouf, Adam, 1534

Knouff, Adam, 599

Knouf, Knouff. *See also* Knauff, Kneff, Neff

Knowles, Shaw, 21

Knox, David H., 183

Knox, John, 1782

Knox, Matthew, 670

Knuesser, Adam, 828

Knull, Christian, 935

Knull, Henry, 931

Knull. *See also* Knoll, Null

Kober, Adam, 747

Koehler, George, 1242

Koehler, John, 50

Koehler. *See also* Kayler, Kohler, Kollar, Koller

Koenig, Christian, 747

Koenner, Henry, 608

Koeplein. *See* Copline

Koerner, Philip, 48

Koerner, Stephen, 1582

Koerner. *See also* Corner

Koester, Conrad, 1161

Koester, Emmanuel, 1049

Koester, Jacob, 991

Koester, John, 877

Koester, William, 1313

Koester. *See also* Custar, Custer, Kaster, Kester

Kohler, William, 1089

Kohler. *See also* Kayler, Koehler, Kollar, Koller

Kolb, Richard, 1243

Kollar, George, 1242

Koller, William, 1089

Kollar, Koller. *See also* Kayler, Koehler, Kohler

Kolly, Darby, 991

Kome, Mary, 552

Komer. *See* Comer, Gombar

Koner, Joseph, 1073

Konkle, Jacob, 294

Konkle. *See also* Concal, Congill, Conkle, Gunckle, Kunckel

Koons, Gaspar, 1195

Koontz, Baltzer, 378

Koontz, John, 430

Koontz. *See also* Coons, Kuntz

Kopf. *See* Copp

Koppel, Jacob, 550

Koppel. *See also* Copple, Kappel

Korbman, George, 385

Korbmann, Jacob, 478

Korfmann, Jacob, 747

Korfmann, Martin, 991

Kortman, George, 174

Koshar, George, 514

Koutz, Jacob, 6

Koutz. *See also* Kautz

Kraehbill, Jonathan, 380

Kraehbill, Kraehbuhl. *See also* Creble, Grable, Grayble

Kraemer, Adam, 1314

Kraemer, Casper, 552

Kraemer, Christopher, 1402

Kraemer, D., 1569

Kraemer, Daniel, 1049

Kraemer, Francis, 991

Kraemer, John, 628

Kraemer, Ludwick, 339, 991

Kraemer, Michael, 514

Kraemer, Valentine, 1569

Kraemer, Zadock, 632

Kraemer. *See also* Cramer, Creamer, Kreamer

Kraft, Abraham, 960, 1049

Kraft, John, 50, 949

Krahner, Michael, 270

Kraider, David, 1029

Kraider. *See also* Crider, Kreider, Kryder

Kraisher, John, 332

Kramlech. *See* Kromlegh

Kramm, Joseph, 992

Kraner, Jacob, 270

Kraner, Michael, 270, 337, 514

Kranwell, Henry, 747

Krater, David, 56

Kraus, Daniel, 339

Kraus, Jacob, 232

Kreager, George, 1709

Kreager. *See also* Creager, Kreger, Krieger, Krueger

Kreamer, Adam, 1314

Kreamer, Christopher, 1402

Kreamer, Francis, 991

Kreamer, Ludwick, 339, 991

Kreamer. *See also* Cramer, Creamer, Kraemer

Krebs, Henry, 473

Krebs, Jacob, 473

Kreger, Jacob, 285

Kreger. *See also* Creager, Kreager, Krieger, Krueger

Kreider, David, 1029

Kreider, John, 732, 1784

Kreider. *See also* Crider, Kraider, Kryder

Kreis, Lewis, 1195

Kreis. *See also* Circle [translation]

Kreischer, John, 332

Kreitz, Henry, 864

Kreitzer, Andrew, 459

Kreitzer, Peter, 459

Krepleber. *See* Creplever

Kress, John, 1486

Kress, William, 1486

Kretzer, Henry, 1108

Kreuter, David, 56

Kribe, John, 212

Kribe. *See also* Chribe, Cribbee

Krieger, Henry, 992

Krieger. *See also* Creager, Kreager, Kreger, Krueger

Kritz, Conrad, 1667

Kroeger, Jacob, 285

Krohn, Henry, 1241

Krohn, John, 1753

Krohn. *See also* Cron, Crown, Krown

Kroll, Henry, 1195

Kroll, John, 91

Kroll. *See also* Croll, Crull

Kromlegh, Christian, 412

Kromley, Christian, 1109

Kromlegh, Kromley. *See also* Cromley, Crumley

Kroninger. *See also* Cronninger

Krown, Henry, 1241

Krown. *See also* Cron, Crown, Krohn

Krueger, George, 1709

Krueger, Henry, 992

Krueger. *See also* Creager, Kreager, Kreger, Krieger

Krumbacher, John, 1394

Krumbacher. *See also* Crumbacker

Krumbein, None, 1056

Krumme, M., 865

Krumrein, Christian, 52

Krumrein, Michael, 1155

Krumrein, Peter, 135

Krydar, John, 1784

Krydar. *See also* Crider, Kraider, Kreider

Kuhn, George, 153

Kuhn, John, 1036, 1753

Kuhn, Philip, 454, 552

Kuhn. *See also* Coon

Kuhnz, Gaspar, 1195

Kuhnz, Isaac, 747

Kuhnz. *See also* Coons, Koons, Koontz, Kuntz

Kulp, Henry, 337, 339

Kulp, Jacob, 1314

Kulp. *See also* Culp

Kunckel, Philip, 544

Kunckel. *See also* Concal, Congill, Conkle, Gunckle, Konkle

Kundell, James, 317

Kunse, George, 130, 187

Kunse, Jacob, 153

Kunse. *See also* Kunze

Kuntz, Baltasar, 378

Kuntz, Henry, 1667

Kuntz, Jacob, 1371

Kuntz, John, 430

Kuntz. *See also* Coons, Koons, Koontz, Kuhnz

Kunze, George, 130, 187

Kunze, Jacob, 153

Kunze. *See also* Kunse

Kurtz, Low, 478

Kurtz, Nicholas, 533

Kyle, Samuel, 1313

Kyle, Thomas B., 710

Kyle. *See also* Kehl, Keil, Kile

Kyles, William S., 529

La Fayette, G. de, 1402

La Fayette, T. de, 1402

Labadi, Medard, 952

Labadie, Alexis, 608

Labady, Medard, 622

Labrose, Dominique, 608

Lackey, Richard, 1265

Lacock, Abner, *Honorable*, 1047, 1459

Lacock, None, *Honorable*, 820, 1365

Lacroix, Hubert, 608, 934

Lacroix, Pierre, 849

Lacy, Samuel, 951

Laderout, Joseph, 966

Lafamboise, Joseph, 966

Laferty, Samuel, 134

Lafontaine, Antoine, 844

Laframboise, Alexis, 966

Laframboise, Joseph, 966

Lajoye, Louis, 313

Lamarre, André, 977

Lamb, James, 456, 1041, 1080

Lamb, John, 22

Lamb, Joseph, 953

Lamb, Philip, 254

Lamb, Thomas, 1718

Lambert, J., 815

Lambert, James, 319, 361, 1485

Lambert, Joseph, 747

Lambert, Josias, 1667

Lamberton, John, 1689

Lambrecht, John, 996

Lame, Joseph, 1488

Lamme, James, 1328

Lamme, None, 1453, 1468

Lamme, William, 1084, 1667

Lancaster, Wright, 642, 1478

Lance, George, 1494

Lance, John, 1130

Lance, None, 1516

Lance, Peter, 1130

Lance. *See also* Lantz, Lintz

Land, Jacob, 1108

Landan, Elisha, 372

Landers, Henry, 459

Landers, Samuel, 1110

Landerson, William, 764

Landies, David, 942

Landis, Barbary, 684

Landis, David, 942

Landis, Martin, 684, 770

Lane, David, 118, 155, 203, 247, 296, 864

Lane, Jesse, 187

Lane, Joseph, 337

Lane, Julius, 1625

Lane, Richard, 557, 737

Lane. *See also* Layn, Layne

Lanert, Boston, 239

Laney, John, 960

Lanfesty, Thomas, 1252

Lanford, Robert, 1507

Lang, Jacob, 935

Langenacker, Jacob, 150

Langenacker. *See also* Longenecker

Langenbock, Jacob, 747

Langford, Robert, 1689

Langham, Elias, 331

Langlois, Ambroise, 901

Langly, William, 758

Langstaff, Samuel, 1490

Langstaff, Thomas, 1490

Lanier, Alexander C., 122

Lanison, John, 557

Lankford, Robert, 1689

Lansing, Garnet, 850

Lantz, Andrew, 996

Lantz. *See also* Lance, Lintz

Lape, Henry, 477

Lapointe, Jean Baptiste, 901

Lapointe, None, 934

Lapp, George, 490, 1072

Lapp, Jacob, 284

Lapp, John, 1220, 1633, 1718

Lapus, St. Vrain, 1738

Laragood, Christian, 758

Larew, John, 992

Larimer, Isaac, 1549

Larkin, David, 828

Laroche, None, 966

Larrick, Isaac, 85

Larrison, John, 1625

Larron, James, 552

Larsh, Paul, 1749

Larue, John, 992

Larwill, Joseph H., 1378

Lasen, A., 1683

Lash, Jacob, 532

Lashley, Samuel, 876, 884

Lasselle, Antoine, Junior, 875

Lasselle, François, 844, 901

Lasselle, Jacques, 608, 844, 901

Lasselle, Jean Baptiste, 901

Lassus, St. Vrain, 1754

Lassus. *See also* Lapus

Latchaw, Joseph, 498

Lees, William, 212

Lees. *See also* Lease

Lefaver, Christian, 740

Lefaver, Daniel, 740

Lefebre, Christian, 740

Lefebre, Daniel, 740

Lefevre, C., 1133

Lefevre, D., 1133

Lefevre, Joseph, *Honorable*, 442, 932

Leffel, Daniel, 556

Lefferts, Jonathan, 1072

Leffler, Jacob, 561

Legast, Leclede, 1184

Lehman, None, 440

Lehmann, David, 1314

Lehmann, Peter, 56, 992

Lehmann. *See also* Lawman, Layman, Lowman

Leibli, None, 1402

Leibli, Peter, 1242

Leibli. *See also* Lepley, Lively

Leichleder, Conrad, 794

Leichleder, Jacob, 794

Leichleder. *See also* Lechleider

Leigler, Andrew, 1108

Leininger, George, 283

Leise, Amasa, 599

Leitenacker, Henry, 109, 594

Leleivre. *See* Le Leivre

Lemasters, Isaac, 1253

Lemert, Joshua, 1748

Lemmon, Lemuel, 1041, 1530, 1710

Lenhart, Christopher, 1196

Lennon, James, 1265, 1328

Lennon, John, 903

Lenon, James, 1265

Lenox, John, 1502

Lenox, Richard, 1502

Leon, None, 1196

Leonard, Francis, 952

Leonard, George, 961

Leonard, J., 961

Lepley, Peter, 1242, 1709

Lepley. *See also* Leibli, Lively

Leporth, George, 536, 828

Leporth. *See also* Leeporth

Lertman, Peter, 1134

Lesh, Jacob, 1582

Lesley, Elisha, 1726

Leslie, John, 1478

Leslie, None, 1073

Lesourd, Peter, 1581

Lett, James, 719, 824

Levell, John, 677

Levengood, Jacob, 1252

Levengood, Magdalene, 1108

Levengood. *See also* Levingood, Livengood

Leverage, Benjamin, 1176

Levering, William, 827

Levering. *See also* Lavering

Levingood, Jacob, 617, 737

Levingood. *See also* Levengood, Livengood

Levingstone, John, 356

Levingstone. *See also* Livingstone

Leviston, James, 1313

Lewis, Abraham, 1041, 1195

Lewis, Caleb, 865

Lewis, James, 132

Lewis, Job, 281, 1085

Lewis, Joseph, 1477

Lewis, Joseph, *Honorable*, 117, 139, 727

Lewis, Joshua, 1292

Lewis, Levi, 1132

Lewis, Paul, 1371

Lewis, Samuel, 381, 458, 508, 1274, 1718

Lewis, William, 632, 951, 983, 1753

Licht, Tice, 403

Lichty, Jacob, 1530

Lidsey, Amasa, 1154

Ligget, Thomas, 787

Liggins, William, 575

Light. *See* Licht

Lilley, David, 1531

Limpus, Enoch, 1161

Limpus. *See also* Lymps, Lympus

Linch, Philip, 1084

Linch. *See also* Lynch

Lindersmith, Joseph, 1030

Lindesmith, Joseph, 561

Lindesmith, Peter, 1626

Lindlay, None, 1096

Lindley, David, 898

Lindley, Isaac, 1251

Lindley, Jesse, 1760

Lindley, Jonathan, 178, 631, 1051, 1151, 1220, 1488, 1557, 1755

Lindley, Owen, 898

Lindley, Thomas, 898, 1220, 1488

Lindley, William, 983, 1051, 1135, 1325, 1376

Lindley, Zachariah, 1376

Lindley, Zacheus, 1051

Lindly, Isaac, 350

Lindly, Jonathan, 605, 636

Lindly, Samuel, 636

Lindly, Thomas, 636

Lindsey, D., 1328

Lindsey, James, 1760

Lindsey, William, 6

Line, Jacob, 1582

Line, Samuel, 927

Lingle, John, 1265

Links, None, 1401

Linn, Daniel, 384

Linn, Hugh, 1750

Linn, None, 339, 1780

Linn. *See also* Lynn

Linton, David, 740, 1487

Lintz, Nicholas, 470

Lintz. *See also* Lance, Lantz

Lirman, Isaac, 1110

Lisle, William, 134

Lisle. *See also* Lyle

List, Andrew, 1711

List, Andrew, Senior, 1781

List, David, 747

Lister, James, 153

Lister, John, 465

Liteanaker, Henry, 109, 594

Little, Alexander, 1551

Little, Jacob, 1371

Little, Jacob, Senior, 680

Little, John T., 1086

Little, Lewis, 723

Little, Peter, *Honorable*, 1166

Little, Samuel, 1556

Little. *See also* Lyttle

Littleberry, Stanley, 323

Littrell, Samuel, 1530

Lively, None, 1402

Livengood, Jacob, 617, 737, 1252

Livengood, Magdalene, 1108

Livengood. *See also* Levengood, Levingood

Livernois, Joseph, Junior, 875

Livesey, Amos, 1761

Livingstone, John, 356

Livingstone. *See also* Levingstone, Leviston

Lochbach, Lewis, 1709

Lock, John, 122, 180, 209, 291, 563, 564, 1239, 1241, 1262, 1287, 1288, 1289, 1344, 1372, 1375, 1508, 1625

Lock, John, Junior, 1251

Lockhart, William, 997

Lockland, Dennis, 867

Lockridge, James, 998

Lockwood, None, 202

Loefel, Daniel, 556

Loefler, Jacob, 561

Loesch. *See* Lesh

Loessle, George, 402

Lofton, William, 1718

Logan, Anthony, 903, 1265

Logan, George, 89, 998

Logan, Samuel, 927, 1133

Logan, William, 89, 677, 1051

Lohmueller, John, 758

Lomiller, John, 758

London, Robert, Senior, 983

Loney, John, 960

Loney. *See also* Looney

Long, Abraham, 1624

Long, Daniel, 57

Long, David, 865

Long, George, 1314, 1756

Long, Jacob, 935

Long, James, 992

Long, John, 1328, 1377

Long, Lewis, 135

Long, None, 1073

Long, Patrick, 1195

Long, Philip, 659, 1195

Long, Robert

Long, William, 931

Longanecker, Ulrich, 548

Longaneker, Jacob, 150

Longenecker, Daniel, 734, 1049

Longenecker, Henry, 594

Longenecker. *See also* Langenacker, Longnecker

Longfellow, Joseph, 1369

Longhead, David, 392, 579

Longly, William, 758

Longnecker, Ulrick, 548

Looker, James, 254, 478

Looker, Jonathan, 254, 991

Looker, Othniel, 56, 953

Lookingbell, Henry, 1755

Looney, Absalom, 1689

Looney. *See also* Loney

Lopp, John, 1220, 1633

Lopp. *See also* Lapp

Lorance, Abraham, 319

Lorance, John, 319

Lorance. *See also* Laurence, Lawrence

Losley, George, 402

Loson, Nicholas, 966

Lott, Robert, 983, 1533

Louden, Thomas, 1624

Loun, Isaac, 1308

Loun, John, 1308

Loury, Archibald, 1481

Loury, David, 1481

Loutsenheiser, Jacob, 1090

Love, George, 1534

Love, Sarah, 1711

Loveland, Joseph, 684

Loveland, Nancy, 684

Loveridge, James, 1314

Loverly, Jane, 991

Low, John, 132

Low, William, 759, 829, 923, 1502

Lowderback, Daniel, 1636

Lowderback. *See also* Lauterbach

Lowell, Jesse, 1151

Lower, John, 1667

Lower, Matthias, 796

Lower, None, 1012

Lowman, None, 294, 440

Lowman. *See also* Lawman, Layman, Lehmann

Lowrey, James, 1569

Lowry, Archibald, 1481

Lowry, David, 1481

Lowry, Fielding, 740

Lowry, James, 1569

Lowry, John, 1036, 1378, 1689

Lowry, Joseph, 1434

Lowther, William, Senior, 380

Loy, John, 1433

Lucas, William, Senior, 1549

Luce, William, 950

Luckenbuehl, Henry, 1755

Ludgrove, James, 6

Ludlow, None, 90, 915

Ludlow, William, 868, 869

Ludwig, Daniel, 1109, 1134

Luke, John, 400

Luts, Jacob, 959

Lutz, Jacob, 286, 959

Lutz, John, 1753

Lybrand, Samuel, 598

Lybrook, Henry, 1029, 1582

Lybrook, John, 1582

Lybrook, Philip, 142, 1161

Lydick, Elizabeth, 829

Lyle, Aaron, *Honorable*, 162, 1045

Lyle, David, 1756

Lyle, James, 1130

Lyle, None, *Honorable*, 423

Lyle. *See also* Lisle

Lymps, Elijah, 457

Lymps, Enoch, 457

Lympus, Elijah, 1041

Lymps, Lympus. *See also* Limpus

Lynch, Philip, 1084

Lynch. *See also* Linch

Lynn, Absalom, 500

Lynn, Robert, 169

Lynn. *See also* Linn

Lyon, Gotham, 680

Lyon, James, 380

Lyon, Jonathan, 861

Lyon, Joseph, 1478

Lyon, Moses, 91

Lyon, None, 983, 997

Lyons, Archibald, 884

Lyons, Matthew, 1315

Lysy, Amasa, 599

Lytle, Aaron, *Honorable*, 1122

Lytle, Robert, 1163

Lytle, William, 1031, 1161

Lytle. *See also* Little

Mace, Edmund, 1549

Mace, None, 1402

Macenterfer, George, 134, 724, 1049

Macenterfer, Jacob, 355, 993

Macenterfer, William, 960

Macenterfer. *See also* McEnterfer

Mack, Jacob, 996

Maclay, John M., 932

Macomb, Alexander, 204, 1178

Macomb, None, 204

Macy, Jacob, 942

Macy, Micajah, 22

Maddock, William, 1710

Martz, Christopher, 1624

Martz, Jacob, 263, 1592

Mason, Christopher, 1029

Mason, Dean, 270

Mason, Dorsey, 1756

Mason, John, 960

Mason, Peleg, 202

Mason, Richard, 1392

Mason, Ruth, 511

Mason, William, 1073

Massie, Henry, 64

Massingale, Solomon, 1689

Mast, Jacob, 953

Mast, John, 606

Masters, Benjamin, 724

Masters, Isaac Less, 751

Maston, Peter, Junior, 569

Mathew, John, 1152

Mathews, George, 132

Mathews, John, 704, 705, 716

Mathews, Philip, 998

Mathias, Daniel, 474

Matson, Enos, 291, 950

Matson, Ezekiel, 950

Matson, James, 1749

Matthews, John, 1238, 1242

Matthews, Joseph, 1689

Matthewson, Elisha, 93

Mattin, Giles, 1625

Mauck, John, Junior, 1310

Mauck, Jonathan, 1151

Maunce, Smith, 284

Maurice, M., 1027, 1449

Maurice, Morris, 1551

Maxwell, D. H., 983

Maxwell, Hugh, 1478

Maxwell, James, 140, 1027

Maxwell, John, 1151, 1636

Maxwell, Joseph, 776, 1477

Maxwell, Richard, 677

Maxwell, Robert, 960

Maxwell, Samuel, 997

Maxwell, William, 1328

May, Andrew, 1436

May, Daniel, 337, 517

May, Ezra, 830, 1196

May, None, 1681

Mayer, Henry, 1090

Mayer, None, 747

Mayer. *See also* Majer, Majers, Major, Meier, Meiers, Meyers, Mier, Miers, Myers

Mayes, Thomas, 1626

Mays, Joseph, 306

Maze, D., 1582

Maze, S., 1582

McAdams, John, 384

McAlexander, James, 1371

McArthur, John, 141, 1549

McBean, Francis, 537

McBean, Hugh, 134

McBeth, Alexander, 950

McBeth, Samuel, 632

McBeth, William, 1161

McBratney, Alexander, 994

McBride, Andrew, 318, 1152, 1552

McBride, James, 961

McBride, John, 222, 1550

McBride, Richard, 318, 1152

McBride, Stephen, 599

McCabe, John, 1029, 1757

McCall, Gabriel, 135

McCalla, Andrew, 368

McCallister, Daniel, 1750

McCallum, Daniel, 1756

McCampbell, William, 1195

McCann, Garrett, 711

McCann, Samuel, 552

McCarland, William, 1568

McCarn, Niel, 1433

McCartey, Benjamin, 1726

McCartney, James, 1718

McCarty, Benjamin, 115, 1031

McCarty, Patrick, 731

McCasher, J., 1667

McCasland, Joseph, 1547

McCaughan, William, 524

McCaughey, Joseph, 1784

McCaulley, Hugh, 47

McCauslin, Thomas, 960

McCay, Abisha, 1783

McCay, Jacob, 537

McCay, Jesse, 978

McCay, Thomas, 1207

McChristy, William, 1779

McClain, Allen, 733

McClain, Elam, 1709

McClain, Joseph, 828

McClaray, John, 132

McClaron, Hugh, 355

McClay. *See* Maclay

McClean, John, 837, 845

McClean, Joseph, 1569

McClean, None, 1543

McClean, None, *Honorable*, 1304

McCleary, J., 1403

McCleary, James, 935

McCleary, John, 1436, 1569

McCleary, None, 1249

McCleary, Robert, 628

McCleery, James, 523

McClellan, John, 931

McClellan, William, 749

McClelland, James, 747

McClelland, Robert, 1090

McClelland, Thomas, 932

McClelland, William, 205, 805, 852

McClintock, A., 815

McClintock, Alexander, 129, 188, 1662

McClintock, James, 573, 698

McCloskey, William, 1626

McClucken, Matthew, 751

McClucken. *See also* McClurken

McClung, Daniel, 459

McClung, David, 459

McClung, Robert, 1756

McClure, James, 1220, 1243, 1481

McClure, John, 677

McClure, Nathaniel, 1002

McClure, Samuel, 751

McClurken, James, 1502

McClurken. *See also* McClucken

McComas, Daniel, 1252

McComb, David, 313, 608

McComb, Hugh, 1490

McComb, John, 313, 608

McComb, William, 313, 608

McComb. *See also* Macomb

McConkle, John, 828

McConneighy, David, 998

McConnel, R., 554

McConnel, William, 1085

McConnell, James, 1784

McConnell, None, 554

McConnell, Robert, 24, 56

McConnell, Samuel, 1135

McConnell, William, 732

McConnels, Alexander, 1371

McConnels, James L., 1371

McConnels, William R., 1371

McConochy, Daniel, 1154

McCoole, Gabriel, 1012

McCord, John, 1478

McCord, Samuel, 1265

McCorkle, John, 828

McCorkle, Joseph, 1012

McCormick, John, 616, 1195, 1401, 1779

McCormick, Robert, 942

McCormick, Samuel, 1626

McCormick, William, 339

McCoy, James, 775

McCoy, John, 134

McCoy, Joseph, 737

McCoy, Margaret, 1160

McCoy, Thomas, 1031, 1478

McCoy, William, 16

McCracken, Elihu, 747

McCrackin, James, 1689

McCraren, Christopher, 828

McCraron, James, 1154

McCrary, John, 1072

McCrary, Thomas, 1689, 1690

McCray, Phinchas, 1313

McCray, Phineas, 359

McCray, Samuel, 1313

McCreary, James, 960, 1154

McCreary, William, 314, 652, 1530

McCreery, William, 257

McCrory, John, 747, 1719

McCullen, M., 1105

McCullough, Hugh, 1661

McCullough, James, 373

McCune, George, 1108

McCune, James, 996

McCune, John, 996

McCune, Joseph, 1521

McCune, Samuel, 733

McCune, Thomas, 1386

McCurdy, Daniel, 1090, 1130

McCutchan, John, 1756

McCutcheon, Alexander, 1517, 1660

McCutcheon, John, 1756

McCutchin, None, 722

McDaniel, James, 1195

McDermott, Edward, 1341

McDevit, Charles, 1130

McDill, David, 153

McKnight, John, 949

McKnight, Roger, 1533

McKnight, William, 1325, 1533

McLaughlin, A., 344

McLaughlin, Charles, 1587

McLaughlin, J., 960

McLaughlin, James, 423

McLaughlin, John, 1750

McLaughlin, Robert, 423, 941

McLay. *See also* Maclay

McLean, John, 926

McLean, John, *Honorable*, 1359

McLean, William, 557

McLelland, John, 953

McLucas, William, 1636

McMaken, Joseph, 669, 829

McMaster, John, 1154

McMillan, John, 28, 260, 1348, 1376

McMillan, Robert, 1196

McMomjak, William, 1036

McMonigal, William, 1011, 1089, 1378

McMullen, Alexander, 614, 1007, 1043

McMullen, John, 13

McMullin, John, 218

McMun, Prudence, 356

McNair, William, 1101, 1313

McNaughten, John, 1662

McNaughten, Neale, 1709

McNeal, John, 319, 747, 905

McNeal, Thomas, 270, 319

McNeal, William A., 270

McNight, Roger, 1533

McNull, Alexander, 677

McNutt, Alexander, 677

McNutt, Todd, 1041

McPeek, Daniel, 1490

McPhaill, Cornelius, 1779

McPherrin, Thomas, 549, 697

McPherson, Adam, 457

McPherson, James, 1750

McPheters, John, 1325

McSherry, Hugh, 1369

McTavish, None, 934

McThibben, D., 969

McVay, Hugh, 1507

McWilliams, John, 960

McWilliams, Samuel, 960, 1198, 1711

McWilliams, William, 1689

Meahan, Neal, 363

Meason, John, 960, 1489

Mechling, Jacob, 1753

Meck, Barzil, 1785

Meck, John, 680

Meck, Samuel, 257

Meck, William, 259

Meek, Barzil, 1785

Meek, Jeremiah, 316

Meek, None, 1401

Meek, Samuel, 570

Meeker, Joseph, 1195

Meeks, Bazel, 633, 747

Meeks, Robert, Senior, 1090

Meier, Daniel, 1756

Meier, Michael, 1784

Meiers, Lambert, 1626

Meier, Meiers. *See also* Majer, Majers, Major, Meyers, Mier, Miers, Myers

Meigs, G., 202

Meigs, J., 1256, 1260

Meigs, Josiah, 1076, 1691

Meigs, Return J., *Colonel*, 1040

Meinhardt, Jacob, 349

Meldford, Gasper, 1002

Meldrum, George, 952

Meldrum, John, 901

Meldrum, None, 844, 901

Melholland, John, 76

Melick, John, 996

Melick, William, 527

Menard, Thomas, 844

Mench, John, 923

Mench. *See also* Mensch, Muench, Munch

Mendenhall, Elijah, 153, 606, 1012, 1029

Mendenhall, John, 1035

Mendenhall, Joseph, 153

Mendenhall, Moses, 395, 692

Mendenhall, Samuel, 95, 462

Mendenhall. *See also* Mandenhall, Manderhall

Mensch, John, 923

Mensch. *See also* Mench, Muench, Munch

Mercer, Archibald, 1161

Mercer, John, 384

Mercer, None, 1405

Meredith, Obediah, 552

Meredith, William, 358, 417

Merkley, Daniel, 531

Merkley. *See also* Maerkel, Maerkle, Markley

Merrick, Peter, 950

Merritt, John, 1636, 1726

Messer, Abraham, 318

Messer, George, 318, 830

Metcalf, Massom, 1531

Metcalf, Vacheal, 1317, 1719

Metozan, John, 967

Metz, John, 281

Metz, Mary, 1782

Metzger, Henry, 1478

Metzger, Peter, 1519

Mevine, Jonathan, 1041

Meyers, C., 830

Meyers. *See also* Maier, Majer, Major, Mayor, Meier, Meiers, Mier, Miers, Myer, Myers

Meyner, John, 1393

Meyner. *See also* Miner

Michael, Jacob, 1073

Middleton, Robertson, 782

Middleton, S., 1105

Midges, Levi, 332

Mier, Daniel, 1756

Miers, Frederick, 452

Mier, Miers. *See also* Maier, Majer, Major, Mayor, Meier, Meiers, Myer, Myers

Miessy, Abraham, 1549

Mikesell, Peter, 1556

Milam, Jarvis, 1507

Milburn, Joseph E., 1625

Miles, David, 1012, 1195

Miles, Thomas, 66

Miles, William, 865, 931

Milhorne, John, 570

Millenger, John, 632, 1073

Millenger, Joseph, 632

Miller, Abraham, 521, 747, 991, 1084, 1108, 1110

Miller, Adam, 1379

Miller, Anthony, 758, 828, 1132

Miller, Benjamin, 960, 1626

Miller, Charles, 775

Miller, Christian, 628

Miller, Christopher, 1195

Miller, Daniel, 1195, 1313

Miller, David, 195, 465, 632, 723, 830, 1049, 1306

Miller, Edward, 430, 1709, 1761

Miller, Emmanuel, 1779

Miller, F., 536

Miller, Frederick, 76, 652, 1371, 1726

Miller, George, 263, 994, 1197, 1610, 1749

Miller, Henry, 751, 996, 1041, 1108, 1196, 1436, 1689, 1709

Miller, Isaac, 9, 142, 1252, 1749, 1785

Miller, J., 865

Miller, Jacob, 263, 329, 996, 1018, 1252, 1582, 1625

Miller, James, 291, 998, 1317, 1371

Miller, Jesse, 829, 1253

Miller, Joash, 1711

Miller, John, 125, 316, 371, 414, 456, 465, 478, 549, 983, 1041, 1156, 1313, 1436, 1478, 1532, 1626, 1636, 1667

Miller, John A., 284

Miller, Jonas, 830

Miller, Joseph, 200, 372, 459, 829

Miller, M., 1638

Miller, M. S., *Honorable*, 1638

Miller, Michael, 1253, 1393, 1717

Miller, Morris, 1342

Miller, Moses, 949

Miller, Nicholas, 57

Miller, None, 211, 339, 628, 1333

Miller, P., 536

Miller, Peter, 337, 747, 775, 1085, 1108, 1557

Miller, Philip, 1753

Miller, Samuel, 478

Miller, Solomon, 1266, 1591

Miller, Susanna, 1012

Miller, Thomas, 306, 659, 1689

Miller, Tobias, 1041

Miller, William, 1313, 1406

Miller, Yost, 1242

Milleson, James, 1049

Millhouse, John, 903

Milligan, Jane, 531

Milligan, John, 474

Milligan, William, 992

Millikan, William, 288

Millinger, John, 677

Millis, Edward, 1551

Mills, Alexander, 1625

Mills, David, 359

Mills, John, 122, 205, 1401

Mills, John R., 3

Mills, None, 117, 205, 530

Mills, Peter, 213, 527, 706, 885

Mills, Reuben, 994

Mills, Richard, 1265

Mills, Seth, 122, 205, 1401

Musselman, John, 931, 1783

Mussey, Abraham, 1549

Mutz. *See* Moots

Myer, Abraham, 953

Myer, Daniel, 1756

Myer, Michael, 1784

Myers, Abraham, 953, 1155

Myers, Christopher, 1719

Myers, Frederick, 452

Myers, George, 1049

Myers, Henry, 996

Myers, Isaiah, 561

Myers, John, 56

Myers, Lambert, 1503, 1626

Myers, None, 294, 440

Myer, Myers. *See also* Maier, Majers, Major, Meier, Meiers, Meyers, Mier, Miers

Nadault, Martin, 853

Nafe, John, 524

Nafzer, John, 1719

Nagel. *See* Nagley, Nail *[translation]*, Naugle

Nagley, Philip, 6

Nail, William, Senior, 680

Nailor, John, 1719

Nalliquet, Francis, 901

Nance, Clement, 403

Nauftzger, John 1717, 1719

Naugle, Henry, 1550

Naugle. *See also* Nagley, Nail

Nava, Peter, 592

Nave, Benjamin, 1502

Nave, J., 815

Nave, Jacob, 659

Nave. *See also* Knave

Neaf, Abraham, 953

Neal, Abraham, 953

Neal, St. Leager, 1002, 1243

Neal, Thomas, 5

Neal. *See also* O'Neal

Nealaris, None, 1286

Neas, George, 537, 549

Neas. *See also* Nees

Neatans, William, 1226

Needles, Philamon, 166

Needless, P., 1402

Needless, Philemon, 121, 1753

Neely, David, 1753

Neely, James, 456, 747

Nees, George, 27

Nees, Peter, 1038, 1213, 1259

Nees. *See also* Neas, Ness

Neff, Abraham, 953

Neff, Henry, 269

Neff, Henry, Junior, 1197

Neff, Jacob, 628, 1436, 1542

Neff, John, 718

Neff, John, Senior, 1035

Neff. *See also* Knauff, Kneff, Knouff

Neighstadt, Conrad, 1036

Neiswanger, David, 1783

Neiswanger. *See also* Nieswanger, Nighswonger

Nellson, Moses, 120

Nelson, Adam, 532

Nelson, John, 1783

Nelson, Jonathan, 966

Nelson, Joseph, 1625, 1783

Nelson, Moses, 120, 198

Nelson, William, 1478

Nesbit, James, 1642

Nesbit, James, Junior, 1719

Nesbitt, James, 1768, 1769

Ness, Peter, 1038

Ness. *See also* Neas, Nees

Nessley, Jacob, 1090, 1130, 1348, 1393, 1490, 1573

Nessley, Jacob, Junior, 1573

Nessley, Jacob, Senior, 1573

Neumann, Henry, 1755

Neumann, John, 1782

Neumann. *See also* Newman, Nowman, Nyman

Neustadt. *See* Neighstadt

Nevel, None, 747

Newcom, Edward, 1667

Newcom, George, 470

Newcom, Matthew, 1757

Newcomb, Daniel, 1436

Newcomer, Peter, 6

Newcorn, George, 316

Newcorner, Peter, 6

Newell, David, 1719

Newell, Hugh, 1726

Newell, Robert, 864, 1050, 1489

Newell, Samuel, 1196, 1379, 1667

Newell, Thomas, 1582, 1667

Newell, William, 1478

Newkirk, Reuben, 141

Newman, Andrew, 378, 1036

O'Dell, James, 1041

Odum, David, 1582

Officer, James, 1085, 1132, 1242

Ogden, Stephen, 1049, 1062

Ogg, George, 747

Ogle, Alexander, 1337, 1673

Ogle, John, 1551, 1626

Ogle, William, 1582

O'Hara, Hugh, 957

O'Hara, James, 319

O'Hara. *See also* Harah

Oilar, V., 1785

O'Key, Levin, 969

O'Key. *See also* Key

Oldham, Isaac, 557

Oldham, James, 830

Oldham, None, 32

Oler, Henry, 10

Olinger, George, 1486

Olinger, John, 751

Oliver, Thomas, 1130

Oliver, William, 639

Olson, Michael, 1195

Oltfather, Henry, 731

O'Neall, Abijah, 1369

O'Neall. *See also* Neal

Ong, Jacob, 100

Opdycke, Henry, 1265, 1436

Oram, Thomas, 1489

Orbison, Robert, 21

Orgam, Marg, 1638

Orgam, None, Mrs., 1342

Organ, William, 527, 747, 1072

Ormsby, S. B., *Honorable*, 619

Orr, Hugh, 592

Orr, Robert, 724

Orr, Samuel, 1761

Orr, Thomas, 815, 919

Orr, William, 960, 985

Ortman, John, 1781

Orts, Henry, 141

Osborn, Cyrus, 992

Osborn, David, 879

Osborn, John, 1436

Osborne, David, 48, 83

Osborne, Isaac, 455, 1036

Osborne, Thomas, 1041

Osbun, Isaac, 455

Osbun, Samuel, 1484

Osburn, Isaac, 1036, 1403

Osburn, Samuel, 1484

Osler, V., 1785

Ostertag, Jacob, 305

Ostertag. *See also* Easterday *[translation]*

Oswalt, Michael, 1489

Ott, Francis, 135, 224, 865

Overholder, Martin, 68

Overmire, John, 331, 1549

Overpeck, John, 1436

Overturff, Martin, 1624

Owen, Benjamin, 26, 356

Owen, Caleb, 1689

Owen, Ephraim, 26, 532

Owen, Joseph, 261

Owens, Bartlett, 701

Owens, Benjamin, 532

Owens, James, 701

Owens, Peter, 751, 1035

Owens, William, 1351

Owings, Patrick, 747, 1756

Ox, John, 1753

Ozman, Isaac, 20

Ozmeier, Isaac, 20

Paddock, Ebenezer, 953

Paddock, Henry, 532, 1313

Paddock, Nathan, 546

Paddock, None, 1283

Paesley, David, 950

Paesley. *See also* Paisley

Page, Jonathan, 1031, 1073

Paine, David, 991

Paine, Elijah, 182

Paine, Isaac, 532

Painter, Jacob, 646

Painter, John, 1625

Painter, Matthias, 1029

Painter. *See also* Penter

Paisley, David, 1490

Paisley. *See also* Paesley

Palmer, Jacob, 632

Palmer, John, 1550

Palmer. *See also* Pollmer

Pancake, John, 452, 472

Pancake. *See also* Pfannkuchen *[translation]*

Pangborn, William, 1568

Paramour, Nathaniel, 134

Penn, Joseph, 1707

Pennock, John, 599

Pennock, William, 960

Penquite, William, 880

Pentecost, John, 953

Pentecost, John, Junior, 1726

Pentecost, Joseph, 911, 1501

Penter, Matthias, 1029

Penter. *See also* Painter

Pentz, John, Senior, 1313

Pentz. *See also* Pence

Penwell, John, 1041

Peppinger, John, 1478

Perkins, Abraham, 1327

Perkins, John, 1549

Perrin, John, 677, 1749

Perrine, Nicholas, 104

Perry, John, 1393

Perry, None, 323, 532

Perry, Samuel, 1489

Persinger, Alexander, 877

Persinger, Jacob, 779, 1048, 1151, 1171, 1207, 1216

Petafish, Christian, 1041

Peter, Jonathan, 983

Peterbaugh, D., 1029

Peterbaugh, David, 546

Peterbaugh. *See also* Puterbaugh

Peters, Abraham, 366, 896

Peterson, Frederick, 239

Peterson, Rulif, 1481

Petit, Antoine Nicholas, 872

Petit, Ignace, 966

Petit, Jean Baptiste

Petro, Leonard, 114

Petticrew, James, 347

Pettier, Phillis, 853

Pettit, Daniel, 440

Pettit, John, 995

Pettway, None, 1554

Petty, George, 546

Petty, John, 1549

Petty, Joseph, 991

Petz, Abraham, 51

Petz. *See also* Betz

Pfannkuchen, Benjamin, 1490

Pfannkuchen, John, 452, 472

Pfannkuchen. *See also* Pancake

Pfautz, Andrew, 26, 1478

Pfautz, David, 942, 1477

Pfautz, Henry, 1110

Pfautz, Jacob, 762, 776, 983, 1477

Pfautz, Jonas, 349

Pfautz, Lewis, 761

Pfautz, Noel, 1592

Pfautz, William, 942

Pfautz. *See also* Fast, Faust, Foht, Fost, Fouts, Pfoutz, Phoutz

Pfeifer, Christopher, 581

Pfeifer. *See also* Fifer, Piper

Pfoutz, Adam, 57

Pfoutz, Andrew, 26

Pfoutz, Daniel, 163, 546

Pfoutz, David, 630

Pfoutz, Jacob, 335, 677

Pfoutz, John, 349

Pfoutz, Lewis, 140

Pfoutz, William, 163, 592, 718

Pfoutz. *See also* Fast, Faust, Foht, Fost, Fouts, Pfautz, Phoutz

Phares, William, 1530

Pharis, John, Senior, 532

Phares, Pharis. *See also* Farris

Philips, David, 337

Philips, J., 1756

Philips, John, 270, 953

Philips, Ralph, 1528

Philips, William, 337, 517

Philips, Zachariah, 1242

Phillips, Frederick, 280

Phillips, Jabish, 1328

Phillips, None, 607, 1545

Phillips, Ralph, 520

Phillips, Samuel, 6

Phipps, Isaac, 1719

Phoutz, Henry, 1110

Phoutz. *See also* Fast, Faust, Foht, Fost, Fouts, Pfautz, Pfoutz

Piatt, John H., 1371

Piatt, None, 1335

Picken, Matthew, 1130

Pickens, John, 225, 339

Pickle, Jacob, 456, 747

Pierce, James, 337, 492

Pierce, Joseph, 132

Pierce, Lewis, 1196

Pierce, Michael, 153

Pierce, Nicholas, 156

Pierce, None, 607, 1328

Pierpoint, Francis, 69

Pierpoint, Obed, 69, 1270, 1393, 1514

Piggot, John, 295, 482

Piggot, Joshua, 212

Piggott, John, 134, 1250

Pigott, John, 49, 881, 1141

Pike, Benjamin, 680

Piles, Elijah, 1084

Pim, Nathan, 1154

Piper, Daniel, 1506

Piper, None, 991, 1002

Piper, None, *Honorable*, 769, 827, 1337, 1587

Piper, William, *Honorable*, 577

Piper. *See also* Fifer, Pfeifer

Pippenger, John, 1478

Pitcher, Abraham, 991

Pitman, John, 959

Pitser, Conrad, 339

Pitt, Andrew, 776

Pittenger, Abraham, 1490

Pittman, John, 898, 1376

Pitts, Andrew, 779

Plank, Adam, 764

Plaskett, None, 997

Plaskett, Robert L., 630

Plaskett, Samuel, 997

Plaskett, William, 1376

Platt, Amelia, 1252

Platt, Richard, 117

Pleasonton, S., 348, 981

Plummer, Abraham, 52

Plummer, J. W., 736

Plummer, John, 1041

Plummer, John W., 897

Plummer, Joseph West, 736

Poe, Jacob, 1014

Poe, Thomas, 503

Poindexter, None, *Honorable*, 1172

Polke, Thomas, 1557

Pollmer, Christopher, 1331

Pollock, John, 1626

Pollock, None, 1172

Pollock. *See also* Ballack

Pontieus, Adam, 1109

Pontius, Adam, 1109

Pontius, Frederick, 559, 747, 1549

Pontius, George, 594

Pontius, Peter, 384

Pontius, Philip, 1314

Pool, John, 677, 942

Pool, William, 1780

Poole, Andrew, 55

Poor, Moses, 1327

Poorman, Daniel, 343, 1016

Pope, George F., 1432

Pope, John, *Honorable*, 912

Pope, None, *Honorable*, 443

Popenoe, James, 448

Port, James, 532

Port, John, 1371

Portenay, None, 1754

Porter, Charles, 960, 1197, 1569

Porter, James, 271, 1569

Porter, John, 1242, 1247, 1354, 1500

Porter, L., 1354

Porter, Lancelot, 1247

Porter, Landlot, 1247

Porter, M., 186

Porter, Nathan, 865

Porter, S., 186

Porter, William, 1750

Porterfield, John, 1626

Porterfield, None, *General*, 915

Porterfield, Robert, 868

Ports, Philip, 1132

Pose, Lloyd, 1373

Posey, Francis, 1681

Posey, Joel, 121, 1063

Posey, Lloyd, 1373

Posey, None, 1670

Posey, Thomas, 1374

Pothier, Toussaint, 849, 872

Potter, Horace, 960, 1393

Potter, Noadiah, 942

Pottinger, John, 654

Pottinger, None, 654

Pottorf, Jacob, 1478

Pottorf, Joseph, 1313

Pottorf, Martin, 1477

Potts, Henry, 1478

Poulson, Thomas, 1718

Poweal, Michael, 1569

Powel, George, 1753

Powell, Abraham, 1195

Powell, Benjamin, 1530

Powell, Esau, 1626

Powell, Jacob, 1626

Powell, Michael, 1569

Power, Nathaniel, 1507

Power, Peter, 531

Powers, Aaron, 677

Powers, Jacob, 267, 546

Powers, John, 1779

Powers, Joseph, 794

Prand, Thomas, 1602

Pratt, J. H., 1397

Prellaman, Jacob, 1667

Pressly, David, 1313

Prestley, David, 367, 1110

Preston, Amos, 569

Prewett, Jacob, 1507, 1689

Prewitt, Jacob, 1689

Price, Benjamin, 1501

Price, David, 950

Price, George, 1625

Price, Henry, 492, 992

Price, Henry R., 946

Price, Jacob, 677

Price, James, 234, 1750

Price, John, Junior, 50

Price, Keith, 120, 199

Price, Rice, 632

Price, Thomas, 1534

Price, William, 925, 946

Priest, Jeremiah, 949, 1726

Prillaman, Jacob, 801, 1667

Prince, George, 482, 882

Pringle, Henry, 711

Prior, Barbara, 774, 1379

Prior, John, 345

Pritchard, James, 837, 845, 1069

Pritchard, John, 490, 758

Pritchard, Rees, 1719

Probst, Jacob, 514

Procter, Izak, 672

Propst, Jacob, 337

Proudfoot, Andrew, 1610

Prough, Samuel, 1711

Provine, William, 585

Pryer, G., 1073

Pryer, J., 1073

Pryer, John, 1779

Puffenberger. See Buffinburgher

Pugh, Caleb, 1041

Pugh, David, 478, 1328

Pugh, John, 22, 134, 994

Pugh, William, 1582

Pulliam, Thomas, 959

Pullian, M. J., 983

Pumphrey, Reason, 1393

Pumphrey, William, 960, 1490

Purcel, Benjamin, 1371

Purcell, Benjamin, 1371

Purcell, Jesse, 766

Purcell, John, 1195

Purcell, Thomas, 1073

Purcell, William, 766

Purdee, John, 337

Purkiser, John, 1755

Pursel, John, 1195

Purviance, David, 1749

Purviance, David P., 829

Purviance, Eleizar. 357

Purviance, John, 532, 829

Purvis, John, 1230

Pusey, Joel, 1312

Puterbaugh, D., 1029

Puterbaugh, David, 1031

Puterbaugh. See also Peterbaugh

Putnam, Aaron W., 1491

Pyle, William, 430

Quakinbush, Peter, 1041

Quick, John, 1749

Quillen, John, 356

Quin, John, 532

Quin, Robert, 135

Quine, Henry, 951

Quinn, James, 1035

Quinn, Matthew, 1029

Raber, John, 1393, 1784

Radcliffe, John, 352

Radley, John, 1783

Ragers, Benjamin, 1055

Ragsdale, B., 1356

Railsback, David, 722, 829

Railsback, John, 521

Railsback, None, 654

Raimer, Rosanna, 1719

Rainey, William, 6

Rairy, Charles, 85, 514

Rairy. See also Rary

Raker, Peter, 56

Raker. See also Reicher, Riker, Ryker

Raley, John, 531

Ralston, Edward, 923

Rambo, Jackson, 1313

Rambo, William, 1489

Ramey, William, 6

Ramsay, Benjamin, 1376

Ramsay, James, 1709

Ramsay, John, 1208, 1709, 1718

Ramsay, Samuel, 332

Ramsey, Allen, 953

Ramsey, Elizabeth, 286

Ramsey, George, 27, 734

Ramsey, James, 747

Ramsey, John, 521, 652, 747, 1178

Ramsey, Lucy, 261, 1390

Ramsey, Samuel, 991, 1044

Ramsey, Thomas, 21, 365, 536

Ramsey, William, 532

Rance, Asaiah, 298

Rand, Thomas, 1602

Randall, James, 1401

Randell, J., 1105

Randle, Jonas, 316

Ranfrew, William, 1719

Ranier, Daniel, 1781

Rankin, Alexander, 1626

Rankin, Thomas, 1393

Rano, Benjamin, 970

Rape, Jacob, 1029

Rapeholst, Anthony, 430

Rapeholts, Anthony, 896

Rapenholst, Anthony, 319

Raper, Daniel, 384

Rapp, Henry, 677

Rary, Charles, 747

Ratchkin, James, 1

Ratckin, James, 380

Ratckin. *See also* Ratekin

Ratherr, Samuel, 677

Ratliff, Cornelius, 731

Ratliff, None, 628

Rats, Henry, 631, 1422

Rats, None, 696

Ratt, John H., 1436, 1502

Ratter, Samuel, 677

Rau, George, 524

Rau, Peter, 617

Rau, Richard, 142

Rau. *See also* Row, Rue

Rauch, George, 747

Rauch, Jacob, 1087

Rauch, Joseph, 787

Rauch, Thomas, 1534

Rauch. *See also* Rouch, Rough, Roush, Ruff, Rush

Raudebusch, George, 56

Raver, Frederick, 1109

Raver. *See also* Reaver, Reber, Rever, Rieber

Rawles, Elisha, 1549

Rawlings, William, 1711

Ray, Hester, 1753

Ray, None, 950

Ray. *See also* Reagh, Wray

Raymond, Colder, 1530

Raynolds, Benjamin, 900

Raynolds, None, 682, 900

Raynolds, William, 745, 922, 1072

Raynolds. *See also* Reynolds, Ruynolds

Razor, Daniel, Senior, 1783

Rea, John, *Honorable*, 147

Reagan, Nicholas, 1779

Reagh, John, 1104

Reah, John, 1152

Reagh, Reah. *See also* Ray, Wray

Ream, Jacob, 132, 830

Ream, Philip, 305

Ream, Samuel, 53, 132, 337, 557, 830

Ream. *See also* Reem

Reardon, Moses, 1667

Reasler, None, 325

Reaver, Thomas, 337

Reaver. *See also* Raver, Reber, Rever, Rieber

Reaves, Joseph, 490

Reber, Conrad, 504, 754

Reber, John, 1393

Reber, Peter, 991

Reber, Thomas, 337, 747

Reber, Valentine, 747

Reber. *See also* Raver, Reaver, Rever, Rieber

Rechtmeier. *See* Rightmire

Rector, Charles, 874

Rector, George, 475

Rector, None, 1691

Reddick, John, 186

Redenbaugh, Adam, 1779

Redenbaugh, Andrew, 903

Redenhour, Peter, 1530

Reece, Jacob, 1486

Reece. *See also* Rees, Reese, Reis, Rice, Ruse

Reed, Abraham, 1391

Reed, Adam, 931, 1030

Reed, Andrew, 910

Reed, Archibald, 1783

Reed, Christopher, 1073

Reed, Daniel, 654, 723

Reed, David, 1049

Reed, Frederick, 748

Reed, James, 1132, 1195, 1530

Reed, Jeremiah, 1242

Reed, John, 646, 763, 991, 998, 1295, 1371, 1719

Reed, Jonathan, 828

Reed, Michael, 131, 549, 599, 828

Reed, None, 553, 1109, 1328

Reed, Philip, *Honorable*, 136

Reed, Rufus Seth, 1013

Reed, Thomas, 1041

Reed, Thomas M., 1452

Reed, William, 863, 1031, 1073

Reed. *See also* Reid

Reeder, Daniel H., 992

Reeder, None, 1133

Reeder, William, 992, 1265

Reeds, Thomas, 677

Reedy, John, 1433

Reem, Abraham, 960, 1750

Reem. *See also* Ream

Rees, David, 239, 628

Rees, James, 1582

Rees, John, 747

Rees, Pritchard, 1719

Rees, Thomas, 75

Reese, David, 48, 171

Reese, John, 140

Rees, Reese. *See also* Reece, Reis, Rice, Ruse

Reeve, Joseph, 209, 593

Reeve, Joshua, 960

Reeves, John, 1253

Reeves, Joseph, 57, 77, 1430, 1455

Reeves, Josias, 960

Reichardt, Abraham, 722

Reicher, John, 997

Reicher, Peter, 56

Reicher. *See also* Raker, Riker, Ryker

Reichle, Conrad, 1109

Reif. *See* Rife

Reid, Joseph, 1132, 1313

Reighle, Conrad, 1109

Reilly, None, 998

Reimann, Joseph, 550

Reimer, Rosanna, 1719

Reinhardt, Valentine, 1750

Reininger, John, 1478

Reis, Henry, 1391

Reis. *See also* Reece, Rees, Reese, Rice, Ruse

Reitenhauer. *See* Ridenhour, Ridinghour

Reiter, Adam, 399

Reitmeier, James, 996

Reley, John, 531

Reley, Robert, 863

Remy, James, 1313

Rench, John, 56, 923, 931

Renfrow, William, 1719

Renick, Felix, 419, 1753

Renick, George, 251, 396

Renick, Robert, 1757

Renton, Thomas, 992

Repp, Daniel, 350, 465

Resener, Benjamin, 557

Resline, Henry, 877

Retter, J., 1133

Retter, Tobias, 992

Retter. *See also* Ratter, Ritter, Rutter

Rever, Peter, 337

Rever, Valentine, 430

Rever. *See also* Raver, Reaver, Reber, Rieber

Rex, Daniel, 931

Rex, George Adam, 323, 1750

Rex, John, 1783

Reynolds, Benjamin, 900

Reynolds, Isaac, 950, 953, 1625

Reynolds, James, 476

Reynolds, John, 950, 1246, 1371

Reynolds, Joseph, 433, 553, 556, 998, 1265, 1478, 1667

Reynolds, Nathaniel, 900

Reynolds, None, 673, 682, 900

Reynolds, Richard, 586

Reynolds, William, 46, 53, 745, 922, 1072, 1692

Reynolds. *See also* Raynolds, Ruynolds

Rhea, John, *Honorable*, 1077, 1352, 1644

Rhea, None, *Honorable*, 1338

Rhea, Robert, 1710

Rheinhold, Matheus, 263

Rhendy, Jacob, 521

Rhoads, Daniel, 486

Rhode, John, 130, 1401

Rhode, William, 1401

Rhodes, J., 1314

Rhodes, Jacob, 586, 1550, 1719

Rhodes, James, 319

Rhodes, Joseph, 493

Rhodes, Philip, 1550

Rhodes, William, 1090

Rhorer, Joseph, 1073

Ricard, Joseph, 872

Ricard, Oliver, 872

Rice, George, 1217

Rice, Jacob, 1602

Rice, John, 1049

Rice, Richard, 134

Rice. *See also* Reece, Rees, Reese, Reis, Ruse

Richard, Henry, 1748

Richards, A., 903

Richards, E., 903

Richards, George, 1314

Richards, Jesse, 1719

Richards, John, 724, 960

Richards, Leonard, 555

Richards, Thomas, 1108

Richardson, Daniel, 520, 1401

Richardson, Fielder, 1090

Richardson, James, 1196, 1242

Richardson, John, 659, 1313, 1393

Richardson, Nathan, 1041

Richardson, Rachel, 1719

Richardson, Robert, 21, 26

Richardt, Abraham, 722

Richey, John, 1163

Rick, H., 574

Rickabaugh, Anne, 747

Ricketts, Edward, 430, 747

Riddle, John, 114, 545, 677, 960

Ridenhour, Joseph, 153

Ridenhour, Peter, 135

Rider, Adam, 399

Ridgely, Absalom, 1569

Ridgeway, Basil, 1626

Ridgeway, David, 1314

Ridinghour, Ludwick, 747

Rieber, Peter, 337

Rieber. *See also* Raver. Reaver, Reber, Rever, Ries. *See* Reece, Rees, Reese, Reis, Rice, Ruse

Riesener, Benjamin, 557

Rife, John, 102, 1049, 1338, 1352

Rifner, Peter, 1783

Riggs, John, 1557

Riggs, John S., 942

Rightmire, James, 996

Rigney, William, 1718

Riker, Samuel, 1636

Riker, Wentworth, 1379

Riker. *See also* Raker, Reicher, Ryker

Riley, John, 400, 533, 592

Rinaman, William, 519

Rinebold, Matheus, 263

Rinehart, Valentine, 1750

Ringold, Samuel, *Honorable*, 909

Riopell, Antoine, 849

Rippey, Joseph, 1090

Rippith, William, 57

Ritchey, George, 747, 991, 1314

Ritchie, George, 53

Ritchie, James, 625

Ritchie, John, 1151

Ritchie, Thomas, 53

Ritchie, W., 642

Rittenhouse, Garret, 654, 731

Rittenhouse, Ludwick, 747

Rittenhouse, Peter, 1530

Rittenhouse, William, 1110

Ritter, Henry, 991

Ritter, Jacob, 378

Ritter, John, 254, 991, 1109, 1756, 1781

Ritter. *See also* Retter, Rutter

Rivard, Antoine, 853

Rivard, Charles, 929

Rivard, François, 929

Rivard, Nicholas, 952

Roach, Jeremiah, 1781

Roads, J., 1314

Roads, Jacob, 1550, 1719

Roads, James, 319

Roads, Philip, 1550

Robb, David, 592

Robbins, Daniel, 1051

Robbins, William, 535

Robe, David, 1196

Robe, Josiah, 552

Robenault, Peter, 414

Robenson, Richard, 545

Robert, Peter, 951

Robert, Thomas, 1031

Roberts, Charles, 216, 404, 542, 870

Roberts, David, 1753

Roberts, Henry, 1590

Sackeiter, Henry, 617

Sackett, Aaron, 829

Sackett, Elizabeth, 1549

Saffer, John, 1718

Saffers, John, 1376

Safford, Robert, 1491

Sagar, Jacob, 1784

Sage, Jeremiah, 779

Sage, John, 1718

Sailor, Christian, 632

Sailor, Jacob, 1089

Sailor, John, 632

Sailor. *See also* Saylor, Seiler, Seller, Siler, Zeiler, Zeller

St. Clair, Arthur, 1401

St. Jean, Joseph, 929, 934

St. Martin, Adhemar, 934

Salcedo, Manuel de, 1333

Salmon, Frederick, 17, 283

Salomon, Frederick, 283

Saltsgaver, Jacob, 319, 1314

Saltsgiver, Peter, 996, 1242

Saltz, Edward, 1781

Saltz. *See also* Saultz, Solt

Salzgeber, Jacob, 319, 1314

Salzgeber, Peter, 996, 1242

Sample, David, 40, 42, 48, 98, 112

Sanders, Francis, 1325

Sanders, Samuel, 1110

Sanderson, George, 747

Sandies, David, 942

Sands, Thomas, 120, 197

Santz, Thomas, 1756

Sapp, Daniel, 1601

Sapp, John, 1569

Sargent, James, 998

Sarver. *See* Server

Sater, Henry, 1195

Sater, John, 1195, 1710

Satterthwaite, Joseph W., 758

Satterthwaite, Joshua W., 4, 758

Satterthwaite, Thomas, 1242

Satterthwaith, Joseph, 732

Sauer, Henry, 1049

Sauer. *See also* Sower

Saultz, Thomas, 1756

Saultz. *See also* Saltz, Solt

Saum, Jacob, 935

Sawyer, Barbary, 1012

Sawyer, Joseph, 616, 671, 1401

Sawyers, L., 1200

Sayers, Ephraim, 1196

Sayers, Thomas, 935

Saylor, Arthur, 992

Saylor, E., 1012

Saylor, Elizabeth, 337, 991

Saylor, J., 1012

Saylor, John, 1314

Saylor. *See also* Sailor, Seiler, Seller, Siler, Zeiler, Zeller

Sayne, Pierson, 1243

Sayre, Leonard, 1625

Sayres, Jonathan, 257

Sayres, Thomas, 546

Sayrs, Jonathan, 257

Scattergood, Benjamin, 57

Schaefer, Friedrich, 21

Schaefer, Jacob, 561

Schaefer, Joseph, 1140

Schaefer, None, 736

Schaefer, Samuel, 736

Schaefer, Simon, 632, 659

Schaeffer, Adam, 22

Schafer, Simon, 632

Schaefer, Schaeffer, Schafer. *See also* Schefer, Schiefer, Shaffer, Sheefer, Sheffer

Schallenberger, David, 332

Schallenberger. *See also* Shallenberger

Schartel. *See also* Shartle

Schauch, John, 512, 1765

Schauck, Henry, 1739, 1740

Schauck, John, 1107

Schauck, John, Junior, 1740

Schauch, Schauck. *See also* Schock, Shauck, Shock

Schauer, Abraham, 1073

Schauer, Benjamin, 1073

Schauer. *See also* Shooer, Shore, Shower

Scheerer, Agness, 1218

Scheerer, Joseph, 1218

Scheerer, Nancy, 1218

Scheerer. *See also* Scherer, Shearer, Sherer

Schefer, Simon, 659

Schefer. *See also* Schaefer, Schaeffer, Schafer, Schiefer, Shaffer, Sheefer, Sheffer

Scheible, Christian, 22, 652

Scheible, Daniel, 1779

Scheible, Jacob, 599, 628

Scheible, Ulrich, 5, 355

Scheibli, Conrad, 1049

Scheible, Scheibli. *See also* Shiveley, Shively

Scheidler, George, 51

Schell, L., 953

Schell, Laurence, 714, 892, 1328

Schell. *See also* Shell

Schenck, C., 651

Schenck, None, 1168

Schenck, Obadiah, 457

Schenck, W. C., 992

Schenck, William C., 457, 520, 759, 784, 1243

Schenck. *See also* Schenk, Shenck, Shenk

Schenenberger, Jacob, 5

Schenenberger. *See also* Schoenenberger, Shennebery

Schenk, William C., 546, 652

Scherer, Valentine, 1749

Scherer. *See also* Scheerer, Shearer, Sherer

Schiefer, Joseph, 1140

Schiefer. *See also* Schaefer, Schaeffer, Schafer, Schefer, Shaffer, Sheefer, Sheffer

Schilds, Matthias, 1750

Schilling, Balzer, 1320

Schillingberger, George, 828

Schimp, George, 478

Schindler, George, 901, 966

Schlegel, John, 546

Schleifer, Jacob, 21

Schleiff, Frederick, 732

Schloesser, Philip, 595, 890, 993, 1030, 1089, 1163

Schlosser, Philip, 46, 296

Schloesser, Schlosser. *See also* Slusher, Slusser

Schluss, John, 22

Schmeier, Frederick, 659

Schmeier, Jacob, 22

Schmitz, Conrad, 592

Schnaebeli, None, 628

Schnaebeli. *See also* Schnibely, Snively

Schneider, Abraham, 927

Schneider, Asa B., 1252

Schneider, Balser, 1161

Schneider, Daniel, 254, 722, 1753

Schneider, David, 1534

Schneider, George, 100, 257, 1253, 1489, 1760

Schneider, Henry, 722, 950

Schneider, John, 447, 478, 959, 1252

Schneider, Joseph, 1090

Schneider, Michael, 942, 1049, 1436

Schneider, None, 1135

Schneider, Peter, 104

Schneider, Philip, 470

Schneider, William, 747

Schneider. *See also* Snider, Snyder

Schneip, Leonard, 1636

Schnell, John, 1313

Schnep, Leonard, 1084

Schnibely, None, 628

Schnibely. *See also* Schnaebeli, Snively

Schnipe, Leonard, 1636

Schober, Daniel, 994

Schober, Jacob, 1717

Schober, John, 294, 440

Schober. *See also* Shaver, Shover

Schock, Christian, 496

Schock, Henry, 1126

Schock, None, 747, 1402

Schock, Simon, 748

Schock, Stephen, 1242

Schock. *See also* Schauch, Schauck, Shauck, Shock

Schoeffler. *See* Shepler

Schoen. *See* Shane

Schoenenberg, John, 1489

Schoenenberger, Jacob, 5, 1377

Schoenenberger. *See also* Schenenberger, Shennebery

Schoenhuber, John, 747

Schoff, Philip, 1709

Schoffield, Seely, 1238

Schofield, Elizabeth, 1085

Schofield, Elnathan, 1109

Scholfield, Elizabeth, 1085

Schoffield, Scholfield. *See also* Scofield

Scholl, Christian, 1130

Scholl, John, 750

Scholl, Samuel, 539

Scholl. *See also* Schule, Schooley, Scioley, Shull

Schooler, Benjamin, 1436

Schooley, Andrew, 1433

Schooley, Henry, 5

Schooley, Richard, 9

Schooley, Samuel, 1548

Schooley. *See also* Scholl, Schule, Scioley, Shull

Schoonhover, John, 747

Schorb, Andrew, 1030

Schorb, Jacob, 503

Schorb, John, 1090, 1782

Schorb. *See also* Shorb

Schott, John, 750

Schreiber, Adam, 394

Schreiber, Elijah, 394

Schreiber, Jacob, 1012

Schreiber, Stacy, 531

Schreiber. *See also* Shriver

Schreiner, Peter, 689

Schroeder, Aaron, 1031

Schroeder, Daniel, 1313

Schroeder, David, 1029

Schroeder, Henry, 1392

Schroeder, Jacob, Junior, 550

Schroeder. *See also* Shrader, Shreader

Schuch, Christopher, 1477

Schuck, Philip, 779

Schuch, Schuck. *See also* Shuck

Schueb. *See* Shoup

Schuett. *See* Schutt, Shut, Shutt

Schuetz, Andrew, 606

Schuetz. *See also* Schutz, Shoots

Schugart, George, 1749

Schule, Peter, 306

Schule, Samuel, 1548

Schule. *See also* Scholl, Schooley, Scioley, Shull

Schuler. *See* Schooler

Schultz, George, 5, 1128

Schultz, Philip, 592, 1718

Schumacher, G., 255

Schumacher, Jacob, 337

Schumacher, John, 431, 434, 747, 808

Schumacher, None, 815

Schumacher. *See also* Shoemaker

Schumann, John, 677

Schurr, John, 1246, 1314

Schuster, Daniel, 960, 994, 1049, 1750

Schuster, G., 1662

Schuster. *See also* Shuster

Schutt, George, 789

Schutt, John, 789

Schutt, Peter, 306

Schutt, Philip, 732

Schutt. *See also* Shut, Shutt

Schutz, Joseph, 319, 1314

Schutz. *See also* Shoots

Schwab. *See* Swope

Schwartzel, Philip, 1073

Schwartzell, Matthias, 350

Schwartzell, Philip, 722

Schwartzle, Philip, 1195

Schweinfurt, Peter, 456, 1080

Schweinfurth, Peter, 1119

Schweinhard, John, 263

Schweinhardt, John, 747, 1314

Schweinhardt, Salome, 475

Schweinhart, Adam, 1636

Schweinhart, Jacob, 1636

Schweinhart, Peter, 1636

Schweitzer, Jacob, 1549

Schweitzer, Jacob, Junior, 331

Schweitzer, Jacob, Senior, 331

Schweitzer, M., 960

Schweitzer, Michaël, 1719

Schweizer, None, 475

Schweizer, William, 449

Schwitzer, M., 960

Schweitzer, Schwitzer. *See also* Swisher, Switzer

Scimey, Frederick, 1084

Scioley, Andrew, 1433

Scioley. *See also* Scholl, Schooley, Schule, Shull

Scoffield, Seely, 716

Scofield, Elijah, 1761

Scofield, Elnathan, 332, 337, 1549

Scofield, Seely, 704, 705, 716, 1238

Scofield. *See also* Schoffield, Schofield, Scholfield

Scothorn, Lewis, 1753

Scott, Abraham, 531

Scott, Allen, 1632

Scott, Andrew, 398

Scott, Charles, 130

Scott, David, 1074

Scott, John, 1031, 1569

Scott, Joseph, 995

Scott, Moses, 262

Scott, None, 1041, 1738

Scott, Patrick, 1534

Scott, Richard, 372

Scott, Robert, 135, 347, 372, 784, 1035

Scott, Samuel, 130

Scott, Thomas, 1086

Scott, William, 57, 1489

Scruggs, James, 1433, 1689

Scudder, Ephraim, 76

Scudder, Matthias, 435

Scudder, Nathaniel, 1651

Scudder, None, 425

Seal, James, 182

Seal, William, 182

Seaman, Henry, 671

Seamans, Gilbert, 885

Searcy, Samuel, 1582

Searey, Samuel, 1582

Sears, David, 1477

Sears, Jacob, 1477

Sears, Joseph, 101, 1783

Sears, William, 1783

Searse, William, 950

Sears, Searse. *See also* Siers

Sebre, None, 1325

Secrist, Frederick, 271

Sedgewick, Richard, 1002

Seear, Henry, 1026

Seefort, Philip, 1090

Seeporth, George, 502

Sefton, Henry, 115

Seghefoost, George, 1569

Seghefoost. *See also* Sickafoose, Zickafuss

Seib, Francis, 1548

Seibert, Adam, 1408

Seibert. *See also* Seybert, Siebert, Sighbert

Seidenbinder, George, 1781

Seiler, E., 1012

Seiler, Henry, 1029

Seiler, J., 1012

Seiler, Jacob, 1089

Seiler, John, 1314

Seiler, Philip, 328, 453, 663

Seiler. *See also* Sailer, Saylor, Seller, Siler, Zeiler, Zeller

Seitz, Lewis, 400

Seitz, Nicholas, 433

Selby, George W., 331

Selby, Zachariah, 535

Seldon, Roger, 184

Self, John, 1306, 1585

Self, William, 1306

Self. *See also* Selp

Sell, John, 1196

Seller, George, 1534

Seller, Joseph, 50, 1132

Seller, Nathan, 91

Sellers, Henry, 747, 1132

Sellers, Isaac, 1242

Sellers, Nathan, 532, 1195

Sellers, Peter, 1328

Sellers, William, 1242

Seller. Sellers. *See also* Sailer, Saylor, Siler, Zeiler, Zeller

Selp, John, 1585

Selp. *See also* Self

Seneff, Jacob, 747

Senff, Michael, 16, 52

Seneff, Senff. *See also* Zenf, Zenft

Senior, John, 957

Sensy, Owen, 1195

Serjeant, Snowden, 1126

Serre, Joseph, 929, 934

Serrere, André, 966

Server, Jacob, 470

Servieres, François M. de, 872

Sevier, John, 648

Sewall, Lewis, 1006

Seward, Daniel, 1582, 1710

Seybert, Adam, *Honorable*, 1621

Seybert. *See also* Seibert, Siebert, Sighbert

Shackford, Josiah, 1134

Shackleford, William, 1690

Shaffer, Jacob, 561

Shaffer, None, 736

Shaffer, Samuel, 736

Shaffer. *See also* Schaefer, Schaeffer, Schafer, Schefer, Schiefer, Sheefer, Sheffer

Shallenberger, David, 332, 684, 686

Shallenberger, Henry, 684, 686

Shallenberger, Michael, 684

Shallenberger, Samuel, 684

Shallenberger. *See also* Schallenberger

Shane, Abraham, 104

Shannon, Chloe, 1000

Shannon, George, 28, 140, 604, 630

Shannon, John, 1154

Shannon, Robert, 617

Shannon, Samuel, 931

Sharp, George, 1284

Sharp, John, 128, 282

Sharp, Robert, 900, 1001

Sharrard, William, 537

Sharrards, Lodowick, 1377

Shartle, Philip, 337

Shauck, Henry, 1739, 1740

Shauck, John, 512, 1107, 1765

Shauck. *See also* Schauch, Schauck, Schock, Shock

Shaver, Daniel, 994

Shaver. *See also* Schober, Shover

Shaw, John, 22, 1073, 1197, 1253, 1371

Shaw, Knowles, 21

Shaw, Nathan, 1569

Shaw, None, 960, 985

Shaw, Samuel, 116

Shay, John, 599

Shearer, David, 1478

Shearer. *See also* Scheerer, Scherer, Sherer

Shearman, John, 1393

Sheefer, Joseph, 1140

Sheefer. *See also* Schaefer, Schaeffer, Schafer, Schefer, Schiefer, Shaffer, Sheffer

Sheerer, Agness, 1218

Sheerer, Joseph, 1218

Sheerer, Nancy, 1218

Sheerer. *See also* Scheerer, Scherer, Shearer, Sherer

Sheetz, Andrew, 606

Sheffer, Frederick, 21

Sheffer. *See also* Schaefer, Schaeffer, Schafer, Schefer, Schiefer, Shaffer, Sheefer

Shelby, David, 332, 337

Sheldon, Daniel, 202

Shell, Christian, 1130

Shell, L., 953

Shell, Laurence, 714, 892, 1328

Shell. *See also* Schell

Shellabarger, John, 1667

Shellabarger, Martin, 1667

Shenck, Obadiah, 457

Shenck, William C., 457

Shenck. *See also* Schenck, Schenk, Shenk

Shenenberger, Jacob, 1377

Shenenberger. *See also* Schoenenberger, Shennebery

Shenep, John, 654

Shenk, William C., 520, 759, 784

Shenk. *See also* Schenck, Schenk, Shenck

Shennebery, John, 1489

Shennebery. *See also* Schoenenberger, Shenenberger

Shepherd, James, 569

Shepherd, John, 536

Shepherd, Nathan, 1090, 1130, 1534

Shepherd, Peter, 787

Shepherd, Thomas, 1377

Shepler, Henry, 132

Sherer, Valentine, 1749

Sherer. *See also* Scheerer, Scherer, Shearer, Sheerer

Sherg, Jacob, 552

Sherg. *See also* Joerg, Shirk, Yarrick, Yerk, York, Yurrick

Sherrard, William, 537

Sherwood, James, 20

Shewman, John, 677

Shewman. *See also* Schumann

Shidler, George, 51, 1012

Shidler. *See also* Schindler, Shindler

Shields, James, 1760

Shields, Joseph, 131, 1079

Shields, Patrick, 403

Shields, Samuel, 961, 1002

Shilds, Mattias, 1750

Shilling, Palser, 1320

Shimp, George, 478

Shindledecker, John, 1265

Shindler, George, 901, 966

Shindler. *See also* Schindler, Shidler

Shingledecker, Isaac, 923

Shingletaker, None, 759

Shipler, Henry, 996

Shiplor, John, 1662

Shirk, Andrew, 942

Shirk. *See also* Joerg, Sherg, Yarrick, Yerk, York, Yurrick

Shirley, Christian, 1551

Shirley, Valentine, 719, 824

Shirlock, Edward, 16

Shirly, Valentine, 824

Shiveley, Christian, 22

Shiveley, Ulrey, 5

Shiveley, Ulrich, 5

Shively, Christian, 652

Shively, Conrad, 1049

Shively, Daniel, 1779

Shively, Jacob, 116, 599, 628

Shively, Ullery, 355

Shiveley, Shively. *See also* Scheible, Scheibli

Shock, Chris., 496

Shock, Henry, 1126

Shock, None, 747, 1402

Shock, Stephen, 1242

Shock. *See also* Schauch, Schauck, Schock, Shauck

Shoemaker, G., 255

Shoemaker, George, 70, 71

Shoemaker, Jacob, 208, 337

Shoemaker, John, 431, 434, 747, 808

Shoemaker, None, 815

Shoemaker. *See also* Schumacher

Sholl, Christian, 1130

Sholl, John, 750

Sholl. *See also* Scholl

Shooer, None, 1012

Shooer. *See also* Schauer, Shore, Shower

Shoots, Joseph, 319, 1314

Shoots. *See also* Schuetz

Shorb, Andrew, 1030

Shorb, Jacob, 503

Shorb, John, 1049, 1090, 1331, 1360, 1393, 1782

Shorb, Peter, 1393

Shorb. *See also* Schorb

Shore, James, 960

Shore. *See also* Schauer, Shooer, Shower

Short, Elihu, 430

Short, Jacob, 1718

Short, John, 1041

Short, John Cleves, 1384, 1385

Short, Peyton, 443, 659, 669, 1133, 1214, 1268, 1779

Short, Thomas, 1197

Short, William, 1073, 1133, 1249, 1251, 1371, 1384, 1487, 1710

Shott, John, 750

Shotwell, Hugh, 1782

Shotwell, John, 1782

Shoup, George, 628, 1328, 1371, 1392, 1548

Shoup, Jacob, 239

Shoup, John, 1134

Shouse, Thomas, 1760

Shover, Jacob, 1717

Shover, John, 294, 440

Shover. *See also* Schober, Shaver

Shower, Abraham, 1073

Shower, Benjamin, 1073

Shower. *See also* Schauer, Shooer, Shore

Shrader, Aaron, 1031

Shraider, David, 1029

Shreader, Jacob, Junior, 550

Shrader, Shraider, Shreader. *See also* Schroeder

Shriver, Adam, 394

Shriver, Elijah, 394

Shriver, Stacy, 531

Shriver. *See also* Schreiber

Shrog, David, 1085

Shropshire, Thomas, 951

Shuck, Philip, 779

Shuck, Simon, 748

Shuck. *See also* Schuech, Schueck

Shugart, George, 1749

Shull, Peter, 306

Shull. *See also* Scholl, Schooley, Schule, Scioley

Shultz, Philip, 592

Shultz. *See also* Schultz

Shurr, John, 1246, 1314

Shuster, Daniel, 960, 994, 1049, 1750

Shuster, G., 1662

Shuster. *See also* Schuster

Shut, George, 789

Shut, John, 789

Shutt, George, 854

Shutt, John, 854

Shutt, Peter, 306

Shutt, Philip, 17, 732

Shutt. *See also* Schutt

Sibbett, Aaron, 1195

Sibley, Solomon, 901

Sickafoose, George, 1569

Sickafoose. *See also* Seghefoost, Zickafuss

Sickles, Garret, 615, 743, 851

Sickman, Barnet, 1408

Sickman, Barnhart, 1550

Siddell, William, 1569

Sidwell, Henry, 1197

Sidwell, N., 1444

Siebert, Adam, 73

Siebert. *See also* Seibert, Seybert, Sighbert

Siers, Joseph, 101, 1783

Siers, William, 1783

Siers. *See also* Sears

Sighbert, Adam, 1408

Sighbert. *See also* Seibert, Seybert, Siebert

Siler, Philip, 328, 453, 663

Siler. *See also* Sailer, Saylor, Seiler, Seller, Zeiler, Zeller

Silliman, Wyllys, 1006

Sills, Joseph, 1636

Sills, Michael, 998

Simmerman, Conrad, 22

Simmerman. *See also* Zimmermann

Simmington, Robert, 997, 1602, 1718

Simmington. *See also* Simonton, Symington

Simmons, Adam, 489

Simmons, John, 6, 212, 356, 448, 652, 1478, 1726

Simmons, William, 469

Simons, Thomas, 1031, 1041

Simonton, None, 475

Simonton. *See also* Simmington, Symington

Simontt, Benjamin, 924

Simpson, William, 1689

Sims, Jeremiah, 1582

Sinclair, James, 503, 1379

Sinclair, James, Senior, 87

Sinclair, William, 724

Singer, Joseph, 142

Singleton, Hiram, 951

Singrey, Jacob, 1719

Sinks, George, 91

Sinks, Jacob, 677

Sinks, None, 1401

Sinnip, Richard, 1265

Sintz, Nicholas, 433

Sintz, Peter, 609

Sipe, Francis, 1548

Sirman, Isaac, 1110

Sites, Lewis, 400

Sivisker, William, 6

Skillman, Jacob, 677, 680

Skinner, George, 1379

Skinner, John, 747

Skinner, Robert, 349, 764

Skinner, Thomas, 545, 680

Skinner, W., 1407

Skinner, William, 202, 747

Skyles, William, 992

Slack, Abel, 1601

Slack, John, 728

Slagle, John, 546

Slater, William, 1550

Slates, Frederick, 1393

Slates, John, 960

Slatton, Reuben, 1195

Slaughter, David, 24

Slaughter, Ezekiel, 1549

Slaughter, R. F., 1056, 1671

Slaughter, Robert F., 157, 332

Sleighter, David, 24

Slidger, George, 614

Slifer, Jacob, 21

Slinger, Mary, 257

Slingluff, None, 29, 138, 297, 996, 1166

Slips, George, 949

Slires, John, 1601

Sloan, John, 1073

Sloan, Richard, 532

Sloan, William, 706, 726

Sloane, John, 1006

Sloo, Thomas, 1006, 1656, 1770

Slooj, Thomas, 943

Slump, Frederick, 1007

Slusher, Philip, 296, 595, 890, 993, 1089, 1163

Slusher. *See also* Schloesser, Schlosser, Slusser

Sluss, John, 22

Slusser, Philip, 46, 1030

Slusser. *See also* Schloesser, Schlosser, Slusher

Slutman, Peter, 1195

Sluts, John, 22

Sluts, Samuel, 599

Slutsman, David, 628

Slythe, Richard, 1624

Small, A., 1582

Small, James, 609

Small, John, 212

Small, Nathan, 1002

Smart, Henry, 268

Smier, Jacob, 22

Smiler, John, 1557

Smiley, Christiana, 316

Smiley, John, 316, 1665

Smiley, John, Junior, 316

Smilie, John, *Honorable*, 111, 150, 155, 177, 871, 1055, 1074

Smilie, None, *Honorable*, 770

Smith, Abraham, 1002

Smith, Adam, 17, 132, 1196, 1393

Smith, Alexander, 828, 938

Smith, Andrew, 747, 1109, 1393, 1750

Smith, Augustine, 1781

Smith, Bell, 1030

Smith, Charles, 535

Smith, Christian, 1163

Smith, Christopher, 1041, 1667

Smith, Conrad, 592

Smith, Daniel, 136, 1610, 1711

Smith, David, 57, 82

Smith, Edward, 1072

Smith, Edwin, 459

Smith, Ephraim, 628

Smith, George, 628, 1040, 1433, 1781

Smith, Goodin, 1549

Smith, Henry, 1030, 1163, 1378, 1478, 1602

Smith, Henry C., 306

Smith, Hosea, 959, 1135

Smith, Hunt, 942

Smith, J., 50, 1614

Smith, Jacob, 294, 440, 628, 932, 970, 992, 1531, 1782

Smith, James, 408, 470, 746, 932, 959, 1032, 1132, 1307, 1325, 1549, 1557, 1558, 1760

Smith, John, 22, 227, 378, 383, 384, 408, 409, 455, 667, 669, 677, 680, 740, 751, 764, 890, 953, 993, 1029, 1030, 1036, 1049, 1116, 1241, 1335, 1397, 1436, 1557, 1710, 1738, 1753, 1754, 1783

Smith, John, *Honorable*, 708, 720

Smith, Joseph, 504, 606, 1478

Smith, Lewis, 1717

Smith, Mahlon,   358, 417, 640

Smith, Maunce,   284

Smith, Michael,   276

Smith, Nicholas,   993, 1050

Smith, None, *Honorable*,   1336

Smith, Peter,   289, 654, 659, 949, 1049, 1133, 1227, 1587

Smith, Philip,   305, 1089

Smith, Robert,   1090

Smith, S.,   1357

Smith, S. H.,   1148

Smith, Samuel,   316, 738, 744, 860, 932, 939, 1006, 1380, 1401

Smith, Samuel H.,   1042, 1577

Smith, Stephen,   1689

Smith, Thomas,   532, 1436

Smith, Thomas R.,   669

Smith, Valentine,   993, 1378

Smith, William,   490, 747, 801, 960, 1090, 1132, 1313, 1534, 1760

Smith, William P.,   6, 135

Smith, Zadock,   1031

Smoot, Benjamin S.,   1734

Smyer, Frederick,   659

Smyer, Jacob,   22

Snell, John,   1313

Snider, Abraham,   927

Snider, Asa B.,   1252

Snider, Balser,   1161

Snider, Daniel,   722

Snider, George,   100, 257, 1253

Snider, Henry,   722, 950

Snider, John,   1252

Snider, Joseph,   1090

Snider, Michael,   942, 1049, 1436

Snider, Peter,   104

Snider, William,   747

Snider. *See also* Schneider, Snyder

Snillinghberger, George,   828

Snively, Joseph,   1393

Snively. *See also* Schnaebeli, Schnibely

Snodgrass, Hugh,   1718

Snodgrass, James,   1481

Snodgrass, John,   448

Snodgrass, Robert,   949

Snodgrass, William,   1436, 1783

Snook, John,   1753

Snuff, Jacob,   1487

Snyder, Daniel,   254, 1753

Snyder, David,   1534

Snyder, George,   1489, 1760

Snyder, John,   447, 478, 959

Snyder, None,   1135

Snyder. *See also* Schneider, Snider

Snysor, Philip,   470

Solliday, Henry,   747

Solman, Peter,   182

Solt, John,   1781

Solt. *See also* Saltz, Saultz

Somerlaird, Valentine,   1049

Sommerlathe, Valentin,   1049

Sontag, John,   269, 332, 364

Sontag. *See also* Sunday [translation]

Sorrell, George,   1406

Sorrels, John,   1719

Sower, Henry,   1049

Sower, Matthias,   796

Sower. *See also* Sauer

Soy, Barbary,   1012

Soyr, Barbary,   1012

Spade, Jacob,   1314

Spahr, John,   1377

Spaight, John,   224

Spangler, Christian,   271

Spangler, David,   617

Spangler, G.,   991

Spangler, G. C.,   1026

Spangler, G. C., Junior,   394

Spangler, George C.,   1108

Spangler, J.,   991

Spangler, John,   394

Spangler, John Jacob,   557

Spangler, Michael,   355

Sparks, Ann,   794

Sparks, Isaac,   1242

Sparks, Leonard,   1636

Sparks, William,   101, 1041, 1369, 1783

Speakman, Willis,   1314

Spears, Friend,   766

Specht, Jacob,   751

Speelman, Jacob,   1130

Speelman. *See also* Speilman, Spielmann

Speer, Alexander,   165

Speer, Hyram,   983

Speer, Robert,   690

Speer, Thomas,   179

Speer, William,   690

Speicher, Christian,   1569

Speilman, Conrad,   1331

States, Frederick, 1303, 1393

Statler, George, 115

Statler. *See also* Stetler

Stauder, Joseph, 1073

Stebelton, John, 1756

Steddam, Henry, 26, 935

Steddem, John, 289

Steddom, Henry, 1313

Stedham, John, 26

Steedham, Henry, 26

Steel, Archibald, 1378

Steel, James, 21, 497

Steel, John K., 1371

Steele, A., 1718

Steele, John, 217

Steele, None, 1328

Steely, Gabriel, 991

Steely, George, 1246

Steely, John, 991

Steel, Steele, Steely. *See also* Stahl, Stall

Steen, John, 1254, 1255

Steen, Richard, 1153

Steen. *See also* Stein, Stone

Steenbarger, Frederick, 942, 1783

Steenbarger. *See also* Steinberger, Stoneberger

Stees, Jacob, 1130

Steger, John P., 679

Steiger, John P., 679

Stein, Felix, 470

Stein, Jacob, 1130

Stein, John, 1180, 1181, 1215, 1254, 1255, 1615, 1617, 1645, 1677, 1712

Stein, Richard, 1153

Stein. *See also* Steen, Stone

Steinberger, Frederick, 942, 1783

Steinberger, John, 50, 924

Steinberger. *See also* Steenbarger, Stoneberger

Steinbrecker, Henry, 834

Steinbrecker, Sebastian, 731

Steiner. *See* Stoner

Steinhacker, John M., 1242

Steinhacker, Michael, 1242

Steinmann, Jesse, 1314

Stenger, George, 1569

Stephens, Christian, 949

Stephens, Elijah, 1379

Stephens, Hazzard, 1073

Stephens, John, 1391

Stephens, Richard, 1073

Stephens, Thomas, 1073

Stephens, William, 1718

Stephenson, Benjamin, *Colonel*, 1708

Stephenson, C., 1397

Stephenson, James, 1265

Stephenson, John, 1488

Stephenson, Joseph, 1667

Stephenson, Thomas, 287

Stephenson. *See also* Stevenson

Sterret, None, 226

Sterrett, Benjamin, 1766

Sterrett, Charles, 1073

Stetler, Abraham, 224

Stetler, George, 115

Stetler. *See also* Statler

Stevens. *See* Stephens

Stevenson, Daniel, 85, 747

Stevenson, William, 15

Stevenson. *See also* Stephenson

Stever, Adam, 632

Steward, William, 1783

Stewart, Adam, 1314

Stewart, Andrew, 949

Stewart, Charles, 949, 1073

Stewart, Duncan, 951, 1651

Stewart, Edie, 1717

Stewart, Galbreath, 1085

Stewart, George, 1625

Stewart, Isaac, 1507

Stewart, James, 332, 433, 545, 609, 632, 796, 1220, 1225

Stewart, James P., 534

Stewart, Jesse, 1030

Stewart, John, 556, 609, 1393

Stewart, Philander B., 920

Stewart, Philip, *Honorable*, 1082

Stewart, Samuel, 556, 1243, 1436

Stewart, Thomas, 1547

Stewart, William, 532, 1147, 1243

Steyer, Samuel, 758

Stibbs, Joseph, 993

Stickler, Martin, 518

Stidger, George, 1007, 1043

Stiess, Jacob, 1130

Stiles, Jonathan, 1085

Still, Samuel, 497, 1392

Stiltz, Philip, 1550

Stinchcomb, David, 935

Stine, John, 1180, 1181, 1215, 1645, 1677, 1712

Tagart, Margaret, 1030

Taggart, John, 1090

Taggart, Thomas, 1750

Taggert, James, 1719

Taillon, Jean Baptiste, 901

Tait, None, *Honorable*, 1293

Tait, Samuel, 115

Talbert, Nathan, 671

Talbert, Sampson, 949

Talbot, Samuel, 536

Talbot, William, 991

Talbott, Demovil, 1436, 1478

Talbott, Rodham, 1436

Tallman, Benjamin, 85

Tallman, James, 1133

Tallman, Samuel, 1109

Taney, Jesse, 751

Tanner, James, 1478, 1783

Tanner, William, 1243

Tappin, Samuel, 677

Tarlow, William, 1041

Tartans, Jacob, 1625

Tartar, Jacob, 1625

Tate, John, 1090

Tatman, James, 1133, 1757

Taylor, Abiathar V., 1001, 1204

Taylor, Abiather S., 1608

Taylor, Abraham, 900

Taylor, Agnes, 718

Taylor, Alexander, 973, 1112

Taylor, Edmund H., 636, 1006, 1396

Taylor, Elizabeth, 337

Taylor, George, 1781

Taylor, Henry, 115

Taylor, Isaac, 750

Taylor, Jacob, 1557

Taylor, James, 24, 677, 680, 970, 1073, 1109, 1679

Taylor, James, *Colonel*, 32

Taylor, John, 55, 114, 182, 276, 550, 605, 747, 877, 900, 1002, 1204, 1314, 1328, 1436, 1608

Taylor, Jonathan, 1253

Taylor, Matthew, 747

Taylor, None, 127, 532

Taylor, Robert, 1313

Taylor, Samuel, 552

Taylor, Thomas, 1665

Taylor, Walter, 683

Taylor, William, 336, 948, 1710

Teagarden, Daniel, 1502, 1783

Teague, Elijah, 942

Teague, Magness, 1507

Teague, Samuel, 710

Teal, Edward, 52, 327

Teelers, Elisha, 960

Teil, Samuel, 135, 153

Teal, Teil. *See also* Deal, Deel, Dell, Dial, Diehl, Dill

Telfer, Alexander, 316, 532, 1195

Telford, None, 1401

Telkurr, Martin, 1671

Teller, John, 1109

Temboss, Isaac, 319

Temboss. *See also* Terboss

Templeton, Robert, 710, 718, 1110

Tener, Adam, 1610

Tener. *See also* Tiner, Tyner

Tent, Jacob, 862

Terboss, Isaac, 434, 747

Terboss. *See also* Temboss

Terrell, John, 324

Terrell, Joseph, 998

Terrence, Joseph, 18

Terril, John, 324, 453, 663

Terry, Enos, 1478

Tessier, Pierre, 875

Testan, Charles, 606

Tester, John, 1130

Tester, Melcher, 1130

Teterick, Daniel, 1750

Teterich. *See also* Diddridge, Dietrich, Ditrick, Doddridge, Titarick, Titerack

Tetter, David, 654

Thain, John, 801

Tharp, James, Senior, 1625

Tharp, John, 1195

Thatcher, Rachel, 1195

Thayer, B., 1641

Thayer, Ephraim, 1641

Themren, David, 1314

Thennermere, Stephen, 1507

Thenton, M., 1133

Thibault, Prospert, 952

Thimmet, David, 1156

Thomas, Abraham, 1073

Thomas, Absalom, 1195

Thomas, Arthur, 1436, 1636

Thomas, Camm, 960

Thomas, Daniel, 338

Thomas, Edward, 751

Thomas, Esther, 433

Thomas, Evan, 942

Thomas, Francis, 1369

Thomas, George, 599

Thomas, Guniel, 949

Thomas, Isaac, 780

Thomas, Jacob, 262, 996

Thomas, John, 997

Thomas, Lemuel, 949

Thomas, Nathaniel, 599

Thomas, None, 950

Thomas, Robert, 1031

Thomas, Samuel, 337

Thomas, Thomas, 677

Thomas, William, 1719

Thompson, Abraham, 758

Thompson, Adam, 1547

Thompson, Andrew, 1252

Thompson, Andrew, Senior, 991

Thompson, D., 1261

Thompson, Ignatius, 995

Thompson, James, 1132

Thompson, John, 337, 1196, 1354, 1760

Thompson, Joshua, 995

Thompson, Mage, 1782

Thompson, Robert, 445, 1448

Thompson, Roger, 140

Thompson, Samuel, 132

Thompson, Sylvester, 1397

Thompson, Thomas, 794, 1694, 1718

Thompson, Thomas M., 123, 217

Thompson, Thomas, Junior, 1325

Thompson, Thomas, Senior, 1325

Thompson, William, 1072, 1151, 1547

Thorn, Azarias, 532

Thorn, Stephen, 1257

Thorn, Thomas, 440

Thorn, William, 1041, 1582, 1625, 1636, 1726

Thornburgh, Amos, 1325

Thornton, Coats, 1390

Thralls, Samuel, 830

Thrift, None, 505

Thrift, William, 741

Thuun, Daniel, 544

Tibbals, Noah, 992

Tibbles, Noah, 1392

Tice, James, 1780

Tickell, John, 485

Tiefenbach, Adam, 1314

Tiefenbach, Daniel, 332, 1044

Tiefenbach, Mary, 452, 472

Tiefenbach. *See also* Deffenbaugh

Tiffin, Edward, 319, 790, 962

Tiffin, Joseph, 319, 337

Tilbrough, Daniel, 1676

Tilford, Alexander, 532

Tilford. *See also* Telfer, Telford, Tillford

Tilghman, None, 583

Tillford, Alexander, 316

Tillford. *See also* Telfer, Telford, Tilford

Tillman, Daniel, 1689

Tillman, John, 1530

Tillman, Lewis, 1507

Tillman, Tobias, 752, 1710

Tilman, Daniel, 1433, 1507

Tilman, John, 135, 475

Tilman, Tobias, 475

Tilton, John, 1072

Tilton, Nehemiah, 1006

Tilton, Richard, 1132

Timmer, Abraham, 1206

Timmer, Henry, 1163, 1206

Timmer, Philip, 1036

Tiner, Adam, 1666

Tiner. *See also* Tener, Tyner

Tingley, John A., 520, 992

Tintsman, John, 380

Tipton, Ns., 960

Tipton, Thomas, 1195

Tislow, Paul, 766

Titarick, Nicholas, 1379

Titerack, Jacob, 318

Titerack, Ns., 996

Titereck, Jacob, 758

Titerick, Balthasar, 688

Titerick, Nicholas, 688

Titarick, Titerick. *See also* Diddridge, Dietrich, Ditrick, Doddridge, Teterick

Titus, Jacob, 1783

Titus, Rachel, 994

Tobert, James, 1109

Todd, Benjamin, 1569

Todd, John, 359

Tolman, Philip, 1206

Tolman. *See also* Dulman, Toulmin

Tomlinson, John, 951, 1264, 1282, 1321, 1322, 1600

Tussing, Nicholas, 747

Tuttle, Sylvanus, 1436

Twigg, John Thomas, 349

Tye, Abraham, 1625

Tyler, Major, 1719

Tyler, William, 935

Tyner, James, 1369

Tyner, Solomon, 654

Tyner. *See also* Tener, Tiner

Uby, Jacob, 654

Uby. *See also* Aebi, Ebey, Ebi, Eby

Uhl, Charles, 1196

Ullery, Daniel, 677, 1029

Ulm, Daniel, 263

Ulrich, John, 430

Ulrich, Stephen, 1783

Ulrick, Joseph, 521

Ulry, Jacob, 1073

Umstol, Peter, 996

Umstot, Abraham, 1242

Underwood, James, 1086

Underwood, Jesse, 1049, 1393

Unger, Michael, 114

Updyke, Henry, 1265, 1436

Uri, Margaret, 1320

Urner, Jonas, 115

Urrly, John, 1671

Urrly. *See also* Early

Vail, Henry, 1582

Vail, Moses, 751

Vail, Stephen, 348

Vail, Thomas, 1002

Vale, James, 1504, 1704

Vale, John, 1629, 1782

Vale, Samuel, 1626

Valentin, Daniel, 1002

Valentine, George, 747

Valentine, Henry, 263

Valentine, None, 327

Valliquet, François, 901

Van Arsdale, John, 108

Van Arsdale, Peter, 1667

Van Buskirk, Isaac, 1602

Van Buskirk. *See also* Vanbuskirk

Van Cleave, Benjamin, 1477

Van Cleve, Benjamin, 904, 1100

Van Cleve, None, 443

Van Cleve. *See also* Vancleave, Vancleve

Van Courtright, Abraham, 337, 1549

Van Grundy, Michael, 1314

Van Gundy, David, 1781

Van Gundy, None, 211

Van Horn, Isaac, 895, 1366, 1379

Van Horne, Isaac, 186

Van Horne. *See also* Vanhorne

Van Kirk, Barnet, 478

Van Nuys, G., 1785

Van Nuys, Garret, 1243

Van Nuys, Isaac, 1328

Van Nuys, John, 634, 772, 829

Van Voorhies, Daniel, 1132

Vanatta, John, 991

Vanausdle, John, 108

Vanbuskirk, George, 1779

Vanbuskirk, John, 978

Vanbuskirk. *See also* Van Buskirk

Vance, Ezekiel, 257, 314, 418

Vance, Jacob, 1029

Vance, John, 130

Vance, Joseph, 124, 437, 768, 935, 1014

Vance, None, 606

Vancell, John, 667

Vanchoyk, Aaron, 1313

Vancleave, John, 983, 1718

Vancleife, Benjamin, 142

Vancleve, Benjamin, 553

Vancleve, John, 1207

Vancleave, Vancleife, Vancleve. *See also* Van Cleave, Van Cleve

Vandamark, Daniel, 1582

Vandavier, Arthur, 1392

Vandeberg, David, 996

Vandenberg, David, 996

Vandenberg. *See also* Funderbaugh, Funderberg, Vonderbach

Vander Horst, None, 1685

Vander Horst, T. C., 1604, 1605

Vanderhorst, Elias, 1025, 1179, 1339, 1605, 1703

Vanderhorst, Thomas Cooper, 1339

Vandershee, William, 1478

Vandeveer, Arthur, 433, 1401, 1481

Vandever, Arthur, 433, 520

Vandola, Joseph, 1371

Vaneaton, Abraham, 931, 1195

Vanfossan, Jacob, 569

Waddel, William, 281

Waddle, James, 1511

Waddle, Thomas, 349

Wade, Abner, 870

Wade, Elijah, 1110

Wade, John, 119, 360, 798, 949, 956, 1240, 1242, 1668, 1669

Wade, Thomas C., 532, 935

Waggaman, Christian, 10

Waggaman, William, 357

Waggoner, Benjamin, 734

Waggoner, John, 931, 1486, 1490, 1546, 1662, 1711

Waggoner, P., 931

Waggoner, Philip, 1108, 1132

Wagnar, George, 747

Wagner, George, 747

Wagner, Joseph, 1478

Wagoner, Michael, 1756

Waider, None, 319

Wailes, Edward L., 1741

Wailes, L., 1302

Wailes, Levin, 1006

Wairam, Harman, 1582

Waiser, Frederick, 1314

Waiser, None, 319

Waldron, Isaac, 710

Waldschmidt, Christian, 1195, 1636

Waldsmith, Christian, 1195, 1636

Walhammer, Christian, 283

Walk, Abraham, 1391

Walker, Abraham, 1379

Walker, Hannah, 1208

Walker, James, 676, 1232, 1279, 1507

Walker, John, 754, 1208

Walker, Joseph, 380

Walker, Mesheck, 404, 542

Walker, Robert, 996

Walker, Samuel, 115, 1195, 1591

Walker, William, 844

Walker, Zadock, 612, 1074

Wall, James, 1371, 1749

Wall, John, 1371

Wallace, A., 1569

Wallace, Adam, 1014

Wallace, Anderson, 948

Wallace, Andrew, 1014

Wallace, Cadwallader, 982

Wallace, D., 1569

Wallace, James, 747

Wallace, John, 284, 1478, 1481

Wallace, Thomas, 923, 927

Wallam, Benjamin, 1314

Waller, George, 1549

Wallers, Jacob, 557

Wallinford, Benjamin, 142

Wallingford, Benjamin, 142

Wallingsford, Benjamin, 659

Wallis, William, 1760

Walls, George, 1135

Walsh, James, 941

Walsh, William Henry, 941

Walter, Adam, 899

Walter, Isaac, 41

Walter, Peter, 558, 571, 637

Walter, William, 1779

Walters, George, 331, 896

Walters, Jacob, 557, 991

Walters, John, 552, 830

Waltman, Isaac, 434

Walton, Benjamin, 355

Walton, Felix, 18, 818, 878, 1139, 1313

Walton, Jonathan, 844, 853

Walton, Jonathan, *Captain*, 849, 872, 875, 884, 901, 934, 952, 966, 972, 977

Walton, Parke, 1006, 1703

Walton. *See also* Welton, Wilton

Wanden, Robert, 1036

Wander, John, 906

Wandner, John, 839

Ward, Abijah, 935

Ward, Benjamin, 1342

Ward, Daniel, 1342

Ward, Edward, 1085, 1132, 1546

Ward, George, 1002

Ward, Isaac, 56

Ward, Jane, 969

Ward, John, 1342

Ward, John A., 659

Ward, None, 552

Ward, None, *Colonel*, 1727

Ward, Peter, 268

Ward, Samuel, 931, 992

Ward, William, 428, 459, 606, 671, 1133, 1265, 1281, 1328, 1481, 1757, 1785

Warden, John, 511

Warden, Robert, 1036

Warder, John, 511, 987

Warne, Abraham, 1748

Warner, Abraham, 738

Warner, Adam, 1197

Warner, Benjamin, 337

Warner, Leonard, Senior, 747

Warner, Leonard, Junior, 625

Warner, Nathan, 1489

Warner, Thomas, 747

Warner, Zebulon, 75

Warnick, Jacob, 668

Warnock, John, 447, 599, 1542

Warnock, Joseph, 1602

Warrack, James, 1242

Warrack. *See also* Warrick, Weihrauch, Wireck, Wirick, Wirrick, Wyrick

Warrall, Jonathan, 503

Warren, B., 747

Warren, Hardick, 1197

Warren, Peter, 1073

Warren, Silas, 747

Warrick, J., 1220

Warrick, Jacob, 1070, 1370, 1391

Warrick, John, 284, 426

Warrick, Robert, 1196

Warrick. *See also* Warrack, Weihrauch, Wireck, Wirick, Wirrick, Wyrick

Warrington, Abraham, Junior, 257

Warschler, George, 57

Wartembe, John, 552

Wartenby, William, 750

Warwick, James Alexander, 1251

Washburn, Isaac, 919

Washburne, None, 815

Washington, George, *General*, 104

Wason, David, 1636

Wason, William, 1290, 1371

Wassermeier, John, 53

Wasson, Joseph, 751

Watermire, John, 53

Waters, Thomas, 496

Watkins, Peregrine, 828

Watkins, William, Senior, 1251

Watson, Abraham, 1488

Watson, Calbert, 992

Watson, Henry, 1665

Watson, James, 51

Watson, John, 1582

Watson, Robert, 374, 1038, 1480, 1564, 1689

Watson, Thomas, 253, 991

Watson, William, 1488, 1556

Watts, Mason, 1376

Watts, Richard, 359, 628, 671

Wavram, Harman, 1582

Waxler, Michael, 277

Way, John, 35, 77

Wead, Ebenezer, Junior, 1478

Wead, Robert, 1478

Weatherhalt, Jacob, 1220

Weatherhead, James, 1757

Weatherington, John, 1549, 1756

Weathers, John, 1636

Weaver, Adam, 75, 747, 808

Weaver, Andrew, 171

Weaver, Anthony, 747

Weaver, Christopher, 101, 1090

Weaver, David, 1753

Weaver, John, 50, 355, 992, 1507

Weaver, Matthew W., 1689

Weaver, None, 747

Weaver, Peter, 927, 1002, 1073

Webb, Edward, 1478, 1783

Webb, Elisha, 992

Webb, James, 1569

Webb, William, 1478

Weber. *See* Weaver [translation]

Webster, Augustine, 222

Webster, John, 1662, 1689

Wechsler, Michael, 277

Weibel, Adam, 786, 1551

Weighbricht, Martin, 1779

Weightbright, Martin, 475

Weighbricht, Weightbright. *See also* Weybrecht

Weihrauch, Jacob, 1370, 1391

Weihrauch, James, 1242

Weihrauch, Martin, 1779

Weihrauch. *See also* Warrack, Warrick, Wireck, Wirick, Wirrick, Wyrick

Weil, Peter, 942

Weimann, Christian, 504

Weimann, Henry, 782, 861

Weimar, Godfrey, 490

Weimer, Godfrey, 1753

Weimar, Weimer. *See also* Weymer, Weymire

Weingaertner, Herbert, 430, 478, 1549

Weingaertner, Martin, 734

Weingaertner, Robert, 598

Weingarten, Stephen, 1371

Weingarten. *See also* Vineyard [translation]

Weingartner, Herbert, 270

White, Ithamar, 1371
White, Jacob, 329, 1251, 1313, 1401, 1481, 1625
White, James, 1073
White, Jesse, 524
White, Joab, 1625
White, John, 1582
White, Jonathan, 672
White, Joseph, 1719
White, Leonard, 1648, 1723
White, None, 114, 628
White, None, *Doctor*, 1342
White, Reuben, 951
White, Stephen, 433
White, Tabitha, 677
White, Tobias, 599
White, William, 1313
White, William Sutherland, 1369
Whitehead, John, 1041
Whitehead, Lazarus, 101, 1401
Whitehead, William, 731, 951, 1170
Whitehill, None, *Honorable*, 1528
Whitehill, Robert, Junior, 477
Whiteleather, Andrew, 754
Whiteman, B., 1401
Whiteman, Benjamin, 1262
Whiteman, Christian, 331, 339, 905
Whiteman, John, 1041
Whitenger, H., 953
Whitesell, Henry, 1582
Whitesell, William, 1325
Whitesill, Tobias, 1481
Whitmar, John, 1530
Whitmer, Peter, 747
Whitsel, Isaac, 991
Whitson, Willis, 101
Wick, William, 464
Wickiser, Andrew, 1753
Wickle, Philip, 1313
Wickliffe, Robert, 1681
Widney, John, 1636
Wiely, Cornelius, 316
Wierman, David, 288, 992
Wierman, Jacob, 1073
Wierman. *See also* Worman
Wiggins, Edward, 750
Wilbahan, G., 991
Wilcox, Joseph, 837, 845
Wildman, Abraham, 9

Wildman, James, 1325
Wildman, Johah, 257
Wildridge, Ralph, 1313
Wilds, John D., 1470
Wile, Peter, 942
Wileman, Mahlon, 1377
Wiley, Cornelius, 316
Wiley, David, 1155
Wiley, Haris, 2
Wiley, Hugh, 991, 1660
Wiley, James, 1530
Wiley, Joseph, 1242
Wiley, William, 747
Wiley. *See also* Viley, Voley, Willey, Willy
Wilhalm, Abraham, 538
Wilhelm, Abraham, 1093
Wilhelm. *See also* Willhelm
Wilie, John, 758
Wilker, Jacob, 474
Wilker, William, 339
Wilkin, Daniel, 318
Wilkin, Robert, 1490
Wilkins, Daniel, 758, 942, 1195
Wilkins, John, 1205
Wilkins, William, 1243
Wilkinson, Gideon, 261, 931, 953
Wilkinson, Joshua, 997
Wilkinson, Solomon, 1314
Will, Daniel, 769, 1337
Will, George, 332
Willaman, Leonard, 780
Willcox, Joseph, 1381
Willcox, Josiah, 297
Wille. *See* Viley, Voley, Wiley, Willey, Willy
Willeman, John, 1245
Willets, James, 747
Willets, Samuel, 625
Willetts, Isaac, 1195
Willetts, John, 754
Willey, John, 210
Willey. *See also* Viley, Voley, Wiley, Willy
Willhelm, Abraham, 1038, 1093
Willhelm. *See also* Wilhalm, Wilhelm
Williams, Abel, 1072
Williams, Abraham, 758
Williams, Benjamin, 1049, 1549
Williams, Daniel, 307
Williams, Daniel, Senior, 1105

Williams, David, 950

Williams, Elmow, 457

Williams, George W., 339

Williams, Henry, 1265

Williams, James, 119, 996

Williams, Jesse, 474

Williams, Joel, 261, 359, 654, 733, 751, 758, 942

Williams, John, 1, 6, 557, 593, 1265, 1532, 1582, 1785

Williams, Joseph, 1486

Williams, Levi, 1501

Williams, Mordecai, 331

Williams, N., 1401

Williams, Nathaniel, 316

Williams, None, 701 702, 1002

Williams, Robert, 1626

Williams, Samuel, 953

Williams, Thomas, 91, 1090, 1393, 1626

Williamson, David, 269

Williamson, J., 747, 950

Williamson, John, 456, 510, 1314, 1538, 1711, 1753

Williamson, Joseph, 992, 1625

Williamson, None, 1725

Williamson, Peter, 1195

Williamson, Samuel, 1478

Williamson, Theodorus, 337, 517

Williamson, W., 950

Williamson, William, 456, 1155, 1756

Willis, Isaiah, 419, 580

Willitz, John, 754

Wills, James, 316, 1371

Willson, James, 931, 953

Willson, John, 50, 552

Willson, John, Junior, 1783

Willson, Joseph, 605

Willson, Thomas, 356

Willson, William, 993

Willy, John, 557

Willy. See also Viley, Voley, Wiley, Willey

Wilmoth, William, 1164

Wilmuth, William, 1162

Wilson, Andrew, 991

Wilson, Ann, 953

Wilson, Benjamin, 130, 142, 1689

Wilson, Charles, 797, 821, 1750

Wilson, D. G., 1313

Wilson, Daniel, 606, 923, 1313

Wilson, Douglas, 569

Wilson, Edward, 7, 17

Wilson, George, 102, 147, 449, 1151, 1313, 1569

Wilson, Hans, 1626

Wilson, Isaac, 1041, 1407

Wilson, Israel, 474, 1090

Wilson, Jacob, 448, 1195, 1487

Wilson, James, 132, 318, 830, 1049

Wilson, Jesper, 1755

Wilson, Jesse, 470, 1029, 1507, 1667, 1689

Wilson, John, 41, 92, 239, 357, 426, 747, 953

Wilson, John L., 114

Wilson, Margaret, 1748

Wilson, Michael, 950

Wilson, Nathan, 1196

Wilson, Nathaniel, 402, 1109

Wilson, None, 840, 1268, 1631, 1754

Wilson, Peter, 1006

Wilson, Richard, 331, 1761

Wilson, Robert, 212

Wilson, Samuel, 625

Wilson, Simeon, 1313

Wilson, Thomas, 787, 863, 1392, 1530

Wilson, Thomas, *Honorable*, 610, 612, 1074

Wilson, W., *Honorable*, 1609

Wilson, William, 480, 747, 764, 927, 993, 1041, 1068, 1582, 1753, 1783

Wilson, William, Junior, 1436, 1476

Wilter, Christopher, 76

Wilton, Felix, 18, 450

Wilton. *See also* Walton, Welton

Wilty, John, 557

Wimans, James, 156

Wimmer, Abraham, 865

Winance, John, 599, 1130

Winans, Richard, 532

Winans, Samuel, 992

Winburn, J., 1105

Windell, John, 995

Winegarder, Herbert, 270,

Winegardner, Herbert, 430, 478, 1549

Winegardner, Robert, 598

Wingar, Martin, 784, 1052

Wingart, Martin, 734

Wingate, Ziba, 1749

Winkelblech, Christian, 1132

Winklebleck, Philip, 1196

Winkler, Lawrence, 1719

Winn, John, 992, 998, 1110, 1478, 1710, 1749

Winn, None, 950

Winrod, George, 863

Winshall, Ruggles, 1726

Winship, Jabes, 1195

Winship, Winn, 337, 559, 1612, 1756

Winston, Lewis, 1278, 1362

Winteringer, Jesse, 644

Winteringer, Nathan, 644

Winteringer. *See also* Wintwringer

Winters, Lewis, 801

Winters, Moses, 923

Winton, None, 1202

Wintwringer, Thomas, 1168

Wintwringer. *See also* Winteringer

Wireck, Jacob, 1012

Wirick, George, 259

Wirick, John, 284

Wirrick, Jacob, 1012

Wireck, Wirick, Wirrick. *See also* Warrack, Warrick, Weihrauch, Wyrick

Wise, Adam, 57

Wise, Daniel, 1569·

Wise, Peter, 257, 259, 447, 537, 1626, 1750

Wise. *See also* Weiss

Wiseman, Abraham, 877

Wiseman, Jacob, 1753

Wiseman, Samuel, 339

Wiseman, William, 1151

Wiseman. *See also* Weissmann

Withers, John, 1689

Witkins, Charles, 1722

Witter, Christopher, 722

Witteracht, Peter, 1784

Woerschler, George, 57

Wohlfarth. *See* Wolford

Wolf, Christian, 270, 430

Wolf, George, 617, 1029, 1481

Wolf, Henry, 536

Wolf, Jacob, 1710

Wolf, John, 50, 1371, 1779, 1781, 1783

Wolf, Leonard, 1549

Wolf, Michael, 459, 1313

Wolf, None, 1402

Wolf, Peter, 337, 487, 778

Wolf, Valentine, 747

Wolf, William, 732

Wolford, Frederick, 1306

Wolford, John, 1623

Wolsley, Ludwick, 75

Wood, Alexander, 654

Wood, Andrew, 546

Wood, Benjamin, 1478

Wood, Bennet, 1261, 1507

Wood, Isaac, 1265, 1403, 1457, 1717

Wood, James, 1436

Wood, John, 1220, 1557

Wood, Jonathan, 1108

Wood, Joseph, 959, 1006

Wood, Joshua, 355

Wood, Mathew, 489

Wood, Nathan, 16, 736

Wood, None, 1133

Wood, Robert, 1377

Wood, Samuel, 221

Wood, Spencer, 1220

Wood, Stephen, 865, 1636

Wood, William, 1477

Woodbridge, William, .758

Woodburn, James, 533

Woodcuck, Joseph, 680

Woodfill, Daniel, 1325

Woodfill, John, 1325

Woodhouse, Henry, 1749

Woodmany, Samuel, 828

Woodruff, John, 991

Woods, Amy, 1667

Woods, Andrew, 609

Woods, Archibald, 126

Woods, Benjamin, 1161

Woods, James, 1433, 1689

Woods, John, 27, 1313

Woods, Samuel, 1371

Woodward, Andrew, 1569

Woody, Lewis, 776

Wooldridge, Ralph, 1313

Wooley, James, 1665

Woollery, J., 1073

Wools, Philip, 1726

Work, Robert, 1781

Work, Samuel, 1761

Workman, Stephen, 1569

Worley, John, 355, 599

Worman, David, 992

Worman, Jacob, 1073

Worman, None, 1397

Worman, Thomas J., 1369

Worman. *See also* Wierman

Worstell, Matthew, 57

Worthington, George, 1012

Worthington, Thomas, 63, 64, 331, 1233, 1662

Worthington, Thomas, *General*, 133, 143, 151, 188, 189, 191, 588, 641, 900, 999, 1091, 1204, 1263, 1516, 1608

Worthington, Thomas, *Honorable*, 157, 164, 166, 170, 396, 416, 429, 452, 468, 515, 523, 554, 559, 568, 573, 591, 597, 607, 613, 626, 643, 673, 690, 698, 739, 807, 1075, 1167, 1192

Wotrines, Peter, 498

Wray, Joseph, 1218

Wray, William, 1218

Wray. *See also* Ray, Reagh

Wright, Amos, 995

Wright, Daniel, 1690

Wright, Eli, 78, 387, 630

Wright, Elijah, 1533

Wright, Jacob, 599

Wright, James, 114, 323, 546, 1376, 1502

Wright, Jeremiah, 747

Wright, John, 747, 1134, 1688, 1690, 1719, 1726

Wright, Jonathan, 1377

Wright, Joseph, 1756

Wright, Lancaster, 632

Wright, Moses, 152

Wright, Philberd, 776, 779

Wright, Philbert, 586

Wright, Reuben, 1551

Wright, Samuel, 1784

Wright, William, 1220, 1477, 1533

Wuertemberger, George, 384

Wyant, Jacob, 1090

Wyatt, Edward, 992

Wyatt, Nathaniel, 1549

Wyble, Adam, 786, 1551

Wygandt, Peter, 1163

Wygandt. *See also* Weygandt

Wylie, John, 732, 758

Wylie, Samuel, 732, 758

Wyman, Christian, 504

Wyman, Henry, 276, 782, 861

Wynans, John, 1130

Wynants, John, 1393

Wynn, William, 767, 1242

Wynne, William, 833

Wyrick, George, 1163

Wyrick, Jacob, 1012, 1370, 1391

Wyrick, James, 1242

Wyrick. *See also* Warrack, Warrick, Weihrauch, Wireck, Wirick, Wirrick

Yakely, Michael, 1530

Yakely. *See also* Jaeckli, Yeagley

Yandt, Abraham, 1154, 1626

Yant, John, 1030, 1154

Yandt, Yant. *See also* Gaunt, Yeant, Yount

Yarger, John, 1085, 1108

Yarrick, Adam, 1547

Yarrick. *See also* Joerg, Sherg, Shirk, Yerk, York, Yurrack

Yates, Benjamin, 319

Yax, Pierre, 844

Ybáñez, Ferdinand, 1291

Yeagel, Abraham, 459

Yeagley, Elias, 1377

Yeagley, Peter, 1626

Yeagley. *See also* Jaeckli, Yakely

Yeaman, John, 993

Yeaman, Samuel, 114, 497

Yeant, Philip, 1750

Yeant. *See also* Gaunt, Yandt, Yant, Yount

Yeatman, Griffin, 329, 667, 998

Yeatman, Griffith, 520

Yeazel, Abraham 459, 1369

Yerk, Hanes, 447

Yerk. *See also* Joerg, Sherg, Shirk, Yarrick, York, Yurrack

Yoder, Christian, 536, 599

Yoder. *See also* Yotter

Yoho, Jacob, 223

Yoke, Jacob, 126

Yoke, Michael, 473

Yoke. *See also* Jauch

Yollen, Christian, 283

Yoller, Christian, 1532

York, Shubel, 1760

York. *See also* Joerg, Sherg, Shirk, Yarrick, Yerk, Yurrack

Yotter, Christian, 1532

Yotter. *See also* Yoder

Youert, James, 953

Young, Aaron, 1378

Young, Baltzer, 59

Young, David, 1391

Young, Edward, 747

Young, Ephraim, 1550

Young, Henry, 632

Young, Jacob, 983, 1376

Young, James, 420, 1151, 1502

Young, John, 298, 1610

Young, John, Junior, 1163

Young, M., 258

Young, Mary M., 1392

Young, Nicholas, 764

Young, None, 652

Young, Robert, 1090

Young, William, 1002, 1130

Young. *See also* Jung

Youngs, Benjamin, 212

Yount, Daniel, 350, 935

Yount, Henry, 420, 769, 1041

Yount, John, 532

Yount. *See also* Gaunt, Yandt, Yant, Yeant

Yulstar, Jacob, 284

Yunker, Joseph, 440

Yunker. *See also* Juncker

Yurrack, Adam, 994

Yurrack. *See also* Joerg, Sherg, Shirk, Yarrick, Yerk, York

Yutzey, Michael, 1717

Zahner, Henry, 358

Zahner, Michael, 57

Zahner. *See also* Zehner

Zane, Isaac, 996

Zane, Joel, 732

Zane, John, 75, 690

Zane, Noah, 75, 154, 157, 588, 591, 828, 1662, 1750

Zane, Silas, 732

Zanes, None, 1072

Zaun, Jacob, 935

Zedeker, David, 1531

Zehner, John, 1755

Zehner. *See also* Zahner

Zehring, John, 747

Zehring, Ludwick, 430

Zeigler, Andrew, 1108

Zeile, Joseph, 332

Zeiler, Christian, 632

Zeiler, John, 632

Zeiler, Philip, 663

Zeiler. *See also* Sailer, Saylor, Seiler, Siler, Zeller

Zelkurr, Martin, 1671

Zeller, Andrew, 865

Zeller, Henry, 265, 293

Zeller, John, 25, 153

Zeller. *See also* Sailer, Saylor, Seiler, Siler, Zeiler

Zenf, Michael, 52

Zenft, Jacob, 747

Zenf, Zenft. *See also* Senef, Senff, Zent

Zenor, John, 1755

Zent, John, 510

Zerbe, John, 1784

Zertman, Samuel, 1753

Zickafuss, George, 1569

Zickafuss. *See also* Seghefoost, Sickafoose

Ziegler, Andrew, 1108

Zimmer, Frederick, 1489

Zimmer, Henry, 1163

Zimmer, Philip, 1036

Zimmerman, George, 1487

Zimmerman, John, 680

Zimmermann, Conrad, 22

Zimmerman, Zimmermann. *See also* Simmerman

Zink. *See* Sinks

Zins, Zinz. *See* Sintz

Zirkel. *See* Circle *[translation]*

SUBJECT INDEX

Accounting entries, instructions regarding, 1193

Act of 21 Apr 1806, cited, 1149
    of 23 Apr 1812, imposes new duties on Land Com-
        missioners at Detroit, 1609; regulations
        implementing, 988
    of 6 Jul 1812, regulations implementing, 988
    of 5 Feb 1813, pre-emption rights of certain Il-
        linois settlers, interpretation of, 1537,
        1736
    of 25 Jan 1814, granting Moses Hook the right of
        pre-emption, 1575
    of 16 Apr 1814, interpretation of, having to do
        with claims to land previous to commence-
        ment of American sovereignty, 1732
    of 18 Apr 1814, for relief of Dennis Clark, 1659
    of --, confirming grants of land in Mississippi
        Territory, 848
    of --, for relief of Daniel Boone, 1589
    of --, for relief of William Crawford, 1606
    of --, for relief of John James Dufour, 1446
    of --, granting further time for registering
        claims to land in Western District of Or-
        leans Territory, newspaper clipping regard-
        ing, 847
    of --, requiring investigation of land claims in
        Missouri, 825

British grants, claims under. *See* Elias Vanderhorst;
    John Ramsay [in *Name Index*]

British patent, confirmed by U.S. Commissioners,
    case of ejectment against, 1687

Budget, for 1813, discussed, 1078

Claims, conflicting, to be determined by law, not
    by GLO, 1380

Claims, instructions regarding, 1382

Claims, rejected, in Louisiana, report to Congress
    regarding, 1333

Claims, of persons having none, based upon British,
    French, or Spanish governmental action,
    917, 1345

Claims, unconfirmed, in West Orleans district, re-
    port of, 1102, 1103

Clark's Grant, fractional sections around, 1652

Coinage, of silver, found in Indiana, 1283

Competition to sale of public lands, in EPR district,
    962, 963

Detroit, performance of Land Commissioners at, re-
    ports not received since June 1811, 1609

Detroit, private land claims at, surveys inaccurate,
    765

Dismissal of Zaccheus Biggs, monies outstanding, 1737

Donation *versus* pre-emption claims, 1149

EPR District, list of townships between Chickasha
    and Tombigbee rivers, 1092

Ejectment, case of, against Charles Carson, from
    land purchased from the United States, 1731;
    on land covered by previous British patent
    confirmed by U.S. Commissioners, 1687

Extension of time for payment, in WPR District,
    needed, 1574

Florida, West, transcripts from records of, 1208,
    1342, 1638

Fort Stoddard, moving LO from St. Stephens, Mississ-
    ippi Territory, to, 1389, 1655

Fractional acreage, calculation of, 1468

Fraud, land, alleged in EPR District, 1614

Fuketchooponta Reserve. *See* Indian Reservation

General Land Office, regeneration of, since death of
    chief clerk, 1413

Graft, possible, in sale of land in LO Cin, 1423

Gulf of Mexico, claim to island in, 1621

Illinois, pre-emption rights in, 1736

Illinois Territory, beginning of land sales in, 1673

Illinois Saline on Wabash River. *See* United States
    Saline on Wabash River (Illinois)

Indian Reservation (Fuketchooponta, Futcheeponta),
    sections in, 947, 989

Indians, land ceded by, between Tombigbee and Ala-
    bama rivers, map of, 1622

Interest, computation of, instructions regarding, 804

Jefferson College, tracts selected for, 947, 989

Land claims, previous to commencement of American
    sovereignty, numbers thereof mentioned,
    1732

Land Commissioners, in Mississippi Territory, in-
    structions regarding, 841

Land Commissioners, at St. Louis, report of, 806,
    807, 808

Land Commissioners, at Vincennes [Indiana], report
    of, 809

Land descriptions, vague, patents cannot issue for,
    1706

Land sales, of land previously sold, instructions
    regarding, 1120; proposal for, in three
    territories west of Ohio, 1603

Lead mines, in Missouri, lease of, 840

Lot, decisions to be made by, 1499; deposits of per-
    sons excluded by, instructions regarding,
    1440; right to land decided by, 1751

Louisiana Territory (near Missouri), claims to land
    in, report regarding, 1083, 1105

Mineral rights, leasing of, by United States Govern-
    ment, 1702

Mines, silver and lead, in Indiana, lease solicited,
    1283

Mississippi Territory land sales, report for period
    1810-1813, plus remaining to sell, 1613

Missouri Territory, land claim of Daniel Boone, 1523;
    mineral rights in, report regarding, 1738;
    rapacious speculation in mineral rights,
    1675; surveys of land in, 1691

Ohio Company, price of reserved sections, 1630

Ohio land sales, report for period 1810-1813, plus
    remaining to sell, 1613

Orleans Territory, Western District, report of uncon-
    firmed claims in, 1102, 1103

Patents, unlisted, recorded in Volume 7, pages 144
    to 237, note regarding, 1570

Pre-emption certificates, in EPR District, 1330

Pre-emption *versus* donation claims, 1149

Public lands, disposal of, plan of citizen rejected, 1649, 1664; records regarding, in State Department, to be transferred to GLO, 793; in War Department, to be transferred to GLO, 792; remaining to be distributed, annual report to Congress, 1544

Pulaski, town of, in Hun LO district, site fixed, 1077

Purchase, land, eligibility for, in EPR district, 1349

Recorder of Land Titles at St. Louis [Missouri], report of, 1627

Roads, accounting method proposed for, 1473

Round Head's Town [Ohio], at headwaters of Scioto River, 1643

St. Stephens LO [Mississippi Territory], moved to Fort Stoddard, 1389, 1655

Salt spring [Ohio], cannot be sold, 1560, 1616; lease of, 1735

School sections, reservation of land for, 1764

Seal of GLO, requested, 791; approved, 800

Seminary, land for, in Illinois, 1771

Shibboleth Mine [Missouri], lease of, 1631; lessees of, 1738; United States title to, 1754

Speculation in mineral rights in Missouri Territory, 1675

Stationery, charges for, in Cin LO, 1267, 1518

Strategic advantage of land sales in three territories west of Ohio, 1603

Suit against sureties of Lemuel Henry (Rec EPR), 1734

Suit to recover $120,710.15 from estate of Lemuel Henry, 1562

Surveyors, appointment of, for lands south of Tennessee, 1766; errors of, to be borne by purchasers, 1215, 1674

Translations of French and Spanish documents, instructions regarding, 1193

Translator, still needed, in Orleans Territory, 1143

Trial of General -- Hull, order to obey summons to attend, 1572

United States Military District [Ohio], vacant lots remaining in, 515, 1148, 1192

United States Saline on Wabash River [Illinois], agreement regarding, 1269, 1280; clause requiring approval by President, 1424; complaint regarding former lessees, 1723; lease of, 1647, 1648; royalty on, 1554

Virginia military service, C. Royston's claim to land for, during Revolutionary War, to be submitted to State, 1644, 1646

Virginia Military District of Ohio, bound volumes and surveys, sent to Benjamin Hough, 1091, 1273, 1663; inquiry regarding boundaries of, 1157, 1643; transmits patents for land in, 948, 970, 971, 975, 978, 984, 986, 990

War, Secretary of, now near Great Lakes, 1456

Witnesses, compulsory attendance of, 916

Woodville, Wilkinson County, Mississippi, requests assistance of postmaster at, 1730

TRACT INDEX

CANTON, OHIO, LAND OFFICE DISTRICT

Can	–	3	14	22	416
Can	–	3	15	12	993
Can	–	7	9	18	1688
Can	–	8	11	25	745
Can	–	9	9	7	1719
Can	–	9	9	17	1719
Can	–	9	9	25	1719
Can	–	9	9	31	1668
Can	–	9	9	36	1719
Can	–	9	10	17	1206, 1489
Can	–	9	10	18	1036
Can	–	9	10	20	1206, 1489
Can	–	9	10	30	1489
Can	–	9	11	19	922
Can	–	9	19	19	1378
Can	–	10	1	8	1378, 1550, 1610
Can	–	10	1	17	1198
Can	–	10	1	18	1610
Can	–	10	1	20	1163, 1378
Can	–	10	1	22	993, 1036
Can	–	10	1	23	993
Can	–	10	1	26	993
Can	–	10	1	27	296, 890, 1163, 1378
Can	–	10	1	28	864, 1163, 1489, 1719
Can	–	10	1	29	1036, 1163
Can	–	10	1	31	1163
Can	–	10	1	32	1163, 1441
Can	–	10	1	33	1089, 1531
Can	–	10	1	34	1163
Can	–	10	1	35	993, 1163
Can	–	10	1	36	1531
Can	–	10	11	3	993
Can	–	10	11	4	890
Can	–	10	11	12	662, 834
Can	–	10	11	17	1198
Can	–	10	11	21	993
Can	–	10	11	23	275
Can	–	10	11	36	1198, 1751
Can	–	10	12	1	1719
Can	–	10	12	2	1089, 1378
Can	–	10	12	3	1036, 1089, 1378
Can	–	10	12	4	993
Can	–	10	12	5	822, 1089, 1489
Can	–	10	12	6	1489
Can	–	10	12	7	624
Can	–	10	12	8	595, 1163
Can	–	10	12	9	395, 578, 1050, 1378
Can	–	10	12	10	1378
Can	–	10	12	11	595, 1036
Can	–	10	12	12	1036, 1089, 1441, 1459
Can	–	10	12	13	993, 1036
Can	–	10	12	14	296, 890, 1489
Can	–	10	12	15	823
Can	–	10	12	18	993
Can	–	10	12	22	1378
Can	–	10	12	24	1550
Can	–	10	12	25	1036
Can	–	10	12	26	814, 954, 1489
Can	–	10	12	27	1007, 1163
Can	–	10	12	28	401, 1053, 1299, 1482, 1610, 1611
Can	–	10	12	29	1489
Can	–	10	12	33	401, 551, 1198
Can	–	10	12	34	383, 864, 1007, 1163
Can	–	10	12	35	1163, 1198
Can	–	11	10	4	383
Can	–	11	15	12	277
Can	–	11	16	1	1550
Can	–	11	16	3	1719
Can	–	11	16	5	1163, 1531, 1610
Can	–	11	16	6	1719
Can	–	11	16	8	993
Can	–	11	16	9	993, 1719
Can	–	11	16	10	1550, 1719
Can	–	11	16	11	820, 1441, 1531
Can	–	11	16	12	1050, 1378
Can	–	11	16	13	1089
Can	–	11	16	14	1531
Can	–	11	16	15	1531
Can	–	11	16	26	1163
Can	–	11	17	3	1550
Can	–	11	17	14	1550
Can	–	11	17	17	1536
Can	–	11	17	23	1163
Can	–	11	17	24	1610
Can	–	11	17	25	1089
Can	–	11	17	28	993
Can	–	11	17	29	993
Can	–	11	17	30	1163, 1719
Can	–	11	17	34	1531
Can	–	11	17	36	1089
Can	–	11	18	34	1550
Can	–	11	18	36	1531
Can	–	12	12	25	1036
Can	–	12	12	36	1036
Can	–	12	15	2	1719
Can	–	12	15	10	1719

Can	– 12 15 11	1719	Can	– 13 15 17	1036
Can	– 12 15 15	1719	Can	– 13 15 23	1531
Can	– 12 15 17	1378	Can	– 13 15 24	1163, 1378
Can	– 12 15 20	1489	Can	– 13 16 5	1036
Can	– 12 15 21	1719	Can	– 13 16 6	1050
Can	– 12 15 33	1610	Can	– 13 16 8	1036, 1050
Can	– 12 16 4	1489	Can	– 13 16 9	1036
Can	– 12 16 5	1036	Can	– 13 16 17	1719
Can	– 12 16 7	1378	Can	– 13 16 21	1489
Can	– 12 16 18	1305, 1489	Can	– 13 16 22	993
Can	– 12 16 19	1378, 1531, 1550	Can	– 13 16 23	993
Can	– 12 16 20	993	Can	– 13 16 26	1036
Can	– 12 16 21	993, 1719	Can	– 13 16 31	1050
Can	– 12 16 22	1719	Can	– 13 16 33	1550
Can	– 12 16 23	1719	Can	– 13 16 34	993
Can	– 12 16 28	1378, 1610	Can	– 13 16 35	993
Can	– 12 16 29	993, 1719	Can	– 13 17 30	1050, 1089
Can	– 12 16 31	1719	Can	– 14 8 15	1036
Can	– 12 17 1	1719	Can	– 14 18 11	1423, 1531, 1758
Can	– 12 17 20	1719	Can	– 14 18 13	1719
Can	– 12 17 22	1719	Can	– 14 18 14	1036, 1666
Can	– 12 17 28	1666	Can	– 14 18 15	1036
Can	– 12 17 31	1448	Can	– 14 19 1	1036, 1531
Can	– 12 17 36	1163	Can	– 14 19 6	1011, 1089
Can	– 12 18 27	1610	Can	– 14 19 19	1719
Can	– 12 18 36	1719	Can	– 14 19 20	993
Can	– 13 13 1	1661	Can	– 14 19 30	1719
Can	– 13 13 2	1378, 1719	Can	– 14 20 24	183
Can	– 13 13 3	1089	Can	– 14 20 35	1610
Can	– 13 13 9	1550	Can	– 14 21 3	1198
Can	– 13 13 10	82, 1206, 1550, 1610	Can	– 14 21 14	1198
Can	– 13 13 11	183	Can	– 14 21 24	1198
Can	– 13 13 12	1661	Can	– 14 21 25	1050, 1198
Can	– 13 13 17	1317	Can	– 15 19 4	993, 1610
Can	– 13 14 20	1489	Can	– 15 19 8	1610
Can	– 13 14 33	1489	Can	– 15 19 13	1499
Can	– 13 15 1	415, 416, 1719	Can	– 15 19 15	1719
Can	– 13 15 2	993, 1036	Can	– 15 20 4	247
Can	– 13 15 3	241, 820, 993, 1378	Can	– 15 20 5	247
Can	– 13 15 4	614, 1043, 1055, 1378	Can	– 15 20 26	1610
Can	– 13 15 5	820	Can	– 15 20 27	1719
Can	– 13 15 6	82, 820, 1489	Can	– 15 20 33	1719
Can	– 13 15 9	422, 1036, 1089, 1163	Can	– 15 21 1	1036
Can	– 13 15 10	820, 823, 1489	Can	– 15 21 3	1036
Can	– 13 15 11	1531, 1550	Can	– 15 21 5	1719
Can	– 13 15 12	1050, 1163	Can	– 15 21 10	1036
Can	– 13 15 13	1089, 1378	Can	– 15 21 13	1489
Can	– 13 15 14	1378	Can	– 15 21 15	1378
Can	– 13 15 15	1489	Can	– 15 21 22	1317, 1489

Can	– 15 21 23	296, 864, 1489
Can	– 15 21 26	1489
Can	– 15 22 6	1550
Can	– 15 22 7	1610
Can	– 15 22 10	1550
Can	– 15 22 17	1719
Can	– 15 22 18	1666, 1719
Can	– 15 22 22	1050
Can	– 15 22 26	1719
Can	– 15 22 36	1378
Can	– 16 18 21	967
Can	– 16 19 4	1616
Can	– 16 19 8	1616
Can	– 16 19 9	1560, 1616
Can	– 16 19 10	1616
Can	– 16 21 24	97, 247, 383, 968, 979, 993
Can	– 16 21 25	97, 247, 383, 968, 979
Can	– 16 21 26	97, 247, 383, 968, 979
Can	– 16 22 5	1050, 1489, 1531
Can	– 16 22 7	1489
Can	– 16 22 9	1206, 1610
Can	– 16 22 21	1089
Can	– 16 22 24	1036
Can	– 16 22 25	864
Can	– 16 22 26	1050, 1089, 1489
Can	– 16 22 27	1089
Can	– 16 22 29	1610
Can	– 16 23 27	1719
Can	– 16 23 28	1719
Can	– 16 23 31	1550
Can	– 16 23 36	1719
Can	– 17 20 32	1163
Can	– 17 21 1	1274, 1412
Can	– 17 21 2	1036, 1050
Can	– 17 21 3	296, 864
Can	– 17 21 18	1489
Can	– 17 22 2	967, 993, 1036
Can	– 17 22 4	1036
Can	– 17 22 6	1531
Can	– 17 22 10	967, 1489
Can	– 17 22 11	967, 1610
Can	– 17 22 27	1550
Can	– 17 22 35	1550
Can	– 17 22 36	1550
Can	– 17 23 10	1206
Can	– 17 23 14	1036
Can	– 17 23 19	1719
Can	– 17 23 22	993, 1206

Can	– 17 23 24	1036, 1206
Can	– 17 23 25	1036
Can	– 17 23 26	241
Can	– 17 23 27	993
Can	– 17 23 28	1719
Can	– 17 23 29	1517, 1660
Can	– 17 23 30	1719
Can	– 17 23 31	118, 296, 864, 993, 1206, 1531
Can	– 17 23 32	993, 1036, 1719
Can	– 17 23 33	1036
Can	– 17 24 23	1719
Can	– 17 24 31	1036
Can	– 17 24 32	993
Can	– 17 24 34	1036, 1116
Can	– 17 25 22	1719
Can	– 17 25 23	1719
Can	– 18 18 2	118
Can	– 18 18 4	1489
Can	– 18 18 5	1719
Can	– 18 18 6	246, 1036, 1206
Can	– 18 19 5	241
Can	– 18 19 9	510, 862
Can	– 18 19 10	1163
Can	– 18 19 13	1489
Can	– 18 19 35	864
Can	– 18 20 5	1317
Can	– 18 20 18	1489
Can	– 18 20 30	1378
Can	– 18 21 7	1719
Can	– 18 21 19	1719
Can	– 18 21 20	1489
Can	– 18 21 21	241, 1036
Can	– 18 21 22	1036
Can	– 18 21 24	1163
Can	– 18 21 25	1550
Can	– 18 21 26	1719, 1724
Can	– 18 21 32	1531
Can	– 18 21 34	1531
Can	– 18 21 35	1163
Can	– 18 21 36	864, 1550
Can	– 18 22 3	993
Can	– 18 22 4	993
Can	– 18 22 9	1715
Can	– 18 22 10	1610
Can	– 18 22 22	1368, 1492
Can	– 18 22 25	1050
Can	– 18 22 26	1484

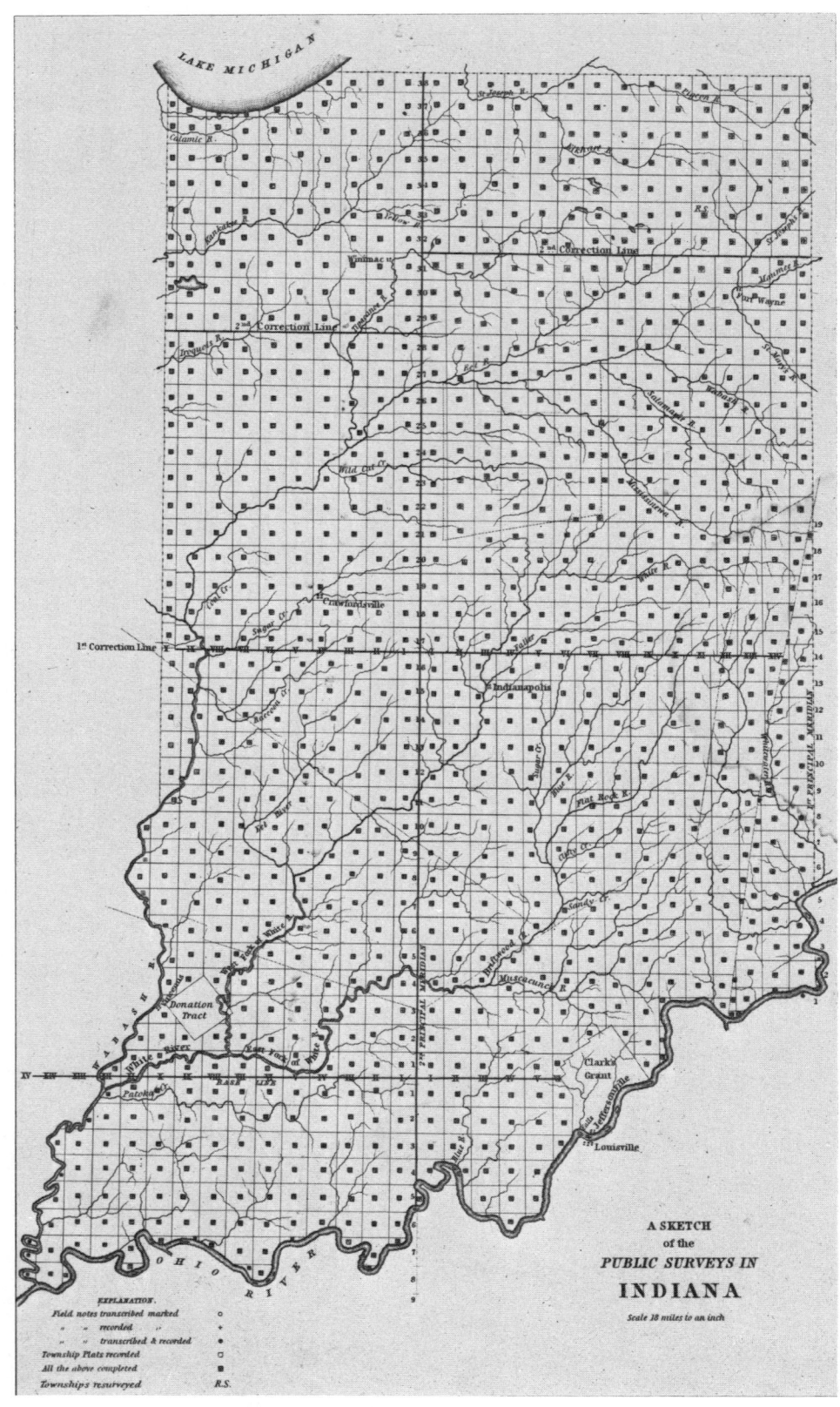

MAP 6. Tract map of Indiana showing range-township numbering system

Map 7. Tract map of Indiana showing counties

[271]

Can	–	18	22	36	1036	Ch1	–	11	16	2	689
Can	–	18	23	32	1719	Ch1	–	12	7	14	504, 741
Can	–	18	23	33	1610	Ch1	–	12	7	15	1600
Can	–	18	24	21	1036	Ch1	–	12	7	16	1600
Can	–	19	18	1	1036	Ch1	–	12	7	25	133, 452
Can	–	19	18	3	1489	Ch1	–	13	7	12	487
Can	–	19	18	4	864, 1378, 1489, 1666	Ch1	–	14	8	12	16, 1314
Can	–	19	18	5	383, 827, 1163	Ch1	–	14	8	19	121
Can	–	19	18	6	1163	Ch1	–	14	8	21	487
Can	–	19	18	8	1036	Ch1	–	14	16	5	747
Can	–	19	18	10	1317	Ch1	–	14	19	23	1109
Can	–	19	18	11	1666	Ch1	–	15	3	18	1756
Can	–	19	18	12	1036	Ch1	–	16	1	26	1781
Can	–	19	19	5	512, 1107, 1310	Ch1	–	16	1	29	764, 812
Can	–	19	19	8	512, 826, 1550	Ch1	–	16	1	32	430
Can	–	19	19	10	512, 826, 1107, 1311	Ch1	–	16	1	33	430
Can	–	19	19	11	1550	Ch1	–	16	2	19	747
Can	–	19	19	12	1036	Ch1	–	16	2	35	269
Can	–	19	19	31	118, 246, 1163	Ch1	–	16	5	24	991
Can	–	19	19	33	1489	Ch1	–	16	6	22	1314
Can	–	19	20	4	1610	Ch1	–	16	6	25	430
Can	–	19	20	11	1317	Ch1	–	16	6	29	400, 1756
Can	–	19	20	12	993	Ch1	–	16	6	36	262
Can	–	19	20	14	1642, 1719, 1768, 1769	Ch1	–	16	7	13	1549
Can	–	19	20	23	1489	Ch1	–	16	7	14	1781
Can	–	19	20	25	1163	Ch1	–	16	7	24	269
Can	–	19	20	28	1198	Ch1	–	16	7	25	269
Can	–	19	20	32	1719	Ch1	–	16	7	27	991
Can	–	19	21	25	890	Ch1	–	16	7	36	1781
Can	–	20	12	15	1719	Ch1	–	16	15	2	991, 1109
Can	–	20	18	25	1463, 1565, 1666	Ch1	–	16	15	4	1711, 1781
Can	–	20	18	36	1463	Ch1	–	16	15	6	747, 1314
						Ch1	–	16	15	8	991
						Ch1	–	16	15	10	1781
						Ch1	–	16	15	11	1781
						Ch1	–	16	15	13	1781
						Ch1	–	16	15	17	1109, 1753
	CHILLICOTHE, OHIO, LAND OFFICE DISTRICT					Ch1	–	16	15	19	121, 194
Ch1	–	–	15	18	15	Ch1	–	16	15	20	1109
Ch1	–	1	3	28	1756	Ch1	–	16	15	31	389, 576
Ch1	–	3	8	21	598	Ch1	–	16	16	1	429
Ch1	–	6	9	6	570	Ch1	–	16	16	2	349, 764
Ch1	–	6	16	34	1056	Ch1	–	16	16	3	263, 570
Ch1	–	7	16	36	570	Ch1	–	16	16	4	331, 1109, 1549, 1753
Ch1	–	7	17	21	430	Ch1	–	16	16	5	808
Ch1	–	9	14	30	501	Ch1	–	16	16	9	402
Ch1	–	9	16	25	788	Ch1	–	16	16	10	1314
Ch1	–	11	8	23	991	Ch1	–	16	16	11	543, 1109

Ch1	–	16	16	12	452, 478
Ch1	–	16	16	13	456, 478, 1781
Ch1	–	16	16	14	364, 747, 1549
Ch1	–	16	16	17	747
Ch1	–	16	16	18	764
Ch1	–	16	16	20	747, 1711, 1753
Ch1	–	16	16	21	1109, 1781
Ch1	–	16	16	22	1109
Ch1	–	16	16	23	263
Ch1	–	16	16	24	747
Ch1	–	16	16	25	1781
Ch1	–	16	16	26	430
Ch1	–	16	16	28	434, 1711
Ch1	–	16	16	29	343, 1016, 1549, 1711
Ch1	–	16	16	30	991, 1134
Ch1	–	16	16	32	270, 991
Ch1	–	16	16	33	991, 1109, 1753
Ch1	–	16	16	34	1155
Ch1	–	16	17	1	1314, 1761
Ch1	–	16	17	2	88, 376, 747, 1109
Ch1	–	16	17	3	286, 991
Ch1	–	16	17	4	39, 325, 747
Ch1	–	16	17	7	253
Ch1	–	16	17	9	286, 327, 1314
Ch1	–	16	17	10	332, 747, 1414, 1402
Ch1	–	16	17	12	764
Ch1	–	16	17	13	456, 559, 747
Ch1	–	16	17	14	747, 1781
Ch1	–	16	17	18	1753
Ch1	–	16	17	19	263
Ch1	–	16	17	20	747
Ch1	–	16	17	23	1753
Ch1	–	16	17	24	991, 1549
Ch1	–	16	17	25	1753
Ch1	–	16	17	26	270, 633, 747
Ch1	–	16	17	27	339, 1549, 1753
Ch1	–	16	17	28	267, 747, 1109
Ch1	–	16	17	30	270
Ch1	–	16	17	32	52
Ch1	–	16	17	33	370, 349
Ch1	–	16	17	34	478, 1549
Ch1	–	16	17	35	747, 764
Ch1	–	16	17	36	747
Ch1	–	17	1	3	541
Ch1	–	17	1	4	541
Ch1	–	17	1	5	85
Ch1	–	17	1	6	541
Ch1	–	17	1	7	541
Ch1	–	17	2	19	184
Ch1	–	17	2	30	240
Ch1	–	17	2	31	240
Ch1	–	17	2	32	52
Ch1	–	17	2	36	1761
Ch1	–	17	6	1	1711
Ch1	–	17	6	6	1753
Ch1	–	17	7	32	1549, 1781
Ch1	–	17	8	2	1395
Ch1	–	17	8	29	1761
Ch1	–	17	9	30	1753
Ch1	–	17	10	8	1753
Ch1	–	17	10	20	991
Ch1	–	17	10	31	991
Ch1	–	17	11	12	1494, 1516
Ch1	–	17	11	29	1494, 1516
Ch1	–	17	11	34	270
Ch1	–	17	12	33	1781
Ch1	–	17	14	4	332, 919
Ch1	–	17	14	5	331, 1109, 1402, 1753
Ch1	–	17	14	6	265, 273, 274, 292, 293, 582
Ch1	–	17	14	8	1549, 1753, 1756
Ch1	–	17	14	9	337, 517
Ch1	–	17	14	10	64
Ch1	–	17	14	12	1753
Ch1	–	17	14	15	1233
Ch1	–	17	14	17	270
Ch1	–	17	15	31	991
Ch1	–	17	16	2	94, 332, 1402, 1753
Ch1	–	17	16	3	430, 747
Ch1	–	17	16	4	1167
Ch1	–	17	16	8	1756
Ch1	–	17	16	9	349, 478
Ch1	–	17	16	10	332, 1402
Ch1	–	17	16	11	747, 991, 1711
Ch1	–	17	16	12	1753, 1781
Ch1	–	17	16	13	319, 747, 1402
Ch1	–	17	16	14	747, 1109
Ch1	–	17	16	15	1753
Ch1	–	17	16	17	543, 747
Ch1	–	17	16	19	339
Ch1	–	17	16	23	747, 1109
Ch1	–	17	16	24	270, 331, 1761
Ch1	–	17	16	25	991
Ch1	–	17	16	26	1549
Ch1	–	17	16	29	239
Ch1	–	17	16	34	339
Ch1	–	17	16	36	1549
Ch1	–	17	17	3	414
Ch1	–	17	17	4	263, 402, 747

[273]

Ch1	–	17	17	5	1781	Ch1	–	18	14	5	226
Ch1	–	17	17	8	991	Ch1	–	18	14	6	226
Ch1	–	17	17	9	1109, 1753, 1761	Ch1	–	18	14	9	501
Ch1	–	17	17	10	991	Ch1	–	18	14	10	501
Ch1	–	17	17	13	85, 747	Ch1	–	18	14	13	1109
Ch1	–	17	17	15	1549	Ch1	–	18	14	14	337, 514
Ch1	–	17	17	21	88, 483, 708, 1336, 1753	Ch1	–	18	14	20	1402
Ch1	–	17	17	22	1756, 1781	Ch1	–	18	14	25	747
Ch1	–	17	17	23	75, 154, 588, 591	Ch1	–	18	14	26	1314, 1711
Ch1	–	17	17	24	339	Ch1	–	18	14	36	400
Ch1	–	17	17	32	52	Ch1	–	18	15	6	70
Ch1	–	17	17	34	16, 248, 598, 991	Ch1	–	18	15	7	159
Ch1	–	17	17	35	747, 1109	Ch1	–	18	15	10	208
Ch1	–	17	17	36	254, 1314	Ch1	–	18	15	15	339, 598
Ch1	–	17	18	1	1109	Ch1	–	18	15	22	240, 478
Ch1	–	17	18	3	747, 1314	Ch1	–	18	16	1	150
Ch1	–	17	18	5	617	Ch1	–	18	16	2	991
Ch1	–	17	18	6	150	Ch1	–	18	16	3	991
Ch1	–	17	18	9	337, 487, 1071	Ch1	–	18	16	4	1753, 1756
Ch1	–	17	18	10	337, 430, 514	Ch1	–	18	16	5	747
Ch1	–	17	18	12	991, 1756	Ch1	–	18	16	6	52, 1023, 1065
Ch1	–	17	18	13	1753	Ch1	–	18	16	7	70, 256, 270, 337, 747
Ch1	–	17	18	14	13, 218	Ch1	–	18	16	8	141, 815, 919, 1753
Ch1	–	17	18	17	94, 141	Ch1	–	18	16	9	991
Ch1	–	17	18	18	747, 1781	Ch1	–	18	16	10	1756
Ch1	–	17	18	19	103, 269	Ch1	–	18	16	12	270, 339, 1314
Ch1	–	17	18	20	1071	Ch1	–	18	16	13	70, 231, 262
Ch1	–	17	18	22	1761	Ch1	–	18	16	14	478, 523
Ch1	–	17	18	24	125, 158, 414, 747, 1134	Ch1	–	18	16	18	478, 747
Ch1	–	17	18	26	263, 1314, 1753	Ch1	–	18	16	20	263
Ch1	–	17	18	27	239, 478, 1402, 1753	Ch1	–	18	16	23	253, 1756
Ch1	–	17	18	28	286, 625, 747, 1781	Ch1	–	18	16	26	331, 430, 456, 896
Ch1	–	17	18	29	103, 400, 1781	Ch1	–	18	16	30	240
Ch1	–	17	18	30	430	Ch1	–	18	16	23	157
Ch1	–	17	18	31	52, 327, 747	Ch1	–	19	2	8	764, 1314
Ch1	–	17	18	32	151, 991	Ch1	–	19	2	15	1314
Ch1	–	17	18	33	103, 254, 747	Ch1	–	19	4	14	1538
Ch1	–	17	18	35	240	Ch1	–	19	6	24	1447
Ch1	–	18	1	31	747	Ch1	–	19	8	7	815, 919
Ch1	–	18	2	9	1711	Ch1	–	19	9	6	991, 1549
Ch1	–	18	2	17	1314	Ch1	–	19	9	20	1756
Ch1	–	18	2	18	1314	Ch1	–	19	10	23	1314
Ch1	–	18	4	18	1711	Ch1	–	19	10	28	1314
Ch1	–	18	6	34	1753	Ch1	–	19	10	29	570
Ch1	–	18	9	36	1781	Ch1	–	19	10	30	352
Ch1	–	18	13	10	270	Ch1	–	19	11	7	85
Ch1	–	18	13	14	270, 430	Ch1	–	19	11	8	430
Ch1	–	18	13	23	270, 442	Ch1	–	19	11	9	52, 747
Ch1	–	18	13	25	1549	Ch1	–	19	11	10	582

Ch1	–	20	8	27	478
Ch1	–	20	8	29	476, 747
Ch1	–	20	8	34	61, 146, 188
Ch1	–	20	8	35	430
Ch1	–	20	8	36	991
Ch1	–	20	9	4	582
Ch1	–	20	9	7	240, 1781
Ch1	–	20	9	9	1109
Ch1	–	20	9	18	991
Ch1	–	20	9	20	747
Ch1	–	20	9	29	476
Ch1	–	20	9	30	747
Ch1	–	20	9	31	430, 698, 896
Ch1	–	20	10	2	337, 487
Ch1	–	20	10	4	1549
Ch1	–	20	10	6	286, 339
Ch1	–	20	10	11	1134, 1314
Ch1	–	20	10	12	991, 1314
Ch1	–	20	10	15	747
Ch1	–	20	10	19	991, 1637
Ch1	–	20	10	21	1314
Ch1	–	20	10	24	747
Ch1	–	20	10	27	747
Ch1	–	20	10	30	617
Ch1	–	20	10	32	478
Ch1	–	20	11	1	577
Ch1	–	20	11	2	96, 747
Ch1	–	20	11	4	52, 434, 594, 598
Ch1	–	20	11	5	337, 570, 641, 747, 1008
Ch1	–	20	11	9	991
Ch1	–	20	11	11	625, 991
Ch1	–	20	11	12	747, 1549
Ch1	–	20	11	15	747
Ch1	–	20	11	17	559, 747, 1549
Ch1	–	20	11	18	208
Ch1	–	20	11	19	1155
Ch1	–	20	11	21	747, 1549
Ch1	–	20	11	27	617
Ch1	–	20	11	28	476, 543, 747, 1314
Ch1	–	20	11	29	487
Ch1	–	20	11	30	337, 559
Ch1	–	20	11	33	1314, 1549, 1711
Ch1	–	20	12	2	452, 1756
Ch1	–	20	12	4	456, 1080, 1119
Ch1	–	20	12	6	337, 487
Ch1	–	20	12	7	337, 514
Ch1	–	20	12	9	33, 570
Ch1	–	20	12	10	319, 366, 517, 896, 1109
Ch1	–	20	12	14	1549
Ch1	–	20	12	17	337, 487, 747, 957, 1155
Ch1	–	20	12	18	121, 181
Ch1	–	20	12	19	128, 991, 1538, 1711
Ch1	–	20	12	20	128
Ch1	–	20	12	21	991, 1314
Ch1	–	20	12	23	476
Ch1	–	20	12	27	1549
Ch1	–	20	12	28	1314
Ch1	–	20	12	30	402, 1756
Ch1	–	20	12	32	1314
Ch1	–	20	12	33	364, 747, 778, 1402
Ch1	–	20	13	2	85, 159
Ch1	–	20	13	3	331, 1134
Ch1	–	20	13	6	1756
Ch1	–	20	13	7	1549
Ch1	–	20	13	9	331, 364, 896
Ch1	–	20	13	11	430, 478, 747
Ch1	–	20	13	12	747, 1044
Ch1	–	20	13	13	625, 747
Ch1	–	20	13	15	349, 747
Ch1	–	20	13	21	991
Ch1	–	20	13	22	121, 991, 1155, 1314, 1753
Ch1	–	20	13	24	501
Ch1	–	20	13	25	501
Ch1	–	20	13	27	251
Ch1	–	20	13	31	430
Ch1	–	20	13	32	747, 991
Ch1	–	20	13	35	270, 747
Ch1	–	20	14	3	337, 514
Ch1	–	20	14	4	543
Ch1	–	20	14	5	430, 617, 991, 1711
Ch1	–	20	14	6	141, 478
Ch1	–	20	14	7	319, 1314
Ch1	–	20	14	9	414
Ch1	–	20	14	10	52, 625, 1134
Ch1	–	20	14	14	253, 747, 991, 1549
Ch1	–	20	14	17	1756
Ch1	–	20	14	18	641, 747, 1756, 1781
Ch1	–	20	14	20	319, 1753
Ch1	–	20	14	21	747, 1781
Ch1	–	20	14	22	747, 1549, 1753
Ch1	–	20	14	23	240, 254, 1549
Ch1	–	20	14	24	269, 487
Ch1	–	20	14	27	1109
Ch1	–	20	14	30	253, 337, 514
Ch1	–	20	14	31	349, 478, 1402, 1485
Ch1	–	20	14	32	1756

Ch1	–	20	14	33	263, 747
Ch1	–	20	14	35	263, 337, 517, 747
Ch1	–	20	14	36	141
Ch1	–	20	15	1	85, 349, 570
Ch1	–	20	15	3	269
Ch1	–	20	15	4	270
Ch1	–	20	15	5	905, 991, 1756
Ch1	–	20	15	6	70, 71, 255, 361, 747, 815, 918
Ch1	–	20	15	7	570
Ch1	–	20	15	8	543, 1314
Ch1	–	20	15	9	254, 1549
Ch1	–	20	15	10	254, 263, 991
Ch1	–	20	15	11	478
Ch1	–	20	15	12	402, 747, 764, 991
Ch1	–	20	15	14	254, 337, 514
Ch1	–	20	15	15	254
Ch1	–	20	15	17	747, 1134
Ch1	–	20	15	18	478, 1756
Ch1	–	20	15	19	85, 339
Ch1	–	20	15	20	201, 431, 747, 808
Ch1	–	20	15	23	430, 747, 1314
Ch1	–	20	15	25	483, 1134, 1509
Ch1	–	20	15	26	1756
Ch1	–	20	15	28	598, 1109
Ch1	–	20	15	29	430, 991, 1314, 1549
Ch1	–	20	15	30	339, 430, 1549
Ch1	–	20	15	31	52, 166, 991
Ch1	–	20	15	32	319, 991, 1402, 1753
Ch1	–	20	15	33	352, 921
Ch1	–	20	15	35	747
Ch1	–	20	18	15	1314
Ch1	–	20	?	1	406
Ch1	–	21	1	7	991
Ch1	–	21	1	8	991
Ch1	–	21	1	9	1128
Ch1	–	21	1	12	1781
Ch1	–	21	2	6	893
Ch1	–	21	2	17	419
Ch1	–	21	2	32	1134
Ch1	–	21	2	33	991
Ch1	–	21	3	33	747, 991
Ch1	–	21	3	34	1109
Ch1	–	21	4	3	747
Ch1	–	21	5	5	292, 747
Ch1	–	21	5	16	292, 747
Ch1	–	21	5	17	598
Ch1	–	21	5	18	991
Ch1	–	21	5	26	991
Ch1	–	21	5	27	263
Ch1	–	21	5	28	1126
Ch1	–	21	5	29	991, 1711
Ch1	–	21	5	32	262, 269
Ch1	–	21	5	33	319, 617, 1155
Ch1	–	21	6	2	991
Ch1	–	21	7	1	344
Ch1	–	21	7	8	991, 1753
Ch1	–	21	8	1	430
Ch1	–	21	8	2	747
Ch1	–	21	8	8	133, 991
Ch1	–	21	8	11	400, 1753
Ch1	–	21	8	14	188, 747, 815, 919
Ch1	–	21	8	15	1314, 1761
Ch1	–	21	8	21	339
Ch1	–	21	8	23	1314
Ch1	–	21	8	24	991
Ch1	–	21	8	25	1109
Ch1	–	21	8	26	747
Ch1	–	21	8	32	269, 573, 1109
Ch1	–	21	9	9	1314
Ch1	–	21	9	22	1567
Ch1	–	21	9	23	747
Ch1	–	21	9	31	319
Ch1	–	21	9	34	1402, 1781
Ch1	–	21	10	3	1314
Ch1	–	21	10	5	1225
Ch1	–	21	10	14	1402, 1485
Ch1	–	21	10	18	152
Ch1	–	21	10	19	327
Ch1	–	21	10	25	991
Ch1	–	21	10	26	991
Ch1	–	21	10	27	327
Ch1	–	21	10	30	339
Ch1	–	21	10	34	991, 1155
Ch1	–	21	11	1	70
Ch1	–	21	11	8	96, 1181, 1617
Ch1	–	21	11	9	1181, 1254, 1255, 1617, 1645
Ch1	–	21	11	18	747
Ch1	–	21	11	24	478, 1402, 1756
Ch1	–	21	11	33	128
Ch1	–	21	11	35	1402
Ch1	–	21	11	36	1314
Ch1	–	22	3	23	1549
Ch1	–	22	4	1	1037, 1065
Ch1	–	22	4	2	1065
Ch1	–	22	4	14	1756
Ch1	–	24	11	8	239

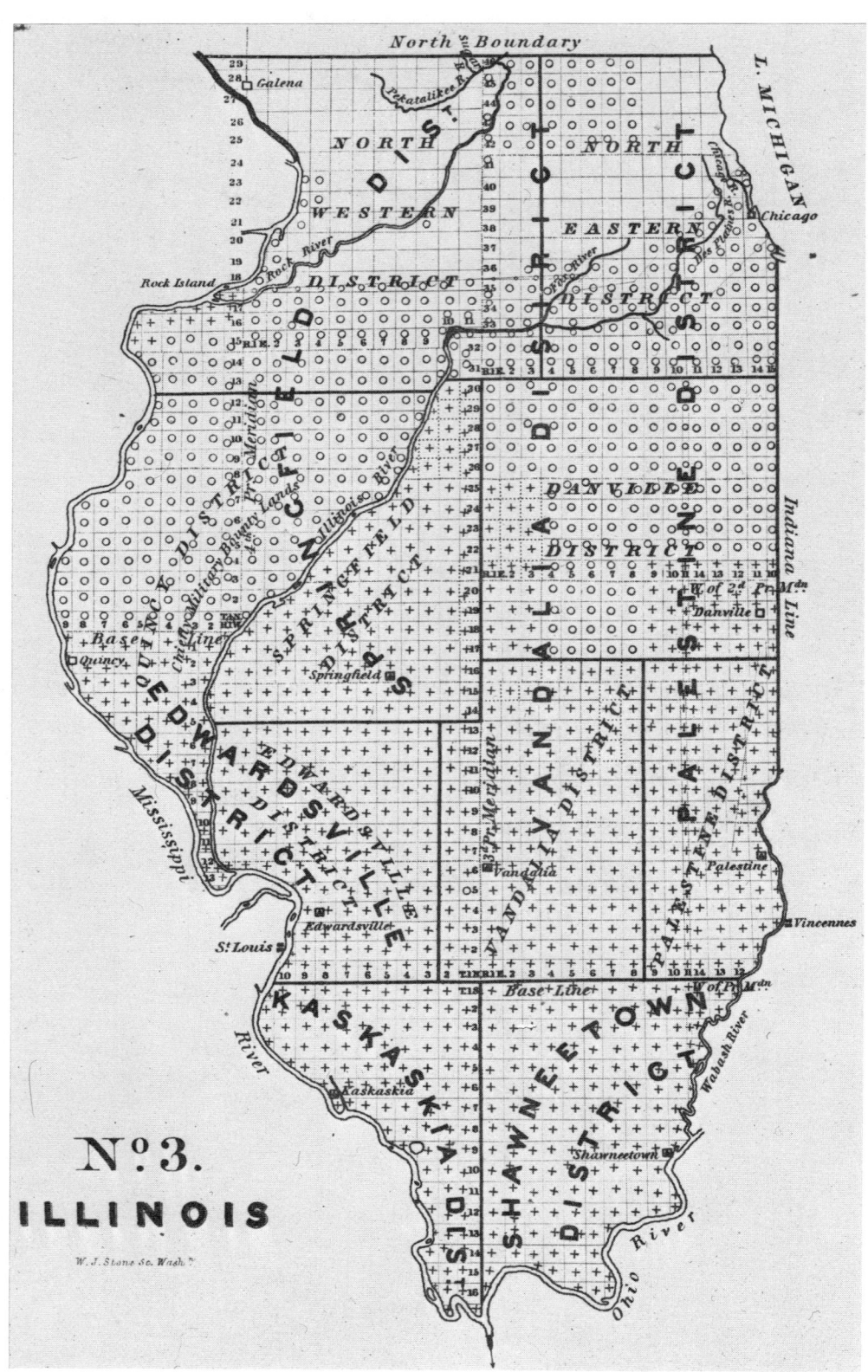

MAP 8. Tract map of Illinois showing land office districts

[278]

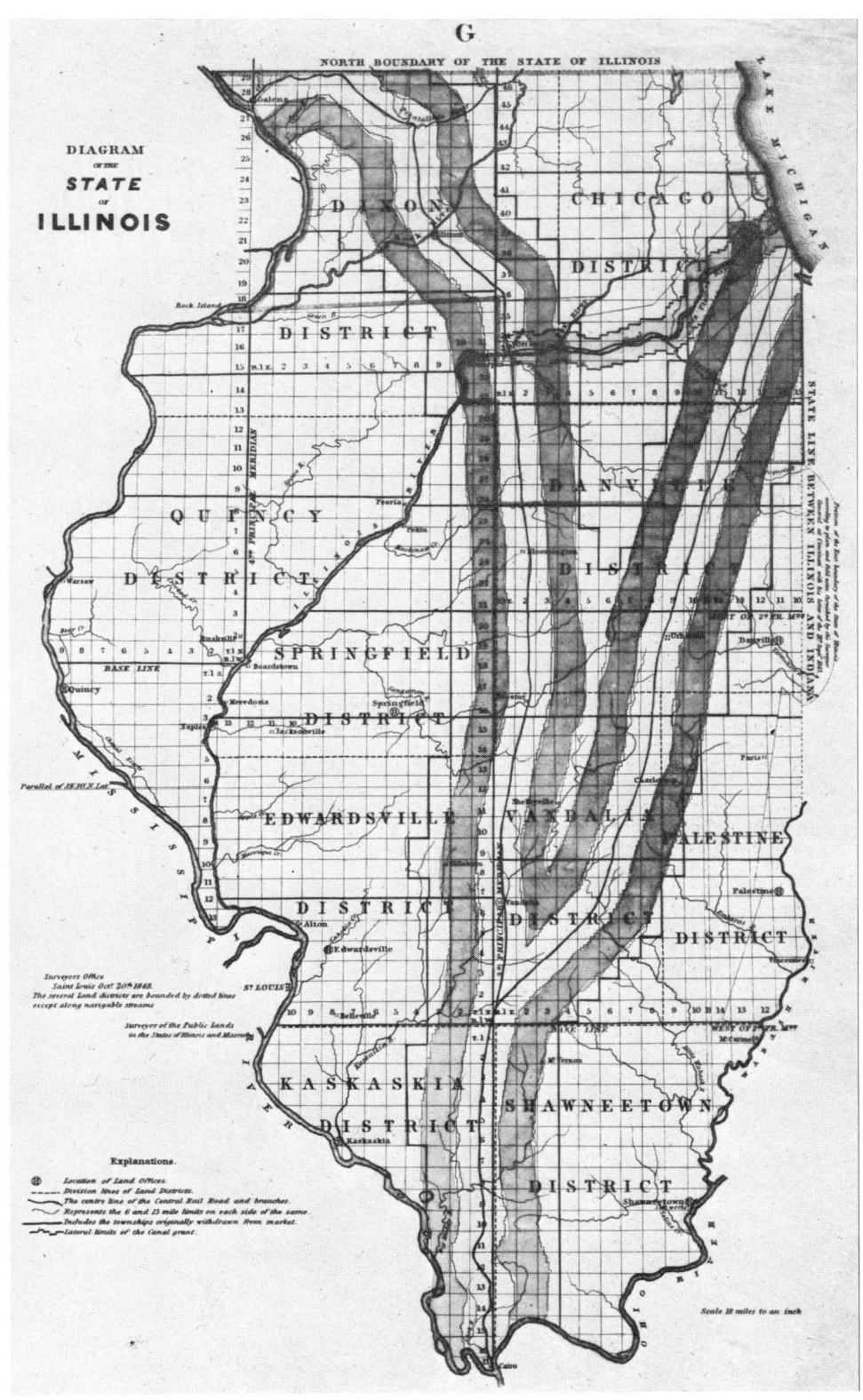

MAP 9. Tract map of Illinois showing range-township numbering system

Langham's Survey

Ch1	LS	20	2	18	331
Ch1	LS	21	2	17	572
Ch1	LS	21	2	18	572
Ch1	LS	21	3	19	991
Ch1	LS	21	3	30	1549
Ch1	LS	22	3	5	747
Ch1	LS	22	3	6	747
Ch1	LS	22	3	7	991
Ch1	LS	22	3	8	1549

Military Land Grants

Ch1	Mil	12	7	16	1282
Ch1	Mil	12	7	24	1632
Ch1	Mil	12	7	25	434, 1314
Ch1	Mil	13	7	2	991
Ch1	Mil	13	7	9	991, 1781
Ch1	Mil	13	7	12	1538
Ch1	Mil	13	7	20	1314
Ch1	Mil	13	7	21	1314
Ch1	Mil	14	8	11	1538
Ch1	Mil	14	8	12	736, 897
Ch1	Mil	14	8	18	598
Ch1	Mil	14	8	19	402, 1312
Ch1	Mil	14	8	20	625
Ch1	Mil	14	8	21	337, 747
Ch1	Mil	15	3	7	1314
Ch1	Mil	15	3	8	1549, 1756
Ch1	Mil	15	3	13	1549
Ch1	Mil	15	3	14	1753
Ch1	Mil	15	3	17	1549
Ch1	Mil	15	3	18	1756
Ch1	Mil	15	3	23	1549
Ch1	Mil	15	3	24	1314
Ch1	Mil	15	3	25	1781
Ch1	Mil	16	2	9	1549, 1711
Ch1	Mil	16	2	10	1711
Ch1	Mil	18	7	12	633
Ch1	Mil	18	7	19	1711
Ch1	Mil	19	6	24	1314
Ch1	Mil	19	7	12	1711
Ch1	Mil	19	7	19	747
Ch1	Mil	19	7	22	434, 1549
Ch1	Mil	19	7	23	598
Ch1	Mil	21	9	11	991
Ch1	Mil	21	9	35	617
Ch1	Mil	21	9	36	760
Ch1	Mil	21	10	1	1284
Ch1	Mil	21	10	12	991
Ch1	Mil	21	10	30	991
Ch1	Mil	22	3	23	991
Ch1	Mil	22	4	2	617

Matthew's Survey

Ch1	MS	1	9	4	263
Ch1	MS	19	16	36	747
Ch1	MS	21	9	1	747, 1753
Ch1	MS	21	9	3	85, 430
Ch1	MS	21	9	4	1711
Ch1	MS	21	9	5	94
Ch1	MS	21	9	6	331
Ch1	MS	21	9	7	747
Ch1	MS	21	9	8	747, 991
Ch1	MS	21	9	9	146
Ch1	MS	21	9	10	896
Ch1	MS	21	9	13	747
Ch1	MS	21	9	15	1756
Ch1	MS	21	9	18	337, 487
Ch1	MS	21	9	19	146, 419, 580
Ch1	MS	21	9	23	239, 262, 1756
Ch1	MS	21	9	26	905, 1134
Ch1	MS	21	9	27	239, 339, 349
Ch1	MS	21	9	29	456, 478, 1155
Ch1	MS	21	9	31	452, 1134
Ch1	MS	21	9	32	1314
Ch1	MS	21	9	34	478, 1314, 1498, 1549
Ch1	MS	21	9	35	957
Ch1	MS	21	9	36	414, 478, 570, 1314
Ch1	MS	21	10	1	339
Ch1	MS	21	10	2	253
Ch1	MS	21	10	3	253
Ch1	MS	21	10	4	514
Ch1	MS	21	10	5	253
Ch1	MS	21	10	7	991
Ch1	MS	21	10	8	1314, 1549, 1781
Ch1	MS	21	10	9	747, 1314
Ch1	MS	21	10	10	52, 253
Ch1	MS	21	10	11	253, 1761
Ch1	MS	21	10	13	269, 764, 991, 1109
Ch1	MS	21	10	14	85, 331, 1753, 1781
Ch1	MS	21	10	18	225, 434, 905
Ch1	MS	21	10	23	1109
Ch1	MS	21	10	24	254, 364, 514
Ch1	MS	21	10	25	240
Ch1	MS	21	10	26	1056
Ch1	MS	21	10	27	414, 430

Ch1	MS	21	10	29	747
Ch1	MS	21	10	31	381, 458, 508, 747
Ch1	MS	21	10	33	337, 747, 991
Ch1	MS	21	10	34	85
Ch1	MS	21	10	35	747, 1109
Ch1	MS	21	10	36	240
Ch1	MS	21	11	1	70, 1109, 1134
Ch1	MS	21	11	2	478, 543, 747, 1109
Ch1	MS	21	11	4	269, 747
Ch1	MS	21	11	5	1753
Ch1	MS	21	11	7	991
Ch1	MS	21	11	8	747
Ch1	MS	21	11	12	747
Ch1	MS	21	11	13	85
Ch1	MS	21	11	14	747
Ch1	MS	21	11	17	269, 434, 747
Ch1	MS	21	11	18	337, 747
Ch1	MS	21	11	20	598
Ch1	MS	21	11	23	239, 747
Ch1	MS	21	11	24	456, 1109
Ch1	MS	21	11	25	339, 747, 1761
Ch1	MS	21	11	26	1155, 1753
Ch1	MS	21	11	27	991
Ch1	MS	21	11	28	200, 747, 1753
Ch1	MS	21	11	30	747
Ch1	MS	21	11	31	1756
Ch1	MS	21	11	32	1109
Ch1	MS	21	11	33	85
Ch1	MS	21	11	36	717
Ch1	MS	22	2	2	570
Ch1	MS	22	2	5	1164
Ch1	MS	22	2	12	747
Ch1	MS	22	2	13	905
Ch1	MS	22	2	25	1162
Ch1	MS	22	2	34	451, 858
Ch1	MS	22	2	35	451, 858
Ch1	MS	22	2	36	184, 239, 251
Ch1	MS	22	3	11	269
Ch1	MS	22	3	13	991
Ch1	MS	22	3	21	251
Ch1	MS	22	3	22	251
Ch1	MS	22	3	26	270
Ch1	MS	22	3	36	331, 633, 747
Ch1	MS	22	4	1	570, 1162
Ch1	MS	22	4	2	1162
Ch1	MS	22	4	3	363
Ch1	MS	22	4	11	339, 363, 764
Ch1	MS	22	4	12	747, 764, 1781
Ch1	MS	22	4	13	747
Ch1	MS	22	4	14	85, 1549
Ch1	MS	22	4	25	263
Ch1	MS	22	4	28	617
Ch1	MS	22	4	34	434
Ch1	MS	22	4	35	269, 747, 764
Ch1	MS	22	4	36	747, 1314
Ch1	MS	26	11	1	239

Worthington's Survey

Ch1	WS	21	4	25	430
Ch1	WS	21	9	2	339, 991
Ch1	WS	21	9	3	339, 747
Ch1	WS	21	9	4	625
Ch1	WS	21	9	6	52, 1314
Ch1	WS	21	9	9	319, 991
Ch1	WS	21	9	22	568, 1781
Ch1	WS	21	9	29	269
Ch1	WS	21	9	33	371, 747, 1781
Ch1	WS	21	9	34	16, 52, 434
Ch1	WS	21	9	35	339, 991
Ch1	WS	21	9	36	747
Ch1	WS	21	10	1	617, 1538, 1756
Ch1	WS	21	10	2	747
Ch1	WS	21	10	10	452, 991
Ch1	WS	21	10	13	240, 1612
Ch1	WS	21	10	14	991, 1590
Ch1	WS	21	10	15	1314
Ch1	WS	21	10	17	991, 1314
Ch1	WS	21	10	18	332
Ch1	WS	21	10	20	991
Ch1	WS	21	10	22	1109
Ch1	WS	21	10	23	1725
Ch1	WS	21	10	24	337
Ch1	WS	21	10	25	52, 253
Ch1	WS	21	10	26	617
Ch1	WS	21	10	27	1109
Ch1	WS	21	10	28	319, 467, 747
Ch1	WS	21	10	30	991
Ch1	WS	21	10	33	262
Ch1	WS	21	10	34	52, 319, 991, 1134, 1756
Ch1	WS	21	10	35	402
Ch1	WS	21	10	36	211, 337, 747
Ch1	WS	21	11	1	617
Ch1	WS	21	11	2	400
Ch1	WS	21	11	3	339
Ch1	WS	21	11	5	559
Ch1	WS	21	11	6	270
Ch1	WS	21	11	7	270, 747, 1519
Ch1	WS	21	11	8	1254, 1255, 1677, 1753

Ch1	WS	21	11	9	1712
Ch1	WS	21	11	11	292, 1017
Ch1	WS	21	11	13	747, 1314
Ch1	WS	21	11	14	625
Ch1	WS	21	11	15	991
Ch1	WS	21	11	17	1109, 1402
Ch1	WS	21	11	18	319, 747, 905
Ch1	WS	21	11	21	1109, 1134
Ch1	WS	21	11	22	617, 747, 1711
Ch1	WS	21	11	24	1364
Ch1	WS	21	11	25	570
Ch1	WS	21	11	26	81, 1549
Ch1	WS	21	11	30	452, 472, 747
Ch1	WS	21	11	34	254, 1711
Ch1	WS	21	11	35	349, 991, 1126
Ch1	WS	21	18	23	1725
Ch1	WS	22	4	1	1314
Ch1	WS	22	4	2	1314
Ch1	WS	22	4	6	1711

CINCINNATI, OHIO, LAND OFFICE DISTRICT

Incomplete and Erroneous Tract Descriptions

Cin	-	1	?	3	1241
Cin	-	1	2	1	329
Cin	-	1	4	30	1353
Cin	-	1	5	5	67, 291
Cin	-	1	5	9	67, 291
Cin	-	1	5	17	18
Cin	-	1	5	19	67, 291
Cin	-	1	12	5	1387
Cin	-	1	14	5	1387
Cin	-	1	15	29	1653
Cin	-	1E	6-	3	1426
Cin	-	1W	12-	18	67
Cin	-	1W	14-	36	67, 90, 1416
Cin	-	2	2	8	1594
Cin	-	2	3	9	1543
Cin	-	2	5	1	432
Cin	-	2	5	18	291
Cin	-	2	6	7	316
Cin	-	2	6	36	67
Cin	-	2	7	6	1195
Cin	-	2	9	8	1401
Cin	-	2	13	26	1401
Cin	-	2E	5-	18	67
Cin	-	3	1	5	1582
Cin	-	3	1	6	1582

Cin	-	3	4	12	18
Cin	-	3	5	15	205, 291, 494
Cin	-	3	5	22	205, 291, 494
Cin	-	3	5	26	1591
Cin	-	3	7	22	1344
Cin	-	3	7	26	291
Cin	-	3	8	24	443
Cin	-	3	8	25	443
Cin	-	3E	7-	23	72
Cin	-	4	2	1	1353
Cin	-	4	2	9	1029
Cin	-	4	2	19	1328
Cin	-	4	3	6	1337
Cin	-	4	3	19	1168
Cin	-	4	3	21	1328
Cin	-	4	3	22	1446
Cin	-	4	3	23	347
Cin	-	4	3	24	347
Cin	-	4	4	5	205, 291, 494
Cin	-	4	4	24	1350
Cin	-	4E	3-	30	67, 90
Cin	-	5	2	12	484, 1401
Cin	-	5	2	27	520
Cin	-	5	3	7	740
Cin	-	5	3	23	392
Cin	-	5	3	24	347, 392
Cin	-	5	3	25	347
Cin	-	5	3	27	801
Cin	-	5	3	28	520
Cin	-	5	3	29	316
Cin	-	5	3	30	1416
Cin	-	5	3	33	1029
Cin	-	5	4	8	475
Cin	-	5	4	15	205, 291, 494, 658
Cin	-	5	4	30	1350
Cin	-	5	5	22	291
Cin	-	5	5	25	1416
Cin	-	5	5	31	1416
Cin	-	5	6	14	291
Cin	-	5	6	31	1224
Cin	-	6	1	9	1353
Cin	-	6	1	10	1353
Cin	-	6	1	19	392
Cin	-	6	1	20	392
Cin	-	6	1	26	1353
Cin	-	6	1	29	392
Cin	-	6	2	11	205
Cin	-	6	2	33	1353
Cin	-	6	3	24	1446

Cin	–	6	3	28	1446
Cin	–	6	4	25	1350
Cin	–	6	4	26	1350
Cin	–	6	4	27	291, 759
Cin	–	6	6	7	316
Cin	–	7	1	4	587
Cin	–	7	2	22	291, 347
Cin	–	7	3	6	1350
Cin	–	7	3	9	1031
Cin	–	7	3	22	759
Cin	–	7	4	30	1029
Cin	–	7	8	9	1168
Cin	–	8	2	6	1446
Cin	–	8	2	26	291
Cin	–	8	2	29	1405
Cin	–	8	3	15	495
Cin	–	8	3	36	1446
Cin	–	9	2	22	1401
Cin	–	9	3	34	1773
Cin	–	9	4	21	1478
Cin	–	9	4	32	1416
Cin	–	10	4	3	1416, 1478
Cin	–	10	5	9	18
Cin	–	10	5	17	18
Cin	–	10	5	21	1563
Cin	–	10	6	9	336
Cin	–	10	6	15	336
Cin	–	11	4	5	1773
Cin	–	11	4	15	1416
Cin	–	11	5	34	1773
Cin	–	11	6	31	1401
Cin	–	12	1	32	1214
Cin	–	12	4	24	973
Cin	–	12	16	13	1561
Cin	– 12E	12N	9		1041
Cin	– 12E	12N	28		1041
Cin	– 12E	12N	36		942
Cin	– 12E	13N	11		1041
Cin	– 12E	13N	23		1041
Cin	– 12E	13N	28		1041
Cin	– 12E	13N	34		1041
Cin	– 12E	14N	24		1041
Cin	– 12E	14N	34		1041
Cin	– 12E	14N	35		1041
Cin	– 12E	14N	36		1041
Cin	– 12E	15N	2		1041
Cin	– 12E	15N	15		1041
Cin	– 12E	15N	25		1041
Cin	– 12E	16N	11		1041
Cin	– 12E	16N	13		1041, 1561
Cin	– 12E	16N	22		1041
Cin	– 12E	16N	27		1041
Cin	– 12E	16N	28		1041
Cin	– 12E	16N	34		1031
Cin	– 12E	16N	35		1031, 1041
Cin	– 12E	16N	36		1041
Cin	– 13	3	9		973
Cin	– 13	4	4		1371
Cin	– 13	5	15		1350
Cin	– 13	5	26		1591
Cin	– 13E	2–	24		1031
Cin	– 13E	11N	5		1041
Cin	– 13E	12N	31		1041
Cin	– 13E	14N	5		1041
Cin	– 13E	14N	18		1031
Cin	– 13E	15N	3		1041
Cin	– 13E	16N	3		1041
Cin	– 13E	16N	8		1041
Cin	– 13E	16N	10		1041
Cin	– 13E	16N	15		1041
Cin	– 13E	16N	18		1031, 1041
Cin	– 13E	16N	19		1041
Cin	– 13E	16N	22		1041
Cin	– 13E	16N	24		1041
Cin	– 13E	16N	28		1041
Cin	– 13E	16N	30		1041
Cin	– 13E	16N	35		1031
Cin	– 13E	17N	17		1073
Cin	– 13E	17N	20		1041
Cin	– 13E	17N	24		1041
Cin	– 13E	17N	32		1031
Cin	– 13E	17N	35		1041
Cin	– 14E	14N	4		1031
Cin	– 14E	14N	5		1031
Cin	– 14E	16N	19		1031
Cin	– 14E	17N	14		1041
Cin	– 14E	17N	18		1041
Cin	– 14E	17N	27		1031
Cin	– 14E	17N	29		1041
Cin	– 14E	17N	33		1031
Cin	– 14E	18N	32		1041

Town of Dayton

Cin Day	–	–	6		1328

East Meridian Line

Cin EML	1	1	island		1405
Cin EML	1	1	1		1029

Cin EML	1	1	2	865, 1035
Cin EML	1	1	8	1073
Cin EML	1	1	9	6, 10, 1156
Cin EML	1	1	10	1530
Cin EML	1	1	11	865
Cin EML	1	1	18	829
Cin EML	1	1	21	50
Cin EML	1	1	22	50
Cin EML	1	1	27	50
Cin EML	1	1	28	50
Cin EML	1	1	30	3, 1405
Cin EML	1	1	31	3, 1405
Cin EML	1	2	1	1073, 1353, 1530
Cin EML	1	2	2	436
Cin EML	1	2	4	751
Cin EML	1	2	7	1783
Cin EML	1	2	8	1035
Cin EML	1	2	9	677, 1073, 1779
Cin EML	1	2	12	10, 115, 357
Cin EML	1	2	13	26, 606
Cin EML	1	2	14	751
Cin EML	1	2	18	677, 1073
Cin EML	1	2	20	56, 532
Cin EML	1	2	23	1161
Cin EML	1	2	30	1073
Cin EML	1	2	33	1701
Cin EML	1	2	34	1749
Cin EML	1	3	1	752
Cin EML	1	3	2	865, 1012, 1749
Cin EML	1	3	3	1073
Cin EML	1	3	4	1783
Cin EML	1	3	6	101, 953
Cin EML	1	3	7	1582, 1779
Cin EML	1	3	9	1625
Cin EML	1	3	10	182, 1110
Cin EML	1	3	11	1012
Cin EML	1	3	12	1530
Cin EML	1	3	17	953
Cin EML	1	3	21	1313
Cin EML	1	3	22	1200, 1625, 1749
Cin EML	1	3	24	224
Cin EML	1	3	28	1313, 1530
Cin EML	1	3	30	1779
Cin EML	1	3	31	1779
Cin EML	1	3	33	91, 1371
Cin EML	1	3	34	356
Cin EML	1	3	36	1073
Cin EML	1	4	1	56, 153, 532
Cin EML	1	4	2	1073
Cin EML	1	4	3	261
Cin EML	1	4	4	1012
Cin EML	1	4	6	224, 680
Cin EML	1	4	8	372, 623, 953, 1029
Cin EML	1	4	9	1073, 1478
Cin EML	1	4	10	1371
Cin EML	1	4	11	1667
Cin EML	1	4	12	350, 1251
Cin EML	1	4	13	76, 953
Cin EML	1	4	14	6, 677, 1313
Cin EML	1	4	17	367, 532, 1073
Cin EML	1	4	18	623, 1195, 1371
Cin EML	1	4	19	759, 1478, 1710, 1779
Cin EML	1	4	20	532, 1436
Ciñ EML	1	4	21	1779
Cin EML	1	4	22	521, 1073
Cin EML	1	4	23	465, 1461, 1530, 1625
Cin EML	1	4	24	76, 710, 1313
Cin EML	1	4	26	942, 1530
Cin EML	1	4	27	723, 1625
Cin EML	1	4	28	101, 1783
Cin EML	1	4	29	1582, 1783
Cin EML	1	4	30	931
Cin EML	1	4	31	101
Cin EML	1	4	33	1582, 1710
Cin EML	1	4	34	261, 680, 1390
Cin EML	1	4	35	677
Cin EML	1	4	36	357, 1195, 1313
Cin EML	1	6	1	1636, 1710
Cin EML	1	6	3	632, 659, 950, 1012
Cin EML	1	6	4	950
Cin EML	1	6	5	420, 532, 1073
Cin EML	1	6	6	659
Cin EML	1	6	7	459
Cin EML	1	6	8	459
Cin EML	1	6	9	532, 1195
Cin EML	1	6	10	1073, 1328
Cin EML	1	6	11	10
Cin EML	1	6	14	532, 1530
Cin EML	1	6	17	115, 1313
Cin EML	1	6	19	532, 931
Cin EML	1	6	20	485, 1313
Cin EML	1	6	23	532
Cin EML	1	6	24	91, 521
Cin EML	1	6	25	135, 1530
Cin EML	1	6	26	91, 953
Cin EML	1	6	28	931, 1419
Cin EML	1	6	29	153, 942, 1073
Cin EML	1	6	30	367, 865

Cin EML	1	6	31	21, 135	Cin EML	1	9	20	677, 829, 1478
Cin EML	1	6	32	10, 722, 1110	Cin EML	1	9	28	1749
Cin EML	1	6	33	135, 221, 1530	Cin EML	1	9	29	357, 632
Cin EML	1	6	35	153	Cin EML	1	9	30	532, 751
Cin EML	1	6	36	677	Cin EML	1	9	31	1749
Cin EML	1	7	1	1582	Cin EML	1	9	32	628, 931, 1625
Cin EML	1	7	3	632, 751	Cin EML	1	9	34	1502
Cin EML	1	7	4	931, 1313, 1783	Cin EML	1	10	23	1203
Cin EML	1	7	5	182	Cin EML	1	10	27	1203
Cin EML	1	7	7	1726	Cin EML	1	10	28	942, 1582
Cin EML	1	7	9	153	Cin EML	1	11	7	1041
Cin EML	1	7	10	356, 359, 1749	Cin EML	1	11	17	1041
Cin EML	1	7	11	751	Cin EML	1	12	19	1041
Cin EML	1	7	12	1436, 1582	Cin EML	1	13	27	520, 953
Cin EML	1	7	14	1478	Cin EML	1	14	14	1041
Cin EML	1	7	19	1029, 1582	Cin EML	2	1	18	623
Cin EML	1	7	23	1779	Cin EML	2	2	6	130, 942, 1195
Cin EML	1	7	24	532, 751, 1034, 1094, 1436	Cin EML	2	2	18	953
Cin EML	1	7	25	1203	Cin EML	2	2	26	1195
Cin EML	1	7	27	261	Cin EML	2	3	2	731, 759, 1073, 1195
Cin EML	1	7	28	367, 535, 1582	Cin EML	2	3	5	359, 751, 1783
Cin EML	1	7	31	1195, 1783	Cin EML	2	3	6	101, 212, 521, 751
Cin EML	1	7	33	187, 1582	Cin EML	2	3	11	101
Cin EML	1	7	35	1582	Cin EML	2	3	12	1582, 1710
Cin EML	1	7	36	1502	Cin EML	2	3	14	101
Cin EML	1	8	3	1478	Cin EML	2	3	15	801, 1195, 1625
Cin EML	1	8	9	1035	Cin EML	2	3	17	1667
Cin EML	1	8	10	1710	Cin EML	2	3	21	1243
Cin EML	1	8	12	1371, 1582	Cin EML	2	3	22	1667
Cin EML	1	8	13	1073	Cin EML	2	3	32	21
Cin EML	1	8	17	372, 632	Cin EML	2	4	3	56
Cin EML	1	8	18	532, 680, 1436	Cin EML	2	4	4	195, 212
Cin EML	1	8	19	654	Cin EML	2	4	5	942
Cin EML	1	8	20	632, 659, 953	Cin EML	2	4	7	829, 1029
Cin EML	1	8	25	1502	Cin EML	2	4	8	372, 751
Cin EML	1	8	28	1478	Cin EML	2	4	9	521, 609, 628, 1749
Cin EML	1	8	29	1313	Cin EML	2	4	10	532, 1161, 1313
Cin EML	1	8	32	532, 942	Cin EML	2	4	11	386
Cin EML	1	8	33	532	Cin EML	2	4	12	1073
Cin EML	1	8	34	135, 142	Cin EML	2	4	13	153, 1160, 1161
Cin EML	1	8	36	659, 1502	Cin EML	2	4	14	475, 1392, 1436, 1625
Cin EML	1	9	4	221, 532	Cin EML	2	4	18	1371
Cin EML	1	9	5	829	Cin EML	2	4	19	182
Cin EML	1	9	9	942, 1012, 1636	Cin EML	2	4	20	654
Cin EML	1	9	10	677	Cin EML	2	4	23	532, 829
Cin EML	1	9	11	931	Cin EML	2	4	24	532
Cin EML	1	9	13	1041	Cin EML	2	4	26	829, 931, 1548
Cin EML	1	9	14	1041	Cin EML	2	4	28	829, 931
Cin EML	1	9	17	359, 680	Cin EML	2	4	29	942, 1073

Cin EML	2	4	30		316, 1436
Cin EML	2	4	34		261, 942
Cin EML	2	4	35		931, 1530
Cin EML	2	5	1		436, 479, 602, 677, 1203, 1530, 1667
Cin EML	2	5	6		448
Cin EML	2	5	7		680
Cin EML	2	5	8		50, 953, 1530
Cin EML	2	5	10		298
Cin EML	2	5	11		91, 657, 942
Cin EML	2	5	12		101, 680, 931
Cin EML	2	5	13		659, 931
Cin EML	2	5	15		628, 1073
Cin EML	2	5	17		829, 1161, 1783
Cin EML	2	5	18		623, 891, 1582, 1749
Cin EML	2	5	19		48, 532, 953, 1625
Cin EML	2	5	20		485
Cin EML	2	5	21		357, 372, 1313, 1371
Cin EML	2	5	22		1502
Cin EML	2	5	26		865, 1035
Cin EML	2	5	27		21, 953
Cin EML	2	5	34		1313
Cin EML	2	5	35		261, 475, 931, 950
Cin EML	2	5	36		115
Cin EML	2	6	3		112, 931
Cin EML	2	6	6		1012
Cin EML	2	6	7		759, 1636
Cin EML	2	6	8		1035
Cin EML	2	6	10		654
Cin EML	2	6	17		1328
Cin EML	2	6	18		1313, 1371
Cin EML	2	6	19		680
Cin EML	2	6	20		677
Cin EML	2	6	21		1313, 1582
Cin EML	2	6	25		115, 931
Cin EML	2	6	26		1625
Cin EML	2	6	28		50
Cin EML	2	6	29		76, 359, 532
Cin EML	2	6	30		40, 42, 48, 372, 535, 953
Cin EML	2	6	31		532, 677, 1783
Cin EML	2	6	32		532
Cin EML	2	6	34		21
Cin EML	2	6	35		187, 1012, 1783
Cin EML	2	6	36		224, 638, 953
Cin EML	2	7	1		953, 1478
Cin EML	2	7	2		6, 50, 1073
Cin EML	2	7	3		56
Cin EML	2	7	4		942, 1110
Cin EML	2	7	5		1161, 1749
Cin EML	2	7	7		1073, 1530, 1710
Cin EML	2	7	9		532, 1667
Cin EML	2	7	10		50, 91
Cin EML	2	7	11		122, 180
Cin EML	2	7	12		135, 359, 931
Cin EML	2	7	13		1726
Cin EML	2	7	14		521, 1582
Cin EML	2	7	18		521, 532, 950, 1073
Cin EML	2	7	19		950
Cin EML	2	7	22		680
Cin EML	2	7	24		1478
Cin EML	2	7	25		654, 677
Cin EML	2	7	26		632
Cin EML	2	7	30		1012, 1478
Cin EML	2	7	31		1012
Cin EML	2	7	34		372, 654, 718
Cin EML	2	7	36		6, 115
Cin EML	2	8	1		1012
Cin EML	2	8	7		1478
Cin EML	2	8	8		1073
Cin EML	2	8	9		359
Cin EML	2	8	10		1029
Cin EML	2	8	11		1625
Cin EML	2	8	13		623
Cin EML	2	8	17		751, 1012
Cin EML	2	8	18		1073, 1313
Cin EML	2	8	19		1749
Cin EML	2	8	24		135, 521
Cin EML	2	8	26		153, 465, 829
Cin EML	2	8	27		1073
Cin EML	2	8	28		677
Cin EML	2	8	29		628, 639
Cin EML	2	8	30		829
Cin EML	2	8	32		609
Cin EML	2	8	33		212, 1012
Cin EML	2	8	34		56, 224, 532
Cin EML	2	8	35		465, 639, 1195
Cin EML	2	9	1		1783
Cin EML	2	9	12		1625
Cin EML	2	9	19		1041
Cin EML	2	9	25		1667
Cin EML	2	9	34		1041
Cin EML	2	9	35		1478
Cin EML	2	11	20		1419, 1710
Cin EML	2	11	22		153, 303
Cin EML	2	11	28		1313
Cin EML	2	12	1		356
Cin EML	2	12	26		1436, 1478
Cin EML	2	12	28		942

Cin EML	2	12	35	1012, 1478
Cin EML	2	12	36	607
Cin EML	3	2	7	829
Cin EML	3	2	11	634, 772, 829
Cin EML	3	2	17	153, 953
Cin EML	3	2	18	135, 532
Cin EML	3	3	2	1161, 1453
Cin EML	3	3	3	628
Cin EML	3	3	6	606, 1243
Cin EML	3	3	8	532, 722
Cin EML	3	3	10	1530
Cin EML	3	3	11	1530
Cin EML	3	3	12	261, 359, 1073
Cin EML	3	3	13	142
Cin EML	3	3	14	369
Cin EML	3	3	17	21, 1313
Cin EML	3	3	21	1073, 1328
Cin EML	3	3	23	76, 101, 751
Cin EML	3	3	24	1369
Cin EML	3	3	25	56
Cin EML	3	3	26	67, 532, 865
Cin EML	3	3	29	953
Cin EML	3	3	31	21
Cin EML	3	3	34	865
Cin EML	3	4	1	632, 1502
Cin EML	3	4	2	449, 1029
Cin EML	3	4	3	212, 865, 1561
Cin EML	3	4	4	135, 153
Cin EML	3	4	5	1035, 1328
Cin EML	3	4	8	632, 1701, 1779
Cin EML	3	4	9	659, 1387
Cin EML	3	4	10	1436
Cin EML	3	4	11	26, 1530
Cin EML	3	4	12	264, 600
Cin EML	3	4	13	1582
Cin EML	3	4	14	10, 350
Cin EML	3	4	17	153, 751, 942
Cin EML	3	4	18	1012
Cin EML	3	4	23	234
Cin EML	3	4	25	457, 1530
Cin EML	3	4	27	1029
Cin EML	3	4	28	1251
Cin EML	3	4	30	718, 953, 1073, 1313
Cin EML	3	4	32	76
Cin EML	3	4	33	628
Cin EML	3	4	34	606
Cin EML	3	4	35	1478
Cin EML	3	4	36	1073
Cin EML	3	5	1	475, 1405, 1478, 1625
Cin EML	3	5	4	350, 1530
Cin EML	3	5	5	942
Cin EML	3	5	7	350, 465, 931
Cin EML	3	5	8	433, 1313
Cin EML	3	5	9	459
Cin EML	3	5	11	1243
Cin EML	3	5	12	1582, 1636
Cin EML	3	5	13	722
Cin EML	3	5	14	532
Cin EML	3	5	15	108
Cin EML	3	5	17	714, 892, 953, 1667
Cin EML	3	5	19	182, 718
Cin EML	3	5	20	677, 1012
Cin EML	3	5	21	1195
Cin EML	3	5	23	6, 465, 710
Cin EML	3	5	24	632
Cin EML	3	5	25	532, 1012
Cin EML	3	5	26	1012, 1625
Cin EML	3	5	27	950
Cin EML	3	5	28	101, 459
Cin EML	3	5	29	115, 950
Cin EML	3	5	30	1195
Cin EML	3	5	31	1073
Cin EML	3	5	32	101, 632
Cin EML	3	5	33	6, 459, 632
Cin EML	3	5	34	632
Cin EML	3	5	36	386, 628
Cin EML	3	6	4	659, 865, 1161
Cin EML	3	6	5	628, 1783
Cin EML	3	6	6	492, 632
Cin EML	3	6	7	1035
Cin EML	3	6	8	1073, 1783
Cin EML	3	6	13	1012
Cin EML	3	6	15	1313, 1332, 1478
Cin EML	3	6	17	532, 1012
Cin EML	3	6	18	1158
Cin EML	3	6	20	135
Cin EML	3	6	21	1749
Cin EML	3	6	22	1195
Cin EML	3	6	23	1029
Cin EML	3	6	24	153
Cin EML	3	6	29	153, 187
Cin EML	3	6	30	532, 1029
Cin EML	3	6	31	135
Cin EML	3	6	32	350, 485, 1313
Cin EML	3	6	33	224
Cin EML	3	6	34	76
Cin EML	3	6	36	465, 931
Cin EML	3	7	3	1530

Cin EML	3	7	7	1530	Cin EML	4	3	27	21, 142, 1478
Cin EML	3	7	10	1783	Cin EML	4	3	28	1195, 1726
Cin EML	3	7	11	1371, 1726	Cin EML	4	3	30	606
Cin EML	3	7	12	135, 475, 953	Cin EML	4	3	31	6
Cin EML	3	7	15	1371	Cin EML	4	3	32	115, 1582
Cin EML	3	7	18	1530	Cin EML	4	3	33	521
Cin EML	3	7	19	865, 1530	Cin EML	4	3	35	153, 359, 942, 1313
Cin EML	3	7	20	224, 752, 1195, 1508, 1625	Cin EML	4	3	36	457, 1313, 1625
Cin EML	3	7	21	1251, 1561	Cin EML	4	4	1	459, 1029
Cin EML	3	7	22	564, 1241, 1288, 1372	Cin EML	4	4	2	1012
Cin EML	3	7	23	1156, 1195	Cin EML	4	4	6	628, 1073
Cin EML	3	7	26	564, 677, 1241, 1288	Cin EML	4	4	7	532
Cin EML	3	7	27	115	Cin EML	4	4	9	1667
Cin EML	3	7	28	212, 931	Cin EML	4	4	10	21, 1012, 1029, 1073
Cin EML	3	7	29	135	Cin EML	4	4	11	1029, 1195, 1779
Cin EML	3	7	31	1313	Cin EML	4	4	12	680, 1029
Cin EML	3	7	32	1029	Cin EML	4	4	13	495, 1401
Cin EML	3	7	33	130, 153, 931	Cin EML	4	4	14	1012, 1029
Cin EML	3	7	34	142	Cin EML	4	4	15	1783
Cin EML	3	7	35	1636	Cin EML	4	4	17	532, 1073
Cin EML	3	8	28	1710	Cin EML	4	4	18	722, 1625, 1636
Cin EML	4	1	7	1625	Cin EML	4	4	19	942, 953
Cin EML	4	2	4	865, 1073	Cin EML	4	4	20	722, 950
Cin EML	4	2	5	953, 1073	Cin EML	4	4	23	26
Cin EML	4	2	8	357, 1110	Cin EML	4	4	24	50, 142, 1029
Cin EML	4	2	9	628, 1783	Cin EML	4	4	25	350, 654, 677
Cin EML	4	2	10	535, 751	Cin EML	4	4	29	56, 1073, 1401, 1502
Cin EML	4	2	11	21	Cin EML	4	4	30	329, 1636
Cin EML	4	2	15	21	Cin EML	4	4	31	10, 654, 677, 1636
Cin EML	4	2	16	21	Cin EML	4	4	34	50, 304, 865
Cin EML	4	2	20	865	Cin EML	4	4	35	953
Cin EML	4	2	31	56	Cin EML	4	5	1	101, 1478
Cin EML	4	2	32	56	Cin EML	4	5	2	521, 1530
Cin EML	4	2	33	56	Cin EML	4	5	4	1779
Cin EML	4	3	2	350	Cin EML	4	5	5	1268
Cin EML	4	3	3	6, 1195	Cin EML	4	5	10	1779
Cin EML	4	3	4	731, 1073	Cin EML	4	5	11	1243, 1371
Cin EML	4	3	5	115, 1313	Cin EML	4	5	12	67, 367, 532
Cin EML	4	3	6	769, 942	Cin EML	4	5	13	135
Cin EML	4	3	7	953	Cin EML	4	5	23	1667
Cin EML	4	3	8	10, 21	Cin EML	4	5	24	628, 1783
Cin EML	4	3	10	357, 1012, 1325	Cin EML	4	5	25	10, 1073
Cin EML	4	3	12	950	Cin EML	4	5	26	723, 1783
Cin EML	4	3	14	372, 628	Cin EML	4	5	27	182
Cin EML	4	3	18	532	Cin EML	4	5	29	1779
Cin EML	4	3	19	448, 532	Cin EML	4	5	33	1029
Cin EML	4	3	23	329, 1502	Cin EML	4	5	34	1783
Cin EML	4	3	25	865	Cin EML	4	5	35	628, 710, 942, 1084
Cin EML	4	3	26	457, 535, 953	Cin EML	4	5	36	357, 632, 1073

Cin EML	4	6	7	1012
Cin EML	4	6	13	1313, 1701
Cin EML	4	6	14	623, 1073, 1313
Cin EML	4	6	18	1203
Cin EML	4	6	23	182, 1195, 1530
Cin EML	4	6	24	56, 953, 1073
Cin EML	4	6	25	1073
Cin EML	4	6	26	816, 942
Cin EML	4	6	27	1548
Cin EML	4	6	35	1478, 1530
Cin EML	4	6	36	1029, 1110
Cin EML	4	7	1	1243
Cin EML	4	7	2	372
Cin EML	4	7	3	1012
Cin EML	4	7	11	865
Cin EML	4	7	12	718
Cin EML	4	9	10	1779
Cin EML	4	9	12	722
Cin EML	4	9	23	751
Cin EML	4	9	24	475
Cin EML	4	9	26	359
Cin EML	4	9	30	903
Cin EML	4	9	33	195, 931
Cin EML	4	9	35	465
Cin EML	4	9	36	1012
Cin EML	4	17	18	953
Cin EML	5	2	7	544
Cin EML	5	2	8	1041, 1200
Cin EML	5	2	18	6
Cin EML	5	2	29	1667
Cin EML	5	2	30	1029
Cin EML	5	2	31	495, 1156, 1203
Cin EML	5	3	1	50
Cin EML	5	3	2	21
Cin EML	5	3	3	135
Cin EML	5	3	4	50
Cin EML	5	3	5	91
Cin EML	5	3	13	50
Cin EML	5	3	15	677, 942
Cin EML	5	3	18	1002
Cin EML	5	3	22	122, 291, 829, 955, 1530
Cin EML	5	3	23	579
Cin EML	5	3	24	579
Cin EML	5	3	30	6, 56, 377, 857
Cin EML	5	3	31	80
Cin EML	5	3	32	25
Cin EML	5	4	1	26, 91, 356, 532
Cin EML	5	4	2	931
Cin EML	5	4	3	10, 659, 1783

Cin EML	5	4	4	153, 654
Cin EML	5	4	6	722
Cin EML	5	4	7	722, 1012, 1653
Cin EML	5	4	8	1779
Cin EML	5	4	10	459, 1195, 1313, 1625
Cin EML	5	4	13	632, 723
Cin EML	5	4	15	1749
Cin EML	5	4	18	1073
Cin EML	5	4	19	187, 628
Cin EML	5	4	20	386, 1436
Cin EML	5	4	21	590, 751, 1073, 1203, 1710
Cin EML	5	4	22	751, 1073, 1478
Cin EML	5	4	26	135
Cin EML	5	4	29	731
Cin EML	5	4	30	606, 722
Cin EML	5	4	31	212, 931
Cin EML	5	4	32	76
Cin EML	5	4	35	329, 1156
Cin EML	5	4	36	931
Cin EML	5	5	1	359, 677, 1073
Cin EML	5	5	2	91, 372
Cin EML	5	5	4	356, 1371
Cin EML	5	5	7	1783
Cin EML	5	5	8	50, 632, 931
Cin EML	5	5	9	135, 865
Cin EML	5	5	10	448
Cin EML	5	5	11	953
Cin EML	5	5	12	751, 953, 1530
Cin EML	5	5	13	532
Cin EML	5	5	14	135, 953, 1243
Cin EML	5	5	15	1636, 1783
Cin EML	5	5	17	10, 465, 659, 723
Cin EML	5	5	19	56, 628
Cin EML	5	5	20	10, 680, 722
Cin EML	5	5	23	261, 677
Cin EML	5	5	24	420
Cin EML	5	5	25	10, 1369
Cin EML	5	5	26	950, 1313
Cin EML	5	5	27	731, 942, 1530
Cin EML	5	5	28	722, 1561
Cin EML	5	5	29	163, 532, 1073
Cin EML	5	5	30	521, 942, 1667
Cin EML	5	5	31	628
Cin EML	5	5	32	84
Cin EML	5	5	34	931, 942, 1161
Cin EML	5	5	35	10, 153, 182, 212, 1478
Cin EML	5	5	36	829
Cin EML	5	6	3	359, 367, 953
Cin EML	5	6	4	606, 680, 1073

Cin EML	5	6	5	261, 532, 659
Cin EML	5	6	6	359, 865, 931
Cin EML	5	6	7	278, 359, 535
Cin EML	5	6	8	356, 1073
Cin EML	5	6	9	680, 718
Cin EML	5	6	10	465, 485, 722
Cin EML	5	6	14	659, 953
Cin EML	5	6	18	953
Cin EML	5	6	19	182
Cin EML	5	6	21	1313, 1530
Cin EML	5	6	23	606, 1110
Cin EML	5	6	25	606, 751, 1073
Cin EML	5	6	26	942
Cin EML	5	6	27	532, 680
Cin EML	5	6	28	606
Cin EML	5	6	29	459, 931, 1029
Cin EML	5	6	30	659, 1548
Cin EML	5	6	31	1060
Cin EML	5	6	32	153, 942
Cin EML	5	6	34	1405, 1710
Cin EML	5	6	35	532, 632, 680
Cin EML	5	6	36	372, 532, 680
Cin EML	5	7	1	1012
Cin EML	5	7	5	521
Cin EML	5	7	6	196, 722
Cin EML	5	7	7	50, 357, 1667
Cin EML	5	7	12	76
Cin EML	5	7	17	931
Cin EML	5	7	18	931
Cin EML	5	7	20	298, 1625
Cin EML	5	7	28	710, 942
Cin EML	5	7	29	135, 953, 1012
Cin EML	5	7	30	829, 1012, 1195
Cin EML	5	7	31	135, 865, 1012
Cin EML	5	7	32	26, 359
Cin EML	5	7	33	21, 1073
Cin EML	5	7	34	931
Cin EML	5	8	1	532
Cin EML	5	8	2	1530
Cin EML	5	8	3	1783
Cin EML	5	8	7	1783
Cin EML	5	8	11	425
Cin EML	5	8	12	10, 425
Cin EML	5	8	13	10, 1530, 1636
Cin EML	5	8	18	680
Cin EML	5	8	19	76, 532, 942
Cin EML	5	8	20	459
Cin EML	5	8	24	359, 677
Cin EML	5	8	25	677
Cin EML	5	8	29	1029
Cin EML	5	8	30	1012, 1073, 1530
Cin EML	5	8	31	359, 865
Cin EML	5	8	38	1397
Cin EML	5	9	2	751
Cin EML	5	9	3	677
Cin EML	5	9	24	1582
Cin EML	5	9	34	1073
Cin EML	5	9	35	942, 1582
Cin EML	5	11	6	532
Cin EML	6	1	3	1096
Cin EML	6	1	4	1096
Cin EML	6	1	5	1096
Cin EML	6	1	6	6, 1096
Cin EML	6	1	9	1096
Cin EML	6	1	10	1096
Cin EML	6	1	17	50
Cin EML	6	1	18	50
Cin EML	6	1	19	579
Cin EML	6	1	20	579
Cin EML	6	1	29	579
Cin EML	6	1	30	579
Cin EML	6	2	1	50
Cin EML	6	2	3	357, 372, 1110, 1582
Cin EML	6	2	4	751, 953, 1436
Cin EML	6	2	6	26, 76, 532
Cin EML	6	2	8	532, 829
Cin EML	6	2	9	953
Cin EML	6	2	10	942, 1195
Cin EML	6	2	17	628, 659, 950
Cin EML	6	2	18	931
Cin EML	6	2	20	368
Cin EML	6	2	21	368
Cin EML	6	2	22	368
Cin EML	6	2	31	1371
Cin EML	6	3	3	1029, 1369, 1530
Cin EML	6	3	4	1591
Cin EML	6	3	7	1195
Cin EML	6	3	10	942
Cin EML	6	3	13	1073
Cin EML	6	3	14	1073
Cin EML	6	3	18	356
Cin EML	6	3	19	372, 829, 1371
Cin EML	6	3	23	457, 1530
Cin EML	6	3	24	1530
Cin EML	6	3	27	367
Cin EML	6	3	28	1073
Cin EML	6	3	29	1073, 1313
Cin EML	6	3	30	67, 261, 350, 532

Cin EML	6	3	32	532, 1369
Cin EML	6	3	33	1073, 1749
Cin EML	6	3	34	1073
Cin EML	6	4	3	115, 1290
Cin EML	6	4	4	677, 953, 1313
Cin EML	6	4	5	101, 234, 359, 829
Cin EML	6	4	6	1012, 1161
Cin EML	6	4	8	261, 829
Cin EML	6	4	9	628, 865
Cin EML	6	4	10	153
Cin EML	6	4	11	135
Cin EML	6	4	14	135
Cin EML	6	4	17	153, 865, 1203
Cin EML	6	4	19	1478
Cin EML	6	4	20	115, 135, 359, 628
Cin EML	6	4	22	1710
Cin EML	6	4	27	931, 1035
Cin EML	6	4	28	142, 1073, 1779
Cin EML	6	4	29	1478, 1591
Cin EML	6	4	30	153, 521, 639, 1710
Cin EML	6	4	31	942
Cin EML	6	4	32	1582
Cin EML	6	4	33	1195, 1371
Cin EML	6	4	34	1029
Cin EML	6	4	35	942
Cin EML	6	4	36	942
Cin EML	6	5	6	357
Cin EML	6	5	7	606
Cin EML	6	5	19	459, 532, 628
Cin EML	6	5	20	10, 931
Cin EML	6	5	21	357
Cin EML	6	5	22	357
Cin EML	6	5	28	135, 359, 639
Cin EML	6	5	29	632, 677, 1749
Cin EML	6	5	30	1073
Cin EML	6	5	31	710, 1313
Cin EML	6	5	32	359, 751, 1161
Cin EML	6	5	33	465, 1073, 1667
Cin EML	6	5	34	1203
Cin EML	6	6	17	359
Cin EML	6	6	19	1012
Cin EML	6	6	24	457
Cin EML	6	6	30	1073
Cin EML	6	6	31	224, 677, 1636
Cin EML	6	7	1	1161
Cin EML	6	7	5	1582
Cin EML	6	7	6	1012, 1636
Cin EML	6	7	7	357, 1478
Cin EML	6	7	10	532, 931
Cin EML	6	7	11	1029
Cin EML	6	7	14	751
Cin EML	6	7	15	751
Cin EML	6	7	17	942
Cin EML	6	7	18	1073, 1401
Cin EML	6	7	19	448, 1195
Cin EML	6	7	29	10, 677, 1073, 1195
Cin EML	6	7	30	632, 1313
Cin EML	6	8	24	1582
Cin EML	6	8	25	101, 751, 1779
Cin EML	6	8	29	1783
Cin EML	6	8	30	1313
Cin EML	6	8	31	942, 1502
Cin EML	6	8	32	1582
Cin EML	6	8	36	1073
Cin EML	6	21	27	553
Cin EML	6	21	28	553
Cin EML	6	21	29	553
Cin EML	7	1	19	1436
Cin EML	7	1	30	659
Cin EML	7	2	26	1304
Cin EML	8	1	12	1783
Cin EML	9	5	10	1371
Cin EML	11	1	30	50
Cin EML	12	12	36	801
Cin EML	12	15	24	1591
Cin EML	13	13	21	1453
Cin EML	16	17	32	771

Between the Miami Rivers

Cin MR	1	1	10	1461
Cin MR	1	2	8	1783
Cin MR	1	3	8	1436, 1625
Cin MR	1	3	11	545, 1243
Cin MR	1	3	26	1436, 1582
Cin MR	1	4	8	609, 632, 950, 1636
Cin MR	1	4	11	1478
Cin MR	1	4	26	927, 1195, 1313, 1779
Cin MR	1	5	26	1636
Cin MR	1	12	33	1084
Cin MR	1	14	36	546
Cin MR	2	1	8	1636, 1710
Cin MR	2	1	11	1582
Cin MR	2	1	26	1110
Cin MR	2	2	6	1002
Cin MR	2	2	8	1195, 1251, 1496, 1563
Cin MR	2	2	22	396
Cin MR	2	2	26	546, 1161, 1195
Cin MR	2	2	34	1405

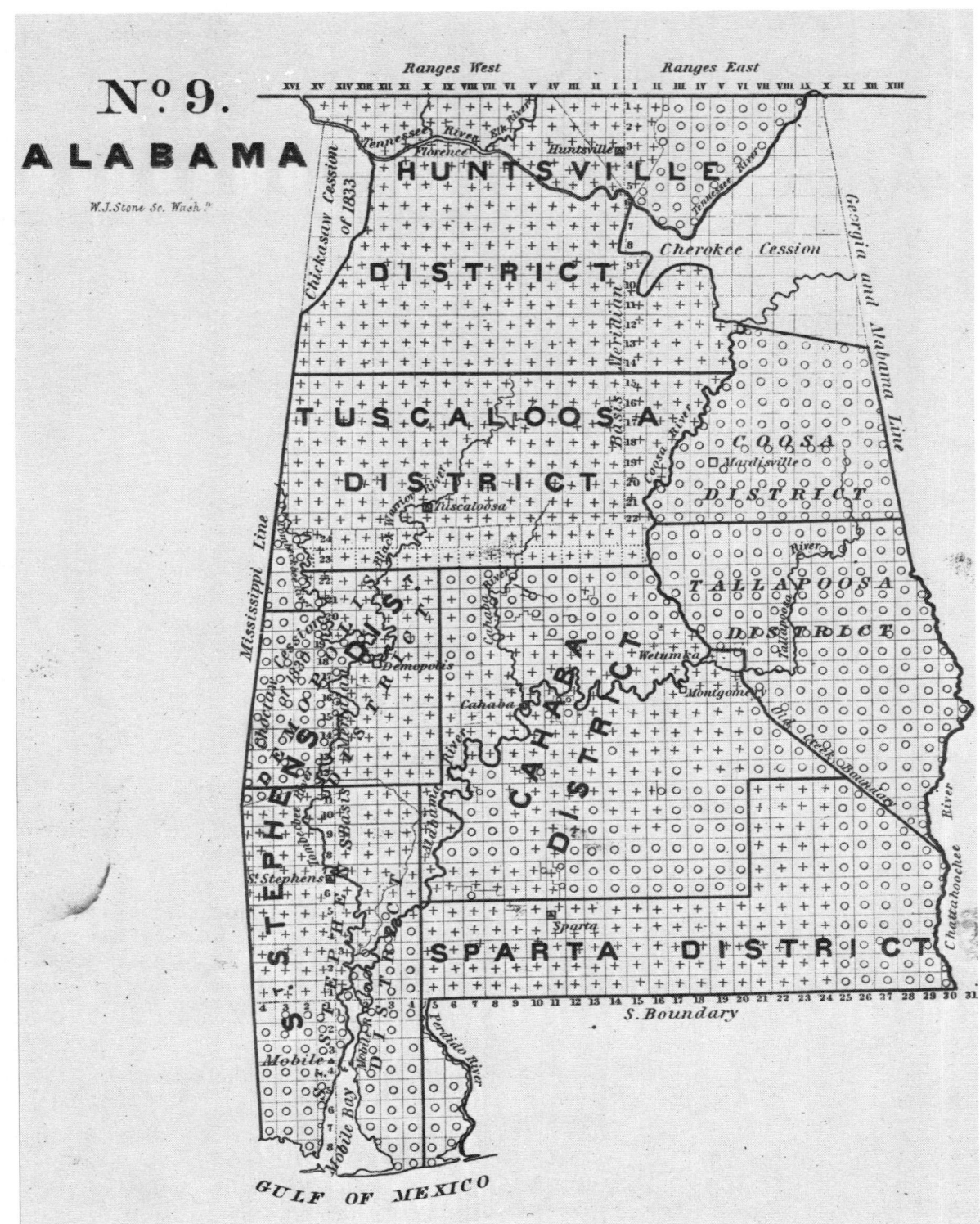

MAP 10. Tract map of Alabama showing land office districts

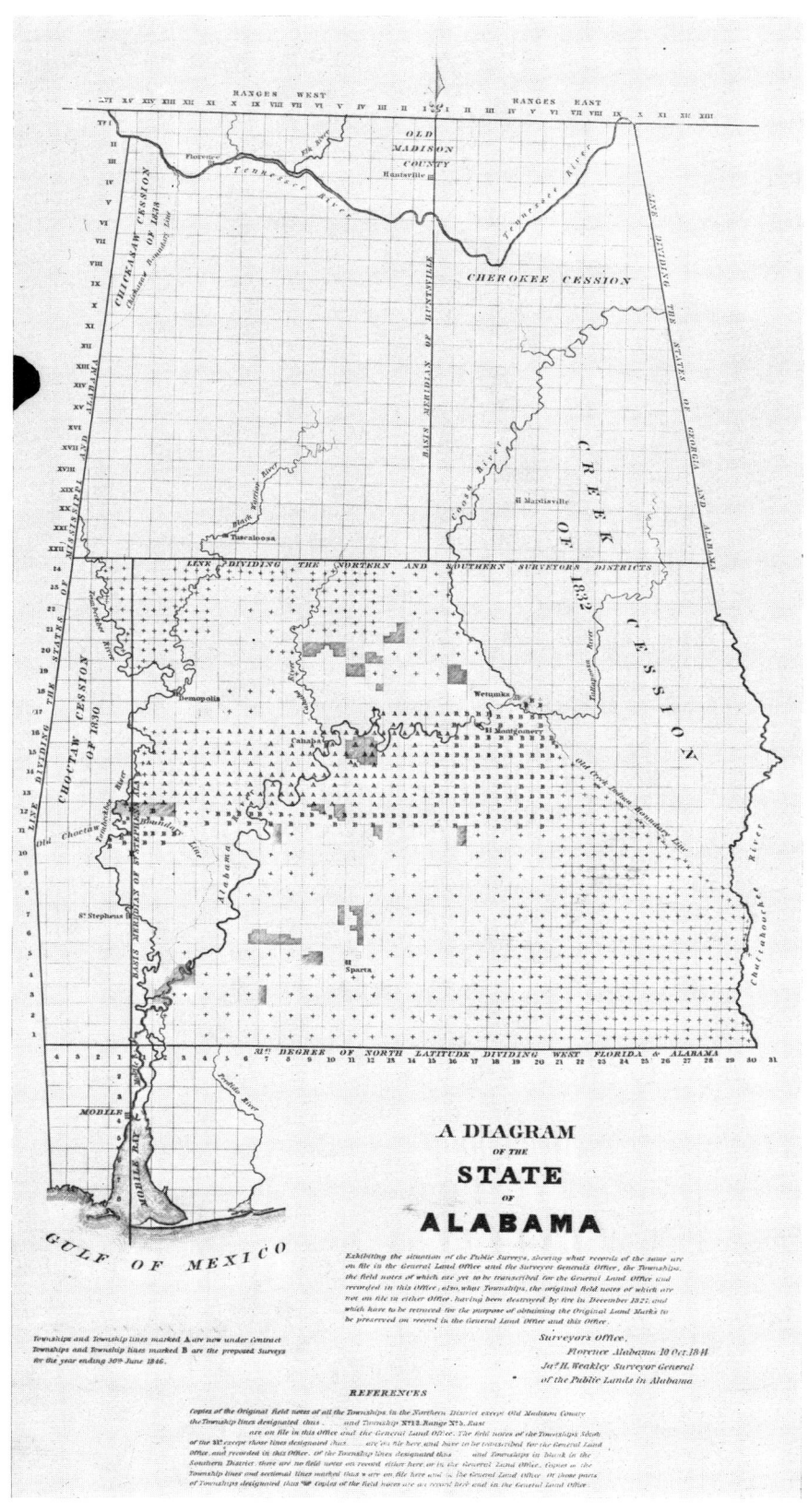

MAP 11. Tract map of Alabama showing range-township numbering system

[293]

Cin	MR	2	3	8	1195, 1530
Cin	MR	2	3	11	114
Cin	MR	2	3	26	1195
Cin	MR	2	4	8	1582
Cin	MR	2	4	22	1667
Cin	MR	2	4	26	1436, 1582
Cin	MR	2	5	5	459
Cin	MR	2	5	20	350
Cin	MR	2	7	26	459
Cin	MR	3	2	8	546, 1667
Cin	MR	3	2	21	1416
Cin	MR	3	2	26	1031, 1195, 1582
Cin	MR	3	3	8	433, 1243, 1436
Cin	MR	3	3	11	433, 1195, 1243
Cin	MR	3	3	26	1301, 1346, 1581
Cin	MR	3	4	11	448, 1195
Cin	MR	4	2	11	142, 1478
Cin	MR	4	2	12	6
Cin	MR	4	2	26	329, 998, 1416, 1502
Cin	MR	4	2	29	632
Cin	MR	4	3	8	903
Cin	MR	4	3	11	6, 1313
Cin	MR	4	3	13	784
Cin	MR	4	3	25	1401, 1502
Cin	MR	4	3	29	56, 114, 1416, 1502
Cin	MR	4	3	31	142
Cin	MR	4	4	26	56, 114, 497, 950
Cin	MR	4	4	29	10, 142
Cin	MR	5	1	7	142
Cin	MR	5	2	8	1636
Cin	MR	5	2	11	101, 1084
Cin	MR	5	2	20	759
Cin	MR	5	2	22	1002
Cin	MR	5	2	26	6, 546, 998
Cin	MR	5	2	28	1168
Cin	MR	5	2	30	114, 457, 1401
Cin	MR	5	3	8	6
Cin	MR	5	3	11	114, 356, 1561, 1625
Cin	MR	5	3	26	470, 950, 1779
Cin	MR	5	3	29	606, 950, 1002
Cin	MR	5	4	29	597
Cin	MR	5	4	30	470
Cin	MR	5	8	29	459
Cin	MR	6	1	2	459
Cin	MR	6	1	8	1625
Cin	MR	6	1	11	1084, 1636
Cin	MR	6	1	12	1084
Cin	MR	6	1	14	1783
Cin	MR	6	1	19	449
Cin	MR	6	1	20	950
Cin	MR	6	1	26	1530
Cin	MR	6	2	1	1478
Cin	MR	6	2	2	950
Cin	MR	6	2	8	114, 130, 448
Cin	MR	6	2	11	142, 411, 805, 852, 998
Cin	MR	6	2	18	459
Cin	MR	6	2	22	656, 658
Cin	MR	6	2	23	1335, 1397
Cin	MR	6	2	26	114, 903
Cin	MR	6	2	28	242
Cin	MR	6	2	29	411, 794, 1436
Cin	MR	6	3	26	623, 1392
Cin	MR	6	3	29	448
Cin	MR	6	3	32	623, 1392
Cin	MR	7	1	5	1779
Cin	MR	7	1	12	1487
Cin	MR	7	2	2	386
Cin	MR	7	2	3	1416
Cin	MR	7	2	11	21, 316, 1401, 1502
Cin	MR	7	2	18	1073
Cin	MR	7	2	19	1779
Cin	MR	7	2	26	707, 903, 1416, 1478
Cin	MR	7	2	29	448, 950
Cin	MR	7	3	6	1359
Cin	MR	7	3	9	10, 659, 1111
Cin	MR	7	3	10	1161
Cin	MR	7	3	11	545, 950, 1478
Cin	MR	7	3	12	659, 1636, 1726, 1779
Cin	MR	7	3	17	142
Cin	MR	7	3	29	1350, 1397, 1502, 1667
Cin	MR	7	3	36	803
Cin	MR	7	4	24	89, 998
Cin	MR	7	4	29	56
Cin	MR	7	4	35	1419, 1530
Cin	MR	7	4	36	1478, 1636
Cin	MR	8	1	4	1710
Cin	MR	8	2	6	546, 998
Cin	MR	8	2	8	329, 1313
Cin	MR	8	2	9	1487
Cin	MR	8	2	11	1313
Cin	MR	8	2	12	556
Cin	MR	8	2	15	1341
Cin	MR	8	2	17	556
Cin	MR	8	2	18	998
Cin	MR	8	2	21	659, 1749
Cin	MR	8	2	23	546, 950, 1031
Cin	MR	8	2	24	546, 950, 1591
Cin	MR	8	2	26	291, 545, 546, 950

Cin	MR	8	2	27	904
Cin	MR	8	2	29	1487
Cin	MR	8	2	30	470, 553, 794
Cin	MR	8	2	36	998
Cin	MR	8	3	2	475, 1002, 1031
Cin	MR	8	3	5	1478
Cin	MR	8	3	8	1783
Cin	MR	8	3	10	759, 1749, 1779
Cin	MR	8	3	12	632
Cin	MR	8	3	15	1371
Cin	MR	8	3	17	1707
Cin	MR	8	3	23	961, 998
Cin	MR	8	3	30	1371
Cin	MR	8	3	31	998
Cin	MR	8	3	33	950
Cin	MR	8	3	34	1419, 1530
Cin	MR	8	4	8	623, 998, 1328, 1371
Cin	MR	8	4	24	1328, 1369
Cin	MR	8	4	26	459, 492, 497
Cin	MR	8	4	29	1667
Cin	MR	8	5	6	545, 1701
Cin	MR	8	5	12	1243
Cin	MR	8	5	15	556
Cin	MR	8	5	17	1726
Cin	MR	8	5	18	448, 632, 1002
Cin	MR	8	5	23	950, 998
Cin	MR	8	5	24	1530
Cin	MR	8	5	27	356, 1110, 1726
Cin	MR	8	5	28	961
Cin	MR	8	5	30	1313
Cin	MR	8	5	33	1359
Cin	MR	8	5	35	659
Cin	MR	8	6	5	142
Cin	MR	8	6	12	1195
Cin	MR	8	6	17	1667
Cin	MR	8	6	35	903
Cin	MR	8	6	36	623, 1313
Cin	MR	9	1	1	1530
Cin	MR	9	2	7	546, 632
Cin	MR	9	2	9	1243
Cin	MR	9	2	13	316, 448, 998
Cin	MR	9	2	15	903, 1195
Cin	MR	9	2	18	546
Cin	MR	9	2	19	497
Cin	MR	9	2	21	950, 1487
Cin	MR	9	2	22	122, 205, 1701
Cin	MR	9	2	25	91, 470, 632, 659
Cin	MR	9	2	27	903, 927
Cin	MR	9	2	28	497, 521, 1667
Cin	MR	9	2	31	961
Cin	MR	9	2	32	903, 1084, 1195
Cin	MR	9	2	34	1478
Cin	MR	9	3	5	535
Cin	MR	9	3	7	1749
Cin	MR	9	3	8	149, 546, 903
Cin	MR	9	3	9	998
Cin	MR	9	3	10	632, 1636
Cin	MR	9	3	12	659, 1002
Cin	MR	9	3	17	1328, 1405, 1487
Cin	MR	9	3	27	903
Cin	MR	9	3	28	1530
Cin	MR	9	3	29	448
Cin	MR	9	3	30	998
Cin	MR	9	3	33	927
Cin	MR	9	4	4	356
Cin	MR	9	4	5	1436
Cin	MR	9	4	7	1653
Cin	MR	9	4	9	1359
Cin	MR	9	4	15	1359
Cin	MR	9	4	17	950
Cin	MR	9	4	18	546, 751, 1636
Cin	MR	9	4	21	1405
Cin	MR	9	4	22	1371, 1436
Cin	MR	9	4	23	470
Cin	MR	9	4	24	556, 609, 1582, 1636
Cin	MR	9	4	30	950
Cin	MR	9	4	32	1625
Cin	MR	9	4	34	663, 903
Cin	MR	9	4	35	316, 1401
Cin	MR	9	5	2	1582
Cin	MR	9	5	3	1548
Cin	MR	9	5	4	927, 1369
Cin	MR	9	5	6	1031
Cin	MR	9	5	9	950
Cin	MR	9	5	10	659
Cin	MR	9	5	13	21, 1436
Cin	MR	9	5	14	1313, 1369
Cin	MR	9	5	15	950
Cin	MR	9	5	19	497, 1749
Cin	MR	9	5	20	1195
Cin	MR	9	5	21	1110
Cin	MR	9	5	27	1002, 1749
Cin	MR	9	6	1	998, 1002
Cin	MR	9	6	2	659, 950, 998, 1002
Cin	MR	9	6	5	1195
Cin	MR	9	6	6	1195
Cin	MR	9	6	7	1002
Cin	MR	9	6	10	546

Cin	MR	9	6	12	1625
Cin	MR	9	6	13	1478
Cin	MR	9	6	17	114
Cin	MR	9	6	18	1478
Cin	MR	9	6	19	751
Cin	MR	9	6	20	1195
Cin	MR	9	6	21	545, 1031
Cin	MR	9	6	23	142, 659
Cin	MR	9	6	24	659, 1195
Cin	MR	9	6	30	903, 927, 1002
Cin	MR	9	6	33	632, 1701
Cin	MR	9	6	35	1436, 1548
Cin	MR	9	6	36	1582
Cin	MR	9	7	32	998
Cin	MR	10	1	1	1436
Cin	MR	10	1	6	1002
Cin	MR	10	1	7	1436
Cin	MR	10	1	8	386, 1667
Cin	MR	10	2	3	1313
Cin	MR	10	2	5	1359
Cin	MR	10	2	10	433, 950
Cin	MR	10	2	15	1359
Cin	MR	10	2	17	632
Cin	MR	10	2	18	1726
Cin	MR	10	2	23	546
Cin	MR	10	2	24	751, 1726
Cin	MR	10	2	33	356, 961
Cin	MR	10	2	36	1371
Cin	MR	10	3	1	545, 759, 1582
Cin	MR	10	3	4	1436
Cin	MR	10	3	7	1073
Cin	MR	10	3	13	1084
Cin	MR	10	3	19	553, 632
Cin	MR	10	3	21	1502, 1625
Cin	MR	10	3	22	1530
Cin	MR	10	3	23	1530
Cin	MR	10	3	25	470, 556
Cin	MR	10	3	27	1726
Cin	MR	10	3	31	1401, 1502
Cin	MR	10	3	32	1478, 1625
Cin	MR	10	3	35	1726
Cin	MR	10	3	36	142, 449, 1636
Cin	MR	10	4	2	903
Cin	MR	10	4	8	6, 609
Cin	MR	10	4	12	101
Cin	MR	10	4	15	89, 998
Cin	MR	10	4	18	1779
Cin	MR	10	4	20	1002
Cin	MR	10	4	22	632
Cin	MR	10	4	23	632
Cin	MR	10	4	25	659
Cin	MR	10	4	29	632, 1195
Cin	MR	10	4	30	372
Cin	MR	10	4	32	1371
Cin	MR	10	4	36	433, 545
Cin	MR	10	5	1	546, 998, 1436, 1530
Cin	MR	10	5	2	545, 1369
Cin	MR	10	5	3	122, 369, 927
Cin	MR	10	5	4	623, 1401
Cin	MR	10	5	5	950
Cin	MR	10	5	6	1203, 1478, 1710
Cin	MR	10	5	9	450, 818, 1139, 1313
Cin	MR	10	5	10	609
Cin	MR	10	5	17	450, 818, 878, 1749
Cin	MR	10	5	18	1625
Cin	MR	10	5	23	950, 1783
Cin	MR	10	5	24	1478
Cin	MR	10	5	25	950
Cin	MR	10	5	26	546
Cin	MR	10	5	31	1625
Cin	MR	10	5	32	927
Cin	MR	10	6	9	1710
Cin	MR	10	6	13	1371
Cin	MR	10	6	14	492
Cin	MR	10	6	15	1710
Cin	MR	10	6	19	998, 1371
Cin	MR	10	6	21	1625
Cin	MR	10	6	23	759, 1783
Cin	MR	10	6	25	950, 998
Cin	MR	10	6	31	459, 470, 1002, 1582
Cin	MR	10	6	32	1031, 1313
Cin	MR	10	6	33	1031, 1073
Cin	MR	11	1	2	142, 632
Cin	MR	11	1	3	998
Cin	MR	11	1	4	449, 950
Cin	MR	11	1	7	1203
Cin	MR	11	1	12	356, 1502
Cin	MR	11	1	15	1530, 1582
Cin	MR	11	1	22	212, 1195
Cin	MR	11	1	23	903, 927, 950
Cin	MR	11	1	24	1726
Cin	MR	11	1	26	1195
Cin	MR	11	1	29	1783
Cin	MR	11	1	36	1073
Cin	MR	11	2	1	998
Cin	MR	11	2	2	998
Cin	MR	11	2	9	420, 998, 1002
Cin	MR	11	2	12	1/83

Cin	MR	11	2	13	903, 998
Cin	MR	11	2	14	1436, 1530
Cin	MR	11	2	17	1478
Cin	MR	11	2	18	1783
Cin	MR	11	2	19	448, 903
Cin	MR	11	2	21	1436
Cin	MR	11	2	23	1667
Cin	MR	11	2	24	553, 1783
Cin	MR	11	2	26	1783
Cin	MR	11	2	28	492, 1478
Cin	MR	11	2	30	546
Cin	MR	11	2	34	1478
Cin	MR	11	2	35	212
Cin	MR	11	2	36	6, 448, 470
Cin	MR	11	3	2	801, 1487
Cin	MR	11	3	3	659
Cin	MR	11	3	5	1667
Cin	MR	11	3	9	1667
Cin	MR	11	3	17	1390
Cin	MR	11	3	28	142
Cin	MR	11	3	31	1478, 1582, 1591
Cin	MR	11	3	32	998, 1636, 1726
Cin	MR	11	3	35	1436
Cin	MR	11	4	2	1031
Cin	MR	11	4	4	1369
Cin	MR	11	4	5	1313, 1636
Cin	MR	11	4	11	1203, 1710, 1783
Cin	MR	11	4	14	1371
Cin	MR	11	4	15	433, 1478
Cin	MR	11	4	17	546, 746, 1032
Cin	MR	11	4	20	950
Cin	MR	11	4	21	953
Cin	MR	11	4	22	1002
Cin	MR	11	4	24	1530
Cin	MR	11	4	25	356, 1625
Cin	MR	11	4	29	1002
Cin	MR	11	4	30	1416, 1478
Cin	MR	11	4	31	553, 556
Cin	MR	11	4	32	433, 1031
Cin	MR	11	4	33	465, 903
Cin	MR	11	4	34	1002
Cin	MR	11	5	1	950
Cin	MR	11	5	7	950, 1110, 1749
Cin	MR	11	5	10	950
Cin	MR	11	5	12	998, 1701
Cin	MR	11	5	14	998
Cin	MR	11	5	15	1478
Cin	MR	11	5	17	1002
Cin	MR	11	5	18	1110
Cin	MR	11	5	20	1371
Cin	MR	11	5	21	459
Cin	MR	11	5	26	746, 927, 1033, 1195
Cin	MR	11	5	28	1313
Cin	MR	11	5	29	659, 746, 1032, 1033, 1195
Cin	MR	11	5	32	1625
Cin	MR	11	5	33	356
Cin	MR	11	5	35	903
Cin	MR	11	5	36	746, 1033
Cin	MR	11	6	28	950
Cin	MR	11	6	32	1002
Cin	MR	11	6	34	546, 998
Cin	MR	11	6	35	369
Cin	MR	11	6	36	369
Cin	MR	12	1	1	1251, 1313, 1478
Cin	MR	12	1	5	101
Cin	MR	12	1	7	1419
Cin	MR	12	1	12	1530
Cin	MR	12	1	14	1436
Cin	MR	12	1	15	212, 609, 927
Cin	MR	12	1	17	1195
Cin	MR	12	1	20	350
Cin	MR	12	1	21	220, 903, 1031
Cin	MR	12	1	22	470, 1002
Cin	MR	12	1	23	435, 448
Cin	MR	12	1	26	1502, 1779
Cin	MR	12	1	27	425, 435
Cin	MR	12	1	28	1328
Cin	MR	12	1	29	470
Cin	MR	12	1	32	1150, 1371
Cin	MR	12	1	33	425
Cin	MR	12	2	6	659
Cin	MR	12	2	25	1726
Cin	MR	12	2	31	903
Cin	MR	12	3	1	546, 1195, 1313
Cin	MR	12	3	2	659, 903, 1328
Cin	MR	12	3	6	632, 927
Cin	MR	12	3	7	1783
Cin	MR	12	3	8	48, 86
Cin	MR	12	3	9	448, 950
Cin	MR	12	3	30	50
Cin	MR	12	4	1	1530
Cin	MR	12	4	8	545
Cin	MR	12	4	9	470
Cin	MR	12	4	10	545
Cin	MR	12	4	12	998
Cin	MR	12	4	14	212, 1582
Cin	MR	12	4	15	1369
Cin	MR	12	4	17	1405, 1710

Cin	MR	12	4	20	91
Cin	MR	12	4	21	196, 469
Cin	MR	12	4	22	1307, 1558
Cin	MR	12	4	23	1369
Cin	MR	12	4	24	546, 1112
Cin	MR	12	4	29	903
Cin	MR	12	4	30	50, 465, 1436
Cin	MR	12	4	31	101, 924
Cin	MR	12	4	35	1667
Cin	MR	12	4	36	212, 1371
Cin	MR	12	5	1	1369
Cin	MR	12	5	7	1243
Cin	MR	12	5	9	48, 83, 879
Cin	MR	12	5	10	127, 173, 182
Cin	MR	12	5	13	1002, 1313, 1436
Cin	MR	12	5	17	242, 903
Cin	MR	12	5	18	961
Cin	MR	12	5	19	998
Cin	MR	12	5	20	950, 998, 1262
Cin	MR	12	5	21	492
Cin	MR	12	5	22	1002
Cin	MR	12	5	23	1436
Cin	MR	12	5	24	1002
Cin	MR	12	5	25	1530
Cin	MR	12	5	27	950
Cin	MR	12	5	28	1084
Cin	MR	12	5	30	546, 927
Cin	MR	12	5	32	1195, 1436, 1636
Cin	MR	12	5	34	356, 1436
Cin	MR	13	1	4	1436
Cin	MR	13	1	9	1478
Cin	MR	13	1	10	1478
Cin	MR	13	2	7	1582
Cin	MR	13	2	14	546
Cin	MR	13	2	20	1161
Cin	MR	13	2	27	1436
Cin	MR	13	2	28	1436
Cin	MR	13	2	34	1478
Cin	MR	13	3	3	903, 1161
Cin	MR	13	3	5	465
Cin	MR	13	3	9	1112
Cin	MR	13	3	14	1726
Cin	MR	13	3	15	998
Cin	MR	13	4	4	1371, 1749
Cin	MR	13	4	7	556
Cin	MR	13	4	13	1002
Cin	MR	13	4	17	1667
Cin	MR	13	4	19	1371, 1582, 1667
Cin	MR	13	4	20	1371
Cin	MR	13	4	23	1002
Cin	MR	13	4	25	470, 1031, 1436
Cin	MR	13	4	32	998, 1436
Cin	MR	13	4	35	632
Cin	MR	13	5	13	1084
Cin	MR	13	5	22	961, 1710
Cin	MR	13	5	25	1636
Cin	MR	13	5	26	1313, 1405
Cin	MR	13	5	27	1387
Cin	MR	13	5	28	1582, 1667
Cin	MR	13	5	32	1478
Cin	MR	13	5	33	632, 961, 1478
Cin	MR	13	5	34	1002, 1161
Cin	MR	14	2	2	998
Cin	MR	14	2	4	228
Cin	MR	14	2	7	1726
Cin	MR	14	2	14	1328
Cin	MR	14	2	15	1328
Cin	MR	14	3	6	1013
Cin	MR	14	3	31	1436
Cin	MR	14	4	27	961
Cin	MR	14	4	28	961
Cin	MR	14	6	23	759

Claimed Under Right of Pre-emption

Cin	Pre	1	10	1	1667
Cin	Pre	1	11	13	1133
Cin	Pre	2	1	26	1328
Cin	Pre	3	2	26	1266
Cin	Pre	4	1	–	1371
Cin	Pre	4	1	2	1371
Cin	Pre	4	2	–	1371
Cin	Pre	4	2	1	1548
Cin	Pre	4	2	4	1392
Cin	Pre	4	2	5	1392
Cin	Pre	4	2	6	923
Cin	Pre	4	2	7	1161, 1265
Cin	Pre	4	2	9	949, 1328
Cin	Pre	4	2	10	1785
Cin	Pre	4	2	12	1785
Cin	Pre	4	2	13	1481
Cin	Pre	4	2	15	992
Cin	Pre	4	2	17	1039
Cin	Pre	4	2	18	1243, 1328
Cin	Pre	4	2	22	628, 935
Cin	Pre	4	2	25	949
Cin	Pre	4	2	27	992
Cin	Pre	4	2	28	671, 992
Cin	Pre	4	2	32	1371

Cin Pre	4	2	33	992	Cin Pre	5	2	6	992
Cin Pre	4	2	34	671	Cin Pre	5	2	10	628
Cin Pre	4	3	1	1481	Cin Pre	5	2	12	1265
Cin Pre	4	3	2	1251	Cin Pre	5	2	14	114, 935
Cin Pre	4	3	3	949	Cin Pre	5	2	15	949
Cin Pre	4	3	4	1265	Cin Pre	5	2	18	935
Cin Pre	4	3	5	288, 289	Cin Pre	5	2	20	628, 651
Cin Pre	4	3	6	935	Cin Pre	5	2	21	1328
Cin Pre	4	3	7	935, 1265, 1667	Cin Pre	5	2	22	654, 1785
Cin Pre	4	3	9	107	Cin Pre	5	2	23	992
Cin Pre	4	3	10	1350, 1392	Cin Pre	5	2	25	616, 671, 1401, 1667
Cin Pre	4	3	12	654, 1304, 1371	Cin Pre	5	2	27	1265, 1401, 1481
Cin Pre	4	3	14	949, 1251	Cin Pre	5	2	28	992, 1328, 1481
Cin Pre	4	3	15	628, 1785	Cin Pre	5	2	34	1328, 1481
Cin Pre	4	3	17	992, 1168	Cin Pre	5	3	1	671
Cin Pre	4	3	19	1243	Cin Pre	5	3	2	1436
Cin Pre	4	3	20	935, 1487	Cin Pre	5	3	3	949, 1436, 1481
Cin Pre	4	3	21	992	Cin Pre	5	3	4	667, 1401
Cin Pre	4	3	22	1328	Cin Pre	5	3	5	628
Cin Pre	4	3	24	992, 1304	Cin Pre	5	3	7	1487
Cin Pre	4	3	25	923, 1487	Cin Pre	5	3	9	677, 1133
Cin Pre	4	3	27	288	Cin Pre	5	3	10	606, 949
Cin Pre	4	3	28	949, 1785	Cin Pre	5	3	12	289, 1241, 1328
Cin Pre	4	3	31	923, 949, 1328	Cin Pre	5	3	13	56
Cin Pre	4	3	32	992, 1133	Cin Pre	5	3	14	511, 906, 992, 1268, 1667
Cin Pre	4	3	33	992, 1392	Cin Pre	5	3	15	677, 992, 1667
Cin Pre	4	3	34	1481	Cin Pre	5	3	17	613
Cin Pre	4	3	35	1029, 1392	Cin Pre	5	3	18	1133, 1251, 1265
Cin Pre	4	3	36	1161	Cin Pre	5	3	19	324, 428, 629, 663, 992, 1481
Cin Pre	4	4	6	1164	Cin Pre	5	3	20	1133
Cin Pre	4	4	7	992	Cin Pre	5	3	21	949, 992
Cin Pre	4	4	9	923	Cin Pre	5	3	22	1481
Cin Pre	4	4	12	1328	Cin Pre	5	3	23	1328
Cin Pre	4	4	13	288, 545	Cin Pre	5	3	24	949
Cin Pre	4	4	14	289, 935	Cin Pre	5	3	25	949, 1243, 1328
Cin Pre	4	4	15	992	Cin Pre	5	3	27	992
Cin Pre	4	4	19	1133	Cin Pre	5	3	28	1133
Cin Pre	4	4	21	1328, 1371	Cin Pre	5	3	30	386, 1200, 1487, 1785
Cin Pre	4	4	22	316, 992, 1243, 1371	Cin Pre	5	3	31	671
Cin Pre	4	4	23	1436	Cin Pre	5	3	33	475, 949, 1243
Cin Pre	4	4	24	1243, 1265, 1762	Cin Pre	5	3	34	949
Cin Pre	4	4	28	1328, 1371	Cin Pre	5	3	35	613
Cin Pre	4	4	34	1328	Cin Pre	5	3	36	626
Cin Pre	4	4	36	949	Cin Pre	5	4	17	626
Cin Pre	5	2	1	935	Cin Pre	5	4	18	1328
Cin Pre	5	2	2	992, 1667, 1757	Cin Pre	5	4	20	1392
Cin Pre	5	2	3	949	Cin Pre	5	4	21	949
Cin Pre	5	2	4	949	Cin Pre	5	4	23	626
Cin Pre	5	2	5	992, 1392	Cin Pre	5	4	24	1328

Cin Pre	5	4	28	671, 1265, 1481	Cin Pre	6	3	31	628, 949, 1487
Cin Pre	5	4	30	1243, 1436	Cin Pre	6	3	34	794
Cin Pre	5	4	32	1328	Cin Pre	6	3	35	628
Cin Pre	5	4	33	992, 1243	Cin Pre	6	3	36	628
Cin Pre	5	4	34	386, 606, 949, 1548	Cin Pre	6	9	1	1667
Cin Pre	5	4	36	935, 1371	Cin Pre	7	1	1	992
Cin Pre	6	1	2	1371	Cin Pre	7	1	2	1359
Cin Pre	6	1	3	1757	Cin Pre	7	1	3	1548
Cin Pre	6	1	4	433, 992	Cin Pre	7	1	4	873, 1251
Cin Pre	6	1	7	386, 1392	Cin Pre	7	1	6	1251
Cin Pre	6	1	9	949, 1453	Cin Pre	7	1	7	992
Cin Pre	6	1	10	1453, 1757	Cin Pre	7	1	9	1548
Cin Pre	6	1	13	1481	Cin Pre	7	1	10	1548
Cin Pre	6	1	17	992	Cin Pre	7	1	13	992, 1133
Cin Pre	6	1	19	794, 1392	Cin Pre	7	2	2	1243
Cin Pre	6	1	21	1392	Cin Pre	7	2	3	949, 1487
Cin Pre	6	1	22	1328	Cin Pre	7	2	4	1265
Cin Pre	6	1	25	1785	Cin Pre	7	2	6	1328
Cin Pre	6	1	27	1392	Cin Pre	7	2	7	1243, 1785
Cin Pre	6	1	28	1392	Cin Pre	7	2	9	759, 1392
Cin Pre	6	1	31	1785	Cin Pre	7	2	10	114, 992
Cin Pre	6	2	2	949	Cin Pre	7	2	13	1147, 1243, 1667
Cin Pre	6	2	3	56, 1328	Cin Pre	7	2	14	923, 1200
Cin Pre	6	2	4	1265	Cin Pre	7	2	15	1371
Cin Pre	6	2	5	935	Cin Pre	7	2	17	1265
Cin Pre	6	2	6	667, 935, 1401	Cin Pre	7	2	18	1265
Cin Pre	6	2	7	992, 1265, 1481	Cin Pre	7	2	19	1328, 1481
Cin Pre	6	2	10	926	Cin Pre	7	2	20	435
Cin Pre	6	2	12	949, 992	Cin Pre	7	2	21	1328, 1548, 1576, 1785
Cin Pre	6	2	13	740, 992, 1265, 1436	Cin Pre	7	2	22	291, 949
Cin Pre	6	2	15	114	Cin Pre	7	2	23	628, 923, 1757
Cin Pre	6	2	17	114	Cin Pre	7	2	24	628, 923, 1251, 1757
Cin Pre	6	2	18	671	Cin Pre	7	2	25	56, 632
Cin Pre	6	2	19	114, 923	Cin Pre	7	2	27	56
Cin Pre	6	2	20	433, 923, 1265, 1474	Cin Pre	7	2	28	992
Cin Pre	6	2	21	628, 671	Cin Pre	7	2	31	288, 949, 1548
Cin Pre	6	2	23	949, 1548	Cin Pre	7	2	33	1100, 1548
Cin Pre	6	2	24	949	Cin Pre	7	2	34	1133
Cin Pre	6	2	25	935, 1265	Cin Pre	7	2	35	1548
Cin Pre	6	2	27	671, 1265, 1481	Cin Pre	7	3	2	1419, 1667
Cin Pre	6	2	28	288, 667, 992, 1401	Cin Pre	7	3	5	924, 992, 1029
Cin Pre	6	2	30	935	Cin Pre	7	3	7	56
Cin Pre	6	2	31	923, 949, 992	Cin Pre	7	3	13	1328, 1392
Cin Pre	6	2	32	935	Cin Pre	7	3	15	1201
Cin Pre	6	2	33	935, 992, 1785	Cin Pre	7	3	18	1029, 1481
Cin Pre	6	2	35	1251	Cin Pre	7	3	19	992, 1328, 1528
Cin Pre	6	3	18	1328	Cin Pre	7	3	20	935, 1405, 1416, 1487
Cin Pre	6	3	24	1328	Cin Pre	7	3	21	677, 1416, 1487
Cin Pre	6	3	30	606, 1328	Cin Pre	7	3	22	949, 1265

Cin Pre	7	3	23	507, 1136, 1328	Cin Pre	8	4	13	1446, 1481
Cin Pre	7	3	25	56, 992	Cin Pre	8	4	14	1548
Cin Pre	7	3	27	507, 909, 923	Cin Pre	8	4	17	671, 1265
Cin Pre	7	3	28	1785	Cin Pre	8	4	18	1243
Cin Pre	7	3	32	1371, 1548	Cin Pre	8	4	19	992
Cin Pre	7	3	33	1481	Cin Pre	8	4	20	1371
Cin Pre	7	3	34	1785	Cin Pre	8	4	30	949
Cin Pre	7	3	36	1548	Cin Pre	8	4	31	671
Cin Pre	7	4	18	935	Cin Pre	8	4	32	1521
Cin Pre	8	1	3	1251	Cin Pre	8	4	34	1548
Cin Pre	8	2	2	1392	Cin Pre	8	5	20	1401
Cin Pre	8	2	3	1249, 1371	Cin Pre	8	5	21	1401
Cin Pre	8	2	4	1481	Cin Pre	8	5	32	288, 1243
Cin Pre	8	2	5	1757	Cin Pre	8	5	34	1265
Cin Pre	8	2	6	1133	Cin Pre	8	5	36	1521
Cin Pre	8	2	7	1133, 1268, 1371	Cin Pre	9	1	2	1667
Cin Pre	8	2	9	1251	Cin Pre	9	2	1	992, 1251, 1481
Cin Pre	8	2	10	1133	Cin Pre	9	2	3	992, 1667
Cin Pre	8	2	13	1133	Cin Pre	9	2	4	1757
Cin Pre	8	2	15	1251, 1481	Cin Pre	9	2	6	1133, 1201, 1265
Cin Pre	8	2	19	1133	Cin Pre	9	2	9	992, 1481
Cin Pre	8	2	22	1200, 1416, 1487	Cin Pre	9	2	12	677, 949, 1251
Cin Pre	8	2	23	1200	Cin Pre	9	2	17	677, 1371, 1387, 1548
Cin Pre	8	2	25	1133	Cin Pre	9	2	18	540, 663
Cin Pre	8	2	28	1481	Cin Pre	9	2	23	433
Cin Pre	8	2	31	1133	Cin Pre	9	2	28	634
Cin Pre	8	2	32	1387	Cin Pre	9	2	30	1785
Cin Pre	8	2	33	992, 1251	Cin Pre	9	2	35	1265
Cin Pre	8	2	34	1133	Cin Pre	9	3	2	114, 1481
Cin Pre	8	3	1	342, 507, 909, 1136, 1371	Cin Pre	9	3	3	1251
Cin Pre	8	3	4	288, 606, 671	Cin Pre	9	3	7	613, 1265
Cin Pre	8	3	5	1268, 1548	Cin Pre	9	3	9	1481
Cin Pre	8	3	7	114	Cin Pre	9	3	10	1133
Cin Pre	8	3	13	671, 677	Cin Pre	9	3	13	457
Cin Pre	8	3	14	910	Cin Pre	9	3	14	1328
Cin Pre	8	3	15	1785	Cin Pre	9	3	15	992, 1328, 1401, 1487
Cin Pre	8	3	17	1241, 1785	Cin Pre	9	3	16	924
Cin Pre	8	3	20	1419, 1667	Cin Pre	9	3	19	1251
Cin Pre	8	3	21	1243, 1405, 1487, 1757	Cin Pre	9	3	20	1251
Cin Pre	8	3	22	1133, 1785	Cin Pre	9	3	22	289, 992
Cin Pre	8	3	23	1785	Cin Pre	9	3	23	949, 992
Cin Pre	8	3	24	1251, 1785	Cin Pre	9	3	25	1384
Cin Pre	8	3	30	1251	Cin Pre	9	3	28	1328
Cin Pre	8	3	31	923	Cin Pre	9	3	30	1265, 1328
Cin Pre	8	3	32	520	Cin Pre	9	3	31	663, 1384
Cin Pre	8	3	34	912	Cin Pre	9	3	32	1251, 1387, 1446
Cin Pre	8	3	35	912	Cin Pre	9	3	34	923, 927
Cin Pre	8	3	36	1251	Cin Pre	9	3	35	1251
Cin Pre	8	4	6	992	Cin Pre	9	3	36	1384, 1481, 1487

Cin Pre	9	4	1	516, 518, 547, 908, 913	Cin Pre	10	4	1	1446, 1757
Cin Pre	9	4	2	529, 992, 1371	Cin Pre	10	4	2	606
Cin Pre	9	4	3	677	Cin Pre	10	4	9	949
Cin Pre	9	4	5	1757	Cin Pre	10	4	12	874
Cin Pre	9	4	6	628, 654	Cin Pre	10	5	4	1481
Cin Pre	9	4	10	433	Cin Pre	10	5	10	1481
Cin Pre	9	4	12	923	Cin Pre	10	5	12	992
Cin Pre	9	4	14	1481	Cin Pre	10	5	13	935
Cin Pre	9	4	15	1487	Cin Pre	10	5	30	1265, 1281, 1328
Cin Pre	9	4	17	1371	Cin Pre	10	5	31	606
Cin Pre	9	4	19	1243	Cin Pre	10	5	32	671
Cin Pre	9	4	20	597	Cin Pre	10	5	33	992, 1265
Cin Pre	9	4	21	1353	Cin Pre	10	6	22	1401
Cin Pre	9	4	23	1392	Cin Pre	10	6	24	794
Cin Pre	9	4	27	949	Cin Pre	10	6	28	1481
Cin Pre	9	4	28	923	Cin Pre	11	1	7	992, 1667
Cin Pre	9	4	32	671, 992	Cin Pre	11	1	10	677
Cin Pre	9	4	33	949	Cin Pre	11	1	13	949, 1268, 1353
Cin Pre	9	5	17	987	Cin Pre	11	1	14	992
Cin Pre	9	5	23	987	Cin Pre	11	1	19	1328, 1371
Cin Pre	9	5	24	987, 1785	Cin Pre	11	1	20	1353, 1436
Cin Pre	9	5	33	1548	Cin Pre	11	2	25	992
Cin Pre	9	5	34	1481	Cin Pre	11	2	27	1757
Cin Pre	9	5	35	1265	Cin Pre	11	2	31	992, 1757
Cin Pre	10	1	2	740, 1133	Cin Pre	11	2	32	1265
Cin Pre	10	1	3	433, 935, 949	Cin Pre	11	2	34	1757
Cin Pre	10	1	4	329, 949	Cin Pre	11	4	3	1265
Cin Pre	10	1	9	1328	Cin Pre	11	4	4	992
Cin Pre	10	1	10	1161	Cin Pre	11	4	6	1133
Cin Pre	10	1	12	794, 935, 1487	Cin Pre	11	4	7	949
Cin Pre	10	1	17	1481	Cin Pre	11	4	9	1351, 1371
Cin Pre	10	1	18	408, 409, 720, 949	Cin Pre	11	4	10	949, 1351
Cin Pre	10	1	23	1481	Cin Pre	11	4	12	935, 949
Cin Pre	10	2	1	671, 935, 992, 1265	Cin Pre	11	4	15	1351
Cin Pre	10	2	7	801, 1667, 1785	Cin Pre	11	4	17	518, 907, 949
Cin Pre	10	2	13	923, 949	Cin Pre	11	4	18	992
Cin Pre	10	2	14	1785	Cin Pre	11	4	22	949
Cin Pre	10	2	17	677, 949	Cin Pre	11	4	23	289, 518, 907
Cin Pre	10	2	23	923, 1200	Cin Pre	11	4	30	1353, 1436
Cin Pre	10	2	27	1481	Cin Pre	11	4	36	289
Cin Pre	10	2	28	935, 1265, 1268, 1328, 1371	Cin Pre	11	5	17	949, 1481
Cin Pre	10	2	30	1392	Cin Pre	11	5	18	949
Cin Pre	10	2	31	992	Cin Pre	11	5	20	108
Cin Pre	10	2	32	1265	Cin Pre	11	5	21	1133, 1328
Cin Pre	10	2	33	1221, 1328	Cin Pre	11	5	22	1328
Cin Pre	10	2	34	923, 1251, 1328	Cin Pre	11	5	23	1265
Cin Pre	10	2	35	935, 1371	Cin Pre	11	5	24	1133
Cin Pre	10	3	31	433	Cin Pre	11	5	25	1265
Cin Pre	10	3	32	1262	Cin Pre	11	5	27	935, 1328

Cin Pre	11	5	30	1481
Cin Pre	11	5	31	1328
Cin Pre	11	5	33	289
Cin Pre	11	5	34	1416
Cin Pre	11	5	36	408
Cin Pre	11	6	31	740, 935
Cin Pre	12	4	1	949
Cin Pre	12	4	3	1328
Cin Pre	12	4	7	1481
Cin Pre	12	4	22	408
Cin Pre	12	5	19	1133
Cin Pre	12	5	25	1133
Cin Pre	13	5	20	1243
Cin Pre	13	5	21	1243

Town of Cincinnati (square and lot)

Cin Twn	-	1	1	1161
Cin Twn	-	1	2	1161
Cin Twn	-	1	3	1161
Cin Twn	-	1	4	1161
Cin Twn	-	2	11	1726
Cin Twn	-	2	15	1313
Cin Twn	-	2	23	1530
Cin Twn	-	3	4	26
Cin Twn	-	3	6	1371
Cin Twn	-	3	7	1502
Cin Twn	-	3	10	1371
Cin Twn	-	3	11	1371
Cin Twn	-	3	14	1195
Cin Twn	-	3	15	1195
Cin Twn	-	3	16	1436
Cin Twn	-	7	1	1031
Cin Twn	-	8	2	998
Cin Twn	-	8	3	998
Cin Twn	-	9	2	998
Cin Twn	-	10	2	998
Cin Twn	-	13	2	998
Cin Twn	-	17	1	998
Cin Twn	-	18	1	998
Cin Twn	-	18	2	998
Cin Twn	-	19	2	1031
Cin Twn	-	21	2	998
Cin Twn	-	29	2	998

Land East of Second Principal Meridian

Cin	2	1E	6-	3	1375
Cin	2	2E	4-	4	1390
Cin	2	3E	7-	22	1262
Cin	2	3E	13-	2	1625

Cin	2	4E	16-	24	1241
Cin	2	12E	12N	33	1582
Cin	2	12E	12N	34	1243
Cin	2	12E	12N	35	1110
Cin	2	12E	12-	3	1369
Cin	2	12E	12-	26	1313
Cin	2	12E	13-	22	1478
Cin	2	12E	13-	28	1530
Cin	2	12E	14N	1	1243
Cin	2	12E	14N	23	1530
Cin	2	12E	14N	31	1243
Cin	2	12E	14-	2	1582
Cin	2	12E	14-	5	1625
Cin	2	12E	14-	12	1478, 1530
Cin	2	12E	14-	20	1436, 1582
Cin	2	12E	14-	21	1478
Cin	2	12E	14-	22	1369
Cin	2	12E	14-	24	1313
Cin	2	12E	15N	25	1313
Cin	2	12E	15N	27	1110, 1436
Cin	2	12E	15N	34	1110
Cin	2	12E	15-	11	1371, 1582
Cin	2	12E	15-	33	1478
Cin	2	12E	16N	23	1110
Cin	2	12E	16-	12	1478, 1582
Cin	2	12E	16-	34	1371
Cin	2	12-	12-	35	1530, 1726
Cin	2	12-	12-	36	1779
Cin	2	12-	13N	34	1161
Cin	2	12-	13-	2	1701, 1779
Cin	2	12-	13-	4	1667
Cin	2	12-	13-	9	1726
Cin	2	12-	13-	12	1783
Cin	2	12-	13-	20	1667
Cin	2	12-	13-	33	1783
Cin	2	12-	14-	12	1636
Cin	2	12-	14-	19	1783
Cin	2	12-	14-	25	1683
Cin	2	12-	14-	26	1667
Cin	2	12-	14-	30	1783
Cin	2	12-	14-	33	1783
Cin	2	12-	15-	1	1749
Cin	2	12-	15-	12	1783
Cin	2	12-	15-	35	1783
Cin	2	12-	16-	13	1726
Cin	2	12-	16-	23	1710, 1779
Cin	2	12-	16-	24	1726
Cin	2	13E	11-	3	1502
Cin	2	13E	11-	4	1313

Cin	2	13E	11-	5	1313	Cin	2	13-	14-	21	1667
Cin	2	13E	12N	19	1243	Cin	2	13-	14-	35	1726
Cin	2	13E	12N	32	1243	Cin	2	13-	14-	36	1779
Cin	2	13E	13N	20	1313	Cin	2	13-	15N	9	1636
Cin	2	13E	13N	27	1582	Cin	2	13-	15-	12	1783
Cin	2	13E	13-	2	1530	Cin	2	13-	15-	15	1783
Cin	2	13E	13-	3	1530, 1625	Cin	2	13-	15-	19	1749
Cin	2	13E	13-	12	1371	Cin	2	13-	15-	22	1779, 1783
Cin	2	13E	13-	13	1582	Cin	2	13-	15-	24	1783
Cin	2	13E	14N	7	1195	Cin	2	13-	15-	27	1667
Cin	2	13E	14N	20	1195	Cin	2	13-	15-	29	1161
Cin	2	13E	14N	22	1195	Cin	2	13-	16-	4	1710
Cin	2	13E	14N	31	1195	Cin	2	13-	16-	9	1749
Cin	2	13E	14-	19	1371	Cin	2	13-	16-	19	1726
Cin	2	13E	14-	22	1203	Cin	2	13-	16-	21	1636
Cin	2	13E	14-	30	1313, 1371	Cin	2	13-	16-	24	1710
Cin	2	13E	14-	31	1313, 1478	Cin	2	13-	17-	21	1726
Cin	2	13E	14-	33	1582	Cin	2	13-	17-	29	1710
Cin	2	13E	15N	10	1371	Cin	2	13-	17-	35	1783
Cin	2	13E	15N	18	1084	Cin	2	13-	18-	29	1726
Cin	2	13E	15N	28	1243	Cin	2	14E	14N	19	1195
Cin	2	13E	15-	6	1478	Cin	2	14E	14-	6	1313
Cin	2	13E	15-	10	1478	Cin	2	14E	14-	19	1313, 1530
Cin	2	13E	15-	15	1371	Cin	2	14E	15-	32	1530
Cin	2	13E	15-	31	1625	Cin	2	14E	16N	17	1502
Cin	2	13E	15-	33	1582	Cin	2	14E	16-	7	1313
Cin	2	13E	16N	18	1436	Cin	2	14E	16-	17	1502
Cin	2	13E	16N	21	1195	Cin	2	14E	16-	21	1371
Cin	2	13E	16N	25	1313	Cin	2	14E	16-	27	1591
Cin	2	13E	16-	17	1369	Cin	2	14E	16-	31	1502
Cin	2	13E	16-	19	1582	Cin	2	14E	17N	15	1478
Cin	2	13E	16-	21	1625	Cin	2	14E	17-	5	1478
Cin	2	13E	16-	26	1313	Cin	2	14E	17-	11	1313
Cin	2	13E	16-	36	1582	Cin	2	14E	17-	12	1369
Cin	2	13E	17N	29	1084	Cin	2	14E	17-	14	1313
Cin	2	13E	17-	23	1582	Cin	2	14E	17-	18	1625
Cin	2	13E	17-	26	1436	Cin	2	14E	17-	22	1313
Cin	2	13E	17-	34	1313, 1436	Cin	2	14E	17-	27	1436, 1582
Cin	2	13-	11-	6	1478	Cin	2	14E	18N	28	1243
Cin	2	13-	12-	2	1710	Cin	2	14E	18-	32	1369
Cin	2	13-	12-	5	1783	Cin	2	14-	16-	17	1636
Cin	2	13-	12-	34	1667	Cin	2	14-	16-	21	1710
Cin	2	13-	13N	6	1161	Cin	2	14-	17-	1	1749
Cin	2	13-	13-	11	1726	Cin	2	14-	18-	28	1636
Cin	2	13-	13-	27	1749						
Cin	2	13-	13-	34	1749	West Meridian Line					
Cin	2	13-	14-	17	1749	Cin	WML	1	2	11	1582
Cin	2	13-	14-	18	1783	Cin	WML	1	2	27	101
Cin	2	13-	14-	19	1667	Cin	WML	1	2	34	628

Cin WML	1	4	4	1502
Cin WML	1	4	14	161
Cin WML	1	4	15	161
Cin WML	1	4	16	161
Cin WML	1	4	19	1783
Cin WML	1	4	22	1530
Cin WML	1	4	23	1530
Cin WML	1	4	34	101
Cin WML	1	5	3	931
Cin WML	1	5	4	1625
Cin WML	1	5	5	463, 1041, 1636
Cin WML	1	5	8	1041
Cin WML	1	5	9	463, 1041
Cin WML	1	5	19	48, 171, 463, 1041
Cin WML	1	5	20	48, 171
Cin WML	1	5	21	48, 171
Cin WML	1	5	22	48, 171
Cin WML	1	5	23	48, 171
Cin WML	1	5	30	1371
Cin WML	1	6	1	1478
Cin WML	1	6	2	234, 1710
Cin WML	1	6	11	1478
Cin WML	1	6	13	659, 953
Cin WML	1	6	14	56, 628
Cin WML	1	6	20	752
Cin WML	1	6	22	1161
Cin WML	1	6	23	950, 1195
Cin WML	1	6	24	1749
Cin WML	1	6	27	130
Cin WML	1	6	28	628
Cin WML	1	6	34	751
Cin WML	1	6	35	1073
Cin WML	1	7	4	1251, 1405
Cin WML	1	7	5	1313
Cin WML	1	7	9	1195
Cin WML	1	7	11	56
Cin WML	1	7	13	6
Cin WML	1	7	14	91
Cin WML	1	7	15	545
Cin WML	1	7	25	752
Cin WML	1	7	27	1195
Cin WML	1	7	28	1478, 1783
Cin WML	1	8	1	1041
Cin WML	1	8	2	1041
Cin WML	1	8	4	1783
Cin WML	1	8	9	6
Cin WML	1	8	10	26, 1749, 1783
Cin WML	1	8	11	101, 1371, 1530
Cin WML	1	8	12	1636, 1710
Cin WML	1	8	13	1195, 1582
Cin WML	1	8	14	1195, 1371
Cin WML	1	8	18	234
Cin WML	1	8	19	865, 1582
Cin WML	1	8	23	1195, 1625
Cin WML	1	8	24	1195
Cin WML	1	8	25	1313
Cin WML	1	8	29	76, 1031
Cin WML	1	8	30	1371
Cin WML	1	8	35	731, 1625
Cin WML	1	9	2	1195
Cin WML	1	9	3	953
Cin WML	1	9	4	953, 1041
Cin WML	1	9	5	931, 1436, 1478
Cin WML	1	9	6	723
Cin WML	1	9	7	654, 1436
Cin WML	1	9	9	931, 1195, 1591
Cin WML	1	9	10	1073, 1313, 1779
Cin WML	1	9	13	942
Cin WML	1	9	14	1667
Cin WML	1	9	18	1110, 1371
Cin WML	1	9	23	1041, 1478, 1530, 1582
Cin WML	1	9	24	677, 1084
Cin WML	1	9	25	182
Cin WML	1	9	26	1371, 1478
Cin WML	1	9	28	1073
Cin WML	1	9	29	1041, 1530
Cin WML	1	9	31	182
Cin WML	1	9	32	623, 1073
Cin WML	1	9	33	1073
Cin WML	1	9	35	1478
Cin WML	1	10	1	316, 1156, 1313
Cin WML	1	10	2	1478, 1636
Cin WML	1	10	3	751, 931
Cin WML	1	10	4	1582
Cin WML	1	10	5	1591
Cin WML	1	10	6	931, 942
Cin WML	1	10	7	1710
Cin WML	1	10	8	1667
Cin WML	1	10	10	1591
Cin WML	1	10	11	931
Cin WML	1	10	12	142, 1436
Cin WML	1	10	13	680, 752, 942, 1041
Cin WML	1	10	14	942, 1041, 1313, 1478
Cin WML	1	10	18	677
Cin WML	1	10	19	680, 1582
Cin WML	1	10	20	1041, 1161
Cin WML	1	10	23	1041, 1749
Cin WML	1	10	24	677

Cin WML	1	10	25		298, 751, 1251
Cin WML	1	10	26		1251
Cin WML	1	10	27		1478
Cin WML	1	10	30		931, 1041, 1502
Cin WML	1	10	31		1779
Cin WML	1	10	32		182
Cin WML	1	10	33		1710
Cin WML	1	10	34		1530, 1582
Cin WML	1	10	36		212, 654, 1710
Cin WML	1	11	1		942, 953
Cin WML	1	11	2		1561, 1710
Cin WML	1	11	4		623, 677, 953, 1073, 1110
Cin WML	1	11	5		677
Cin WML	1	11	7		710
Cin WML	1	11	8		677
Cin WML	1	11	9		1726
Cin WML	1	11	12		677, 1667
Cin WML	1	11	13		76, 1502
Cin WML	1	11	17		759
Cin WML	1	11	20		1369, 1582
Cin WML	1	11	23		953
Cin WML	1	11	24		677
Cin WML	1	11	26		680, 1561
Cin WML	1	11	27		1041, 1110
Cin WML	1	11	28		1749
Cin WML	1	11	29		1478
Cin WML	1	11	30		677
Cin WML	1	11	31		1779
Cin WML	1	11	32		101, 1779
Cin WML	1	11	34		632, 677, 1582
Cin WML	1	11	35		680, 1110
Cin WML	1	11	36		56
Cin WML	1	12	3		718, 1195
Cin WML	1	12	4		659, 1041, 1387, 1667
Cin WML	1	12	5		680
Cin WML	1	12	6		659, 723, 1478
Cin WML	1	12	7		130, 680, 1582
Cin WML	1	12	8		794
Cin WML	1	12	9		91, 677, 1041, 1195
Cin WML	1	12	10		654, 950, 1041
Cin WML	1	12	11		1002, 1041, 1478
Cin WML	1	12	12		1502
Cin WML	1	12	14		1625
Cin WML	1	12	17		654, 1726
Cin WML	1	12	18		163, 546, 751
Cin WML	1	12	20		234
Cin WML	1	12	24		942, 1436
Cin WML	1	12	25		1161
Cin WML	1	12	26		1582
Cin WML	1	12	27		1530
Cin WML	1	12	28		606, 1041, 1625
Cin WML	1	12	30		1313
Cin WML	1	12	31		1710
Cin WML	1	12	32		680
Cin WML	1	12	33		420, 1041
Cin WML	1	12	34		751
Cin WML	1	12	36		142
Cin WML	1	13	1		130, 609, 1073
Cin WML	1	13	2		26, 663, 677, 680
Cin WML	1	13	3		677, 1002
Cin WML	1	13	4		722, 751, 1436
Cin WML	1	13	5		677, 751
Cin WML	1	13	6	316, 677, 680, 1401, 1478, 1779
Cin WML	1	13	7		680
Cin WML	1	13	8		677, 865
Cin WML	1	13	9		26, 115, 632, 950
Cin WML	1	13	10		1002, 1195, 1478
Cin WML	1	13	11		677, 1002, 1749
Cin WML	1	13	12		677, 1002, 1195
Cin WML	1	13	13		163, 751, 942, 1110
Cin WML	1	13	17		50
Cin WML	1	13	18		1160
Cin WML	1	13	19		943, 1002, 1041
Cin WML	1	13	20		632, 1667
Cin WML	1	13	22		1313
Cin WML	1	13	23		1041, 1436
Cin WML	1	13	24		1313
Cin WML	1	13	26		329, 953, 1530
Cin WML	1	13	27		520, 1530, 1548
Cin WML	1	13	28		953, 1478
Cin WML	1	13	29		680, 752
Cin WML	1	13	30		91, 142, 659
Cin WML	1	13	31		101, 1041, 1313
Cin WML	1	13	33		1041
Cin WML	1	13	34		677, 680, 903
Cin WML	1	14	1		731, 1002
Cin WML	1	14	4		1002
Cin WML	1	14	5		1002, 1478
Cin WML	1	14	8		212, 718, 953
Cin WML	1	14	9		1636
Cin WML	1	14	11		677, 723
Cin WML	1	14	12		623, 1002, 1041
Cin WML	1	14	14		718, 1625
Cin WML	1	14	17		718, 1110
Cin WML	1	14	20		212, 1073, 1667
Cin WML	1	14	25		677, 751
Cin WML	1	14	26		545, 1371
Cin WML	1	14	27		171, 261, 628, 1502

Cin WML	1	14	28	171, 212	Cin WML	2	9	11	1783
Cin WML	1	14	29	171, 212, 628, 731	Cin WML	2	9	17	1195, 1783
Cin WML	1	14	30	628, 1002	Cin WML	2	9	19	91, 234
Cin WML	1	14	31	677, 718, 1478	Cin WML	2	9	20	115, 1073
Cin WML	1	14	32	261, 677, 731, 953	Cin WML	2	9	21	115, 1313
Cin WML	1	14	33	261, 677, 752, 1073	Cin WML	2	9	22	1502
Cin WML	1	14	34	632, 680	Cin WML	2	9	27	654
Cin WML	1	14	35	751, 829, 942, 1726	Cin WML	2	9	28	1726
Cin WML	1	14	36	545, 677	Cin WML	2	9	29	26, 115
Cin WML	1	15	17	623	Cin WML	2	9	30	953
Cin WML	1	15	32	1243	Cin WML	2	9	32	56
Cin WML	1	15	36	1073	Cin WML	2	9	33	10
Cin WML	1	16	28	1779	Cin WML	2	10	3	865
Cin WML	2	1	4	1436	Cin WML	2	10	5	751
Cin WML	2	2	25	1313	Cin WML	2	10	9	677, 710
Cin WML	2	2	35	1591	Cin WML	2	10	10	710
Cin WML	2	2	36	1636	Cin WML	2	10	11	1041
Cin WML	2	3	2	759, 1110	Cin WML	2	10	12	1041, 1313
Cin WML	2	3	24	1726	Cin WML	2	10	13	1002
Cin WML	2	4	1	1625	Cin WML	2	10	17	84, 234
Cin WML	2	4	10	356, 1625	Cin WML	2	10	21	632, 1041
Cin WML	2	4	11	168	Cin WML	2	10	24	142, 1110, 1161
Cin WML	2	4	22	1203	Cin WML	2	10	28	710
Cin WML	2	4	23	130	Cin WML	2	10	33	677, 1502, 1584
Cin WML	2	4	29	1200, 1636	Cin WML	2	10	34	829
Cin WML	2	4	30	953	Cin WML	2	11	2	1478
Cin WML	2	4	31	1073	Cin WML	2	11	3	1041
Cin WML	2	5	1	1084, 1371, 1667	Cin WML	2	11	9	659
Cin WML	2	5	2	1530	Cin WML	2	11	13	1478
Cin WML	2	5	23	677	Cin WML	2	11	14	931
Cin WML	2	5	24	1530	Cin WML	2	11	21	722
Cin WML	2	5	25	1625	Cin WML	2	11	22	299, 677, 710
Cin WML	2	5	35	751, 1502	Cin WML	2	11	23	659
Cin WML	2	5	36	1667	Cin WML	2	11	24	130
Cin WML	2	6	35	1667	Cin WML	2	11	26	677
Cin WML	2	7	4	1073	Cin WML	2	11	27	10, 710
Cin WML	2	8	2	101, 1749	Cin WML	2	11	28	234, 632, 722, 731
Cin WML	2	8	3	76, 130	Cin WML	2	11	29	1591
Cin WML	2	8	4	609	Cin WML	2	11	32	632
Cin WML	2	8	10	731, 1530	Cin WML	2	11	34	101, 1478
Cin WML	2	8	11	1243	Cin WML	2	11	35	677
Cin WML	2	8	12	1371	Cin WML	2	12	1	654, 677
Cin WML	2	8	13	623, 1002, 1195, 1243	Cin WML	2	12	2	829
Cin WML	2	8	14	953, 1243	Cin WML	2	12	10	601
Cin WML	2	9	3	718	Cin WML	2	12	11	26, 632
Cin WML	2	9	4	710, 718, 1110	Cin WML	2	12	12	545, 609, 942
Cin WML	2	9	7	680	Cin WML	2	12	13	545
Cin WML	2	9	8	740, 953, 1195	Cin WML	2	12	14	1478
Cin WML	2	9	9	680	Cin WML	2	12	15	632

Cin	WML	2	12	22	1582	EPR	–	2W 10–	9	947
Cin	WML	2	12	24	628, 751, 1436	EPR	–	2W 10–	10	947
Cin	WML	2	12	25	1041	EPR	–	2W 10–	11	947
Cin	WML	2	12	26	1313, 1667	EPR	–	2W 10–	12	947
Cin	WML	2	12	36	1031, 1667	EPR	–	2W 10–	13	947
Cin	WML	2	13	11	1243	EPR	–	2W 10–	14	947
Cin	WML	2	13	12	457, 1073, 1243	EPR	–	2W 10–	15	947
Cin	WML	2	13	23	751	EPR	–	2W 10–	16	947
Cin	WML	2	13	25	752, 1478	EPR	–	2W 10–	17	947
Cin	WML	2	13	26	1710	EPR	–	2W 10–	18	947
Cin	WML	2	13	35	722	EPR	–	2W 10–	19	947
Cin	WML	2	13	36	115, 130, 632, 731	EPR	–	2W 10–	20	947
Cin	WML	2	14	13	1243	EPR	–	2W 10–	21	947
Cin	WML	2	14	24	1243	EPR	–	2W 10–	22	947
Cin	WML	3	1	5	333, 334, 351	EPR	–	2W 10–	23	947
Cin	WML	3	1	6	333, 334, 351	EPR	–	2W 10–	24	947
Cin	WML	3	2	15	1596	EPR	–	2W 10–	25	947
Cin	WML	3	2	22	1596	EPR	–	2W 10–	26	947
Cin	WML	3	2	27	1596	EPR	–	2W 10–	27	947
Cin	WML	3	2	31	1783	EPR	–	2W 10–	28	947
Cin	WML	3	3	34	751	EPR	–	2W 10–	29	947
Cin	WML	3	4	1	1478	EPR	–	2W 10–	30	947
Cin	WML	3	4	9	623	EPR	–	2W 10–	31	947
Cin	WML	3	4	25	457	EPR	–	2W 10–	32	947
Cin	WML	3	5	36	1371	EPR	–	2W 10–	33	947
Cin	WML	3	10	25	731	EPR	–	2W 10–	34	947
Cin	WML	4	1	2	794, 1694	EPR	–	2W 10–	35	947
Cin	WML	4	4	14	91	EPR	–	2W 10–	36	947
Cin	WML	5	3	31	91	EPR	–	3– 8–	26	941
Cin	WML	5	3	34	91	EPR	–	4– 10–	7	941
Cin	WML	5	5	28	931	EPR	–	4– 10–	18	941
Cin	WML	5	7	36	1313	EPR	–	10– 3–	15	941
Cin	WML	7	2	7	91	EPR	–	18– 3–	34	941
Cin	WML	11	4	18	91					

LAND OFFICE DISTRICT EAST OF PEARL RIVER

HUNTSVILLE (ALABAMA) LAND OFFICE DISTRICT

EPR	–	1– 11–	21	1022		Hun	–	–	2– 25	1690
EPR	–	1W 10–	30	947, 989		Hun	–	1	3 22	1169
EPR	–	1W 10–	31	947, 989		Hun	–	1	3 23	1169
EPR	–	2W 10–	1	947		Hun	–	1E	1– 17	1689
EPR	–	2W 10–	2	947		Hun	–	1E	1– 19	1689
EPR	–	2W 10–	3	947		Hun	–	1E	1– 20	1689
EPR	–	2W 10–	4	947		Hun	–	1E	1– 26	1689
EPR	–	2W 10–	5	947		Hun	–	1E	2– 2	1690
EPR	–	2W 10–	6	947		Hun	–	1E	2– 3	1689
EPR	–	2W 10–	7	947		Hun	–	1E	2– 17	1689
EPR	–	2W 10–	8	947		Hun	–	1E	2– 21	1689
						Hun	–	1E	2– 23	1689, 1690

Hun	–	1E	2–	24	1690
Hun	–	1E	2–	26	1690
Hun	–	1E	2–	28	1689
Hun	–	1E	2–	29	1689
Hun	–	1E	2–	34	1690
Hun	–	1E	3–	1	1409
Hun	–	1E	3–	3	1689
Hun	–	1E	3–	7	1106, 1689
Hun	–	1E	3–	8	1689
Hun	–	1E	3–	9	1689
Hun	–	1E	3–	12	1689
Hun	–	1E	3–	13	1689
Hun	–	1E	3–	14	1689
Hun	–	1E	3–	15	1451
Hun	–	1E	3–	19	1261
Hun	–	1E	3–	21	1362, 1689
Hun	–	1E	3–	23	1689
Hun	–	1E	3–	24	1689
Hun	–	1E	3–	30	1232
Hun	–	1E	4–	8	1689
Hun	–	1E	4–	28	1689
Hun	–	1E	5–	2	1689
Hun	–	1E	5–	17	1689
Hun	–	1W	1–	13	1689
Hun	–	1W	1–	24	1689
Hun	–	1W	2–	23	1698
Hun	–	1W	2–	31	1689
Hun	–	1W	3–	1	1689
Hun	–	1W	3–	3	1689
Hun	–	1W	3–	11	1689
Hun	–	1W	3–	13	1409
Hun	–	1W	3–	14	1409
Hun	–	1W	3–	29	1689
Hun	–	1W	3–	31	1689
Hun	–	1W	3–	32	1689
Hun	–	1W	3–	35	1690
Hun	–	1W	4–	2	1689
Hun	–	1W	4–	3	1689
Hun	–	1W	4–	4	1689
Hun	–	1W	4–	8	1689
Hun	–	1W	4–	10	1689
Hun	–	1W	4–	11	1106
Hun	–	1W	4–	12	1689
Hun	–	1W	4–	22	1689, 1409
Hun	–	1W	4–	23	1689
Hun	–	2E	1–	4	1690
Hun	–	2E	1–	9	1689
Hun	–	2E	1–	10	1689
Hun	–	2E	1–	15	1409
Hun	–	2E	1–	17	1409
Hun	–	2E	1–	29	1690
Hun	–	2E	1–	33	1040
Hun	–	2E	1–	34	1040
Hun	–	2E	2–	32	1689
Hun	–	2E	3–	27	1689
Hun	–	2E	3–	30	1689
Hun	–	2E	3–	31	1690
Hun	–	2E	4–	32	1689
Hun	–	2W	1–	27	1689
Hun	–	2W	1–	29	1689
Hun	–	2W	2–	2	1689
Hun	–	2W	2–	13	1689
Hun	–	2W	2–	24	1689
Hun	–	2W	3–	5	1689
Hun	–	2W	3–	24	1689
Hun	–	2W	3–	25	1689
Hun	–	2W	4–	12	1689
Hun	–	3W	1–	25	1689
Hun	–	3W	1–	26	1689
Hun	–	3W	1–	36	1689
Hun	–	3W	2–	12	1689
Hun	–	3W	2–	14	1689
Hun	–	8–	3–	34	1418
Hun	EML	1	1	26	1507
Hun	EML	1	1	34	1507
Hun	EML	1	1	35	1507
Hun	EML	1	2	20	1507
Hun	EML	1	2	21	1507
Hun	EML	1	2	30	1433, 1507
Hun	EML	1	2	31	1433
Hun	EML	1	2	35	1507
Hun	EML	1	3	1	1279
Hun	EML	1	3	2	1507
Hun	EML	1	3	8	1237
Hun	EML	1	3	11	1507
Hun	EML	1	3	12	1433
Hun	EML	1	3	17	1327
Hun	EML	1	3	18	1433
Hun	EML	1	3	21	1507
Hun	EML	1	3	25	1433, 1507
Hun	EML	1	3	30	1507
Hun	EML	1	4	7	1433
Hun	EML	1	4	18	1327
Hun	EML	1	4	32	1546
Hun	EML	1	5	1	1507
Hun	EML	2	1	8	1507
Hun	EML	2	1	15	1279
Hun	EML	2	1	17	1279, 1507

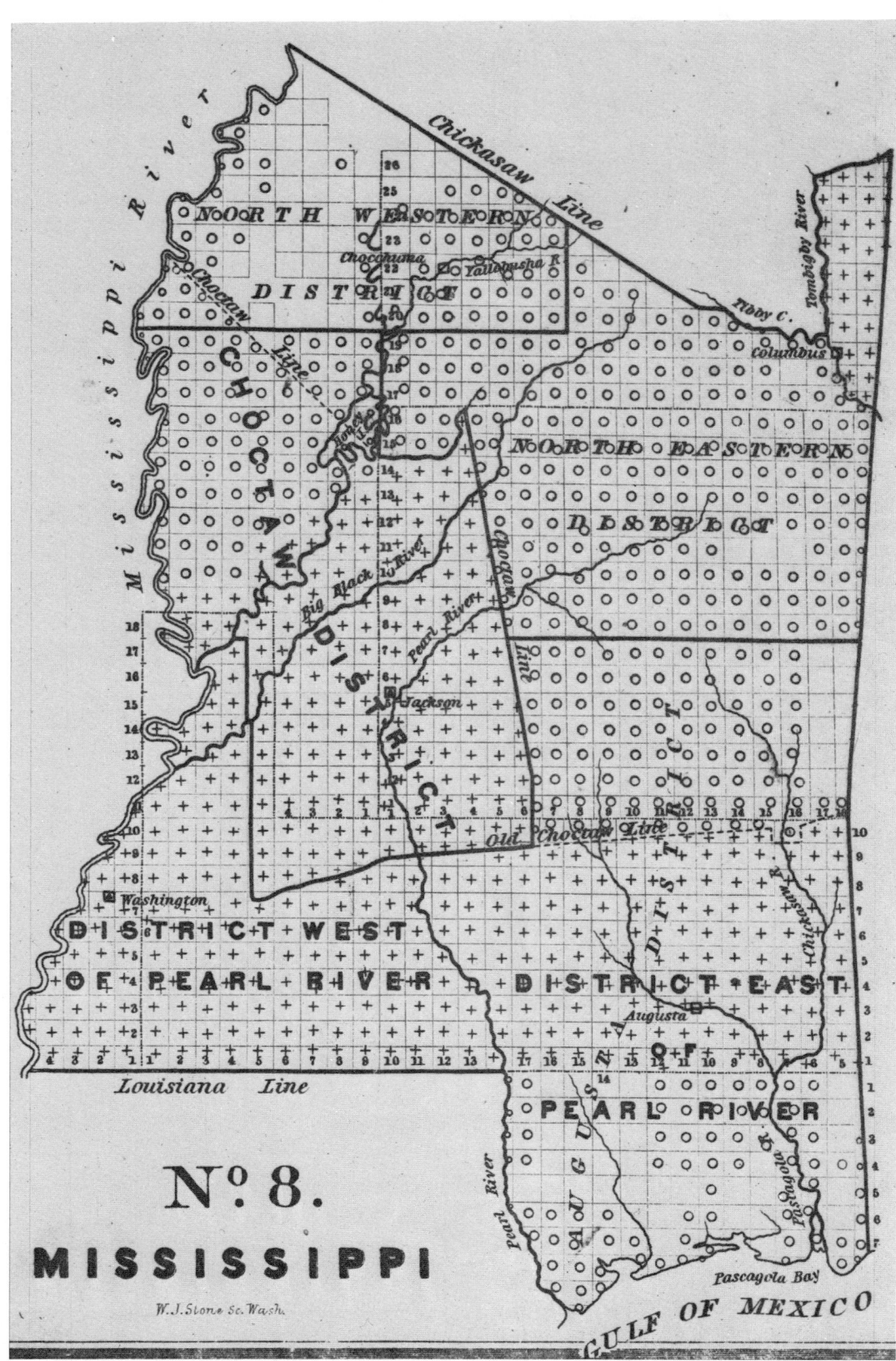

MAP 12. Tract map of Mississippi showing land office districts

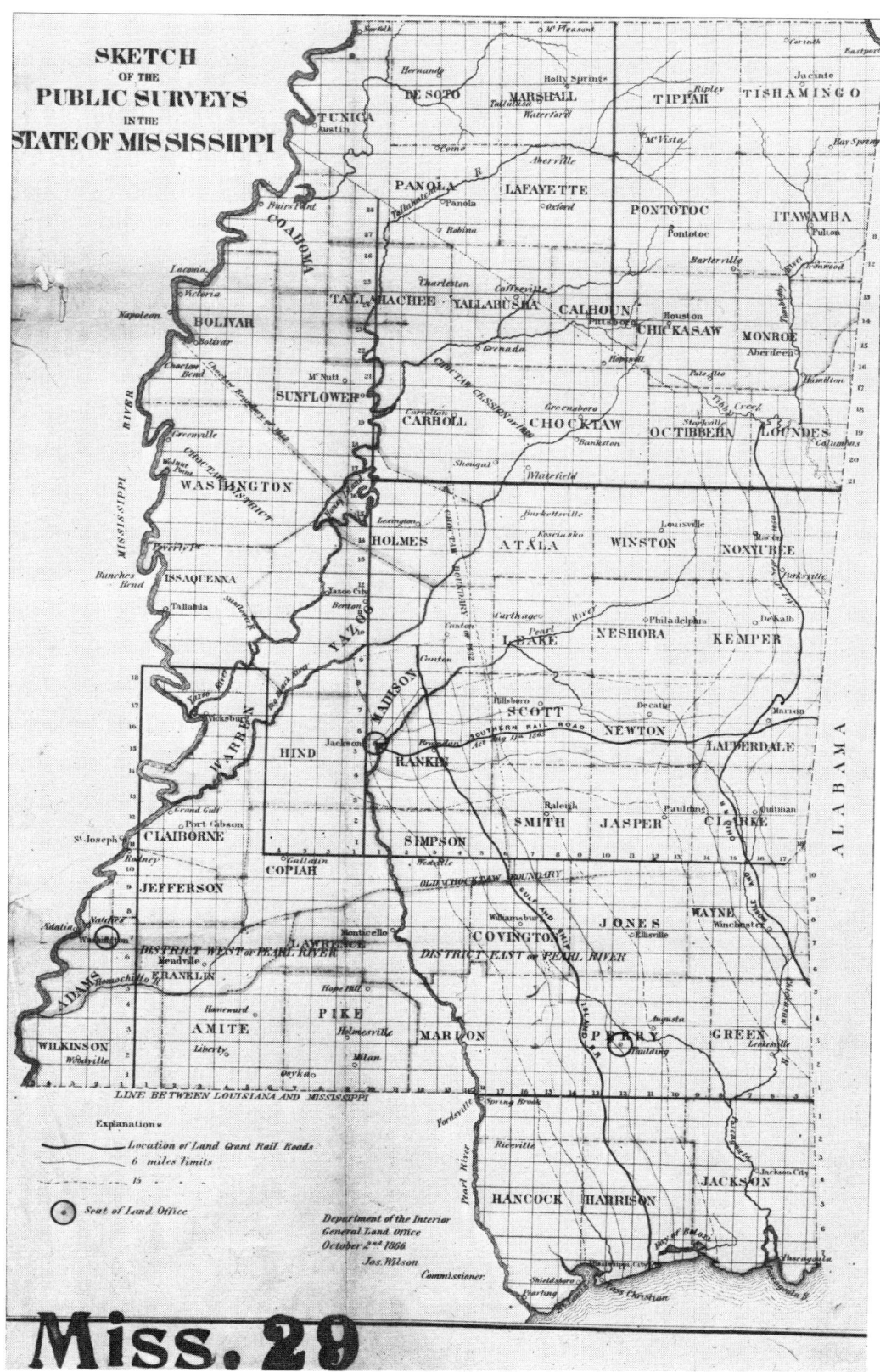

MAP 13. Tract map of Mississippi showing range-township numbering system

[311]

Hun	EML	2	1	28	1327
Hun	EML	2	1	33	1433
Hun	EML	2	1	34	1433
Hun	EML	2	2	5	1327
Hun	EML	2	3	6	1507
Hun	EML	2	3	7	1433
Hun	EML	2	3	8	1433, 1507
Hun	EML	2	3	19	1507
Hun	EML	2	3	21	1507
Hun	EML	2	3	24	1650
Hun	EML	2	3	31	1433
Hun	EML	2	3	34	1327, 1650
Hun	WML	1	1	10	1507
Hun	WML	1	1	12	1507
Hun	WML	1	1	15	1507
Hun	WML	1	1	24	1507
Hun	WML	1	2	23	1507
Hun	WML	1	2	24	1507
Hun	WML	1	2	25	1327, 1433
Hun	WML	1	2	30	1433
Hun	WML	1	2	33	1507
Hun	WML	1	2	36	1507
Hun	WML	1	3	13	1279, 1507
Hun	WML	1	3	14	1279
Hun	WML	1	3	20	1507
Hun	WML	1	3	24	1327
Hun	WML	1	3	25	1507
Hun	WML	1	3	26	1433
Hun	WML	1	3	32	1507
Hun	WML	1	3	33	1433, 1507
Hun	WML	1	3	36	1507
Hun	WML	1	4	3	1507
Hun	WML	1	4	7	1433, 1507
Hun	WML	1	4	10	1433
Hun	WML	1	4	13	1433, 1507
Hun	WML	1	4	15	1433, 1507
Hun	WML	1	4	22	1546
Hun	WML	2	1	35	1433
Hun	WML	2	1	36	1433
Hun	WML	2	2	4	1507
Hun	WML	2	2	19	1327
Hun	WML	2	2	23	1507
Hun	WML	2	3	26	1546
Hun	WML	3	1	14	1507
Hun	WML	3	1	23	1507
Hun	WML	3	1	26	1219
Hun	WML	3	2	1	1507
Hun	WML	3	2	13	1507
Hun	WML	3	2	23	1507

Hun	WML	3	2	24	1507
Hun	WML	3	2	26	1507

JEFFERSONVILLE (INDIANA) LAND OFFICE DISTRICT

Jef	–	1E	1N	2	779
Jef	–	1E	1N	6	1325
Jef	–	1E	1N	8	178, 631, 1051
Jef	–	1E	1N	9	1051, 1207, 1488
Jef	–	1E	1N	17	898
Jef	–	1E	1N	20	898
Jef	–	1E	1N	21	898
Jef	–	1E	2N	1	280
Jef	–	1E	2N	2	776, 983, 1592
Jef	–	1E	2N	3	983, 997
Jef	–	1E	2N	4	983, 1477, 1665
Jef	–	1E	2N	5	140
Jef	–	1E	2N	7	983
Jef	–	1E	2N	8	983
Jef	–	1E	2N	12	280
Jef	–	1E	2N	18	1551
Jef	–	1E	2N	20	1488
Jef	–	1E	2N	25	1477
Jef	–	1E	2N	31	1207, 1325
Jef	–	1E	2N	35	983, 1568
Jef	–	1E	3N	19	1551
Jef	–	1E	3N	34	898
Jef	–	1E	3N	35	1624
Jef	–	1E	5S	17	995
Jef	–	1E	5S	18	1488
Jef	–	1W	1N	2	605
Jef	–	1W	1N	11	605
Jef	–	1W	2N	34	762
Jef	–	2E	1N	4	1325, 1551
Jef	–	2E	1N	5	786, 1477, 1568
Jef	–	2E	1N	10	995
Jef	–	2E	1N	13	786
Jef	–	2E	1N	18	983
Jef	–	2E	1N	23	605
Jef	–	2E	1N	24	983
Jef	–	2E	1S	4	782, 898
Jef	–	2E	1S	29	983
Jef	–	2E	2N	7	983
Jef	–	2E	2N	10	1477
Jef	–	2E	2N	32	280, 1086
Jef	–	2E	2N	33	1207
Jef	–	2E	2S	34	1086
Jef	–	2E	4S	29	1602

Jef	– 2E	5S	4	1602
Jef	– 3E	1N	1	1477
Jef	– 3E	1N	11	779, 1207
Jef	– 3E	1N	12	317, 776, 1488
Jef	– 3E	1N	26	1624
Jef	– 3E	1S	9	983
Jef	– 3E	1S	11	1602
Jef	– 3E	1S	14	721, 1325
Jef	– 3E	1S	15	983, 1207
Jef	– 3E	2N	24	1699
Jef	– 3E	2N	25	995
Jef	– 3E	2N	27	779
Jef	– 3E	2N	34	1592
Jef	– 3E	3N	12	1592
Jef	– 3E	3N	24	1592
Jef	– 3E	4N	1	898
Jef	– 3E	4N	13	983
Jef	– 3E	4N	29	586
Jef	– 3E	4S	9	898
Jef	– 3E	4S	28	630
Jef	– 3E	4S	33	1602
Jef	– 3E	5N	25	605
Jef	– 3E	5N	36	605
Jef	– 3E	5S	4	995
Jef	– 3E	5S	7	630, 1665
Jef	– 3E	5S	8	1556, 1665
Jef	– 3E	5S	9	1477, 1488
Jef	– 3E	5S	10	1488
Jef	– 3E	5S	18	1551, 1568
Jef	– 3E	5S	19	1477
Jef	– 3E	5S	23	779
Jef	– 3E	5S	35	877
Jef	– 4-	5-	22	1207
Jef	– 4E	1N	2	898, 1488, 1624
Jef	– 4E	1N	6	631, 1422
Jef	– 4E	1N	31	276, 983, 1018
Jef	– 4E	1N	34	782
Jef	– 4E	1S	2	861, 1477
Jef	– 4E	1S	3	276, 861
Jef	– 4E	1S	9	1325
Jef	– 4E	1S	10	140, 631
Jef	– 4E	1S	14	630, 1592
Jef	– 4E	2N	1	140
Jef	– 4E	2N	2	604, 776, 983
Jef	– 4E	2N	3	140, 983, 995
Jef	– 4E	2N	4	140, 776, 1086
Jef	– 4E	2N	5	550
Jef	– 4E	2N	8	786, 877, 898
Jef	– 4E	2N	9	[28], 1027
Jef	– 4E	2N	10	776, 1272, 1356
Jef	– 4E	2N	11	983, 1477, 1551
Jef	– 4E	2N	12	631, 995
Jef	– 4E	2N	13	276, 1325, 1556
Jef	– 4E	2N	14	1207, 1624, 1665
Jef	– 4E	2N	17	776, 1325
Jef	– 4E	2N	18	1477
Jef	– 4E	2N	19	1325, 1477, 1488
Jef	– 4E	2N	21	1207, 1488
Jef	– 4E	2N	23	1665
Jef	– 4E	2N	24	1624
Jef	– 4E	2N	25	1602
Jef	– 4E	2N	28	983, 1325, 1624
Jef	– 4E	2N	29	779
Jef	– 4E	2N	30	983, 1592
Jef	– 4E	2N	31	586, 1477
Jef	– 4E	2N	32	776, 1477
Jef	– 4E	2N	33	779, 1488
Jef	– 4E	2S	5	1624
Jef	– 4E	2S	23	1624
Jef	– 4E	3N	9	1602
Jef	– 4E	3N	17	1051
Jef	– 4E	3N	27	1665
Jef	– 4E	3N	32	1325
Jef	– 4E	3N	33	1477
Jef	– 4E	3N	34	1488, 1551
Jef	– 4E	3N	35	1325, 1477
Jef	– 4E	3S	1	1665
Jef	– 4E	3S	2	983
Jef	– 4E	3S	31	1556
Jef	– 4E	4N	6	877
Jef	– 4E	4S	2	585
Jef	– 4E	5N	20	776
Jef	– 4E	5N	21	776
Jef	– 4E	5N	22	779, 1048, 1171, 1207, 1488
Jef	– 4E	5N	29	1488
Jef	– 4E	5N	31	585, 995
Jef	– 4E	5S	4	1086
Jef	– 4E	5S	17	1592
Jef	– 4E	5S	29	1592
Jef	– 4N	2E	9 [erroneous]	28
Jef	– 5E	1S	31	1551
Jef	– 5E	1S	32	995
Jef	– 5E	1S	33	995
Jef	– 5E	1S	34	1477
Jef	– 5E	2N	6	1477
Jef	– 5E	2N	7	1325, 1556
Jef	– 5E	2N	8	1325
Jef	– 5E	2N	18	776, 1551, 1556, 1568

Jef	–	5E	2N	19	995, 1488, 1624	Jef	–	8E	5N	10	997
Jef	–	5E	2S	1	779	Jef	–	8E	5N	15	786
Jef	–	5E	2S	5	1556	Jef	–	8E	5N	21	1086
Jef	–	5E	2S	6	317, 776	Jef	–	8E	5N	30	1624
Jef	–	5E	2S	7	1624	Jef	–	9–	3–	2	513
Jef	–	5E	2S	8	1602	Jef	–	9E	1N	1	762
Jef	–	5E	2S	10	1477	Jef	–	9E	1N	2	877
Jef	–	5E	2S	14	1551	Jef	–	9E	1N	3	317, 782
Jef	–	5E	2S	19	280	Jef	–	9E	1N	4	605
Jef	–	5E	2S	20	1477	Jef	–	9E	1N	5	140, 317, 630, 1551
Jef	–	5E	2S	22	1551	Jef	–	9E	1N	8	877
Jef	–	5E	2S	26	1602	Jef	–	9E	1N	9	586, 1488
Jef	–	5E	2S	27	280	Jef	–	9E	1N	10	721, 997, 1086
Jef	–	5E	2S	29	995	Jef	–	9E	1N	11	631, 983
Jef	–	5E	2S	30	630	Jef	–	9E	1N	12	1325
Jef	–	5E	2S	32	776	Jef	–	9E	1N	13	605, 1051
Jef	–	5E	2S	33	983	Jef	–	9E	1N	14	605, 630, 877
Jef	–	5E	2S	35	983	Jef	–	9E	1N	15	[28], 1086
Jef	–	5E	2S	36	983	Jef	–	9E	1N	23	786, 995
Jef	–	5E	3S	1	1551	Jef	–	9E	1N	27	786, 1602
Jef	–	5E	3S	4	776	Jef	–	9E	1N	28	581
Jef	–	5E	4S	10	1477	Jef	–	9E	2N	3	317, 1624
Jef	–	5E	4S	11	1477	Jef	–	9E	2N	12	65, 280, 1477
Jef	–	5E	4S	36	1568	Jef	–	9E	2N	19	1411
Jef	–	5E	5S	13	1086	Jef	–	9E	2N	24	1624
Jef	–	6E	1S	5	1086	Jef	–	9E	2N	26	983, 1325
Jef	–	6E	2S	6	1551	Jef	–	9E	2N	28	1477
Jef	–	6E	2S	20	1477	Jef	–	9E	2N	30	140, 1325, 1592
Jef	–	6E	3S	18	1624	Jef	–	9E	2N	31	140, 779
Jef	–	6E	3S	20	776	Jef	–	9E	2N	32	550, 1086
Jef	–	6E	3S	21	776	Jef	–	9E	2N	33	140, 995
Jef	–	8E	2N	12	65, 280	Jef	–	9E	2N	35	604, 997, 1477
Jef	–	8E	2N	13	983	Jef	–	9E	2N	36	605, 779, 877
Jef	–	8E	2N	23	335, 776, 983	Jef	–	9E	3N	2	207, 1086, 1568
Jef	–	8E	2N	24	762, 1477	Jef	–	9E	3N	5	776, 997
Jef	–	8E	3N	15	877	Jef	–	9E	3N	8	983
Jef	–	8E	3N	19	1452	Jef	–	9E	3N	9	997
Jef	–	8E	3N	20	877	Jef	–	9E	3N	11	1602
Jef	–	8E	3N	25	1477	Jef	–	9E	3N	12	604, 630, 1051
Jef	–	8E	3N	26	1477	Jef	–	9E	3N	13	983
Jef	–	8E	3N	28	1325	Jef	–	9E	3N	14	997
Jef	–	8E	3N	33	550, 1477	Jef	–	9E	3N	15	1051, 1665
Jef	–	8E	4N	3	1665	Jef	–	9E	3N	19	861, 877, 1207
Jef	–	8E	4N	8	581, 782, 1624	Jef	–	9E	3N	24	[25], 140, 630
Jef	–	8E	4N	10	1325	Jef	–	9E	3N	35	786
Jef	–	8E	4N	13	779	Jef	–	9E	3N	36	1051
Jef	–	8E	4N	14	776	Jef	–	9E	4N	3	877
Jef	–	8E	4N	17	630	Jef	–	9E	4N	9	140
Jef	–	8E	4N	21	1551	Jef	–	9E	4N	10	1207

Jef	–	9E	4N	13		1602	Jef	– 10E	4N	27	861, 1051
Jef	–	9E	4N	15		1592, 1624	Jef	– 10E	4N	29	1051, 1488, 1665
Jef	–	9E	4N	22		983	Jef	– 10E	4N	32	550, 877, 1325
Jef	–	9E	4N	24		1602	Jef	– 10E	4N	33	[28], 1325, 1477
Jef	–	9E	4N	29		605	Jef	– 10E	4N	34	276, 997, 1051, 1624
Jef	–	9E	4N	30		983	Jef	– 10E	4N	35	877, 983
Jef	–	9E	4N	32		983	Jef	– 10E	4N	36	[28], 1477
Jef	–	9E	5N	24		1624	Jef	– 10E	4S	28	898
Jef	–	9E	5N	33		1624	Jef	– 10E	5N	36	1488
Jef	–	9N	1E	15	[erroneous]	28	Jef	– 10E	6N	3	1665
Jef	–	9N	3E	24	[erroneous]	25	Jef	– 10E	7N	36	1665
Jef	–	10E	1N	4		997	Jef	– 10N	4E	33	[erroneous] 28
Jef	–	10E	1N	6		721, 983, 995	Jef	– 10N	4E	36	[erroneous] 28
Jef	–	10E	1N	7		776, 861, 995, 997	Jef	– 11E	3N	1	605
Jef	–	10E	1N	8		997	Jef	– 11E	3N	2	605
Jef	–	10E	1N	9		997	Jef	– 11E	3N	12	605
Jef	–	10E	1N	17		997	Jef	– 11E	4N	5	1665
Jef	–	10E	1N	18		983	Jef	– 11E	4N	9	983
Jef	–	10E	1N	19		983	Jef	– 11E	4N	18	983, 1325
Jef	–	10E	2N	5		995	Jef	– 11E	4N	19	877, 1051, 1551
Jef	–	10E	2N	6		276, 550, 983, 1051	Jef	– 11E	4N	20	983, 1086
Jef	–	10E	2N	7		786, 1207	Jef	– 11E	4N	23	721, 1325
Jef	–	10E	2N	8		995	Jef	– 11E	4N	24	1086
Jef	–	10E	2N	17		280	Jef	– 11E	4N	30	997
Jef	–	10E	2N	19		983	Jef	– 11E	4N	31	983, 997
Jef	–	10E	2N	20		280	Jef	– 11E	4N	36	877
Jef	–	10E	2N	30		280	Jef	– 11E	5N	2	983
Jef	–	10E	2N	31		983, 1325, 1556	Jef	– 11E	5N	3	631
Jef	–	10E	2N	32		1602	Jef	– 11E	5N	9	1325
Jef	–	10E	3N	1		997	Jef	– 11E	5N	19	586
Jef	–	10E	3N	2		983	Jef	– 11E	5N	21	1477
Jef	–	10E	3N	3		983	Jef	– 11E	5N	28	983
Jef	–	10E	3N	4		550	Jef	– 11E	5N	29	276, 1551
Jef	–	10E	3N	5		550	Jef	– 11E	5N	32	1325
Jef	–	10E	3N	18		630	Jef	– 11E	6N	26	1325, 1624
Jef	–	10E	3N	19		995	Jef	– 11E	6N	34	140
Jef	–	10E	3N	30		1551	Jef	– 11E	6N	35	631, 779
Jef	–	10E	3N	31		1602	Jef	– 12E	3N	7	1051
Jef	–	10E	3N	32		1602	Jef	– 12E	3N	16	983
Jef	–	10E	3N	33		1602	Jef	– 12E	3N	17	983
Jef	–	10E	4N	1		1325	Jef	– 12E	3N	18	1051
Jef	–	10E	4N	7		983	Jef	– 12E	3N	20	983
Jef	–	10E	4N	13		1325	Jef	– 12E	3N	21	983
Jef	–	10E	4N	14		605, 1477	Jef	– 12E	6N	3	1602
Jef	–	10E	4N	20		1325, 1477	Jef	2	1E	1N	5	1151
Jef	–	10E	4N	23		1086	Jef	2	1E	1N	11	1376
Jef	–	10E	4N	24		1051	Jef	2	1E	1N	21	1376
Jef	–	10E	4N	25		1051, 1477	Jef	2	1E	2N	3	1533
Jef	–	10E	4N	26		995, 1325	Jef	2	1E	2N	7	1533

Jef	2	1E	2N	8	1376	Jef	2	4-	1S	1	1718
Jef	2	1E	2N	25	1151	Jef	2	4-	1S	2	1755
Jef	2	1E	2N	29	1151	Jef	2	4-	1S	4	1755
Jef	2	1E	3N	31	1376	Jef	2	4-	2N	9	1718
Jef	2	1W	1N	1	1151	Jef	2	4-	2N	18	1755
Jef	2	1-	1N	7	1718	Jef	2	4-	2N	22	1718
Jef	2	1-	1N	8	1755	Jef	2	4-	2S	32	1718
Jef	2	1-	2N	34	1718	Jef	2	4-	4N	8	1718
Jef	2	1-	3N	30	1718	Jef	2	4-	4S	5	1718
Jef	2	2E	1N	33	1376	Jef	2	4-	5N	13	1718
Jef	2	2E	1S	3	1376	Jef	2	4-	5N	31	1718
Jef	2	2E	1S	4	1533	Jef	2	5E	2N	8	1533
Jef	2	2E	3N	5	1533	Jef	2	5E	2N	19	1533
Jef	2	2-	1N	8	1718	Jef	2	5E	2S	4	1151
Jef	2	2-	1N	32	1755	Jef	2	5E	5S	5	1376
Jef	2	2-	2N	8	1718	Jef	2	5-	1N	20	1755
Jef	2	2-	2N	32	1755	Jef	2	5-	1S	26	1718
Jef	2	2-	2N	33	1718	Jef	2	5-	2S	9	1718
Jef	2	2-	4S	20	1718	Jef	2	5-	2S	34	1755
Jef	2	2-	5S	13	1755	Jef	2	5-	2S	36	1718
Jef	2	3E	1S	1	1533	Jef	2	5-	3N	37	1718
Jef	2	3E	2N	13	1376	Jef	2	5-	4S	22	1755
Jef	2	3E	4S	8	1376	Jef	2	5-	5S	8	1718
Jef	2	3E	4S	17	1151	Jef	2	8E	3N	33	550
Jef	2	3E	5S	27	1151	Jef	2	8E	3N	34	1718
Jef	2	3-	1N	14	1718	Jef	2	8E	4N	24	1718
Jef	2	3-	1S	10	1718	Jef	2	9E	1N	2	1151
Jef	2	3-	1S	21	1718	Jef	2	9E	1N	5	1533
Jef	2	3-	2N	15	1718	Jef	2	9E	1N	27	1533
Jef	2	3-	2N	34	1718	Jef	2	9E	2N	6	1533
Jef	2	3-	2S	33	1718	Jef	2	9E	2N	13	1376
Jef	2	3-	4S	8	1718	Jef	2	9E	2N	20	1533
Jef	2	4E	1N	6	1533	Jef	2	9E	2N	26	1778
Jef	2	4E	1S	2	1376	Jef	2	9E	2N	28	1533
Jef	2	4E	2N	4	1151	Jef	2	9E	2N	32	550
Jef	2	4E	2N	5	550, 1376	Jef	2	9E	2N	34	1151
Jef	2	4E	2N	6	1533	Jef	2	9E	3N	2	1151
Jef	2	4E	2N	9	1533	Jef	2	9E	3N	4	1151, 1376
Jef	2	4E	2N	17	1151	Jef	2	9E	3N	15	1151
Jef	2	4E	2N	18	1376	Jef	2	9E	3N	23	1376
Jef	2	4E	2N	20	1376	Jef	2	9E	4N	33	1151
Jef	2	4E	2N	24	1151	Jef	2	9-	1N	24	1718
Jef	2	4E	3N	32	550	Jef	2	9-	1N	25	1718
Jef	2	4E	3N	33	1151	Jef	2	9-	2N	1	1718
Jef	2	4E	3S	11	1533	Jef	2	9-	2N	3	1755
Jef	2	4E	3S	12	1533	Jef	2	9-	2N	11	1755
Jef	2	4E	5N	12	1533	Jef	2	9-	3N	3	1718
Jef	2	4E	5N	22	1151	Jef	2	9-	3N	4	1718
Jef	2	4E	5N	30	1376	Jef	2	9-	3N	36	1718

Jef	2	9-	4N	30	1718
Jef	2	9-	5N	33	1718
Jef	2	10E	1N	8	1376
Jef	2	10E	2N	6	550
Jef	2	10E	2N	18	1376
Jef	2	10E	2N	19	1376
Jef	2	10E	3N	4	550
Jef	2	10E	3N	5	550
Jef	2	10E	3N	6	1376
Jef	2	10E	4N	28	1376
Jef	2	10E	4N	32	550
Jef	2	10E	5N	13	1376
Jef	2	10-	3N	6	1718
Jef	2	10-	4N	11	1718
Jef	2	10-	4N	35	1533
Jef	2	10-	4N	15	1376
Jef	2	11E	5N	21	1533
Jef	2	11-	4N	17	1533
Jef	2	11-	4N	22	1718
Jef	2	11-	4N	25	1718, 1755
Jef	2	11-	4N	29	1718
Jef	2	12-	5N	17	1718
Jef	2	12-	5N	20	1718

MADISON (COUNTY) LAND OFFICE DISTRICT

Mad	-	1E	2-	28	679
Mad	-	1E	3-	1	676
Mad	-	1E	3-	13	679
Mad	-	1E	3-	15	679
Mad	-	1E	3-	17	679
Mad	-	1E	3-	21	1278
Mad	-	1W	2-	32	679
Mad	-	1W	2-	33	679
Mad	-	1W	3-	13	676
Mad	-	1W	3-	14	676
Mad	-	2E	1-	15	676
Mad	-	2E	1-	17	676
Mad	-	2E	1-	28	679

MARIETTA (OHIO) LAND OFFICE DISTRICT

Mar	-	3	1	26	222
Mar	-	3	4	6	202
Mar	-	3	4	21	969
Mar	-	3	4	30	1780
Mar·	-	4	2	2	920
Mar	-	4	3	6	969
Mar	-	4	3	24	969
Mar	-	4	5	3	338
Mar	-	4	5	10	969
Mar	-	4	5	22	1491, 1588
Mar	-	4	5	28	1588
Mar	-	5	1	17	202
Mar	-	5	1	23	202
Mar	-	5	1	27	685, 755
Mar	-	5	2	2	338
Mar	-	5	2	3	338
Mar	-	5	3	3	1491
Mar	-	5	3	13	1308
Mar	-	5	3	25	969
Mar	-	5	3	36	1673
Mar	-	5	5	11	1780
Mar	-	5	5	32	1639, 1759
Mar	-	5	6	4	969
Mar	-	5	6	7	1780
Mar	-	5	6	18	1491
Mar	-	5	6	29	969
Mar	-	5	6	33	969
Mar	-	5	6	34	407, 1174
Mar	-	6	2	2	413
Mar	-	6	2	7	1407
Mar	-	6	3	20	1780
Mar	-	6	7	12	969
Mar	-	7	2	35	222, 969
Mar	-	7	3	26	969
Mar	-	7	3	31	282, 969
Mar	-	7	7	30	969
Mar	-	7	8	6	1780
Mar	-	7	8	21	1491
Mar	-	7	8	24	969
Mar	-	7	8	27	1131, 1415
Mar	-	7	8	33	233, 969
Mar	-	7	17	11	969
Mar	-	9	1	26	969
Mar	-	10	2	8	1491
Mar	-	12	4	8	222
Mar	-	13	5	8	1678
Mar	-	14	4	8	1491
Mar	-	14	4	11	172
Mar	-	14	5	8	1087

LAND GRANTS FOR MILITARY SERVICE
(See also Chl Mil *and* Zan Mil *land grants)*

Mil	–	1	2	21	1176
Mil	–	1	5	21	1176
Mil	–	1	6	2	1257
Mil	–	1	6	11	615
Mil	–	1	7	19	615
Mil	–	1	9	2	229
Mil	–	1	9	10	106, 144, 177
Mil	–	1	9	11	106
Mil	–	1	9	13	106, 155
Mil	–	1	10	1	575
Mil	–	1	19	11	155
Mil	–	2	1	1	179
Mil	–	2	5	2	1257
Mil	–	2	7	4	1257
Mil	–	2	7	13	174
Mil	–	2	7	17	615
Mil	–	2	7	18	615
Mil	–	2	7	19	615
Mil	–	2	10	2	713, 1257
Mil	–	3	1	21	4
Mil	–	3	2	3	176
Mil	–	3	7	1	138, 670, 1257
Mil	–	3	8	1	29
Mil	–	3	8	2	29
Mil	–	3	8	3	29
Mil	–	3	8	4	137, 138, 539, 914, 1257
Mil	–	3	8	16	615
Mil	–	3	9	1	148
Mil	–	3	9	9	148
Mil	–	4	7	16	615
Mil	–	4	10	1	603
Mil	–	4	10	3	539, 867
Mil	–	5	1	1	179
Mil	–	5	1	13	106
Mil	–	5	1	18	106
Mil	–	5	3	3	214, 704, 870, 1238
Mil	–	5	4	24	223
Mil	–	5	9	3	138
Mil	–	6	2	1	124, 870, 1641
Mil	–	7	1	9	258
Mil	–	7	3	19	4
Mil	–	7	4	2	213, 655
Mil	–	7	9	2	627, 1767
Mil	–	8	4	3	1728
Mil	–	8	4	4	193
Mil	–	8	5	16	727
Mil	–	8	9	1	575
Mil	–	8	9	2	217
Mil	–	8	9	3	217
Mil	–	9	1	19	186
Mil	–	9	5	12	727
Mil	–	9	5	20	727
Mil	–	9	7	3	136
Mil	–	10	3	1	4
Mil	–	10	3	10	4
Mil	–	10	4	21	4
Mil	–	11	6	1	236, 851, 946, 1082
Mil	–	12	2	4	62
Mil	–	12	7	16	1264
Mil	–	12	7	25	143
Mil	–	14	8	3	1587
Mil	–	15	1	3	32
Mil	–	15	8	3	574
Mil	–	16	6	1	213, 1014
Mil	–	16	7	2	124, 139
Mil	–	16	7	4	32
Mil	–	17	7	1	1014
Mil	–	17	7	2	124
Mil	–	17	7	4	117, 139
Mil	–	19	7	2	124, 999
Mil	–	19	7	19	319
Mil	–	21	8	8	143

NASHVILLE (TENNESSEE) LAND OFFICE DISTRICT

Nas	–	1	2	33	445
Nas	–	1	3	33	445
Nas	W	1	2	12	445

CANADIAN AND NOVA SCOTIAN REFUGEE TRACT (OHIO)

Ref	–	17	19	7	900
Ref	–	18	17	26	900
Ref	–	18	17	29	900
Ref	–	21	12	8	900
Ref	–	21	12	18	1608
Ref	–	21	12	20	900
Ref	–	21	12	26	900

STEUBENVILLE (OHIO) LAND OFFICE DISTRICT

Stu	–	1	3	26	592
Stu	–	1	4	27	799, 960, 1030, 1058

Stu	–	1	4	31	1717
Stu	–	1	4	33	799, 960, 1030, 1058
Stu	–	1	6	3	1750
Stu	–	1	6	4	314, 960
Stu	–	1	6	5	863, 1323
Stu	–	1	6	7	592
Stu	–	1	6	8	380
Stu	–	1	6	9	863
Stu	–	1	6	15	355
Stu	–	1	6	17	1569
Stu	–	1	6	18	22, 323, 775
Stu	–	1	6	19	960, 1049, 1717
Stu	–	1	6	20	287, 323
Stu	–	1	6	21	1090, 1542, 1717
Stu	–	1	6	22	724, 1253
Stu	–	1	6	23	1090
Stu	–	1	6	33	162
Stu	–	1	6	35	57
Stu	–	1	7	1	355, 1377
Stu	–	1	7	3	134, 960, 1090
Stu	–	1	7	4	1626
Stu	–	1	7	8	1717
Stu	–	1	7	9	384, 418
Stu	–	1	7	10	1253, 1444, 1717
Stu	–	1	7	17	1049, 1393
Stu	–	1	7	18	474, 561
Stu	–	1	7	19	503
Stu	–	1	7	20	134, 1504, 1629
Stu	–	1	7	21	1782
Stu	–	1	7	24	1750
Stu	–	1	7	26	1393
Stu	–	1	7	27	1490
Stu	–	1	7	28	131, 1049, 1573
Stu	–	1	7	29	1569
Stu	–	1	7	30	735, 960, 1323, 1393
Stu	–	1	7	31	1504, 1626
Stu	–	1	7	32	294, 440, 1049, 1234, 1315
Stu	–	1	7	33	1315
Stu	–	1	7	34	384, 599, 1049
Stu	–	1	8	15	1569
Stu	–	1	8	21	51
Stu	–	1	8	22	1626
Stu	–	1	8	34	134
Stu	–	1	8	35	131
Stu	–	1	8	36	447, 1090
Stu	–	1	9	3	519, 642
Stu	–	1	9	7	5, 35
Stu	–	1	9	15	1049, 1393
Stu	–	1	9	21	589, 796, 828
Stu	–	1	9	22	533, 592, 1784
Stu	–	1	9	31	1595
Stu	–	2	3	26	599
Stu	–	2	3	31	738
Stu	–	2	3	32	22
Stu	–	2	5	5	489
Stu	–	2	5	8	473, 489, 1750
Stu	–	2	5	26	960, 1122, 1490
Stu	–	2	5	29	531, 1130
Stu	–	2	6	13	960, 1750
Stu	–	2	6	15	787, 1393
Stu	–	2	6	19	1626
Stu	–	2	6	22	1130, 1782
Stu	–	2	6	25	9, 994
Stu	–	2	6	36	1782
Stu	–	2	7	8	1049
Stu	–	2	7	11	1717
Stu	–	2	7	26	691, 1049
Stu	–	2	7	29	1713
Stu	–	2	8	1	1501, 1569
Stu	–	2	8	6	314
Stu	–	2	8	12	1490
Stu	–	2	8	15	380, 960, 1130
Stu	–	2	8	17	1569
Stu	–	2	8	21	994, 1049, 1069
Stu	–	2	8	22	1377, 1393, 1626
Stu	–	2	8	23	489, 1547, 1626
Stu	–	2	8	27	592, 1490
Stu	–	2	8	28	724
Stu	–	2	8	31	384, 1090
Stu	–	2	8	32	738
Stu	–	2	8	34	599, 754
Stu	–	2	9	8	1348, 1393, 1573
Stu	–	2	9	14	1348, 1393, 1573
Stu	–	2	9	22	1717
Stu	–	2	9	25	1130
Stu	–	2	9	28	305
Stu	–	2	9	29	938
Stu	–	2	9	30	373, 439
Stu	–	2	9	34	57
Stu	–	2	9	35	305, 378
Stu	–	2	9	36	960, 1098
Stu	–	2	10	1	960
Stu	–	2	10	2	268
Stu	–	2	10	3	305, 734
Stu	–	2	10	4	323, 1049
Stu	–	2	10	5	549, 1750
Stu	–	2	10	6	960
Stu	–	2	10	8	960, 1090, 1393

Stu	–	2	10	9	1130
Stu	–	2	10	11	5, 23
Stu	–	2	10	12	592, 599
Stu	–	2	10	13	599, 1090
Stu	–	2	10	14	775, 1030
Stu	–	2	10	17	380
Stu	–	2	10	18	257, 863
Stu	–	2	10	19	1626
Stu	–	2	10	23	569, 1626
Stu	–	2	10	26	960, 985
Stu	–	2	10	27	77, 1123
Stu	–	2	10	28	373
Stu	–	2	10	29	960
Stu	–	2	10	31	561
Stu	–	2	10	34	134, 537
Stu	–	2	11	5	9, 27
Stu	–	2	11	9	323
Stu	–	2	11	14	5, 22
Stu	–	2	11	17	355, 880
Stu	–	2	11	23	1030
Stu	–	2	11	24	960
Stu	–	2	11	25	398
Stu	–	2	11	26	5, 305, 536
Stu	–	2	11	27	1626
Stu	–	2	11	28	592, 1626
Stu	–	2	11	29	561, 1626
Stu	–	2	11	30	355, 440
Stu	–	2	11	31	57, 828, 1130, 1490
Stu	–	2	11	32	323
Stu	–	2	11	33	474
Stu	–	2	11	34	1569
Stu	–	2	11	35	1030, 1377
Stu	–	2	11	36	994
Stu	–	2	12	9	1490
Stu	–	2	12	11	1490
Stu	–	2	12	12	474
Stu	–	2	12	15	134, 268
Stu	–	2	12	21	1684
Stu	–	2	12	22	440, 533, 1782
Stu	–	2	13	1	380
Stu	–	2	13	3	134
Stu	–	2	13	15	660, 1513, 1569, 1672
Stu	–	2	13	18	134
Stu	–	2	13	21	960
Stu	–	2	13	22	120, 960, 1049
Stu	–	3	5	4	1569
Stu	–	3	5	13	828
Stu	–	3	5	18	440
Stu	–	3	5	23	1049
Stu	–	3	5	26	1784
Stu	–	3	5	27	828, 1784
Stu	–	3	5	29	531, 592
Stu	–	3	5	30	1197
Stu	–	3	5	36	259
Stu	–	3	6	15	1569, 1750
Stu	–	3	6	19	1154, 1197, 1253, 1522
Stu	–	3	6	20	1542
Stu	–	3	6	21	1490, 1717
Stu	–	3	6	25	828, 960
Stu	–	3	6	26	1626
Stu	–	3	6	32	781, 964, 965
Stu	–	3	7	15	960, 1253
Stu	–	3	7	21	828, 960, 1049, 1197
Stu	–	3	7	22	828, 1049, 1490, 1784
Stu	–	3	8	15	1030, 1626
Stu	–	3	8	21	678
Stu	–	3	8	22	1030
Stu	–	3	9	6	960, 1750
Stu	–	3	9	11	100
Stu	–	3	9	15	533, 599, 724, 960
Stu	–	3	9	18	734, 810, 1030, 1090
Stu	–	3	9	21	960, 1130, 1377, 1393
Stu	–	3	9	22	1626
Stu	–	3	9	23	724, 1049
Stu	–	3	9	24	27
Stu	–	3	9	29	384, 418, 618
Stu	–	3	9	30	134, 259
Stu	–	3	9	35	1784
Stu	–	3	9	36	1569
Stu	–	3	10	1	1490, 1569
Stu	–	3	10	6	134
Stu	–	3	10	7	1569
Stu	–	3	10	8	488
Stu	–	3	10	11	960
Stu	–	3	10	13	599, 1090
Stu	–	3	10	14	134, 537
Stu	–	3	10	15	294, 440, 960
Stu	–	3	10	17	994, 1569
Stu	–	3	10	19	994
Stu	–	3	10	23	1090, 1154
Stu	–	3	10	24	410
Stu	–	3	10	25	51
Stu	–	3	10	30	504
Stu	–	3	10	31	51
Stu	–	3	11	3	960, 1782
Stu	–	3	11	8	1377
Stu	–	3	11	9	1377
Stu	–	3	11	27	384, 473

Stu	—	3	11	32	57, 503, 1626	Stu	—	4	6	18	1534
Stu	—	3	11	34	1735	Stu	—	4	6	24	1569
Stu	—	3	12	4	528, 643	Stu	—	4	6	28	463
Stu	—	3	12	5	1393	Stu	—	4	6	33	1315
Stu	—	3	12	9	1750	Stu	—	4	6	34	1197
Stu	—	3	12	17	1393	Stu	—	4	6	35	345, 754, 1784
Stu	—	3	12	27	1626	Stu	—	4	7	1	994, 1049, 1569
Stu	—	3	12	33	378	Stu	—	4	7	7	438, 828, 899, 1626
Stu	—	3	13	1	1393	Stu	—	4	7	8	724
Stu	—	3	13	2	1569	Stu	—	4	7	12	59
Stu	—	3	13	3	1750	Stu	—	4	7	26	531, 1253
Stu	—	3	13	4	1717	Stu	—	4	7	29	734, 994, 1024, 1717
Stu	—	3	13	6	259, 1750	Stu	—	4	7	30	362
Stu	—	3	13	12	960, 1047, 1253	Stu	—	4	8	3	599, 734, 775
Stu	—	3	13	13	1049	Stu	—	4	8	9	73
Stu	—	3	14	7	461, 994	Stu	—	4	8	15	1393, 1534, 1569, 1750
Stu	—	3	14	15	533, 960	Stu	—	4	8	21	1045, 1090, 1315, 1534
Stu	—	3	14	18	14, 110, 1090	Stu	—	4	8	22	960, 1130
Stu	—	3	14	19	131	Stu	—	4	9	15	1049, 1253
Stu	—	3	14	20	599, 960, 1569	Stu	—	4	9	21	780, 1197
Stu	—	3	14	21	1501, 1626	Stu	—	4	9	22	100, 1393
Stu	—	3	14	22	322, 410, 1393, 1626	Stu	—	4	10	3	305
Stu	—	3	14	25	828	Stu	—	4	10	6	22
Stu	—	3	14	27	281	Stu	—	4	10	11	474, 775
Stu	—	3	14	28	398, 1534	Stu	—	4	10	15	531, 1626
Stu	—	3	14	29	828	Stu	—	4	10	18	599
Stu	—	3	14	30	960	Stu	—	4	10	21	455, 1393, 1403, 1569
Stu	—	3	14	31	754, 1130	Stu	—	4	10	22	268, 1049, 1253
Stu	—	3	14	32	27	Stu	—	4	10	23	589, 960, 1626
Stu	—	3	14	33	503	Stu	—	4	10	28	724, 985
Stu	—	3	14	35	1626	Stu	—	4	10	29	440, 504
Stu	—	3	14	36	1090	Stu	—	4	10	30	489
Stu	—	3	15	15	77, 1455	Stu	—	4	10	32	1030
Stu	—	3	15	22	57, 1455	Stu	—	4	10	34	960
Stu	—	3	15	25	57	Stu	—	4	10	35	27, 1130, 1784
Stu	—	3	15	28	960	Stu	—	4	11	4	1090, 1315, 1784
Stu	—	3	15	29	715, 1049	Stu	—	4	11	8	5, 489, 1049, 1534
Stu	—	3	16	3	1090	Stu	—	4	11	12	22, 1197
Stu	—	3	16	5	1569	Stu	—	4	11	15	380, 960, 1130, 1377
Stu	—	3	16	12	1569	Stu	—	4	11	18	1626
Stu	—	3	16	21	1626	Stu	—	4	11	21	599, 1130, 1253
Stu	—	4	6	4	1569	Stu	—	4	11	22	294, 440, 787, 1513, 1628
Stu	—	4	6	5	384, 960, 1784	Stu	—	4	11	30	489
Stu	—	4	6	6	2, 994	Stu	—	4	11	31	380
Stu	—	4	6	9	734	Stu	—	4	11	34	960, 1303, 1393, 1717
Stu	—	4	6	10	504, 599	Stu	—	4	11	35	775, 994, 1569
Stu	—	4	6	11	599, 960, 1542, 1573	Stu	—	4	11	36	268
Stu	—	4	6	12	447	Stu	—	4	12	1	346, 1090
Stu	—	4	6	17	787	Stu	—	4	12	2	1090

Stu	–	4	12	4	477, 1003	Stu	–	4	17	8	960
Stu	–	4	12	7	537	Stu	–	4	17	9	69
Stu	–	4	12	9	281, 569	Stu	–	4	17	10	41
Stu	–	4	12	10	1569	Stu	–	4	17	12	257
Stu	–	4	12	13	1049, 1626	Stu	–	4	17	13	1090
Stu	–	4	12	14	134, 1377	Stu	–	4	17	14	69, 1030
Stu	–	4	12	26	787	Stu	–	4	17	17	569, 1784
Stu	–	4	12	28	9	Stu	–	4	17	18	1377, 1490
Stu	–	4	12	33	592	Stu	–	4	17	19	531
Stu	–	4	13	31	423	Stu	–	4	17	27	134
Stu	–	4	13	32	504, 1154	Stu	–	4	17	28	474
Stu	–	4	14	1	5, 305, 1750	Stu	–	4	17	29	134
Stu	–	4	14	2	1030, 1750	Stu	–	4	17	30	555, 960
Stu	–	4	14	4	1154	Stu	–	4	17	31	257, 395, 599, 692
Stu	–	4	14	10	821	Stu	–	5	6	14	522
Stu	–	4	14	11	599, 960, 1534	Stu	–	5	7	3	599
Stu	–	4	14	14	474	Stu	–	5	7	8	384, 1030, 1510
Stu	–	4	14	19	1197	Stu	–	5	7	9	522
Stu	–	4	15	4	599	Stu	–	5	7	10	384
Stu	–	4	15	11	592	Stu	–	5	7	11	384, 960, 1626
Stu	–	4	15	14	780, 960, 1118	Stu	–	5	7	13	219, 569
Stu	–	4	15	17	9, 355	Stu	–	5	7	14	1326
Stu	–	4	15	18	1090	Stu	–	5	7	18	87, 503
Stu	–	4	15	19	561, 796	Stu	–	5	7	19	489, 537, 549
Stu	–	4	15	20	863, 1445	Stu	–	5	7	20	455, 524, 537
Stu	–	4	15	21	268, 863, 1030, 1547	Stu	–	5	7	21	1626
Stu	–	4	15	23	22	Stu	–	5	7	26	134
Stu	–	4	15	24	57, 503	Stu	–	5	7	27	754
Stu	–	4	15	25	232, 561	Stu	–	5	7	29	134, 295
Stu	–	4	15	26	1090	Stu	–	5	7	30	134, 504, 1340, 1490, 1497
Stu	–	4	15	28	268, 537, 960, 1090	Stu	–	5	7	32	405, 424, 828
Stu	–	4	15	29	599	Stu	–	5	7	33	340, 566, 902, 1130
Stu	–	4	15	30	215, 323, 599	Stu	–	5	7	35	1784
Stu	–	4	15	31	116, 1090	Stu	–	5	8	8	1469
Stu	–	4	15	32	493, 599	Stu	–	5	8	10	358, 417, 640
Stu	–	4	15	34	1626	Stu	–	5	8	15	1130, 1146
Stu	–	4	15	35	384	Stu	–	5	8	17	100
Stu	–	4	16	2	1559	Stu	–	5	8	23	131, 960
Stu	–	4	16	3	960	Stu	–	5	8	25	134
Stu	–	4	16	6	323	Stu	–	5	8	26	27
Stu	–	4	16	10	57	Stu	–	5	8	27	100
Stu	–	4	16	19	536	Stu	–	5	8	29	9, 960, 1784
Stu	–	4	16	29	268, 828, 1090	Stu	–	5	8	30	384, 592
Stu	–	4	16	31	1090, 1501, 1619	Stu	–	5	8	32	504
Stu	–	4	16	32	1784	Stu	–	5	8	33	960
Stu	–	4	17	1	57	Stu	–	5	8	34	323
Stu	–	4	17	3	960	Stu	–	5	8	36	1717
Stu	–	4	17	4	69	Stu	–	5	9	15	828, 1154
Stu	–	4	17	7	323, 724, 775, 828	Stu	–	5	9	19	455, 960

Stu	–	5	9	23	134, 754
Stu	–	5	9	24	384, 1090
Stu	–	5	9	25	599
Stu	–	5	9	26	49
Stu	–	5	9	27	27, 504, 599
Stu	–	5	9	28	281, 748, 1090, 1377
Stu	–	5	9	29	314, 828, 1490
Stu	–	5	9	30	960
Stu	–	5	9	32	323, 370, 378
Stu	–	5	9	33	599, 1090
Stu	–	5	9	35	1784
Stu	–	5	9	36	447
Stu	–	5	10	13	57
Stu	–	5	10	15	960, 1393
Stu	–	5	10	17	754, 863, 960, 994
Stu	–	5	10	19	131, 134
Stu	–	5	10	20	51, 1348, 1393
Stu	–	5	10	21	1393, 1784
Stu	–	5	10	24	828, 1547
Stu	–	5	10	25	384, 1030, 1049
Stu	–	5	10	27	796
Stu	–	5	10	28	268, 1154, 1569
Stu	–	5	10	30	561
Stu	–	5	10	31	960, 1253, 1393
Stu	–	5	10	32	960
Stu	–	5	10	33	599, 994
Stu	–	5	10	34	268, 1348, 1393
Stu	–	5	10	35	1490
Stu	–	5	10	37	474
Stu	–	5	11	2	738, 744, 960
Stu	–	5	11	3	257
Stu	–	5	11	4	257, 268, 524
Stu	–	5	11	5	537, 828, 1393
Stu	–	5	11	6	5
Stu	–	5	11	7	828, 960
Stu	–	5	11	8	134, 1030, 1750
Stu	–	5	11	9	305, 1090, 1377
Stu	–	5	11	10	524, 1626
Stu	–	5	11	11	1253, 1490
Stu	–	5	11	12	787
Stu	–	5	11	13	440, 1030
Stu	–	5	11	14	259, 1090
Stu	–	5	11	15	1253
Stu	–	5	11	17	57, 828, 1784
Stu	–	5	11	18	9, 1403, 1457, 1490, 1717
Stu	–	5	11	19	131, 257, 960
Stu	–	5	11	20	100
Stu	–	5	11	23	775
Stu	–	5	11	24	257, 592
Stu	–	5	11	25	268
Stu	–	5	11	27	1197
Stu	–	5	11	28	1782
Stu	–	5	11	33	384
Stu	–	5	12	2	1315
Stu	–	5	12	3	1784
Stu	–	5	12	6	257
Stu	–	5	12	7	384
Stu	–	5	12	8	1393
Stu	–	5	12	12	418, 1569
Stu	–	5	12	14	1049
Stu	–	5	12	17	562, 567
Stu	–	5	12	18	244
Stu	–	5	12	20	1253, 1534, 1597, 1626
Stu	–	5	12	25	355, 1569
Stu	–	5	12	31	259, 1717
Stu	–	5	12	32	384
Stu	–	5	12	33	1030, 1095, 1137
Stu	–	5	13	6	423, 1090
Stu	–	5	13	11	960, 1090
Stu	–	5	13	17	244, 1090
Stu	–	5	13	18	1547
Stu	–	5	13	23	5, 268, 775
Stu	–	5	13	35	1626
Stu	–	5	14	2	536
Stu	–	5	14	7	1090
Stu	–	5	14	25	1717
Stu	–	5	14	26	1782
Stu	–	5	14	31	775
Stu	–	5	14	32	1393
Stu	–	5	15	1	828, 1253
Stu	–	5	15	14	1393, 1714
Stu	–	5	15	16	1030
Stu	–	5	15	23	1393, 1501
Stu	–	5	15	24	856, 1049
Stu	–	5	15	26	1377
Stu	–	5	15	27	1377, 1503, 1626
Stu	–	5	16	1	828
Stu	–	5	16	2	57
Stu	–	5	16	3	724
Stu	–	5	16	13	134
Stu	–	5	16	14	1569, 1750
Stu	–	5	16	15	1393
Stu	–	5	16	18	1444
Stu	–	5	16	20	1747
Stu	–	5	16	21	1393
Stu	–	5	16	24	120, 199, 796
Stu	–	5	16	25	116, 1326
Stu	–	5	16	26	110, 447, 569

Stu	–	5	16	27	120, 197
Stu	–	5	16	31	87, 113
Stu	–	5	16	34	1154
Stu	–	5	16	35	1049, 1062
Stu	–	5	16	36	134, 1049
Stu	–	5	17	1	355
Stu	–	5	17	3	524
Stu	–	5	17	10	534
Stu	–	5	17	11	131, 1079
Stu	–	5	17	13	69, 380
Stu	–	5	17	19	131, 134, 378
Stu	–	5	17	20	474
Stu	–	5	17	23	754, 1130
Stu	–	5	17	26	558, 571, 637
Stu	–	5	17	30	592, 724
Stu	–	5	17	34	323
Stu	–	5	17	35	22
Stu	–	5	18	4	1393
Stu	–	5	18	6	524
Stu	–	5	18	9	41, 92
Stu	–	5	18	19	524, 589
Stu	–	5	18	20	268
Stu	–	5	18	23	1253
Stu	–	5	18	24	384, 1253
Stu	–	5	18	25	51, 561
Stu	–	5	18	27	534
Stu	–	5	18	29	569
Stu	–	5	18	32	355
Stu	–	5	18	33	22
Stu	–	5	18	35	592
Stu	–	5	19	15	1064
Stu	–	6	1	28	374
Stu	–	6	4	12	1095, 1137
Stu	–	6	8	1	57
Stu	–	6	8	2	994, 1393
Stu	–	6	8	5	1444
Stu	–	6	8	7	599, 960
Stu	–	6	8	13	257
Stu	–	6	8	15	100, 1099
Stu	–	6	8	18	754
Stu	–	6	8	19	1090
Stu	–	6	8	20	257
Stu	–	6	8	21	1038, 1099, 1130, 1480, 1564
Stu	–	6	8	22	257
Stu	–	6	8	23	22, 1090
Stu	–	6	8	24	960, 1547
Stu	–	6	8	27	57
Stu	–	6	8	30	1154
Stu	–	6	8	31	504, 646
Stu	–	6	8	34	1750, 1784
Stu	–	6	8	35	960, 1154
Stu	–	6	9	1	738
Stu	–	6	9	5	1030
Stu	–	6	9	6	537
Stu	–	6	9	10	22
Stu	–	6	9	11	1348, 1393
Stu	–	6	9	12	1750
Stu	–	6	9	14	1717
Stu	–	6	9	18	257, 787
Stu	–	6	9	19	474, 561
Stu	–	6	9	20	1626
Stu	–	6	9	23	569
Stu	–	6	9	26	748, 775
Stu	–	6	9	27	960
Stu	–	6	9	28	960, 994
Stu	–	6	9	29	994, 1626
Stu	–	6	9	34	533, 599
Stu	–	6	10	2	482, 881
Stu	–	6	10	3	134, 314
Stu	–	6	10	5	1626
Stu	–	6	10	6	522, 1154
Stu	–	6	10	7	355, 537
Stu	–	6	10	8	116
Stu	–	6	10	9	134, 489, 599, 1717
Stu	–	6	10	10	828
Stu	–	6	10	11	314, 1377
Stu	–	6	10	12	22, 1049
Stu	–	6	10	14	30, 828, 863
Stu	–	6	10	17	305
Stu	–	6	10	18	9, 1049
Stu	–	6	10	20	960
Stu	–	6	10	24	828, 994, 1130
Stu	–	6	10	25	1534
Stu	–	6	10	27	116, 379
Stu	–	6	10	28	1782
Stu	–	6	10	33	379
Stu	–	6	10	35	474
Stu	–	6	11	1	489, 960, 994
Stu	–	6	11	2	134
Stu	–	6	11	3	828
Stu	–	6	11	4	960
Stu	–	6	11	8	524, 1393
Stu	–	6	11	10	9, 22
Stu	–	6	11	19	994
Stu	–	6	11	27	9, 257, 592
Stu	–	6	11	31	1626
Stu	–	6	11	33	994
Stu	–	6	12	4	1090

Stu	–	6	12	7	599	Stu	–	6	17	3	1393, 1717
Stu	–	6	12	9	549	Stu	–	6	17	4	828, 960
Stu	–	6	12	14	536, 828	Stu	–	6	17	6	268
Stu	–	6	12	20	1569	Stu	–	6	17	7	1154, 1750
Stu	–	6	12	27	473, 787	Stu	–	6	17	8	960
Stu	–	6	12	28	549, 775	Stu	–	6	17	10	69, 599
Stu	–	6	12	33	473	Stu	–	6	17	13	268
Stu	–	6	12	34	473, 592, 1049	Stu	–	6	17	17	960, 1154, 1315, 1393
Stu	–	6	13	2	522, 738, 1049, 1490	Stu	–	6	17	18	1049
Stu	–	6	13	7	592	Stu	–	6	17	19	1049
Stu	–	6	13	8	77, 268, 599	Stu	–	6	17	20	724
Stu	–	6	13	9	599	Stu	–	6	17	23	1154
Stu	–	6	13	14	561, 828, 1090	Stu	–	6	17	26	1049
Stu	–	6	13	20	1393	Stu	–	6	17	33	1717
Stu	–	6	13	27	305, 960	Stu	–	6	17	36	87, 113, 1253
Stu	–	6	13	28	355	Stu	–	6	18	1	620, 700
Stu	–	6	13	30	1	Stu	–	6	18	5	69
Stu	–	6	13	33	738, 1750	Stu	–	6	18	8	471, 506, 699
Stu	–	6	13	34	536, 599, 621, 883	Stu	–	6	18	9	471, 699
Stu	–	6	13	35	1784	Stu	–	6	18	10	1393
Stu	–	6	14	6	1717	Stu	–	6	18	11	440
Stu	–	6	14	11	1547	Stu	–	6	18	12	1717
Stu	–	6	14	18	960, 1270, 1514	Stu	–	6	18	13	531, 1626
Stu	–	6	14	24	599, 1534	Stu	–	6	18	14	69, 503, 1049, 1393
Stu	–	6	14	25	323, 1569	Stu	–	6	18	23	646
Stu	–	6	14	28	5, 380, 1054, 1090, 1483	Stu	–	6	18	24	536
Stu	–	6	14	29	1030, 1782	Stu	–	6	18	25	715
Stu	–	6	14	30	646, 649	Stu	–	6	18	30	116, 599
Stu	–	6	14	33	1197, 1377	Stu	–	6	18	32	1253
Stu	–	6	14	34	380	Stu	–	6	18	33	384
Stu	–	6	14	36	1030	Stu	–	6	18	34	69
Stu	–	6	15	1	960, 1782	Stu	–	6	19	4	257, 754, 1019
Stu	–	6	15	13	649	Stu	–	6	19	5	35, 77, 257
Stu	–	6	15	19	1784	Stu	–	6	19	8	27
Stu	–	6	15	23	734	Stu	–	6	19	9	384
Stu	–	6	15	25	1784	Stu	–	6	19	10	775
Stu	–	6	15	26	1030	Stu	–	6	19	11	22, 257
Stu	–	6	15	27	1784	Stu	–	6	19	12	22, 533
Stu	–	6	16	1	649, 1782	Stu	–	6	19	13	268
Stu	–	6	16	2	649, 960	Stu	–	6	19	17	323, 489
Stu	–	6	16	3	1626	Stu	–	6	19	20	524
Stu	–	6	16	7	1747	Stu	–	6	19	23	536, 1049
Stu	–	6	16	10	643, 1626	Stu	–	6	19	24	599
Stu	–	6	16	11	976	Stu	–	6	19	25	384, 489
Stu	–	6	16	12	12, 650	Stu	–	6	19	26	599, 1777
Stu	–	6	16	17	110, 441, 446, 466, 1775	Stu	–	7	7	1	533
Stu	–	6	16	19	12, 650	Stu	–	7	7	14	341, 446
Stu	–	6	17	1	1782	Stu	–	7	9	4	257, 378, 440
Stu	–	6	17	2	1377	Stu	–	7	9	5	314, 524

Stu	–	7	9	6	787, 1090
Stu	–	7	9	7	131
Stu	–	7	9	10	257
Stu	–	7	9	11	418, 828, 1154
Stu	–	7	9	13	131
Stu	–	7	9	16	1547
Stu	–	7	9	17	1197
Stu	–	7	9	20	440, 1154
Stu	–	7	9	28	592, 911, 1049, 1490
Stu	–	7	9	30	305, 504
Stu	–	7	9	32	524
Stu	–	7	9	33	57, 828
Stu	–	7	9	35	828, 1534
Stu	–	7	10	1	504
Stu	–	7	10	2	1626
Stu	–	7	10	3	1626
Stu	–	7	10	7	5
Stu	–	7	10	13	5
Stu	–	7	10	17	775, 1393, 1547
Stu	–	7	10	23	1490
Stu	–	7	10	27	1253
Stu	–	7	10	31	724
Stu	–	7	10	33	1490
Stu	–	7	10	34	1490
Stu	–	7	10	35	1490, 1784
Stu	–	7	10	36	1700
Stu	–	7	11	5	1090
Stu	–	7	11	6	555
Stu	–	7	11	9	1141, 1250
Stu	–	7	11	12	1154, 1626
Stu	–	7	11	17	116
Stu	–	7	11	18	27, 599, 960
Stu	–	7	11	20	1490
Stu	–	7	11	23	1626
Stu	–	7	11	24	1776
Stu	–	7	11	26	748, 1750
Stu	–	7	12	1	1784
Stu	–	7	12	2	1784
Stu	–	7	12	3	5, 1090
Stu	–	7	12	7	1253, 1750
Stu	–	7	12	8	1784
Stu	–	7	12	9	1784
Stu	–	7	12	14	504, 994, 1253, 1782
Stu	–	7	12	19	134
Stu	–	7	12	20	1090
Stu	–	7	12	21	1782
Stu	–	7	12	23	724, 960
Stu	–	7	12	24	131
Stu	–	7	12	27	1784
Stu	–	7	12	31	1569, 1717
Stu	–	7	13	19	646
Stu	–	7	14	5	57
Stu	–	7	14	13	748
Stu	–	7	14	17	1315
Stu	–	7	14	18	473
Stu	–	7	14	19	1490
Stu	–	7	14	20	1393
Stu	–	7	14	25	522, 734, 1569
Stu	–	7	14	26	1130
Stu	–	7	14	31	960, 1750
Stu	–	7	15	1	1
Stu	–	7	15	6	533, 561, 960
Stu	–	7	15	8	355
Stu	–	7	15	9	1049, 1393
Stu	–	7	15	10	1393
Stu	–	7	15	11	1030
Stu	–	7	15	12	12, 650, 773, 960, 1030, 1154
Stu	–	7	15	14	69
Stu	–	7	15	17	1090
Stu	–	7	15	23	549, 697
Stu	–	7	15	27	1049, 1750
Stu	–	7	15	29	314, 440, 960
Stu	–	7	15	30	1534
Stu	–	7	15	36	569, 599, 994
Stu	–	7	16	11	355
Stu	–	7	16	24	1030
Stu	–	7	16	31	1154
Stu	–	7	16	32	960, 1501
Stu	–	7	16	36	257
Stu	–	7	17	3	536, 537
Stu	–	7	17	5	1569
Stu	–	7	17	6	1490, 1750
Stu	–	7	17	10	27, 592, 734
Stu	–	7	17	13	1747
Stu	–	7	17	14	341, 353, 354, 748, 1540
Stu	–	7	17	19	1626
Stu	–	7	17	20	131
Stu	–	7	17	23	12, 599, 650
Stu	–	7	17	28	1750
Stu	–	7	17	30	960
Stu	–	7	18	1	100, 134
Stu	–	7	18	4	305
Stu	–	7	18	5	51, 305, 378
Stu	–	7	18	6	323, 734, 1746
Stu	–	7	18	7	305
Stu	–	7	18	8	116
Stu	–	7	18	9	305, 1049
Stu	–	7	18	11	524, 549, 828, 960

Stu	–	7	18	12	22, 1197	Stu	–	8	9	1	1750
Stu	–	7	18	14	259	Stu	–	8	9	2	1030
Stu	–	7	18	18	1315	Stu	–	8	9	3	748
Stu	–	7	18	19	22, 355	Stu	–	8	9	5	599, 1626
Stu	–	7	18	24	12, 650, 773	Stu	–	8	9	6	1569
Stu	–	7	18	30	398	Stu	–	8	9	7	1090
Stu	–	7	18	31	473, 589	Stu	–	8	9	8	102, 147, 789, 854
Stu	–	7	18	32	384, 569	Stu	–	8	9	9	561
Stu	–	7	18	34	599	Stu	–	8	9	10	1377
Stu	–	7	18	35	1197	Stu	–	8	9	11	116
Stu	–	7	19	1	599	Stu	–	8	9	12	1030
Stu	–	7	19	3	358, 474	Stu	–	8	9	17	734, 960, 1049
Stu	–	7	19	5	257	Stu	–	8	9	19	1393
Stu	–	7	19	6	257, 259	Stu	–	8	9	20	410, 473, 1750
Stu	–	7	19	7	100, 257	Stu	–	8	9	21	1154
Stu	–	7	19	9	373	Stu	–	8	9	23	474
Stu	–	7	19	10	531	Stu	–	8	9	24	1197
Stu	–	7	19	11	729, 1777	Stu	–	8	9	26	1501, 1626
Stu	–	7	19	12	592, 724	Stu	–	8	9	27	1750
Stu	–	7	19	13	51	Stu	–	8	9	28	1049
Stu	–	7	19	17	259, 358	Stu	–	8	9	29	960
Stu	–	7	19	18	384, 1090	Stu	–	8	10	1	305, 447
Stu	–	7	19	23	355	Stu	–	8	10	2	27
Stu	–	7	19	24	57	Stu	–	8	10	3	131, 455, 461
Stu	–	7	19	26	1501	Stu	–	8	10	4	305, 1393
Stu	–	7	19	29	5, 259	Stu	–	8	10	5	116, 305, 1030, 1393
Stu	–	7	19	30	537, 1049, 1427	Stu	–	8	10	6	314, 960
Stu	–	7	19	31	1746	Stu	–	8	10	7	1607, 1747
Stu	–	7	19	33	373, 1784	Stu	–	8	10	8	1030, 1782
Stu	–	7	19	34	734	Stu	–	8	10	9	828, 1393
Stu	–	7	19	35	1154	Stu	–	8	10	11	384, 665
Stu	–	7	19	36	646	Stu	–	8	10	12	22, 960
Stu	–	7	20	1	9, 134, 257, 531	Stu	–	8	10	15	482, 882, 1377, 1393, 1501
Stu	–	7	20	2	531, 1534	Stu	–	8	10	17	268, 370, 378
Stu	–	7	20	10	531	Stu	–	8	10	18	1607, 1747
Stu	–	7	20	11	259, 531, 1130	Stu	–	8	10	19	775, 1717
Stu	–	7	20	13	440	Stu	–	8	10	20	12, 1540
Stu	–	7	20	14	960	Stu	–	8	10	21	305, 889
Stu	–	7	20	20	5	Stu	–	8	10	22	1030, 1626, 1784
Stu	–	7	20	23	34, 268, 1377	Stu	–	8	10	23	1049
Stu	–	7	20	24	9, 398, 493	Stu	–	8	10	24	1049
Stu	–	7	20	25	44, 69, 748	Stu	–	8	10	25	27, 314, 1410
Stu	–	7	20	26	1393	Stu	–	8	10	27	257, 373, 1081, 1154
Stu	–	7	20	27	1393	Stu	–	8	10	29	341, 353, 354, 384, 446, 473, 1540
Stu	–	7	20	29	410						
Stu	–	7	20	31	537	Stu	–	8	10	30	27, 549, 599
Stu	–	7	20	32	355	Stu	–	8	10	31	536, 599
Stu	–	7	20	34	1129, 1393	Stu	–	8	10	32	410, 555
Stu	–	7	20	35	1377, 1569	Stu	–	8	10	33	780, 1490, 1529

Stu	–	8	10	34		691, 828, 1626
Stu	–	8	10	35		1030, 1408
Stu	–	8	10	36		473
Stu	–	8	11	1		27, 1750
Stu	–	8	11	2		440
Stu	–	8	11	3		9, 1049
Stu	–	8	11	4		960
Stu	–	8	11	5		524, 1030, 1090
Stu	–	8	11	6		373
Stu	–	8	11	8		474, 754
Stu	–	8	11	9		1130, 1393
Stu	–	8	11	10		1534
Stu	–	8	11	11		259
Stu	–	8	11	12		599, 1393, 1717
Stu	–	8	11	15		1377, 1784
Stu	–	8	11	17		780, 960
Stu	–	8	11	19		57, 592, 828
Stu	–	8	11	20		473, 549, 775, 1393
Stu	–	8	11	21		1049, 1258, 1377, 1693, 1774
Stu	–	8	11	22		1197, 1319, 1377, 1393, 1750
Stu	–	8	11	23		22, 281
Stu	–	8	11	24		355, 524
Stu	–	8	11	25		373, 1049
Stu	–	8	11	26		22, 447, 1090, 1331
Stu	–	8	11	27		5, 355, 599
Stu	–	8	11	28		323, 1090, 1197
Stu	–	8	11	29		22, 355
Stu	–	8	11	30		1049, 1258, 1377
Stu	–	8	11	31		1750
Stu	–	8	11	32		1393
Stu	–	8	11	34		134, 355
Stu	–	8	11	35		5, 120, 198
Stu	–	8	11	36		549
Stu	–	8	12	5		1547
Stu	–	8	12	6		1393
Stu	–	8	12	8		1049, 1393, 1784
Stu	–	8	12	9		1393
Stu	–	8	12	17		235, 1626, 1750
Stu	–	8	12	18		489, 1090, 1569
Stu	–	8	12	19		384, 1626
Stu	–	8	12	20		504, 1154, 1782
Stu	–	8	12	21		1049
Stu	–	8	12	25		724, 1782
Stu	–	8	12	26		1154
Stu	–	8	12	28		440, 1393, 1784
Stu	–	8	12	29		474
Stu	–	8	12	30		294, 440, 665, 1130
Stu	–	8	12	31		1746
Stu	–	8	12	33		1777
Stu	–	8	12	35		380
Stu	–	8	12	36		724
Stu	–	8	18	1		960
Stu	–	9	8	7		960
Stu	–	9	9	1		503, 1534
Stu	–	9	9	2		69, 102, 548, 1049, 1338, 1352
Stu	–	9	9	3		69, 219, 378, 569
Stu	–	9	9	4		69, 314
Stu	–	9	9	10		22, 378, 592
Stu	–	9	9	11		599
Stu	–	9	9	12		1038, 1213, 1245
Stu	–	9	9	13		257, 1393
Stu	–	9	9	14		9, 1090
Stu	–	9	9	22		69
Stu	–	9	9	23		69
Stu	–	9	9	24		1154, 1626, 1750
Stu	–	9	10	2		1607, 1747
Stu	–	9	10	3		1607, 1747, 1784
Stu	–	9	10	4		1534, 1717
Stu	–	9	10	5		1717
Stu	–	9	10	7		524
Stu	–	9	10	8		1534, 1717
Stu	–	9	10	9		1717
Stu	–	9	10	10		1784
Stu	–	9	10	12		1527, 1607, 1747
Stu	–	9	10	13		1197, 1607, 1747
Stu	–	9	10	14		524, 561, 1534
Stu	–	9	10	17		960
Stu	–	9	10	18		960
Stu	–	9	10	22		1475, 1566, 1782
Stu	–	9	10	23		1626
Stu	–	9	10	25		1049, 1090, 1393
Stu	–	9	10	26		503, 960, 1393
Stu	–	9	10	27		537
Stu	–	9	10	28		537, 592, 775
Stu	–	9	10	33		314, 536
Stu	–	9	10	34		116, 1030
Stu	–	9	10	35		250, 504, 754, 1331
Stu	–	9	10	36		1393
Stu	–	9	11	1		1090, 1130
Stu	–	9	11	6		724
Stu	–	9	11	7		960, 1569
Stu	–	9	11	9		960, 1052
Stu	–	9	11	10		1052
Stu	–	9	11	14		1052
Stu	–	9	11	18		1030
Stu	–	9	11	29		1626
Stu	–	9	11	31		1717
Stu	–	9	11	32		1717

Stu	–	9	11	33	1319, 1393
Stu	–	9	11	34	1049
Stu	–	9	11	36	1607, 1747
Stu	–	9	12	1	1784
Stu	–	9	12	4	754
Stu	–	9	12	5	1049
Stu	–	9	12	8	1547
Stu	–	9	12	9	754
Stu	–	9	12	10	592, 1049
Stu	–	9	12	11	1049, 1569
Stu	–	9	12	12	1569
Stu	–	9	12	13	960
Stu	–	9	12	14	724
Stu	–	9	12	17	57, 592
Stu	–	9	12	22	538, 1038, 1093
Stu	–	9	12	23	380, 397, 994
Stu	–	9	12	24	57, 384, 754, 1569
Stu	–	9	12	25	447
Stu	–	9	12	27	538
Stu	–	9	12	34	1501
Stu	–	9	12	35	477
Stu	–	9	12	36	477
Stu	–	10	1	4	69
Stu	–	10	1	9	69
Stu	–	10	1	12	1090
Stu	–	10	1	13	1782, 1784
Stu	–	10	1	14	1501, 1784
Stu	–	10	1	22	1626
Stu	–	10	1	24	1782
Stu	–	10	2	14	1038, 1213, 1259
Stu	–	10	2	24	1782
Stu	–	10	2	26	524, 1049
Stu	–	10	2	27	524, 1782
Stu	–	10	2	34	1501
Stu	–	10	2	35	355
Stu	–	10	4	38	960
Stu	–	10	12	15	1569
Stu	–	11	9	29	828
Stu	–	11	15	1	1772
Stu	–	11	15	11	1772
Stu	–	11	15	12	1772
Stu	–	11	15	15	1772
Stu	–	11	15	21	1772
Stu	–	11	15	22	1772
Stu	–	11	15	23	1772
Stu	–	12	1	27	960
Stu	–	12	5	20	1578
Stu	–	16	16	10	528
Stu	–	16	17	2	370
Stu	–	16	17	18	1315
Stu	–	16	19	23	365
Stu	–	17	17	7	1569
Stu	–	17	19	6	257
Stu	–	20	12	32	569

UNKNOWN LAND OFFICE DISTRICT

Unk	–	1	8	2	999
Unk	–	2	3	31	742
Unk	–	2	11	32	260
Unk	–	3E	6S	4	160
Unk	–	3E	6S	5	160
Unk	–	4	4	3	170
Unk	–	4	17	4	31
Unk	–	4	17	9	31
Unk	–	4	17	14	31
Unk	–	4E	3S	18	403
Unk	–	4E	3S	25	403
Unk	–	5	7	30	1535
Unk	–	5	9	23	111
Unk	–	5	9	36	111
Unk	–	5	10	14	111
Unk	–	5	10	20	111
Unk	–	5	15	24	802
Unk	–	5	17	13	31
Unk	–	5E	2S	33	403
Unk	–	5E	3S	15	403
Unk	–	5E	3S	19	403
Unk	–	6	2	11	749
Unk	–	6	17	10	31
Unk	–	6	18	34	31
Unk	–	7	15	14	31
Unk	–	7	20	25	31
Unk	–	8	10	10	46
Unk	–	9	9	2	31
Unk	–	9	9	3	31
Unk	–	9	9	5	31
Unk	–	9	9	6	31
Unk	–	9	9	8	31
Unk	–	9	9	22	31
Unk	–	9	9	23	31
Unk	–	9	9	26	31
Unk	–	10	1	4	31
Unk	–	10	1	5	31
Unk	–	10	1	6	31
Unk	–	10	1	9	31
Unk	–	16	7	4	169

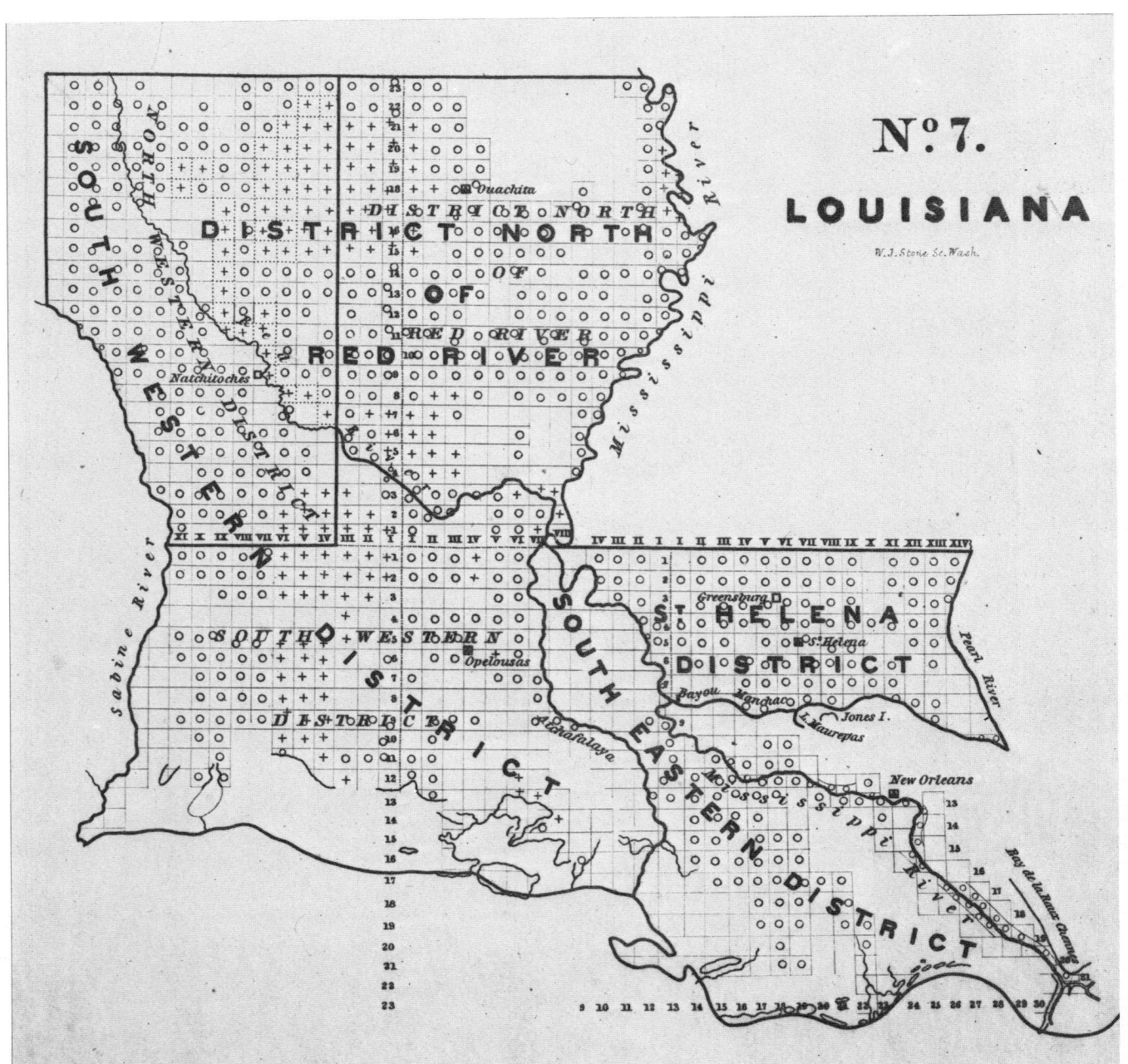

Map 14. Tract map of Louisiana showing land office districts

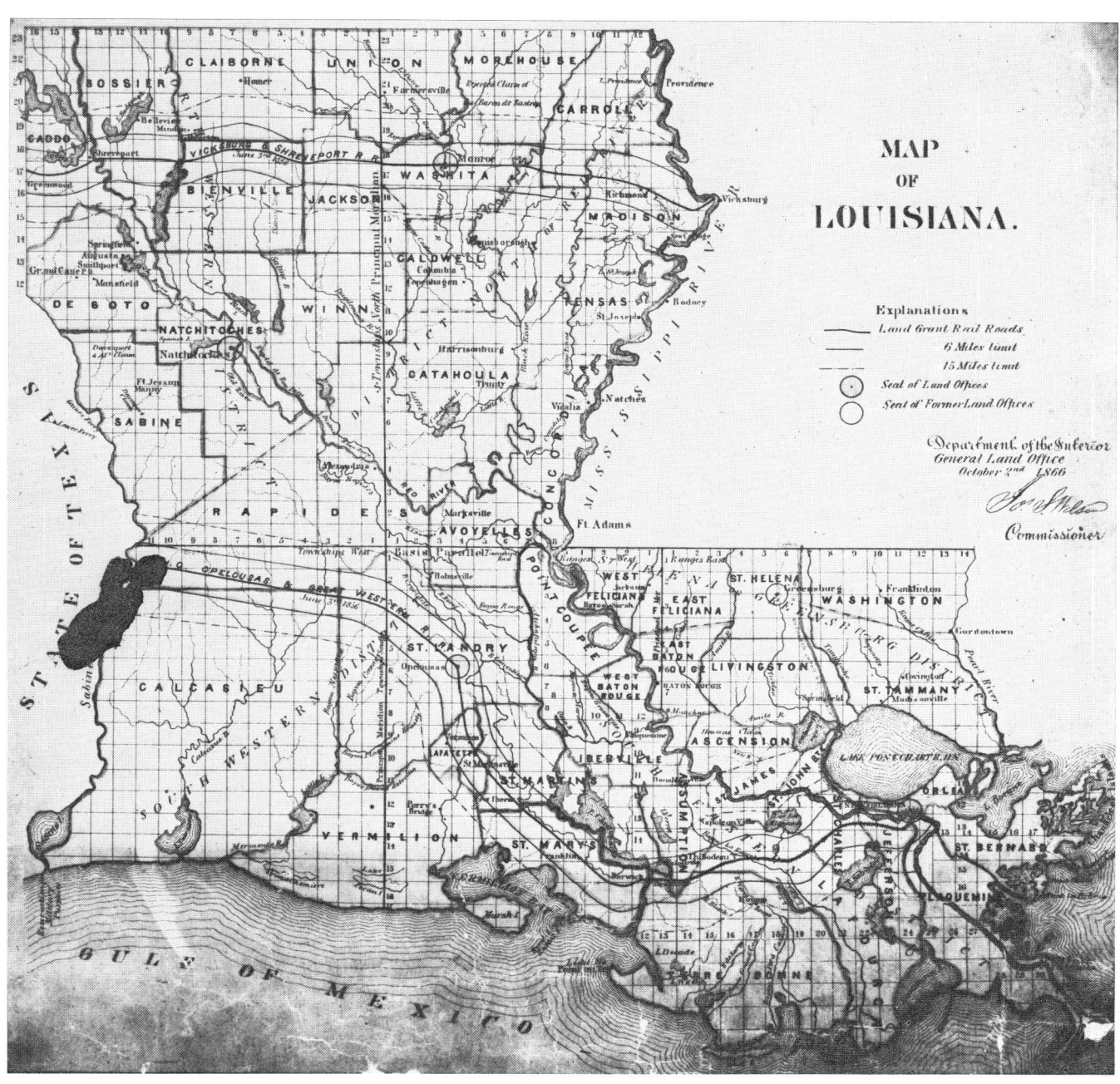

MAP 15. Tract map of Louisiana showing range-township numbering system

Unk	–	17	7	1	999
Unk	–	20	6	3	437
Unk	Pre	9	2	18	328

VINCENNES (INDIANA) LAND OFFICE DISTRICT

Vin	–	1E	1S	2	1557
Vin	–	1E	1S	11	1557
Vin	–	1E	5S	3	284
Vin	–	1E	5S	4	284
Vin	–	1W	1N	3	1051
Vin	–	1W	1N	11	1220
Vin	–	1W	2N	7	719, 824
Vin	–	1W	2N	13	1220
Vin	–	1W	2N	14	1557
Vin	–	1W	2N	24	1220
Vin	–	1W	2N	36	1220
Vin	–	1W	6S	9	1153
Vin	–	1W	6S	28	1557
Vin	–	1W	7S	3	1153
Vin	–	1W	7S	6	1557
Vin	–	1W	7S	10	1153
Vin	–	2E	1S	35	486
Vin	–	2E	3S	13	1557
Vin	–	2E	3S	26	1220
Vin	–	2E	3S	36	959
Vin	–	2E	4S	7	683, 894, 1021
Vin	–	2E	4S	8	683, 894, 1021
Vin	–	2E	4S	17	683, 894, 1021
Vin	–	2E	5S	2	43, 719, 824
Vin	–	2E	5S	13	1220
Vin	–	2E	5S	23	284
Vin	–	2E	5S	25	284
Vin	–	2E	5S	26	284
Vin	–	2W	7S	21	1557
Vin	–	2W	8S	3	1220
Vin	–	2W	8S	4	1220
Vin	–	3–	5–	31	1097
Vin	–	3–	5–	32	1097
Vin	–	3E	1S	15	279
Vin	–	3E	3S	31	959
Vin	–	3E	3S	35	78, 79
Vin	–	3E	3S	36	1220, 1557
Vin	–	3E	4S	13	1046
Vin	–	3E	5S	3	1220
Vin	–	3E	5S	7	959
Vin	–	3E	5S	22	1220
Vin	–	3E	5S	24	719, 824

Vin	–	3E	5S	30	763
Vin	–	3E	5S	31	[1525], 1705
Vin	–	3E	5S	32	[1525], 1705
Vin	–	3E	5S	34	1220
Vin	–	3E	6S	2	1370
Vin	–	3E	6S	11	1370
Vin	–	3S	5E	31 [erroneous]	1525
Vin	–	3S	5E	32 [erroneous]	1525
Vin	–	4–	3–	31	1300
Vin	–	4E	2N	10	761
Vin	–	4E	2S	1	486, 687
Vin	–	4E	2S	2	619
Vin	–	4E	2S	14	1633, 1635
Vin	–	4E	2S	34	1580
Vin	–	4E	3S	8	1220
Vin	–	4E	3S	10	1557
Vin	–	4E	3S	19	1153
Vin	–	4E	3S	22	1557
Vin	–	4E	3S	25	719
Vin	–	4E	3S	31	1347
Vin	–	4E	3S	32	185
Vin	–	4E	3S	34	421
Vin	–	4E	4S	3	496
Vin	–	4E	4S	4	78, 766
Vin	–	4E	5S	21	766
Vin	–	4E	5S	24	1557
Vin	–	4E	5S	28	1153
Vin	–	4E	6S	26	1720
Vin	–	4E	6S	27	1720
Vin	–	4W	3S	32	763
Vin	–	5E	2S	20	1153
Vin	–	5E	2S	21	596, 1088
Vin	–	5E	2S	26	959
Vin	–	5E	2S	34	488, 1557
Vin	–	5E	3S	15	1220
Vin	–	5E	3S	21	1432
Vin	–	5E	4S	10	496
Vin	–	5E	5S	1	959
Vin	–	5E	5S	6	730
Vin	–	5E	5S	12	730
Vin	–	5E	5S	24	730
Vin	–	5E	5S	25	730
Vin	–	5E	5S	26	730, 1557
Vin	–	5E	6S	3	763
Vin	–	5E	6S	7	1070
Vin	–	5W	4S	10	486
Vin	–	6E	2S	26	1450
Vin	–	6E	2S	35	1142, 1450
Vin	–	6E	3S	2	1115

Vin	–	6E	3S	28	730
Vin	–	6E	3S	31	1557
Vin	–	6E	3S	32	1153
Vin	–	6E	4S	6	496
Vin	–	6E	4S	7	496
Vin	–	6W	7S	26	763
Vin	–	6W	8S	2	1220
Vin	–	6W	8S	11	1220
Vin	–	6W	8S	28	1153
Vin	–	7W	2N	3	766
Vin	–	7W	2N	4	1153
Vin	–	7W	2N	5	766, 1070
Vin	–	7W	2N	8	766
Vin	–	7W	2N	9	284, 959, 1220
Vin	–	7W	2N	17	486, 959
Vin	–	7W	2N	20	486, 719, 824, 1220
Vin	–	8W	1N	19	766
Vin	–	8W	1N	27	1153
Vin	–	8W	1N	28	766, 959
Vin	–	8W	1N	29	766
Vin	–	8W	1N	34	959
Vin	–	8W	7S	9	486
Vin	–	9E	1N	3	761
Vin	–	9E	1N	6	761
Vin	–	9W	1N	1	959
Vin	–	9W	7S	3	763
Vin	–	10W	2S	6	719, 824
Vin	–	10W	2S	7	1220
Vin	–	10W	2S	18	1220
Vin	–	10W	7S	11	185
Vin	–	11W	1S	13	675, 959
Vin	–	11W	1S	14	719, 824
Vin	–	11W	1S	24	284, 500
Vin	–	11W	1S	25	1220, 1370
Vin	–	11W	1S	26	284
Vin	–	11W	1S	34	78
Vin	–	11W	1S	35	284, 959
Vin	–	11W	1S	36	284, 486, 500
Vin	–	11W	3S	4	284, 426
Vin	–	11W	3S	19	426
Vin	–	11W	6S	25	763
Vin	–	11W	8S	1	959
Vin	–	11W	8S	12	959
Vin	–	12E	3S	4	279
Vin	–	12W	1N	1	1115, 1220
Vin	–	12W	1N	11	766
Vin	–	12W	1N	12	284
Vin	–	12W	1N	23	959
Vin	–	12W	1N	24	284, 959
Vin	–	12W	1N	32	1557
Vin	–	12W	2S	34	766, 959
Vin	–	12W	2S	35	766
Vin	–	12W	3S	1	1220
Vin	–	12W	3S	2	486, 959, 1153
Vin	–	12W	3S	3	766, 1493
Vin	–	12W	3S	4	[252], 496
Vin	–	12W	3S	5	284
Vin	–	12W	3S	10	1220
Vin	–	12W	3S	11	1070
Vin	–	12W	3S	12	1370
Vin	–	12W	3S	13	1070, 1153
Vin	–	12W	3S	14	1153
Vin	–	12W	3S	15	1153
Vin	–	12W	3S	17	1220
Vin	–	12W	3S	22	1153
Vin	–	12W	3S	24	284, 1070
Vin	–	12W	3S	25	959
Vin	–	12W	3S	27	1153
Vin	–	12W	4S	7	1557
Vin	–	12W	4S	11	1557
Vin	–	12W	4S	19	959
Vin	–	12W	7S	11	959
Vin	–	12W	35–	4 [erroneous]	252
Vin	–	13W	1N	36	1220
Vin	–	13W	4S	17	1557
Vin	–	13W	4S	31	1370
Vin	–	13W	4S	32	959
Vin	–	13W	5S	18	959, 1153
Vin	–	13W	6S	17	959
Vin	–	13W	6S	31	959
Vin	–	13W	7S	5	243
Vin	–	13W	7S	6	500, 766
Vin	–	13W	7S	7	464, 894
Vin	–	13W	7S	18	763
Vin	–	13W	7S	19	763
Vin	–	14W	5S	1	1557
Vin	–	14W	7S	9	1220
Vin	–	14W	7S	15	1220
Vin	–	14W	8S	1	426
Vin	–	14W	8S	7	284
Vin	2	1W	1N	11	1391
Vin	2	1W	1N	13	1135
Vin	2	1W	1N	14	1391
Vin	2	1W	2N	30	1760
Vin	2	1W	3N	32	1760
Vin	2	2E	2S	6	1760
Vin	2	2E	3S	1	1760
Vin	2	2E	3S	12	1760

Vin	2	2E	4S	35	1135
Vin	2	2W	7S	7	1391
Vin	2	3E	3S	19	1135
Vin	2	3E	3S	29	1760
Vin	2	3E	4S	32	1391
Vin	2	4E	2S	27	1391
Vin	2	4E	3S	3	1760
Vin	2	4E	3S	5	1760
Vin	2	4E	3S	19	1135
Vin	2	4E	4S	1	1391
Vin	2	4E	4S	35	1391
Vin	2	4E	5S	17	1760
Vin	2	4E	5S	21	1760
Vin	2	4E	5S	22	1760
Vin	2	4E	5S	25	1391
Vin	2	5E	2S	15	1391
Vin	2	5E	2S	28	1760
Vin	2	5E	2S	32	1135
Vin	2	5E	2S	36	1391
Vin	2	5E	5S	35	1391
Vin	2	5W	1N	29	1760
Vin	2	5W	1N	35	1135
Vin	2	6E	3S	2	1760
Vin	2	6E	3S	3	1135
Vin	2	6W	1N	7	1760
Vin	2	6W	7S	35	1760
Vin	2	6W	8S	10	1760
Vin	2	6W	8S	15	1135
Vin	2	7W	2N	4	1135, 1760
Vin	2	7W	2N	9	1760
Vin	2	7W	2N	17	1760
Vin	2	7W	2N	29	1760
Vin	2	8W	1N	19	1760
Vin	2	8W	1N	28	1135
Vin	2	8W	2N	1	1135
Vin	2	8W	2N	6	1135
Vin	2	8W	5S	26	1391
Vin	2	8W	5S	29	1760
Vin	2	11W	1S	13	1760
Vin	2	11W	1S	14	1760
Vin	2	11W	1S	25	1391
Vin	2	11W	1S	36	1135
Vin	2	11W	3S	13	1760
Vin	2	12W	2S	26	1391
Vin	2	12W	3S	23	1391
Vin	2	12W	3S	24	1135, 1760
Vin	2	12W	3S	34	1760
Vin	2	12W	4S	8	1760
Vin	2	12W	4S	18	1760

Vin	2	13W	4S	9	1760
Vin	2	13W	4S	15	1760
Vin	2	13W	4S	22	1760
Vin	2	13W	4S	34	1135
Vin	2	13W	5S	6	1760
Vin	2	13W	7S	6	1391
Vin	2	13W	7S	8	1135
Vin	2	14W	5S	1	1391
Vin	2	14W	6S	28	1760
Vin	2	14W	7S	10	1135
Vin	2	14W	8S	35	1135
Vin	2	14W	9S	2	1135

LAND OFFICE DISTRICT WEST OF PEARL RIVER

WPR	–	1E	1–	10	1721
WPR	–	2E	3–	28	1105
WPR	–	2E	11–	28	1105
WPR	–	3–	1–	–	859
WPR	–	3E	5–	5	1105
WPR	–	3E	5–	14	1105
WPR	–	3E	15–	29	1230
WPR	–	4E	2–	1	1105
WPR	–	4E	2–	4	1230
WPR	–	4E	3–	30	1230
WPR	–	5E	2–	28	1230
WPR	EML	1	1	2	951
WPR	EML	1	1	11	1651
WPR	EML	1	1	12	951
WPR	EML	1	1	24	1651
WPR	EML	1	1	25	951
WPR	EML	1	1	33	951
WPR	EML	1	2	14	951
WPR	EML	1	2	27	1651
WPR	EML	1	6	36	951
WPR	EML	1	7	16	951
WPR	EML	1	7	24	951
WPR	EML	1	9	4	951
WPR	EML	2	1	9	951
WPR	EML	2	2	36	1651
WPR	EML	2	2	37	1500
WPR	EML	2	2	41	1651
WPR	EML	2	3	16	1434
WPR	EML	2	3	24	951
WPR	EML	2	3	25	951
WPR	EML	2	11	17	951
WPR	EML	2	11	26	951
WPR	EML	3	1	7	951

WPR	EML	3	1	30	951
WPR	EML	3	1	41	951
WPR	EML	3	1	47	951
WPR	EML	3	2	27	1434
WPR	EML	3	5	1	1500
WPR	EML	3	5	13	1434
WPR	EML	3	6	45	1500
WPR	EML	3	15	30	951
WPR	EML	4	1	12	1651
WPR	EML	4	2	20	1434
WPR	EML	4	5	37	1500
WPR	EML	4	6	30	1434
WPR	EML	4	6	37	1500
WPR	EML	5	2	33	1651
WPR	EML	8	2	11	951
WPR	EML	9	3	3	1651
WPR	EML	9	3	10	1651
WPR	EML	11	6	35	1170
WPR	EML	11	6	36	951
WPR	EML	11	7	16	951
WPR	EML	11	7	24	951
WPR	WML	1	1	2	951
WPR	WML	1	1	9	951
WPR	WML	1	1	20	951
WPR	WML	1	1	28	1170
WPR	WML	1	1	44	951
WPR	WML	1	2	37	951
WPR	WML	2	1	7	951
WPR	WML	2	1	11	951
WPR	WML	2	1	40	951
WPR	WML	2	10	9	951
WPR	WML	3	2	24	951

WASHINGTON (MISSISSIPPI TERRITORY) LAND OFFICE DISTRICT

Wsh	-	1W	1-	7	1226
Wsh	-	2E	3-	32	1406
Wsh	-	2W	2-	31	1406
Wsh	-	3E	1-	6	1406
Wsh	-	3E	2-	41	1406
Wsh	-	3-	2-	29	1406
Wsh	-	4-	2-	6	1354
Wsh	-	4-	3-	32	1354
Wsh	-	4E	2-	34	1406
Wsh	-	4W	5-	3	1399
Wsh	-	4W	5-	8	1399
Wsh	-	5-	1-	8	1654

Wsh	-	5-	2-	8	1354, 1406
Wsh	-	5-	2-	15	1354, 1406
Wsh	-	6-	2-	34	1406
Wsh	EML	2	3	32	1470
Wsh	EML	2	5	27	1470
Wsh	EML	2	6	6	1752
Wsh	EML	2	7	41	1752
Wsh	EML	3	1	6	1470
Wsh	EML	3	2	29	1470
Wsh	EML	3	2	41	1470
Wsh	EML	4	2	34	1470
Wsh	EML	4	13	20	1470
Wsh	EML	5	1	8	1553
Wsh	EML	5	2	8	1470
Wsh	WML	2	2	21	1752
Wsh	WML	2	2	31	1470

ZANESVILLE (OHIO) LAND OFFICE DISTRICT

Zan	-	?	14	36	54
Zan	-	1	2	25	1524
Zan	-	1	3	8	36, 1417
Zan	-	1	8	8	209
Zan	-	1	9	1	17
Zan	-	2	2	20	245
Zan	-	2	7	12	210, 1520
Zan	-	2	7	13	385
Zan	-	2	8	25	1640
Zan	-	2	8	28	1271
Zan	-	3	1	20	1601
Zan	-	3	1	29	1512
Zan	-	3	2	4	164
Zan	-	3	2	8	167
Zan	-	3	2	13	164
Zan	-	3	2	14	167
Zan	-	3	2	15	164
Zan	-	3	4	14	1436
Zan	-	3	8	5	1506
Zan	-	3	8	25	1512
Zan	-	3	9	3	1669
Zan	-	3	10	12	693
Zan	-	3	10	14	1506
Zan	-	3	10	16	119, 360, 1140
Zan	-	3	10	18	360
Zan	-	3	10	19	119
Zan	-	3	10	24	1140
Zan	-	3	10	25	350

Zan	–	4	2	22	165	Zan	–	9	8	5	1072
Zan	–	4	8	6	390	Zan	–	9	8	7	283
Zan	–	4	8	12	17	Zan	–	9	8	8	1252
Zan	–	4	15	11	552	Zan	–	9	8	9	1108
Zan	–	4	16	8	290, 1026	Zan	–	9	8	10	271
Zan	–	5	1	1	706	Zan	–	9	8	13	1108
Zan	–	5	1	2	732	Zan	–	9	8	25	1697
Zan	–	5	1	6	1306, 1585	Zan	–	9	8	28	1479
Zan	–	5	9	21	1252	Zan	–	10	1	19	17
Zan	–	6	1	4	554	Zan	–	10	1	21	17
Zan	–	6	1	7	24	Zan	–	10	1	22	17
Zan	–	6	1	9	767	Zan	–	10	2	16	1417
Zan	–	6	1	20	1252	Zan	–	10	3	25	1252
Zan	–	6	2	8	1601	Zan	–	10	6	31	527, 1242
Zan	–	6	2	15	1601	Zan	–	10	6	32	527, 1242
Zan	–	7	1	8	554	Zan	–	10	7	5	830, 1114, 1196
Zan	–	7	4	14	1252	Zan	–	10	8	6	1486
Zan	–	8	2	4	1252	Zan	–	10	9	6	1108
Zan	–	8	3	12	68	Zan	–	10	9	14	758
Zan	–	8	4	4	119, 290	Zan	–	10	9	18	1072
Zan	–	8	4	10	53	Zan	–	10	9	28	1242
Zan	–	8	4	21	871	Zan	–	10	9	31	758, 1244, 1709
Zan	–	8	4	24	871	Zan	–	10	9	32	830, 1196
Zan	–	8	5	7	1379	Zan	–	10	9	33	1379
Zan	–	8	5	17	1242	Zan	–	11	3	17	480, 1068, 1476
Zan	–	8	5	18	1601	Zan	–	11	5	7	1152
Zan	–	8	8	3	1132	Zan	–	11	5	25	1252
Zan	–	8	8	4	733, 758	Zan	–	11	6	23	1252
Zan	–	8	8	6	53	Zan	–	11	10	30	1196
Zan	–	8	8	7	1552	Zan	–	11	12	1	1316
Zan	–	8	8	10	593	Zan	–	11	12	29	733
Zan	–	8	8	12	126, 223	Zan	–	11	12	32	733
Zan	–	8	8	25	1524	Zan	–	11	13	2	53, 1108
Zan	–	8	10	10	209	Zan	–	11	13	3	1085
Zan	–	9	1	8	1196	Zan	–	11	13	5	1132
Zan	–	9	1	13	7, 17	Zan	–	11	13	6	1132, 1242
Zan	–	9	1	19	119	Zan	–	11	13	8	1132
Zan	–	9	3	13	95	Zan	–	11	13	9	1196
Zan	–	9	3	18	95	Zan	–	11	13	12	758, 1085, 1242
Zan	–	9	3	19	95, 1252	Zan	–	11	13	13	132, 996, 1748
Zan	–	9	3	23	1252	Zan	–	11	13	14	996, 1252
Zan	–	9	6	2	593	Zan	–	11	13	17	1132
Zan	–	9	6	3	53	Zan	–	11	13	19	1748
Zan	–	9	7	2	1242	Zan	–	11	13	20	1196
Zan	–	9	7	20	1132	Zan	–	11	13	23	1379
Zan	–	9	7	28	1132	Zan	–	11	13	29	1709
Zan	–	9	7	29	1132	Zan	–	11	14	17	1486
Zan	–	9	8	2	758	Zan	–	12	10	3	733
Zan	–	9	8	4	758	Zan	–	12	10	10	554

Zan	–	12	10	11	554	Zan	–	14	14	10	186, 399, 996
Zan	–	12	10	24	554	Zan	–	14	14	17	996
Zan	–	12	11	5	557	Zan	–	14	14	32	132, 1242
Zan	–	12	11	28	552	Zan	–	14	15	1	318, 557, 1152
Zan	–	12	11	33	1709	Zan	–	14	15	2	132, 733
Zan	–	12	12	5	480, 1486	Zan	–	14	15	3	132, 385, 593, 1379
Zan	–	12	12	8	237, 480, 1486	Zan	–	14	15	7	223, 1486
Zan	–	12	12	17	527, 1196	Zan	–	14	15	8	1132, 1379
Zan	–	12	12	20	527, 1196	Zan	–	14	15	9	132
Zan	–	12	13	1	557, 1085	Zan	–	14	15	10	1196
Zan	–	12	13	2	557, 1748	Zan	–	14	15	11	132, 1072
Zan	–	12	13	3	17, 37, 38, 106, 144, 156, 174	Zan	–	14	15	12	1242
Zan	–	12	13	4	1072	Zan	–	14	15	17	1085
Zan	–	12	13	5	1242, 1748	Zan	–	14	15	18	186
Zan	–	12	13	6	318, 593, 830	Zan	–	14	15	20	711
Zan	–	12	13	8	132	Zan	–	14	15	22	1242
Zan	–	12	13	9	1242	Zan	–	14	15	23	1108
Zan	–	12	13	10	645, 706, 712	Zan	–	14	15	26	53
Zan	–	12	13	11	1601	Zan	–	14	15	27	132, 830, 1072
Zan	–	12	13	12	132	Zan	–	14	15	31	186
Zan	–	12	13	17	132, 557	Zan	–	14	15	32	1242
Zan	–	12	13	18	132, 271, 1132	Zan	–	14	15	33	271, 996
Zan	–	12	13	27	1601	Zan	–	14	15	34	53, 271
Zan	–	13	2	3	733	Zan	–	14	15	35	996
Zan	–	13	10	5	1252	Zan	–	14	16	2	1379
Zan	–	13	11	7	145, 830	Zan	–	14	16	6	1072
Zan	–	13	11	8	145, 830	Zan	–	14	16	7	758
Zan	–	13	11	10	245	Zan	–	14	16	8	227, 272, 318
Zan	–	13	11	14	725, 1555	Zan	–	14	16	11	552, 688, 996
Zan	–	13	11	17	1379, 1464, 1598, 1599, 1709	Zan	–	14	16	14	1196
Zan	–	13	12	1	552, 557, 711	Zan	–	14	16	15	385, 527, 557, 1486
Zan	–	13	12	2	271, 711	Zan	–	14	16	17	552
Zan	–	13	12	3	758	Zan	–	15	6	1	996
Zan	–	13	12	6	186	Zan	–	15	6	8	996
Zan	–	13	12	7	557, 1486	Zan	–	15	14	13	681
Zan	–	13	12	8	271, 830, 1028, 1175, 1586	Zan	–	15	14	26	1176
Zan	–	13	12	9	733	Zan	–	15	15	3	1132
Zan	–	13	12	10	132, 1072, 1132	Zan	–	15	15	18	1709
Zan	–	13	12	11	271, 1132	Zan	–	15	16	1	688, 1242
Zan	–	13	12	13	1379	Zan	–	15	16	2	132, 1242
Zan	–	13	12	14	758, 1072	Zan	–	15	16	3	1132
Zan	–	13	12	15	385, 527, 1196	Zan	–	15	16	5	1085, 1242
Zan	–	13	15	2	1072	Zan	–	15	16	6	1132
Zan	–	14	6	2	996	Zan	–	15	16	7	733, 758
Zan	–	14	13	3	527	Zan	–	15	16	8	318, 830, 1132
Zan	–	14	13	12	974, 1121, 1173	Zan	–	15	16	9	490
Zan	–	14	14	3	557	Zan	–	15	16	10	1252
Zan	–	14	14	4	1108	Zan	–	15	16	11	758
Zan	–	14	14	9	271, 1486	Zan	–	15	16	14	996, 1601

Zan	–	15	16	18	132, 557
Zan	–	15	16	19	1379
Zan	–	15	16	31	1085
Zan	–	15	16	34	830, 1242
Zan	–	15	17	1	1532
Zan	–	15	17	3	1132
Zan	–	15	17	4	186, 283
Zan	–	15	17	5	557
Zan	–	15	17	7	552, 711, 1085
Zan	–	15	17	9	1196
Zan	–	15	17	10	186
Zan	–	15	17	12	175
Zan	–	15	17	13	132
Zan	–	15	17	17	53, 271, 1486
Zan	–	15	17	18	271, 1242
Zan	–	15	17	20	1196
Zan	–	15	17	23	552
Zan	–	15	17	24	271, 1085, 1196
Zan	–	15	17	25	552, 830
Zan	–	15	17	26	1145, 1285
Zan	–	15	17	27	1552
Zan	–	15	17	28	132, 557, 1196, 1242
Zan	–	15	17	30	552
Zan	–	15	17	31	53, 557
Zan	–	15	17	32	53, 552
Zan	–	15	17	33	1072
Zan	–	15	17	36	53, 132, 1108
Zan	–	15	18	3	283
Zan	–	15	18	5	1085
Zan	–	15	18	6	490, 1196
Zan	–	15	18	7	711, 733, 1242
Zan	–	15	18	9	593, 733
Zan	–	15	18	10	1252
Zan	–	15	18	12	271, 1242
Zan	–	15	18	15	132, 1085, 1242
Zan	–	15	18	17	1431
Zan	–	15	18	18	1132, 1379, 1486, 1601
Zan	–	16	7	4	709
Zan	–	16	14	13	681
Zan	–	17	1	11	830
Zan	–	19	9	28	1132
Zan	–	30	12	7	210
Zan Mil	1	1	1		1486
Zan Mil	1	1	2		132, 1196
Zan Mil	1	1	3		732
Zan Mil	1	1	8		552
Zan Mil	1	1	9		552, 732
Zan Mil	1	1	10		758, 1601
Zan Mil	1	1	11		1132
Zan Mil	1	1	21		1132
Zan Mil	1	1	22		1132
Zan Mil	1	1	23		318, 552
Zan Mil	1	2	4		737, 996, 1242
Zan Mil	1	2	5		737, 1242
Zan Mil	1	2	14		1072
Zan Mil	1	2	15		1379
Zan Mil	1	2	16		552, 1132
Zan Mil	1	2	17		557
Zan Mil	1	2	18		996, 1748
Zan Mil	1	2	19		996
Zan Mil	1	2	20		1748
Zan Mil	1	2	21		758
Zan Mil	1	2	22		1108
Zan Mil	1	2	23		557, 1085
Zan Mil	1	2	24		527, 996
Zan Mil	1	2	25		557, 732
Zan Mil	1	3	14		132, 1242
Zan Mil	1	3	15		318, 758, 1132
Zan Mil	1	3	25		552
Zan Mil	1	4	24		391
Zan Mil	1	6	1		996
Zan Mil	1	6	2		996
Zan Mil	1	8	8		563, 1239
Zan Mil	1	9	1		283, 1085, 1242
Zan Mil	1	9	2		132, 757, 1196, 1623
Zan Mil	1	9	3		1072
Zan Mil	1	9	5		1108
Zan Mil	1	9	9		1242
Zan Mil	1	9	10		732, 830, 1072
Zan Mil	1	9	12		830
Zan Mil	1	9	13		1132
Zan Mil	1	9	20		1306
Zan Mil	1	10	5		1108
Zan Mil	1	10	6		758, 996
Zan Mil	1	10	7		1108
Zan Mil	1	10	15		557
Zan Mil	2	1	1		996
Zan Mil	2	1	2		1196
Zan Mil	2	1	11		1242
Zan Mil	2	1	19		1072
Zan Mil	2	1	20		1108, 1486
Zan Mil	2	1	21		895
Zan Mil	2	2	4		1379
Zan Mil	2	2	5		1196
Zan Mil	2	2	8		318, 758
Zan Mil	2	2	11		996
Zan Mil	2	2	18		996
Zan Mil	2	2	19		1196

Zan Mil	2	2	20	525, 694, 758, 1486
Zan Mil	2	2	21	557
Zan Mil	2	3	1	318, 557, 758
Zan Mil	2	3	17	1085
Zan Mil	2	3	18	1623
Zan Mil	2	3	23	996, 1072
Zan Mil	2	4	21	1196
Zan Mil	2	7	11	732
Zan Mil	2	7	12	382, 393
Zan Mil	2	8	14	1132
Zan Mil	2	8	15	1132
Zan Mil	2	8	16	552, 750
Zan Mil	2	8	17	1108
Zan Mil	2	8	25	454
Zan Mil	3	1	19	394
Zan Mil	3	1	20	1196
Zan Mil	3	1	21	1709
Zan Mil	3	2	3	557
Zan Mil	3	2	8	552
Zan Mil	3	3	5	1709
Zan Mil	3	3	8	711
Zan Mil	3	3	12	1532
Zan Mil	3	3	13	1196, 1379
Zan Mil	3	3	18	830
Zan Mil	3	4	18	758
Zan Mil	3	4	23	1108, 1379
Zan Mil	3	8	1	996
Zan Mil	3	8	2	283
Zan Mil	3	8	4	1242
Zan Mil	3	8	6	758
Zan Mil	3	8	8	1108, 1132
Zan Mil	3	9	11	732
Zan Mil	3	9	12	1227
Zan Mil	3	9	19	1132
Zan Mil	3	9	21	830
Zan Mil	3	9	22	557, 996
Zan Mil	3	10	12	427, 509
Zan Mil	3	10	16	798, 996, 1242
Zan Mil	3	10	18	798, 1240
Zan Mil	3	10	19	1379
Zan Mil	3	10	21	758
Zan Mil	3	10	24	399
Zan Mil	3	10	25	798, 1242
Zan Mil	4	1	23	1532
Zan Mil	4	2	18	732
Zan Mil	4	2	21	690
Zan Mil	4	2	22	1231
Zan Mil	4	2	23	732
Zan Mil	4	2	25	758
Zan Mil	4	4	3	996, 1103
Zan Mil	4	4	4	732, 996, 1103
Zan Mil	4	4	5	1072, 1085, 1132
Zan Mil	4	4	6	1132
Zan Mil	4	4	7	1085
Zan Mil	4	4	8	552
Zan Mil	4	4	18	1103
Zan Mil	4	4	19	1316, 1709
Zan Mil	4	4	21	1709
Zan Mil	4	4	22	552
Zan Mil	4	5	11	1103
Zan Mil	4	8	1	283
Zan Mil	4	8	2	1072
Zan Mil	4	8	3	1242
Zan Mil	4	8	6	560
Zan Mil	4	8	7	1709
Zan Mil	4	8	8	758
Zan Mil	4	8	10	732, 995
Zan Mil	4	8	11	758
Zan Mil	4	8	12	732, 1709
Zan Mil	4	8	13	758
Zan Mil	4	8	14	1108
Zan Mil	4	8	16	285, 1026
Zan Mil	4	9	12	557
Zan Mil	4	9	15	1532
Zan Mil	4	9	16	830
Zan Mil	4	9	17	830
Zan Mil	4	9	18	1196
Zan Mil	4	9	19	1709
Zan Mil	4	9	20	732
Zan Mil	4	9	21	996, 1132
Zan Mil	4	9	22	732, 996, 1252
Zan Mil	4	9	23	1196
Zan Mil	4	9	25	1108, 1242
Zan Mil	5	1	1	1242
Zan Mil	5	1	2	690, 732, 758
Zan Mil	5	1	3	1532, 1623
Zan Mil	5	1	7	996
Zan Mil	5	1	8	750, 1623
Zan Mil	5	1	9	888, 1085
Zan Mil	5	1	10	705
Zan Mil	5	1	11	132, 557
Zan Mil	5	1	12	995
Zan Mil	5	1	13	995
Zan Mil	5	1	14	394, 732
Zan Mil	5	1	15	732
Zan Mil	5	1	16	1132
Zan Mil	5	1	17	1132
Zan Mil	5	1	23	318, 758

Zan Mil	5	1	24	1379, 1486	Zan Mil	7	8	25	1709
Zan Mil	5	3	3	542	Zan Mil	7	9	19	1196
Zan Mil	5	4	1	1072	Zan Mil	7	9	23	1196
Zan Mil	5	4	10	1132	Zan Mil	8	2	1	490
Zan Mil	5	4	11	750	Zan Mil	8	2	3	732
Zan Mil	5	4	16	1242	Zan Mil	8	2	4	1108
Zan Mil	5	6	24	1108	Zan Mil	8	2	5	1072, 1552
Zan Mil	5	8	19	394, 557, 1108	Zan Mil	8	2	6	996, 1132
Zan Mil	5	8	20	375, 695	Zan Mil	8	2	7	490, 552
Zan Mil	5	9	11	1085	Zan Mil	8	2	12	557
Zan Mil	5	9	12	1252	Zan Mil	8	2	15	774, 1379
Zan Mil	5	9	19	1532	Zan Mil	8	2	19	750, 1132
Zan Mil	5	9	20	283, 1379	Zan Mil	8	2	20	283, 1486
Zan Mil	5	9	21	1379	Zan Mil	8	2	21	552, 732, 1552
Zan Mil	5	9	33	1085	Zan Mil	8	2	22	737, 756
Zan Mil	5	10	10	726	Zan Mil	8	3	8	557, 732
Zan Mil	6	1	2	1108, 1532, 1623	Zan Mil	8	4	4	767
Zan Mil	6	1	3	1196	Zan Mil	8	4	8	1132
Zan Mil	6	1	5	1196, 1242	Zan Mil	8	4	10	996, 1709
Zan Mil	6	1	6	552, 737, 758	Zan Mil	8	4	12	283, 557, 737
Zan Mil	6	1	7	318, 758	Zan Mil	8	4	13	758
Zan Mil	6	1	8	732, 1748	Zan Mil	8	4	21	552
Zan Mil	6	1	9	750, 1108, 1242	Zan Mil	8	4	22	394
Zan Mil	6	1	10	833, 1242	Zan Mil	8	5	6	1072
Zan Mil	6	1	11	1132	Zan Mil	8	5	17	1108
Zan Mil	6	1	12	737, 1252	Zan Mil	8	5	18	996, 1623
Zan Mil	6	1	20	1379	Zan Mil	8	6	6	557
Zan Mil	6	1	22	552	Zan Mil	8	6	15	996, 1108
Zan Mil	6	1	23	750	Zan Mil	8	8	5	1697
Zan Mil	6	2	22	1623	Zan Mil	8	8	10	490
Zan Mil	6	2	25	1108, 1379	Zan Mil	9	1	15	1748
Zan Mil	6	4	18	758	Zan Mil	9	1	20	1108
Zan Mil	7	1	1	737, 758	Zan Mil	9	3	4	732, 1196
Zan Mil	7	1	2	552, 758, 1085	Zan Mil	9	3	12	394
Zan Mil	7	1	3	737	Zan Mil	9	3	13	462
Zan Mil	7	1	7	318	Zan Mil	9	3	16	1601
Zan Mil	7	1	8	732	Zan Mil	9	3	18	462, 732
Zan Mil	7	1	9	552	Zan Mil	9	3	19	462, 1196
Zan Mil	7	1	10	132, 996	Zan Mil	9	3	22	1085
Zan Mil	7	1	11	557	Zan Mil	9	3	23	732, 737
Zan Mil	7	1	12	728	Zan Mil	9	3	25	1108
Zan Mil	7	3	20	1108	Zan Mil	9	4	12	1709, 1748
Zan Mil	7	3	23	1379	Zan Mil	9	4	22	1601
Zan Mil	7	4	2	1242	Zan Mil	9	5	3	1085
Zan Mil	7	4	15	1072	Zan Mil	9	5	4	1196, 1532
Zan Mil	7	4	16	996, 1132	Zan Mil	9	5	5	1196
Zan Mil	7	4	25	737	Zan Mil	9	6	21	552
Zan Mil	7	5	1	132	Zan Mil	9	6	22	758
Zan Mil	7	5	2	552	Zan Mil	9	7	15	1108

Zan Mil	9	7	34	732	
Zan Mil	10	1	19	132, 1479, 1709	
Zan Mil	10	1	20	1709	
Zan Mil	10	1	21	132, 552	
Zan Mil	10	1	22	132, 1242	
Zan Mil	10	3	10	996	
Zan Mil	10	3	12	996	
Zan Mil	10	3	18	557	
Zan Mil	10	3	23	732	
Zan Mil	10	4	21	996	
Zan Mil	10	5	3	1379	
Zan Mil	10	6	3	1196	
Zan Mil	10	6	20	750	
Zan Mil	10	6	21	1085, 1108	
Zan Mil	10	6	24	1242	
Zan Mil	10	7	4	1072, 1601, 1748	
Zan Mil	10	7	5	490, 836	
Zan Mil	10	7	6	1072, 1486, 1532	
Zan Mil	10	7	7	1532, 1623	
Zan Mil	10	7	13	644, 1196, 1709	
Zan Mil	10	7	14	1196, 1532	
Zan Mil	10	7	16	1379	
Zan Mil	10	7	20	1196	
Zan Mil	10	7	24	996	
Zan Mil	10	7	25	552	
Zan Mil	10	8	16	1579	

Zan Mil	–	10	9	19	1196
Zan Mil	–	10	9	22	1196, 1242
Zan Mil	–	11	1	12	732
Zan Mil	–	11	1	19	1486
Zan Mil	–	11	1	22	996
Zan Mil	–	11	3	16	318, 758, 1132
Zan Mil	–	11	3	17	758
Zan Mil	–	11	5	3	732
Zan Mil	–	11	5	4	1072
Zan Mil	–	11	5	5	1486
Zan Mil	–	11	6	14	732
Zan Mil	–	11	6	18	1108
Zan Mil	–	11	6	25	1085
Zan Mil	–	11	8	11	1579
Zan Mil	–	11	8	20	1579
Zan Mil	–	11	8	21	1579
Zan Mil	–	11	13	11	1108
Zan Mil	–	13	12	15	690
Zan Mil	–	14	16	8	728
Zan Mil	–	14	16	14	490
Zan Mil	–	15	16	4	552
Zan Mil	–	15	16	14	490
Zan Mil	–	15	16	30	1108
Zan Mil	–	15	18	11	996
Zan Pre	–	15	18	3	1026

MAY 28 '80 0

OVERSIZE
KF5675
S6   REFERENCE ROOM   F51509   OCLC
          Smith, Clifford Neal
              Federal land series; a calendar of archival materials on
          the land patents issued by the United States Government,
          with subject, tract, and name indexes. Chicago, American
          Library Association, 1972-

              v. maps. 29 cm.

              CONTENTS: v. 1. 1788-1810.-v. 2. 1799-1835. —v. 3.
          810-1814. —

              1. Land grants—United States.   I. Title.

          KF5675.S6   333.1'6'0973   72-3238
          ISBN 0-8389-0138-7   548057   MARO
          Library of Congress   72 (10-2)Library has 41,23
                                    FOR VOLUMES IN LIBRARY SEE AUTHOR CARD

P9-AGN-545

Swimming in Chocolate

Poems and Drawings by

Mr. Mike

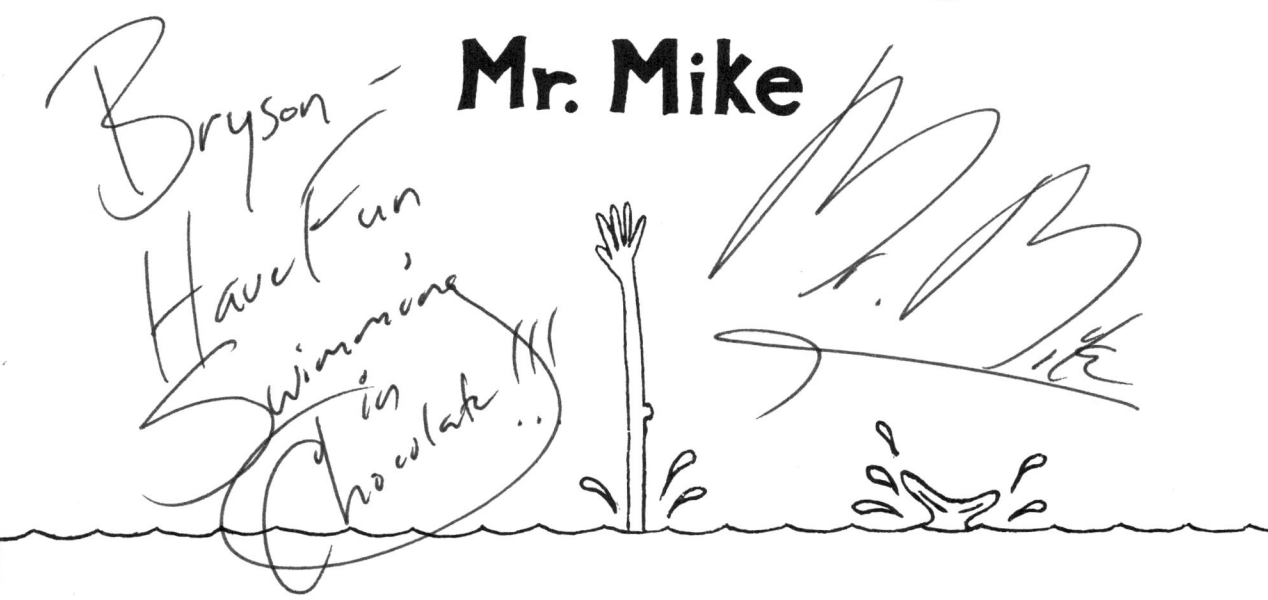

Bryson - Have Fun Swimming in Chocolate!!!

Mr. Mike

Beetle Bug Books

SWIMMING IN CHOCOLATE

Copyright © 1998, 2004 by Mr. Mike

All rights reserved. No part of this book may be used or reproduced in any manner whatsoever without written permission except in the case of brief quotations embodied in critical articles and reviews. Printed in the United States of America. For information address Beetle Bug Books, Box 4636 San Clemente, CA 92674 or visit www.BeetleBugBooks.com.

Copyediting: Royal Literary Publications, Laguna Niguel, CA
Cover design and art: Mr. Mike
Cover color and effects: Robert Howard, Fort Collins, CO
Photography: Scott B. Mantecon, San Clemente, CA
Printing and binding: Delta Printing Solutions, Inc., Valencia, CA
Creative consulting: Kersti E. Rydell, San Clemente, CA

10 9 8 7 6 5 4

Library of Congress Cataloging-in-Publication Data

Mike, Mr.
    Swimming in chocolate : poems and drawings /
by Mr. Mike. – 1st ed.
        p. cm.
    Includes index
    ISBN: 0-9658365-4-1
    SUMMARY: Humorous rhyming poems about a variety of child and animal subjects.
    1. Children's poetry, American.   I. Title.
PS3563.I37155S95   1998   811'.54   97-93905
                                               CIP

For all children, young and old.

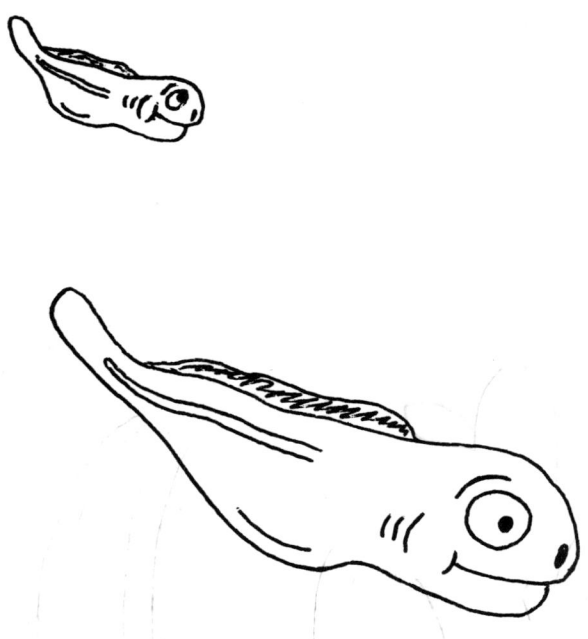

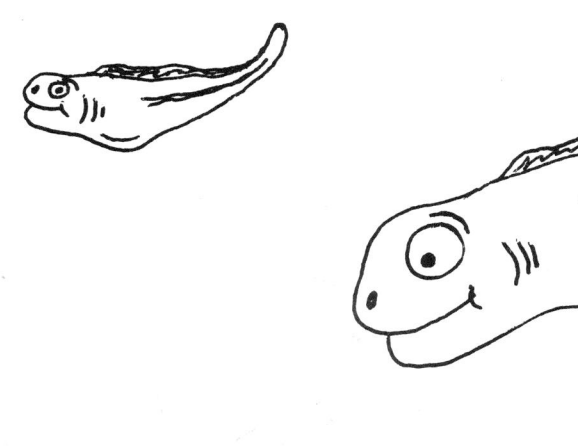

CUTE POLLIWOGS

Cute polliwogs grow up to be frogs.
Little kittens grow up to be cats.
Pigletts to hogs—
Puppies to dogs.
But do mice grow up to be rats?

MY CROWN

I found me a crown.
It fit well upside down,
But I didn't like points in my head.

So I tossed out the jewels,
Added some spools,
And now I wear nothing instead.

SUNFLOWER

I look up to the sky and try and try
And higher and higher and way up high
I see near the clouds a bright bloom—I do spy,
Beaming and gleaming—a glint in its eye,
A great, great sunflower.

HOCUS POCUS

Welcome to the mystery magic show—
A tap of the wand, away we go.
Want to try the card trick "Find the Ace"?
In my crystal ball, I see your funny face.

Here's a little rabbit, watch him disappear.
Hey, look at this—there's a quarter in your ear.
I'll lock up my assistant and hide her with my cape.
No one's ever seen this magnificent escape.

Isn't it incredible—no trap door?
Are you having fun, wanna see some more?
Test my psychic powers—insight from the stars.
You like playing games and eating ice-cream bars.

I know you're stumped with wonder, you're dazzled by my ring.
Stand back as I gulp this sword—it doesn't even sting!
Here's a mystic rope—it turns into a snake.
You there, are you watching, are you still awake?

For the grand finale, a special trick you'll love
A burning flame in a pan, POOF—becomes a dove!
Thank you all for coming—it has really been a pleasure
Spending an enchanting time of magic tricks together.

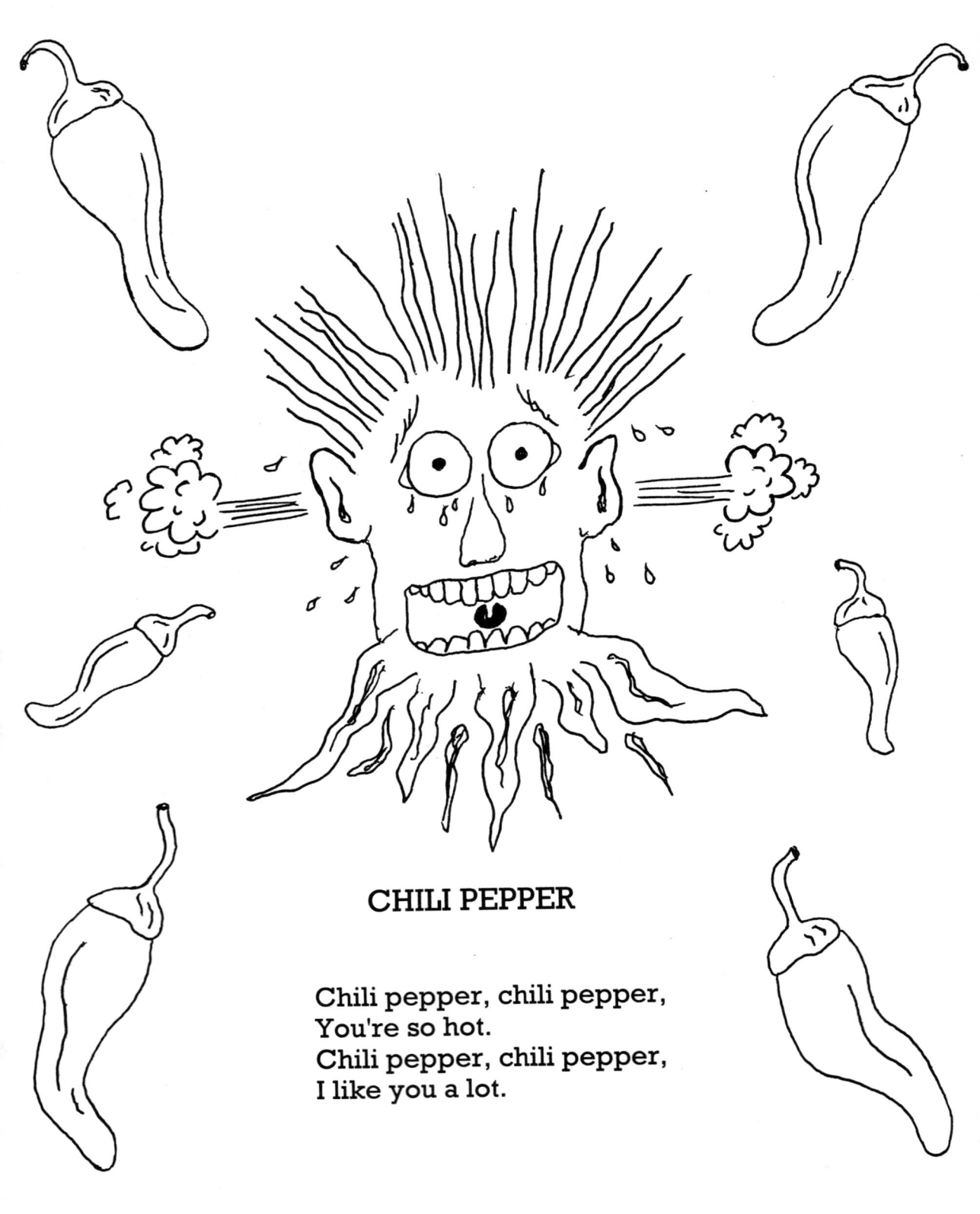

CHILI PEPPER

Chili pepper, chili pepper,
You're so hot.
Chili pepper, chili pepper,
I like you a lot.

Monday—glum day, the inevitable day after Sunday.
Tuesday—blues day, the everyone wants to snooze day.
Wednesday—again day, the day we miss our friends day.
Thursday—the worst day, the everything starts to blur day.
Friday—my day, the totally yours and my day.
Saturday—nothin' matters day,
   the ice cream and chocolate splatter day.
Sunday—fun day, the barbecue, hot dog and bun day.
   Enjoy your time in the sun day
   'cause tomorrow is . . . MONDAY!

GOOD AND BAD

If we all did good
And a lot less bad,
We'd be much more happy
And a lot less sad.

HARD TO LET GO

A hug from a grandma or grandpa or friend—
An excellent book with no logical end.
A 'lectronic game with a million-point score—
The old funky sweater you don't use any more.
The bar on the seat of a big roller coaster—
The up-and-down lever that turns on the toaster.
A dollar you saved for a week and a half—
Your belly that aches when you laugh and you laugh.
A tug-of-war game when you've just about won—
A big bag of candy that weighs 'bout a ton.
A cute little puppy with nowhere to go—
I tell you sometimes it's just hard to let go.

CIRCUS

Circus! Circus! Comin' to town.
Gotta run and see it—don't slow down!
Lots of cotton candy, twizzles and balloons.
Look out for the elephants with piggyback baboons.

Clowns in funky colors like purple, pink and green
Jump and flip and spin around like folks have never seen.
The fire breather blows a flame that's brighter than the sun.
He goes to take a second breath, and people start to run.

The place is gettin' crazy—we're jumpin' up and down,
Throwin' lots of streamers and confetti all around.
The juggler's got some bowling pins, balls and other stuff.
Out come forty monkeys screamin' loud and playin' rough.

High up in the big top swings a group of acrobats.
The lion roars the loudest roar of all the great big cats.
KABOOM! Through the air shoots the human cannon ball.
I wonder how they do that stunt—it doesn't hurt at all.

A muscle man sure shows he can bend anything in sight.
The fortune-teller tells the past of each of us just right.
Circus! Circus! Go and see it while it's here.
Get your ticket now or you'll be waitin' one more year.

HIDE AND SEEK

Hide and seek,
Hide and seek—

Close your eyes and please don't peek!

Count to ten,
Count to ten—

Don't come out till I say when!

Hiding spot,
Hiding spot—

Stay out of sight, don't get caught!

Here I come,
Here I come—

I see you there—you'd better run!

PAINTING OF AIR

This is my painting of air.
Please don't stare.

MY LITTLE RED POT WITH THE BLUE POLKA DOT

My little red pot
With the blue polka dot
Grows beautiful flowers
In spring when it's hot.
I'll never part with it
'Cause I like it a lot.
My little red pot
With the blue polka dot.

BEAVER

Have you ever seen
A tap-dancing beaver?
I guess I haven't either.

NEW AND IMPROVED

Better than ever.
New and improved.
Nothin' else like it.
Perfect for you.
Special enhancer.
Patented part.
Easy to open.
Simple to start.
Additional feature—
The old one is gone.
Incredibly 'fficient.
A cinch to put on.
Won't need a hammer.
Works fine in the rain.
Ready to go.
Don't need a brain.
Better than others.
Passed a big test.
Fine workmanship.
Absolutley the best.
Washable, squashable.
Won't ever break.
Commendable, bendable.
Real, not a fake.
Durable, stirable
Big warranty.
Made like no other.
Try it for free.
Years of fine service.
Just what you need.
Satisfaction forever.
Of course, guaranteed.
Easy assembly.
Superior choice.
Sold with a smile—
'Cause I just lost my voice.

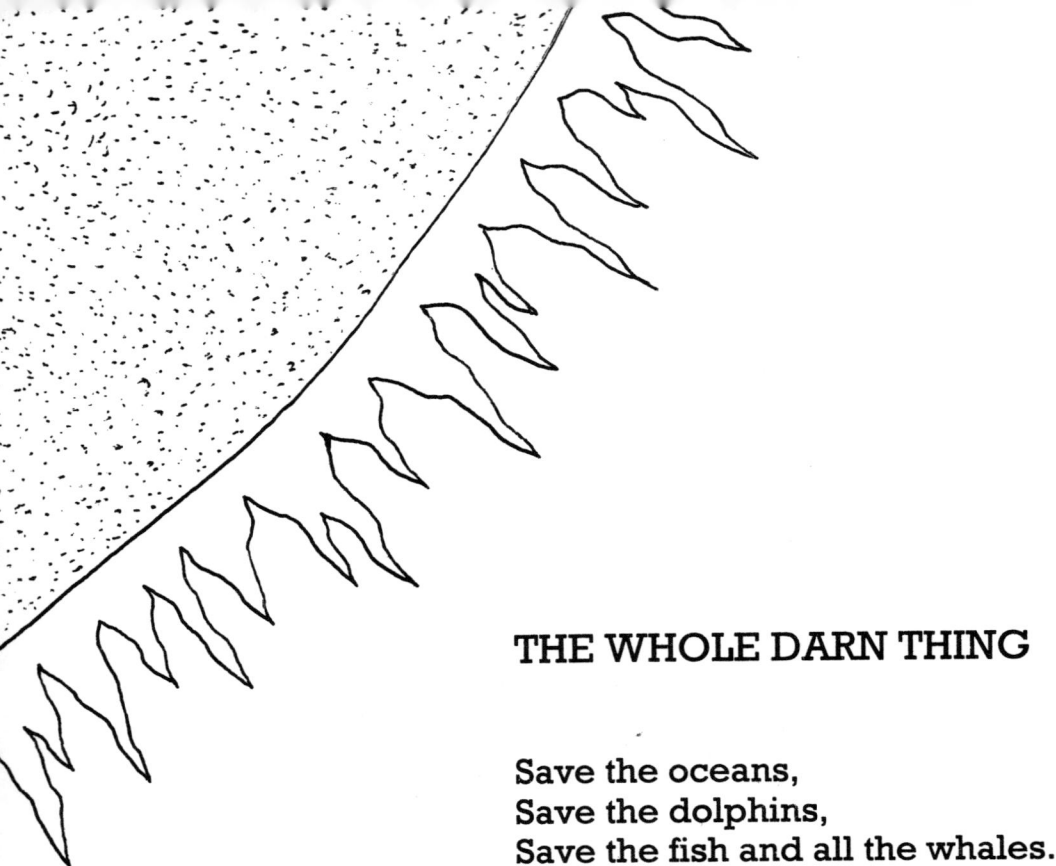

THE WHOLE DARN THING

Save the oceans,
Save the dolphins,
Save the fish and all the whales.

Save the jungles,
Save the vines,
Save the monkeys and their tails.

Save the swamps,
Save the gators,
Save the fireflies and frogs.

Save the moors,
Save the dew drops,
Save the mossy, ancient bogs.

Save the mountains,
Save the forests,
Save the bears and skeeters, too.

Save the caves,
Save the spiders,
Save the bats and Boogey Boo.

Save the deserts,
Save the camels,
Save the sand and all the dunes.

Save the stars,
Save the comets,
Save the planets and their moons.

Save the people, save the kitties,
Save the dogs and birds that sing.
Hey, I've got a question—
Why not save the whole darn thing?

THE FISH AND THE WORM

"Hey, little worm, I see you squirm,
But why do you sit on a hook?"
"It's a new thing, called a swing—
Come closer, take a look."
"Well," thought the fish, "I really wish
That worm wouldn't trick me this way."
So, from behind, he shook the line
And had his first meal of the day.

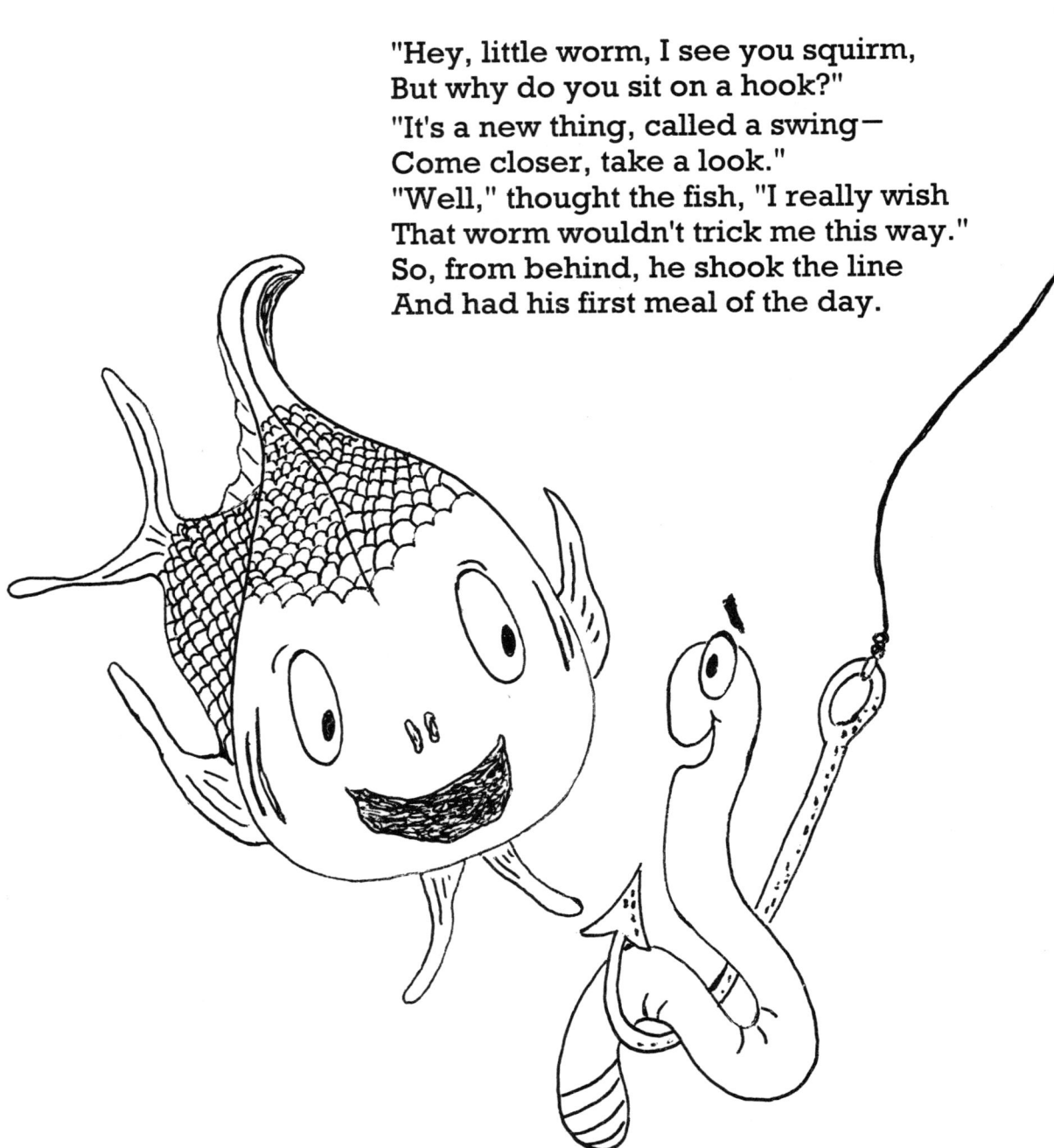

ELMO D. UNCE

Elmo D. Unce never did brush
He had an excuse, "I'm in a rush!"
So, his teeth fell out, like the other chums.
Now he sorely chews with soft, pink gums.

THE WEED

I've heard a lot of stories, and the one I know is true
Is about a little kid and a weed that grew and grew.
To protect the young and innocent, I'll have to change some names.
The weed we'll call 'the weed' of course—
  the kid we'll just call James.

James had responsibilities and pickin' weeds was one.
On his hands and knees he'd work—it wasn't any fun.
Right back in the corner under two big blades of grass
Sprouted that gigantic weed—hence, this story comes to pass.

It grew an inch in April and a couple more in May.
After that it grew a foot every other day.
But James just kept on pickin'—too bad he didn't see
That weed grew tall behind him just as tall as one could be.

It was thick and green and prickly, and it didn't make much sound.
Its roots were tough and sturdy and dug deep in the ground.
It overtook the garden, squeezing trees and plants.
The bugs moved out in panic with a colony of ants.

Through the house it winded up the stairs and down the walls.
In and out the chimney till it clogged up all the halls.
The neighbor folks got nervous and their dogs began to bark.
The sun sank low behind the weed and soon it got real dark.

James looked up and suddenly he realized his fate.
"There ain't no way to pick that weed—it's just too way darn late."
That's the very end my friend—there's nothing more to say.
It's amazing how one unpicked weed can mess up your whole day.

HAIR

It's really a dread, there's no hair on my head.
People shout, "Baldy and Slick."
What can I do to make me look new?
There are many solutions to pick.
A blob of spaghetti, it sticks when it's ready,
But you know it's really not "me."
I'd find an old mop, plop it on top,
But that makes it harder to see.
Seaweed could work, but people would smirk
'Cause I'd smell like a stinky sardine.
What about grass, for hair it could pass?
I tried, but it's wormy and green.
Maybe it's better to glue on some feathers
But what would the birdies think?
This spot on my head is making me red.
It isn't as funny as you think.

THE CIRCLE WHO WANTED TO BE A SQUARE

There once was a circle who felt a bit sad,
Thinkin' that being a circle was bad.
It pulled in its sides, bottom and top
And proclaimed, "I'm a square!", although it was *not.*
The other shapes looked with amazement and awe.
It took them a while to believe what they saw.
They jumped and waived and cheered out loud.
Rectangles strained to see over the crowd.
It admired itself from six different angles.
Compliments came from jealous triangles.
Some of the squares quickly came calling.
The circles, of course, found the new square appalling.
Up on its corner it spun like a top,
But it couldn't slow down when it wanted to stop.
It got stuck on its side when it wanted to roll,
And it couldn't fit into the usual hole.
After a while, it started to wonder,
"Is this a mistake—a great big ol' blunder?
I've no circle friends—the other shapes stare.
It's been a long time since I rolled here to there."
It didn't take long for the new square to know
That being a square when you're not doesn't go.
So, it let out its sides, bottom and top
And started off rolling and never did stop.
If you ever start feelin' a little bit sad
Or thinkin' that bein' a person is bad,
Don't pull in your sides, bottom and top.
You just be *you* and DON'T EVER STOP!

NOT TO DO NOR TO SAY

A list of things not to do nor to say:
Lighting a match to a big pile of hay,
Teasing a dog when you know it should stay,
Yelling "STICK-UP!" and making them pay,
Peeking at people as they sit and pray,
Piling up toys to block the way,
Saying it's March when you know that it's May,
Going with strangers is *never* okay.
I'll warn you right now, if I may.
Never forget not to do nor to say.

CUCKOO

What does the Cuckoo in the clock
Do between the tick and the tock?
Have you ever peeked to spy?
I guarantee it's worth a try.
I took a look—yes, I did,
Long ago, when I was a kid.
In that little house of wood,
Many interesting things there stood.
A kitchen table and wooden chair,
Cookies and cakes were sitting there.

Little cups and miniature dishes—
A perfect arrangement to suit cuckoo's wishes.
Clean wooden floors, shiny and bright,
A quaint little study and reading light,
Fancy spring flowers dried on the walls,
Fine crystal lamps lighted the halls.
A vase with rosebuds and little books.
Pictures hung up with tiny hooks.

Back in the corner, a little bed—
A perfect place to rest one's head.
Behind the wall, the gears of the clock
Snapped and clacked, teetered and rocked.
A tiny white note was pinned on the door:
"Don't forget to cuckoo at four."
The Cuckoo, however, could not be found.
No squeek, no peep, nor any sound.
Seeing the Cuckoo is really a trick,
But not a problem that you can't lick.
My advice is simply to wait,
'Cause we know the Cuckoo is *never* late!

LIZARD

There's a lizard in my gizzard, it's true.
It slipped into my stew.
It wiggles and scriggles and jiggles.
I don't know what to do.

FREE

Hey, little friend,
A monkey's tail does bend.
The animals live in the zoo.

Take me away.
We can run and play
Where the ocean's water is blue.

UNAWARE BEAR

He didn't know where he was going
Or where he had been.
He never finished a job because
He always started again.

He went into a honey shop
But couldn't remember why.
He dressed up in his favorite suit
And always forgot his tie.

He couldn't guess where the sun went
When it slipped away at night.
And when the moon came up, he thought,
"Well, that's an interesting sight."

He forgot that questions always have answers
And letters need a reply—
And when you talk about yourself
The word for "me" is "I."

He waited long outside the door
Because he forgot to knock.
Inside his shoe his foot was bare
Because he forgot his sock.

Unaware Bear had many friends,
But he didn't know who they were.
Unaware Bear knew who *he* was,
But didn't know *why* he had fur.

SECRET

Firefly, tell me a secret,
A special one I will keep.
Firefly, I will keep it,
If you tell me a special secret.

DARING DAVE AND THE GIANT WAVE

It was super hot and sunny
On that Sunday afternoon,
When a daring boy named Dave
Took a wave a bit too soon.

He started out by paddling
On his board way out to sea.
And there he caught the biggest wave,
As big as one could be.

It roared up from the ocean,
Moving fish and sand,
Dragging boats and buoys
And seaweed toward the land.

Dave, he saw it coming
And gave a mighty kick.
He skimmed along the ocean,
Really, really quick.

Blasts of frothy water
Blew sand crabs through his hair.
He dodged a bunch of driftwood
As the lifeguard stood to stare.

Down the wave came crashin'
While the beach umbrellas shook.
The seagulls watched in wonder,
And the starfish wouldn't look.

There was so much swishy swashing
Like clothes in a machine.
It was easily the biggest splash
That folks had ever seen.

Now, you musn't waste a worry
On famous Daring Dave.
He turned around and paddled out
To catch the next big wave.

QUIET LITTLE MOLLY AND THE GREAT BIG HOT TAMALE

It was quiet little Molly and her great big hot tamale
That sent everybody runnin' far away.
She took a great big bite—it hit the spot just right.
It's what happened *later* that I cannot dare to say.

ME

I hated washing clothes
Till I wore a dirty shirt.

I hated eating broccoli
Till I didn't get dessert.

I never cleaned my room
Till I lost my python snake.

I never saved my money
Till a coin I got was fake.

I didn't do my homework
Till I couldn't spell my name.

I didn't dump the trash
Till the health inspector came.

I couldn't keep a secret
Till one was told of me.

I couldn't do a lot of things
But that's what made me, ME.

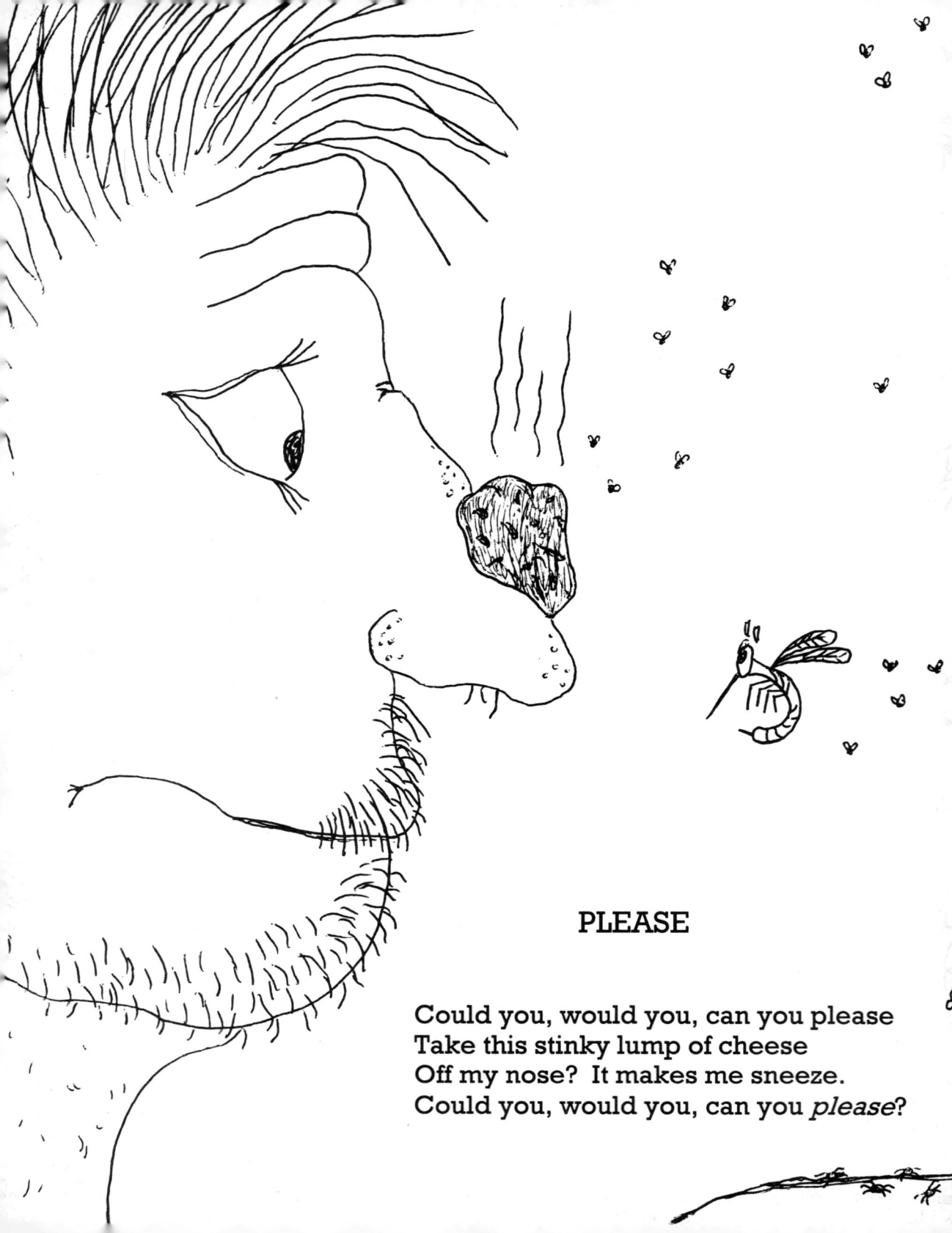

PLEASE

Could you, would you, can you please
Take this stinky lump of cheese
Off my nose? It makes me sneeze.
Could you, would you, can you *please*?

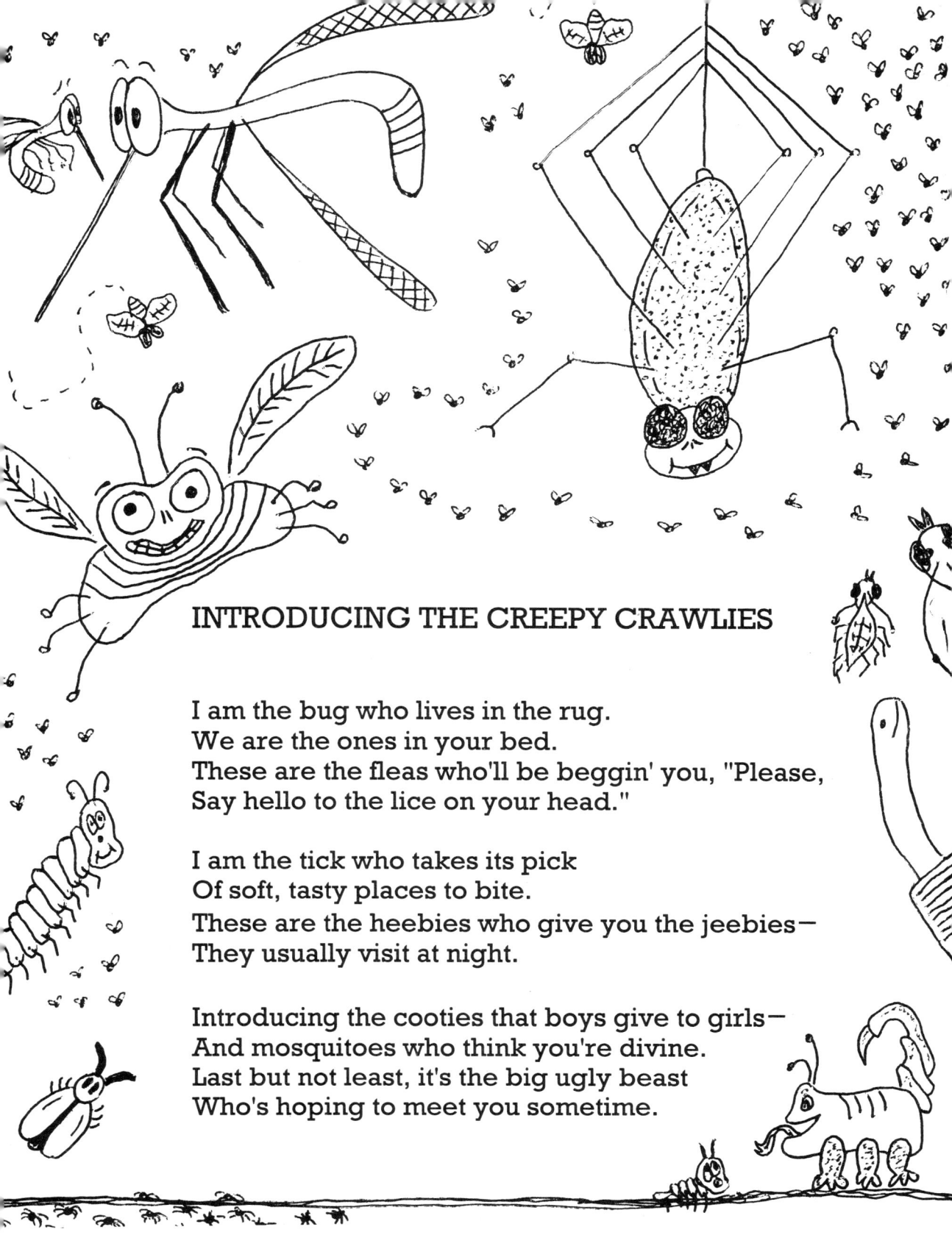

INTRODUCING THE CREEPY CRAWLIES

I am the bug who lives in the rug.
We are the ones in your bed.
These are the fleas who'll be beggin' you, "Please,
Say hello to the lice on your head."

I am the tick who takes its pick
Of soft, tasty places to bite.
These are the heebies who give you the jeebies—
They usually visit at night.

Introducing the cooties that boys give to girls—
And mosquitoes who think you're divine.
Last but not least, it's the big ugly beast
Who's hoping to meet you sometime.

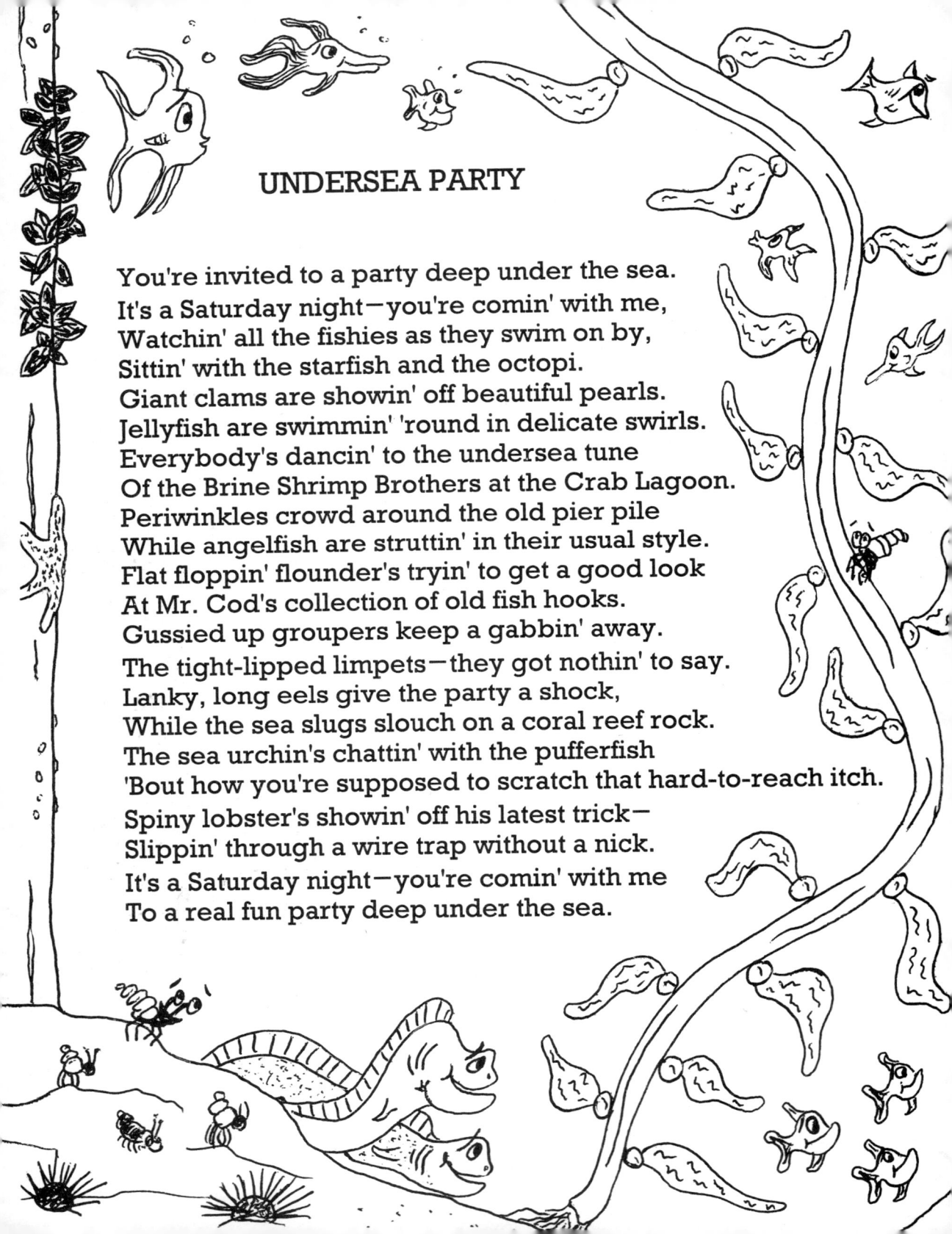

UNDERSEA PARTY

You're invited to a party deep under the sea.
It's a Saturday night—you're comin' with me,
Watchin' all the fishies as they swim on by,
Sittin' with the starfish and the octopi.
Giant clams are showin' off beautiful pearls.
Jellyfish are swimmin' 'round in delicate swirls.
Everybody's dancin' to the undersea tune
Of the Brine Shrimp Brothers at the Crab Lagoon.
Periwinkles crowd around the old pier pile
While angelfish are struttin' in their usual style.
Flat floppin' flounder's tryin' to get a good look
At Mr. Cod's collection of old fish hooks.
Gussied up groupers keep a gabbin' away.

The tight-lipped limpets—they got nothin' to say.
Lanky, long eels give the party a shock,
While the sea slugs slouch on a coral reef rock.
The sea urchin's chattin' with the pufferfish
'Bout how you're supposed to scratch that hard-to-reach itch.

Spiny lobster's showin' off his latest trick—
Slippin' through a wire trap without a nick.

It's a Saturday night—you're comin' with me
To a real fun party deep under the sea.

GREEDY GRETTLE

Greedy Grettle would never settle
For just one piece of pie.
She wanted it all—one piece was too small.
If she didn't get it, she'd cry.
Grettle was spoiled—her parents toiled.
It was they who made her that way.
That's what they got for raising a snot.
It happens *every* day.

DANCIN' MAN

Dancin' man, dancin' man—
Dances the dances that nobody can.
Taps the tap, jitters the bug,
Won't slow down on an old shag rug.
Look out, here comes the dancin' man.

47

THE SCRUFFYMADOODLE NUT

What? What? WHAT?
A Scruffymadoodle nut?
You've got to be kidding—
There's really no way.
What kind of a nut
Is this that you say
Comes from a Scruffymadoodle nut tree
That grows two nuts a year and sometimes three?
Well, I don't believe it—no surely not me.
I get my nuts from the Ufamungungalo tree.

MARSHMALLOW GOO VOLCANO

You're climbin' to the top, to the very, very top
Of the Marshmallow Goo volcano.
And you like it a lot, a very, very lot
On the Marshmallow Goo volcano.
You hear a grumblin' rumblin' and to keep yourself from stumblin',
You glop marshmallow goo on your feet.
To keep yourself from slidin' down the slippery, sloppery sides,
You sit down and goo up your seat.
The marshmallow goometer reads "SuperGoo Warning,"
Which means "Get a move on and go!"
But you're stuck at the top, the very, very top
Of the Marshmallow Goo volcanoooooooooooo !!!

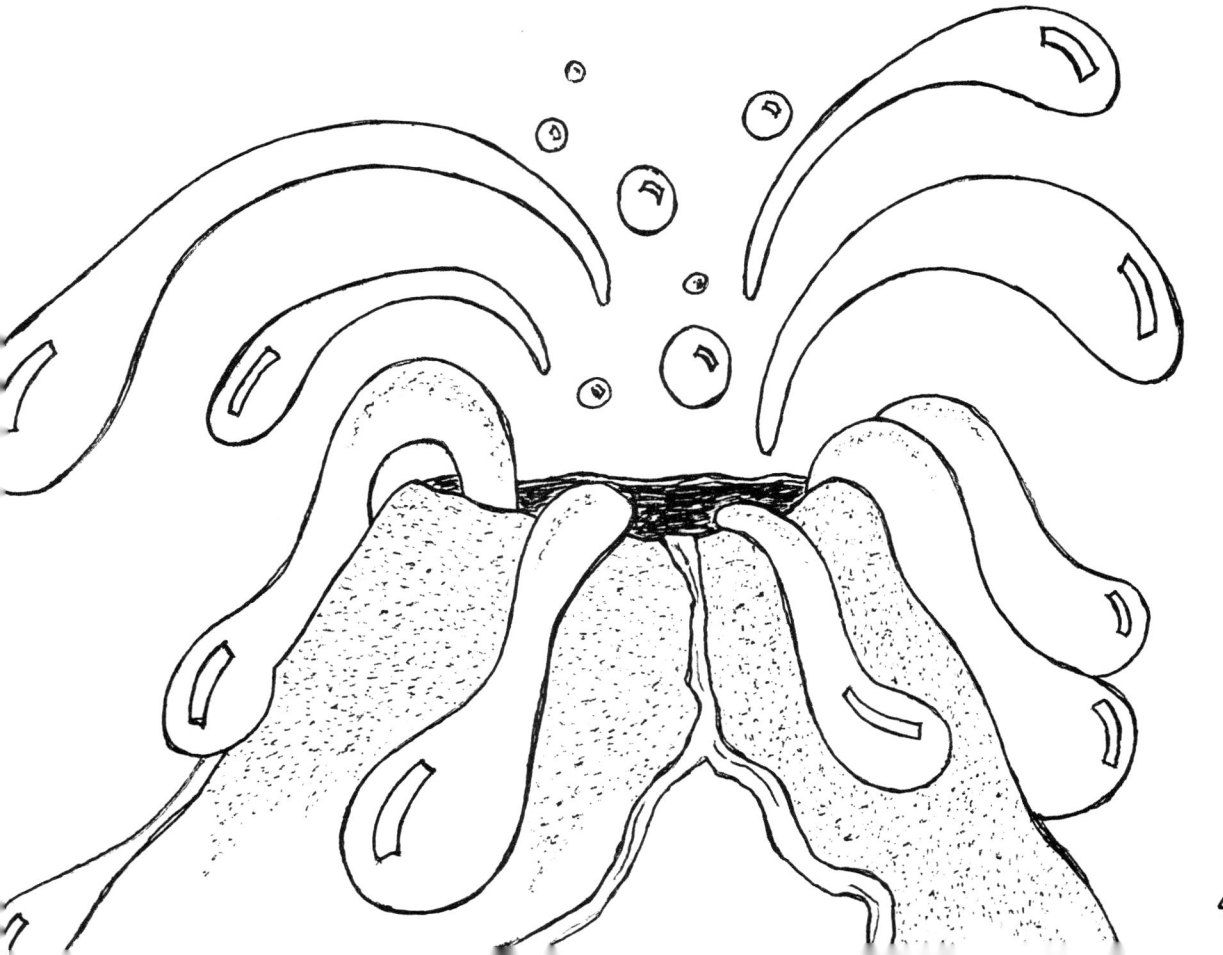

SEARCHIN' FOR TREASURE

We're sailin' out on the high open sea.
Searchin' for treasure if you can believe.
Rockin' and rollin' in this little boat,
It's really a wonder we're stayin' afloat.

Jolly ol' Roger is flyin' up high.
Days of all fun have quickly passed by.
It's a dangerous voyage, we might not come back.
The passage is long and quite hard to track.

There's a tropical island and cold foggy bay.
An old treasure map will show us the way
Through jungles of darkness and tunnels of rats,
The Temple of Mystery guarded by bats—

The Reef of Destruction, Cliff of Despair.
"**X**" marks the spot, the treasure lies there!
Cutting through swarms of beetles and bugs—
Wading through pools of snails and slugs.

Under dry bones of the pirates before,
The ancient chest lies, hidden no more.
Digging and digging through rocks and thick mud,
Shovels pierce deep till we hear a loud thud.

Yes! It's the treasure—"Yippee!" we all shout,
Moping and groping—it's tough to pull out.
We smash off the lock and lift the big lid.
Think, all this treasure just for us kids!

Beautiful diamonds, red rubies and gold,
Crystal and silver bars too big to hold.
Off in the distance we hear a loud hoot.
It's pirate ghosts coming back for their loot!

With nowhere to go and no place to hide,
We jump in the hole and cling to the side.
Laughing and howling all over the treasure,
They gather it up and take off together.

Somehow we manage our way to the boat.
Safely we push off to sea—we all float.
In the hot sun, we fall fast asleep.
Dreaming of pirates and treasures they keep.

Tossing and turning from this side to that,
I wake up and wonder how I got back
Safe in my bed, clothes covered in sand—
How did I get this gold coin in my hand?

FROG

There's a frog in my throat, it's so.
How it got there, I don't know.
I hate eating flies
And bugs with big eyes.
So, I *really* wish it would go.

GREEN LEMONADE

Gringy old, grungy old, green lemonade.
Folks watched me make it, but none of 'em stayed.
Had it for sale, but nobody paid.
Couldn't swap for it 'cause no one would trade.
Now, I admit, I regret that I've made
Gringy old, grungy old, *green* lemonade.

DREAMIN'

I had a dream I was eatin' ice cream.
Alas, it was only a dream!

I had a dream that I danced with a queen.
Alas, it was only a dream!

I had a dream things weren't what they seem.
Alas, it was only a dream!

I had a dream that I dreamt that I dreamed.
Alas, it was only a dream!

CLOTHESPIN EARRINGS

Clothespin earrings—they're so fine.
I'll try yours, you try mine.
Me, oh my, you look divine
In fancy clothespin earrings.

JACK

Candle Jack, Candle Jack,
Jumped over the candle—
But *didn't* jump back.

CALVIN C. CLAYTON

Say, have you heard of Calvin C. Clayton?
'Twas a wild and crazy machine he was makin'.
It took him a year or two or three.
That super invention was somethin' to see.

Go forward in time or back real fast.
See your future and visit your past.
No one believed that Calvin was sane,
But that didn't wash his hopes down the drain.

He hammered and clamored until it was ready—
Then loaded up food like bread and spaghetti.
Calvin proclaimed, "I'm ready to go.
What will happen, I really don't know."

He climbed up and in and locked the door tight,
Put on his helmet and turned on the light.
"Which way shall I go on my journey through time?"
He decided and set the date: Two Nine Nine Nine.

It rattled and rocked and pitched here and there.
Smoke came from the sides as everyone stared.
Grinding and whining, it spun all around.
Jerking and quirking, it tossed off the ground.

All of a sudden a huge lightening flash
Blew everyone's hair off and scattered the trash.
When the dust cleared, all the folks saw,
Calvin went nowhere, nowhere at all.

People made jokes and some even sneered.
They made funny faces and said he was weird.
But Calvin C. Clayton held tightly on—
With the blink of your eye, POOF—he was gone.

CAKE

The biggest chocolate cake
Anyone dared to bake
Was bigger than a house
And the Alabama state.

I often sit and wonder
Just who might have made it.
The thing I know for sure
Is *I'm* the one who ate it.

TEN O'CLOCK SCREAM

It's the eight o'clock, nine o'clock, ten o'clock scream.
Lean out your open window,
You'll hear what I mean.
When the time is right, we'll break the night—
It's not a nightmare dream.
It's the eight o'clock, nine o'clock, ten o'clock scream.

STALE MAIL

Do you know who delivers the mail
Through rain, sleet, snow and hail,
Tornado winds and a gale?
I gotta know 'cause this time it's stale.

BEST

Never ever try to guess
What you think is best
For somebody else
Till you've tried it yourself.

LIE

I cannot tell a lie.
I couldn't even try.
It wasn't I who ate the pie.
I cannot tell a lie.

STUCK

What do you do when you're stuck in your shoes?
How do you get yourself out?
What if you find yourself in this bind?
Will it do any good to shout?
How would they feel, your toes and heel,
When they hear you starting to pout?
What do you do when you're stuck in your shoes?
How do you get yourself out?

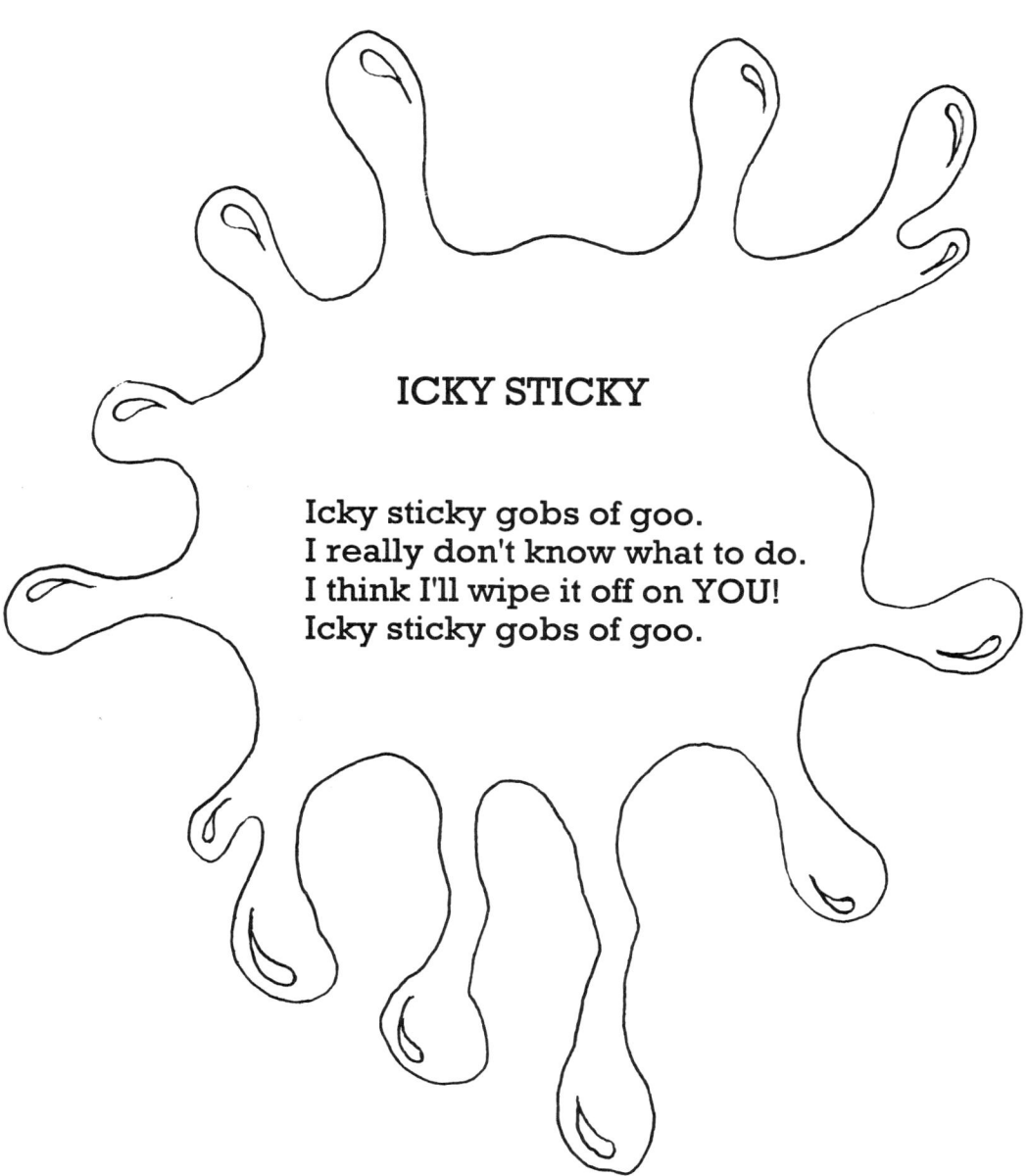

ICKY STICKY

Icky sticky gobs of goo.
I really don't know what to do.
I think I'll wipe it off on YOU!
Icky sticky gobs of goo.

TELEPHONE TALKER

Did you hear?
You don't say.
Oh, my gosh,
Just today?
Who told you?
I won't tell.
How and where?
Well, well, well!
You won't believe.
Have you heard?
I just found out.
That's absurd!
Who and what,
Why and when?
Well, I'll be!
Say again?
Cross my heart.
Cross my toes.
It's a secret.
No one knows!
It's a wonder.
Me, oh my.
My lips are sealed.
Stick my eye!
Gotta go.
Got things to do . . .
. . . Hello, friend,
Guess what I heard about you!

JUMP

Fiona jumped so high
She bumped into the sky.
It came right down
And broke the ground.
She ran away to cry.

STINKY

There was an old woman who lived in a shoe.
How did she do it? I wish that I knew.
It must have been stinky and dark in there, too.
I doubt if that's anything I'd ever do.

SPREE

Way, way off in the Caribbean Sea
You'll find a dog named Shanty on a little boat named Spree.
Spree has got a captain, Captain Bob, mind you me,
Who loves to sail the waters of that Caribbean sea.

Shanty keeps a watchful eye on all that's going on—
Barking at the tack and turn so nothing happens wrong.
Captain Bob drops anchor near the famous Pirate Rock,
Where you might spy a gold doubloon as seagulls look and squawk.

If you take a swim, and I recommend you do,
You'll see a lot of fishes and a turtle—maybe two.
The coral reef is delicate—be careful not to touch.
The conch and all the crabs and eels will thank you very much.

Shanty likes to splash and swim in waters crystal clear.
She jumps right in and paddles 'round—that dog has got no fear.
Captain Bob will serve you up a very tasty lunch.
Shanty gets a biscuit—it's her favorite thing to munch.

"It'll soon be time to sail!" says friendly Captain Bob.
"Watch your head and hold on tight while Shanty does her job!"
The sail it starts to flutter as the boom swings quickly by.
"Wanna steer the boat a while? Come up and have a try!"

When the evening comes and the sky turns red and pink,
A gentle breeze, warm and soft, will make you start to think.
Remember Captain Bob and little Shanty on the Spree
Sailing through the islands in the Caribbean Sea.

WONDER

Can you take a color picture
When a zebra's black and white?
If the moon comes out in daytime,
Why's the sun not out at night?
Can you dowse a burning fire
With some water boiling hot?
I often wonder 'bout these things.
I often wonder a lot.

MR. MISTAKE

Mr. Mistake tried to bake
A pickle in a pan.
When it burned, he quickly learned—
It's better to eat from a can.

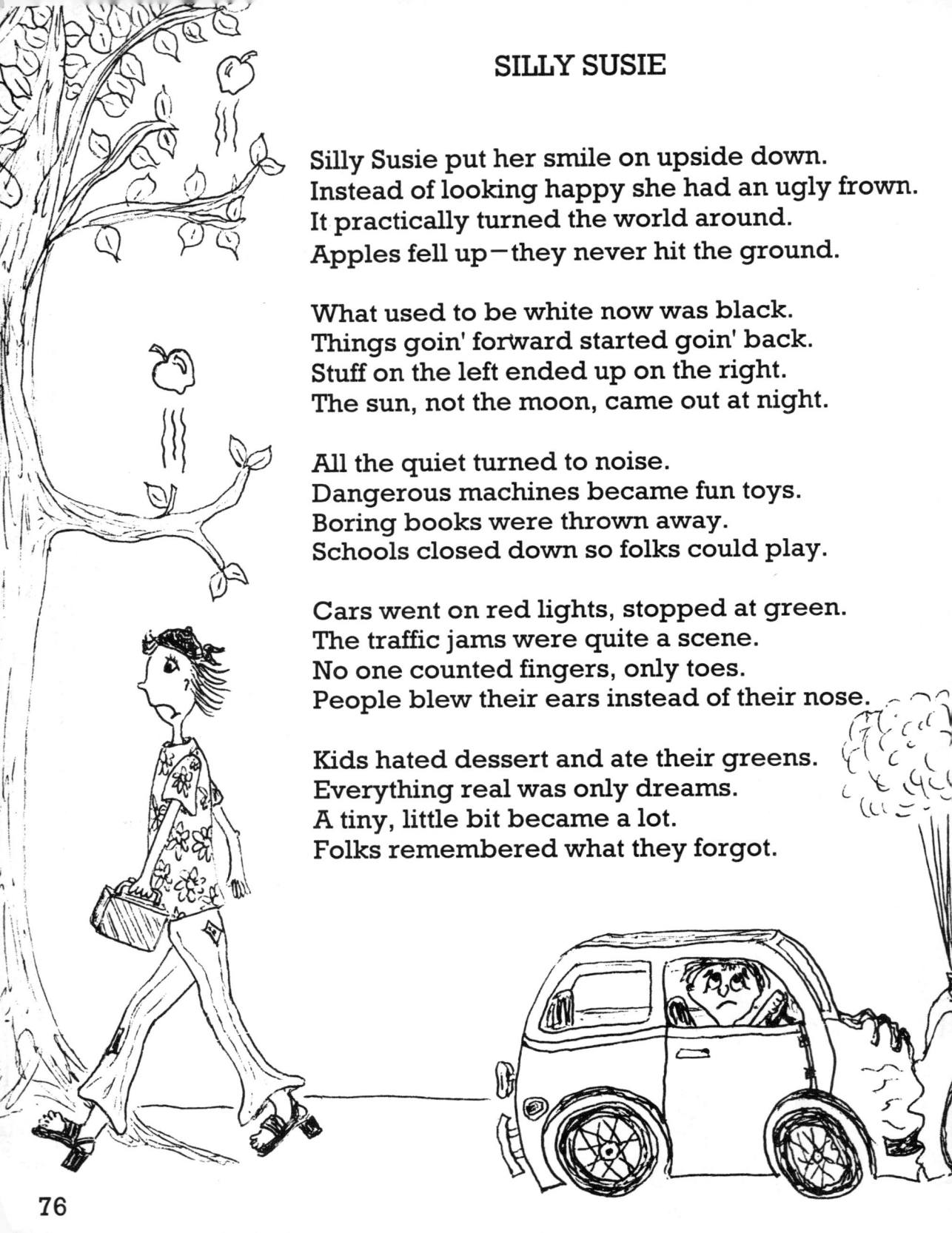

SILLY SUSIE

Silly Susie put her smile on upside down.
Instead of looking happy she had an ugly frown.
It practically turned the world around.
Apples fell up—they never hit the ground.

What used to be white now was black.
Things goin' forward started goin' back.
Stuff on the left ended up on the right.
The sun, not the moon, came out at night.

All the quiet turned to noise.
Dangerous machines became fun toys.
Boring books were thrown away.
Schools closed down so folks could play.

Cars went on red lights, stopped at green.
The traffic jams were quite a scene.
No one counted fingers, only toes.
People blew their ears instead of their nose.

Kids hated dessert and ate their greens.
Everything real was only dreams.
A tiny, little bit became a lot.
Folks remembered what they forgot.

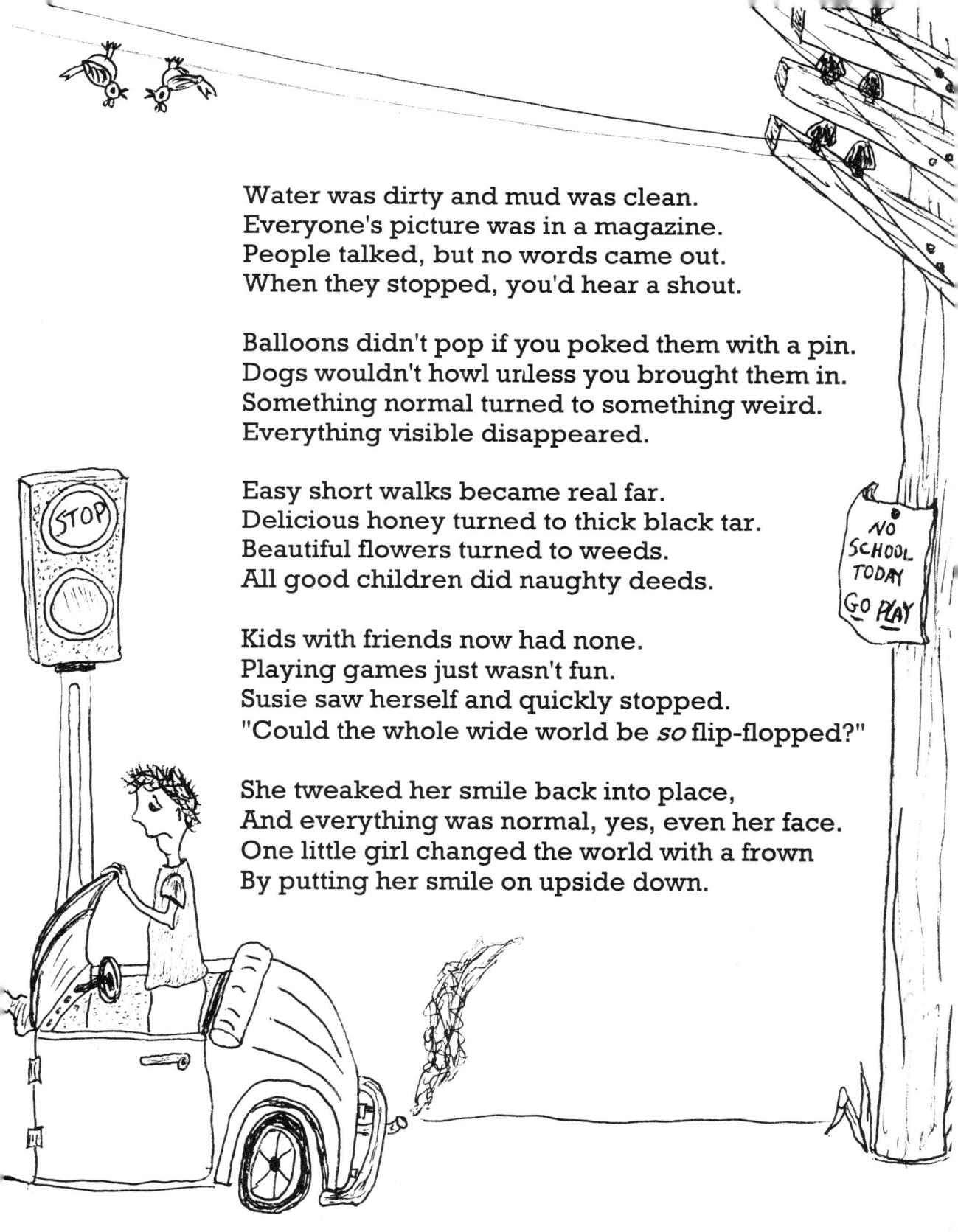

Water was dirty and mud was clean.
Everyone's picture was in a magazine.
People talked, but no words came out.
When they stopped, you'd hear a shout.

Balloons didn't pop if you poked them with a pin.
Dogs wouldn't howl unless you brought them in.
Something normal turned to something weird.
Everything visible disappeared.

Easy short walks became real far.
Delicious honey turned to thick black tar.
Beautiful flowers turned to weeds.
All good children did naughty deeds.

Kids with friends now had none.
Playing games just wasn't fun.
Susie saw herself and quickly stopped.
"Could the whole wide world be *so* flip-flopped?"

She tweaked her smile back into place,
And everything was normal, yes, even her face.
One little girl changed the world with a frown
By putting her smile on upside down.

FRIENDS

Said the tugboat to the lighthouse,
"Thanks for shining clear and bright!"

Said the lighthouse to the tugboat,
"Thanks for visiting at night!"

ICE BLOCKIN'

Very late at night when the moon is glowing nice,
There comes a group of crazy kids with ten-pound blocks of ice.
They climb right up the highest hill—that one over there
And start their wild screamin' as the neighbors peek and stare.
One by one they plop the ice down upon the ground.
The first kid sits down on it as the others crowd around.
She shouts when she is ready, and they give her one good push.
Down the hill she slides so fast—right into a bush!
The others take off down the hill, through the plants and flowers.
Crashin' here and tumblin' there—they're doin' it for hours.
A neighbor with a flashlight yells, "I'm gonna call the cops!"
The kids just keep on screamin' and no one really stops.
Clothes are wet, rumps are cold, someone lost a stockin'.
They don't care 'cause that's the fun of late-at-night ice blockin'.

FAIRIES

There're fairies in the garden,
But no one seems to care.
There're fairies in the garden—
I've seen them dancing there.
There're fairies in the garden,
But no one comes to see.
There're fairies in the garden—
Now they're smiling at me.

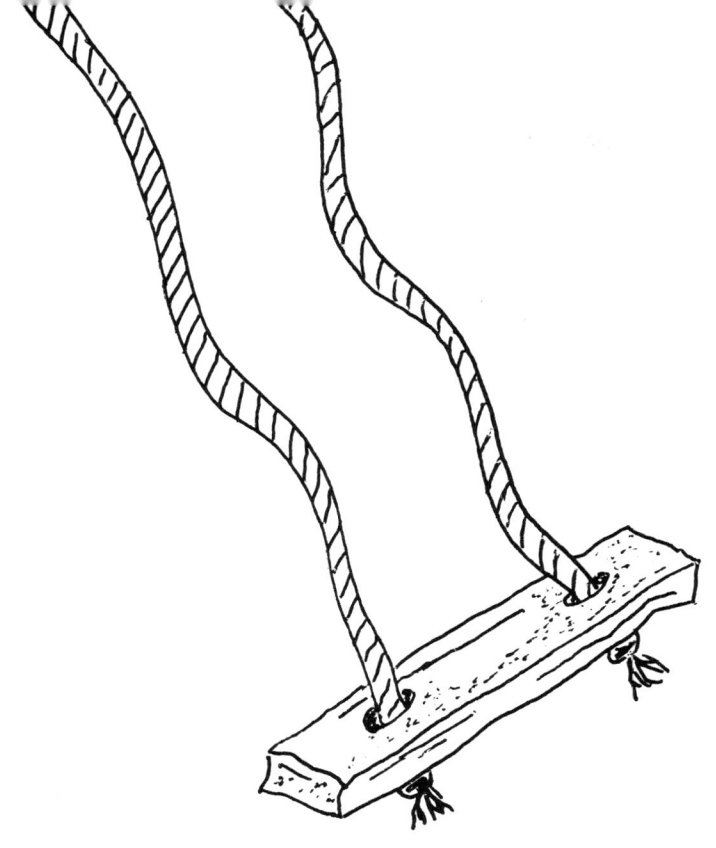

SWINGING

I swing on my swing so high.
If I swing any higher, I'll fly.
I look down at the ground.
I don't want to come down.
I'd rather be high in the sky.

SWIMMING IN CHOCOLATE

Swimming in chocolate.
Oh, what a treat.
Isn't it wonderful?
Isn't it neat?

A little sip here—
A giant gulp there.
Gobs of thick chocolate
All stuck in our hair.

Semi-sweet, super-sweet
Milk chocolate, white.
This swimmin' hole's open
All day and all night.

A swan dive, a jackknife
A belly flop flump.
Stand back and watch
This big cannonball jump.

Swimming in chocolate,
Come on and see,
But remember, it's over
If anyone pees.

SPECIAL

You are something special.
Yes, you are—yes, you are.

You are something special.
And I know that you'll go far.

You are something special.
It's so true, it's so true.

You are something special.
You can do it—yes, *you.*

You are something special.
Head to toe, head to toe.

You are something special.
And I think that you should know.

ANCHOVIE PIE

Can you eat a whole anchovie pie
Without getting a fishbone in your eye?
Little heads and tiny tails—
Crunchy fins and crispy scales.
I'd surely like to see you try
To eat a whole anchovie pie.

JUNK YARD

Junk yard, klunk yard,
Watch out for the skunk yard.
It's lots of fun to climb junk piles,
But you'd better watch out for Old Man Stiles!

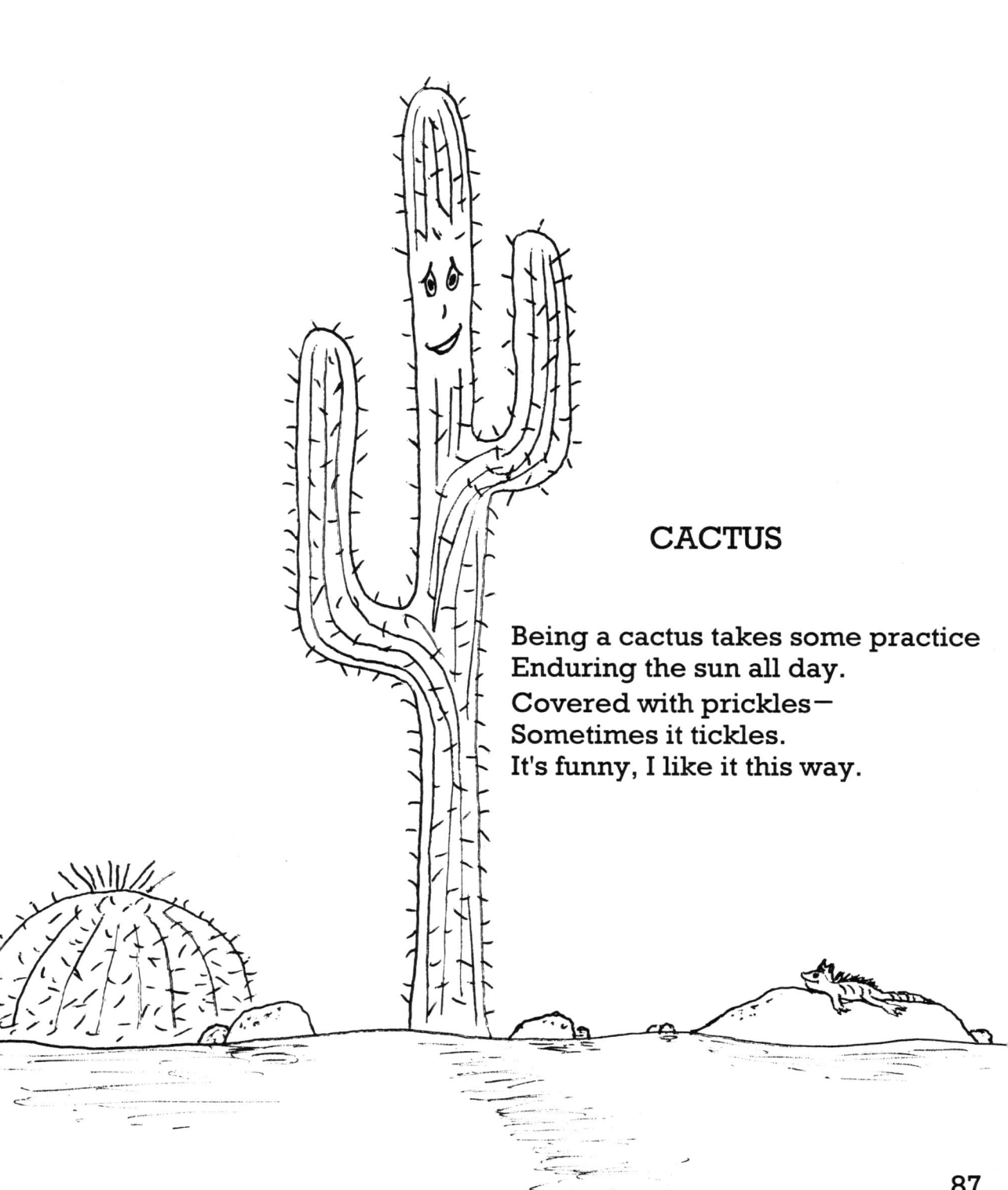

CACTUS

Being a cactus takes some practice
Enduring the sun all day.
Covered with prickles—
Sometimes it tickles.
It's funny, I like it this way.

THIRTY-TWO SNAILS

Thirty-two snails in an old metal pail,
Slimin' and grimin' and smellin' quite stale,
Escape to the world from that old metal jail,
Leavin' nothin' but one big ol' slimy snail trail.

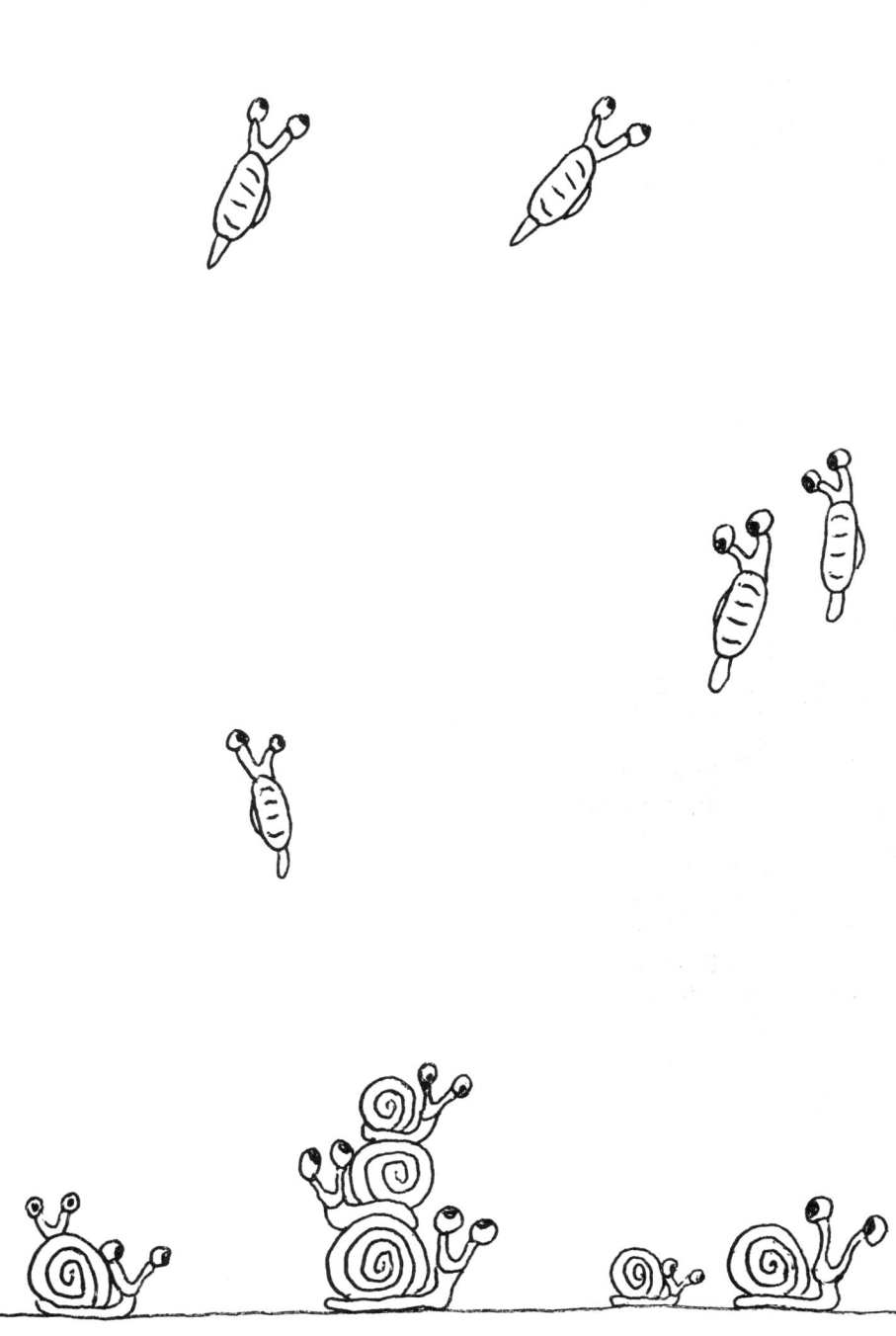

KABOOM!

A porcupine and a balloon
Sat together on a stone.
The porcupine sneezed.
The balloon went KABOOM!
Now the porcupine sits alone.

SCANDALOUS SANDALESS SUE

I'm not wearin' shoes—I flatly refuse!
I'm Scandalous Sandaless Sue.

I'm not wearin' slippers or rubber beach flippers.
I'm Scandalous Sandaless Sue.

I'm not wearin' slip-ons or weird, funny clip-ons.
I'm Scandalous Sandaless Sue.

I'm not wearin' socks or big Birkenstocks.
I'm Scandalous Sandaless Sue.

I'm not wearin' clogs or shoes for long jogs.
I'm Scandalous Sandaless Sue.

My feet, bare and flat, will stay just like that.
Say, have I told you I won't wear a hat?

TICKLE MACHINE

The tickle machine is outta control!
The tickle machine is outta control!!
Everyone's laughin', the young and the old.
It's the tickle machine and it's outta control.

The way it's designed, unpredictably wild.
No one escapes, no kid, no child.
You cannot break loose, down on your knees
You'll be laughin' and beggin'—oh, please, oh, please!

It starts with your toes and goes and goes
Then up like a feather under your nose.
Around your arms, legs and neck,
Under your chin and sides—oh, heck!

The tickle machine is outta control!
The tickle machine is outta control!!
The tickle machine like a bright pink giraffe
Will get you to giggle and force you to laugh.

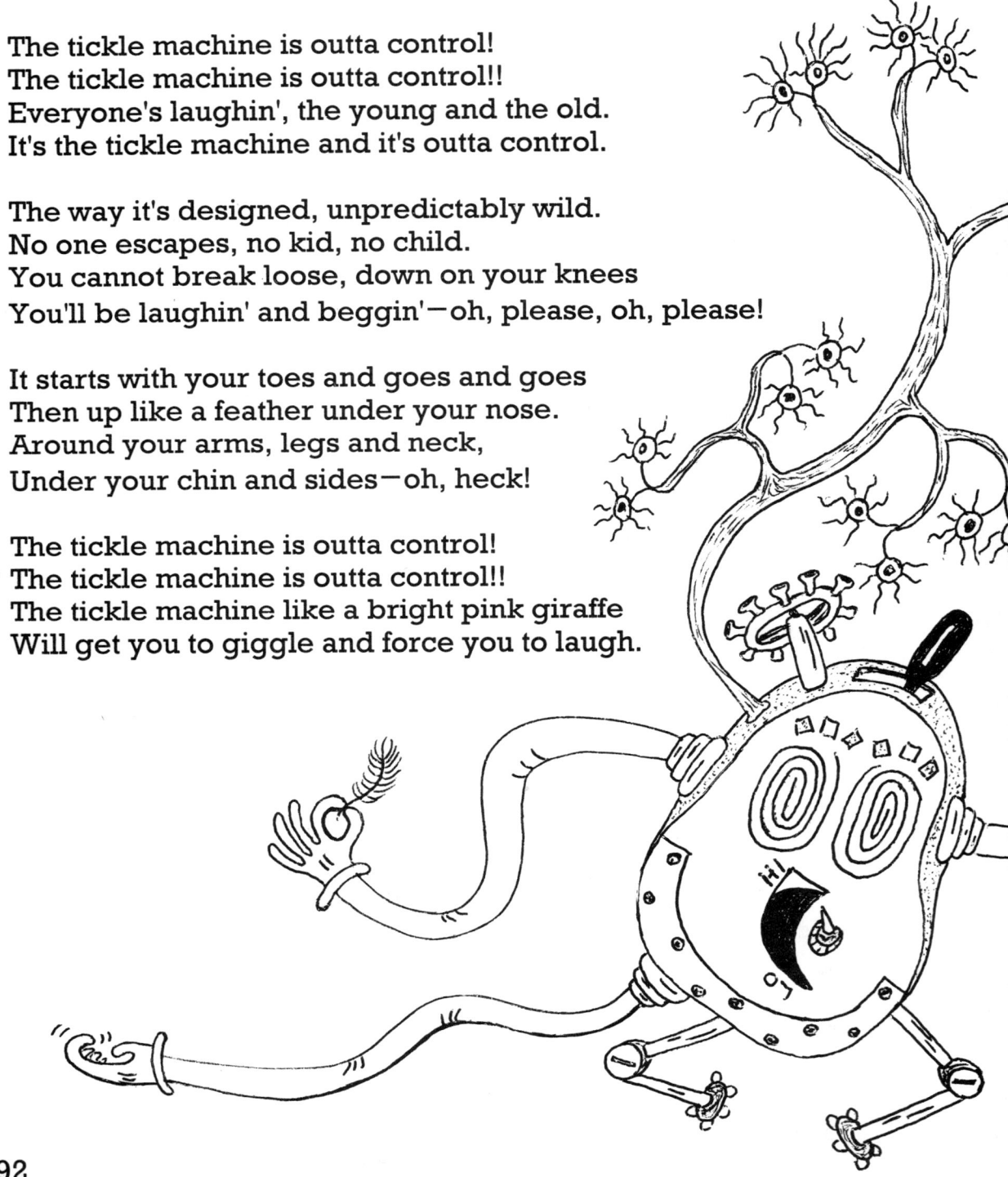

JENNY

Jenny Ann Sarah May Wanda Q. Whirl
Had one of the longest names in the world.
Her friend made it short for only a penny.
Now when we call her, we say simply," Jenny."

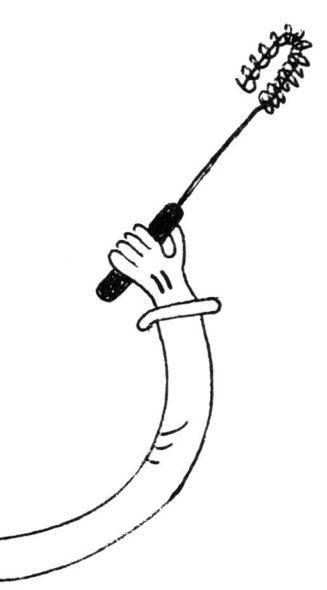

EATING

A spoon and a fork will do
For eatin' a pile of food.
A napkin and bib are best
To keep you from makin' a mess.
But if you *really* wanna have fun,
Your fingers will get the job done.

RUBBER BAND

The world's longest rubber band
Stretches from here to another land
And I'll tell you, it sure can
Hurt when it snaps back on your hand.

SPIN ME

I get so dizzy when you spin me around
and around
and around.

I get kind of queezy and feel uneasy
when you spin me around
and around
and around.

I'm not sure what I'll do, but it could get on you,
when you spin me around.
and around
and around.

The world's in a tumble — my body's a jumble.
I think I'd better lie down!

TATTLETALE

Tattletale, tattletale,
Your mouth is bigger than a whale.
Tattletale, tattletale,
You'll make friends slower than a snail.

DETERMINED

Joey built a spaceship to fly to the sun.
We laughed and joked that it couldn't be done.
"You'll get almost there—then you'll burn up in flight!"
Joey smiled and said, "I'm going at *night*."

BORED

I'm stuck in my bedroom with nothin' to do.
It's cold, it's rainy—I'm really bored, too.
Comic-book stacks about twenty feet high,
A big telescope and a map of the sky.
A Super Bake oven with ten recipes,
Cool roller skates with pads for your knees.
Marbles and checkers—a big hoola hoop,
Clobs of fresh clay and buckets of goop.
A fancy new train, still in the box,
A miniature pickax and two big ol' rocks.
A cool microscope and plenty of bugs,
An old pickle jar with snails and slugs.
A jump rope, a skip rope, a brand new kazoo,
All sorts of markers, ink pens and glue.
Boxes of nails, a hammer and wood,
A hundred-tooth saw—it's perfectly good.
A neat science kit to grow colored crystals,
A Western outfit with two plastic pistols.
Two pinball machines—play them for free,
A video movie 'bout fish in the sea.
Special trick Frisbees for girls and boys.
I know what *you're* thinkin'—I need some new toys.

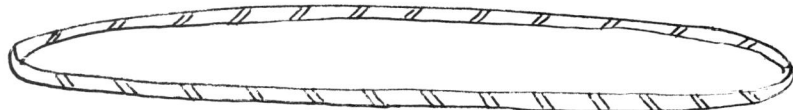

DRAGONFLY

I am the dragonfly.
Blue, blue sky,
Cattails growing high,
A breeze and a quiet sigh—
I am the dragonfly.

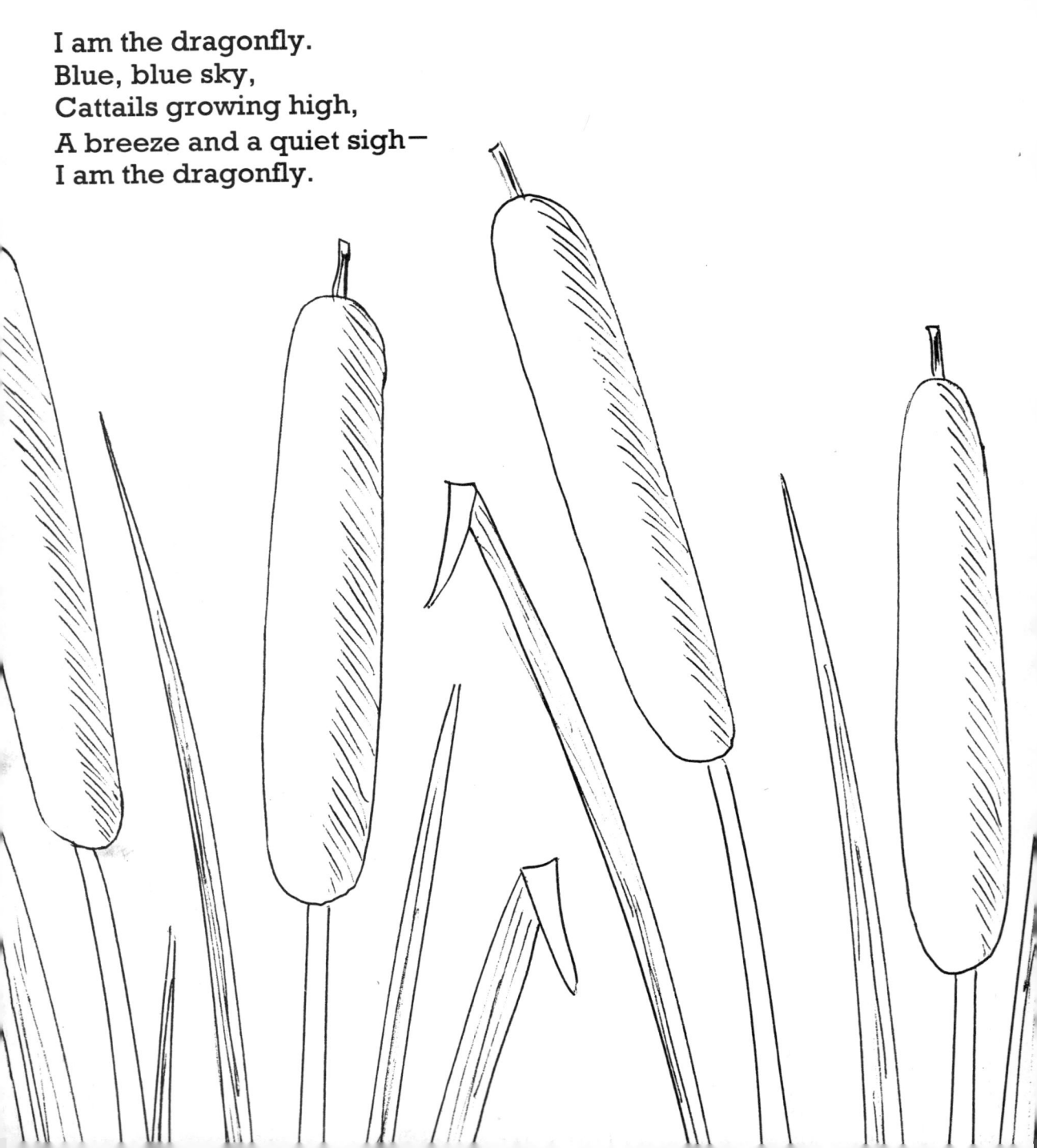

LONELY

Here I am, all alone—
With nobody to talk to.
Here I am, all alone—
I guess no one really wants to.

AGATHA ROSE

A purple umbrella for Agatha Rose
Turns yellow in springtime and white when it snows.
When the cool autumn comes and the Wiley Wind blows,
It turns red like the bud of a fancy primrose.
And from far, far away everyone knows
It's a purple unbrella for Agatha Rose.

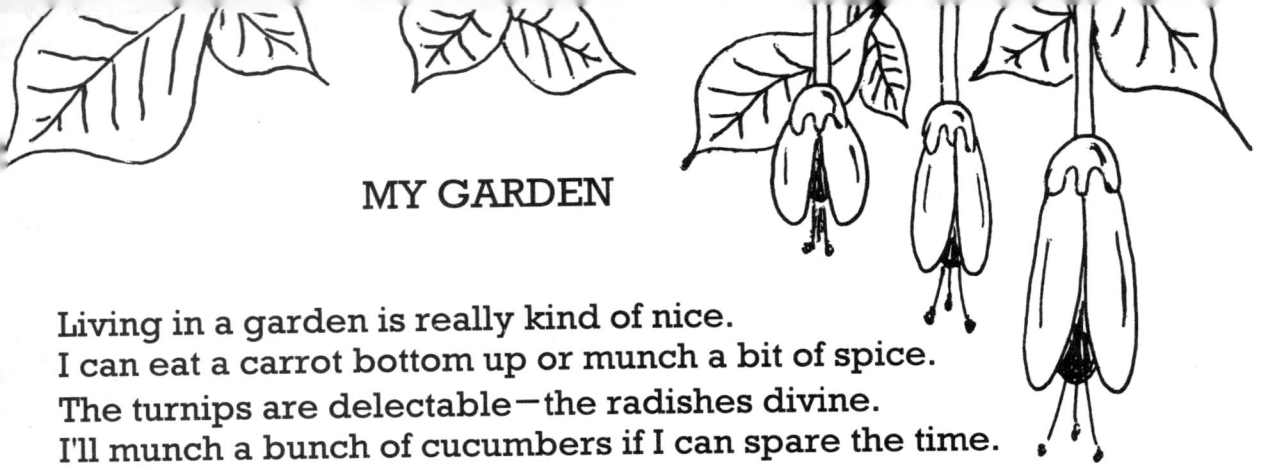

MY GARDEN

Living in a garden is really kind of nice.
I can eat a carrot bottom up or munch a bit of spice.
The turnips are delectable—the radishes divine.
I'll munch a bunch of cucumbers if I can spare the time.

Tomatoes are my favorite, juicy, red and ripe.
I can down a head of lettuce, depending on the type.
Zucchinis are so tasty—I leave little ones alone.
I just can't bring myself to eat the ones that aren't full grown.

The watermelons tempt me, so I take a great big bite.
I love those giant, gooshy chunks—they hit the spot just right.
I pass the peas and limas, their taste just isn't good.
I don't believe in eatin' things that taste like rotten wood.

Now corn is really somethin'—I'll always make the climb.
Grapes and berries turn me on—I love a curly vine.
When the night is over, I'll search for something sweet.
It sure is fun to live where there's a lot of food to eat.

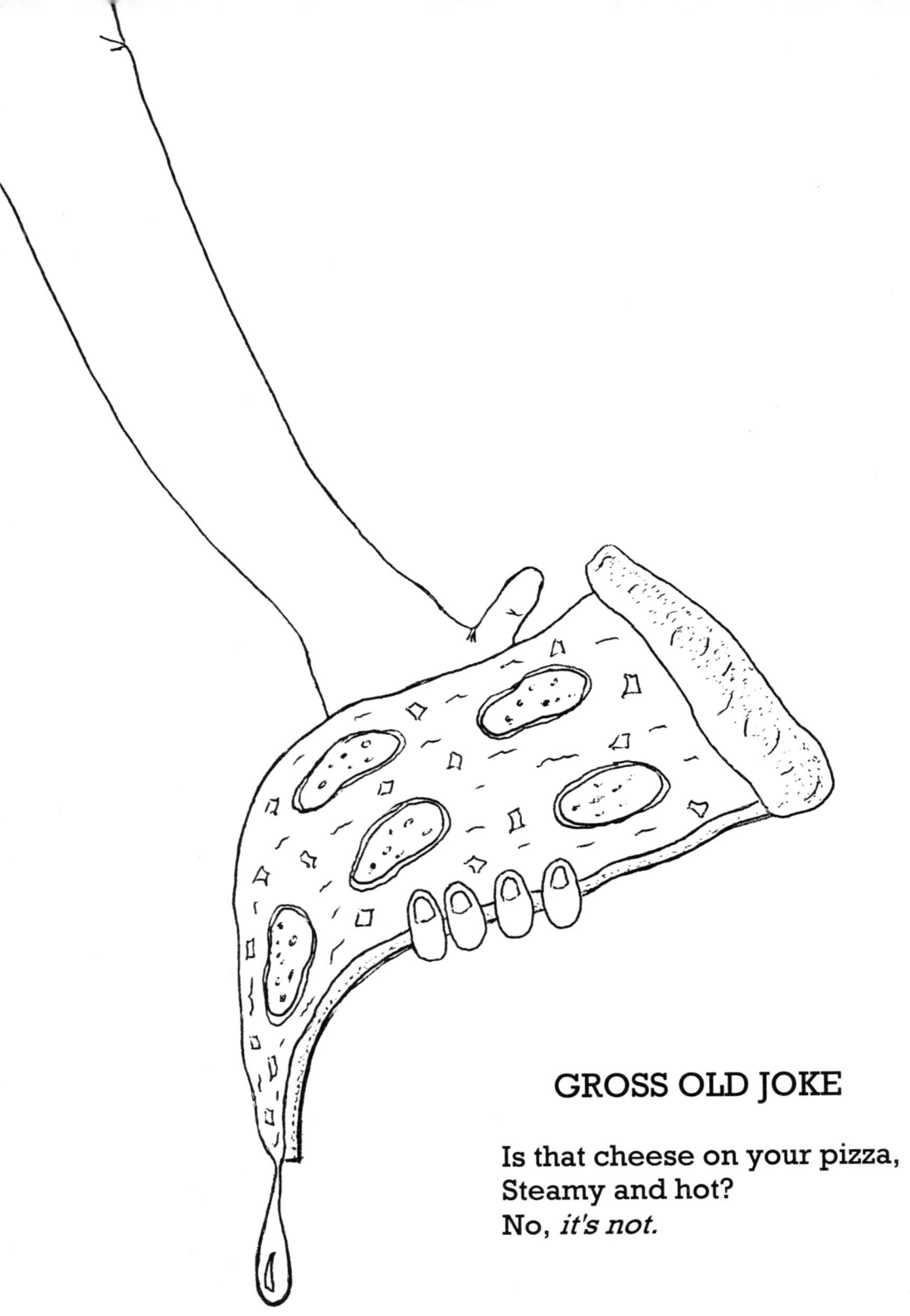

GROSS OLD JOKE

Is that cheese on your pizza,
Steamy and hot?
No, *it's not.*

NORM

Tall guy, small guy,
You just can't have it all, guy.
Funny folks in funny form,
I guess it's true there is no norm.

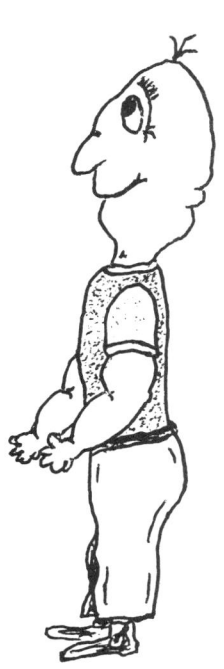

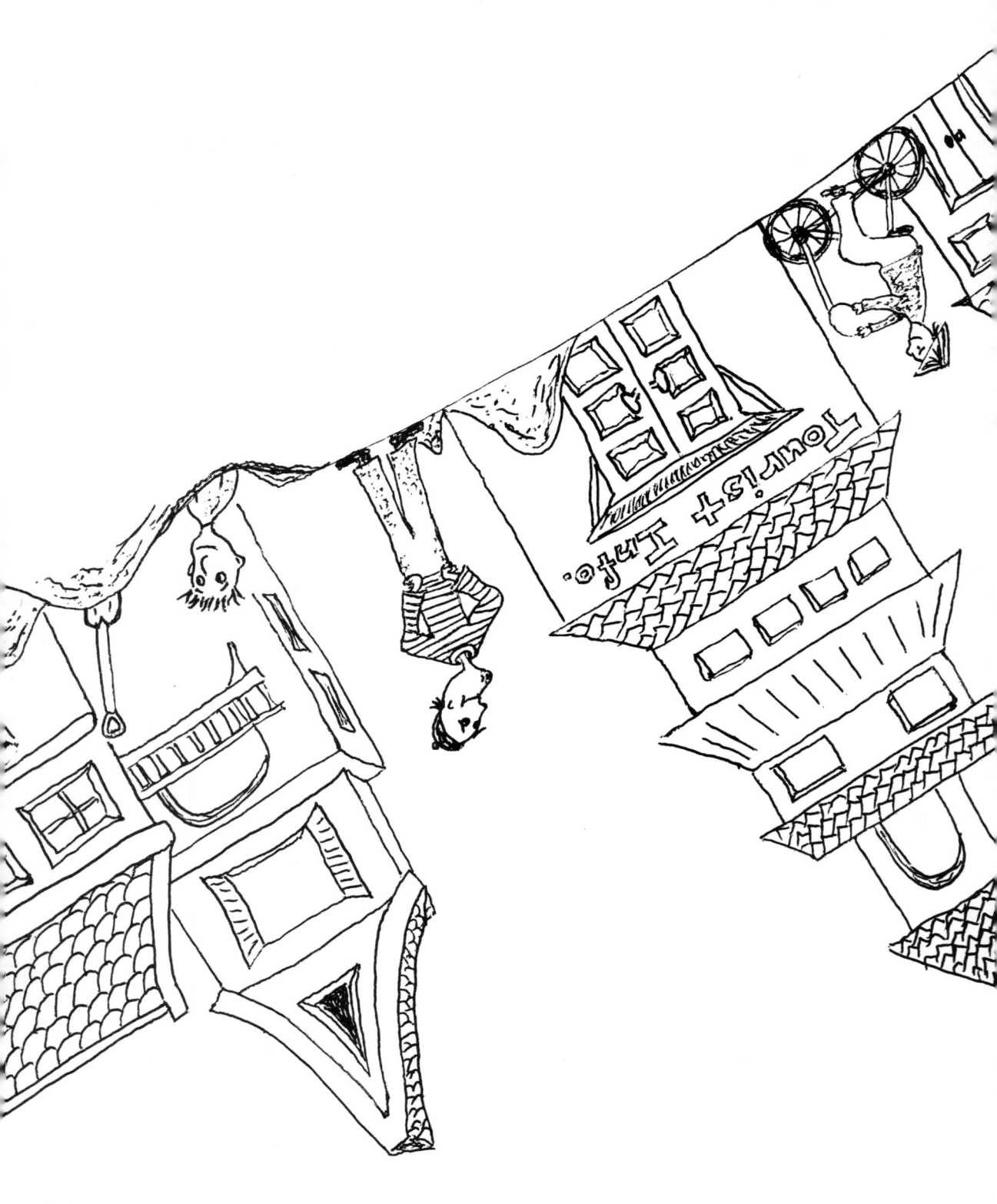

DIGGIN' TO CHINA

We're diggin' to China—let's pack up and go.
You take the shovel, I'll take the hoe.

We're diggin' to China—it can be done.
It's you and me friend on a journey of fun.

We're diggin' to China—ya, we sure are.
I know how to get there but don't know how far.

We're diggin' to China—we'll be the first.
What if we missed? That'd be the worst.

We're diggin' to China—we're goin' on through.
When we arrive, there'll be much to do.

We're diggin' to China—to prove that we can
Meet interesting people and see a new land.

We're diggin' to China—they'll see us and say,
"How did you get here, who showed you the way?"

We're diggin' to China—to eat the good food,
See the old palace, great wall and bamboo.

We're diggin' to China—then comin' on back
With lots of fun toys, like jump ropes and jacks.

We're diggin' to China—we'll travel for free,
Eat fresh fortune cookies, drink hot mystic tea.

We're diggin' to China—another day soon.
But before we go back, we'll climb to the moon.

FAKE

Cheese on a cracker.
Butter on bread.
Scales on a fishy.
Hair on your head.
Snow on a shovel.
Leaves on a rake.
I like diamonds,
But this one's fake.

SORRY SAM

Excuse me, ma'am,
I'm Sorry Sam.
I really am
Sorry, ma'am.
So, if you can
Excuse me, ma'am,
I'm really, really,
Sorry Sam.

WELL PLANNED

The ocean is filled with lots of water.
The desert is loaded with sand.
Clouds are white—the sun is bright.
I guess they were very well planned.

I WANNA IGUANA

I wanna iguana with scales and spikes.
I wanna iguana so people scream, "Yikes!"
I wanna iguana to climb all around.
I wanna iguana to dig in the ground.
I wanna iguana 'bout twenty feet long.
I wanna iguana—they do nothin' wrong.
I wanna iguana to have lots of fun.
I wanna iguana to lie in the sun.
I wanna iguana, friendly and green.
I wanna iguana, you know what I mean?

LISTEN

Listen to the voice in your head, friend.
The one that says, "Be good."
Listen to the voice in your head, friend.
Everyone wishes you would.

BUNGEE JUMPIN'

I'm goin' bungee jumpin'.
I've seen it on TV.
Tie a rope around my foot
And one end to a tree.

Get the movie camera.
Come on now, crowd around.
Here I go, OOPS, oh no!
Gosh, I hit the GROUND!

BELIEVE

I believe in shooting stars, luck and wishing wells.
I believe in Santa Claus and jingly, jangly bells.

I believe in changelings, leprechauns and nymphs.
I believe in gypsies, trolls and little imps.

I believe in fairies, pixies and their dust.
I believe in genies, dreaming, truth and trust.

I believe in magic, mystery and dreams.
They're the most real of reality, it seems.

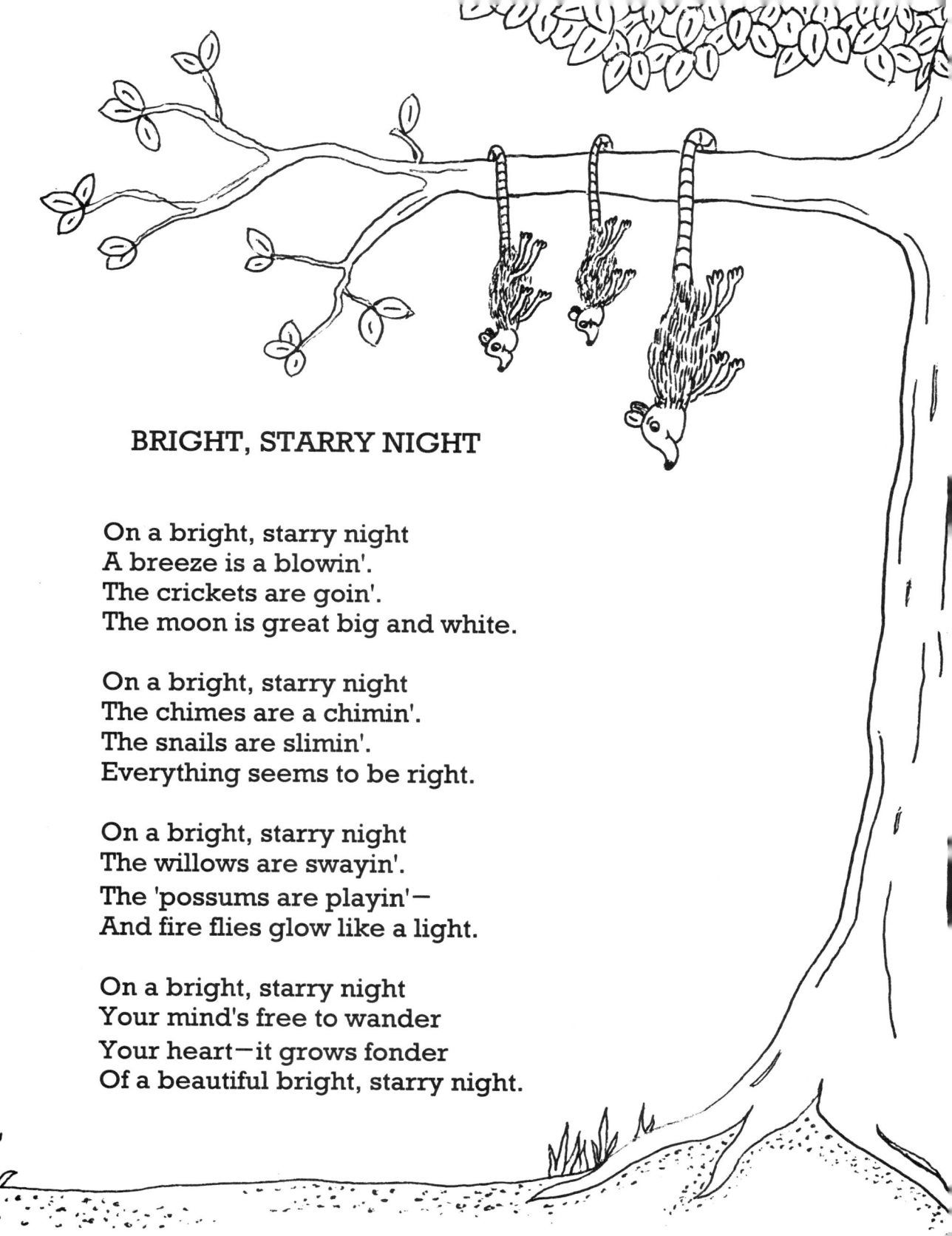

BRIGHT, STARRY NIGHT

On a bright, starry night
A breeze is a blowin'.
The crickets are goin'.
The moon is great big and white.

On a bright, starry night
The chimes are a chimin'.
The snails are slimin'.
Everything seems to be right.

On a bright, starry night
The willows are swayin'.
The 'possums are playin'—
And fire flies glow like a light.

On a bright, starry night
Your mind's free to wander
Your heart—it grows fonder
Of a beautiful bright, starry night.

ODD

Isn't it odd—the things that we say?
"Don't bite off your nose to spite your face."
Isn't it odd—the things that we do?
Hiding our eyes and asking, "Guess who?"
Isn't it odd—the things that we hear?
Bumps in the night and steps coming near.
Isn't it odd—the things that we see?
Small dogs in sweaters, a circus for fleas.
Isn't it odd that we all get along
When folks think they're right,
 and we know that they're wrong?

BRAGGER

My arm is so long
I reach to Hong Kong
If I want to.

My eyes are so good
I look right through wood
If I want to.

My tongue is so keen
I taste ice in ice cream
If I want to.

My ears work so well
I hear secrets you tell
If I want to.

My legs run so fast
I'll leave you aghast
If I want to.

My mouth is so wide
A brick fits inside
If you want to.

SURPRISE

We're mixin' and fixin' before your big eyes
A glubbery, rubbery, sloppy surprise.
Toss in an onion, throw in some flour.
Add a few lemons to make it taste sour.
A can of black beans, a rotten ol' pickle,
A handful of feathers to give it some tickle.
Mix in some snails with your bare hand.
What did you do with that bucket of sand?
When it gets thick, we'll dump in some oil
And pieces of pizza so it won't spoil.
How 'bout some mustard or ketchup, instead?
A lump of horseradish to clear up your head.
A teaspoon of pepper, a gallon of salt.
If it doesn't turn out, it isn't my fault.
Add Crackle Crisp Crunchies, but keep the free prize.
You'll get a great color with fancy egg dyes.
We're just about ready, a bit more to do.
I guess if you want, you can squirt in some glue.
I'll turn on the oven to three-fifty-four.
You dump it and spread it all over the floor.
Together we'll lift it and roll it up tight—
Then shake it and bake it one day and a night.
When the bell rings, get ready for fun.
We'll stick it and prick it to check if it's done.
Isn't it beautiful? Oh, what a sight!
Too bad that no one will take the first bite.

JELLYBEAN

Jellybean, jellybean—
Pink, red, yellow, blue and green.
It tastes so good it makes me SCREAM!
I love a tasty jellybean.

SIGNS

Signs, signs, everywhere.
Stop, Go, Caution, Wild Bear,
Open, Closed, Park in Back,
Watch Your Step, Railroad Track,
Push, Pull, Danger, Falling Rocks,
Winding Trail, Electric Shocks,
Take a Number, Start of Line,
Slippery, Icy, Standard Time,
School, Crosswalk, Take a Seat,
Watch Your Head, Wipe Your Feet,
Do Not Enter, Exit Here,
Right Turn, Left Turn, Road is Clear,
Gusty Winds Next Half Mile,
Keep the Line in Single File,
No Talking, Walking, Safe to Pass,
No Spitting, Sitting, Keep Off Grass,
Come Again, Thanks a Bunch,
We'll Be Back, Out to Lunch,
Order Here, Pick up There,
This Side Up, Lift with Care,
No Jumping, Fishing, Throwing Rocks,
Keep Out Stranger, Private Dock,
Reward for Lost Dog, Missing Cat,
Do you know where they're at?
Discount Price, Special Sale,
Third Class Package, First Class Mail,
North, South, East and West,
Good, Bad, Better and Best.
Signs, signs, everywhere.
Then, again, we don't care!

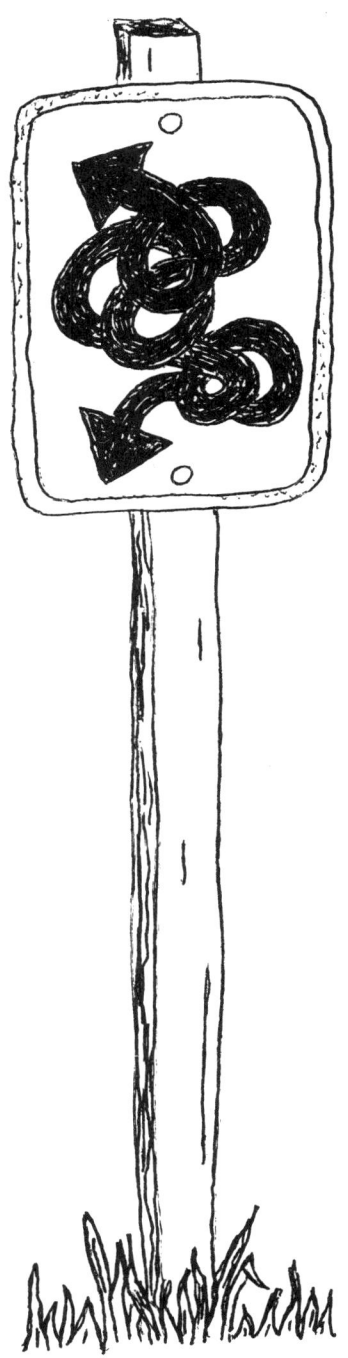

ASTONISHING ANN

Astonishing Ann had an alternate plan:
Plan B after A, so to say.
For all of those things that you'd normally do
Ann had a different way.

Let's say, for example, her bike didn't work.
Then she'd fly on a kite, instead.
And if she got dizzy and couldn't stand up,
She'd flip over and stand on her head.

Once she came to a fork in the road.
It was smart that she carried a spoon.
Ann took a piano on all of her trips,
So she never did hum out of tune.

When she felt sad it wasn't too bad
'Cause she'd saved up some happy in case.
Ann knew the girl who changed the whole world
When the smile got flipped on her face.

When she got tired of walking up hills,
She'd kick up her heels and run.
Ann never remembered her ounces and pounds,
So candy she bought by the ton.

Astonishing Ann had an alternate plan:
Plan B after A, so to say.
Whenever you do what you normally do,
Try it an alternate way.

UNFUN DAY

An unfun day—A day with no fun—
A supposed-to-be-sunny day with no sun.
A day when things that aren't fun get done—
We've said it, we dread it—a day with no fun.

EATIN' ITALIAN TONIGHT

"Hey, lasagna is on ya!" yelled ticklish Tanya.
"The spaghetti is ready!" screamed Pete.
Crazy ol' Fred made his great garlic bread.
Then everyone sat down to eat.
Pitiful Paul lost his meatball—
It rolled 'cross the table and floor.
Teresa asked, "Please, pass the Parmisan cheese—
It's delicious—I've got to have more!"
"I am the boss of the vinegar sauce—
Don't touch it!" exclaimed little Joe.
Marco's linguini turned out kind of teeny,
But no one complained, even so.
The cannoli was best—it passed our test.
The meal exceeded our wishes.
We're piled on the floor—can't eat anymore.
So, *who's* gonna clean up the dishes?

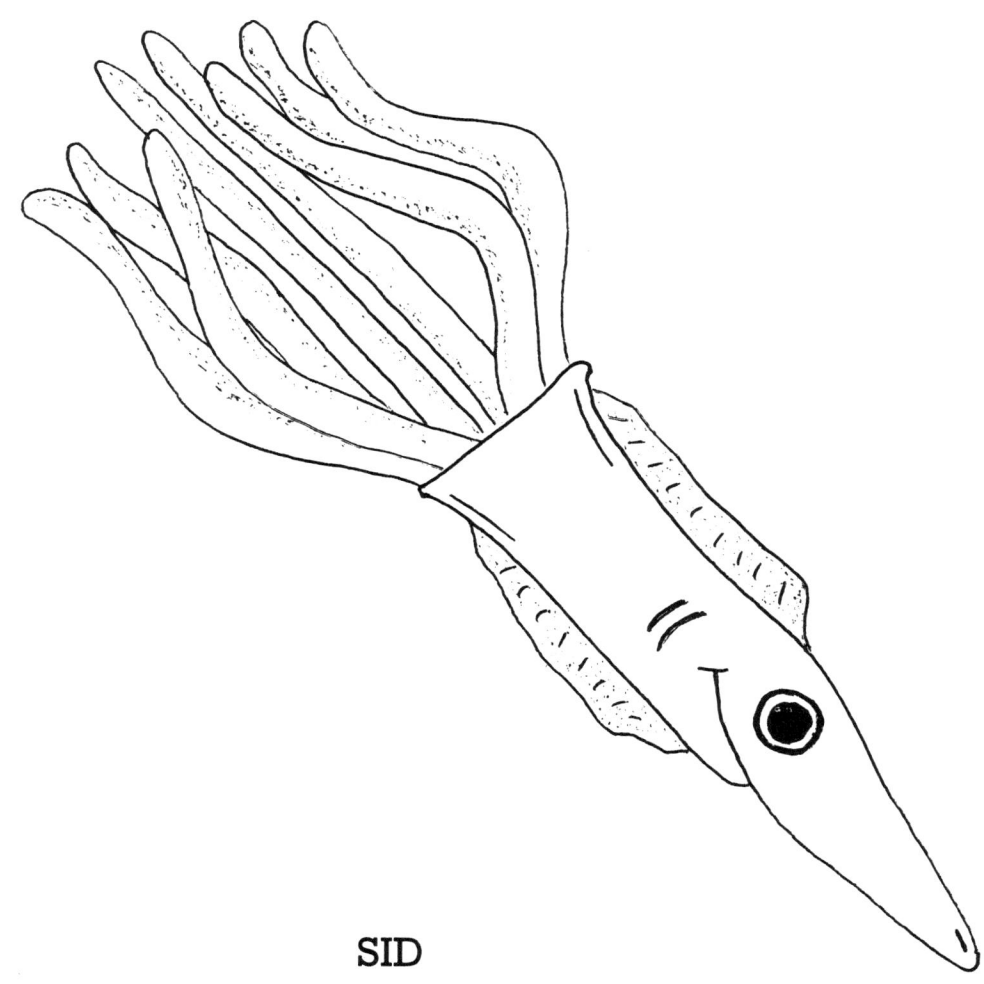

SID

Can you think of a better name for a squid than Sid?
I thought and thought, and I never did
Think of a better name for a squid than Sid.

BEACH BALL

I blew it up and gave it to Lou,
Who thumped it and bumped it to two-year-old Sue.
She licked it and kicked it to crazy ol' Pete,
Who scrunched it and bunched it with his stinky ol' feet.
Then Billy Boy got it and jounced it to Jen.
She thoinked it and boinked it to her very best friend.
He gooshed it and smooshed it—it almost went flat.
Wilber was screamin', "Gimme that, gimme that!"
Glenda decided to sit on it rough.
Wilber was screamin', "Enough is enough!"
Heather said softly, "You might wanna stop."
"That poor ol' beach ball will probably . . ."

QUICKSAND

Here I am
Stuck in the sand,
Up to my knees
Over my hands.
From my toes
To my nose,
Down under
I goes.
It isn't fair.
Everyone stares.
Up to my ears—
It was a dare.

IN MY POUCH

In my pouch I bounce about.
I bounce, I bounce, I bounce about.

I am sure I won't fall out.
I bounce, I bounce, I bounce about.

Hopping in and hopping out,
I bounce, I bounce, I bounce about.

In my pouch I bounce about.
I bounce, I bounce, I bounce about.

GOOGILY ROO

I'm hot on the trail of the Googily Roo.
To where has it gone?
I wish that I knew.
I've got a sure feelin'
I'm just about through
Searchin' around for that Googily Roo.

MANNERS

Can you crunch a cookie quietly
While sipping soda silently?
If you do them both politely
Then you've got manners.

LOSING FACE

A moment ago I laid my face there.
Now I search all around, but it ain't anywhere.
I've misplaced my elbows, my knees and my thighs.
What will I do with no mouth, nose or eyes?
My arms wiggled loose and my toes dropped right off.
I was missing my neck when I needed to cough.
Somehow my fingers walked off and away.
How my hand disappeared I can't honestly say.
What an unlikely trouble and unfortunate bind.
Now I'm afraid that I've just lost my mind!

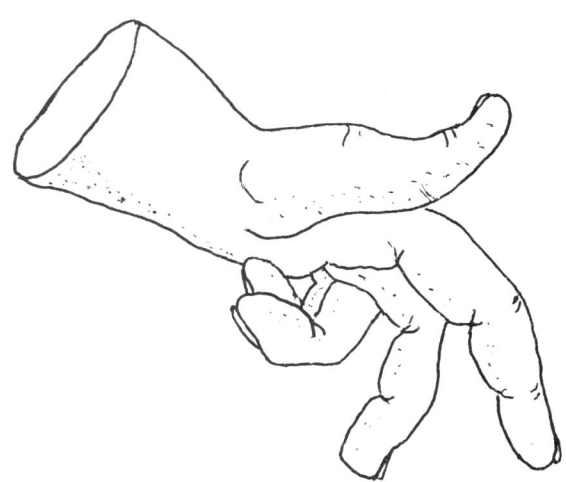

DREAM WORLD

I live in a dream world.
I really like it here.
Anything can happen—
Any time of year.
I often practice flying
Or search for pots of gold.
I meet with noble kings
In castles big and old.
You've got to come and visit me—
It's totally the best.
I'll show you all around the place—
You'll really be impressed.
I'll be a ragged pirate,
And you a shiply mate.
We'll climb right up a mountain
And down we'll roller-skate.
We'll learn to do a tap dance
And sing a crazy song.
You'll jump up to a star,
And I'll come right along.
You could turn invisible,
And we'll play hide and seek.
I doubt that I would find you,
Even when I peek.
We'll dive beneath the ocean
In a purple submarine
Or fly up over clouds
In a blimp of red and green.
Come on now and visit me—
Get your things and pack.
Take a lot of munchy food.
'Cause most folks don't come back.

CAN'T

"Will" always did
And "could" often would,
But "can't" never did anything.

Julius
Wheezer
(the 1st)

ROCK IN MY SOCK

There's a rock in my sock—it's rollin' around.
It sticks in my heel when I step on the ground.
I hope it comes out 'fore I trip and fall down.
There's a rock in my sock—it's rollin' around.

SLOW MORRIS

Slow Morris was so slow
You could hardly see him go
From the corner to the edge of the room.

He took a walk to town.
His feet barely touched the ground
As the snails that passed him went VROOOOM!

CORY CLUMP

Did you ever hear the story 'bout little Cory Clump?
He got so gross and dirty he was taken to the dump.
He didn't wash his hands when they started to grow mold.
He didn't clean his ears and neck just as he was told.

The stink was bad—it filled the air everywhere he went.
People stared, dogs were scared of the nauseating scent.
Piles of flaky filth came off in great big dusty loads.
I can't begin to tell you what came dripping from his nose.

His hair was fully filled with lots of slippy, sloppy slime.
His toes were tightly packed with clods of grungy, grimy grime.
On his back there lived a mound of murky, mangy muck.
In his ear a chunk of gunk was permanently stuck.

Finally, late one day, the trash folks from the dump
Picked up all the bags of junk and cruddy Cory Clump.
That's *exactly* how it was, I cross my heart it's true.
If you ever get that dirty, they might come and pick up you!

HAPPY BIRTHDAY

Hey, Happy Birthday!
Are you havin' fun?
Lots of cake and ice cream?
Gifts from everyone?

A little cup of candy,
Balloons and pixie sticks,
Crazy games and music,
Prizes you can pick.

Here comes little Johnny
In a suit today.
Tanya's hair is curly,
She hates it done that way.

Wilber's got his finger
Too far up his nose.
Exactly what you wanted,
A brand new pair of clothes!

Here's the entertainment,
It's a funny clown.
Watch him blow a bubble—
Jumping all aroun'.

Time to do some singin'.
Someone's out of tune.
Wait, don't blow the candles now.
It's a bit too soon!

Happy Birthday to you
And many, many more.
Now you blow the candles out—
Oops, you got one more!

What a crazy party.
You've got a pointy hat,
Little horn and shaker,
Where's the camera at?

We like havin' birthdays.
They're always such a blast.
The only problem is
They always go too fast!

WAYTOOSMALL

In the teeny, tiny town of little Waytoosmall
They don't have room for anything—not anything at all.
Everybody's clothes seem to fit a bit too tight.
Their feet stick out from the bed when they sleep at night.
Be careful not to sneeze—you could blow it off the map.
Some folks say that Waytoosmall is just a tourist trap.
Thomas Thumb grew up there and so did Tiny Tim.
See the little stream where Thumbelina took a swim.
The population grew last year from barely three to four.
Crowd Control's been screamin'—they just can't take no more.
Now you know a tiny bit 'bout little Waytoosmall.
There's no use in visiting—you're prob'ly *waytootall.*

THE KID WHO GOT STUCK IN A TIRE

Somewhere, out there, rollin' all around
'Cross the hills and through the valleys,
Bouncin' up and bouncin' down,
Wobblin' through the cities—in and out of little towns,
Rollin' over, over, over, never, never, slowin' down
Is a kid who got stuck in a tire.

THE BOTTLE

I picked up a bottle and pulled out the cork.
Out popped a lanky, cranky old stork.
He said, "Thanks for the spoon, but I needed a fork."
And climbed back in the bottle and pulled down the cork.

LUCKY PENNY

It's a penny—pick it up.
People say it brings good luck.
Rub it once and roll it twice.
Hold it tight and close your eyes.
Think about what makes you glad.
Wish it on someone who's sad.
Now good luck will come your way.
Run along—enjoy the day!

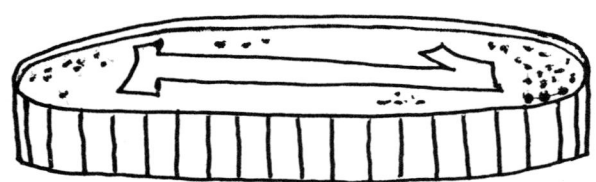

JOE'S

We wiggle our toes
And sniff our nose
To the wonderful, wafting
Flavors of Joe's.

Don't eat at Minnie's.
Don't eat at Moe's.
Don't eat at places
Where nobody goes.

We're waiting in rows
Where nobody knows
When our favorite, flavorite
Hangout will close.

No shiny red bows,
No fancy new clothes,
No TV or music,
Or swank dinner shows.

We wiggle our toes
And sniff our nose
To the wonderful, wafting
Flavors of Joe's.

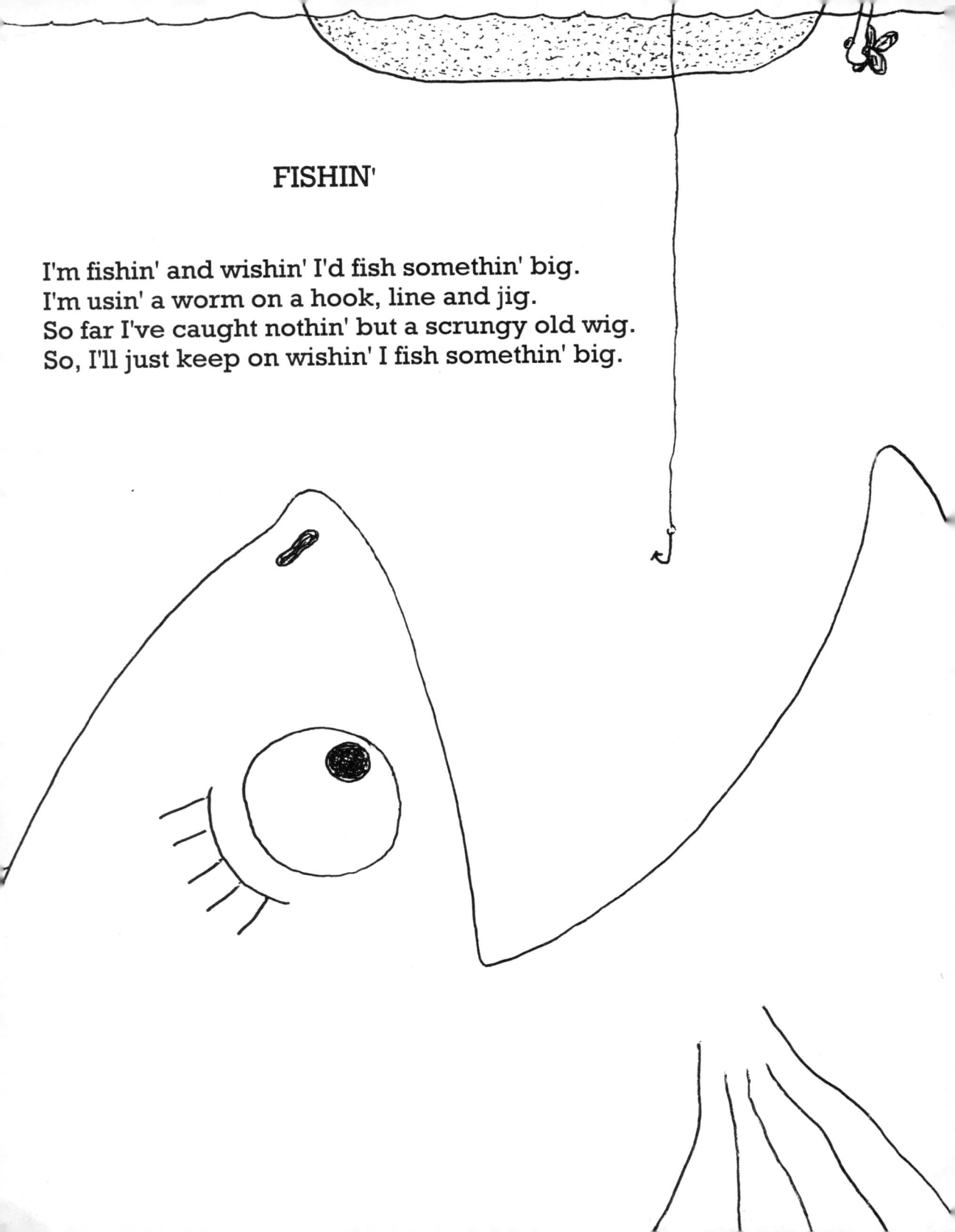

FISHIN'

I'm fishin' and wishin' I'd fish somethin' big.
I'm usin' a worm on a hook, line and jig.
So far I've caught nothin' but a scrungy old wig.
So, I'll just keep on wishin' I fish somethin' big.

OBNOXIOUS ARNOLD

Obnoxious Arnold was so proud
Of dirty words he said out loud.
He shouted out, rude and strong.
He sweared and cursed like nothin' was wrong.
Then late one day, he disappeared.
It was strangely silent, totally weird.
Perhaps the words took him away
Or maybe he's lost out in the fray.
Late at night you will sometimes hear
A faraway foul mouth coming near.
Remember Arnold—he's the one
Who thought bad words were lots of fun.

DO YOU?

Do you know what time it is?
Can you tie your shoe?
Do you see the difference 'tween
Aqua and light blue?
Do you see the shining stars
While you sleep in bed?
Do you eat your vegetables—
Or chocolate cake instead?

CAN'T SLEEP

Can't sleep, can't sleep,
Can't even get a wink.
I try to close my eyes
But I always start to blink.
I'd fill my mind with nothin',
But I always start to think.
Can't sleep, can't sleep,
Can't even get a wink.

SHARING

Give your cookies all to me.
You get one—
I get two.
That's what we're supposed to do.

Give your cookies all to me.
You get two—
I get three.
It's so nice that you agree.

Give your cookies all to me.
You get three—
I get four.
If you're nice you'll feed me more.

Give your cookies all to me.
You get four—
I get five.
I've got to eat to stay alive.

Give your cookies all to me.
You get five—
I get six.
This is better than Pick-Up Sticks.

Give your cookies all to me.
You get six—
I get seven.
I feel like I'm in cookie heaven.

Give your cookies all to me.
You get seven—
I get eight.
Pile them up, I just can't wait.

Give your cookies all to me.
You get eight—
I get nine.
Don't you think that sounds fine?

Give your cookies all to me.
You get nine—
I get ten.
Aren't you happy I'm your friend?

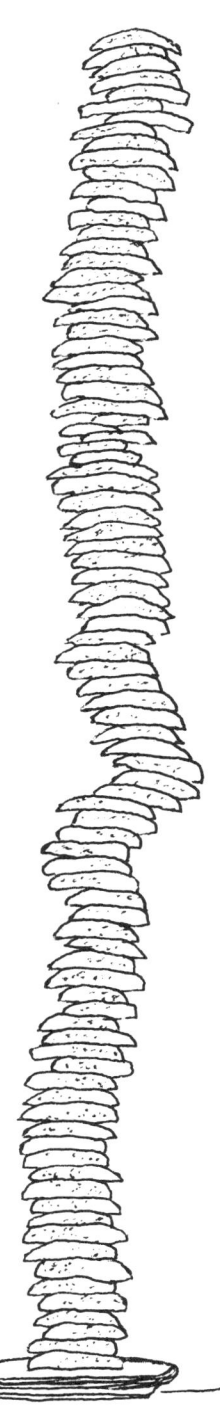

THE RIDE

We'd waited forever.
Our turn finally came.
Said the kid right behind me,
"This ride is so lame."

He was shakin' and sweatin'—
That, I could see.
I think he was fakin'
And scared just like me.

Around from the corner
The coaster machine
Came clickin' and clackin'—
Bright red splattered green.

It stopped for a moment.
Our eyes opened wide.
The safety bar snapped—
I just about died.

Kids started cryin'.
Some turned around.
Said a loud, shaky voice
In a monotone sound,

"Get on, keep your feet in,
Your hands should be down.
No jumpin' or thumpin',
No messin' around."

With an unsettling jerk
And the clank of the lever,
We were off on a ride
We'd remember forever.

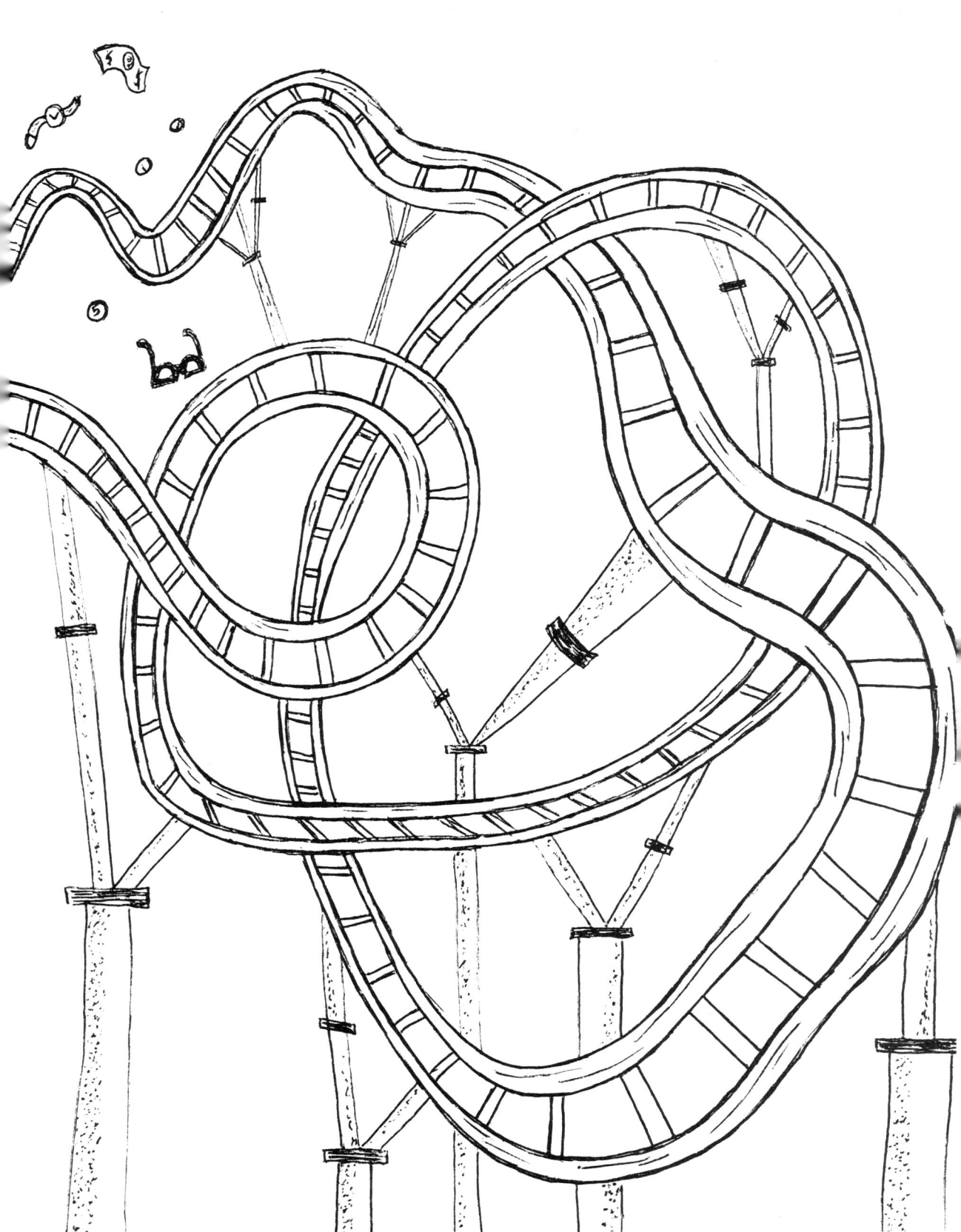

IN MY CLOSET

The monster in my closet
Is over ten feet high.
It's got hairy paws, gnarly claws
And one big rolling eye.

I lie here in my bed—
I just can't go to sleep.
I hear its goozy oozing
As it slowly starts to creep.

I smell it and I tell it
That I know it's hiding there.
The door it starts to jiggle
As I lie here stiff and stare.

It sure sounds like it's hungry
And wants something good to eat.
I imagine if it wanted
It could prob'ly reach my feet.

All this thumpy bumping
Sends a chill right up my spine.
I'd better think of something
Or I'll be its feast to dine.

I grab my fluffy pillow
And my favorite safety blanket.
I hop right out of bed
Toward the hall—I hope I'll make it.

I run right past the closet
As the door swings open wide.
I flip the bedroom light
And quickly glance inside.

With innocent amazement
I see sitting on my chair,
A pile of musty clothing
And a happy teddy bear.

DOUBTER

Ollie said I couldn't do it,
But I knew I could.
I stuffed my mouth with bubble gum
To prove to him I would.
I chewed and chewed and chewed the blob
Until I could no more.
I blew such a great, big bubble
From the ceiling to the floor.
Ollie stood way back and cried,
"I believe you now!"
Then it was too late, you see,
And Ollie's sorry now.

AUNT ANGELINE AND THE GREEN LIMA BEAN

I'd eaten it all, most everything;
A pile of potatoes and hot chicken wing.
And with much despise I tried to disguise
A green lima bean from Aunt Angeline's eyes.

Just as the plates were about to be cleared,
I looked at my aunt and she looked back and sneered.
"What's that on your plate you hid, little sneak!"
My body froze stiff and my tummy felt weak.

"I think it's a lima," I said with a scruff.
"I can't eat anymore—I've eaten enough."
"I just cannot do it, I've tried but no way.
I can't eat that lima, I honestly say."

"My hand it won't move and my mouth it stays shut.
The entrance is locked to my stomach and gut."
She looked at me hard and her face it grew red.
She leaned 'cross the table and quietly said,

"What would the children who starve have to say
As you sit there complaining and whining this way?"
"You won't eat a lima—just one little bean,
More food than most kids in this world have seen."

My heart—it grew sad as I stared at the wall.
Eatin' a lima ain't bad after all.
So my mouth opened wide, and my tongue it did savor
The bland gooshy taste of that lima bean's flavor.

SHOW AND TELL

This is my rock, it's gray and hard.
I found it down by the lake.
"Wait!" screamed Lyle, in the third aisle,
"How do we know it's not fake?"

Today I've got my sister's book.
I'll pass it for all to see.
I read it for fun—see page twenty-one,
The title is "My Diary."

I like to play out in the garden.
I've got my own shovel and hoe.
Here in this pail I've got thirty-two snails.
Uh-oh, where did they go?

A warning to those sitting up front—
This is a dangerous plant.
It's like a trap—watch it snap!
I know, 'cause it ate up my aunt.

I caught the monster under my bed.
It's the ultimate show and tell.
Come here and help me open this up.
RING! Sounds like you're saved by the bell.

Gee, what a drag they missed me again.
It seems like it's always this way.
So much for the whale I caught by the tail.
Maybe some other day.

WHAT?

Potatoes have eyes
Other vegies despise
'Cause they can't see a thing.

Birds fly around—
Penguins sit on the ground
Even though they have wings.

Hippies have hair—
Bald men go bare,
We all take a second look.

Your chocolate mousse
Is running loose.
Where did you learn how to cook?

GO-CART

Go-cart, slow cart,
When we gonna go, cart?
You can't imagine how it feels
To go in a cart that has *no* wheels.

PICNIC

We're goin' to a picnic
To have some food and fun—
Right up on that grassy hill.
Come on, everyone!
Oh, this sure is tasty—
Munchy food galore,
There's enough to feed an army.
We've gotta have some more!
Pass the big ol' sandwich.
Try the watermelon.
Take seconds, thirds and fourths.
That's chocolate I keep smellin'!
A perfect day to picnic—
A breeze and friendly sun.
We're feeling really satisfied
And *people* haven't come!

HURRY

Come on, hurry—we're gonna be late
Never stops to say,
Come on, hurry—we're gonna be late
"Did you have a good day?"
Come on, hurry—we're gonna be late
Won't sing a happy song.
Come on, hurry—we're gonna be late
Because it takes too long.
Come on, hurry—we're gonna be late
Is losing all its hair.
Come on, hurry—we're gonna be late
Doesn't really care.
Come on, hurry—we're gonna be late
Will let you take your pick.
Come on, hurry—we're gonna be late
Only if you're quick.
Come on, hurry—we're gonna be late
Does everything in haste.
Come on, hurry—we're gonna be late
Has no time to waste.
Come on, hurry—we're gonna be late
Says, "Hurry up, let's go."
Come on, hurry—we're gonna be late
Wonders why you're slow.

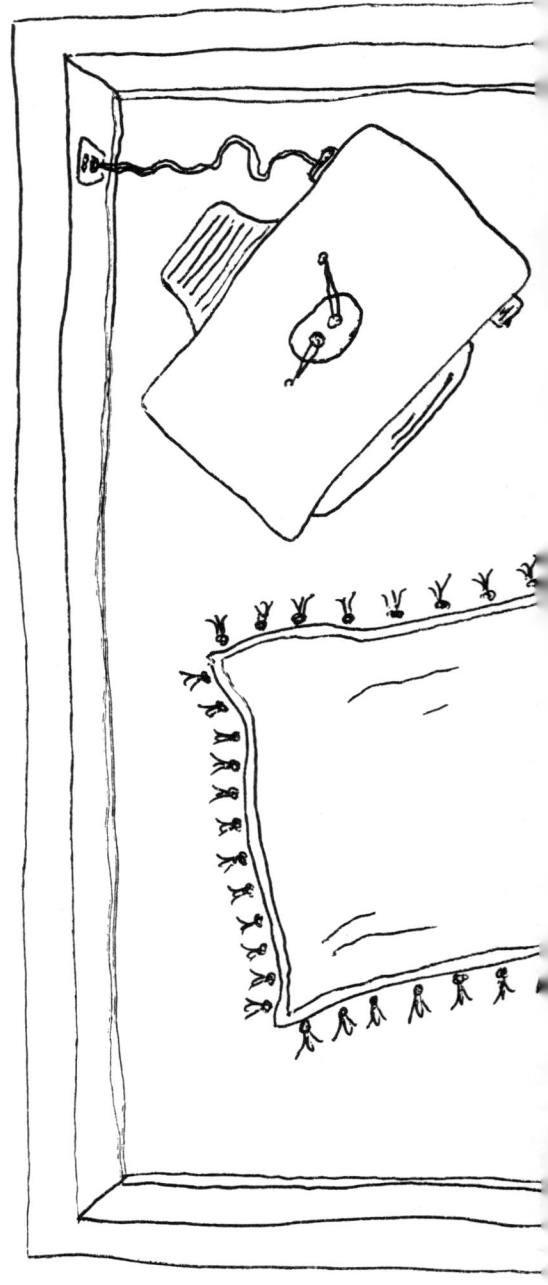

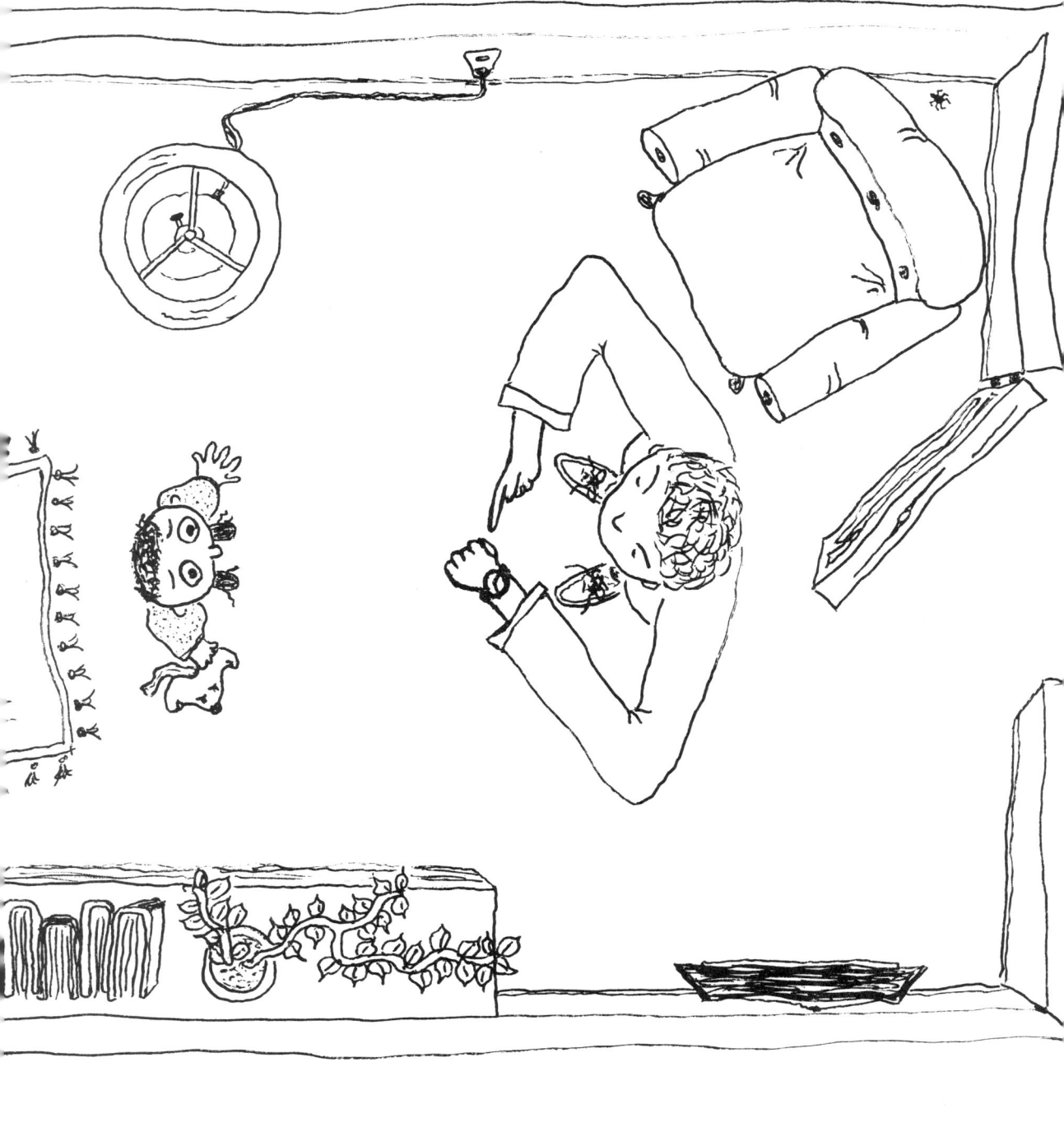

FARM

Hey, piggy wiggy, you're sure havin' fun,
Sloppin' in the mud in the warm summer sun.
Say, Mr. Rooster, you're cacklin' away.
Don't you have anything better to say?
Well, billy goat, what 'ya chewin' on now?
Isn't that the seat off Farmer John's plow?
Moo, old cow, it's just another day.
Does that green gob of grass taste okay?
Hey, granny goose, are you still here?
I thought you'd flown away for another year.
Now, tell me, little chickie, in a peep or two—
Which came first, the egg or you?

SWEET TOOTH

Eat it up, sweet tooth, don't slow down.
There's plenty of goodies to go around.
Chocolate chips and ice-cream bars,
Peppermint sticks in candy jars,

Sugar-dipped pinwheels, icicle pops,
Loads and loads of lemon drops,
Marshmallow men with licorice eyes,
One hundred different fruit cream pies,

Cotton candy, cinnamon rolls,
Bubble gum gobs, donut holes,
Fat cream puffs and long eclairs,
Sour balls, white chocolate bears,

Chunky chews and big sweet tarts,
Tasty gum drops, red-hot hearts,
Frosty milk shakes, root beer floats,
Peanut butter cookies on banana boats,

Chunks of brownies, strawberry slop,
Buckets and buckets of butterscotch glop,
Giant jaw breakers, hard rock candy,
Take a bite, ain't it dandy?

Thick whipped cream, vanilla clumps,
Lots of colored sugar bumps.
Carmel corn and pixie sticks,
Blocks of toffee, honeycomb bricks,

Cherry bon-bons, walnut brittle,
Go ahead, take a little.
Eat it up, sweet tooth, don't slow down.
There's plenty of goodies to go around.

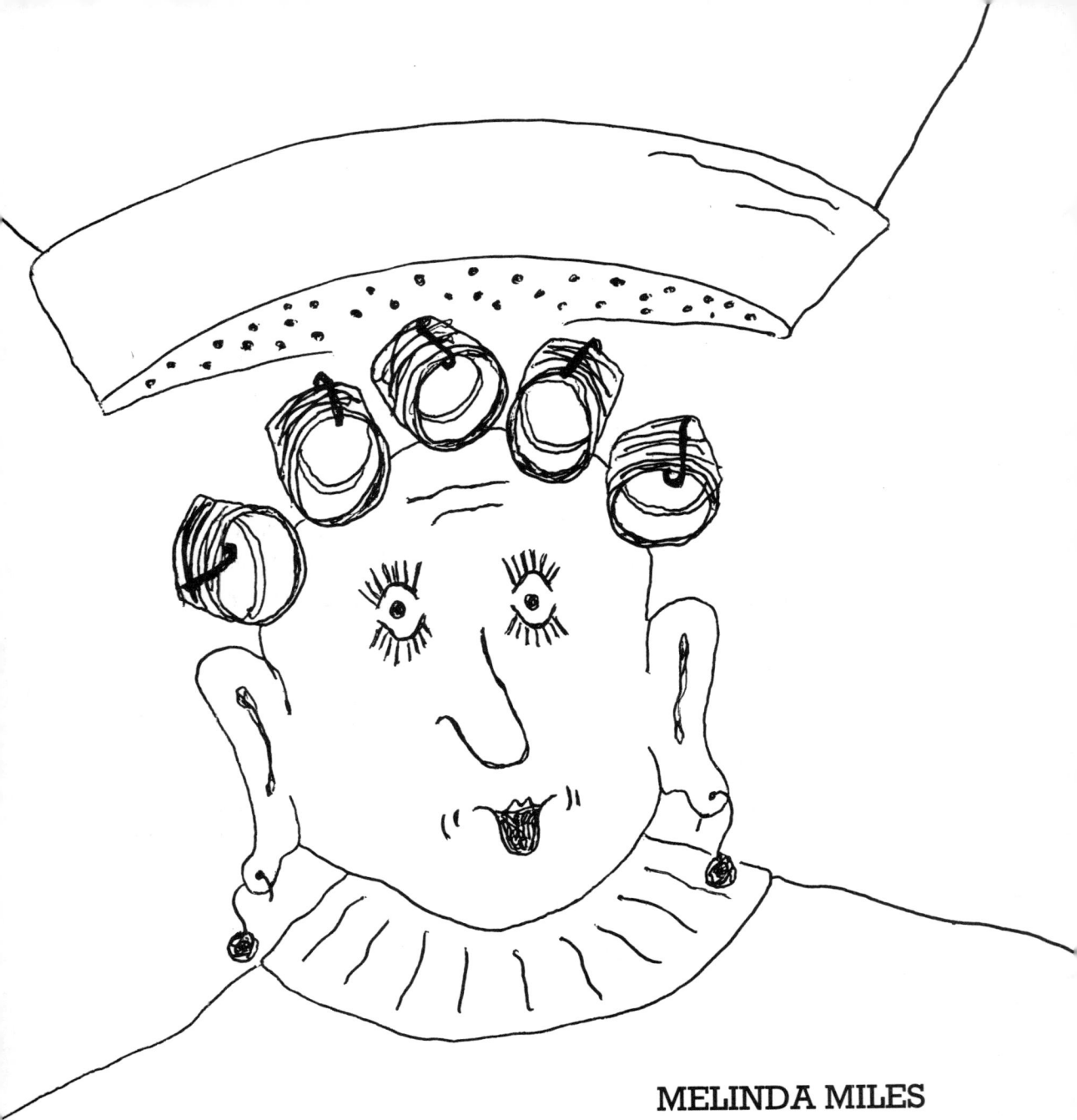

MELINDA MILES

"I want my hair in funny styles—
Curly, whirly, up in piles—
So all the people flash me smiles!"
Said, Melinda Miles.

BEST TRICK

I was gettin' some shade by a great big ol' tree
When a little smart kid came up and asked me,
"What kind of trick can you do for a penny?
Show me your best one or can you do any?"
So I stood on my head and crossed my toes.
I wiggled my ears and popped my nose.
I twisted my legs together tight
And flipped right over, landing upright.
I stuck out my tongue and rolled my eyes,
Cracked my knuckles and jiggled my thighs.
I walked on my hands and clapped my feet—
Sat on my head instead of my seat.
I wove my arms real tight in a knot—
Rolled down the hill and bounced a lot.
I twirled in circles and shook my hair.
You should have seen that kid stare.
At the end of the trick he gave me my penny.
I said, "The encore's a nickle or have you got any?"

HELLO!

Earth calling Mars, Earth calling Mars.
Come in, moon—come in, stars.
Attention, all 'telligent forms of life
And even those that aren't so smart.
We're sendin' a message loud and clear—
Hello, out there, do you hear?
Earth calling Mars, Earth calling Mars.
Come in, moon—come in, stars . . .

INDEX

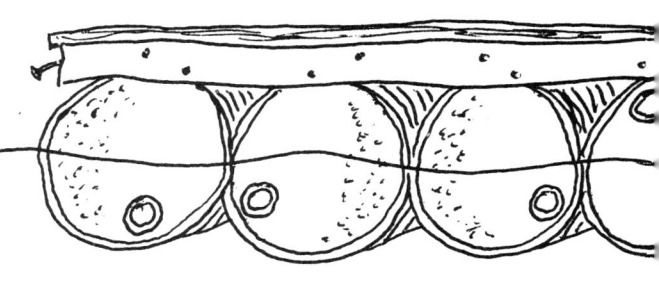

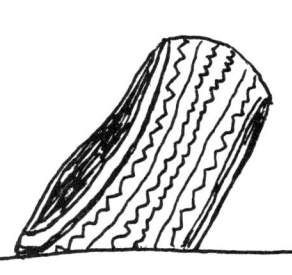

Mr. Mike lives in a little house by the ocean.
He likes going places and having lots of fun.

Hey, have you seen *Lemon Drop Rain*?

Lemon Drop Rain is another hilarious collection of
wacky poems and drawings by Mr. Mike!
If you like *Swimming in Chocolate*,
You've gotta check out *Lemon Drop Rain*!

You can order any of Mr. Mike's books by visiting
BeetleBugBooks.com
Or you can send the order form below (or a copy)
with a check or money order in U.S. dollars to:

Beetle Bug Books – P.O. Box 4636 – San Clemente, CA 92674 – USA

- -

Name: _____

Address: _____

City: _____ State: _____ Zip: _____

Email: _____

Favorite Dessert: _____

Lemon Drop Rain - $14.95   # of books _____
Swimming in Chocolate - $14.95   # of books _____

Sales Tax: Add sales tax for books shipped to California addresses
Shipping: For one or two books is free and $2.00 for each additional book
Please allow up to 15 working days for delivery

Hey, have you seen *Lemon Drop Rain*?

Lemon Drop Rain is another hilarious collection of
wacky poems and drawings by Mr. Mike!
If you like *Swimming in Chocolate*,
You've gotta check out *Lemon Drop Rain*!

You can order any of Mr. Mike's books by visiting
BeetleBugBooks.com
Or you can send the order form below (or a copy)
with a check or money order in U.S. dollars to:

Beetle Bug Books – P.O. Box 4636 – San Clemente, CA 92674 – USA

- -

Name: _____

Address: _____

City: _____ State: _____ Zip: _____

Email: _____

Favorite Dessert: _____

Lemon Drop Rain - $14.95   # of books _____
Swimming in Chocolate - $14.95   # of books _____

**Sales Tax: Add sales tax for books shipped to California addresses
Shipping: For one or two books is free and $2.00 for each additional book
Please allow up to 15 working days for delivery**